ATL Internals
Second Edition

The Addison-Wesley Object Technology Series

Grady Booch, Ivar Jacobson, and James Rumbaugh, Series Editors
For more information, check out the series web site at www.awprofessional.com/otseries.

Ahmed/Umrysh, *Developing Enterprise Java Applications with J2EE™ and UML*

Arlow/Neustadt, *Enterprise Patterns and MDA: Building Better Software with Archetype Patterns and UML*

Arlow/Neustadt, *UML 2 and the Unified Process, Second Edition*

Armour/Miller, *Advanced Use Case Modeling: Software Systems*

Bellin/Simone, *The CRC Card Book*

Bergström/Råberg, *Adopting the Rational Unified Process: Success with the RUP*

Binder, *Testing Object-Oriented Systems: Models, Patterns, and Tools*

Bittner/Spence, *Managing Iterative Software Development Projects*

Bittner/Spence, *Use Case Modeling*

Booch, *Object Solutions: Managing the Object-Oriented Project*

Booch, *Object-Oriented Analysis and Design with Applications, 2E*

Booch/Bryan, *Software Engineering with ADA, 3E*

Booch/Rumbaugh/Jacobson, *The Unified Modeling Language User Guide, Second Edition*

Box et al., *Effective COM: 50 Ways to Improve Your COM and MTS-based Applications*

Buckley/Pulsipher, *The Art of ClearCase® Deployment*

Carlson, *Modeling XML Applications with UML: Practical e-Business Applications*

Clarke/Baniassad, *Aspect-Oriented Analysis and Design*

Collins, *Designing Object-Oriented User Interfaces*

Conallen, *Building Web Applications with UML, 2E*

Denney, *Succeeding with Use Cases*

D'Souza/Wills, *Objects, Components, and Frameworks with UML: The Catalysis(SM) Approach*

Douglass, *Doing Hard Time: Developing Real-Time Systems with UML, Objects, Frameworks, and Patterns*

Douglass, *Real-Time Design Patterns: Robust Scalable Architecture for Real-Time Systems*

Douglass, *Real Time UML, 3E: Advances in The UML for Real-Time Systems*

Eeles et al., *Building J2EE™ Applications with the Rational Unified Process*

Fowler, *Analysis Patterns: Reusable Object Models*

Fowler, *UML Distilled, 3E: A Brief Guide to the Standard Object Modeling Language*

Fowler et al., *Refactoring: Improving the Design of Existing Code*

Gomaa, *Designing Concurrent, Distributed, and Real-Time Applications with UML*

Gomaa, *Designing Software Product Lines with UML*

Heinckiens, *Building Scalable Database Applications: Object-Oriented Design, Architectures, and Implementations*

Hofmeister/Nord/Dilip, *Applied Software Architecture*

Jacobson/Booch/Rumbaugh, *The Unified Software Development Process*

Jacobson/Ng, *Aspect-Oriented Software Development with Use Cases*

Jordan, *C++ Object Databases: Programming with the ODMG Standard*

Kleppe/Warmer/Bast, *MDA Explained: The Model Driven Architecture™: Practice and Promise*

Kroll/Kruchten, *The Rational Unified Process Made Easy: A Practitioner's Guide to the RUP*

Kroll/MacIsaac, *Agility and Discipline Made Easy: Practices from OpenUP and RUP*

Kruchten, *The Rational Unified Process, 3E: An Introduction*

LaLonde, *Discovering Smalltalk*

Lau, *The Art of Objects: Object-Oriented Design and Architecture*

Leffingwell/Widrig, *Managing Software Requirements, 2E: A Use Case Approach*

Manassis, *Practical Software Engineering: Analysis and Design for the .NET Platform*

Marshall, *Enterprise Modeling with UML: Designing Successful Software through Business Analysis*

McGregor/Sykes, *A Practical Guide to Testing Object-Oriented Software*

Mellor/Balcer, *Executable UML: A Foundation for Model-Driven Architecture*

Mellor et al., *MDA Distilled: Principles of Model-Driven Architecture*

Naiburg/Maksimchuk, *UML for Database Design*

Oestereich, *Developing Software with UML, 2E: Object-Oriented Analysis and Design in Practice*

Page-Jones, *Fundamentals of Object-Oriented Design in UML*

Pohl, *Object-Oriented Programming Using C++, 2E*

Quatrani, *Visual Modeling with Rational Rose 2002 and UML*

Rector/Sells, *ATL Internals*

Reed, *Developing Applications with Visual Basic and UML*

Rosenberg/Scott, *Applying Use Case Driven Object Modeling with UML: An Annotated e-Commerce Example*

Rosenberg/Scott, *Use Case Driven Object Modeling with UML: A Practical Approach*

Royce, *Software Project Management: A Unified Framework*

Rumbaugh/Jacobson/Booch, *The Unified Modeling Language Reference Manual*

Schneider/Winters, *Applying Use Cases, 2E: A Practical Guide*

Smith, *IBM Smalltalk*

Smith/Williams, *Performance Solutions: A Practical Guide to Creating Responsive, Scalable Software*

Tavares/Fertitta/Rector/Sells, *ATL Internals, Second Edition*

Tkach/Fang/So, *Visual Modeling Technique*

Unhelkar, *Process Quality Assurance for UML-Based Projects*

Warmer/Kleppe, *The Object Constraint Language, 2E: Getting Your Models Ready for MDA*

White, *Software Configuration Management Strategies and Rational ClearCase®: A Practical Introduction*

The Component Software Series

Clemens Szyperski, Series Editor
For more information, check out the series web site at www.awprofessional.com/csseries.

Cheesman/Daniels, *UML Components: A Simple Process for Specifying Component-Based Software*

Szyperski, *Component Software, 2E: Beyond Object-Oriented Programming*

ATL Internals
Second Edition

Working with ATL 8

Christopher Tavares

Kirk Fertitta

Brent Rector

Chris Sells

✦ Addison-Wesley

Upper Saddle River, NJ • Boston • Indianapolis • San Francisco
New York • Toronto • Montreal • London • Munich • Paris • Madrid
Capetown • Sydney • Tokyo • Singapore • Mexico City

The publisher offers excellent discounts on this book when ordered in quantity for bulk purchases or special sales, which may include electronic versions and/or custom covers and content particular to your business, training goals, marketing focus, and branding interests. For more information, please contact:

> U.S. Corporate and Government Sales
> (800) 382-3419
> corpsales@pearsontechgroup.com

For sales outside the United States please contact:

> International Sales
> international@pearsoned.com

 This Book Is Safari Enabled

The Safari Enabled icon on the cover of your favorite technology book means the book is available through Safari Bookshelf. When you buy this book, you get free access to the online edition for 45 days.

Safari Bookshelf is an electronic reference library that lets you easily search thousands of technical books, find code samples, download chapters, and access technical information whenever and wherever you need it.

To gain 45-day Safari Enabled access to this book:

- Go to http://www.awprofessional.com/safarienabled
- Complete the brief registration form
- Enter the coupon code QLCN-98WD-9EFH-UTD1-T4P8

If you have difficulty registering on Safari Bookshelf or accessing the online edition, please e-mail customer-service@safaribooksonline.com.

Visit us on the Web: www.awprofessional.com

Library of Congress Cataloging-in-Publication Data

ATL internals : working with ATL 8 / Chris Tavares... [et al.]. — 2nd ed.
    p. cm.
  Previous ed. by Brent Rector.
  ISBN 0-321-15962-4 (pbk. : alk. paper) 1. Application software—Development. 2. Active template library. I. Tavares, Chris. II. Rector, Brent. ATL internals.

  QA76.76.D47R43 2006
  005.3—dc22

                        2006008998

ISBN 0-321-15962-4
Text printed in the United States on recycled paper at Edwards Brothers in Ann Arbor, Michigan.
First printing, July 2006

Chris Tavares:

For Wendy, who believed in me even when I didn't believe in myself.

Kirk Fertitta:

To Mom and Ed, for their unwavering faith and encouragement.

Brent Rector:

To Lisa, for being there from the start and providing encouragement constantly, for nearly three decades now.
To Carly and Sean, who don't think it's that big of a deal that their dad writes books; it's all they've ever known.

Chris Sells:

This edition is dedicated to the native Windows programmers that .NET has left behind. I hope that .NET will serve your needs in the future, but until then, this book is for you.

Contents

Foreword to the Second Edition

Wow. It has been a long time since I wrote the foreword for the first edition of *ATL Internals*. Reading through the old introduction really takes me down memory lane; I can hardly believe that it has been almost eight years. Not long after I wrote it, I moved on to the Windows team at Microsoft and then on out of Microsoft a year later. I came back to Microsoft (and the Visual C++ team) a few years ago, and I am now managing several development teams in Visual C++. One of these is the libraries team, of which ATL is a part, and it is fun to be involved in ATL again. Jan and Christian have both moved on, although Nenad expanded the windowing classes from ATL that I mentioned in the first introduction into a separate library called WTL (Windows Template Library[1]). WTL is now a Microsoft open-source project that Nenad manages.

ATL has changed in ways I never could have predicted, and it has been bitter-sweet to see it continue to grow without being personally involved. There have been many great people who have worked on ATL over the years. Some of them I have known quite well and others I never knew.

When I mentioned "some new ways of accessing the ATL functionality" in the first foreword, I was referring to attributes. This technology was delivered in Visual Studio .NET 2002, but it never really developed into what we envisioned. ATL attributes still work in the current release and they can be quite powerful, but there are no plans to expand their use. This new version of ATL Internals provides lots of updates and does cover attributes, but doesn't assume that you're going to depend on this feature. This edition also includes a very nice introduction to ATL Server, which provides a flexible, high-performance way to create web applications. If performance is a critical requirement, ATL Server was built for you. Other ATL 8 improvements include better security, full 64-bit support, better scalability, debugging improvements, support for C++/CLI, and managed ATL components.

What has become the .NET ecosystem was just getting underway back in 1998. It has revolutionized programming for many developers and will continue to deliver improvements in the years to come. However, COM programming (and

---

[1] http://wtl.sourceforge.net

ATL) is still very much alive and is very important to many developers both inside and outside of Microsoft. The second edition of this book, like the first, provides the details you need to maximize your investment in those technologies.

Jim Springfield
April, 2006

Foreword to the First Edition

When I first saw the title of this book, I told Chris Sells that it sounded like the book I always wanted to write. Ever since we released ATL, some of us have been saying, "We should write a book on how ATL works." After reading *ATL Internals*, I don't think there would be much left for me to write about. Actually, this is kind of a relief. At this point, I think most aspects of ATL have been covered, and *ATL Internals* provides an excellent source of information of the inner workings of ATL. So, Chris asked me to provide some information that can't be deduced by looking at the ATL source code.

A Brief History of ATL

I first got into templates in late 1995, while I was a developer on the MFC team. A friend of mine here was evaluating various STL vendors for the Visual C++ product, and he talked to me a lot about templates. I played around with templates a bit, but didn't do much with them. Soon after, the VC team split off an enterprise team to focus solely on Visual C++ 4.2 Enterprise (our first VC enterprise product). I moved over to head up the libraries work for VCEE. At the time, we explored several different ideas. Microsoft Transaction Server was just getting started then, and we talked a lot with them about COM, transactions, databases, and middle-tier business objects. Pretty quickly, we realized that we needed a better mechanism for creating COM objects from C++. Jan Falkin and Christian Beaumont were working for me at that time. Jan was working on an automation interface to ODBC data sources, and Christian was working on a template-based access method to ODBC data sources (a forerunner of our current OLEDB consumer templates). I was working on the COM infrastructure, since everything was already pointing to COM back then.

Initially, I was just playing around with COM and templates, but slowly it started to stabilize around a few important concepts. From the beginning I wanted to support all threading models, but I didn't want to pay for it unless it was needed. The same was true for aggregation. I didn't want anyone to have an excuse not to use ATL. (I didn't want to hear, "Well, ATL is cool, but I can save a couple of bytes if I do this myself.") So, performance and flexibility came before ease of use when that decision had to be made. One of the main concepts that came out of this was that the class a user writes is not the class that was actually instantiated. This allowed many optimizations that otherwise could not have occurred. Some of the other concepts were multiple inheritance for interfaces, "creator" functions, and a data-driven COM map. We started to show this around and got a lot of good feedback on it. Several people thought we should get this out to customers as soon as possible, so we decided to RTW (release to the web) in the early summer of '96. That was ATL 1.0. Our working name for our libraries was MEC (Microsoft Enterprise Classes), but our marketing person thought we should have something that more reflected what we were doing. Because of our COM focus and the fact that at the time, everything was being called "Active" something or other, we selected the name *Active Template Library*. We got a good reception for it and in late summer of '96 we released ATL 1.1. By this time, Jan and Christian had started working directly on ATL. ATL 1.1 had bug fixes and support for a few more features such as connection points, NT services, RGS registry support, and security.

After ATL 1.1, we started working on ATL 2.0. Its primary focus was the creation of ActiveX controls. Jan and Christian did much of the work on this, while I still focused on the core stuff (such as rewriting the connection points to make them smaller). Nenad Stefanovic also joined us at that time and started work on the windowing support in ATL, as well as doing the composite control support in VC 6.0. We were originally planning on ATL 2.0 to be shipped on the web targeting VC 4.2. However, our plans changed and we changed ATL 2.0 to ship in VC 5.0 (12/96), and shipped ATL 2.1 with the Alpha version of Visual C++ 5.0. The only difference between ATL 2.0 and 2.1 were some bug fixes for Alpha, MIPS, and PowerPC. We also simultaneously shipped ATL 2.1 on the web with AppWizard and ObjectWizard support for VC 4.2. After a couple of months of working on ATL 3.0 (called ATL 2.5 at the time), Christian and I were burned out and took some time off from ATL, while Jan took over as ATL lead. A few months later, we came back, and Christian became the ATL lead while I moved on to explore some other things for Visual C++, although I do still get into the source code every now and then.

We shipped VC 6.0 in June '98 and are currently working on the next release. Expect to see lots of cool new stuff in ATL as well as some new ways of accessing the ATL functionality. I am glad to see ATL continue to evolve, while at the same time maintaining the original goals of generating small, efficient code. So, take a look at this book, learn some new tricks, and gain a deeper understanding of how it all works.

Jim Springfield
October, 1998

Preface

.NET has hit the Windows programmer community like a tornado, tipping over the trailer homes of the ways that we used to do things. It's pretty much swept up the needs of most web applications and service applications, as well of most of the line-of-business applications for which we previously used Visual Basic and MFC.

However, a few stubborn hold-outs in their root cellars will give up their native code only at the end of a gun. These are the folks with years of investment in C++ code who don't trust some new-fangled compiler switches to make their native code "managed." Those folks won't ever move their code, whether there are benefits to be gained or not. This book is partially for them, if they can be talked into moving their ATL 3/Visual C++ 6 projects forward to ATL 8 and Visual Studio 2005.

Another class of developers that inhabit downtown Windows city aren't touched by tornados and barely notice them when they happen. These are the ones shipping applications that have to run fast and well on Windows 95 on up, that don't have the CPU or the memory to run a .NET application or the bandwidth to download the .NET Framework even if they wanted to. These are the ones who also have to squeeze the maximum out of server machines, to take advantage of every resource that's available. These are the ones who don't have the luxury of the CPU, memory or storage resources provided by the clear weather of modern machines needed for garbage collection, just-in-time compilation, or a giant class library filled with things they don't need. These developers value load time, execution speed, and direct access to the platform in rain, sleet, or dark of night. For them, any framework they use must have a strict policy when it comes to zero-overhead for features they don't use, maximum flexibility for customization, and hard-core performance. For these developers, there's ATL 8, the last, best native framework for the Windows platform.

For clients, ATL provides windowing, COM client smart types, extensive COM control and control hosting, MFC integration (including several MFC classes that no longer require the rest of MFC), and web service proxy generation. For servers, ATL provides full COM server and object services, and extensive support for high-throughput, high-concurrency web applications and services. For both clients and services, ATL makes aggressive use of macros and templates to give you maximum flexibility and low overhead, making sure you pay for only the features you use and giving you full transparency via the source code into how those classes map their functions to the platform. For productivity, ATL provides a full set of wizards for starting and building client and server projects.

Attributes

Pushing the productivity idea, in ATL 7 and Visual Studio 2003, the ATL team introduced attributed ATL, allowing ATL programmers to annotate their code using the same techniques that you would use to add metadata to IDL interfaces and coclasses (such as the uuid attribute). In fact, the wizards were so happy to show you this style of code that, in VS03, the Attributed option was on by default. However, all is not sunshine and bluebirds with attributes. In .NET and IDL, attributes are a real part of the programming model; support for them exists all the way down. In ATL, attributes are more of a compiler trick, like super-macros, generating base classes, macro maps, Registry scripts, and IDL files.

Unlike macros, however, ATL attributes are not transparent—you can't see what is going on very well. A compiler switch is included to show a representation of generated code, such as what base classes were added, but it has regressed in VS05. This has led to problems in understanding and debugging issues, which was not helped by bugs in the attribute-generated code. That's not to say that the rest of ATL is bug free (or that any software is bug free), but when it comes to problems in base classes or macros, ATL has always enabled you to replace problem functionality in several ways. In fact, code to work around problems was a big part of the first edition of this book because you could so easily sidestep problems.

Cues in VS05 indicate that attributes are no longer a major part of the ATL team's focus. For example, the compiler switch shows less information, not more, about what attributes generate. Most telling, however, is that the Attributed option in the VS05 wizards is no longer checked by default.[1] For that reason, although we cover the principles of ATL attributes in Appendix D, "Attributed ATL," you won't find them sprinkled throughout the book. We believe that half-hearted attributes won't make ATL 8 programmers the happiest with their native framework of choice.

Audience

This book is for the C++/COM programmer moving to ATL 8, as provided with Visual Studio 2005. ATL was built with a set of assumptions, so to be an effective ATL programmer, you need to understand not only how ATL is built, but also why.

---

[1] Except for when generating an ATL Server Web Service project, when the Attributed Code option is checked and disabled so that you can't uncheck it.

Of course, to understand the why of ATL, you must understand the environment in which ATL was developed: COM. Instead of attempting to compress all required COM knowledge into one or two chapters, this book assumes that you already know COM and spends all its time showing you the design, use, and internals of ATL. Don Box's *Essential COM* (Addison-Wesley Professional, 1997) is a good source of COM knowledge, if you'd like to brush up before diving into ATL.

Outline

With the exception of the first chapter, this book is arranged from the lowest levels of ATL to the highest; each chapter builds on knowledge in previous chapters. The first chapter is a brief overview of some of the more common uses for ATL and the wizards that aid in those uses. Whenever things get too detailed in the first chapter, however, we refer you to a subsequent chapter that provides more in depth coverage.

Chapters 2 through 5 present the core of ATL. Chapter 2, "Strings and Text," covers the messy world of string handling in C++, COM, and ATL. Chapter 3, "ATL Smart Types," discusses ATL smart types, such as `CComPtr`, `CComQIPtr`, `CComBSTR`, and `CComVariant`. Chapter 4, "Objects in ATL," discusses how objects are implemented in ATL and concentrates on the great range of choices you have when implementing `IUnknown`. Chapter 5, "COM Servers," discusses the glue code required to expose COM objects from COM servers. Chapter 6, "Interface Maps," delves into the implementation of `IUnknown` again, this time concentrating on how to implement `QueryInterface`; this chapter shows techniques such as tear-off interfaces and aggregation. Chapters 7, "Persistence in ATL"; 8, "Collections and Enumerators"; and 9, "Connection Points," discuss canned interface implementations that ATL provides to support object persistence, COM collections and enumerators, and connection points, respectively. These services can be used by components that might or might not provide a user interface. Chapters 10, "Windowing"; 11, "ActiveX Controls"; and 12, "Control Containment," concentrate on building both standalone applications and user interface components. These chapters cover the ATL window classes, controls, and control containment, respectively. Finally, Chapters 13, "Hello, ATL Server," and 14, "ATL Server Internals," cover ATL Server, which lets you build web applications on IIS. Chapter 13 introduces ISAPI and ATL Server, and Chapter 14 looks under the hood of ATL Server.

Much of what makes the ATL source difficult to read is its advanced use of templates. Appendix A, "C++ Templates by Example," provides a set of examples that illustrate how templates are used and built. If you've seen ATL source code and wondered why you pass the name of a deriving class to a base class template, you will find this appendix useful. Appendix B, "ATL Header Files," provides a list of the ATL header files, along with descriptions to help you track down your favorite parts of the ATL implementation. If you're already an ATL 3 programmer and you want to hit the ground running on what's new in ATL 8, Appendix C, "Moving to ATL 8," is for you. Finally, if you'd like an introduction to attributes (and a bit more information about why we've relegated attribute coverage to a lowly appendix), you'll want to read Appendix D, "Attributed ATL."

Conventions

When writing these chapters, it became necessary to show you not only diagrams and sample code, but also internal ATL implementation code. This book often becomes your personal tour guide through the ATL source code. To help you distinguish author-generated code from Microsoft-employee-generated code, we've adopted the following convention:

```
// This code is author-generated and is an example of what you'd type.
// Bold-faced code requires your particular attention.
CComBSTR bstr = OLESTR("Hello, World.");
```

```
// Code with a gray background is part of ATL or Windows.
CComBSTR(LPCOLESTR pSrc) { m_str = ::SysAllocString(pSrc); }
```

Because the ATL team didn't write its code to be published in book form, we often had to reformat it or even abbreviate it. Every effort has been made to retain the essence of the original code, but, as always, the ATL source code is the final arbiter.

Sample Code and Further Information

More information about this book, including the sample source code, is available at www.sellsbrothers.com/writing/atlbook. On that site, you'll also find contact information so that you can report errors or give feedback.

Acknowledgments

We have a large number of people to thank for their contributions to this book. Chris Sells would like to thank his wife, Melissa, and his boys, John and Tom, for sparing him countless evenings and weekends to work on this project. Chris would also like to thank Brent Rector for letting him horn in on the first edition of this book, Kirk Fertitta for updating a large portion of this book to ATL 7, and Chris Tavares for bringing this project home.

Brent would like to thank his wife, Lisa, and his children, Carly and Sean, for delaying the delivery of this book significantly. If it weren't for them, he would never have left the computer some days. Brent would also like to thank Chris Sells for his intelligence, patience, and general good looks.[2]

Kirk Fertitta would like to thank the following: the readers, who, after all, make book writing a worthwhile and rewarding endeavor; Chris Sells, for getting him involved in this book project and for his insights into ATL and into the writing process itself; Brad Handa and Hugues Valois, for countless hours working on real projects unraveling COM and ATL mysteries; all the subscribers to DevelopMentor's ATL discussion list for their sharing their perspectives and experiences with many of the new ATL features; MusicMatch (now Yahoo!) employees and contractors for all their feedback on using ATL in a very large commercial application (many of the caveats of using some of the attributed ATL features were exposed by this talented and patient group of developers); and Stephane Thomas, of Addison-Wesley, for her patience in getting this project started.

Chris Tavares would like to thank his long-suffering wife, Wendy, for her understanding, love, and support. The late-night glasses of water and bowls of ice cream were instrumental in finishing this book and keeping Chris sane. Thanks also go to his son, Matthew, who didn't mind too much when Daddy disappeared into his office for days at a time. Chris would also like to thank Chris Sells for the opportunity to help get the second edition out to the ATL community.

Chris, Kirk, Brent, and Chris would like to thank several folks together, starting first with the reviewers: Bill Craun, Johan Ericsson, Igor Tandetnik, Kim Gräsman,

---

[2] You get only one guess as to who wrote that part, and he doesn't have my initials or my good looks. BER

Jeff Galinovsky, Igor Tandetnik, and Nenad Stefanovic. Special thanks go to the members of the ATL team, including Christian Beaumont, Jim Springfield, Walter Sullivan, and Mark Kramer, for suffering nagging questions and taking the time to answer them. More special thanks to Don Box for his MSJ ATL feature, which so heavily influenced the ATL short-course and, in turn, this book. Thanks to reviewers Don Box, Keith Brown, Jon Flanders, Mike Francis, Kevin Jones, Stanley Lippman, Dharma Shukla, Jim Springfield, Jeff Stalls, Jaganathan Thangavelu, and Jason Whittington. Special thanks go to Dharma for his especially thorough and educational reviews. Thanks to Fritz Onion for his groundbreaking work delving into the depths of ATL control containment. Thanks to a former student, Valdan Vidakovic, for inspiring Chris to delve a bit more into the HTML control. Thanks to Tim Ewald, Jim Springfield, and Don Box for their help in developing the forwarding shims trick. Thanks to the members of the ATL and DCOM mailing lists, especially Don Box, Tim Ewald, Charlie Kindel, Valery Pryamikov, Mark Ryland, and Zane Thomas. Also, we'd like to thank George Shepherd for his initial research and even a little writing for the ATL Server chapters. And last, but not least, thanks to Addison-Wesley, especially Karen Gettman, Lori Lyons, and Kim Boedigheimer, for providing an environment in which we actually want to write (although not as quickly or as concisely as they might prefer. . .).

About the Authors

Chris Tavares is currently a software development engineer in the Microsoft patterns and practices group, where he strives to help developers learn the best way to develop on the Microsoft platform. He first touched a computer in third grade, doing hand-assembly of machine code on an Intel 8080 machine with 512 bytes (yes, bytes) of memory, a hex keypad, and 7 segment LCD display. He's been digging into computers and software ever since.

Kirk Fertitta is CTO of Pacific MindWorks, a leading provider of tools and services for electronic test and measurement. With his team at Pacific MindWorks, Kirk works extensively on code generation technology and Visual Studio extensibility. He is also a .NET/C# instructor for Pluralsight.

Brent Rector, president and founder of Wise Owl Consulting, is a noted speaker, consultant, and author, specializing in .NET, ASP.NET, XML, COM+, and ATL.

Chris Sells is a program manager for the Connected Systems Division. He's written several books, including *Programming Windows Presentation Foundation*, *Windows Forms Programming in C#*, and *ATL Internals*. In his free time, Chris hosts various conferences and makes a pest of himself on Microsoft internal product team discussion lists. More information about Chris, and his various projects, is available at http://www.sellsbrothers.com

1 | Hello, ATL

Welcome to the Active Template Library (hereafter referred to as ATL). In this chapter, I present a few of the tasks that you'll probably want to perform using ATL and the integrated wizards. This is by no means all of what ATL can accomplish, nor is it meant to be exhaustive coverage of the wizards or their output. In fact, the rest of this book focuses on how ATL is implemented to provide the Component Object Model (COM) glue that holds together this example (as well as several others). This chapter is actually just a warm-up to get you familiar with the support that the Visual Studio environment provides the ATL programmer.

What Is ATL?

Expanding the acronym doesn't completely describe what ATL is or why we have it. The *Active* part is actually residue from the marketing age at Microsoft, when "ActiveX"[1] meant all of COM. As of this writing, "ActiveX" means controls. And although ATL does provide extensive support for building controls, it offers much more than that.

ATL provides:

- Class wrappers around high-maintenance data types such as interface pointers, VARIANTs, BSTRs, and HWNDs

- Classes that provide implementations of basic COM interfaces such as IUnknown, IClassFactory, IDispatch, IPersistXxx, IConnectionPointContainer, and IEnumXxx

- Classes for managing COM servers—that is, for exposing class objects, performing self-registration, and managing the server lifetime

- Classes for building COM controls and COM control containers, as well as for building plain old Windows applications

---

[1] The original expansion of ATL was ActiveX Template Library.

- An enormous library of classes for building web applications and XML web services
- Wizards, to save you typing

ATL was inspired by the current model citizen in the world of C++ class libraries, the C++ Standard Library. ATL is meant to be a set of small, efficient, and flexible classes. However, all this power requires a bit of skill to fully harness. As with the standard C++ library, only an experienced C++ programmer can use ATL effectively.

Of course, because we'll be programming COM, experience using and implementing COM objects and servers is absolutely required. For those of you hoping for a way to build your COM objects without COM knowledge, ATL is not for you (nor is Visual Basic, MFC, or anything else, for that matter). In fact, using ATL means being intimately familiar with COM in C++, as well as with some of the implementation details of ATL itself.

Still, ATL is packaged with several wizards that are helpful for generating the initial code. In the rest of this chapter, I present the various wizards available for ATL programmers as of Visual Studio 2005. Feel free to follow along.

Creating a COM Server

Creating an ATL Project

The first step in any Visual Studio development endeavor is to build the solution and the initial project. Choosing File, New Project displays the New Project dialog box shown in Figure 1.1, which focuses on Visual C++ projects.

Selecting the Visual C++ Projects folder displays the various types of C++ project templates available. The name of the project (shown in the figure as PiSvr) is the name of your generated DLL or EXE server.

The job of the ATL Project Template is to build a project for your COM server. A COM server is either a dynamic link library (DLL) or an executable (EXE). Furthermore, the EXE can be a standalone application or an NT service. The ATL Project Template supports all three of these server types. By default, a DLL server is selected as shown in Figure 1.2.

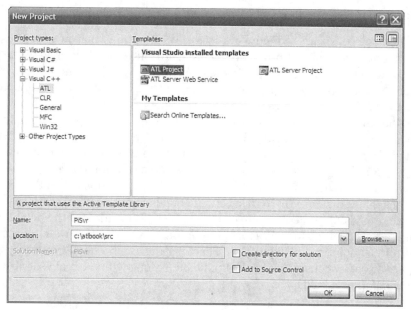

Figure 1.1 Creating a new Visual Studio project

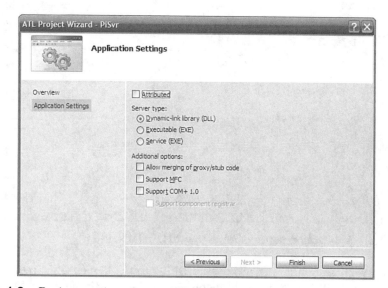

Figure 1.2 Project settings for an ATL project

ATL Project Wizard Options

The ATL Project Wizard in Figure 1.2 lists several options that merit discussion. The first option sets up the project to use ATL attributes. As described in the Preface, nonattributed projects are preferred in ATL 8, so we concentrate on nonattributed projects in this book. If you decide to use attributes anyway, see Appendix D, "Attributed ATL," for coverage of attributed projects.

In the Additional Options section, the first option enables you to bundle your custom proxy/stub code with your DLL server. By default, this option is not selected. As a result, Visual Studio generates a separate project named `<project-name>PS.vcproj` for the proxy/stub and adds it to the solution for your server. This project is for building a separate proxy/stub DLL to distribute to all client and server machines that need to marshal and unmarshal your custom interfaces. However, the proxy/stub project is not selected to be built in either of the default build configurations (Debug, Release) for the solution, as you can see from the property pages for the solution in Figure 1.3. Checking the Build check box next to the proxy/stub project causes this project to be built along with the main server whenever the solution is built.

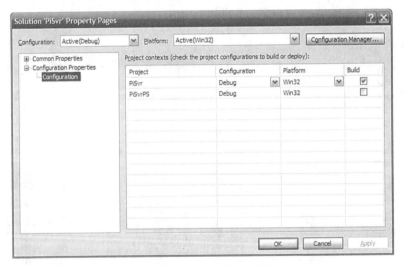

Figure 1.3   Application settings for a new ATL COM server

If you want to bundle the proxy/stub DLL into the server DLL (requiring the server to be installed on the client machine), you can check the Allow Merging of Proxy/Stub Code option (for nonattributed projects). Doing so results in a solution with only a single project (the one for your main server), with a bunch of conditionally compiled statements inserted into your server code to merge the proxy/stub code. The preprocessor definition `_MERGE_PROXYSTUB` controls whether the proxy/stub code is compiled into the server; this definition is added to all project configurations by default.

Unless you have a good reason (which is beyond the scope of this book), you'll want to avoid the option to merge the proxy/stub code into your server, instead preferring dual or oleautomation-compatible custom interfaces.

The second ATL Project Wizard option enables you to use the Microsoft Foundation Classes (MFC). Frankly, you should avoid this option. The following are a few common objections developers have to turning off this check box:

- **"I can't live without CString (or CMap, CList, and so on)."** The MFC utility classes were built as a stopgap until the C++ standards committee defined a standard library. They've done it, so we can stop using the MFC versions. The classes string, map, list, and so on provided in the standard library are more flexible and more robust than their MFC equivalents. Moreover, CString is now a shared class between MFC and ATL, and thus is available in ATL projects without having to include the rest of MFC and link to the MFC library. Other MFC utility classes have also been made shared, including CPoint and CRect. And for those who liked the MFC collections classes, ATL now includes MFC style collections (CAtlMap, CAtlList, and so on).

- **"I can't live without the wizards."** This chapter is all about the wizards that Visual Studio provides for ATL programmers. The ATL wizards are arguably as extensive as the ones MFC provides.

- **"I already know MFC, and I can't learn anything new."** Luckily, none of these people are reading this book.

The third ATL COM AppWizard option, Support COM+, causes your project to link to the COM+ component services library comsvcs.dll and includes the appropriate header file comsvcs.h so that your server can access the various interfaces that comprise COM+. With Support COM+ selected, you can also check the option Support Component Registrar, which generates an additional coclass in your project that implements the IComponentRegistrar interface.[2]

Results of the ATL Project Wizard

With or without these three options, every COM server that the ATL Project Wizard generates supports the three jobs of every COM server: self-registration, server lifetime control, and class objects exposure. As an additional convenience, the wizard adds a post-build event that registers the COM server upon each successful build. This step runs either regsvr32.exe <project>.dll or <project>.exe /regserver, depending on whether it is a DLL or EXE server.

---

[2] The IComponentRegistrar interface was thrown in for early implementations of COM+ but isn't actually used, as far as we know.

For more information about ATL's support for the three jobs of every COM server, as well as how you can extend it for more advanced concurrency and lifetime needs, see Chapter 5, "COM Servers."

Inserting a COM Class

Adding an ATL Simple Object

When you have an ATL COM server, you'll probably want to insert a new COM class. This is accomplished by selecting the Add Class item in the Project menu. When inserting an ATL class, you first have to choose the type of class you want, as shown in Figure 1.4.

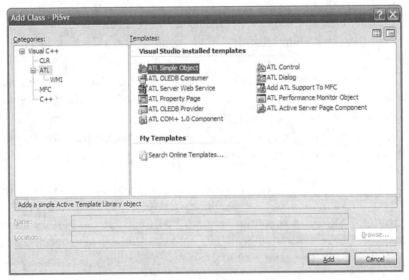

Figure 1.4 Adding an ATL COM class

If you're following along, you might want to take a moment to explore the various types of classes available. Each of these classes results in a specific set of code being generated, using the ATL base classes to provide most of the functionality and then generating the skeleton for your own custom functionality. The wizard for a particular class type is your chance to decide which interfaces you want your COM class to implement. Unfortunately, the wizard doesn't provide access to all the functionality of ATL (or even most of it), but the generated code is designed to be easy for you to add or subtract functionality after it has gotten you started. Experimentation is the best way to get familiar with the various wizard-generated class types and their options.

After you choose one of the class types (and press OK), Visual Studio generally asks for some specific information from you. Some of the classes have more options than the ATL Simple Object (as selected in Figure 1.4), but most of the COM classes require at least the information shown in Figures 1.5 and 1.6.[3]

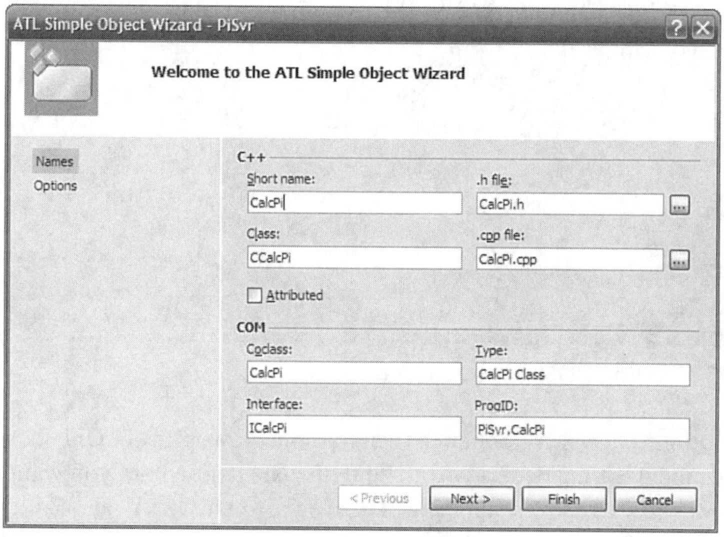

Figure 1.5   Setting COM class names

The Names tab of the ATL Simple Object Wizard dialog box requires you to type in only the short name, such as CalcPi. This short name is used to compose the rest of the information in this dialog box (which you can override, if you choose). The information is divided into two categories. The necessary C++ information is the name of the C++ class and the names of the header and implementation files. The necessary COM information is the coclass name (for the Interface Definition Language [IDL]); the name of the default interface (also for the IDL); the friendly name, called the Type (for the IDL and the registration settings); and finally the version-independent programmatic identifier (for the registration settings). The versioned ProgID is just the version-independent ProgID with the ".1" suffix. Note that the Attributed option is not selected. In a nonattributed project, we have the option of selectively adding attributed classes to our project via the Attributed check box in Figure 1.5.

---

[3] I should note that the ATL team got the terminology wrong here. The ATL Simple Object Wizard inserts a "class," not an "object."

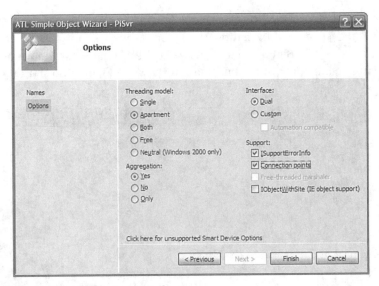

Figure 1.6   Setting COM class attributes

The Options page is your chance to make some lower-level COM decisions. The Threading model setting describes the kind of apartment where you want instances of this new class to live: a single-threaded apartment (STA, also known as the Apartment model), or a multithreaded apartment (MTA, also known as the Free-Threaded model). The Single model is for the rare class that requires all its objects to share the application's main STA, regardless of the client's apartment type. The Both model is for objects that you want to live in the same apartment as their clients, to avoid the overhead of a proxy/stub pair. The Neutral threading model is available only on Windows 2000 (and later) and is useful for objects that can safely execute on the thread of the caller. Calls to components marked as Neutral often execute more quickly because a thread switch is not required, whereas a thread switch always occurs with cross-apartment calls between other types of apartments. The Threading model setting that you choose determines the value for the `ThreadingModel` named value placed in the Registry for your server; it determines just how thread safe you need your object's implementation of `AddRef` and `Release` to be.

The Interface setting enables you to determine the kind of interface you want the class's default interface to be: Custom (it needs a custom proxy/stub and does not derive from `IDispatch`) or Dual (it uses the type library marshaler and derives from `IDispatch`). This setting determines how the IDL that defines your default interface is generated. Custom interfaces can further be qualified by selecting the Automation Compatible option. This option adorns the IDL interface definition with the `[oleautomation]` attribute, which restricts the variable types that your interface's methods can use to OLE Automation-compatible types. For instance, [oleautomation] interface methods must use the SAFEARRAY type instead of conventional C-style arrays. If you plan to use your ATL COM object from several different client environments, such as Visual Basic, it is a good idea to check this option. Moreover, accessing COM objects from code running in the Microsoft .NET framework is much simpler if [oleautomation] interfaces are used. Deploying your COM object might also be simpler with the use of [oleautomation] interfaces because these interfaces always use the universal marshaler to pass interface references across apartments. The type library marshaler always is present on a machine that supports COM, so you don't need to distribute a proxy/stub DLL with your component.

The Aggregation setting enables you to determine whether you want your objects to be aggregatable—that is, whether to participate in aggregation as the controlled inner. This setting does not affect whether objects of your new class can use aggregation as the controlling outer. See Chapter 4, "Objects in ATL," for more details about being aggregated, and Chapter 6, "Interface Maps," about aggregating other objects.

The Support ISupportErrorInfo setting directs the wizard to generate an implementation of ISupportErrorInfo. This is necessary if you want to throw COM exceptions. COM exceptions (also called COM Error Information objects) enable you to pass more detailed error information across languages and apartment boundaries than can be provided with an HRESULT alone. See Chapter 5, "COM Servers," for more information about raising and catching COM exceptions.

The Support Connection Points setting directs the wizard to generate an implementation of IConnectionPoint, which allows your object to fire events into scripting environments such as those hosted by Internet Explorer. Controls also use connection points to fire events into control containers, as discussed in Chapter 9, "Connection Points."

The Help information for the Free-Threaded Marshaler setting reads as follows: "Allows clients in the same interface to get a raw interface even if their threading model doesn't match." This description doesn't begin to describe how dangerous it is for you to choose it. Unfortunately, the Free Threaded Marshaler (FTM) is like an expensive car: If you have to ask, you can't afford it. See Chapter 6, "Interface Maps," for a description of the FTM *before* checking this box.

The Support IObjectWithSite setting directs the wizard to generate an implementation of IObjectWithSite. Objects being hosted inside containers such as Internet Explorer use this interface. Containers use this interface to pass interface pointers to the objects they host so that these objects can directly communicate with their container.

Results of the ATL Simple Object Wizard

After you specify the options, the Simple Object Wizard generates the skeleton files for you to start adding your implementation. For the class, there is a newly generated header file containing the class definition, a .cpp file for the implementation, and an .RGS file containing registration information.[4] In addition, the IDL file is updated to contain the new interface definition.

The generated class definition looks like this:

```
// CalcPi.h : Declaration of the CCalcPi

#pragma once
#include "resource.h"        // main symbols

#include "PiSvr.h"
#include "_ICalcPiEvents_CP.h"

// CCalcPi

class ATL_NO_VTABLE CCalcPi :
    public CComObjectRootEx<CComSingleThreadModel>,
    public CComCoClass<CCalcPi, &CLSID_CalcPi>,
    public ISupportErrorInfo,
    public IConnectionPointContainerImpl<CCalcPi>,
    public CProxy_ICalcPiEvents<CCalcPi>,
    public IDispatchImpl<ICalcPi, &IID_ICalcPi, &LIBID_PiSvrLib,
        /*wMajor =*/ 1, /*wMinor =*/ 0>
{
public:
    CCalcPi() { }
DECLARE_REGISTRY_RESOURCEID(IDR_CALCPI)

BEGIN_COM_MAP(CCalcPi)
    COM_INTERFACE_ENTRY(ICalcPi)
    COM_INTERFACE_ENTRY(IDispatch)
    COM_INTERFACE_ENTRY(ISupportErrorInfo)
    COM_INTERFACE_ENTRY(IConnectionPointContainer)
END_COM_MAP()

BEGIN_CONNECTION_POINT_MAP(CCalcPi)
    CONNECTION_POINT_ENTRY(__uuidof(_ICalcPiEvents))
```

---

[4] See Chapters 4 and 5 for more information on COM class registration.

```
END_CONNECTION_POINT_MAP()
// ISupportsErrorInfo
    STDMETHOD(InterfaceSupportsErrorInfo)(REFIID riid);

    DECLARE_PROTECT_FINAL_CONSTRUCT()

    HRESULT FinalConstruct() {
        return S_OK;
    }

    void FinalRelease() {
    }

public:

};


OBJECT_ENTRY_AUTO(__uuidof(CalcPi), CCalcPi)
```

The first thing to notice is the list of base classes. In this instance, ATL takes advantage of both templates and multiple inheritance. Each base class provides a separate piece of the common code needed for a COM object:

- CComObjectRootEx provides the implementation of the IUnknown interface.
- CComCoClass provides the class factory implementation.
- ISupportErrorInfo is the interface; implementation for the one method is in the .cpp file.
- IConnectionPointContainerImpl provides the implementation I requested by checking the Support Connection Points check box.
- CProxy_ICalcPiEvents is part of the connection point implementation.
- IDispatchImpl provides the implementation of IDispatch needed for the object's dual interface.

The other important thing to note here is the COM_MAP macros. This is an instance of an ATL *map*: a set of macros that generate code (typically to fill in a lookup table). The COM_MAP, in particular, is used to implement the QueryInterface method that all COM objects are required to support.

For more information about the base classes that ATL uses to implement basic COM functionality and how you can leverage this implementation for building object hierarchies and properly synchronizing multithreaded objects, see Chapter 4, "Objects in ATL." For more information about how to make full use of the COM_MAP, see Chapter 6, "Interface Maps."

Adding Properties and Methods

One of the things that make a C++ programmer's life hard is the separation of the class declaration (usually in the .h file) and the class definition (usually in the .cpp file). This can be a pain because of the maintenance required between the two. Any time a member function is added in one, it has to be replicated in the other. Manually, this can be a tedious process, and it is made even more tedious for a C++ COM programmer who must maintain the same definitions in an .idl file. When I'm adding properties and methods to my interfaces, I'd like my C++ development environment to help translate an IDL method definition into C++ (with the appropriate ATL attributes, if necessary) and drop it into my .h and .cpp files for me, leaving me a nice place to provide my implementation. That's just what Visual Studio provides.

By right-clicking on a COM interface in Class view, you can choose to add a new property or method from the Add submenu of the context menu that appears. Figure 1.7 shows the dialog box that enables you to add a property to a COM interface. Parameters to the property can be added by specifying the parameter data type and the parameter direction (for example, [in] or [out]).

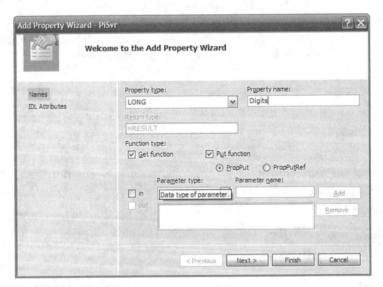

Figure 1.7   Adding a property

Figure 1.8 shows the options available on the IDL Attributes tab for the Add Property Wizard. Selected attributes are inserted into the appropriate interface definition, in your project's IDL file. In either case, the effect on the type library is identical. Many of these attributes apply in rare circumstances, so the default selections and values shown in the figure are often suitable. In any event, adding, deleting, or modifying these attributes directly in the IDL file afterward is a simple matter.

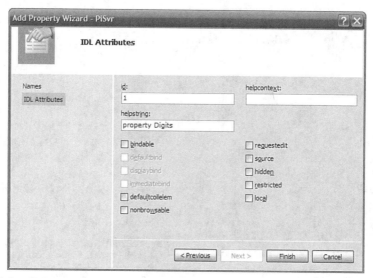

Figure 1.8   IDL attributes for a property

The following shaded code shows the implementation skeleton that the wizard generates. We have to provide only the appropriate behavior (shown as unshaded code).

```
STDMETHODIMP CCalcPi::get_Digits(LONG* pVal) {
    *pVal = m_nDigits;
    return S_OK;
}


STDMETHODIMP CCalcPi::put_Digits(LONG newVal) {
    if( newVal < 0 )
        return Error(L"Can't calculate negative digits of PI");
    m_nDigits = newVal;
    return S_OK;
}
```

Similarly, we can add a method by right-clicking an interface in Class view and choosing Add Method. Figure 1.9 shows the Add Method Wizard. Input and output parameters are added individually using the Parameter Type combo box, the Parameter Name text box, and the Add/Remove buttons.

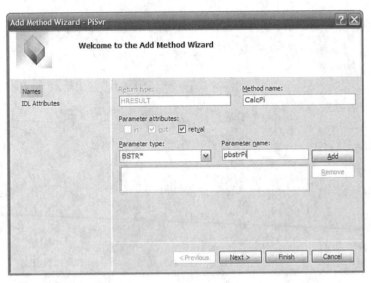

Figure 1.9 Adding a method

Again, the wizard updates the interface definition in either the IDL file or the header file, generates the appropriate C++ code, and places us in the implementation skeleton to do our job. The shaded code is what remains of the wizard-generated C++ code after I added the code to implement the method:

```
STDMETHODIMP CCalcPi::CalcPi(BSTR* pbstrPi) {
  _ASSERTE(m_nDigits >= 0);

  if( m_nDigits ) {
    *pbstrPi = SysAllocStringLen(L"3.", m_nDigits+2);
    if( *pbstrPi ) {
      for( int i = 0; i < m_nDigits; i += 9 ) {
        long nNineDigits = NineDigitsOfPiStartingAt(i+1);
        swprintf(*pbstrPi + i+2, 10, L"%09d", nNineDigits);
      }

      // Truncate to number of digits
      (*pbstrPi)[m_nDigits+2] = 0;
    }
  }
  else {
    *pbstrPi = SysAllocString(L"3");
  }

  return *pbstrPi ? S_OK : E_OUTOFMEMORY;
}
```

For a description of COM exceptions and the ATL `Error` function (used in the `put_Digits` member function), see Chapter 4, "Objects in ATL."

Implementing Additional Interfaces

Interfaces are the core of COM, and most COM objects implement more than one. Even the wizard-generated ATL Simple Object, shown earlier, implements four interfaces (one custom interface and three standard interfaces). If you want your ATL-based COM class to implement another interface, you must first have a definition of it. For example, you can add the following interface definition to your project's IDL file:

```
[
    object,
    uuid("27ABEF5D-654F-4D85-81C7-CC3F06AC5693"),
    helpstring("IAdvertiseMyself Interface"),
    pointer_default(unique)
]
interface IAdvertiseMyself : IUnknown {
    [helpstring("method ShowAd")]
    HRESULT ShowAd(BSTR bstrClient);
};
```

To implement this interface in your project, you simply add the new interface to your C++ class inheritance list and add the interface to the COM_MAP:

```
class ATL_NO_VTABLE CCalcPi :
    public ICalcPi,
    public IAdvertiseMyself {

BEGIN_COM_MAP(CCalcPi)
    COM_INTERFACE_ENTRY(ICalcPi)
    COM_INTERFACE_ENTRY(IAdvertiseMyself)
    ...
END_COM_MAP()
```

If methods in the `IAdvertiseMyself` interface need to throw COM exceptions, the generated implementation of `ISupportErrorInfo` must be modified as well. This is accomplished by simply adding the IID to the array in the generated implementation:

```
STDMETHODIMP CCalcPi::InterfaceSupportsErrorInfo(REFIID riid) {
    static const IID* arr[] = {
        &IID_ICalcPi,
        &IID_IAdvertiseMyself
    };

    for (int i=0; i < sizeof(arr) / sizeof(arr[0]); i++) {
        if (InlineIsEqualGUID(*arr[i],riid))
            return S_OK;
    }
    return S_FALSE;
}
```

After you make the updates, you have to implement the new interface's methods.

```
STDMETHODIMP CCalcPi::ShowAd(BSTR bstrClient) {
    CComBSTR  bstrCaption = OLESTR("CalcPi hosted by ");
    bstrCaption += (bstrClient && *bstrClient ?
        bstrClient : OLESTR("no one"));
    CComBSTR  bstrText =
        OLESTR("These digits of pi brought to you by CalcPi!");

    MessageBox(0, COLE2CT(bstrText), COLE2CT(bstrCaption),
        MB_SETFOREGROUND);

    return S_OK;
}
```

VS provides a convenient wizard to make this process simpler. Right-clicking the class from Class View and selecting Implement Interface from the Add submenu brings up the Implement Interface Wizard, shown in Figure 1.10. This wizard enables you to implement interfaces defined in an existing type library. The wizard is smart enough to pull type libraries from the current project. Alternatively, you can define interfaces in IDL, compile them using MIDL, and implement those interfaces by referencing the resulting type library. The radio buttons enable you to use the type library from the current project, registered type libraries (Registry), or unregistered type libraries (File) that you locate with the Browse button. For our PiSvr project, the type library built from the generated IDL makes the interfaces we've defined available to the Implement Interface Wizard.

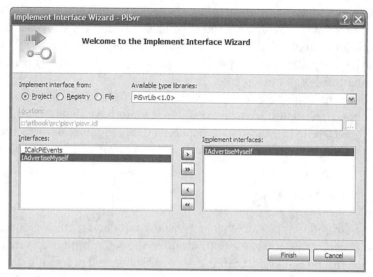

Figure 1.10 The Implement Interface Wizard

Note that interfaces that have already been implemented (ICalcPi, in our case) do not appear in the list of implementable interfaces. Unfortunately, the Implement Interface Wizard does not support interfaces that don't exist in type libraries; this leaves out most of the standard COM interfaces, such as IPersist, IMarshal, and IOleItemContainer.

Unfortunately, there's a bug in this wizard. The wizard did this to our base class list:

```
class ATL_NO_VTABLE CCalcPi :
    ... the usual stuff …
    public IDispatchImpl<ICalcPi, &IID_ICalcPi, &LIBID_PiSvrLib,
        /*wMajor =*/ 1, /*wMinor =*/ 0>,
    public IDispatchImpl<IAdvertiseMyself,
        &__uuidof(IAdvertiseMyself), &LIBID_PiSvrLib,
        /* wMajor = */ 1, /* wMinor = */ 0>
{
...
```

The added code is in bold. The wizard added the IDispatchImpl template as a base class. This is used when implementing dual interfaces. IAdvertiseMyself is *not* a dual interface. The wizard should have just derived from the interface directly. The fix is easy: Change the previous bold line to this:

```
    public IAdvertiseMyself
```

Even with this bug, the Implement Interface Wizard is still worth using for large interfaces. In addition to updating the base class list and the `COM_MAP`, the wizard provides skeleton implementation for all the methods in the interface; for a large interface, this can save a ton of typing. Unfortunately, the skeletons are added only to the header file, not to the .cpp file.

For more information about the various ways that ATL allows your COM classes to implement interfaces, see Chapter 6, "Interface Maps." For more information about `CCom-BSTR` and the string-conversion routines used in the `ShowAd` method, see Chapter 2, "Strings and Text."

Support for Scripting

Any time you run the ATL Simple Object Wizard and choose Dual as the interface type, ATL generates an interface definition for the default interface that derives from `IDispatch` and is marked with the `dual` attribute, and places it in the IDL file. Because it derives from `IDispatch`, our dual interface can be used by scripting clients such as Active Server Pages (ASP), Internet Explorer (IE), and Windows Script Host (WSH). When our COM class supports `IDispatch`, we can use objects of that class from scripting environments. Here's an example HTML page that uses an instance of the `CalcPi` object:

```
<object classid="clsid:859512CF-E4D8-450C-AF09-6578FE2F6DC2"
        id=objPiCalculator>
</object>

<script language=vbscript>
  ' Set the digits property
  objPiCalculator.digits = 5

  ' Calculate pi
  dim pi
  pi = objPiCalculator.CalcPi

  ' Tell the world!
  document.write "Pi to " & objPiCalculator.digits & _
    " digits is " & pi
</script>
```

For more information about how to handle the inconvenient data types associated with scripting—namely, `BSTR`s and `VARIANT`s—see Chapter 2, "Text and Strings," and Chapter 3, "ATL Smart Types."

Adding Persistence

ATL provides base classes for objects that want to be persistent—that is, saved to some persistence medium (such as a disk) and restored later. COM objects expose this support by implementing one of the COM persistence interfaces, such as IPersistStreamInit, IPersistStorage, or IPersistPropertyBag. ATL provides implementation of these three persistence interfaces—namely, IPersistStreamInitImpl, IPersistStorageImpl, and IPersistPropertyBagImpl. Your COM object supports persistence by deriving from any of these base classes, adding the interface to your COM_MAP, and adding a data member called m_bRequiresSave that each of these base classes expects.

```
class ATL_NO_VTABLE CCalcPi :
  public ICalcPi,
  public IAdvertiseMyself,
  public IPersistPropertyBagImpl<CCalcPi> {
public:
  ...

  // ICalcPi
public:
  STDMETHOD(CalcPi)(/*[out, retval]*/ BSTR* pbstrPi);
  STDMETHOD(get_Digits)(/*[out, retval]*/ long *pVal);
  STDMETHOD(put_Digits)(/*[in]*/ long newVal);

public:
  BOOL m_bRequiresSave; // Used by persistence base classes

private:
  long m_nDigits;
};
```

However, that's not quite all there is to it. ATL's implementation of persistence needs to know which parts of your object need to be saved and restored. For that information, ATL's implementations of the persistent interfaces rely on a table of object properties that you want to persist between sessions. This table, called a PROP_MAP, contains a mapping of property names and dispatch identifiers (as defined in the IDL file). So, given the following interface:

```
[
object,
...
]
```

```
interface ICalcPi : IDispatch {
    [propget, id(1)] HRESULT Digits([out, retval] LONG* pVal);
    [propput, id(1)] HRESULT Digits([in] LONG newVal);
};
```

the `PROP_MAP` would be contained inside our implementation of `ICalcPi` like this:

```
class ATL_NO_VTABLE CCalcPi : ...
{
  ...
public:
BEGIN_PROP_MAP(CCalcPi)
  PROP_ENTRY("Digits", 1, CLSID_NULL)
END_PROP_MAP()
};
```

Given an implementation of `IPersistPropertyBag`, our IE sample code can be expanded to support initialization of object properties via persistence using the <param> tag:

```
<object classid="clsid:E5F91723-E7AD-4596-AC90-17586D400BF7"
        id=objPiCalculator>
        <param name=digits value=5>
</object>

<script language=vbscript>
  ' Calculate pi
  dim pi
  pi = objPiCalculator.CalcPi

  ' Tell the world!
  document.write "Pi to " & objPiCalculator.digits & _
    " digits is " & pi
</script>
```

For more information about ATL's implementation of persistence, see Chapter 7, "Persistence in ATL."

Adding and Firing Events

When something interesting happens in a COM object, we'd like to be able to spontaneously notify its client without the client polling the object. COM provides a standard mechanism for sending these notifications to clients (normally called "firing an event") using the connection-point architecture.

Connection-point events are actually methods on an interface. To support the widest variety of clients, an event interface is often defined as a dispinterface. Choosing Support Connection Points in the ATL Simple Object Wizard generates an event in our IDL file. The following is an example of the wizard-generated code augmented with a single event method (shown in bold):

```
[
    uuid(B830F523-D87B-434F-933A-623CEF6FC4AA),
    helpstring("_ICalcPiEvents Interface")
]
dispinterface _ICalcPiEvents {
    properties:
    methods:
    [id(1)] void OnDigit([in] short nIndex,
        [in] short nDigit);
};
```

In addition to changing the IDL file, the Support Connection Points option makes several changes to the class definition. The IConnectionPointContainerImpl base class is added. This class implements the IConnectionPointContainer interface, providing functionality for managing multiple event interfaces on the class. The IConnectionPointImpl base class implements a connection point for a specific event interface: _ICalcPiEvents, in this case. The COM_MAP is also modified to include an entry for IConnectionPointContainer, and a new map, the CONNECTION_MAP, is added to the class.

The wizard also generates a proxy class for the connection point. This proxy class is added to the base class list and provides a convenient way to actually fire the events (that is, call the methods on the connection point). This is very helpful because the typical connection point is a dispinterface.

For example:

```
STDMETHODIMP CCalcPi::CalcPi(BSTR *pbstrPi) {
    // (code to calculate pi removed for clarity)
    ...
```

```
  // Fire each digit
  for( short j = 0; j != m_nDigits; ++j ) {
    Fire_OnDigit(j, (*pbstrPi)[j+2] - L'0');
  }


  ...

}
```

Objects of the CCalcPi class can now send events that can be handled in a page of HTML:

```
<object classid="clsid:E5F91723-E7AD-4596-AC90-17586D400BF7"
        id=objPiCalculator>
          <param name=digits value=50>
</object>

<input type=button name=cmdCalcPi value="Pi to 50 Digits:">
<span id=spanPi>unknown</span>

<p>Distribution of first 50 digits in pi:
<table border cellpadding=4>
... <!- table code removed for clarity ->
</table>

<script language=vbscript>
  ' Handle button click event
  sub cmdCalcPi_onClick
    spanPi.innerText = objPiCalculator.CalcPi
  end sub

  ' Handle calculator digit event
  sub objPiCalculator_onDigit(index, digit)
    select case digit
    case 0: span0.innerText = span0.innerText + 1
    case 1: span1.innerText = span1.innerText + 1
    ... <!- etc ->
    end select
    spanTotal.innerText = spanTotal.innerText + 1
  end sub
</script>
```

The sample HTML page handles these events to provide the first 50 digits of pi and their distribution, as shown in Figure 1.11.

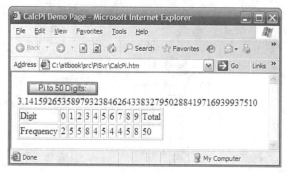

Figure 1.11   Pi to 50 digits

For more information about ATL's support for connection points, see Chapter 9, "Connection Points."

Using a Window

Because this is Microsoft Windows we're developing for, sometimes it's handy to be able to put up a window or a dialog box. For example, the `MessageBox` call we made earlier yielded a somewhat boring advertisement, as shown in Figure 1.12.

Figure 1.12   Boring message box

Normally, putting up a custom dialog box is kind of a pain. For the average Win32 programmer, either it involves lots of procedural code, which we don't like, or it involves building a bunch of forwarding code to map Windows messages to member functions (a dialog box is an object, after all). As with MFC, ATL has a great deal of functionality for building windows and dialog boxes. To add a new dialog box, select Add Class from the Project menu and then select ATL Dialog from the list of available templates, as shown in Figure 1.13.

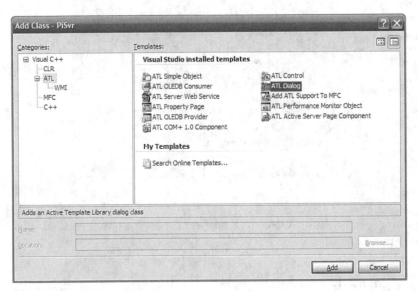

Figure 1.13   Inserting a dialog box class

The ATL Dialog Wizard (see Figure 1.14) is much simpler than many other ATL class templates. It allows you to enter only C++ name information because a dialog box is a Win32 object, not a COM object.

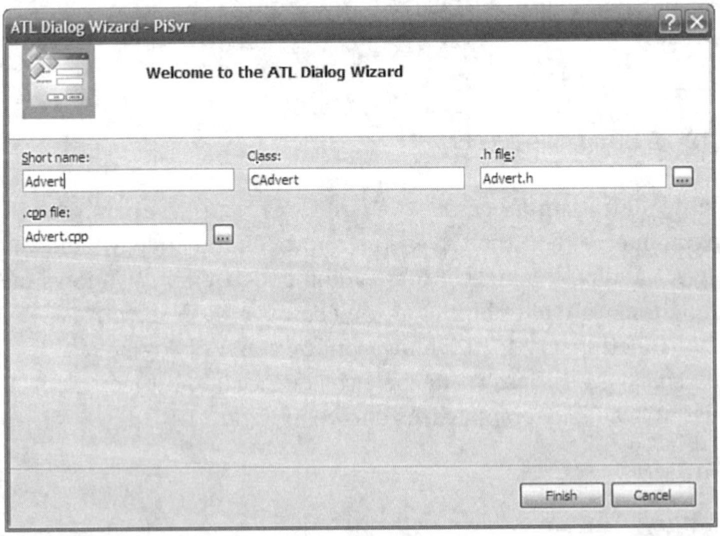

Figure 1.14   ATL Dialog Wizard

The generated code creates a class that derives from `CAxDialogImpl` and uses a new dialog box resource, also provided by the wizard. The derived class routes messages to handlers using the `MSG_MAP` macros, as shown here:

```cpp
class CAdvert : public CAxDialogImpl<CAdvert> {
public:
  CAdvert() {}
  ~CAdvert() {}
  enum { IDD = IDD_ADVERT };


BEGIN_MSG_MAP(CAdvert)
    MESSAGE_HANDLER(WM_INITDIALOG, OnInitDialog)
    COMMAND_HANDLER(IDOK, BN_CLICKED, OnClickedOK)
    COMMAND_HANDLER(IDCANCEL, BN_CLICKED, OnClickedCancel)
    CHAIN_MSG_MAP(CAxDialogImpl<CAdvert>)
END_MSG_MAP()

  LRESULT OnInitDialog(UINT uMsg, WPARAM wParam, LPARAM lParam,
                       BOOL& bHandled) {
    if( m_bstrClient.Length() ) {
      CComBSTR  bstrCaption = OLESTR("CalcPi sponsored by ");
      bstrCaption += m_bstrClient;

      USES_CONVERSION;
      SetWindowText(OLE2CT(bstrCaption));
    }
    return 1;  // Let the system set the focus
  }

  LRESULT OnClickedOK(WORD wNotifyCode, WORD wID, HWND hWndCtl,
    BOOL& bHandled) {
    EndDialog(wID);
    return 0;
  }

  LRESULT OnClickedCancel(WORD wNotifyCode, WORD wID,
    HWND hWndCtl, BOOL& bHandled) {
    EndDialog(wID);
    return 0;
  }

  CComBSTR  m_bstrClient;
};
```

If you want to handle another message, you can add the appropriate entries to the message map and add the handler member functions by hand. If you prefer, you can add a message handler by right-clicking the name of the CAxDialogImpl-based class in Class view, choosing Properties, and clicking the Messages toolbar button. Figure 1.15 shows the resulting window.

Figure 1.15   Adding a Windows message handler

For more information on ATL's extensive support for windowing, including building standalone Windows applications, see Chapter 10, "Windowing."

COM Controls

COM controls are objects that provide their own user interface (UI), which is closely integrated with that of their container. ATL provides extensive support for COM controls via the CComControl base class, as well as various other base IXxxImpl classes. These base classes handle most of the details of being a basic control (although there's plenty of room for advanced features, as shown in Chapter 11, "ActiveX Controls"). Had you chosen ATL Control from the Add Class dialog box when generating the CalcPi class, you could have provided the UI merely by implementing the OnDraw function:

```
HRESULT CCalcPi::OnDraw(ATL_DRAWINFO& di) {
  CComBSTR  bstrPi;
  if( SUCCEEDED(this->CalcPi(&bstrPi)) ) {
```

```
    DrawText(di.hdcDraw, COLE2CT(bstrPi), -1,
      (RECT*)di.prcBounds,
      DT_SINGLELINE | DT_CENTER | DT_VCENTER);
  }

  return S_OK;
}
```

The wizard would also have generated a sample HTML page, which I've augmented to take up the entire browser window and to set the initial number of digits to 50:

```
<HTML>
<HEAD>
<TITLE>ATL 8.0 test page for object CalcPiControl</TITLE>
</HEAD>
<BODY>

<OBJECT ID="CalcPi"
    CLASSID="CLSID:9E7ABA7A-C106-4813-A50C-B15C967264B6"
    height="100%" width="100%">
    <param name="Digits" value="50">
</OBJECT>

</BODY>
</HTML>
```

Displaying this sample page in Internet Explorer yields a view of a control (see Figure 1.16). For more information about building controls in ATL, see Chapter 11, "ActiveX Controls."

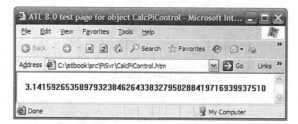

Figure 1.16   The `CalcPi` control hosted in Internet Explorer

Hosting a Control

If you want to host a control, you can do so with ATL's control-hosting support. For example, the `Ax` in `CAxDialogImpl` stands for ActiveX control and indicates that the dialog box is capable of hosting controls. To host a control in a dialog box, right-click the dialog box resource and choose Insert ActiveX Control.[5] This produces a dialog box that lists the controls installed on your system, as shown in Figure 1.17.

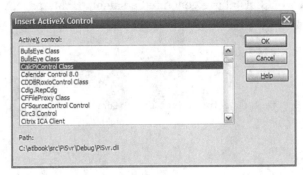

Figure 1.17   Insert ActiveX Control dialog box

After you insert the control, you can click on it and set its properties in the Properties window, as shown in Figure 1.18.

Figure 1.18   Control Properties dialog box

---

[5] For commonly used ActiveX controls, it's usually easier to add them to your Visual Studio toolbox than to go through this dialog box every time. Right-click the toolbox, select Choose Items, wait approximately 37 minutes for the dialog box to appear, select the COM Components tab, and select the controls you want on your toolbox.

By clicking the Control Events toolbar button, you also can choose to handle a control's events, as shown in Figure 1.19.

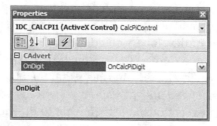

Figure 1.19 Choosing which control events to handle

When the dialog box is shown, the control is created and initialized based on the properties set at development time. Figure 1.20 shows an example of a dialog box hosting a control.

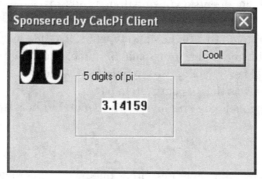

Figure 1.20 A dialog box hosting a COM control

ATL provides support for hosting ATL controls not only in dialog boxes, but also in other windows, in controls that have a UI declared as a dialog box resource (called composite controls), and in controls that have a UI declared as an HTML resource (called HTML controls). For more information about control containment, see Chapter 12, "Control Containment."

Being a C++ COM Client

COM and C++ go hand in hand—at least, theoretically. A COM interface maps directly to a C++ abstract class. All you need to do to use a COM object is run its IDL file through the MIDL compiler, and you've got a header file with all the information you need.

This worked well until the VB team asked if it could play with this COM stuff, too.

VB developers generally neither know nor want to know C++. And IDL is a language that's very much in the C++ tradition, with lots of support for C/C++-specific things in it (such as arrays and pointers) VB needed a way to store type information about COM objects that VB developers could use and understand easily.

Thus was born the *type library* (a.k.a. *typelib*). A typelib stores information about a COM object: The classid, the interfaces that the object supports, the methods on those interfaces, and so on—just about everything you'd find in an IDL file (with some unfortunate exceptions, mostly having to do with C-style arrays). The COM system includes a set of COM objects that lets you programmatically walk through the contents of a typelib. Best of all, the typelib can be embedded into a DLL or EXE file directly, so you never have to worry about the type information getting lost.

The typelib was so successful for VB developers that many COM components these days aren't shipped with an IDL file; the type library includes everything needed to use the components. Only one thing is missing: How do we use typelibs in C++?

The C++ language doesn't understand typelibs. It wants header files. This was such a serious problem that, back in Visual Studio 6, Microsoft extended the compiler so that it could use type libraries in much the same way that you use header files. This extension was the `#import` statement.

`#import` is used much like `#include` is. The general form is shown here:

```
#import "pisvr.dll" <options>
```

The `#import` statement generates either one or two C++ header files, depending on the options you use. These header files have the extensions `.tlh` (for "typelib header") and `.tli` (for "typelib inline") and are generated into your project output directory (by default, Debug for a debug build, Release for a release build).

The options on the `#import` line give you a great deal of control over the contents of the generated files. Check the Visual Studio documentation for the full list; we talk about some of the more commonly used options here.

The `no_namespace` option tells the compiler that we don't want the contents of the generated files to be placed into a C++ namespace. By default, the contents of the generated files are placed in a C++ namespace named after the type library.

`named_guids` instructs the compiler that we want to have named symbols for the GUIDs in the type library. By default, this would not compile because the name `CLSID_PISvr` would not be defined:

```
::CoCreateInstance( CLSID_PISvr, ... );
```

Instead, you have to do this:

```
::CoCreateInstance( __uuidof( PISvr ), ... );
```

You also need to use __uuidof( ) to get the IID for interfaces.

The `raw_interfaces_only` option requires the most explanation. By default, when the #import statement generates the header file, it doesn't just spit out class definitions for interfaces. It actually generates wrapper classes that attempt to make a COM interface easier to use. For example, given the interface:

```
interface ICalcPi : IDispatch {
  [propget, id(1), helpstring("property Digits")]
  HRESULT Digits([out, retval] LONG* pVal);
  [propput, id(1), helpstring("property Digits")]
  HRESULT Digits([in] LONG newVal);
  [id(2), helpstring("method CalcPi")]
  HRESULT CalcPi([out,retval] BSTR* pbstrPi);
};
```

Normal use of this interface would be something like this:

```
HRESULT DoStuff( long nDigits, ICalcPi *pCalc ) {
    HRESULT hr = pCalc->put_Digits( nDigits );
    if( FAILED( hr ) ) return hr;

    BSTR bstrResult;
    hr = pCalc->CalcPi( &bstrResult );
    if( FAILED( hr ) ) return hr;

    std::cout << "PI to " << nDigits << " digits is "
        << CW2A( bstrResult );

    ::SysFreeString( bstrResult );
    return S_OK;
}
```

When using the #import statement, on the other hand, using this interface looks like this:

```
void DoStuff( long nDigits, ICalcPiPtr spCalc ) {
  spCalc->Digits = nDigits;
  _bstr_t bstrResults = spCalc->CalcPi();
  std::cout << "PI to " << spCalc->Digits << " digits is "
    << ( char * )bstrResults;
}
```

The `ICalcPiPtr` type is a smart pointer expressed as a typedef for the `_com_ptr_t` class. This class is *not* part of ATL; it's part of the Direct-To-COM extensions to the compiler and is defined in the system header file `comdef.h` (along with all the other types used by the wrapper classes). The smart pointer automatically manages the reference counting, and the `_bstr_t` type manages the memory for a BSTR (which we discuss in Chapter 2, "Strings and Text").

The most remarkable thing about the wrapper classes is that the HRESULT testing is gone. Instead, the wrapper class translates any failed HRESULTs into a C++ exception (the `_com_error` class, to be precise). This lets the generated code use the method's [`retval`] variable as the actual return value, which eliminates a lot of temporary variables and output parameters.

The wrapper classes can immensely simplify writing COM clients, but they have their downsides. The biggest is that they require the use of C++ exceptions. Some projects aren't willing to pay the performance penalties that exception handling brings, and throwing exceptions means that developers have to pay very careful attention to exception safety.

Another downside to the wrappers for ATL developers is that ATL also has wrapper classes for COM interfaces (see Chapter 3, "ATL Smart Types") and BSTRs (see Chapter 2). The ATL wrappers are arguably better than the ones defined in `comdef.h`; for example, you can accidentally call the `Release()` method on an `ICalcPiPtr`, but if you use the ATL wrapper, that would be a compile error.

By default, you get the wrappers when you use `#import`. If you decide that you don't want them, or if for some reason they don't compile (which has been known to happen to at least one of your humble authors on very complex and strange typelibs), you can turn off the wrapper classes and just get straight interface definitions by using the `raw_interfaces_only` option.

ATL Server Web Projects

Without a doubt, the most dramatic recent addition to the ATL library is a suite of classes and tools collectively termed ATL Server. ATL Server accounts for nearly all of the fourfold increase in the overall size of ATL from ATL 3. This extensive class library provides comprehensive support for building web applications and XML web services. Although traditional ASP and the ASP.NET platform offer compelling and easy-to-use frameworks for web-based development, many application developers must still resort to raw ISAPI programming for applications that demand low-level control and maximum performance. ATL Server is designed to provide the performance and control of ISAPI with the feel and productivity of ASP. To that end, ATL Server follows the design model that has made conventional ATL development so effective over the years: namely small, fast, flexible code.

VS provides excellent wizard support for building web applications and web services. Walking through the numerous options available for ATL Server projects is actually quite insightful in understanding both the architecture and the sheer scope of the support provided. VS provides a wizard to help you get started building a web application with ATL Server. You launch this wizard by selecting the ATL Server Project option from the Visual C++ folder of the New Project dialog box.

The Project Settings tab shown in Figure 1.21 displays the selected options for generating and deploying the DLLs that comprise our web application.

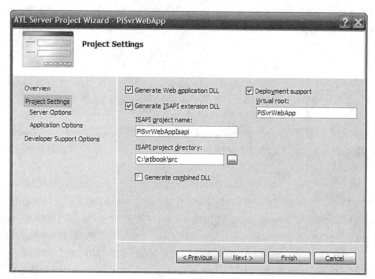

Figure 1.21   Project settings for ATL Server project

By default, ATL Server generates two projects in your solution: a web application DLL and an ISAPI extension DLL. ISAPI extension DLLs are loaded into the IIS process (`inetinfo.exe`) and logically sit between IIS and your web application DLL. Although ISAPI extensions can handle HTTP requests themselves, it is more common for them to provide generic infrastructure services such as thread pooling and caching, leaving web application DLLs to provide the real HTTP response logic. The ATL Server Project Wizard generates an ISAPI extension implementation that communicates with special functions in your web application called handlers. Figure 1.22 depicts this arrangement.

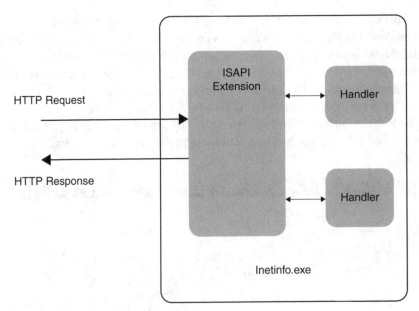

Figure 1.22   Basic ISAPI architecture

The Generate Combined DLL check box enables you to combine everything into a single DLL. This might be an appropriate option if the ISAPI extension is not intended to be used in other web applications. Conversely, developers can opt to leverage ATL Server's extensibility features by creating specialized ISAPI extensions with such options as custom thread pooling, highly tuned caching schemes, or optimized state management. These ISAPI extensions would then likely be reused across multiple web applications. Furthermore, keeping the ISAPI extension as a separate DLL gives us the flexibility to add handlers to our web application without restarting the web server (handler classes are discussed shortly). We'll leave the box unchecked for our first web application and allow VS to generate separate projects.

The Deployment Support check box enables the VS web-deployment tool. With this option selected, the Visual Studio build process automatically performs additional steps for properly deploying your web application so that it is served by IIS. You'll see in a moment how convenient these integrated deployment features can be. A brief word of caution at this point is in order, however. The default setting to enable deployment support causes VS to deploy the built project files in a subdirectory of your default web site, typically `<drive>:\inetpub\wwwroot`. In a real-world development scenario, it might be more desirable to deploy in a different directory on the machine (such as the project directory). Several steps are required to accomplish this, so for now, we're sticking with the default setting just so that we can focus on developing our application.

The Server Options tab shown in Figure 1.23 enables you to select various performance-oriented options for your web application. Several types of caching are supported, including support for arbitrary binary data (Blob cache), file caching, and database connection caching (Data source cache). Additionally, high-availability sites rely upon robust session-state management. ATL Server provides two mechanisms for persisting session state. The OLE DB-backed session-state services radio button includes support for persisting session state in a database (or other OLE DB data source), which is an option suited to applications running on web farms.

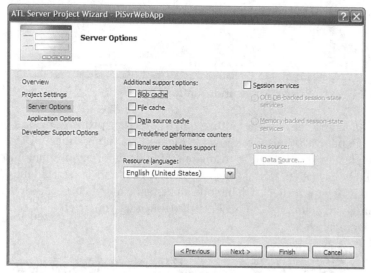

Figure 1.23   Server Options tab for ATL Server project

Figure 1.24 shows the selections available under the Application Options tab. Validation Support generates the necessary code for validating items in the HTTP request from the client, such as query parameters and form variables. Stencil Processing Support generates skeleton code for using HTML code templates known as server response files (SRF). These text files (also known as stencils) end with an .srf extension and intermix static HTML content with special replacement tags that your code processes to generate dynamic content at runtime. With stencil processing enabled, the wizard also allows you to select the locale and codepage for properly localizing responses. This simply inserts locale and codepage tags into the generated SRF file. (More on using SRF files comes shortly.) The Create as Web Service option also is discussed further in the following section. Because we're developing a web application, we leave this box unchecked for now.

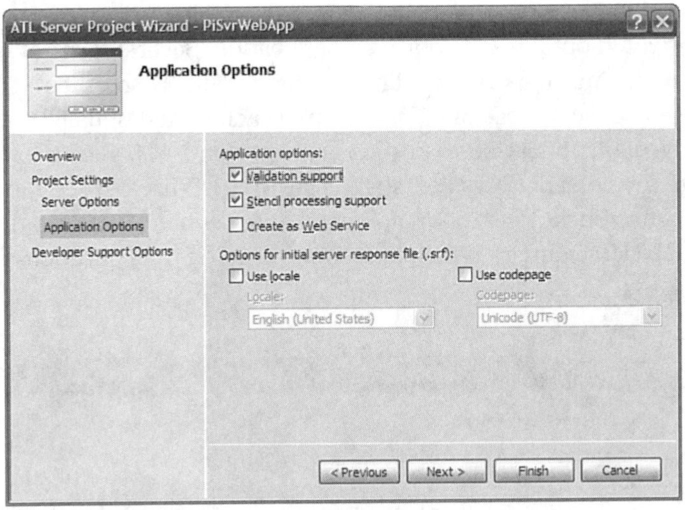

Figure 1.24   ATL Server Application Options tab

The remaining set of options for your ATL Server project appears under the Developer Support Options tab, shown in Figure 1.25. Generating TODO comments simply helps alert the developer to regions of code where additional implementation should be provided. If you select Custom Assert and Trace Handling Support, debug builds of your project will include an instance of the CDebugReportHook class, which can greatly simplify the process of debugging your web application—even from a remote machine.

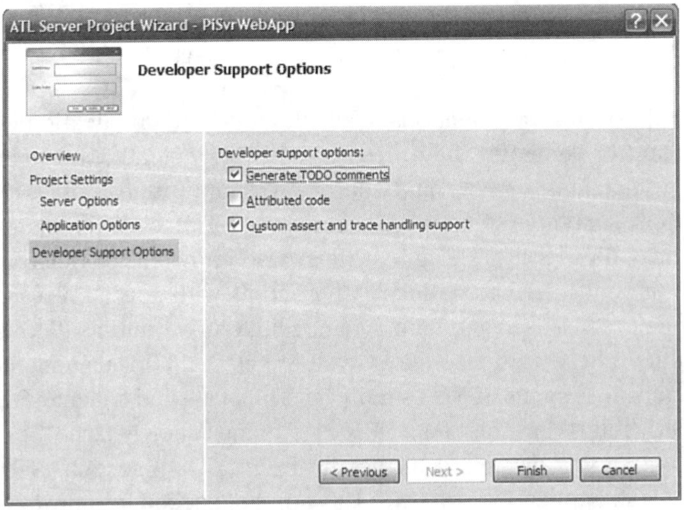

Figure 1.25   ATL Server Developer Support Options tab

Pressing Finish causes the wizard to generate a solution that contains two projects: one for your web application DLL (with a name matching the <projectname> entered in the New Project dialog box) and one for your ISAPI extension (with a name <projectname>Isapi). Let's take a look at the code generated in the ISAPI extension project. The generated .cpp file for our ISAPI extension looks like the following:

```cpp
class CPiSvrWebAppModule :
public CAtlDllModuleT<CPiSvrWebAppModule> {
public:
};


CPiSvrWebAppModule _AtlModule;


typedef CIsapiExtension<> ExtensionType;

// The ATL Server ISAPI extension
ExtensionType theExtension;

// Delegate ISAPI exports to theExtension
//
extern "C"
DWORD WINAPI HttpExtensionProc(LPEXTENSION_CONTROL_BLOCK lpECB) {
    return theExtension.HttpExtensionProc(lpECB);
}


extern "C"
BOOL WINAPI GetExtensionVersion(HSE_VERSION_INFO* pVer) {
    return theExtension.GetExtensionVersion(pVer);
}


extern "C" BOOL WINAPI TerminateExtension(DWORD dwFlags) {
    return theExtension.TerminateExtension(dwFlags);
}


// DLL Entry Point
//
extern "C"
BOOL WINAPI DllMain(HINSTANCE hInstance, DWORD dwReason,
    LPVOID lpReserved) {
    hInstance;
    return _AtlModule.DllMain(dwReason, lpReserved);
}
```

Because the ISAPI extension uses the services of ATL for object creation, it needs an ATL Module object. Also included in the generated code are implementations of the three well-known entry points IIS uses to communicate HTTP request information to the ISAPI extension: `HttpExtensionProc`, `GetExtensionVersion`, and `TerminateExtension`. These implementations simply delegate to a global instance of `CIsapiExtension`, whose definition is given here:

```
template <
  class ThreadPoolClass=CThreadPool<CIsapiWorker>,
  class CRequestStatClass=CNoRequestStats,
  class HttpUserErrorTextProvider=CDefaultErrorProvider,
  class WorkerThreadTraits=DefaultThreadTraits,
  class CPageCacheStats=CNoStatClass,
  class CStencilCacheStats=CNoStatClass
>
class CIsapiExtension :
  public IServiceProvider,
  public IIsapiExtension,
  public IRequestStats
{ ... }
```

This class provides boilerplate functionality for implementing the ISAPI extension. The template parameters to this class provide pluggable implementation for things such as threadpool management, error reporting, and caching statistics. By replacing this class in the `.cpp` file with your own `CIsapiExtension`-derived class and providing your own classes as template parameters, you can highly customize the behavior of your ISAPI extension. Techniques for doing this are presented in Chapter 13, "Hello, ATL Server." The default implementation of the ISAPI extension is suitable for our demonstration purposes here.

Most of the action takes place in the web application project. The wizard generated a skeleton SRF file for us and placed it in the project. The HTML editor integrated into VS provides a convenient means of viewing and manipulating the contents of this file.

```
<html>
{{ handler PiSvrWebApp.dll/Default }}
    <head>
    </head>
    <body>
        This is a test:   {{Hello}}<br>
    </body>
</html>
```

Items that appear within double braces indicate commands that are passed to the stencil processor. The {{handler}} command specifies the name of the DLL that houses our handler classes for processing replacement tags that appear in the SRF file. The /Default specifier identifies the default request-handler class to use for processing replacement tags. In general, an application DLL can contain multiple handler classes for processing SRF commands, and these classes can even exist in multiple DLLs. We use only a single handler class in a single application DLL, so all commands destined for handler classes will be routed to the same handler class. In the earlier wizard-generated skeleton, the {{Hello}} tag will be passed on to a handler class and replaced by the HTML produced from that class's replacement method.

ATL Server uses several macros to map commands in the SRF file to handler classes in our application DLL. The class definition generated for us in the <projectname>.h file shows how these macros are used:

```
class CPiSvrWebAppHandler
    : public CRequestHandlerT<CPiSvrWebAppHandler>
{
public:
    BEGIN_REPLACEMENT_METHOD_MAP(CPiSvrWebAppHandler)
        REPLACEMENT_METHOD_ENTRY("Hello", OnHello)
    END_REPLACEMENT_METHOD_MAP()

    HTTP_CODE ValidateAndExchange() {
        // Set the content-type
        m_HttpResponse.SetContentType("text/html");
        return HTTP_SUCCESS;
    }

protected:
    HTTP_CODE OnHello(void) {
        m_HttpResponse << "Hello World!";
        return HTTP_SUCCESS;
    }
};
```

The CRequestHandlerT base class provides the implementation for a request-handler class. It uses the REPLACEMENT_METHOD_MAP to map the strings in replacements in the SRF file to the appropriate functions in the class.

In addition to the request-handler class itself, in the handler DLL's .cpp file, you'll find this additional global map:

```
BEGIN_HANDLER_MAP()
    HANDLER_ENTRY("Default", CPiSvrWebAppHandler)
END_HANDLER_MAP()
```

The HANDLER_MAP is used to determine which class to use to process substitutions given with a particular name. In this case, the string "Default" as used in the handler tag in the SRF file is mapped to the CPiSvrWebAppHandler class. When the {{Hello}} tag is encountered in the SRF file, the OnHello method is invoked (via the REPLACEMENT_METHOD_MAP). It uses an instance of CHttpResponse declared as a member variable of the CRequestHandlerT to generate replacement text for the tag.

Let's modify the wizard-generated code to display pi to the number of digits specified in the query string of the HTTP request. First, we modify the SRF file to the following:

```
<html>
{{ handler PiSvrWebApp.dll/Default }}
    <head>
    </head>
    <body>
        PI = {{Pi}}<br>
    </body>
</html>
```

We then add a replacement method called OnPi to our existing handler class and apply the [tag_name] attribute to associate this method with the {{Pi}} replacement tag. In the implementation of the OnPi method, we retrieve the number of digits requested from the query string. The CHttpRequest class stored in m_HttpRequest member variable exposes an instance of CHttpRequestParams. This class provides a simple Lookup method to retrieve individual query parameters from the query string as name-value pairs, so processing requests such as the following is a simple matter:

```
http://localhost/PiSvrWebApp/PiSvrWebApp.srf?digits=6
```

The OnPi method implementation to field such requests follows:

```
class CPiSvrWebAppHandler {
...
    HTTP_CODE OnPi(void) {
        LPCSTR pszDigits = m_HttpRequest.m_QueryParams.Lookup("digits");
        long nDigits = 0;
        if (pszDigits)
```

```
        nDigits = atoi(pszDigits);
    BSTR bstrPi = NULL;
    CalcPi(nDigits, &bstrPi);

    m_HttpResponse << CW2A(bstrPi);
    return HTTP_SUCCESS;
    }
...
};
```

When we build our solution, VS performs a number of convenient tasks on our behalf. Because this is a web application, simply compiling the code into DLLs doesn't quite do the trick. The application must be properly deployed on our web server and registered with IIS. This involves creating a virtual directory, specifying an appropriate level of process isolation, and mapping the `.srf` file extension to our ISAPI extension DLL. Recall that when we created the project, we chose to include deployment support on the Project Settings tab of the ATL Server Project Wizard, shown previously in Figure 1.25. As a result, VS invokes the VCDeploy.exe utility to automatically perform all the necessary web-deployment steps for us. Simply compiling our solution in the normal manner places our application DLL, our ISAPI extension DLL, and our SRF file in a directory under our default web site, typically ending up in the directory `<drive>:\inetpub\wwwroot\<projectName>`. VS uses our web application project name as the virtual directory name, so browsing to `http://localhost/PiSvrWebApp/PiSvrWebApp.srf?digits=50` produces the result in Figure 1.26.

Figure 1.26   Web application for displaying pi to 50 digits

For more information about building ISAPI applications, including web services, with ATL Server, see Chapter 13, "Hello, ATL Server."

Summary

This chapter has been a whirlwind tour through some of the functionality of ATL that the wizards expose, as well as some of the basic interface implementations of ATL. Even with the wizards, it should be clear that ATL is no substitute for solid COM knowledge. You still need to know how to design and implement your interfaces. As you'll see throughout the rest of this book, you still have to know about interface pointers, reference counting, runtime type discovery, threading, persistence . . . the list goes on. ATL can help, but you still need to know COM.

It should also be clear that the wizard is not a substitute for intimate knowledge of ATL or web application development. For every tidbit of ATL information shown in this chapter, there are 10 more salient details, extensions, and pitfalls. And although the wizard saves you typing, it can't do everything. It can't make sure your design and implementation goals are met: That's up to you.

Strings and Text

Strings come in a number of different character sets. COM components often need to use multiple character sets and occasionally need to convert from one set to another. ATL provides a number of string conversion classes that convert from one character set to another, if necessary, and do nothing when they are not needed.

The CComBSTR class is a smart string class. This class properly allocates, copies, and frees a string according to the BSTR string semantics. CComBSTR instances can be used in most, but not all, of the places you would use a BSTR.

The CString class is a new addition to ATL, with roots in MFC. This class handles allocation, copying, formatting, and offers a host of advanced string-processing features. It can manage ANSI and Unicode data, and convert strings to and from BSTRs for use in processing Automation method parameters. With CString, you can even control and customize the way memory is managed for the class's string data.

String Data Types, Conversion Classes, and Helper Functions

A Review of Text Data Types

The text data type is somewhat of a pain to deal with in C++ programming. The main problem is that there isn't just one text data type; there are many of them. I use the term *text data type* here in the general sense of an array of characters. Often, different operating systems and programming languages introduce additional semantics for an array of characters (for example, NUL character termination or a length prefix) before they consider an array of characters a text string.

When you select a text data type, you must make a number of decisions. First, you must decide what type of characters constitute the array. Some operating systems require you to use ANSI characters when you pass a string (such as a file name) to the operating system. Some operating systems prefer that you use Unicode characters but will accept ANSI characters. Other operating systems require you to use EBCDIC characters. Stranger character sets are in use as well, such as the Multi/Double Byte Character Sets (MBCS/DBCS); this book largely doesn't discuss those details.

Second, you must consider what character set you want to use to manipulate text within your program. No requirement states that your source code must use the same character set that the operating system running your program prefers. Clearly, it's more convenient when both use the same character set, but a program and the operating system can use different character sets. You "simply" must convert all text strings going to and coming from the operating system.

Third, you must determine the length of a text string. Some languages, such as C and C++, and some operating systems, such as Windows 9x/NT/XP and UNIX, use a terminating NUL character to delimit the end of a text string. Other languages, such as the Microsoft Visual Basic interpreter, Microsoft Java virtual machine, and Pascal, prefer an explicit length prefix specifying the number of characters in the text string.

Finally, in practice, a text string presents a resource-management issue. Text strings typically vary in length. This makes it difficult to allocate memory for the string on the stack—and the text string might not fit on the stack at all. Therefore, text strings are often dynamically allocated. Of course, this means that a text string must be freed eventually. Resource management introduces the idea of an owner of a text string. Only the owner frees the string—and frees it only once. Ownership becomes quite important when you pass a text string between components.

To make matters worse, two COM objects can reside on two different computers running two different operating systems that prefer two different character sets for a text string. For example, you can write one COM object in Visual Basic and run it on the Windows XP operating system. You might pass a text string to another COM object written in C++ running on an IBM mainframe. Clearly, we need some standard text data type that all COM objects in a heterogeneous environment can understand.

COM uses the OLECHAR character data type. A COM text string is a NUL-character-terminated array of OLECHAR characters; a pointer to such a string is an LPOLESTR.[1] As a rule, a text string parameter to a COM interface method should be of type LPOLESTR. When a method doesn't change the string, the parameter should be of type LPCOLESTR—that is, a constant pointer to an array of OLECHAR characters.

Frequently, though not always, the OLECHAR type isn't the same as the characters you use when writing your code. Sometimes, though not always, the OLECHAR type isn't the same as the characters you must provide when passing a text string to the operating system. This means that, depending on context, sometimes you

---

[1] Note that the actual underlying character data type for OLECHAR on one operating system can be different from the underlying character data type for OLECHAR on a different operating system. The COM remoting infrastructure performs any necessary character set conversion during marshaling and unmarshaling. Therefore, a COM component always receives text in its expected OLECHAR format.

need to convert a text string from one character set to another—and sometimes you won't.

Unfortunately, a change in compiler options (for example, a Windows XP Unicode build or a Windows CE build) can change this context. As a result, code that previously didn't need to convert a string might require conversion, or vice versa. You don't want to rewrite all string-manipulation code each time you change a compiler option. Therefore, ATL provides a number of string-conversion macros that convert a text string from one character set to another and are sensitive to the context in which you invoke the conversion.

Windows Character Data Types

Now let's focus specifically on the Windows platform. Windows-based COM components typically use a mix of four text data types:

- **Unicode.** A specification for representing a character as a "wide-character," 16-bit multilingual character code. The Windows NT/XP operating system uses the Unicode character set internally. All characters used in modern computing worldwide, including technical symbols and special publishing characters, can be represented uniquely in Unicode. The fixed character size simplifies programming when using international character sets. In C/C++, you represent a wide-character string as a `wchar_t` array; a pointer to such a string is a `wchar_t*`.

- **MBCS/DBCS.** The Multi-Byte Character Set is a mixed-width character set in which some characters consist of more than 1 byte. The Windows $9x$ operating systems, in general, use the MBCS to represent characters. The Double-Byte Character Set (DBCS) is a specific type of multibyte character set. It includes some characters that consist of 1 byte and some characters that consist of 2 bytes to represent the symbols for one specific locale, such as the Japanese, Chinese, and Korean languages.

  In C/C++, you represent an MBCS/DBCS string as an `unsigned char` array; a pointer to such a string is an `unsigned char*`. Sometimes a character is one `unsigned char` in length; sometimes, it's more than one. This is loads of fun to deal with, especially when you're trying to back up through a string. In Visual C++, MBCS always means DBCS. Character sets wider than 2 bytes are not supported.

- **ANSI.** You can represent all characters in the English language, as well as many Western European languages, using only 8 bits. Versions of Windows that support such languages use a degenerate case of MBCS, called the Microsoft Windows ANSI character set, in which no multibyte characters are present.

The Microsoft Windows ANSI character set, which is essentially ISO 8859/*x* plus additional characters, was originally based on an ANSI draft standard.

The ANSI character set maps the letters and numerals in the same manner as ASCII. However, ANSI does not support control characters and maps many symbols, including accented letters, that are not mapped in standard ASCII. All Windows fonts are defined in the ANSI character set. This is also called the Single-Byte Character Set (SBCS), for symmetry.

In C/C++, you represent an ANSI string as a char array; a pointer to such a string is a char*. A character is always one char in length. By default, a char is a signed char in Visual C++. Because MBCS characters are unsigned and ANSI characters are, by default, signed characters, expressions can evaluate differently when using ANSI characters, compared to using MBCS characters.

- **TCHAR/_TCHAR.** This is a Microsoft-specific generic-text data type that you can map to a Unicode character, an MBCS character, or an ANSI character using compile-time options. You use this character type to write generic code that can be compiled for any of the three character sets. This simplifies code development for international markets. The C runtime library defines the _TCHAR type, and the Windows operating system defines the TCHAR type; they are synonymous.

  tchar.h, a Microsoft-specific C runtime library header file, defines the generic-text data type _TCHAR. ANSI C/C++ compiler compliance requires implementer-defined names to be prefixed by an underscore. When you do not define the __STDC__ preprocessor symbol (by default, this macro is not defined in Visual C++), you indicate that you don't require ANSI compliance. In this case, the tchar.h header file also defines the symbol TCHAR as another alias for the generic-text data type if it isn't already defined. winnt.h, a Microsoft-specific Win32 operating system header file, defines the generic-text data type TCHAR. This header file is operating system specific, so the symbol names don't need the underscore prefix.

Win32 APIs and Strings

Each Win32 API that requires a string has two versions: one that requires a Unicode argument and another that requires an MBCS argument. On a non-MBCS-enabled version of Windows, the MBCS version of an API expects an ANSI argument. For example, the SetWindowText API doesn't really exist. There are actually two functions: SetWindowTextW, which expects a Unicode string argument, and SetWindow-TextA, which expects an MBCS/ANSI string argument.

The Windows NT/2000/XP operating systems internally use only Unicode strings. Therefore, when you call SetWindowTextA on Windows NT/2000/XP, the function translates the specified string to Unicode and then calls `SetWindowTextW`. The Windows $9x$ operating systems do not support Unicode directly. The `SetWindowTextA` function on the Windows $9x$ operating systems does the work, while `SetWindowTextW` returns an error. The MSLU library from Microsoft[2] provides implementations of almost all the Unicode functions on Win$9x$.

This gives you a difficult choice. You could write a performance-optimized component using Unicode character strings that runs on Windows 2000 but not on Windows $9x$. You could use MSLU for Unicode strings on both families and lose performance on Windows $9x$. You could write a more general component using MBCS/ANSI character strings that runs on both operating systems but *not* optimally on Windows 2000. Alternatively, you could hedge your bets by writing source code that enables you to decide at compile time what character set to support.

A little coding discipline and some preprocessor magic let you code as if there were a single API called `SetWindowText` that expects a `TCHAR` string argument. You specify at compile time which kind of component you want to build. For example, you write code that calls `SetWindowText` and specifies a `TCHAR` buffer. When compiling a component as Unicode, you call `SetWindowTextW`; the argument is a `wchar_t` buffer. When compiling an MBCS/ANSI component, you call `SetWindowTextA`; the argument is a `char` buffer.

When you write a Windows-based COM component, you should typically use the `TCHAR` character type to represent characters used by the component internally. Additionally, you should use it for all characters used in interactions with the operating system. Similarly, you should use the `TEXT` or `_TEXT` macro to surround every literal character or string.

`tchar.h` defines the functionally equivalent macros `_T` , `__T`, and `_TEXT`, which all compile a character or string literal as a generic-text character or literal. `winnt.h` also defines the functionally equivalent macros `TEXT` and `__TEXT`, which are yet more synonyms for `_T`, `__T`, and `_TEXT`. (There's nothing like five ways to do exactly the same thing.) The examples in this chapter use `__TEXT` because it's defined in `winnt.h`. I actually prefer `_T` because it's less clutter in my source code.

An operating-system-agnostic coding approach favors including `tchar.h` and using the `_TCHAR` generic-text data type because that's somewhat less tied to the Windows operating systems. However, we're discussing building components with text handling optimized at compile time for specific versions of the Windows operating systems. This argues that we should use `TCHAR`, the type defined in `winnt.h`. Plus, `TCHAR` isn't as jarring to the eyes as `_TCHAR` and it's easier to type. Most code already implicitly includes the `winnt.h` header file via `windows.h`, and you must

---

[2] More information on MSLU is available at http://www.microsoft.com/globaldev/handson/dev/mslu_announce.mspx (http://tinysells.com/49).

explicitly include `tchar.h`. All sorts of good reasons support using TCHAR, so the examples in this book use this as the generic-text data type.

This means that you can compile specialized versions of the component for different markets or for performance reasons. These types and macros are defined in the `winnt.h` header file.

You also must use a different set of string runtime library functions when manipulating strings of TCHAR characters. The familiar functions `strlen`, `strcpy`, and so on operate only on `char` characters. The less familiar functions `wcslen`, `wcscpy`, and so on work on `wchar_t` characters. Moreover, the totally strange functions `_mbslen`, `_mbscpy`, and so on work on multibyte characters. Because TCHAR characters are sometimes `wchar_t`, sometimes `char`-holding ANSI characters, and sometimes `char`-holding (nominally `unsigned`) multibyte characters, you need an equivalent set of runtime library functions that work with TCHAR characters.

The `tchar.h` header file defines a number of useful generic-text mappings for string-handling functions. These functions expect TCHAR parameters, so all their function names use the `_tcs` (the `_t` character set) prefix. For example, `_tcslen` is equivalent to the C runtime library `strlen` function. The `_tcslen` function expects TCHAR characters, whereas the `strlen` function expects `char` characters.

Controlling Generic-Text Mapping Using the Preprocessor

Two preprocessor symbols and two macros control the mapping of the TCHAR data type to the underlying character type the application uses.

- **UNICODE/_UNICODE.** The header files for the Windows operating system APIs use the UNICODE preprocessor symbol. The C/C++ runtime library header files use the _UNICODE preprocessor symbol. Typically, you define either both symbols or neither of them. When you compile with the symbol _UNICODE defined, `tchar.h` maps all TCHAR characters to `wchar_t` characters. The _T, __T, and _TEXT macros prefix each character or string literal with a capital L (creating a Unicode character or literal, respectively). When you compile with the symbol UNICODE defined, `winnt.h` maps all TCHAR characters to `wchar_t` characters. The TEXT and __TEXT macros prefix each character or string literal with a capital L (creating a Unicode character or literal, respectively). The _tcsXXX functions are mapped to the corresponding _wcsXXX functions.

- **_MBCS.** When you compile with the symbol _MBCS defined, all TCHAR characters map to `char` characters, and the preprocessor removes all the _T and __TEXT macro variations. It leaves the character or literal unchanged (creating an MBCS character or literal, respectively). The _tcsXXX functions are mapped to the corresponding _mbsXXX versions.

- **None of the above.** When you compile with neither symbol defined, all TCHAR characters map to char characters and the preprocessor removes all the _T and __TEXT macro variations, leaving the character or literal unchanged (creating an ANSI character or literal, respectively). The _tcsXXX functions are mapped to the corresponding strXXX functions.

You write generic-text-compatible code by using the generic-text data types and functions. An example of reversing and concatenating to a generic-text string follows:

```
TCHAR *reversedString, *sourceString, *completeString;
reversedString = _tcsrev (sourceString);
completeString = _tcscat (reversedString, __TEXT("suffix"));
```

When you compile the code without defining any preprocessor symbols, the preprocessor produces this output:

```
char *reversedString, *sourceString, *completeString;
reversedString = _strrev (sourceString);
completeString = strcat (reversedString, "suffix");
```

When you compile the code after defining the _UNICODE preprocessor symbol, the preprocessor produces this output:

```
wchar_t *reversedString, *sourceString, *completeString;
reversedString = _wcsrev (sourceString);
completeString = wcscat (reversedString, L"suffix");
```

When you compile the code after defining the _MBCS preprocessor symbol, the preprocessor produces this output:

```
char *reversedString, *sourceString, *completeString;
reversedString = _mbsrev (sourceString);
completeString = _mbscat (reversedString, "suffix");
```

COM Character Data Types

COM uses two character types:

- **OLECHAR.** The character type COM uses on the operating system for which you compile your source code. For Win32 operating systems, this is the wchar_t character type.[3] For Win16 operating systems, this is the char character type. For the Mac OS, this is the char character type. For the Solaris OS, this is the wchar_t character type. For the as yet unknown operating system, this is who knows what. Let's just pretend there is an abstract data type called OLECHAR. COM uses it. Don't rely on it mapping to any specific underlying data type.

- **BSTR.** A specialized string type some COM components use. A BSTR is a length-prefixed array of OLECHAR characters with numerous special semantics.

Now let's complicate things a bit. You want to write code for which you can select, at compile time, the type of characters it uses. Therefore, you're manipulating strictly TCHAR strings internally. You also want to call a COM method and pass it the same strings. You must pass the method either an OLECHAR string or a BSTR string, depending on its signature. The strings your component uses might or might not be in the correct character format, depending on your compilation options. This is a job for Supermacro!

ATL String-Conversion Classes

ATL provides a number of string-conversion classes that convert, when necessary, among the various character types described previously. The classes perform no conversion and, in fact, do nothing, when the compilation options make the source and destination character types identical. Seven different classes in atlconv.h implement the real conversion logic, but this header also uses a number of typedefs and preprocessor #define statements to make using these converter classes syntactically more convenient.

These class names use a number of abbreviations for the various character data types:

- **T** represents a pointer to the Win32 TCHAR character type—an LPTSTR parameter.
- **W** represents a pointer to the Unicode wchar_t character type—an LPWSTR parameter.
- **A** represents a pointer to the MBCS/ANSI char character type—an LPSTR parameter.
- **OLE** represents a pointer to the COM OLECHAR character type—an LPOLESTR parameter.
- **C** represents the C/C++ const modifier.

---

[3] Actually, you can change the Win32 OLECHAR data type from the default wchar_t (which COM uses internally) to char by defining the preprocessor symbol OLE2ANSI. This lets you pretend that COM uses ANSI. MFC once used this feature, but it no longer does and neither should you.

All class names use the form C<source-abbreviation>2<destination-abbreviation>. For example, the CA2W class converts an LPSTR to an LPWSTR. When there is a C in the name (not including the first C—that stands for "class"), add a const modification to the following abbreviation; for example, the CT2CW class converts a LPTSTR to a LPCWSTR.

The actual class behavior depends on which preprocessor symbols you define (see Table 2.1). Note that the ATL conversion classes and macros treat OLE and W as equivalent.

Table 2.1. Character Set Preprocessor Symbols

Preprocessor Symbol Defined	T Becomes . . .	OLE Becomes . . .
None	A	W
_UNICODE	W	W

Table 2.2 lists the ATL string-conversion macros.

Table 2.2. ATL String-Conversion Classes

CA2W	COLE2T	CT2CA	CT2W	CW2T
CA2WEX	COLE2TEX	CT2CAEX	CT2WEX	CW2TEX
CA2T	COLE2CT	CT2OLE	CT2CW	CW2CT
CA2TEX	COLE2CTEX	CT2OLEEX	CT2CWEX	CW2CTEX
CA2CT	CT2A	CT2COLE	CW2A	
CA2CTEX	CT2AEX	CT2COLEEX	CW2AEX	

As you can see, no BSTR conversion classes are listed in Table 2.2. The next section of this chapter introduces the CComBSTR class as the preferred mechanism for dealing with BSTR-type conversions.

When you look inside the atlconv.h header file, you'll see that many of the definitions distill down to a fairly small set of six actual classes. For instance, when _UNICODE is defined, CT2A becomes CW2A, which is itself typedef'd to the CW2AEX template class. The type definition merely applies the default template parameters to CW2AEX. Additionally, all the previous class names always map OLE to W, so COLE2T becomes CW2T, which is defined as CW2W under Unicode builds. Because the source and destination types for CW2W are the same, this class performs no conversions. Ultimately, the only six classes defined are the template classes CA2AEX, CA2CAEX, CA2WEX, CW2AEX, CW2CWEX, and CW2WEX. Only CA2WEX and CW2AEX have different source and destination types, so these are the only two classes doing any real work. Thus, our expansive list of conversion classes in Table 2.2 has distilled down to only two interesting ones. These two classes are both defined and implemented similarly, so we look at only CA2WEX to glean an understanding of how they both work.

```
template< int t_nBufferLength = 128 >
class CA2WEX {
    CA2WEX( LPCSTR psz );
    CA2WEX( LPCSTR psz, UINT nCodePage );

    ...
public:
    LPWSTR m_psz;
    wchar_t m_szBuffer[t_nBufferLength];
    ...
};
```

The class definition is actually pretty simple. The template parameter specifies the size of a fixed static buffer to hold the string data. This means that most string-conversion operations can be performed without allocating any dynamic storage. If the requested string to convert exceeds the number of characters passed as an argument to the template, CA2WEX uses malloc to allocate additional storage.

Two constructors are provided for CA2WEX. The first constructor accepts an LPCSTR and uses the Win32 API function MultiByteToWideChar to perform the conversion. By default, the class uses the ANSI code page for the current thread's locale to perform the conversion. The second constructor can be used to specify an alternate code page that governs how the conversion is performed. This value is passed directly to MultiByteToWideChar, so see the online documentation for details on code pages accepted by the various Win32 character conversion functions.

The simplest way to use this converter class is to accept the default value for the buffer size parameter. Thus, ATL provides a simple typedef to facilitate this:

```
typedef CA2WEX<> CA2W;
```

To use this converter class, you need to write only simple code such as the following:

```
void PutName (LPCWSTR lpwszName);

void RegisterName (LPCSTR lpsz) {
    PutName (CA2W(lpsz));
}
```

Two other use cases are also common in practice:

1. Receiving a generic-text string and passing to a method that expects an OLESTR as input
2. Receiving an OLESTR and passing it to a method that expects a generic-text string

The conversion classes are easily employed to deal with these cases:

```
void PutAddress(LPOLESTR lpszAddress);

void RegisterAddress(LPTSTR lpsz) {
    PutAddress(CT2OLE(lpsz));
}

void PutNickName(LPTSTR lpszName);

void RegisterAddress(LPOLESTR lpsz) {
    PutNickName(COLE2T(lpsz));
}
```

A Note on Memory Management

As convenient as the conversion classes are, you can run into some nasty pitfalls if you use them incorrectly. The conversion classes allocate the memory for the converted text automatically and clean it up in the class destructor. This is useful because you don't have to worry about buffer management. However, it also means that code like this is a crash waiting to happen:

```
LPOLESTR ConvertString(LPTSTR lpsz) {
    return CT2OLE(lpsz);
}
```

You've just returned either a pointer to the stack of the called function (which is trashed when the function returns) if the string was short, or a pointer to an array on the heap that will be deallocated before the function returns.

The worst part is that, depending on your macro selection, the code might work just fine but will crash when you switch from ANSI to Unicode for the first time (usually two days before ship). To avoid this, make sure that you copy the converted string to a separate buffer (or use a string class) first if you need it for more than a single expression.

ATL String-Helper Functions

Sometimes you want to copy a string of OLECHAR characters. You also happen to know that OLECHAR characters are wide characters on the Win32 operating system. When writing a Win32 version of your component, you might call the Win32 operating system function lstrcpyW, which copies wide characters. Unfortunately, Windows NT/2000, which supports Unicode, implements lstrcpyW, but Windows 95 does not. A component that uses the lstrcpyW API doesn't work correctly on Windows 95.

Instead of lstrcpyW, use the ATL string-helper function ocscpy to copy an OLECHAR character string. It works properly on both Windows NT/2000 and Windows 95. The ATL string-helper function ocslen returns the length of an OLECHAR string. This is nice for symmetry, although the lstrlenW function it replaces does work on both operating systems.

```
OLECHAR* ocscpy(LPOLESTR dest, LPCOLESTR src);
size_t ocslen(LPCOLESTR s);
```

Similarly, the Win32 CharNextW operating system function doesn't work on Windows 95, so ATL provides a CharNextO string-helper function that increments an OLECHAR* by one character and returns the next character pointer. It does not increment the pointer beyond a NUL termination character.

```
LPOLESTR CharNextO(LPCOLESTR lp);
```

ATL String-Conversion Macros

The string-conversion classes discussed previously were introduced in ATL 7. ATL 3 (and code written with ATL 3) used a set of macros instead. In fact, these macros are still in use in the ATL code base. For example, this code is in the atlctl.h header:

```
STDMETHOD(Help)(LPCOLESTR pszHelpDir) {
    T* pT = static_cast<T*>(this);
    USES_CONVERSION;
```

```
ATLTRACE(atlTraceControls,2,
  _T("IPropertyPageImpl::Help\n"));
CComBSTR szFullFileName(pszHelpDir);
CComHeapPtr<OLECHAR>
  pszFileName(LoadStringHelper(pT->m_dwHelpFileID));
if (pszFileName == NULL)
  return E_OUTOFMEMORY;
szFullFileName.Append(OLESTR("\\"));
szFullFileName.Append(pszFileName);
WinHelp(pT->m_hWnd, OLE2CT(szFullFileName),
    HELP_CONTEXTPOPUP, NULL);
return S_OK;
}
```

The macros behave much like the conversion classes, minus the leading C in the macro name. So, to convert from tchar to olechar, you use T2OLE(s).

Two major differences arise between the macros and the conversion classes. First, the macros require some local variables to work; the USES_CONVERSION macro is required in any function that uses the conversion macros. (It declares these local variables.) The second difference is the location of the conversion buffer.

In the conversion classes, the buffer is stored either as a member variable on the stack (if the buffer is small) or on the heap (if the buffer is large). The conversion macros always use the stack. They call the runtime function _alloca, which allocates extra space on the local stack.

Although it is fast, _alloca has some serious downsides. The stack space isn't freed until the function exits, which means that if you do conversion in a loop, you might end up blowing out your stack space. Another nasty problem is that if you use the conversion macros inside a C++ catch block, the _alloca call messes up the exception-tracking information on the stack and you crash.[4]

The ATL team apparently took two swipes at improving the conversion macros. The final solution is the conversion classes. However, a second set of conversion macros exists: the _EX flavor. These are used much like the original conversion macros; you put USES_CONVERSION_EX at the top of the function. The macros have an _EX suffix, as in T2A_EX. The _EX macros are different, however: They take two parameters, not one. The first parameter is the buffer to convert from as usual. The second parameter is a threshold value. If the converted buffer is smaller than this threshold, the memory is allocated via _alloca. If the buffer is larger, it is allocated on the heap instead. So, these macros give you a chance to avoid the stack overflow.

---

[4] For this reason, the _alloca function is deprecated in favor of _malloca, but ATL still uses _alloca.

(They still won't help you in a `catch` block.) The ATL code uses the `_EX` macros extensively; the previous example is the only one left that still uses the old macros.

We don't go into the details of either macro set here; the conversion classes are much safer to use and are preferred for new code. We mention them only so that you know what you're looking at if you see them in older code or the ATL sources themselves.

The CComBSTR Smart BSTR Class

A Review of the COM String Data Type: BSTR

COM is a language-neutral, hardware-architecture-neutral model. Therefore, it needs a language-neutral, hardware-architecture-neutral text data type. COM defines a generic text data type, `OLECHAR`, that represents the text data COM uses on a specific platform. On most platforms, including all 32-bit Windows platforms, the `OLECHAR` data type is a typedef for the `wchar_t` data type. That is, on most platforms, the COM text data type is equivalent to the C/C++ wide-character data type, which contains Unicode characters. On some platforms, such as the 16-bit Windows operating system, `OLECHAR` is a `typedef` for the standard C `char` data type, which contains ANSI characters. Generally, you should define all string parameters used in a COM interface as `OLECHAR*` arguments.

COM also defines a text data type called `BSTR`. A `BSTR` is a length-prefixed string of `OLECHAR` characters. Most interpretive environments prefer length-prefixed strings for performance reasons. For example, a length-prefixed string does not require time-consuming scans for a `NUL` character terminator to determine the length of a string. Actually, the `NUL`-character-terminated string is a language-specific concept that was originally unique to the C/C++ language. The Microsoft Visual Basic interpreter, the Microsoft Java virtual machine, and most scripting languages, such as VBScript and JScript, internally represent a string as a `BSTR`.

Therefore, when you pass a string to or receive a string from a method parameter to an interface defined by a C/C++ component, you'll often use the `OLECHAR*` data type. However, if you need to use an interface defined by another language, frequently string parameters will be the `BSTR` data type. The `BSTR` data type has a number of poorly documented semantics, which makes using `BSTR`s tedious and error prone for C++ developers.

A `BSTR` has the following attributes:

- A `BSTR` is a pointer to a length-prefixed array of `OLECHAR` characters.
- A `BSTR` is a pointer data type. It points at the first character in the array. The length prefix is stored as an integer immediately preceding the first character in the array.

- The array of characters is NUL character terminated.
- The length prefix is in bytes, not characters, and does not include the terminating NUL character.
- The array of characters may contain embedded NUL characters.
- A BSTR must be allocated and freed using the SysAllocString and SysFree-String family of functions.
- A NULL BSTR pointer implies an empty string.
- A BSTR is not reference counted; therefore, two references to the same string content must refer to separate BSTRs. In other words, copying a BSTR implies making a duplicate string, not simply copying the pointer.

With all these special semantics, it would be useful to encapsulate these details in a reusable class. ATL provides such a class: CComBSTR.

The CComBSTR Class

The CComBSTR class is an ATL utility class that is a useful encapsulation for the COM string data type, BSTR. The atlcomcli.h file contains the definition of the CComBSTR class. The only state maintained by the class is a single public member variable, m_str, of type BSTR.

```
/////////////////////////////////////////////////////
// CComBSTR

class CComBSTR {
public:
  BSTR m_str;
...
} ;
```

Constructors and Destructor

Eight constructors are available for CComBSTR objects. The default constructor simply initializes the m_str variable to NULL, which is equivalent to a BSTR that represents an empty string. The destructor destroys any BSTR contained in the m_str variable by calling SysFreeString. The SysFreeString function explicitly documents that the function simply returns when the input parameter is NULL so that the destructor can run on an empty object without a problem.

```
CComBSTR() { m_str = NULL; }
~CComBSTR() { ::SysFreeString(m_str); }
```

Later in this section, you will learn about numerous convenience methods that the CComBSTR class provides. However, one of the most compelling reasons for using the class is so that the destructor frees the internal BSTR at the appropriate time, so you don't have to free a BSTR explicitly. This is exceptionally convenient during times such as stack frame unwinding when locating an exception handler.

Probably the most frequently used constructor initializes a CComBSTR object from a pointer to a NUL-character-terminated array of OLECHAR characters—or, as it's more commonly known, an LPCOLESTR.

```
CComBSTR(LPCOLESTR pSrc) {
    if (pSrc == NULL) m_str = NULL;
    else {
        m_str = ::SysAllocString(pSrc);
        if (m_str == NULL)
                AtlThrow(E_OUTOFMEMORY);
    }
}
```

You invoke the preceding constructor when you write code such as the following:

```
CComBSTR str1 (OLESTR ("This is a string of OLECHARs")) ;5
```

The previous constructor copies characters until it finds the end-of-string NULL character terminator. When you want some lesser number of characters copied, such as the prefix to a string, or when you want to copy from a string that contains embedded NULL characters, you must explicitly specify the number of characters to copy. In this case, use the following constructor:

```
CComBSTR(int nSize, LPCOLESTR sz);
```

This constructor creates a BSTR with room for the number of characters specified by nSize; copies the specified number of characters, including any embedded NULL characters, from sz; and then appends a terminating NUL character. When sz is

---

[5] The OLESTR macro is similar to the _T macros; it guarantees that the string literal is of the proper type for an OLE string, depending on compile options.

NULL, SysAllocStringLen skips the copy step, creating an uninitialized BSTR of the specified size. You invoke the preceding constructor when you write code such as the following:

```
// str2 contains "This is a string"
CComBSTR str2 (16, OLESTR ("This is a string of OLECHARs"));

// Allocates an uninitialized BSTR with room for 64 characters
CComBSTR str3 (64, (LPCOLESTR) NULL);

// Allocates an uninitialized BSTR with room for 64 characters
CComBSTR str4 (64);
```

The CComBSTR class provides a special constructor for the str3 example in the preceding code, which doesn't require you to provide the NULL argument. The preceding str4 example shows its use. Here's the constructor:

```
CComBSTR(int nSize) {
    ...
    m_str = ::SysAllocStringLen(NULL, nSize);
    ...
}
```

One odd semantic feature of a BSTR is that a NULL pointer is a valid value for an empty BSTR string. For example, Visual Basic considers a NULL BSTR to be equivalent to a pointer to an empty string—that is, a string of zero length in which the first character is the terminating NUL character. To put it symbolically, Visual Basic considers IF p = "", where p is a BSTR set to NULL, to be true. The SysStringLen API properly implements the checks; CComBSTR provides the Length method as a wrapper:

```
unsigned int Length() const { return ::SysStringLen(m_str); }
```

You can also use the following copy constructor to create and initialize a CComBSTR object to be equivalent to an already initialized CComBSTR object:

```
CComBSTR(const CComBSTR& src) {
    m_str = src.Copy();
    ...
}
```

In the following code, creating the str5 variable invokes the preceding copy constructor to initialize their respective objects:

```
CComBSTR str1 (OLESTR("This is a string of OLECHARs")) ;
CComBSTR str5 = str1 ;
```

Note that the preceding copy constructor calls the Copy method on the source CComBSTR object. The Copy method makes a copy of its string and returns the new BSTR. Because the Copy method allocates the new BSTR using the length of the existing BSTR and copies the string contents for the specified length, the Copy method properly copies a BSTR that contains embedded NUL characters.

```
BSTR Copy() const {
    if (!*this) { return NULL; }
    return ::SysAllocStringByteLen((char*)m_str,
        ::SysStringByteLen(m_str));
}
```

Two constructors initialize a CComBSTR object from an LPCSTR string. The single argument constructor expects a NUL-terminated LPCSTR string. The two-argument constructor permits you to specify the length of the LPCSTR string. These two constructors are functionally equivalent to the two previously discussed constructors that accept an LPCOLESTR parameter. The following two constructors expect ANSI characters and create a BSTR that contains the equivalent string in OLECHAR characters:

```
CComBSTR(LPCSTR pSrc) {
    ...
    m_str = A2WBSTR(pSrc);
    ...
}
CComBSTR(int nSize, LPCSTR sz) {
    ...
    m_str = A2WBSTR(sz, nSize);
    ...
}
```

The final constructor is an odd one. It takes an argument that is a GUID and produces a string containing the string representation of the GUID.

```
CComBSTR(REFGUID src);
```

This constructor is quite useful when building strings used during component registration. In a number of situations, you need to write the string representation of a GUID to the Registry. Some code that uses this constructor follows:

```
// Define a GUID as a binary constant
static const GUID GUID_Sample = { 0x8a44e110, 0xf134, 0x11d1,
    { 0x96, 0xb1, 0xBA, 0xDB, 0xAD, 0xBA, 0xDB, 0xAD } };

// Convert the binary GUID to its string representation
CComBSTR str6 (GUID_Sample) ;
// str6 contains "{8A44E110-F134-11d1-96B1-BADBADBADBAD}"
```

Assignment

The CComBSTR class defines three assignment operators. The first one initializes a CComBSTR object using a different CComBSTR object. The second one initializes a CComBSTR object using an LPCOLESTR pointer. The third one initializes the object using a LPCSTR pointer. The following operator=() method initializes one CComBSTR object from another CComBSTR object:

```
CComBSTR& operator=(const CComBSTR& src) {
    if (m_str != src.m_str) {
        ::SysFreeString(m_str);
        m_str = src.Copy();
        if (!!src && !*this) { AtlThrow(E_OUTOFMEMORY); }
    }
    return *this;
}
```

Note that this assignment operator uses the Copy method, discussed a little later in this section, to make an exact copy of the specified CComBSTR instance. You invoke this operator when you write code such as the following:

```
CComBSTR str1 (OLESTR("This is a string of OLECHARs"));
CComBSTR str7 ;

str7 = str1; // str7 contains "This is a string of OLECHARs"
str7 = str7; // This is a NOP. Assignment operator
             // detects this case
```

The second operator=() method initializes one CComBSTR object from an LPCOLESTR pointer to a NUL-character-terminated string.

```
CComBSTR& operator=(LPCOLESTR pSrc) {
    if (pSrc != m_str) {
        ::SysFreeString(m_str);
        if (pSrc != NULL) {
            m_str = ::SysAllocString(pSrc);
            if (!*this) { AtlThrow(E_OUTOFMEMORY); }
        } else {
            m_str = NULL;
        }
    }
    return *this;
}
```

Note that this assignment operator uses the SysAllocString function to allocate a BSTR copy of the specified LPCOLESTR argument. You invoke this operator when you write code such as the following:

```
CComBSTR str8 ;

str8 = OLESTR ("This is a string of OLECHARs");
```

It's quite easy to misuse this assignment operator when you're dealing with strings that contain embedded NUL characters. For example, the following code demonstrates how to use and misuse this method:

```
CComBSTR str9 ;
str9 = OLESTR ("This works as expected");

// BSTR bstrInput contains "This is part one\0and here's part two"
CComBSTR str10 ;
str10 = bstrInput; // str10 now contains "This is part one"
```

To properly handle situations such as this one, you should turn to the AssignBSTR method. This method is implemented very much like operator=(LPCOLESTR), except that it uses SysAllocStringByteLen.

```
HRESULT AssignBSTR(const BSTR bstrSrc) {
    HRESULT hr = S_OK;
    if (m_str != bstrSrc) {
        ::SysFreeString(m_str);
        if (bstrSrc != NULL) {
            m_str = ::SysAllocStringByteLen((char*)bstrSrc,
                ::SysStringByteLen(bstrSrc));
```

```
            if (!*this) { hr = E_OUTOFMEMORY; }
        } else {
            m_str = NULL;
        }
    }

    return hr;
}
```

You can modify the code as follows:

```
CComBSTR str9 ;
str9 = OLESTR ("This works as expected");


// BSTR bstrInput contains
// "This is part one\0and here's part two"
CComBSTR str10 ;
str10.AssignBSTR(bstrInput);    // works properly


// str10 now contains "This is part one\0and here's part two"
```

The third `operator=()` method initializes one `CComBSTR` object using an `LPCSTR` pointer to a `NUL`-character-terminated string. The operator converts the input string, which is in ANSI characters, to a Unicode string; then it creates a `BSTR` containing the Unicode string.

```
CComBSTR& operator=(LPCSTR pSrc) {
    ::SysFreeString(m_str);
    m_str = A2WBSTR(pSrc);
    if (!*this && pSrc != NULL) { AtlThrow(E_OUTOFMEMORY); }
    return *this;
}
```

The final assignment methods are two overloaded methods called `LoadString`.

```
bool LoadString(HINSTANCE hInst, UINT nID) ;
bool LoadString(UINT nID) ;
```

The first loads the specified string resource `nID` from the specified module `hInst` (using the instance handle). The second loads the specified string resource `nID` from the current module using the global variable `_AtlBaseModule`.

CComBSTR Operations

Four methods give you access, in varying ways, to the internal BSTR string that is encapsulated by the CComBSTR class. The operator BSTR() method enables you to use a CComBSTR object in situations where a raw BSTR pointer is required. You invoke this method any time you cast a CComBSTR object to a BSTR implicitly or explicitly.

```
operator BSTR() const { return m_str; }
```

Frequently, you invoke this operator implicitly when you pass a CComBSTR object as a parameter to a function that expects a BSTR. The following code demonstrates this:

```
HRESULT put_Name (/* [in] */ BSTR pNewValue) ;

CComBSTR bstrName = OLESTR ("Frodo Baggins");
put_Name (bstrName); // Implicit cast to BSTR
```

The operator&() method returns the address of the internal m_str variable when you take the address of a CComBSTR object. Use care when taking the address of a CComBSTR object. Because the operator&() method returns the address of the internal BSTR variable, you can overwrite the internal variable without first freeing the string. This causes a memory leak. However, if you define the macro ATL_CCOMB-STR_ADDRESS_OF_ASSERT in your project settings, you get an assertion to help catch this error.

```
#ifndef ATL_CCOMBSTR_ADDRESS_OF_ASSERT
// Temp disable CComBSTR::operator& Assert
#define ATL_NO_CCOMBSTR_ADDRESS_OF_ASSERT
#endif

BSTR* operator&() {
#ifndef ATL_NO_CCOMBSTR_ADDRESS_OF_ASSERT
    ATLASSERT(!*this);
#endif
    return &m_str;
}
```

This operator is quite useful when you are receiving a BSTR pointer as the output of some method call. You can store the returned BSTR directly into a CComBSTR object so that the object manages the lifetime of the string.

```
HRESULT get_Name (/* [out] */ BSTR* pName);

CComBSTR bstrName ;
get_Name (&bstrName); // bstrName empty so no memory leak
```

The `CopyTo` method makes a duplicate of the string encapsulated by a `CComBSTR` object and copies the duplicate's `BSTR` pointer to the specified location. You must free the returned `BSTR` explicitly by calling `SysFreeString`.

```
HRESULT CopyTo(BSTR* pbstr);
```

This method is handy when you need to return a copy of an existing `BSTR` property to a caller. For example:

```
STDMETHODIMP SomeClass::get_Name (/* [out] */ BSTR* pName) {
  // Name is maintained in variable m_strName of type CComBSTR
  return m_strName.CopyTo (pName);
}
```

The `Detach` method returns the `BSTR` contained by a `CComBSTR` object. It empties the object so that the destructor will not attempt to release the internal `BSTR`. You must free the returned `BSTR` explicitly by calling `SysFreeString`.

```
BSTR Detach() { BSTR s = m_str; m_str = NULL; return s; }
```

You use this method when you have a string in a `CComBSTR` object that you want to return to a caller and you no longer need to keep the string. In this situation, using the `CopyTo` method would be less efficient because you would make a copy of a string, return the copy, and then discard the original string. Use `Detach` as follows to return the original string directly:

```
STDMETHODIMP SomeClass::get_Label (/* [out] */ BSTR* pName) {
  CComBSTR strLabel;
  // Generate the returned string in strLabel here
  *pName = strLabel.Detach ();
  return S_OK;
}
```

The `Attach` method performs the inverse operation. It attaches a `BSTR` to an empty `CComBSTR` object. Ownership of the `BSTR` now resides with the `CComBSTR` object, and the object's destructor will eventually free the string. Note that if the `CComBSTR` already contains a string, it releases the string before it takes control of the new `BSTR`.

```
void Attach(BSTR src) {
    if (m_str != src) {
        ::SysFreeString(m_str);
        m_str = src;
    }
}
```

Use care when using the Attach method. You must have ownership of the BSTR you are attaching to a CComBSTR object because eventually the object will attempt to destroy the BSTR. For example, the following code is incorrect:

```
STDMETHODIMP SomeClass::put_Name (/* [in] */ BSTR bstrName) {
    // Name is maintained in variable m_strName of type CComBSTR
    m_strName.Attach (bstrName); // Wrong! We don't own bstrName
    return E_BONEHEAD;
}
```

More often, you use Attach when you're given ownership of a BSTR and you want a CComBSTR object to manage the lifetime of the string.

```
STDMETHODIMP SomeClass::get_Name (/* [out] */ BSTR* pName);
...
BSTR bstrName;
pObj->get_Name (&bstrName); // We own and must free the raw BSTR

CComBSTR strName;
strName.Attach(bstrName);  // Attach raw BSTR to the object
```

You can explicitly free the string encapsulated in a CComBSTR object by calling Empty. The Empty method releases any internal BSTR and sets the m_str member variable to NULL. The SysFreeString function explicitly documents that the function simply returns when the input parameter is NULL so that you can call Empty on an empty object without a problem.

```
void Empty() { ::SysFreeString(m_str); m_str = NULL; }
```

CComBSTR supplies two additional interesting methods. These methods enable you to convert BSTR strings to and from SAFEARRAYs, which might be useful for converting to and from string data to adapt to a specific method signature. Chapter 3, "ATL Smart Types," presents a smart class for handling SAFEARRAYs.

```
HRESULT BSTRToArray(LPSAFEARRAY *ppArray) {
    return VectorFromBstr(m_str, ppArray);
}

HRESULT ArrayToBSTR(const SAFEARRAY *pSrc) {
    ::SysFreeString(m_str);
    return BstrFromVector((LPSAFEARRAY)pSrc, &m_str);
}
```

As you can see, these methods merely serve as thin wrappers for the Win32 functions `VectorFromBstr` and `BstrFromVector`. `BSTRToArray` assigns each character of the encapsulated string to an element of a one-dimensional `SAFEARRAY` provided by the caller. Note that the caller is responsible for freeing the `SAFEARRAY`. `ArrayTo-BSTR` does just the opposite: It accepts a pointer to a one-dimensional `SAFEARRAY` and builds a `BSTR` in which each element of the `SAFEARRAY` becomes a character in the internal `BSTR`. `CComBSTR` frees the encapsulated `BSTR` before overwriting it with the values from the `SAFEARRAY`. `ArrayToBSTR` accepts only `SAFEARRAY`s that contain `char` type elements; otherwise, the function returns a type mismatch error.

String Concatenation Using CComBSTR

Eight methods concatenate a specified string with a `CComBSTR` object: six over-loaded `Append` methods, one `AppendBSTR` method, and the `operator+=()` method.

```
HRESULT Append(LPCOLESTR lpsz, int nLen);
HRESULT Append(LPCOLESTR lpsz);
HRESULT Append(LPCSTR);
HRESULT Append(char ch);
HRESULT Append(wchar_t ch);

HRESULT Append(const CComBSTR& bstrSrc);
CComBSTR& operator+=(const CComBSTR& bstrSrc);

HRESULT AppendBSTR(BSTR p);
```

The `Append(LPCOLESTR lpsz, int nLen)` method computes the sum of the length of the current string plus the specified `nLen` value, and allocates an empty `BSTR` of the correct size. It copies the original string into the new `BSTR` and then con-catenates `nLen` characters of the `lpsz` string onto the end of the new `BSTR`. Finally, it frees the original string and replaces it with the new `BSTR`.

```
CComBSTR strSentence = OLESTR("Now is ");
strSentence.Append(OLESTR("the time of day is 03:00 PM"), 9);
// strSentence contains "Now is the time "
```

The remaining overloaded `Append` methods all use the first method to perform the real work. They differ only in the manner in which the method obtains the string and its length. The `Append(LPCOLESTR lpsz)` method appends the contents of a `NUL`-character-terminated string of `OLECHAR` characters. The `Append(LPCSTR lpsz)` method appends the contents of a `NUL`-character-terminated string of ANSI characters. Individual characters can be appended using either `Append(char ch)` or `Append(wchar_t ch)`. The `Append(const CComBSTR& bstrSrc)` method appends the contents of another `CComBSTR` object. For notational and syntactic convenience, the `operator+=()` method also appends the specified `CComBSTR` to the current string.

```
CComBSTR str11 (OLESTR("for all good men "));
// calls Append(const CComBSTR& bstrSrc);
strSentence.Append(str11);
// strSentence contains "Now is the time for all good men "
// calls Append(LPCOLESTR lpsz);
strSentence.Append((OLESTR("to come ")));
// strSentence contains "Now is the time for all good men to come "
// calls Append(LPCSTR lpsz);
strSentence.Append("to the aid ");
// strSentence contains
// "Now is the time for all good men to come to the aid "

CComBSTR str12 (OLESTR("of their country"));
StrSentence += str12; // calls operator+=()
// "Now is the time for all good men to come to
// the aid of their country"
```

When you call `Append` using a `BSTR` parameter, you are actually calling the `Append(LPCOLESTR lpsz)` method because, to the compiler, the `BSTR` argument *is* an `OLECHAR*` argument. Therefore, the method appends characters from the `BSTR` until it encounters the first `NUL` character. When you want to append the contents of a `BSTR` that possibly contains embedded `NULL` characters, you must explicitly call the `AppendBSTR` method.

One additional method exists for appending an array that contains binary data:

```
HRESULT AppendBytes(const char* lpsz, int nLen);
```

`AppendBytes` does not perform a conversion from ANSI to Unicode. The method uses `SysAllocStringByteLen` to properly allocate a `BSTR` of `nLen` bytes (not characters) and append the result to the existing `CComBSTR`.

You can't go wrong following these guidelines:

- When the parameter is a `BSTR`, use the `AppendBSTR` method to append the entire `BSTR`, regardless of whether it contains embedded `NUL` characters.

- When the parameter is an LPCOLESTR or an LPCSTR, use the Append method to append the NUL-character-terminated string.
- So much for function overloading. . .

Character Case Conversion

The two character case-conversion methods, ToLower and ToUpper, convert the internal string to lowercase or uppercase, respectively. In Unicode builds, the conversion is actually performed in-place using the Win32 CharLowerBuff API. In ANSI builds, the internal character string first is converted to MBCS and then CharLower-Buff is invoked. The resulting string is then converted back to Unicode and stored in a newly allocated BSTR. Any string data stored in m_str is freed using Sys-FreeString before it is overwritten. When everything works, the new string replaces the original string as the contents of the CComBSTR object.

```
HRESULT ToLower() {
        if (m_str != NULL) {
#ifdef _UNICODE
            // Convert in place
            CharLowerBuff(m_str, Length());
#else
        UINT _acp = _AtlGetConversionACP();
        ...
        int nRet = WideCharToMultiByte(
            _acp, 0, m_str, Length(),
            pszA, _convert, NULL, NULL);
        ...

        CharLowerBuff(pszA, nRet);

        nRet = MultiByteToWideChar(_acp, 0, pszA, nRet,
                                pszW, _convert);
            ...

        BSTR b = ::SysAllocStringByteLen(
            (LPCSTR) (LPWSTR) pszW,
            nRet * sizeof(OLECHAR));
        if (b == NULL)
                return E_OUTOFMEMORY;
        SysFreeString(m_str);
        m_str = b;
#endif
```

```
        }
        return S_OK;
}
```

Note that these methods properly do case conversion, in case the original string contains embedded NUL characters. Also note, however, that the conversion is potentially lossy, in the sense that it cannot convert a character when the local code page doesn't contain a character equivalent to the original Unicode character.

CComBSTR Comparison Operators

The simplest comparison operator is `operator!()`. It returns `true` when the CComB-STR object is empty, and `false` otherwise.

```
bool operator!() const { return (m_str == NULL); }
```

There are four overloaded versions of the `operator<()` methods, four of the `operator>()` methods, and five of the `operator==()` and `operator!=()` methods. The additional overload for `operator==()` simply handles special cases comparison to NULL. The code in all these methods is nearly the same, so I discuss only the `operator<()` methods; the comments apply equally to the `operator>()` and `operator==()` methods.

These operators internally use the `VarBstrCmp` function, so unlike previous versions of ATL that did not properly compare two CComBSTRs that contain embedded NUL characters, these new operators handle the comparison correctly most of the time. So, the following code works as expected. Later in this section, I discuss properly initializing CComBSTR objects with embedded NULs.

```
BSTR bstrIn1 =
    SysAllocStringLen(
        OLESTR("Here's part 1\0and here's part 2"), 35);
BSTR bstrIn2 =
    SysAllocStringLen(
        OLESTR("Here's part 1\0and here is part 2"), 35);

CComBSTR bstr1(::SysStringLen(bstrIn1), bstrIn1);
CComBSTR bstr2(::SysStringLen(bstrIn2), bstrIn2);

bool b = bstr1 == bstr2; // correctly returns false
```

In the first overloaded version of the `operator<()` method, the operator compares against a provided CComBSTR argument.

```
bool operator<(const CComBSTR& bstrSrc) const {
    return VarBstrCmp(m_str, bstrSrc.m_str,
        LOCALE_USER_DEFAULT, 0) ==
    VARCMP_LT;
}
```

In the second overloaded version of the `operator<()` method, the operator compares against a provided `LPCSTR` argument. An `LPCSTR` isn't the same character type as the internal `BSTR` string, which contains wide characters. Therefore, the method constructs a temporary `CComBSTR` and delegates the work to `operator<(const CComBSTR& bstrSrc)`, just shown.

```
bool operator<(LPCSTR pszSrc) const {
    CComBSTR bstr2(pszSrc);
    return operator<(bstr2);
}
```

The third overload for the `operator<()` method accepts an `LPCOLESTR` and operates very much like the previous overload:

```
bool operator<(LPCOLESTR pszSrc) const {
    CComBSTR bstr2(pszSrc);
    return operator<(bstr2);
}
```

The fourth overload for the `operator<()` accepts an `LPOLESTR`; the implementation does a quick cast and calls the `LPCOLESTR` version to do the work:

```
bool operator>(LPOLESTR pszSrc) const {
    return operator>((LPCOLESTR)pszSrc);
}
```

CComBSTR Persistence Support

The last two methods of the `CComBSTR` class read and write a `BSTR` string to and from a stream. The `WriteToStream` method writes a `ULONG` count containing the numbers of bytes in the `BSTR` to a stream. It writes the `BSTR` characters to the stream immediately following the count. Note that the method does not tag the stream with an indication of the byte order used to write the data. Therefore, as is frequently the case for stream data, a `CComBSTR` object writes its string to the stream in a hardware-architecture-specific format.

```
HRESULT WriteToStream(IStream* pStream) {
    ATLASSERT(pStream != NULL);
    if(pStream == NULL)
        return E_INVALIDARG;

    ULONG cb;
    ULONG cbStrLen = ULONG(m_str ?
        SysStringByteLen(m_str)+sizeof(OLECHAR) : 0);
    HRESULT hr = pStream->Write((void*) &cbStrLen,
        sizeof(cbStrLen), &cb);
    if (FAILED(hr))
        return hr;
    return cbStrLen ?
        pStream->Write((void*) m_str, cbStrLen, &cb) :
        S_OK;
}
```

The ReadFromStream method reads a ULONG count of bytes from the specified stream, allocates a BSTR of the correct size, and then reads the characters directly into the BSTR string. The CComBSTR object must be empty when you call ReadFromStream; otherwise, you will receive an assertion from a debug build or will leak memory in a release build.

```
HRESULT ReadFromStream(IStream* pStream) {
    ATLASSERT(pStream != NULL);
    ATLASSERT(!*this); // should be empty
    ULONG cbStrLen = 0;
    HRESULT hr = pStream->Read((void*) &cbStrLen,
        sizeof(cbStrLen), NULL);
    if ((hr == S_OK) && (cbStrLen != 0)) {
        //subtract size for terminating NULL which we wrote out
        //since SysAllocStringByteLen overallocates for the NULL
        m_str = SysAllocStringByteLen(NULL,
            cbStrLen-sizeof(OLECHAR));
        if (!*this) hr = E_OUTOFMEMORY;
        else hr = pStream->Read((void*) m_str, cbStrLen, NULL);
        ...
    }
    if (hr == S_FALSE) hr = E_FAIL;
    return hr;
}
```

Minor Rant on BSTRs, Embedded NUL Characters in Strings, and Life in General

The compiler considers the types BSTR and OLECHAR* to be synonymous. In fact, the BSTR symbol is simply a typedef for OLECHAR*. For example, from wtypes.h:

```
typedef /* [wire_marshal] */ OLECHAR __RPC_FAR *BSTR;
```

This is more than somewhat brain damaged. An arbitrary BSTR is not an OLECHAR*, and an arbitrary OLECHAR* is not a BSTR. One is often misled on this regard because frequently a BSTR works just fine as an OLECHAR*.

```
STDMETHODIMP SomeClass::put_Name (LPCOLESTR pName) ;

BSTR bstrInput =  ...
pObj->put_Name (bstrInput) ; // This works just fine… usually
SysFreeString (bstrInput) ;
```

In the previous example, because the bstrInput argument is defined to be a BSTR, it can contain embedded NUL characters within the string. The put_Name method, which expects a LPCOLESTR (a NUL-character-terminated string), will probably save only the characters preceding the first embedded NUL character. In other words, it will cut the string short.

You also cannot use a BSTR where an [out] OLECHAR* parameter is required. For example:

```
STDMETHODIMP SomeClass::get_Name(OLECHAR** ppName) {
  BSTR bstrOutput =... // Produce BSTR string to return
  *ppName = bstrOutput ; // This compiles just fine
  return S_OK ;          // but leaks memory as caller
                         // doesn't release BSTR
}
```

Conversely, you cannot use an OLECHAR* where a BSTR is required. When it does happen to work, it's a latent bug. For example, the following code is incorrect:

```
STDMETHODIMP SomeClass::put_Name (BSTR bstrName) ;
// Wrong! Wrong! Wrong!
pObj->put_Name (OLECHAR("This is not a BSTR!")) ;
```

If the put_Name method calls SysStringLen to obtain the length of the BSTR, it will try to get the length from the integer preceding the string—but there is no such integer. Things get worse if the put_Name method is remoted—that is, lives out-of-process. In this case, the marshaling code will call SysStringLen to obtain the number of characters to place in the request packet. This is usually a huge number (4 bytes from the preceding string in the literal pool, in this example) and often causes a crash while trying to copy the string.

Because the compiler cannot tell the difference between a BSTR and an OLECHAR*, it's quite easy to accidentally call a method in CComBSTR that doesn't work correctly when you are using a BSTR that contains embedded NUL characters. The following discussion shows exactly which methods you must use for these kinds of BSTRs.

To construct a CComBSTR, you must specify the length of the string:

```
BSTR bstrInput =
  SysAllocStringLen (
    OLESTR ("This is part one\0and here's part two"),
    36) ;

CComBSTR str8 (bstrInput) ; // Wrong! Unexpected behavior here
                            // Note: str2 contains only
                            // "This is part one"

CComBSTR str9 (::SysStringLen (bstrInput),
    bstrInput); // Correct!
// str9 contains "This is part one\0and here's part two"
```

Assigning a BSTR that contains embedded NUL characters to a CComBSTR object never works. For example:

```
// BSTR bstrInput contains
// "This is part one\0and here's part two"
CComBSTR str10;
str10 = bstrInput; // Wrong! Unexpected behavior here
                   // str10 now contains "This is part one"
```

The easiest way to perform an assignment of a BSTR is to use the Empty and AppendBSTR methods:

```
str10.Empty();                  // Insure object is initially empty
str10.AppendBSTR (bstrInput); // This works!
```

In practice, although a BSTR can potentially contain embedded NUL characters, most of the time it doesn't. Of course, this means that, most of the time, you don't see the latent bugs caused by incorrect BSTR use.

The CString Class

CString Overview

For years now, ATL programmers have glared longingly over the shoulders of their MFC brethren slinging character data about in their programs with the grace and dexterity of Barishnikov himself. MFC developers have long enjoyed the ubiquitous CString class provided with the library—so much so that when they ventured into previous versions of ATL, they often found themselves tempted to check that wizard option named Support MFC and suck in a 1MB library just to allow them to continue working with their bread-'n-butter string class. Sure, ATL programmers have CComBSTR, which is fine for code at the "edges" of a method's implementation—that is, either receiving a BSTR input parameter at the beginning of a method or returning some sort of BSTR output parameter at the end of a method. But compared to CString's extensive support for everything from sprintf-style formatting to search-and-replace, CComBSTR is woefully inadequate for any serious string processing. And, sure, ATL programmers have had STL's string<> template class for years, but it also falls short of CString in functionality. In addition, because it is a standard, platform-independent class, it can't possibly provide such useful functionality as integrating with the Windows resource architecture.

Well, the long wait is over: CString is available as of ATL 7. In fact, CString is a shared class between MFC and ATL, along with a number of other classes. You'll note that there are no longer separate \MFC\Include and \ATL\Include directories within the Visual Studio file hierarchy. Instead, both libraries maintain code in \ATLMFC\Include. I think it's *extraordinarily* insightful to examine just how and where the shared CString class is defined. First, all the header files are under a directory named \ATLMFC, *not* \MFCATL. CString used to be defined in afx.h, the prefix that has identified MFC from its earliest beginnings. Now the definition appears in a file that simply defines CString as a typedef to a template class called CStringT that does all the work. This template class is actually in the ATL namespace. That's right—one of the last bastions of MFC supremacy is now found under the ATL moniker.

CString Anatomy

Now that CString is template-based, it follows the general ATL design pattern of supporting pluggable functionality through template parameters that specialize in CString behavior. As the first sections of this chapter revealed, a number of different types of strings exist, with different mechanisms for manipulating them. Templates are very well suited to this kind of scenario, in which exposing flexibility is important. But usability is also important, so ATL uses a convenient combination of typedefs and default template parameters to simplify using CString.

Understanding what's under the covers of a CString instance is important in understanding not only how the methods and operators work, but also how CString can be extended and specialized to fit particular requirements or to facilitate certain optimizations. When you declare an instance of CString, you are actually instantiating a template class called CStringT. The file atlstr.h provides typedefs for CString, as well as for ANSI and Unicode versions—CStringA and CStringW, respectively.

```
typedef CStringT< wchar_t, StrTraitATL<
    wchar_t, ChTraitsCRT< wchar_t > > >
    CAtlStringW;
typedef CStringT< char, StrTraitATL<
    char, ChTraitsCRT< char > > >
    CAtlStringA;
typedef CStringT< TCHAR, StrTraitATL<
    TCHAR, ChTraitsCRT< TCHAR > > >
    CAtlString;

typedef CAtlStringW CStringW;
typedef CAtlStringA CStringA;
typedef CAtlString CString;
```

Strictly speaking, these typedefs are generated only if the ATL project is linking to the CRT, which ATL projects now do by default. Otherwise, the ChTraitsCRT template class is not used as a parameter to CStringT because it relies upon CRT functions to manage character-level manipulation.

Because the CStringT template class is the underlying class doing all the work, the remainder of the discussion is in terms of CStringT. This class is defined in cstringt.h as follows:

```
template< typename BaseType, class StringTraits >
class CStringT :
    public CSimpleStringT< BaseType > {
    // ...
}
```

The behavior of the CStringT class is governed largely by three things: 1) the CSimpleStringT base class, 2) the BaseType template parameter, and 3) the StringTraits template parameter. CSimpleStringT provides a lot of basic string functionality that CStringT inherits. The BaseType template parameter is used to establish the underlying character data type of the string. The only state CStringT holds is a pointer to a character string of the type BaseType. This data is held in the m_psz Data private member defined in the CSimpleStringT base class. The StringTraits parameter is an interesting one. This parameter establishes three things: 1) the module from which resource strings will be loaded, 2) the string manager used to allocate string data, and 3) the class that will provide low-level character manipulation. The `atlstr.h` header file contains the definition for this template class.

```
template< typename _BaseType = char, class StringIterator =
                                ChTraitsOS< _BaseType > >
class StrTraitATL : public StringIterator {
public:
    static HINSTANCE FindStringResourceInstance(UINT nID) {
        return( AtlFindStringResourceInstance( nID ) );
    }

    static IAtlStringMgr* GetDefaultManager() {
        return( &g_strmgr );
    }
};
```

`StrTraitATL` derives from the `StringIterator` template parameter passed in. This parameter implements low-level character operations that `CStringT` ultimately will invoke when application code calls methods on instances of `CString`. Two choices of ATL-provided classes encapsulate the character traits: `ChTraitsCRT` and `ChTraitsOS`. The former uses functions that require you to link to the CRT in your project, so you would use it if you were already linking to the CRT. The latter does not require the CRT to implement its character-manipulation functions. Both expose a common set of functions that `CStringT` uses in its internal implementation.

Note that in the definition of the `StrTraitATL`, we see the first evidence of the extensibility of `CStringT`. The `GetDefaultManager` method returns a reference to a string manager via the `IAtlStringMgr` interface. This interface enforces a generic pattern for managing string memory. `atlsimpstr.h` provides the definition for this interface.

```
__interface IAtlStringMgr {
public:
    CStringData* Allocate( int nAllocLength, int nCharSize );
    void Free( CStringData* pData );
    CStringData* Reallocate( CStringData* pData,
        int nAllocLength, int nCharSize );

    CStringData* GetNilString();
    IAtlStringMgr* Clone();
};
```

ATL supplies a default string manager that is used if the user does not specify another. This default string manager is a concrete class called CAtlStringMgr that implements IAtlStringMgr. Abstracting string management into a separate class enables you to customize the behavior of the string-management functions to suit specific application requirements. Two mechanisms exist for customizing string management for CStringT. The first mechanism involves merely using CAtlString-Mgr with a specific memory manager. Chapter 3, "ATL Smart Types," discusses the IAtlMemMgr interface, a generic interface that encapsulates heap memory management. Associating a memory manager with CAtlStringMgr is as simple as passing a pointer to the memory manager to the CAtlStringMgr constructor. CStringT must be instructed to use this CAtlStringMgr in its internal implementation by passing the string manager pointer to the CStringT constructor. ATL provides five built-in heap managers that implement IAtlMemMgr. We use CWin32Heap to demonstrate how to use an alternate memory manager with CStringT.

```
// create a thread-safe process heap with zero initial size
// and no max size
// constructor parameters are explained later in this chapter
CWin32Heap heap(0, 0, 0);

// create a string manager that uses this memory manager
CAtlStringMgr strMgr(&heap);

// create a CString instance that uses this string manager
CString str(&strMgr);

// ... perform some string operations as usual
```

If you want more control over the string-management functions, you can supply your own custom string manager that fully implements IAtlStringMgr. Instead of passing a pointer to CAtlStringMgr to the CString constructor, as in the previous code, you would simply pass a pointer to your custom IAtlStringMgr implementation. This custom string manager might use one of the existing memory managers or a custom implementation of IAtlMemMgr. Additionally, a custom string manager might want to enforce a different buffer-sharing policy than CAtlStringMgr's default copy-on-write policy. Copy-on-write allows multiple CStringT instances to read the same string memory, but a duplicate is created before any writes to the buffer are performed.

Of course, the simplest thing to do is to use the defaults that ATL chooses when you use a simple CString declaration, as in the following:

```
// declare an empty CString instance
CString str;
```

With this declaration, ATL will use `CAtlStringMgr` to manage the string data. `CAtlStringMgr` will use the built-in `CWin32Heap` heap manager for supplying string data storage.

Constructors

`CStringT` provides 19 different constructors, although one of the constructors is compiled into the class definition only if you are building a managed C++ project for the .NET platform. These types of ATL specializations are not discussed in this book. In general, however, the large number of constructors present represents the various different sources of string data with which a `CString` instance can be initialized, along with the additional options for supplying alternate string managers. We examine these constructors in related groups.

Before going further into the various methods, let's look at some of the notational shortcuts that `CStringT` uses in its method signatures. To properly understand even the method declarations with `CStringT`, you must be comfortable with the typedefs used to represent the character types in `CStringT`. Because `CStringT` uses template parameters to represent the base character type, the syntax for expressing the various allowed character types can become cumbersome or unclear in places. For instance, when you declare a `CStringW`, you create an instance of `CStringT` that encapsulates a series of `wchar_t` characters. From the definition of the `CStringT` template class, you can easily see that the `BaseType` template parameter can be used in method signatures that need to specify a `wchar_t` type parameter—but how would you specify methods that need to accept a `char` type parameter? Certainly, I need to be able to append `char` strings to a `wchar_t`-based `CString`. Conversely, I must have the ability to append `wchar_t` strings to a `char`-based `CString`. Yet I have only one template class in which to accomplish all this. `CStringT` provides six type definitions to deal with this syntactic dichotomy. They might seem somewhat arbitrary at first, but you'll see as we look closer into `CStringT` that their use actually makes a lot of sense. Table 2.3 summarizes these typedefs.

Table 2.3. CStringT Character Traits Type Definitions

Typedef	BaseType is `char`	BaseType is `wchar_t`	Meaning
XCHAR	char	wchar_t	Single character of the *same type* as the `CStringT` instance
PXSTR	LPSTR	LPWSTR	Pointer to character string of the *same type* as `CStringT` instance

continues

Table 2.3.   CStringT Character Traits Type Definitions (Continued)

Typedef	BaseType is char	BaseType is wchar_t	Meaning
PCXSTR	LPCSTR	LPCWSTR	Pointer to constant character string of the *same type* as the CStringT instance
YCHAR	wchar_t	Char	Single character of the *opposite type* as the CStringT instance
PYSTR	LPWSTR	LPSTR	Pointer to character string of the *opposite type* as CStringT instance
PCYSTR	LPCWSTR	LPCSTR	Pointer to constant character string of the *opposite type* as the CStringT instance

Two constructors enable you to initialize a CString to an empty string:

```
CStringT();
explicit CStringT( IAtlStringMgr* pStringMgr );
```

Recall that the data for the CString is kept in the m_pszData data member. These constructors simply initialize the value of this member to be either a NUL character or two NUL characters if the BaseType is wchar_t. The second constructor accepts a pointer to a string manager to use with this CStringT instance. As stated previously, if the first constructor is used, the CStringT instance will use the default string manager CAtlStringMgr, which relies upon an underlying CWin32Heap heap manager to allocate storage from the process heap.

The next two constructors provide two different copy constructors that enable you to initialize a new instance from an existing CStringT or from an existing CSimpleStringT.

```
CStringT( const CStringT& strSrc );
CStringT( const CThisSimpleString& strSrc );
```

The second constructor accepts a CThisSimpleString reference, but this is simply a typedef to CSimpleString<BaseType>. Exactly what these copy constructors do depends upon the policy established by the string manager that is associated with the CStringT instance. Recall that if no string manager is specified, such as with the constructor shown previously that accepts an `IAtlStringMgr` pointer, `CAtlStringMgr` will be used to manage memory allocation for the instance's string data. This default string manager implements a copy-on-write policy that allows multiple `CStringT` instances to share a string buffer for reading, but automatically creates a copy of the buffer whenever another `CStringT` instance tries to perform a write operation. The following code demonstrates how these copy semantics work in practice:

```
// "Fred" memcpy'd into strOrig buffer
CString strOrig("Fred");
// str1 points to strOrig buffer (no memcpy)
CString str1(strOrig);
// str2 points to strOrig buffer (no memcpy)
CString str2(str1);
// str3 points to strOrig buffer (no memcpy)
CString str3(str2);
// new buffer allocated for str2
// "John" memcpy'd into str2 buffer
str2 = "John";
```

As the comments indicate, `CAtlStringMgr` creates no additional copies of the internal string buffer until a write operation is performed with the assignment statement of `str2`. The storage to hold the new data in `str2` is obtained from `CAtlString-Mgr`. If we had specified another custom string manager to use via a constructor, that implementation would have determined how and when data is allocated. Actually, `CAtlStringMgr` simply increments `str2`'s buffer pointer to "allocate" memory within its internal heap. As long as there is room in the `CAtlStringMgr`'s heap, no expansion of the heap is required and the string allocation is fast and efficient.

Several constructors accept a pointer to a character string of the same type as the `CStringT` instance—that is, a character string of type `BaseType`.

```
CStringT( const XCHAR* pszSrc );
CStringT( const XCHAR* pch, int nLength );
CStringT( const XCHAR* pch, int nLength, IAtlStringMgr* pStringMgr );
```

The first constructor should be used when the character string provided is NUL terminated. `CStringT` determines the size of the buffer needed by simply looking for the terminating NUL. However, the second and third forms of the constructor can accept an array of characters that is not NUL terminated. In this case, the length of the character array (in characters, not bytes), not including the terminating NUL that will be added, must be provided. You can improperly initialize your `CString` if you don't feed these constructors the proper length or if you use the first form with a string that's not NUL terminated. For instance:

```
char rg[4] = { 'F', 'r', 'e', 'd' };

// Wrong! Wrong! – rg not NULL-terminated
// str1 contains junk
CString str1(rg);

// ok, length provided to invoke correct ctor
CString str2(rg, 4);

char* sz  = "Fred";
// ok, sz NULL-terminated => no length parameter needed
CString str3(sz);
```

You can also initialize a CStringT instance with a character string of the opposite type of BaseType.

```
CSTRING_EXPLICIT CStringT( const YCHAR* pszSrc );
CStringT( const YCHAR* pch, int nLength );
CStringT( const YCHAR* pch, int nLength,
    IAtlStringMgr* pStringMgr );
```

These constructors work in an analogous manner to the XCHAR-based constructors just shown. The difference is that these constructors convert the source string to the BaseType declared for the CStringT instance, if it is required. For example, if the BaseType is wchar_t, such as when you explicitly declare a CStringW instance, and you pass the constructor a char*, CStringT will use the Windows API function MultiByteToWideChar to convert the source string.

```
CStringT( LPCSTR pszSrc, IAtlStringMgr* pStringMgr );
CStringT( LPCWSTR pszSrc, IAtlStringMgr* pStringMgr );
```

You can also initialize a CStringT instance with a repeated series of characters using the following constructors:

```
CSTRING_EXPLICIT CStringT( char ch, int nLength = 1 );
CSTRING_EXPLICIT CStringT( wchar_t ch, int nLength = 1 );
```

Here, the nLength specifies the number of copies of the ch character to replicate in the CStringT instance, as in the following:

```
CString str('z', 5);    // str contains "zzzzz"
```

CStringT also enables you to initialize a CStringT instance from an unsigned char string, which is how MBCS strings are represented.

```
CSTRING_EXPLICIT CStringT( const unsigned char* pszSrc );
CStringT( const unsigned char* pszSrc,
    IAtlStringMgr* pStringMgr );
```

Finally, CStringT provides two constructors that accept a VARIANT as the string source:

```
CStringT( const VARIANT& varSrc );
CStringT( const VARIANT& varSrc, IAtlStringMgr* pStringMgr );
```

Internally, CStringT uses the COM API function VariantChangeType to attempt to convert varSrc to a BSTR. VariantChangeType handles simple conversion between basic types, such as numeric-to-string conversions. However, the varSrc VARIANT cannot contain a complex type, such as an array of double. In addition, these two constructors truncate a BSTR that contains an embedded NUL.

```
// BSTR bstr contains "This is part one\0and here's part two"
VARIANT var;
var.vt = VT_BSTR;
var.bstrVal = bstr;
// var contains "This is part one\0 and here's part two"
CString str(var);   // str contains "This is part one"
```

Assignment

CStringT defines eight assignment operators. The first two enable you to initialize an instance from an existing CStringT or CSimpleStringT:

```
CStringT& operator=( const CStringT& strSrc );
CStringT& operator=( const CThisSimpleString& strSrc );
```

With both of these constructors, the copy policy of the string manager in use dictates how these operators behave. By default, CStringT instances use the copy-on-write policy of the CAtlStringMgr class. See the previous discussion of the CStringT constructors for more information.

The next two assignment operators accept pointers to string literals of the same type as the CStringT instance or of the opposite type, as indicated by the PCXSTR and PCYSTR source string types:

```
CStringT& operator=( PCXSTR pszSrc );
CStringT& operator=( PCYSTR pszSrc );
```

Of course, no conversions are necessary with the first operator. However, CStringT invokes the appropriate Win32 conversion function when the second operator is used, as in the following code:

```
CStringA str;          // declare an empty ANSI CString
str = L"Hello World";  // operator=(PCYSTR) invoked
                       // characters converted via
                       // WideCharToMultiByte
```

CStringT also enables you to assign instances to individual characters. In these cases, CStringT actually creates a string of one character and appends either a 1- or 2-byte NUL terminator, depending on the type of character specified and the Base-Type of the CStringT instance. These operators then delegate to either operator=(PCXSTR) or operator=(PCYSTR) so that any necessary conversions are performed.

```
CStringT& operator=( char ch );
CStringT& operator=( wchar_t ch );
```

Yet another CStringT assignment operator accepts an unsigned char* as its argument to support MBCS strings. This operator simply casts pszSrc to a char* and invokes either operator=(PCXSTR) or operator=(PCYSTR):

```
CStringT& operator=( const unsigned char* pszSrc );
```

Finally, instances of CStringT can be assigned to VARIANT types. The use and behavior here are identical to that described previously for the corresponding CStringT constructor:

```
CStringT& operator=( const VARIANT& var );
```

String Concatenation Using CString

CStringT defines eight operators used to append string data to the end of an existing string buffer. In all cases, storage for the new data appended is allocated using the underlying string manager and its encapsulated heap. By default, this means that CAtlStringMgr is employed; its underlying CWin32Heap instance will be used to invoke the Win32 `HeapReAlloc` API function as necessary to grow the `CStringT` buffer to accommodate the data appended by these operators.

```
CStringT& operator+=( const CThisSimpleString& str );
CStringT& operator+=( PCXSTR pszSrc );
CStringT& operator+=( PCYSTR pszSrc );
template< int t_nSize >
CStringT& operator+=( const CStaticString<
    XCHAR, t_nSize >& strSrc );
CStringT& operator+=( char ch );
CStringT& operator+=( unsigned char ch );
CStringT& operator+=( wchar_t ch );
CStringT& operator+=( const VARIANT& var );
```

The first operator accepts an existing `CStringT` instance, and two operators accept `PCXSTR` strings or `PCYSTR` strings. Three other operators enable you to append individual characters to an existing `CStringT`. You can append a `char`, `wchar_t`, or `unsigned char`. One operator enables you to append the string contained in an instance of `CStaticString`. You can use this template class to efficiently store immutable string data; it performs no copying of the data with which it is initialized and merely serves as a convenient container for a string constant. Finally, you can append a `VARIANT` to an existing `CStringT` instance. As with the `VARIANT` constructor and assignment operator discussed previously, this operator relies upon `VariantChangeType` to convert the underlying `VARIANT` data into a `BSTR`. To the compiler, a `BSTR` looks just like an `OLECHAR*`, so this operator will ultimately end up calling either `operator+=(PCXSTR)` or `operator+=(PCYSTR)`, depending on the `BaseType` of the `CStringT` instance. The same issues with embedded `NUL`s in the source `BSTR` that we discussed earlier in the "Assignment" section apply here.

Three overloads of `operator+()` enable you to concatenate multiple strings conveniently.

```
friend CSimpleStringT operator+(
    const CSimpleStringT& str1,
    const CSimpleStringT& str2 );
friend CSimpleStringT operator+(
    const CSimpleStringT& str1,
    PCXSTR psz2 );
friend CSimpleStringT operator+(
    PCXSTR psz1,
    const CSimpleStringT& str2 );
```

These operators are invoked when you write code such as the following:

```
CString str1("Every good "); // str1: "Every good"
CString str2("boy does ");   // str2: "boy does "
CString str3;                // str3: empty
str3 = str1 + str3 + "fine"; // str3: "Every good boy does fine"
```

String concatenation is also supported through several Append methods. Four of these methods are defined on the CSimpleStringT base class and actually do the real work for the operators just discussed. Indeed, the only additional functionality offered by these four Append methods over the operators appears in the overload that accepts an nLength parameter. This enables you to append only a portion of an existing string. If you specify an nLength greater than the length of the source string, space will be allocated to accommodate nLength characters. However, the resulting CStringT data will be NUL terminated in the same place as pszSrc.

```
void Append( PCXSTR pszSrc );
void Append( PCXSTR pszSrc, int nLength );
void AppendChar( XCHAR ch );
void Append( const CSimpleStringT& strSrc );
```

Three additional methods defined on CStringT enable you to append formatted strings to existing CStringT instances. Formatted strings are discussed more later in this section when we cover CStringT's Format operation. In short, these types of operations enable you to employ sprintf-style formatting to CStringT instances. The three methods shown here differ only from FormatMessage in that the CStringT instance is appended with the constructed string instead of being overwritten by it.

```
void __cdecl AppendFormat( UINT nFormatID, ... );
void __cdecl AppendFormat( PCXSTR pszFormat, ... );
void AppendFormatV( PCXSTR pszFormat, va_list args );
```

Character Case Conversion

Two CStringT methods support case conversion: MakeUpper and MakeLower.

```
CStringT& MakeUpper() {
    int nLength = GetLength();
    PXSTR pszBuffer = GetBuffer( nLength );
    StringTraits::StringUppercase( pszBuffer );
    ReleaseBufferSetLength( nLength );

    return( *this );
}
```

```
CStringT& MakeLower() {
    int nLength = GetLength();
    PXSTR pszBuffer = GetBuffer( nLength );
    StringTraits::StringLowercase( pszBuffer );
    ReleaseBufferSetLength( nLength );

    return( *this );
}
```

Both of these methods delegate their work to the ChTraitsOS or ChTraitsCRT class, depending on which of these was specified as the template parameter when the CStringT instance was declared. Simply instantiating a variable of type CString uses the default character traits class supplied in the typedef for CString. If the preprocessor symbol _ATL_CSTRING_NO_CRT is defined, the ChTraitsOS class is used; and the Win32 functions CharLower and CharUpper are invoked to perform the conversion. If _ATL_CSTRING_NO_CRT is not defined, the ChTraitsCRT class is used by default, and it uses the appropriate CRT function: _mbslwr, _mbsupr, _wcslwr, or _wcsupr.

CString Comparison Operators

CString defines a whole slew of comparison operators (that's a *metric* slew, not an imperial slew). Seven versions of operator== enable you to compare CStringT instances with other instances, with ANSI and Unicode string literals, and with individual characters.

```
friend bool operator==( const CStringT& str1,
    const CStringT& str2 );
friend bool operator==( const CStringT& str1, PCXSTR psz2 );
friend bool operator==( PCXSTR psz1, const CStringT& str2 );
friend bool operator==( const CStringT& str1, PCYSTR psz2 );
friend bool operator==( PCYSTR psz1, const CStringT& str2 );
friend bool operator==( XCHAR ch1, const CStringT& str2 );
friend bool operator==( const CStringT& str1, XCHAR ch2 );
```

As you might expect, a corresponding set of overloads for operator!= is also provided.

```
friend bool operator!=( const CStringT& str1,
    const CStringT& str2 );
friend bool operator!=( const CStringT& str1, PCXSTR psz2 );
friend bool operator!=( PCXSTR psz1, const CStringT& str2 );
friend bool operator!=( const CStringT& str1, PCYSTR psz2 );
friend bool operator!=( PCYSTR psz1, const CStringT& str2 );
friend bool operator!=( XCHAR ch1, const CStringT& str2 );
friend bool operator!=( const CStringT& str1, XCHAR ch2 );
```

And, of course, a full battalion of relational comparison operators is available in CStringT.

```
friend bool operator<( const CStringT& str1,
    const CStringT& str2 );
friend bool operator<( const CStringT& str1, PCXSTR psz2 );
friend bool operator<( PCXSTR psz1, const CStringT& str2 );
friend bool operator>( const CStringT& str1,
    const CStringT& str2 );
friend bool operator>( const CStringT& str1, PCXSTR psz2 );
friend bool operator>( PCXSTR psz1, const CStringT& str2 );
friend bool operator<=( const CStringT& str1,
    const CStringT& str2 );
friend bool operator<=( const CStringT& str1, PCXSTR psz2 );
friend bool operator<=( PCXSTR psz1, const CStringT& str2 );
friend bool operator>=( const CStringT& str1,
    const CStringT& str2 );
friend bool operator>=( const CStringT& str1, PCXSTR psz2 );
friend bool operator>=( PCXSTR psz1, const CStringT& str2 );
```

All the operators use the same method to perform the actual comparison: CStringT::Compare. A brief inspection of the operator= overload that takes two CStringT instances reveals how this is accomplished:

```
friend bool operator==( const CStringT& str1,
    const CStringT& str2 ) {
    return( str1.Compare( str2 ) == 0 );
}
```

Similarly, the same overload for operator!= is defined as follows:

```
friend bool operator!=( const CStringT& str1,
    const CStringT& str2 ) {
    return( str1.Compare( str2 ) != 0 );
}
```

The relational operators use Compare like this:

```
friend bool operator<( const CStringT& str1,
    const CStringT& str2 ) {
    return( str1.Compare( str2 ) < 0 );
}
```

Compare returns -1 if str1 is lexicographically (say *that* ten times fast while standing on your head) less than str2, and 1 if str1 is lexicographically greater than str1. Strings are compared character by character until an inequality occurs or the end of one of the strings is reached. If no inequalities are detected and the strings are the same length, they are considered equal. Compare returns 0 in this case. If an inequality is found between two characters, the result of a lexical comparison between the two characters is returned as the result of the string comparison. If the characters in the strings are the same except that one string is longer, the shorter string is considered to be less than the longer string. It is important to note that all these comparisons are case-sensitive. If you want to perform noncase-sensitive comparisons, you must resort to using the CompareNoCase method directly, as discussed in a moment.

As with many of the character-level operations invoked by various CStringT methods and operators, the character traits class does the real heavy lifting. The CStringT::Compare method delegates to either ChTraitsOS or ChTraitsCRT, as discussed previously.

```
int Compare( PCXSTR psz ) const {
    ATLASSERT( AtlIsValidString( psz ) );
    return( StringTraits::StringCompare( GetString(), psz ) );
}

int CompareNoCase( PCXSTR psz ) const {
    ATLASSERT( AtlIsValidString( psz ) );
    return( StringTraits::StringCompareIgnore(
        GetString(), psz ) );
}
```

Assuming that CString is used to declare the instance and the project defaults are in use (_ATL_CSTRING_NO_CRT is not defined), the Compare method delegates to ChTraitsCRT::StringCompare. This function uses one of the CRT functions lstrcmpA or wcscmp. Correspondingly, CompareNoCase invokes either lstrcmpiA or _wcsicmp.

Two additional comparison methods provide the same functionality as Compare and CompareNoCase, except that they perform the comparison using language rules. The CRT functions underlying these methods are _mbscoll and _mbsicoll, or their Unicode equivalents, depending again on the underlying character type of the CStringT.

```
int Collate( PCXSTR psz ) const
int CollateNoCase( PCXSTR psz ) const
```

One final operator that bears mentioning is operator[]. This operator enables you to use convenient arraylike syntax to access individual characters in the CStringT string buffer. This operator is defined on the CSimpleStringT base class as follows:

```
XCHAR operator[]( int iChar ) const {
    ATLASSERT( (iChar >= 0) && (iChar <= GetLength()) );
    return( m_pszData[iChar] );
}
```

This function merely does some simple bounds checking (note that you can index the NUL terminator if you want) and then returns the character located at the specified index. This enables you to write code like the following:

```
CString str("ATL Internals");
char c1 = str[2];    // 'L'
char c2 = str[5];    // 'n'
char c3 = str[13];   // '\0'
```

CString Operations

CStringT instances can be manipulated and searched in a variety of ways. This section briefly presents the methods CStringT exposes for performing various types of operations. Three methods are designed to facilitate searching for strings and characters within a CStringT instance.

```
int Find( XCHAR ch, int iStart = 0 ) const
int Find( PCXSTR pszSub, int iStart = 0 ) const
int FindOneOf( PCXSTR pszCharSet ) const
int ReverseFind( XCHAR ch ) const
```

The first version of Find accepts a single character of BaseType and returns the zero-based index of the first occurrence of ch within the CStringT instance. Find starts the search at the index specified by iStart. If the character is not found, -1 is returned. The second version of Find accepts a string of characters and returns either the index of the first character of pszSub within the CStringT or -1 if pszSub does not occur in its entirety within the instance. As with many character-level operations, the character traits class performs the real work. With ChTraitsCRT in use, the first two versions of Find delegate ultimately to the CRT functions _mbschr and _mbsstr, respectively. The FindOneOf method looks for the first occurrence of any character within the pszCharSet parameter. This method invokes the CRT function _mbspbrk to do the search. Finally, the ReverseFind method operates similarly to Find, except that it starts its search at the end of the CStringT and looks "backward." Note that all these operations are case-sensitive. The following examples demonstrate the use of these search operations.

```
CString str("Show me the money!");

int n = str.Find('o');       // n = 2
n = str.Find('O');           // n = -1, case-sensitivity
n = str.ReverseFind('o');    // n = 13, 'o' in "money" found
                             // first
n = str.Find("the");         // n = 8
n = str.FindOneOf("aeiou");  // n = 2
n = str.Find('o', 4);        // n = 13, started search after
                             // first 'o'
```

Nine different Trim functions enable you to remove characters from the beginning and or end of a CStringT. The first Trim function removes all leading and trailing whitespace characters from the string. The second overload of Trim accepts a character and removes all leading and trailing instances of chTarget from the string; the third overload of Trim removes leading and trailing occurrences of any character in the pszTargets string parameter. The three overloads for TrimLeft behave similarly to Trim, except that they remove the desired characters only from the beginning of the string. As you might guess, TrimRight removes only trailing instances of the specified characters.

```
CStringT& Trim()
CStringT& Trim( XCHAR chTarget )
CStringT& Trim( PCXSTR pszTargets )
CStringT& TrimLeft()
CStringT& TrimLeft( XCHAR chTarget )
CStringT& TrimLeft( PCXSTR pszTargets )
CStringT& TrimRight()
CStringT& TrimRight( XCHAR chTarget )
CStringT& TrimRight( PCXSTR pszTargets )
```

CStringT provides two useful functions for extracting characters from the encapsulated string:

```
CStringT SpanIncluding( PCXSTR pszCharSet ) const
CStringT SpanExcluding( PCXSTR pszCharSet ) const
```

SpanIncluding starts from the beginning of the CStringT data and returns a new CStringT instance that contains all the characters in the CStringT that are included in the pszCharSet string parameter. If no characters in pszCharSet are found, an empty CStringT is returned. Conversely, SpanExcluding returns a new CStringT that contains all the characters in the original CStringT, up to the first one in pszCharSet. In this case, if no character in pszCharSet is found, the entire original string is returned.

You can insert individual characters or entire strings into a CStringT instance using the overloaded Insert method:

```
int Insert( int iIndex, PCXSTR psz )
int Insert( int iIndex, XCHAR ch )
```

These methods insert the specified character or string into the CStringT instance starting at iIndex. The string manager associated with the CStringT allocates additional storage to accommodate the new data. Similarly, you can delete a character or series of characters from a string using either the Delete or Remove methods:

```
int Delete( int iIndex, int nCount = 1 )
int Remove( XCHAR chRemove )
```

Delete removes from the CStringT nCount characters starting at iIndex. Remove deletes all occurrences of the single character specified by chRemove.

```
CString str("That's a spicy meatball!");
str.Remove('T');    // str contains "hat's a spicy meatball!"
str.Remove('a');    // str contains "ht's  spicy metbll!"
```

Individual characters or strings can be replaced using the overloaded Replace method:

```
int Replace( XCHAR chOld, XCHAR chNew )
int Replace( PCXSTR pszOld, PCXSTR pszNew )
```

These methods search the CStringT instance for every occurrence of the specified character or string and replace each occurrence with the new character or string provided. The methods return either the number of replacements performed or -1 if no occurrences were found.

You can extract substrings of a CStringT using the Left, Mid, and Right functions:

```
CStringT Left( int nCount ) const
CStringT Mid( int iFirst ) const
CStringT Mid( int iFirst, int nCount ) const
CStringT Right( int nCount ) const
```

These functions are quite simple. `Left` returns in a new `CStringT` instance the first `nCount` characters of the original `CStringT`. `Mid` has two overloads. The first returns a new `CStringT` instance that contains all characters in the original starting at `iFirst` and continuing to the end. The second overload of `Mid` accepts an `nCount` parameter so that only the specified number of characters starting at `iFirst` are returned in the new `CStringT`. Finally, `Right` returns the rightmost `nCount` characters of the `CStringT` instance.

`CStringT`'s `MakeReverse` method enables you to reverse the characters in a `CStringT`:

```
CStringT& MakeReverse();

CString str("Let's do some ATL");
str.MakeReverse();    // str contains "LTA emos od s'teL"
```

`Tokenize` is a very useful method for breaking a `CStringT` into tokens separated by user-specified delimiters:

```
CStringT Tokenize( PCXSTR pszTokens, int& iStart ) const
```

The `pszTokens` parameter can include any number of characters that will be interpreted as delimiters between tokens. The `iStart` parameter specifies the starting index of the tokenization process. Note that this parameter is passed by reference so that the `Tokenize` implementation can update its value to the index of the first character following a delimiter. The function returns a `CStringT` instance containing the string token found. When no more tokens are found, the function returns an empty `CStringT` and `iStart` is set to -1. `Tokenize` is typically used in code like the following:

```
CString str("Name=Jenny; Ph: 867-5309");
CString tok;
int nPos = 0;
LPCSTR pszDelims = "; =:-";
tok = str.Tokenize(pszDelims, nPos);
while (tok != "") {
printf("Found token: %s\n", tok);
    tok = str.Tokenize(pszDelims, nPos);
}
```

```
// Prints the following:
// Found token: Name
// Found token: Jenny
// Found token: Ph
// Found token: 867
// Found token: 5309
```

Three methods enable you to populate a CStringT with string data embedded in the component DLL (or EXE) as a Windows resource:

```
BOOL LoadString( UINT nID )
BOOL LoadString( HINSTANCE hInstance, UINT nID )
BOOL LoadString( HINSTANCE hInstance, UINT nID,
    WORD wLanguageID )
```

The first overload retrieves the string from the module containing the calling code and stores it in CStringT. The second and third overloads enable you to explicitly pass in a handle to the module from which the resource string should be loaded. Additionally, the third overload enables you to load a string in a specific language by specifying the LANGID via the wLanguageID parameter. The function returns TRUE if the specified resource could be loaded into the CStringT instance; otherwise, it returns FALSE.

CStringT also provides a very thin wrapper function on top of the Win32 function GetEnvironmentVariable:

```
BOOL GetEnvironmentVariable( PCXSTR pszVar )
```

With this simple function, you can retrieve the value of the environment variable indicated by pszVar and store it in the CStringT instance. The functions return TRUE if it succeeded and FALSE otherwise.

Formatted Data

One of the most useful features of CStringT is its capability to construct formatted strings using sprintf-style format specifiers. CStringT exposes four methods for building formatted string data. The first two methods wrap underlying calls to the CRT function vsprintf or vswprintf, depending on whether the CStringT's Base-Type is char or wchar_t.

```
void __cdecl Format( PCXSTR pszFormat, ... );
void __cdecl Format( UINT nFormatID, ... );
```

The first overload for the Format method accepts a format string directly. The second overload retrieves the format string from the module's string table by looking up the resource ID nFormatID.

Two other closely related methods enable you to build formatted strings with CStringT instances. These methods wrap the Win32 API function FormatMessage:

```
void __cdecl FormatMessage( PCXSTR pszFormat, ... );
void __cdecl FormatMessage( UINT nFormatID, ... );
```

As with the Format methods, FormatMessage enables you to directly specify the format string by using the first overload or to load it from the module's string table using the second overload. It is important to note that the format strings allowed for Format and FormatMessage are different. Format uses the format strings vsprintf allows; FormatMessage uses the format strings the Win32 function FormatMessage allows. The exact syntax and semantics for the various format specifiers allowed are well documented in the online documentation, so this is not repeated here.

You use these methods in code like the following:

```
CString strFirst = "John";
CString strLast = "Doe";
CString str;

// str will contain "Doe, John: Age = 45"
str.Format("%s, %s: Age = %d", strLast, strFirst, 45);
```

Working with BSTRs and CString

You've seen that CStringT is great for manipulating char or wchar_t strings. Indeed, all the operations we've presented so far operate in terms of these two fundamental character types. However, we're going to be using ATL to build COM components, and that means we'll often be dealing with Automation types such as BSTR. So, we must have a convenient mechanism for returning a BSTR from a method while doing all the processing with our powerful CStringT class. As it happens, CStringT supplies two methods for precisely that purpose:

```
BSTR AllocSysString() const {
    BSTR bstrResult = StringTraits::AllocSysString( GetString(),
        GetLength() );
    if( bstrResult == NULL ) {
        ThrowMemoryException();
    }
}
```

```
    return( bstrResult );
}

BSTR SetSysString( BSTR* pbstr ) const {
    ATLASSERT( AtlIsValidAddress( pbstr, sizeof( BSTR ) ) );

    if( !StringTraits::ReAllocSysString( GetString(), pbstr,
        GetLength() ) ) {
        ThrowMemoryException();
    }

    ATLASSERT( *pbstr != NULL );
    return( *pbstr );
}
```

AllocSysString allocates a BSTR and copies the CStringT contents into it. CStringT delegates this work to the character traits class, which ultimately uses the COM API function SysAllocString. The resulting BSTR is returned to the caller. Note that AllocSysString transfers ownership of the BSTR, so the burden is on the caller to eventually call SysFreeString. CStringT also provides SetSysString, which provides the same capability as AllocSysString, except that SetSysString works with an existing BSTR and uses ReAllocSysString to expand the storage of the pbstr argument and then copies the CStringT data into it. This process also frees the original BSTR passed in.

The following example demonstrates how AllocSysString can be used to return a BSTR from a method call.

```
STDMETHODIMP CPhoneBook::LookupName( BSTR* pbstrName) {
    // ... do some processing

  CString str("Kirk");

  *pbstrName = str.AllocString(); // pbstrName contains "Kirk"

    // caller must eventually call SysFreeString
}
```

Summary

You must be especially careful when using the BSTR string type because it has numerous special semantics. The ATL CComBSTR class manages many of the special semantics for you and is quite useful. However, the class cannot compensate for the poor decision that, to the C++ compiler, equates the OLECHAR* and BSTR types. You always must use care when using the BSTR type because the compiler will not warn you of many pitfalls.

The CString class is poised to become the new workhorse for string processing in ATL. It is now a shared class with the MFC library and offers a host of powerful functions for manipulating strings in ways that would be very cumbersome and error prone with other string classes. Additionally, CString provides for the customization of string allocation via the IAtlStringMgr interface and a default implementation of that interface in CAtlStringMgr.

3 | ATL Smart Types

VARIANTs, SAFEARRAYs, and Interface Pointers

COM has a number of data types beyond the numeric types available in the C and C++ languages. Three such data types are the VARIANT data type, interface pointers, and the SAFEARRAY data type. ATL provides useful classes that encapsulate each of these data types and their special idiosyncrasies.

The CComVariant class is a smart VARIANT class. The class implements the special initialization, copy, and destruction semantics of the COM VARIANT data type. CComVariant instances can be used in most, but not all, of the places you would use a VARIANT.

The CComPtr, CComQIPtr, and CComGITPtr classes are smart pointer classes. Smart pointer classes are definitions of objects that "act" like a pointer—specifically, a pointer with extra semantics. The major additional semantic for the ATL smart pointer classes is automatic reference counting, which eliminates entire classes of errors.

The CComSafeArray class manages the Automation array type SAFEARRAY. These arrays require special handling with dedicated API functions for allocating, deallocating, and interrogating members of the array.

The CComVariant Smart VARIANT Class

A Review of the COM VARIANT Data Type

Occasionally while using COM, you'll want to pass parameters to a method without any knowledge of the data types the method requires. For the method to be capable of interpreting its received parameters, the caller must specify the format of the data as well as its value.

Alternatively, you can call a method that returns a result that consists of varying data types, depending on context. Sometimes it returns a string, sometimes a long, and sometimes even an interface pointer. This requires the method to return data in a self-describing data format. For each value transmitted, you send two fields: a code specifying a data type and a value represented in the specified data type. Clearly, for this to work, the sender and receiver must agree on the set of possible formats.

COM specifies one such set of possible formats (the VARTYPE enumeration) and specifies the structure that contains both the format and an associated value (the VARIANT structure). The VARIANT structure looks like this:

```
typedef struct FARSTRUCT tagVARIANT VARIANT;
typedef struct FARSTRUCT tagVARIANT VARIANTARG;

typedef struct tagVARIANT {
    VARTYPE vt;
    unsigned short wReserved1;
    unsigned short wReserved2;
    unsigned short wReserved3;
    union {
        unsigned char          bVal;        // VT_UI1
        short                  iVal;        // VT_I2
        long                   lVal;        // VT_I4
        float                  fltVal;      // VT_R4
        double                 dblVal;      // VT_R8
        VARIANT_BOOL           boolVal;     // VT_BOOL
        SCODE                  scode;       // VT_ERROR
        CY                     cyVal;       // VT_CY
        DATE                   date;        // VT_DATE
        BSTR                   bstrVal;     // VT_BSTR
        IUnknown        FAR*   punkVal;     // VT_UNKNOWN
        IDispatch       FAR*   pdispVal;    // VT_DISPATCH
        SAFEARRAY       FAR*   parray;      // VT_ARRAY|*
        unsigned char   FAR*   pbVal;       // VT_BYREF|VT_UI1
        short           FAR*   piVal;       // VT_BYREF|VT_I2
        long            FAR*   plVal;       // VT_BYREF|VT_I4
        float           FAR*   pfltVal;     // VT_BYREF|VT_R4
        double          FAR*   pdblVal;     // VT_BYREF|VT_R8
        VARIANT_BOOL    FAR*   pboolVal;    // VT_BYREF|VT_BOOL
        SCODE           FAR*   pscode;      // VT_BYREF|VT_ERROR
        CY              FAR*   pcyVal;      // VT_BYREF|VT_CY
        DATE            FAR*   pdate;       // VT_BYREF|VT_DATE
        BSTR            FAR*   pbstrVal;    // VT_BYREF|VT_BSTR
        IUnknown FAR*   FAR*   ppunkVal;    // VT_BYREF|VT_UNKNOWN
        IDispatch FAR*  FAR*   ppdispVal;   // VT_BYREF|VT_DISPATCH
        SAFEARRAY FAR*  FAR*   pparray;     // VT_ARRAY|*
        VARIANT         FAR*   pvarVal;     // VT_BYREF|VT_VARIANT
        void            FAR*   byref;       // Generic ByRef
    };
};
```

You initialize the VARIANT structure by storing a value in one of the fields of the tagged union and then storing the corresponding type code for the value in the vt member of the VARIANT structure. The VARIANT data type has a number of semantics that make using it tedious and error prone for C++ developers.

Correctly using a VARIANT requires that you remember the following rules:

- A VARIANT must be initialized before use by calling the VariantInit function on it. Alternatively, you can initialize the type and associated value field to a valid state (such as setting the vt field to VT_EMPTY).

- A VARIANT must be copied by calling the VariantCopy function on it. This performs the proper shallow or deep copy, as appropriate for the data type stored in the VARIANT.

- A VARIANT must be destroyed by calling the VariantClear function on it. This performs the proper shallow or deep destroy, as appropriate for the data type stored in the VARIANT. For example, when you destroy a VARIANT containing a SAFEARRAY of BSTRs, VariantClear frees each BSTR element in the array and then frees the array itself.

- A VARIANT can optionally represent, at most, one level of indirection, which is specified by adding the VT_BYREF bit setting to the type code. You can call VariantCopyInd to remove a single level of indirection from a VARIANT.

- You can attempt to change the data type of a VARIANT by calling VariantChangeType[Ex].

With all these special semantics, it is useful to encapsulate these details in a reusable class. ATL provides such a class: CComVariant.

The CComVariant Class

The CComVariant class is an ATL utility class that is a useful encapsulation for the COM self-describing data type, VARIANT. The atlcomcli.h file contains the definition of the CComVariant class. The only state the class maintains is an instance of the VARIANT structure, which the class obtains by inheritance from the tagVARIANT structure. Conveniently, this means that a CComVariant instance is a VARIANT structure, so you can pass a CComVariant instance to any function that expects a VARIANT structure.

```
class CComVariant: public tagVARIANT {
    ...
} ;
```

You often use a CComVariant instance when you need to pass a VARIANT argument to a COM method. The following code passes a string argument to a method that expects a VARIANT. The code uses the CComVariant class to do the conversion from a C-style string to the required VARIANT:

```
STDMETHODIMP put_Name(/* [in] const VARIANT* name);

HRESULT SetName (LPCTSTR pszName) {
    // Initializes the VARIANT structure
    // Allocates a BSTR copy of pszName
    // Sets the VARIANT to the BSTR
    CComVariant v (pszName);

    // Pass the raw VARIANT to the method
    return pObj->put_Name(&v);

    // Destructor clears v freeing the BSTR
}
```

Constructors and Destructor

Twenty-three constructors are available for CComVariant objects. The default constructor simply invokes the COM function VariantInit, which sets the vt flag to VT_EMPTY and properly initializes the VARIANT so that it is ready to use. The destructor calls the Clear member function to release any resources potentially held in the VARIANT.

```
CComVariant() {
    ::VariantInit(this);
}

~CComVariant() {
    Clear();
}
```

The other 22 constructors initialize the VARIANT structure appropriately, based on the type of the constructor argument.

Many of the constructors simply set the vt member of the VARIANT structure to the value representing the type of the constructor argument, and store the value of the argument in the appropriate member of the union.

```
CComVariant(BYTE nSrc) {
    vt = VT_UI1;
    bVal = nSrc;
}
CComVariant(short nSrc)  {
    vt = VT_I2;
    iVal = nSrc;
}
CComVariant(long nSrc, VARTYPE vtSrc = VT_I4)  {
    ATLASSERT(vtSrc == VT_I4 || vtSrc == VT_ERROR);
    vt = vtSrc;
    lVal = nSrc;
}
CComVariant( float fltSrc)  {
    vt = VT_R4;
    fltVal = fltSrc;
}
```

A few of the constructors are more complex. An SCODE looks like a long to the compiler. Therefore, constructing a CComVariant that specifies an SCODE or a long initialization value invokes the constructor that accepts a long. To enable you to distinguish these two cases, this constructor also takes an optional argument that allows you to specify whether the long should be placed in the VARIANT as a long or as an SCODE. When you specify a variant type other than VT_I4 or VT_ERROR, this constructor asserts in a debug build.

Windows 16-bit COM defined an HRESULT (a handle to a result code) as a data type that contained an SCODE (a status code). Therefore, you'll occasionally see older legacy code that considers the two data types to be different. In fact, some obsolete macros convert an SCODE to an HRESULT and extract the SCODE from an HRE-SULT. However, the SCODE and HRESULT data types are identical in 32-bit COM applications. The VARIANT data structure contains an SCODE field instead of an HRESULT because that's the way it was originally declared:

```
CComVariant(long nSrc, VARTYPE vtSrc = VT_I4) ;
```

The constructor that accepts a bool initialization value sets the contents of the VARIANT to VARIANT_TRUE or VARIANT_FALSE, as appropriate, not to the bool value specified. A logical TRUE value, as represented in a VARIANT , must be VARIANT_TRUE (–1 as a 16-bit value), and logical FALSE is VARIANT_FALSE (0 as a 16-bit value). The Microsoft C++ compiler defines the bool data type as an 8-bit (0 or 1) value. This constructor provides the conversion between the two representations of a Boolean value:

```
CComVariant(bool bSrc) {
    vt = VT_BOOL;
    boolVal = bSrc ? ATL_VARIANT_TRUE : ATL_VARIANT_FALSE;
}
```

Two constructors accept an interface pointer as an initialization value and produce a CComVariant instance that contains an AddRef'ed copy of the interface pointer. The first constructor accepts an IDispatch* argument. The second accepts an IUnknown* argument.

```
CComVariant(IDispatch* pSrc) ;
CComVariant(IUnknown* pSrc) ;
```

Two constructors enable you to initialize a CComVariant instance from another VARIANT structure or CComVariant instance:

```
CComVariant(const VARIANT& varSrc) {
    vt = VT_EMPTY; InternalCopy (&varSrc);
}
CComVariant(const CComVariant& varSrc); { /* Same as above */ }
```

Both have identical implementations, which brings up a subtle side effect, so let's look at the InternalCopy helper function both constructors use:

```
void InternalCopy(const VARIANT* pSrc) {
    HRESULT hr = Copy(pSrc);
    if (FAILED(hr)) {
        vt = VT_ERROR;
        scode = hr;
#ifndef _ATL_NO_VARIANT_THROW
        AtlThrow(hr);
#endif
    }
}
```

Notice how InternalCopy attempts to copy the specified VARIANT into the instance being constructed; when the copy fails, InternalCopy initializes the CComVariant instance as holding an error code (VT_ERROR). The Copy method used to attempt the copy returns the actual error code. This seems like an odd approach until you realize that a constructor cannot return an error, short of throwing an exception. ATL doesn't require support for exceptions, so this constructor must initialize the instance even when the Copy method fails. You can enable exceptions in this code via the _ATL_NO_VARIANT_THROW macro shown in the code.

I once had a CComVariant instance that always seemed to have a VT_ERROR code in it, even when I thought it shouldn't. As it turned out, I was constructing the CComVariant instance from an uninitialized VARIANT structure that resided on the stack. Watch out for code like this:

```
void func () {        // The following code is incorrect
  VARIANT v;          // Uninitialized stack garbage in vt member
  CComVariant sv(v);  // Indeterminate state
}
```

Three constructors accept a string initialization value and produce a CComVariant instance that contains a BSTR. The first constructor accepts a CComBSTR argument and creates a CComVariant that contains a BSTR copied from the CComBSTR argument. The second accepts an LPCOLESTR argument and creates a CComVariant that contains a BSTR that is a copy of the specified string of OLECHAR characters. The third accepts an LPCSTR argument and creates a CComVariant that contains a BSTR that is a converted-to-OLECHAR copy of the specified ANSI character string. These three constructors also possibly can "fail." In all three constructors, when the constructor cannot allocate memory for the new BSTR, it initializes the CComVariant instance to VT_ERROR with SCODE E_OUTOFMEMORY. The constructors also throw exceptions if the project settings are set appropriately.

```
CComVariant(const CComBSTR& bstrSrc);
CComVariant(LPCOLESTR lpszSrc);
CComVariant(LPCSTR lpszSrc);
```

Although both the first and second constructors logically accept the same fundamental data type (a string of OLECHAR), only the first constructor properly handles BSTRs that contain an embedded NUL—and only then if the CComBSTR object supplied has been properly constructed so that it has properly handled embedded NULs. The following example makes this clear:

```
LPCOLESTR osz = OLESTR("This is a\0BSTR string");
BSTR bstrIn = ::SysAllocStringLen(osz, 21) ;
// bstrIn contains "This is a\0BSTR string"

CComBSTR bstr(::SysStringLen(bstrIn), bstrIn);

CComVariant v1(bstr); // Correct - v1 contains
                      // "This is a\0BSTR string"
```

```
CComVariant v2(osz);  // Wrong! - v2 contains "This is a"

::SysFreeString (bstrIn) ;
```

Assignment

The CComVariant class defines an army of assignment operators—33 in all. All the assignment operators do the following actions:

- Clear the variant of its current contents
- Set the vt member of the VARIANT structure to the value representing the type of the assignment operator argument
- Store the value of the argument in the appropriate member of the union

```
CComVariant& operator=(char cSrc);              // VT_I1
CComVariant& operator=(int nSrc);               // VT_I4
CComVariant& operator=(unsigned int nSrc);      // VT_UI4
CComVariant& operator=(BYTE nSrc);              // VT_UI1
CComVariant& operator=(short nSrc);             // VT_I2
CComVariant& operator=(unsigned short nSrc);    // VT_UI2
CComVariant& operator=(long nSrc);              // VT_I4
CComVariant& operator=(unsigned long nSrc);     // VT_UI4

CComVariant& operator=(LONGLONG nSrc);          // VT_I8
CComVariant& operator=(ULONGULONG nSrc);        // VT_UI8
CComVariant& operator=(float fltSrc);           // VT_R4
CComVariant& operator=(double dblSrc);          // VT_R8
CComVariant& operator=(CY cySrc);               // VT_CY
```

Other overloads accept a pointer to all the previous types. Internally, these produce a vt value that is the bitwise OR of VT_BYREF and the vt member listed earlier. For example, operator=(long*) sets vt to VT_I4 | VT_BYREF.

The remaining operator= methods have additional semantics. Like the equivalent constructor, the assignment operator that accepts a bool initialization value sets the contents of the VARIANT to VARIANT_TRUE or VARIANT_FALSE, as appropriate, not to the bool value specified.

```
CComVariant& operator=(bool bSrc) ;
```

Two assignment operators accept an interface pointer and produce a CComVariant instance that contains an AddRef'ed copy of the interface pointer. One assignment operator accepts an IDispatch* argument. Another accepts an IUnknown* argument.

```
CComVariant& operator=(IDispatch* pSrc) ;
CComVariant& operator=(IUnknown* pSrc) ;
```

Two assignment operators allow you to initialize a CComVariant instance from another VARIANT structure or CComVariant instance. They both use the InternalCopy method, described previously, to make a copy of the provided argument. Therefore, these assignments can "fail" and produce an instance initialized to the VT_ERROR type (and possibly an exception).

```
CComVariant& operator=(const CComVariant& varSrc);
CComVariant& operator=(const VARIANT& varSrc);
```

One version of operator= accepts a SAFEARRAY as an argument:

```
CComVariant& operator=(const SAFEARRAY *pSrc);
```

This method uses the COM API function SafeArrayCopy to produce an independent duplicate of the SAFEARRAY passed in. It properly sets the vt member to be the bitwise OR of VT_ARRAY and the vt member of the elements of pSrc.

The remaining three assignment operators accept a string initialization value and produce a CComVariant instance that contains a BSTR. The first assignment operator accepts a CComBSTR argument and creates a CComVariant that contains a BSTR that is a copy of the specified CComBSTR's string data. The second accepts an LPCOLESTR argument and creates a CComVariant that contains a BSTR that is a copy of the specified string of OLECHAR characters. The third accepts an LPCSTR argument and creates a CComVariant that contains a BSTR that is a converted-to-OLECHAR copy of the specified ANSI character string.

```
CComVariant& operator=(const CComBSTR& bstrSrc);
CComVariant& operator=(LPCOLESTR lpszSrc);
CComVariant& operator=(LPCSTR lpszSrc);
```

The previous remarks about the constructors with a string initialization value apply equally to the assignment operators with a string initialization value. In fact, the constructors actually use these assignment operators to perform their initialization.

One final option to set the value of a CComVariant is the SetByRef method:

```
template< typename T >
void SetByRef( T* pT ) {
    Clear();
    vt = CVarTypeInfo< T >::VT|VT_BYREF;
    byref = pT;
}
```

This method clears the current contents and then sets the vt field to the appropriate type with the addition of the VT_BYREF flag; this indicates that the variant contains a pointer to the actual data, not the data itself. The CVarTypeInfo class is
another *traits* class. The generic version follows:

```
template< typename T >
class CVarTypeInfo {
// VARTYPE corresponding to type T
//    static const VARTYPE VT;
// Pointer-to-member of corresponding field in VARIANT struct
//    static T VARIANT::* const pmField;
};
```

The comments indicate what each template specialization does: provides the
VT constant that gives the appropriate VARTYPE value to use for this type and the
pmField pointer that indicates which field of a variant stores this type. These are
two of the specializations:

```
template<>
class CVarTypeInfo< unsigned char > {
public:
    static const VARTYPE VT = VT_UI1;
    static unsigned char VARIANT::* const pmField;
};

__declspec( selectany ) unsigned char VARIANT::* const
    CVarTypeInfo< unsigned char >::pmField = &VARIANT::bVal;

template<>
class CVarTypeInfo< BSTR > {
public:
    static const VARTYPE VT = VT_BSTR;
    static BSTR VARIANT::* const pmField;
};
```

```
__declspec( selectany ) BSTR VARIANT::* const
    CVarTypeInfo< BSTR >::pmField = &VARIANT::bstrVal;
```

The initializers are necessary to set the `pmField` pointers appropriately. The `pmField` value is not currently used anywhere in ATL 8, but it could be useful for writing your own code that deals with VARIANTs.

CComVariant Operations

It's important to realize that a VARIANT is a resource that must be managed properly. Just as memory from the heap must be allocated and freed, a VARIANT must be initialized and cleared. Just as the ownership of a memory block must be explicitly managed so it's freed only once, the ownership of the contents of a VARIANT must be explicitly managed so it's cleared only once. Four methods give you control over any resources a `CComVariant` instance owns.

The `Clear` method releases any resources the instance contains by calling the `VariantClear` function. For an instance that contains, for example, a `long` or a similar scalar value, this method does nothing except set the variant type field to `VT_EMPTY`. However, for an instance that contains a BSTR, the method releases the string. For an instance that contains an interface pointer, the method releases the interface pointer. For an instance that contains a SAFEARRAY, this method iterates over each element in the array, releasing each element, and then releases the SAFEARRAY itself.

```
HRESULT Clear() { return ::VariantClear(this); }
```

When you no longer need the resource contained in a `CComVariant` instance, you should call the `Clear` method to release it. The destructor does this automatically for you. This is one of the major advantages of using `CComVariant` instead of a raw VARIANT: automatic cleanup at the end of a scope. So, if an instance will quickly go out of scope when you're finished using its resources, let the destructor take care of the cleanup. However, a `CComVariant` instance as a global or static variable doesn't leave scope for a potentially long time. The `Clear` method is useful in this case.

The `Copy` method makes a unique copy of the specified VARIANT. The `Copy` method produces a `CComVariant` instance that has a lifetime that is separate from the lifetime of the VARIANT that it copies.

```
HRESULT Copy(const VARIANT* pSrc)
    { return ::VariantCopy(this, const_cast<VARIANT*>(pSrc)); }
```

Often, you'll use the Copy method to copy a VARIANT that you receive as an [in] parameter. The caller providing an [in] parameter is loaning the resource to you. When you want to hold the parameter longer than the scope of the method call, you must copy the VARIANT:

```
STDMETHODIMP SomeClass::put_Option (const VARIANT* pOption) {
    // Option saved in member m_Option of type CComVariant
    return m_varOption.Copy (pOption) ;
}
```

When you want to transfer ownership of the resources in a CComVariant instance from the instance to a VARIANT structure, use the Detach method. It clears the destination VARIANT structure, does a memcpy of the CComVariant instance into the specified VARIANT structure, and then sets the instance to VT_EMPTY. Note that this technique avoids extraneous memory allocations and AddRef/Release calls.

```
HRESULT Detach(VARIANT* pDest);
```

Do not use the Detach *method to update an* [out] VARIANT *argument without special care!* An [out] parameter is uninitialized on input to a method. The Detach method clears the specified VARIANT before overwriting it. Clearing a VARIANT filled with random bits produces random behavior.

```
STDMETHODIMP SomeClass::get_Option (VARIANT* pOption) {
    CComVariant varOption ;
    ... Initialize the variant with the output data

    // Wrong! The following code can generate an exception,
    // corrupt your heap, and give at least seven years bad luck!
    return varOption.Detach (pOption);
}
```

Before detaching into an [out] VARIANT argument, be sure to initialize the output argument:

```
// Special care taken to initialize [out] VARIANT
::VariantInit (pOption) ;
// or
pOption->vt = VT_EMPTY ;

return vOption.Detach (pOption); // Now we can Detach safely.
```

When you want to transfer ownership of the resources in a VARIANT structure from the structure to a CComVariant instance, use the Attach method. It clears the current instance, does a memcpy of the specified VARIANT into the current instance, and then sets the specified VARIANT to VT_EMPTY. Note that this technique avoids extraneous memory allocations and AddRef/Release calls.

```
HRESULT Attach(VARIANT* pSrc);
```

Client code can use the Attach method to assume ownership of a VARIANT that it receives as an [out] parameter. The function providing an [out] parameter transfers ownership of the resource to the caller.

```
STDMETHODIMP SomeClass::get_Option (VARIANT* pOption);

void VerboseGetOption () {
    VARIANT v;
    pObj->get_Option (&v) ;

    CComVariant cv;
    cv.Attach (&v);    // Destructor now releases the VARIANT
}
```

Somewhat more efficiently, but potentially more dangerously, you could code this differently:

```
void FragileGetOption() {
    CComVariant v;          // This is fragile code!!
    pObj->get_Option (&v) ; // Directly update the contained
                            // VARIANT. Destructor now releases
                            // the VARIANT.
}
```

Note that, in this case, the get_Option method overwrites the VARIANT structure contained in the CComVariant instance. Because the method expects an [out] parameter, the get_Option method does not release any resources contained in the provided argument. In the preceding example, the instance was freshly constructed, so it is empty when overwritten. The following code, however, causes a memory leak:

```
void LeakyGetOption() {
    CComVariant v (OLESTR ("This string leaks!")) ;
    pObj->get_Option (&v) ; // Directly updates the contained
                            // VARIANT. Destructor now releases
                            // the VARIANT.
}
```

When you use a `CComVariant` instance as an [out] parameter to a method that expects a `VARIANT`, you must first clear the instance if there is any possibility that the instance is not empty.

```
void NiceGetOption() {
    CComVariant v (OLESTR ("This string doesn't leak!")) ;
    ...
    v.Clear ();
    pObj->get_Option (&v) ; // Directly updates the contained
                            // VARIANT. Destructor now releases
                            // the VARIANT.


}
```

The `ChangeType` method converts a `CComVariant` instance to the new type specified by the `vtNew` parameter. When you specify a second argument, `ChangeType` uses it as the source for the conversion. Otherwise, `ChangeType` uses the `CComVariant` instance as the source for the conversion and performs the conversion in place.

```
HRESULT ChangeType(VARTYPE vtNew, const VARIANT* pSrc = NULL);
```

`ChangeType` converts between the fundamental types (including numeric-to-string and string-to-numeric coercions). `ChangeType` coerces a source that contains a reference to a type (that is, the `VT_BYREF` bit is set) to a value by retrieving the referenced value. `ChangeType` always coerces an object reference to a value by retrieving the object's `Value` property. This is the property with the `DISPID_VALUE DISPID`. The `ChangeType` method can be useful not only for COM programming, but also as a general data type conversion library.

CComVariant Comparison Operators

The `operator==()` method compares a `CComVariant` instance for equality with the specified `VARIANT` structure:

```
bool operator==(const VARIANT& varSrc) const ;
bool operator!=(const VARIANT& varSrc) const ;
```

When the two operands have differing types, the operator returns `false`. If they are of the same type, the implementation calls the VarCmp API function[1] to do the

---

[1] A number of operating system functions manipulate VARIANTs. The functions `VarAbs`, `VarAdd`, `VarAnd`, `VarCat`, `VarCmp`, `VarDiv`, `VarEqv`, `VarFix`, `VarIdiv`, `VarImp`, `VarInt`, `VarMod`, `VarMul`, `VarNeg`, `VarNot`, `VarOr`, `VarPow`, `VarRound`, `VarSub`, and `VarXor` collectively comprise the Variant Math API.

proper comparison based on the underlying type. The operator!=() method returns the negation of the operator==() method.

Both the operator<() and operator>() methods perform their respective comparisons using the Variant Math API function VarCmp:

```
bool operator<(const VARIANT& varSrc) const ;
bool operator>(const VARIANT& varSrc) const ;
```

CComVariant Persistence Support

You can use the last three methods of the CComVariant class to read and write a VARIANT to and from a stream:

```
HRESULT WriteToStream(IStream* pStream);
HRESULT ReadFromStream(IStream* pStream);
ULONG GetSize() const;
```

The WriteToStream method writes the vt type code to the stream. For simple types such as VT_I4, VT_R8, and similar scalar values, it writes the value of the VARIANT to the stream immediately following the type code. For an interface pointer, WriteToStream writes the GUID CLSID_NULL to the stream when the pointer is NULL. When the interface pointer is not NULL, WriteToStream queries the referenced object for its IPersistStream interface. If that fails, it queries for IPersistStreamInit. When the object supports one of these interfaces, WriteToStream calls the COM OleSaveToStream function to save the object to the stream. When the interface pointer is not NULL and the object does not support either the IPersistStream or IPersistStreamInit interfaces, WriteToStream fails.

For complex types, including VT_BSTR, all by-reference types, and all arrays, WriteToStream attempts to convert the value, if necessary, to a BSTR and writes the string to the stream using CComBSTR::WriteToStream.

The ReadFromStream method performs the inverse operation. First, it clears the current CComVariant instance. Then it reads the variant type code from the stream. For the simple types, such as VT_I4, VT_R8, and similar scalar values, it reads the value of the VARIANT from the stream. For an interface pointer, it calls the COM OleLoadFromStream function to read the object from the stream, requesting the IUnknown or IDispatch interface, as appropriate. When OleLoadFromStream returns REGDB_E_CLASSNOTREG (usually because of reading CLSID_NULL), ReadFromStream silently returns an S_OK status.

For all other types, including VT_BSTR, all by-reference types, and all arrays, ReadFromStream calls CComBSTR::ReadFromStream to read the previously written string from the stream. The method then coerces the string back to the original type.

GetSize provides an estimate of the amount of space that the variant will require in the stream. This is needed for implementing various methods on the persistence interfaces. The size estimate is exactly correct for simple types (int, long, double, and so on). For variants that contain interface pointers, CComVariant does a QueryInterface for the IPersistStream or IPersistStreamInit interfaces and uses the GetSizeMax( ) method to figure out the size. For other types, the variant is converted to a BSTR and the length of the string is used.

In general, the GetSize( ) method is used as an initial estimate for things such as buffer sizes. When the code inside ATL calls GetSize( ) (mainly in persistence support, discussed in Chapter 7, "Persistence in ATL") it correctly grows the buffers if the estimate is low. In your own use, be aware that sometimes the Get-Size( ) method won't be exactly correct.

The CComSafeArray Smart SAFEARRAY Class

A Review of the COM SAFEARRAY Data Type

IDL provides several attributes for specifying arrays in COM interfaces. Attributes such as [size_is] and [length_is] enable you to adorn method definitions with information required to marshal these arrays across COM boundaries. Yet not all languages support arrays in the same way. For instance, some languages support zero-based arrays, while others require one-based arrays. Still others, such as Visual Basic, allow the application itself to decide whether the arrays it references are zero-based or one-based. Array storage varies from language to language as well: Some languages store elements in row-major order, and others use column-major order. To make the situation even worse, type libraries don't support the IDL attributes needed to marshal C-style IDL arrays; the MIDL compiler silently drops these attributes when generating type libraries.

To address the challenges of passing arrays between COM clients in a language-agnostic manner, Automation defines the SAFEARRAY data type. In much the same way as VARIANTs are self-describing generic data types, SAFEARRAYs are self-describing generic arrays. SAFEARRAYs are declared in IDL as follows:

```
interface IMyInterface : IUnknown {
    HRESULT  GetArray([out,retval]
        SAFEARRAY(VARIANT_BOOL)* myArray);
};
```

The VARIANT_BOOL parameter to the SAFEARRAY declaration indicates the data type of the elements in the SAFEARRAY. This type must be an Automation-compatible type as well, meaning that it must be one of the data types that can be contained in a VARIANT. The MIDL compiler preserves this information in the type library so that clients can discover the underlying type of the SAFEARRAY.

The C++ binding for the SAFEARRAY type is actually a struct that represents a self-describing array. It contains a description of the contents of the array, including the upper and lower bounds and the total number of elements in the array. The SAFEARRAY struct is defined in oaidl.h as follows:

```
typedef struct tagSAFEARRAY {
    USHORT cDims;
    USHORT fFeatures;
    ULONG cbElements;
    ULONG cLocks;
    PVOID pvData;
    SAFEARRAYBOUND rgsabound[ 1 ];
} SAFEARRAY;
```

The upper and lower bounds for the SAFEARRAY are stored in the rgsabound array. Each element in this array is a SAFEARRAYBOUND structure.

```
typedef struct tagSAFEARRAYBOUND {
    ULONG cElements;
    LONG lLbound;
} SAFEARRAYBOUND;
```

The leftmost dimension of the array is contained in rgsabound[0], and the rightmost dimension is in rgsabound[cDims - 1]. For example, an array declared with C-style syntax to have dimensions of [3][4] would have two elements in the rgsabound array. The first element at offset zero would have a cElements value of 3 and an lLbound value of 0; the second element at offset one would have a cElements value of 4 and also an lLbound value of 0.

The pvData field of the SAFEARRAY struct points to the actual data in the array. The cbElements array indicates the size of each element. As you can see, this data type is flexible enough to represent an array with an arbitrary number of elements and dimensions.

COM provides a number of APIs for managing SAFEARRAYs. These functions enable you to create, access, and destroy SAFEARRAYs of various dimensions and sizes. The following code demonstrates how to use these functions to manipulate two-dimensional SAFEARRAYs of double. The first step is to create an array of SAFEARRAYBOUND structures to indicate the number and size of the array dimensions:

```
SAFEARRAYBOUND rgsabound[2];
rgsabound[0].cElements = 3;
```

```
rgsabound[0].lLbound = 0;
rgsabound[1].cElements = 4;
rgsabound[1].lLbound = 0;
```

This code specifies a two-dimensional array with three elements in the first dimension (three rows) and four elements in the second dimension (four columns). This array is then passed to the `SafeArrayCreate` function to allocate the appropriate amount of storage:

```
SAFEARRAY* psa = ::SafeArrayCreate(VT_R8, 2, rgsabound);
```

The first parameter to this function indicates the data type for the elements of the array. The second parameter specifies the number of elements in the `rgsabound` array (for example, the number of dimensions). The final parameter is the array of `SAFEARRAYBOUND` structures describing each dimension of the `SAFEARRAY`. You can retrieve elements of the SAFEARRAY using the `SafeArrayGetElement` function, like this:

```
long rgIndices[] = { 2, 1 };
double lElem;
::SafeArrayGetElement(psa, rgIndices, (void*)&lElem);
```

This code retrieves the element stored at location `[1][2]`—that is, the second row, third column. Confusingly, the `rgIndices` specifies the `SAFEARRAY` indices in reverse order: The first element of the `rgIndices` array specifies the rightmost dimension of the `SAFEARRAY`. You must manually free the `SAFEARRAY` and the data it contains using the `SafeArrayDestroy` function.

```
::SafeArrayDestroy(psa);
```

As you can see, manipulating `SAFEARRAY`s with these APIs is a bit tedious. Fortunately, ATL provides some relief in the form of a templatized wrapper class called `CComSafeArray`. This class is defined in `atlsafe.h` as follows:

```
template <typename T,
    VARTYPE _vartype = _ATL_AutomationType<T>::type>
class CComSafeArray {
  ...
public:
    LPSAFEARRAY m_psa;
}
```

This template class encapsulates a pointer to a SAFEARRAY as its only state. The first template parameter is the C++ type that will be stored in the internal SAFEARRAY. Recall that SAFEARRAYs can hold only Automation-compatible types as elements—that is, data types that can be stored in a VARIANT. So, the second template parameter to CComSafeArray indicates the VARTYPE of the elements to be stored. Only a subset of the VARIANT-compatible types are supported with CComSafeArray. These are listed in Table 3.1.

Table 3.1 ARTYPEs CComSafeArray Supports

VARTYPE	C++ Type
VT_I1	char
VT_I2	short
VT_I4	int
VT_I4	long
VT_I8	longlong
VT_UI1	byte
VT_UI2	ushort
VT_UI4	uint
VT_UI4	ulong
VT_UI8	ulonglong
VT_R4	float
VT_R8	double
VT_DECIMAL	decimal
VT_VARIANT	variant
VT_CY	currency
VT_BSTR	BSTR
VT_DISPATCH	IDispatch pointer
VT_UNKNOWN	IUnknown pointer

The documentation indicates that the last three VARTYPEs—BSTR, IDispatch, and IUnknown pointers—are not supported. The documentation is wrong; CComSafeArray uses template specialization to accommodate the unique semantics of these data types. More on this comes later in this section.

The default value for the second template parameter employs a clever combination of templates and macros to automatically associate the C++ data type with the VARTYPE that the SAFEARRAY API functions must use internally. The default parameter value uses the _ATL_AutomationType dummy template, defined as follows:

```
template <typename T>
struct _ATL_AutomationType { };
```

The DEFINE_AUTOMATION_TYPE_FUNCTION macro generates type mappings from the C++ data type to the appropriate VARTYPE. The type enum member holds the VARTYPE that CComSafeArray ultimately will use:

```
#define DEFINE_AUTOMATION_TYPE_FUNCTION(ctype,
 typewrapper, oleautomationtype) \
    template <> \
    struct _ATL_AutomationType<ctype> { \
    typedef typewrapper _typewrapper;\
    enum { type = oleautomationtype }; \
    static void* GetT(const T& t)  { \
        return (void*)&t; \
    } \
};
```

A series of these macros are declared in atlsafe.h to map CComSafeArray-supported types to the appropriate VARTYPE. Note that these macros include as the second macro parameter a typewrapper. This is interesting only for the four supported data types that require special handling: VARIANT, BSTR, IDispatch*, and IUnknown*.

```
DEFINE_AUTOMATION_TYPE_FUNCTION(CHAR, CHAR, VT_I1)
DEFINE_AUTOMATION_TYPE_FUNCTION(SHORT, SHORT, VT_I2)
DEFINE_AUTOMATION_TYPE_FUNCTION(INT, INT, VT_I4)
DEFINE_AUTOMATION_TYPE_FUNCTION(LONG, LONG, VT_I4)
DEFINE_AUTOMATION_TYPE_FUNCTION(LONGLONG, LONGLONG, VT_I8)
DEFINE_AUTOMATION_TYPE_FUNCTION(BYTE, BYTE, VT_UI1)
DEFINE_AUTOMATION_TYPE_FUNCTION(USHORT, USHORT, VT_UI2)
DEFINE_AUTOMATION_TYPE_FUNCTION(UINT, UINT, VT_UI4)
DEFINE_AUTOMATION_TYPE_FUNCTION(ULONG, ULONG, VT_UI4)
DEFINE_AUTOMATION_TYPE_FUNCTION(ULONGLONG, ULONGLONG, VT_UI8)
DEFINE_AUTOMATION_TYPE_FUNCTION(FLOAT, FLOAT, VT_R4)
DEFINE_AUTOMATION_TYPE_FUNCTION(DOUBLE, DOUBLE, VT_R8)
DEFINE_AUTOMATION_TYPE_FUNCTION(DECIMAL, DECIMAL, VT_DECIMAL)
DEFINE_AUTOMATION_TYPE_FUNCTION(VARIANT, CComVariant, VT_VARIANT)
DEFINE_AUTOMATION_TYPE_FUNCTION(CY, CY, VT_CY)
```

With these definitions in hand, declaring an instance of CComSafeArray<long> would generate a second parameter of _ATL_Automation_Type<long>::type, where the exposed type member is equal to VT_I4.

Constructors and Destructor

The template parameter you pass to CComSafeArray establishes only the data type of the SAFEARRAY elements, not the number of dimensions or the size of each dimension. This information is established through one of the seven CComSafeArray constructors. The first constructor is the default (parameterless) constructor and simply initializes m_psa to NULL. Three other constructors create a new CComSafeArray instance from dimension and size information. The first of these constructors creates a one-dimensional array with ulCount elements and is indexed starting with lLBound:

```
explicit CComSafeArray(ULONG ulCount, LONG lLBound = 0);
```

Internally, this constructor uses these arguments to create an instance of a class that serves as a thin wrapper for the SAFEARRAYBOUND structure discussed earlier. The CComSafeArrayBound class exposes simple methods for manipulating the number of elements in a particular CComSafeArray dimension, as well as the starting index (lower bound) for that dimension. Note that this class derives directly from the SAFEARRAYBOUND structure, so it can be passed to methods that expect either a CComSafeArrayBound class or a SAFEARRAYBOUND structure.

```
class CComSafeArrayBound : public SAFEARRAYBOUND {
    CComSafeArrayBound(ULONG ulCount = 0, LONG lLowerBound = 0)
    { ... }
    CComSafeArrayBound&
    operator=(const CComSafeArrayBound& bound)
    { ... }
    CComSafeArrayBound& operator=(ULONG ulCount)  { ... }
    ULONG GetCount() const  { ... }
    ULONG SetCount(ULONG ulCount)  { ... }
    LONG GetLowerBound() const  { ... }
    LONG SetLowerBound(LONG lLowerBound)  { ... }
    LONG GetUpperBound() const  { ... }
};
```

A quick look at the implementation for the CComSafeArray(ULONG, LONG) constructor demonstrates how all the nondefault constructors use the CComSafeArrayBound wrapper class:

```
explicit CComSafeArray(ULONG ulCount, LONG lLBound = 0)
    : m_psa(NULL) {
    CComSafeArrayBound bound(ulCount, lLBound);
    HRESULT hRes = Create(&bound);
    if (FAILED(hRes))
        AtlThrow(hRes);
}
```

An instance of CComSafeArrayBound is created and passed to the Create member function, which is itself a thin wrapper over the SAFEARRAY API functions. As shown in the following code fragment, Create uses the SafeArrayCreate API to support building a SAFEARRAY with any number of dimensions:

```
HRESULT Create(const SAFEARRAYBOUND *pBound, UINT uDims = 1) {
    ATLASSERT(m_psa == NULL);
    ATLASSERT(uDims > 0);
    HRESULT hRes = S_OK;
    m_psa = SafeArrayCreate(_vartype, uDims,
    const_cast<LPSAFEARRAYBOUND>(pBound));
    if (NULL == m_psa)
        hRes = E_OUTOFMEMORY;
    else
        hRes = Lock();
    return hRes;
}
```

This first constructor just shown is probably the most frequently used. One-dimensional SAFEARRAYs are much more common than multidimensional SAFEARRAYs, and C++ developers are accustomed to zero-based array indexing. You make use of this simple constructor with code such as the following:

```
// create a 1-D zero-based SAFEARRAY of long with 10 elements
CComSafeArray<long> sa(10);

// create a 1-D one-based SAFEARRAY of double with 5 elements
CComSafeArray<double> sa(5,1);
```

The second CComSafeArray constructor enables you to pass in a SAFEARRAYBOUND structure or a CComSafeArrayBound instance:

```
explicit CComSafeArray(const SAFEARRAYBOUND& bound);
```

This constructor is invoked when you write code similar to the following:

```
CComSafeArrayBound bound(5,1);     // 1-D one-based array
CComSafeArray<long> sa(bound);
```

This constructor is arguably less useful and less succinct than passing the bounds information directly via the first constructor shown. You use the third constructor to create a multidimensional SAFEARRAY. This constructor accepts an array of SAFEARRAYBOUND structures or CSafeArrayBound instances, along with a UINT parameter to indicate the number of dimensions:

```
explicit CComSafeArray(const SAFEARRAYBOUND *pBound, UINT uDims = 1);
```

You create a multidimensional CComSafeArray with this constructor as follows:

```
// 3-D array with all dimensions
// left-most dimension has 3 elements
CComSafeArrayBound bound1(3);
// middle dimension has 4 elements
CComSafeArrayBound bound2(4);
// right-most dimension has 5 elements
CComSafeArrayBound bound3(5);

// equivalent C-style array indices would be [3][4][5]
CComSafeArrayBound rgBounds[] = { bound1, bound2, bound3 };
CComSafeArray<int> sa(rgBounds, 3);
```

Note that nothing prevents you from creating different starting indices for the different dimensions of the SAFEARRAY—nothing but your conscience that is. This would be extraordinarily confusing for any code that uses this type. In any event, as mentioned previously, multidimensional SAFEARRAYs are pretty rare creatures in reality, so we won't belabor the point.

The remaining three CComSafeArray constructors create an instance from an existing SAFEARRAY or CComSafeArray. They are declared as follows:

```
CComSafeArray(const SAFEARRAY *psaSrc) : m_psa(NULL);
CComSafeArray(const SAFEARRAY& saSrc) : m_psa(NULL);
CComSafeArray(const CComSafeArray& saSrc) : m_psa(NULL);
```

All three constructors do the same thing: check for a NULL source and delegate to the CopyFrom method to duplicate the contents of the source instance. CopyFrom accepts a SAFEARRAY* and CComSafeArray provides a SAFEARRAY* cast operator, so the third constructor delegates to the CopyFrom method as well. This produces a clone of the source array. The following code demonstrates how it instantiates a CComSafeArray from an existing instance:

```
CComSafeArray<int> saSrc(5);      // source is 1-D array of 5 ints
// allocate storage for 1-D array of 5 ints
// and copy contents of source
CComSafeArray<int> saDest(saSrc);
```

The destructor for CComSafeArray is quite simple as well. It automatically releases the resources allocated for the SAFEARRAY when the instance goes out of scope. The implementation simply delegates to the Destroy method, which is defined as follows:

```
HRESULT Destroy() {
    HRESULT hRes = S_OK;
    if (m_psa != NULL) {
        hRes = Unlock();
        if (SUCCEEDED(hRes)) {
            hRes = SafeArrayDestroy(m_psa);
            if (SUCCEEDED(hRes))
                m_psa = NULL;
        }
    }
    return hRes;
}
```

The Destroy method first calls Unlock to decrement the lock count on the internal SAFEARRAY and then simply delegates to the SafeArrayDestroy method. The significance of lock counting SAFEARRAYs is discussed shortly.

Assignment

CComSafeArray defines two assignment operators. Both duplicate the contents of the right-side instance, clearing the contents of the left-side instance beforehand. These operators are defined as follows:

```
CComSafeArray<T>& operator=(const CComSafeArray& saSrc) {
    *this = saSrc.m_psa;
    return *this;
}
CComSafeArray<T>& operator=(const SAFEARRAY *psaSrc) {
    ATLASSERT(psaSrc != NULL);
```

```
      HRESULT hRes = CopyFrom(psaSrc);
      if (FAILED(hRes))
          AtlThrow(hRes);
      return *this;
}
```

The assignment statement in the first line of the first operator delegates immediately to the second operator that accepts a SAFEARRAY* parameter. CopyFrom clears the contents of the destination SAFEARRAY by eventually calling SafeArrayDestroy to free resources allocated when the target SAFEARRAY was created. This code gets invoked with code such as the following:

```
CComSafeArray<long> sa1(10);
// do something interesting with sa1
CComSafeArray<long> sa2(5);


// free contents of sa1, duplicate contents
// of sa2 and put into sa1
sa1 = sa2;
```

The Detach and Attach Methods

As with the CComVariant and CComBSTR classes discussed earlier, the CComSafeArray class wraps a data type that must be carefully managed if resource leaks are to be avoided. The storage allocated for the encapsulated SAFEARRAY must be explicitly created and freed using the SAFEARRAY API functions. In fact, two chunks of memory must be managed: the SAFEARRAY structure itself and the actual data contained in the SAFEARRAY.

Just as with CComVariant and CComBSTR, the CComSafeArray class provides Attach and Detach methods to wrap a preallocated SAFEARRAY:

```
HRESULT Attach(const SAFEARRAY *psaSrc) {
    ATLENSURE_THROW(psaSrc != NULL, E_INVALIDARG);

    VARTYPE vt;
    HRESULT hRes = ::ATL::AtlSafeArrayGetActualVartype(
        const_cast<LPSAFEARRAY>(psaSrc), &vt);
    ATLENSURE_SUCCEEDED(hRes);
    ATLENSURE_THROW(vt == GetType(), E_INVALIDARG);
    hRes = Destroy();
    m_psa = const_cast<LPSAFEARRAY>(psaSrc);
    hRes = Lock();
```

```
    return hRes;
}

LPSAFEARRAY Detach() {
    Unlock();
    LPSAFEARRAY pTemp = m_psa;
    m_psa = NULL;
    return pTemp;
}
```

The `Attach` operation first checks to see if the type contained in the `SAFEARRAY` being attached matches the type passed as a template parameter. If the type is correct, the method next releases its reference to the encapsulated `SAFEARRAY` by calling `Destroy`. We glossed over the `Destroy` method when we presented it previously, but you'll note that the first thing `Destroy` did was call the `CComSafeArray`'s `Unlock` method. The lock count in the `SAFEARRAY` structure is an interesting historical leftover.

Back in the days of 16-bit Windows, the OS couldn't rely on having a virtual memory manager. Every chunk of memory was dealt with as a direct physical pointer. To fit into that wonderful world of 640KB, memory management required an extra level of indirection. The `GlobalAlloc` API function that's still with us is an example. When you allocate memory via `GlobalAlloc`, you don't get an actual pointer back. Instead, you get an `HGLOBAL`. To get the actual pointer, you call `GlobalLock` and pass it the `HGLOBAL`. When you're done working with the pointer, you call `GlobalUnlock`. This doesn't actually free the memory; if you call `GlobalLock` again on the same `HGLOBAL`, your data will still be there, but on 16-bit Windows the pointer you got back could be different. While the block is unlocked, the OS is free to change the physical address where the block lives by copying the contents.

Today, of course, the virtual memory managers inside modern CPUs handle all this. Still, some vestiges of those old days remain. The `SAFEARRAY` is one of those vestiges. You are not allowed to do this to access a `SAFEARRAY`'s data:

```
SAFEARRAY *psa = ::SafeArrayCreateVector(VT_I4, 0, 10);
// BAD - this pointer may not be valid!
int *pData = reinterpret_cast<int *>(pda->pvData);
// BOOM (maybe)
pData[0] = 5;
```

Instead, you need to first lock the `SAFEARRAY`:

```
SAFEARRAY *psa = ::SafeArrayCreateVector(VT_I4, 0, 10);
// GOOD - this will allocate the actual storage for the data
::SafeArrayLock(psa);
```

```
// Now the pointer is valid
int *pData = ( int * )(pda->pvData);
pData[0] = 5;
// Unlock after we're done
::SafeArrayUnlock( psa );
```

Locking the SAFEARRAY actually allocates the storage for the data if it doesn't already exist and sets the pvData field of the SAFEARRAY structure. Several different APIs perform this function. You can't just do psa->cLocks++; you must call an appropriate API function.

In the bad old days, it was important that handles got unlocked as quickly as possible; if they didn't, the OS couldn't move memory around and eventually everything ground to a halt as memory fragmentation grew. These days, there's no need to worry about unlocking, but the API remains. So, the CComSafeArray takes a simple approach: It locks the data as soon as it gets the SAFEARRAY and doesn't unlock it until the SAFEARRAY is either Destroyed or Detached.

You usually use Attach inside a method implementation to wrap a SAFEARRAY that has been passed to you:

```
STDMETHODIMP SomeClass::AverageArray(/* [in] */ SAFEARRAY* psa,
    /* [out] */ LONG* plAvg) {
    if (!plAvg) return E_POINTER;
    CComSafeArray<long> sa; // Note: no type check is done
                            // against psa type
    sa.Attach(psa);         // we're pointing at the same
                            // memory as psa

    ... perform some calculations

    sa.Detach(); // Must detach here or risk a crash
    return S_OK;
}
```

When you want to return a SAFERRAY from a method call, turn to the Detach operation, as in the following example:

```
STDMETHODIMP SomeClass::get_Array(/* [out] */ SAFEARRAY** ppsa) {
    if (!ppsa) return E_POINTER;
    CComSafeArray<long> sa(10);

    ... populate sa instance

    // no resources released when we leave scope
```

```
        // and no copying performed
        *ppsa = sa.Detach();
        return S_OK;
    }
```

Attach and Detach don't do any copying of the SAFEARRAY, and with the lock count in place, you might be tempted to think of the lock count as a kind of reference counting. Unfortunately, ATL 8 has a bug in the implementation of the Destroy method that makes this use of CComSafeArray problematic. Consider this code sample:

```
STDMETHODIMP SomeClass::DontDoThis(SAFEARRAY* psa) {
    // We have two references to the safearray
    CComSafeArray<long> sa1, sa2;
    sa1.Attach(psa);
    sa2.Attach(psa);

    // manipulate the array here
    // BUG: Don't do this
    sa2.Destroy( );
}
```

The explicit call to sa2.Destroy() will not actually destroy the underlying SAFEARRAY; this makes sense because there are still outstanding references (and locks) on the underlying data structure. It did, however, call Unlock(). Here's the bug: Even though Destroy was called, sa2 thinks that it's holding on to a valid reference to a SAFEARRAY. As a result, the destructor of sa2 calls Destroy() *again*, resulting in too many calls to Unlock(). The results afterward are potentially not pretty. To avoid this bug, when you're using CComSafeArray, never Attach multiple CComSafeArray objects to the same SAFEARRAY pointer.

CComSafeArray Operations

Several methods are provided for retrieving information about the size and shape of a CComSafeArray instance:

```
LONG GetLowerBound(UINT uDim = 0) const;
LONG GetUpperBound(UINT uDim = 0) const;
ULONG GetCount(UINT uDim = 0) const;
UINT GetDimensions() const;
VARTYPE GetType() const ;
bool IsSizable() const;
```

All these methods are fairly simple and self-explanatory. GetLowerBound and GetUpperBound return the lower and upper bounds of a particular dimension of the SAFEARRAY. The GetCount method takes a specific dimension number and returns the number of elements in that dimension. GetDimensions returns the total number of dimensions in the SAFEARRAY, also known as the array *rank*. You can query the Automation VARTYPE with the GetType method. IsSizable indicates whether the SAFEARRAY can be resized. Recall that the definition of the SAFEARRAY data type included an fFeatures bit field that stores information about how the array is allocated.

```
typedef struct tagSAFEARRAY {
    ...
    USHORT fFeatures;
    ...
} SAFEARRAY;
```

The SAFEARRAY API functions use this information to properly release elements when the SAFEARRAY is destroyed. The FADF_FIXEDSIZE bit indicates whether the SAFEARRAY can be resized. By default, the SAFEARRAY created with an instance of CComSafeArray is resizable, so the IsSizable method returns TRUE. CComSafeArray doesn't expose any methods for directly manipulating the fFeatures flags, so they would change from their default values only if you directly access the encapsulated SAFEARRAY, if the SAFEARRAY passed to the CComSafeArray constructor has different values, or if an Attach is performed on a SAFEARRAY that manipulated the fFeatures field. You can access the internal SAFEARRAY directly with the GetSafeArrayPtr method:

```
LPSAFEARRAY* GetSafeArrayPtr()  {
    return &m_psa;
}
```

If a CComSafeArray instance is resizable, clients can use two different Resize methods to grow or shrink a SAFEARRAY:

```
HRESULT Resize(ULONG ulCount, LONG lLBound = 0);
HRESULT Resize(const SAFEARRAYBOUND *pBound);
```

The first version takes the new number of elements and lower bound, constructs a SAFEARRAYBOUND structure from the supplied parameters, and delegates the real work to the second version that accepts a SAFEARRAYBOUND* parameter. This second version of Resize first verifies that the SAFEARRAY is resizable and then relies upon the SAFEARRAY API SafeArrayRedim to do the heavy lifting. The first thing to note is that only the least-significant (rightmost) dimension of a SAFEARRAY can be resized. So, you can change the size of a SAFEARRAY with dimensions [3][5][7] to one with dimensions [3][5][4], but you cannot change it to have dimensions [6][5][7]. If the resizing operation reduces the size of the SAFEARRAY, SafeArrayRedim deallocates the elements beyond the new bounds. If the operation increases the size of the SAFEARRAY, SafeArrayRedim allocates and initializes the appropriate number of new elements.

Be warned, there's a nasty bug in the implementation of the Resize method:

```
HRESULT Resize(const SAFEARRAYBOUND *pBound) {
    ATLASSUME(m_psa != NULL);
    ATLASSERT(pBound != NULL);
    if (!IsSizable()) {
        return E_FAIL;
    }
    HRESULT hRes = Unlock();
    if (SUCCEEDED(hRes)) {
        hRes = SafeArrayRedim(m_psa, const_cast<LPSAFEARRAYBOUND>(pBound));
        if (SUCCEEDED(hRes)) {
            hRes = Lock();
        }
    }
    return hRes;
}
```

If the underlying call to SafeArrayRedim fails, the call to relock the SAFEARRAY is never made. When that happens, everything falls apart, and the destructor might even fail. If you call Resize, be *very* careful to check the return HRESULT. If it's a failure, you really can't assume anything about the state of the encapsulated SAFEARRAY. The best bet is to Detach it and clean up manually.

Microsoft has agreed that this is a bug but was unable to fix it in time for the Visual Studio 2005 release. Hopefully, it'll be officially fixed soon.

CComSafeArray also provides three useful Add functions that you can use to append elements in a SAFEARRAY to the end of an existing CComSafeArray instance. Note that these methods work for only one-dimensional SAFEARRAYs. All three versions will assert if the Add method is invoked on a CComSafeArray instance that contains a multidimensional SAFEARRAY.

```
HRESULT Add(const T& t, BOOL bCopy = TRUE);
HRESULT Add(ULONG ulCount, const T *pT, BOOL bCopy = TRUE);
HRESULT Add(const SAFEARRAY *psaSrc);
```

The first version of Add tacks on a single element to the end of the SAFEARRAY. If the SAFEARRAY is NULL, Add first invokes the Create method to allocate an empty SAFEARRY. Resize then increases the size of the SAFEARRAY by one, and the SetAt method is called to insert the value of the t parameter into the last element of the SAFEARRAY. The bCopy parameter is discussed further in a moment when we examine the CComSafeArray accessors: SetAt and GetAt. For now, simply understand that this parameter controls whether the CComSafeArray is appended with an independent duplicate of the new item or whether it actually takes ownership of the item. The second version of Add accepts a count and an array of items to append. It works similar to the single-element version: First, it creates an empty SAFEARRAY, if necessary; then, it calls Resize to grow the SAFEARRAY by ulCount elements. SetAt is invoked within a loop to initialize the new SAFEARRAY elements with the value of the items supplied in the pT parameter. Finally, the third version of Add accepts a pointer to a SAFEARRAY and appends all elements that it contains to the end of the CComSafeArray instance. This version of Add relies upon Resize and SetAt to do its work in exactly the same manner as do the other two versions. Here's how you might use these methods in your own code:

```
CComSafeArray<int> sa;   // sa::m_psa is NULL
sa.Add(7);               // sa allocated and now contains { 7 }

int rgVal[] = { 8, 9 };
sa.Add(2, rgVal);        // sa now contains { 7, 8, 9 }

sa.Add(sa);              // sa now contains { 7, 8, 9, 7, 8, 9 }
                         // see discussion of cast operators to
                         // understand what makes this line work
```

Warning: The various Add overloads call the Resize method under the hood, so they're subject to the same buggy behavior if Resize fails.

CComSafeArray Element Accessors

CComSafeArray provides five methods for reading and writing individual elements of the encapsulated SAFEARRAY. Three of these methods are used for accessing one-dimensional SAFEARRAYs. The GetAt method comes in two flavors.

```
const typename _ATL_AutomationType<T>::_typewrapper&
GetAt(LONG lIndex) const {
    ATLASSUME(m_psa != NULL);
    if(m_psa == NULL)
        AtlThrow(E_FAIL);
```

```
    LONG lLBound = GetLowerBound();
    ATLASSERT(lIndex >= lLBound);
    ATLASSERT(lIndex <= GetUpperBound());
    if ((lIndex < lLBound) || (lIndex > GetUpperBound()))
        AtlThrow(E_INVALIDARG);


    return ( (_ATL_AutomationType<T>::_typewrapper*)
        m_psa->pvData )[lIndex-lLBound];
}


_ATL_AutomationType<T>::_typewrapper& GetAt(LONG lIndex) {
    // code identical to const version
}
```

The two `GetAt` methods differ only in that the first version uses the `const` qualifier to enforce read-only semantics for the accessed element. The methods retrieve the upper and lower bounds and validate the specified index against these bounds. Note that the `lIndex` passed in is the index relative to the `lLBound` defined for the `CComSafeArray` instance, which might or might not be zero. To retrieve the requested element, the `pvData` field of the encapsulated `SAFEARRAY` is cast to the element type; conventional C-style pointer arithmetic does the rest.

At this point, it's worth examining the significance of the `_typewrapper` field of the `_ATL_AutomationType` template class presented earlier. Recall that a series of `DEFINE_AUTOMATION_TYPE_FUNCTION` macros associated the supported C++ data types with both their corresponding Automation `VARTYPE` as well as a wrapper class. Only one `DEFINE_AUTOMATION_TYPE_FUNCTION` macro actually supplied a real wrapper class for the C++ data type—all the others shown so far simply use the actual C++ type as the wrapper type. The one macro mapped the `VARIANT` data type to the `CComVariant` wrapper class and to a `VARTYPE` value of `VT_VARIANT`. This internally sets `_typewrapper` to `CComVariant` and allows `CComSafeArray` to both leverage the convenient semantics of `CComVariant` in its internal implementation and return `CComVariant` elements of the `SAFEARRAY` to the client. Using a wrapper class in the typecasting code within `GetAt` relies upon the fact that `CComVariant` holds the encapsulated `VARIANT` as its only state, as discussed in the previous section on the `CComVariant` class. An instance of `CComVariant` resides at precisely the same memory address and occupies precisely the same storage as the encapsulated `VARIANT`. So, `CComSafeArray` can seamlessly deal in terms of the `_typewrapper` type internally and expose the wrapper type to the client as a convenience. Note that wrapper classes for element types must hold the encapsulated type as their only state if this scheme is to work correctly. You'll see in a moment that the `GetAt` method isn't the only method that breaks down if this isn't the case.

The list of DEFINE_AUTOMATION_TYPE_FUNCTION macros didn't generate type mappings support for two other important SAFEARRAY element types that CComSafeArray actually supports, even though the current ATL documentation doesn't mention them. Instead of macros, CComSafeArray provides support for elements of type BSTR, IDispatch*, and IUnknown* through template specialization. The template specialization for all three data types looks very similar; we examine the one for BSTR as an example because you're already familiar with the associated wrapper class: CComBSTR. The wrapper class for IDispatch* and IUnknown* is CComPtr, presented in detail in the later section "The CComPtr and CComQIPtr Smart Pointer Classes." The specialization for BSTR fills the role of the DEFINE_AUTOMATION_TYPE_FUNCTION macro, in that it sets the _typewrapper member of _ATL_AutomationType to the CComBSTR wrapper class and sets the type member to VT_BSTR, as you can see in the following code:

```
template <>
struct _ATL_AutomationType<BSTR> {
    typedef CComBSTR _typewrapper ;
    enum { type = VT_BSTR};
    static void* GetT(const BSTR& t)  {
        return t;
    }
};
```

Similarly, the specialization for IDispatch* sets type to VT_DISPATCH and _typewrapper to CComPtr; the one for IUnknown* sets type to VT_UNKNOWN and _typewrapper to CComPtr.

You should recall that, like CComVariant, CComBSTR holds in its m_str member the encapsulated BSTR as its only state. Thus, the code shown previously in the GetAt method works fine for CComSafeArrays that contain BSTR elements. Also note that the specialization shown earlier defines the GetT method differently than the other supported data types. This method is only used by the element accessor functions for multidimensional SAFEARRAYs, in which a void* pointer to the destination buffer must be provided to the SafeArrayGetElement API. The GetT implementation that the DEFINE_AUTOMATION_TYPE_FUNCTION macro generates for all the other data types returns the address of the encapsulated data. In the case of a BSTR, the data type is already a pointer to the data, so GetT is specialized to return the encapsulated type itself instead of a pointer to the encapsulated type. The specializations for IDispatch* and IUnknown* implement GetT in precisely the same way as well because they are also inherently pointer types.

CComSafeArray provides the SetAt method for writing to specific elements. The method is defined as follows:

```
HRESULT SetAt(LONG lIndex, const T& t, BOOL bCopy = TRUE) {
    bCopy;
    ATLASSERT(m_psa != NULL);
    LONG lLBound = GetLowerBound();
    ATLASSERT(lIndex >= lLBound);
    ATLASSERT(lIndex <= GetUpperBound());
    ((T*)m_psa->pvData)[lIndex-lLBound] = t;
    return S_OK;
}
```

SetAt first ensures that the encapsulated SAFEARRAY is non-NULL and then validates the index passed in against the upper and lower bounds defined for the SAFEARRAY. The assignment statement copies the element data provided into the appropriate location in the encapsulated SAFEARRAY. Assigning a new value to a SAFEARRAY element is accomplished with code like the following:

```
CComSafeArray<long> sa(5);
long lNewVal = 14;
// replace the 4th element with the value 14
sa.SetAt(3, lNewVal);
```

The relevance of the bCopy parameter becomes evident only when you turn to the four specializations of the SetAt parameter that are provided for SAFEARRAYs: BSTR, VARIANT, IDispatch*, and IUnknown*. Each of these data types requires special handling when performing assignment, so CComSafeArray specializes SetAt to enforce the correct semantics. The specialization for BSTR first uses SysFreeString to clear the existing element in the array and then assigns it either to a copy of the provided BSTR or to the BSTR parameter itself, depending on the value of the bCopy parameter.

```
template<>
HRESULT CComSafeArray<BSTR>::SetAt(LONG lIndex,
    const BSTR& strData, BOOL bCopy) {
    // validation code omitted for clarity

    BSTR strOrg = ((BSTR*)m_psa->pvData)[lIndex-lLBound];
    if (strOrg)
        ::SysFreeString(strOrg);

    if (bCopy) {
        BSTR strTemp = ::SysAllocString(strData);
        if (NULL == strTemp)
```

```
            return E_OUTOFMEMORY;
        ((BSTR*)m_psa->pvData)[lIndex-lLBound] = strTemp;
    }
    else
        ((BSTR*)m_psa->pvData)[lIndex-lLBound] = strData;

    return S_OK;
}
```

When bCopy is TRUE, the caller maintains ownership of the strData BSTR parameter, because CComSafeArray will be working with its own private copy. When bCopy is FALSE, CComSafeArray takes ownership of the strData BSTR; the caller must not attempt to free it, or errors will occur when this element is accessed from the SAFEARRAY. The following code snippet demonstrates this important difference:

```
BSTR bstr1 = ::SysAllocString(OLESTR("Go Longhorns!"));
BSTR bstr2 = ::SysAllocString(OLESTR("ATL Rocks!"));

CComSafeArray<BSTR> sa(5);
sa.SetAt(2, bstr1, true);   // sa generates its own copy of bstr1
sa.SetAt(3, bstr2, false);  // sa assigns element to bstr2
::SysFreeString(bstr1);     // ok, sa still has a copy
::SysFreeString(bstr2);     // wrong!!! we don't own bstr2
```

VARIANT elements in SAFEARRAYs require special handling as well. The code for the specialized version of SetAt for VARIANTs is very similar to that shown earlier for BSTR. The main differences are that the original element is cleared using VariantClear and the copy is performed using VariantCopyInd if bCopy is TRUE. The code that implements SetAt for IDispatch* and IUnknown* type elements is identical (okay, the variable names *are* different—pDisp for IDispatch* and pUnk for IUnknown*). In either case, the original interface pointer element is Release'd before assignment and then is AddRef'd if bCopy is TRUE. Again, this means that the caller is transferring ownership of the interface pointer to the CComSafeArray if bCopy is FALSE and should not then call Release on the pointer passed to the SetAt method. CComSafeArray ultimately generates a call to Release on each element in the SAFEARRAY when the instance is destroyed, so improper handling leads to a double release of the interface pointer and the all-too-familiar exception as a reward. Both proper and improper interface pointer element assignment are demonstrated in the following code:

```
IUnknown* pUnk1, pUnk2;
// assign both pointers to refer to an object
```

```
CComSafeArray<IUnknown*> sa(5);
sa.SetAt(2, pUnk1, true);  // sa calls AddRef on pUnk1
sa.SetAt(3, pUnk2, false); // sa assigns element to pUnk2
                           // without AddRefing
pUnk1->Release();          // ok, refcount non-zero because
                           // of sa AddRef
pUnk2->Release();          // wrong!!! we don't own pUnk2
```

The remaining two methods for accessing SAFEARRAY elements apply to multidimensional SAFEARRAYs. MultiDimGetAt and MultiDimSetAt provide read-and-write access to SAFEARRAY elements housed in a multidimensional SAFEARRAY. Both methods are very thin wrappers on top of the SafeArrayGetElement and SafeArrayPutElement API functions, respectively.

```
HRESULT MultiDimGetAt(const LONG *alIndex, T& t) {
    ATLASSERT(m_psa != NULL);
    return SafeArrayGetElement(m_psa,
        const_cast<LONG*>(alIndex), &t);
}
HRESULT MultiDimSetAt(const LONG *alIndex, const T& t) {
    ATLASSERT(m_psa != NULL);
    return SafeArrayPutElement(m_psa, const_cast<LONG*>(alIndex),
    _ATL_AutomationType<T>::GetT(t));
}
```

The alIndex parameter specifies an array of SAFEARRAY indices. The first element in the alIndex array is the index of the rightmost dimension; the last element is the index of the leftmost dimension. You make use of these functions like this:

```
// 2-D array with all dimensions
// left-most dimension has 3 elements
CComSafeArrayBound bound1(3);
// right-most dimension has 4 elements
CComSafeArrayBound bound2(4);

// equivalent C-style array indices would be [3][4]
CComSafeArrayBound rgBounds[] = { bound1, bound2 };
CComSafeArray<int> sa(rgBounds, 2);

int rgIndElement1[] = { 0, 1 };    // access element at sa[1][0]
int rgIndElement2[] = { 3, 2 };    // access element at sa[2][3]

long lVal = 0;
// retrieve value at sa[1][0]
```

```
sa.MultiDimGetAt(rgIndElement1, lVal);

// multiply value by 2 and store it
// in element located at sa[2][3]
sa.MultiDimSetAt(rgIndElement2, lVal*=2);
```

CComSafeArray Operators

CComSafeArray defines four operators that provide some syntactic convenience for accessing elements of a SAFEARRAY:

```
const typename
_ATL_AutomationType<T>::_typewrapper&
operator[](int nIndex) const {
    return GetAt(nIndex);
}
typename
_ATL_AutomationType<T>::_typewrapper&
operator[](int nIndex) {
    return GetAt(nIndex);
}
const typename
_ATL_AutomationType<T>::_typewrapper&
operator[](LONG nIndex)
    const {
    return GetAt(nIndex);
}
typename
_ATL_AutomationType<T>::_typewrapper&
operator[](LONG nIndex) {
    return GetAt(nIndex);
}
```

As you can see, all these operators simply delegate to the GetAt accessor method, discussed in the previous section. They differ only in the type of index and whether the const qualifier is specified. These operators enable you to write code with CComSafeArray that looks very much like the code you use to manipulate C-style array elements.

```
CComSafeArray<int> sa(5);
ATLASSERT(sa[2] == 0);
sa[2] = 17;
ATLASSERT(sa[2] == 17);
```

CComSafeArray also provides two cast operators. Both implementations are trivial, serving only to expose the encapsulated SAFEARRAY. Nevertheless, they provide some syntactic convenience in some situations, such as when you want to pass a CComSafeArray instance to a function that expects a SAFEARRAY*.

```
operator const SAFEARRAY *() const  {
    return m_psa;
}
operator LPSAFEARRAY()  {
    return m_psa;
}
```

Unfortunately, CComSafeArray does not supply one operator: an overload of operator&. Without it, you can't use CComSafeArray as a wrapper for an out parameter like this:

```
HRESULT CreateANewSafeArray( SAFEARRAY** ppsa ) {
    *ppsa = SafeArrayCreateVector(VT_I4, 1, 15 );
    return S_OK;
}
HRESULT UseCreatedSafeArray( ) {
    CComSafeArray< int > sa;
    HRESULT hr = CreateANewSafeArray( &sa );
}
```

The previous code will not compile but will fail with this error:

```
error C2664: CreateANewSafeArray : cannot convert
parameter 1 from
    ATL::CComSafeArray<T> *__w64  to SAFEARRAY **
        with
        [
            T=int
        ]
        Types pointed to are unrelated;
        conversion requires reinterpret_cast,
        C-style cast or function-style cast
```

This use differs from most of the other ATL smart types, which let you do exactly this, but there's a good reason for the disparity. Imagine that the ATL team had included the overloaded operator&. What happens in this case?

```
HRESULT CreateANewSafeArray( SAFEARRAY** ppsa ) {
    *ppsa = SafeArrayCreateVector(VT_BSTR, 1, 15 );
```

```
        return S_OK;
    }


    HRESULT UseCreatedSafeArray( ) {
        CComSafeArray< int > sa;
        HRESULT hr = CreateANewSafeArray( &sa );
    }
```

The C++ compiler can't tell what the returned SAFEARRAY actually contains; that information is available only at runtime. The compiler would have to allow the conversion, and we now have a CComSafeArray<int> wrapping a SAFEARRAY that actually contains BSTRs. Nothing good can come of this, so the operator& overload was left out. Instead, you can do this:

```
    HRESULT UseCreatedSafeArray( ) {
        SAFEARRAY *psa = null;
        HRESULT hr = CreateANewSafeArray( &psa );
        CComSafeArray< int > sa;
        sa.Attach( psa );
    }
```

The error will now be detected at runtime inside the CComSafeArray::Attach method.

The GetSafeArrayPtr() method, mentioned earlier, explicitly retrieves a pointer to the stored SAFEARRAY. It can be used like this:

```
    HRESULT UseCreatedSafeArray( ) {
        CComSafeArray< int > sa;
        HRESULT hr = CreateANewSafeArray(sa.GetSafeArrayPtr());
    }
```

However, this use bypasses the runtime type check in the Attach method and is not recommended for this reason.

The CComPtr and CComQIPtr Smart Pointer Classes

A Review of Smart Pointers

A *smart pointer* is an object that behaves like a pointer. That is, you can use an instance of a smart pointer class in many of the places you normally use a pointer.

However, using a smart pointer provides some advantages over using a *raw* pointer. For example, a smart interface pointer class can do the following:

- Release the encapsulated interface pointer when the class destructor executes.
- Automatically release its interface pointer during exception handling when you allocate the smart interface pointer on the stack. This reduces the need to write explicit exception-handling code.
- Release the encapsulated interface pointer before overwriting it during an assignment operation.
- Call AddRef on the interface pointer received during an assignment operation.
- Provide different constructors to initialize a new smart pointer through convenient mechanisms.
- Be used in many, *but not all,* the places where you would conventionally use a raw interface pointer.

ATL provides two smart pointer classes: CComPtr and CComQIPtr. The CComPtr class is a smart COM interface pointer class. You create instances tailored for a specific type of interface pointer. For example, the first line of the following code creates a smart IUnknown interface pointer. The second line creates a smart INamedObject custom interface pointer:

```
CComPtr<IUnknown>       punk;
CComPtr<INamedObject>   pno;
```

The CComQIPtr class is a smarter COM interface pointer class that does everything CComPtr does and more. When you assign to a CComQIPtr instance an interface pointer of a different type than the smart pointer, the class calls QueryInterface on the provided interface pointer:

```
CComPtr<IUnknown>       punk = /* Init to some IUnknown* */ ;
CComQIPtr<INamedObject> pno = punk; // Calls punk->QI
                                    // (IID_INamedObject, ...)
```

The CComPtr and CComQIPtr Classes

The CComPtr and CComQIPtr classes are similar, with the exception of initialization and assignment. In fact, they're so similar that CComQIPtr actually derives from CComPtr and CComPtr, in turn, derives from another class, CComPtrBase. This latter class defines the actual storage of the underlying raw pointer, and the actual reference-counting operations on that raw pointer. CComPtr and CComQIPtr add constructors and assignment operators. Because of the inheritance relationship between these classes, all the following comments about the CComPtr class apply equally to the CComQIPtr class unless specifically stated otherwise.

The atlcomcli.h file contains the definition of all three classes. The only state each class maintains is a single public member variable, T* p. This state is defined in the CComPtrBase base class:

```
template <class T>
class CComPtrBase {
    ...
    T* p;
};

template <class T>
class CComPtr : public CComPtrBase<T>
{ ... };

template <class T, const IID* piid = &__uuidof(T)>
class CComQIPtr : public CComPtr<T>
{ ... };
```

The first (or, in the case of CComPtr, only) template parameter specifies the type of the smart interface pointer. The second template parameter to the CComQIPtr class specifies the interface ID for the smart pointer. By default, it is the globally unique identifier (GUID) associated with the class of the first parameter. Here are a few examples that use these smart pointer classes. The middle three examples are all equivalent:

```
CComPtr<IUnknown> punk;    // Smart IUnknown*
CComPtr<INamedObject> pno; // Smart INamedObject*

CComQIPtr<INamedObject> pno;
CComQIPtr<INamedObject, &__uuidof(INamedObject)> pno;
CComQIPtr<INamedObject, &IID_INamedObject> pno;

CComQIPtr<IDispatch, &IID_ISomeDual> pdisp;
```

Constructors and Destructor

A CComPtr object can be initialized with an interface pointer of the appropriate type. That is, a CComPtr<IFoo> object can be initialized using an IFoo* or another CComPtr<IFoo> object. Using any other type produces a compiler error. The actual implementation of this behavior is in the CComPtrBase class. The default constructor initializes the internal interface pointer to NULL. The other constructors initialize the internal interface pointer to the specified interface pointer. When the specified value is non-NULL, the constructor calls the AddRef method. The destructor calls the Release method on a non-NULL interface pointer.

CComPtr has a special copy constructor that pulls out the underlying raw interface pointer and passes it to the CComPtrBase base class, thus guaranteeing proper AddRef and Release calls.

```
CComPtrBase()    { p = NULL; }
CComPtrBase(T* p) { if ((p = lp) != NULL) p->AddRef(); }
~CComPtrBase()    { if (p) p->Release(); }

CComPtr(const CComPtr<T>& lp) : CComPtrBase<T>(lp.p) { }
```

A CComQIPtr object can be initialized with an interface pointer of any type. When the initialization value is the same type as the smart pointer, the constructor simply AddRef's the provided pointer via the base class's constructor:

```
CComQIPtr(T* lp) :
    CComPtr<T>(lp)
    {}

CComQIPtr(const CComQIPtr<T,piid>& lp) :
    CComPtr<T>(lp.p)
    {}
```

However, specifying a different type invokes the following constructor, which queries the provided interface pointer for the appropriate interface:

```
CComQIPtr(IUnknown* lp)
    { if (lp != NULL) lp->QueryInterface(*piid, (void **)&p); }
```

A constructor can never fail. Nevertheless, the QueryInterface call might not succeed. The CComQIPtr class sets the internal pointer to NULL when it cannot obtain the required interface. Therefore, you use code such as the following to test whether the object initializes:

```
void func (IUnknown* punk) {
    CComQIPtr<INamedObject> pno (punk);
    if (pno) {
        // Can call SomeMethod because the QI worked
        pno->SomeMethod ();
    }
}
```

You can tell whether the query failed by checking for a NULL pointer, but you cannot determine why it fails. The constructor doesn't save the HRESULT from a failed QueryInterface call.

Initialization

The CComPtr class defines three assignment operators; the CComQIPtr class defines three slightly different ones. All the assignment operators do the same actions:

- Release the current interface pointer when it's non-NULL.
- AddRef the source interface pointer when it's non-NULL.
- Save the source interface pointer as the current interface pointer.

The CComPtr assignment operators are shown here:

```
// CComPtr assignment operators
T* operator=(T* lp);
template <typename Q> T* operator=(const CComPtr<Q>& lp);
T* operator=(const CComPtr<T>& lp);
```

The templated version of operator= is interesting. It enables you to assign arbitrary CComPtrs to each other with proper QueryInterface calls made, if necessary. For example, this is now legal:

```
CComPtr< IFoo > fooPtr = this;
CComPtr< IBar > barPtr;

barPtr = fooPtr;
```

This begs the question: Why have CComQIPtr at all if CComPtr does the work, too? It appears that the ATL team is moving toward having a single smart interface pointer instead of two and is leaving CComQIPtr in place for backward compatibility.

The CComQIPtr assignment operators are mostly the same. The only one that does any interesting work is the overload that takes an IUnknown*. This queries a non-NULL source interface pointer for the appropriate interface to save. You receive a NULL pointer when the QueryInterface calls fail. As with the equivalent constructor, the HRESULT for a failed query is not available.

```
// CComQIPtr assignment operators
T* operator=(T* lp);
T* operator=(const CComQIPtr<T>& lp);
T* operator=(IUnknown* lp);
```

Typically, you use the `CComQIPtr` assignment operator to perform a `QueryInterface` call. You immediately follow the assignment with a `NULL` pointer test, as follows:

```
// Member variable holding object
CComQIPtr<IExpectedInterface> m_object;

STDMETHODIMP put_Object (IUnknown* punk) {
                        // Releases current object, if any, and
    m_object = punk;  // queries for the expected interface
    if (!m_object)
        return E_UNEXPECTED;
    return S_OK;
}
```

Object Instantiation Methods

The `CComPtrBase` class provides an overloaded method, called `CoCreateInstance`, that you can use to instantiate an object and retrieve an interface pointer on the object. The method has two forms. The first requires the class identifier (`CLSID`) of the class to instantiate. The second requires the programmatic identifier (`ProgID`) of the class to instantiate. Both overloaded methods accept optional parameters for the controlling unknown and class context for the instantiation. The controlling unknown parameter defaults to `NULL`, the normal case, which indicates no aggregation. The class context parameter defaults to `CLSCTX_ALL`, indicating that any available server can service the request.

```
HRESULT CoCreateInstance (REFCLSID rclsid,
                          LPUNKNOWN pUnkOuter = NULL,
                          DWORD dwClsContext = CLSCTX_ALL) {
    ATLASSERT(p == NULL);
    return ::CoCreateInstance(rclsid, pUnkOuter,
        dwClsContext, __uuidof(T), (void**)&p);
}

HRESULT CoCreateInstance (LPCOLESTR szProgID,
                          LPUNKNOWN pUnkOuter = NULL,
                          DWORD dwClsContext = CLSCTX_ALL);
```

Notice how the preceding code for the first `CoCreateInstance` method creates an instance of the specified class. It passes the parameters of the method to the `CoCreateInstance` COM API and, additionally, requests that the initial interface be the interface that the smart pointer class supports. (This is the purpose of the _uuidof(T) expression.) The second overloaded CoCreateInstance method translates the provided ProgID to a CLSID and then creates the instance in the same manner as the first method.

Therefore, the following code is equivalent (although the smart pointer code is easier to read, in my opinion). The first instantiation request explicitly uses the CoCreateInstance COM API. The second uses the smart pointer CoCreateInstance method.

```
ISpeaker* pSpeaker;
HRESULT hr =
 ::CoCreateInstance (__uuidof (Demagogue), NULL, CLSCTX_ALL,
                      __uuidof (ISpeaker_, (void**) &pSpeaker);
... Use the interface
pSpeaker->Release () ;



CComPtr<ISpeaker> pSpeaker;
HRESULT hr = pSpeaker.CoCreateInstance (__uuidof (Demogogue));
... Use the interface. It releases when pSpeaker leaves scope
```

CComPtr and CComQIPtr Operations

Because a smart interface pointer should behave as much as possible like a raw interface pointer, the CComPtrBase class defines some operators to make the smart pointer objects act like pointers. For example, when you dereference a pointer using operator*(), you expect to receive a reference to whatever the pointer points. So dereferencing a smart interface pointer should produce a reference to whatever the underlying interface pointer points to. And it does:

```
T& operator*() const { ATLENSURE(p!=NULL); return *p; }
```

Note that the operator*() method kindly asserts (via the ATLENSURE macro[2]) when you attempt to dereference a NULL smart interface pointer in a debug build of your component. Of course, I've always considered the General Protection Fault message box to be an equivalent assertion. However, the ATLENSURE macro produces a more programmer-friendly indication of the error location.

To maintain the semblance of a pointer, taking the address of a smart pointer object—that is, invoking operator&()—should actually return the address of the

---

[2] ATLENSURE asserts if assertions are turned on and throws either a C++ exception (if exceptions are enabled) or a Windows Structured Exception (if C++ exceptions are disabled) if the condition is false.

underlying raw pointer. Note that the issue here isn't the actual binary value returned. A smart pointer contains only the underlying raw interface pointer as its state. Therefore, a smart pointer occupies exactly the same amount of storage as a raw interface pointer. The address of a smart pointer object and the address of its internal member variable are the same binary value.

Without overriding `CComPtrBase<T>::operator&()`, taking the address of an instance returns a `CComPtrBase<T>*`. To have a smart pointer class maintain the same pointer semantics as a pointer of type `T*`, the `operator&()` method for the class must return a `T**`.

```
T** operator&() { ATLASSERT(p==NULL); return &p; }
```

Note that this operator asserts when you take the address of a non-`NULL` smart interface pointer because you might dereference the returned address and over-write the internal member variable without properly releasing the interface pointer. It asserts to protect the semantics of the pointer and keep you from accidentally stomping on the pointer. This behavior, however, keeps you from using a smart interface pointer as an `[in,out]` function parameter.

```
STDMETHODIMP SomeClass::UpdateObject (
    /* [in, out] */ IExpected** ppExpected);

CComPtr<IExpected> pE = /* Initialize to some value */ ;

pobj->UpdateObject (&pE); // Asserts in debug build because
                          // pE is non-NULL
```

When you really want to use a smart pointer in this way, take the address of the member variable:

```
pobj->UpdateObject (&pE.p);
```

CComPtr and CComQIPtr Resource-Management Operations

A smart interface pointer represents a resource, albeit one that tries to manage itself properly. Sometimes, though, you want to manage the resource explicitly. For example, you must release all interface pointers before calling the `CoUninitialize` method. This means that you can't wait for the destructor of a `CComPtr` object to release the interface pointer when you allocate the object as a global or static variable—or even a local variable in `main()`. The destructor for global and static variables executes only after the main function exits, long after `CoUninitialize` runs.

You can release the internal interface pointer by assigning `NULL` to the smart pointer. Alternatively and more explicitly, you can call the `Release` method.

```
int main( ) {
    HRESULT hr = CoInitialize( NULL );
    If (FAILED(hr)) return -1;  // Something is seriously wrong

    CComPtr<IUnknown> punk = /* Initialize to some object */ ;
    ...
    punk.Release( ); // Must Release before CoUninitialize!

    CoUninitialize( );
}
```

Note that the previous code calls the smart pointer object's CComPtr <T>::Release method because it uses the dot operator to reference the object. It does not directly call the underlying interface pointer's IUnknown::Release method, as you might expect. The smart pointer's CComPtrBase<T>::Release method calls the underlying interface pointer's IUnknown::Release method and sets the internal interface pointer to NULL. This prevents the destructor from releasing the interface again. Here is the smart pointer's Release method:

```
void Release()  {
    T* pTemp = p;
    if (pTemp) {
        p = NULL;
        pTemp->Release();
    }
}
```

It's not immediately obvious why the CComPtrBase<T>::Release method doesn't simply call IUnknown::Release using its p member variable. Instead, it copies the interface pointer member variable into the local variable, sets the member variable to NULL, and then releases the interface using the temporary variable. This approach avoids a situation in which the interface the smart pointer holds is released twice.

For example, assume that the smart pointer is a member variable of class A and that the smart pointer holds a reference to object B. You call the smart pointer's .Release method. The smart pointer releases its reference to object B. Object B, in turn, holds a reference to the class A instance containing the smart pointer. Object B decides to release its reference to the class A instance. The class A instance decides to destruct, which invokes the destructor for the smart pointer member variable. The destructor detects that the interface pointer is non-NULL, so it releases the interface again.[3]

In releases of ATL earlier than version 3, the following code would compile successfully and would release the interface pointer twice. Note the use of the arrow operator.

```
punk->Release( );          // Wrong! Wrong! Wrong!
```

In those releases of ATL, the arrow operator returned the underlying interface pointer. Therefore, the previous line actually called the IUnknown::Release function, not the CComPtr<T>::Release method, as expected. This left the smart pointer's interface pointer member variable non-NULL, so the destructor would eventually release the interface a second time.

This was a nasty bug to find. A smart pointer class encourages you to think about an instance as if it were an interface pointer. However, in this particular case, you shouldn't use the arrow operator (which you would if it actually was a pointer); you had to use the dot operator because it was actually an object. What's worse, the compiler didn't tell you when you got it wrong.

This changed in version 3 of ATL. Note that the current definition of the arrow operator returns a _NoAddRefReleaseOnCComPtr<T>* value:

```
_NoAddRefReleaseOnCComPtr<T>* operator->() const {
    ATLASSERT(p!=NULL); return (_NoAddRefReleaseOnCComPtr<T>*)p;
}
```

This is a simple template class whose only purpose is to make the AddRef and Release methods inaccessible:

```
template <class T>
class _NoAddRefReleaseOnCComPtr : public T {
    private:
        STDMETHOD_(ULONG, AddRef)()=0;
        STDMETHOD_(ULONG, Release)()=0;
};
```

The _NoAddRefReleaseOnCComPtr<T> template class derives from the interface being returned. Therefore, it inherits all the methods of the interface. The class then overrides the AddRef and Release methods, making them private and purely virtual. Now you get the following compiler error when you use the arrow operator to call either of these methods:

---

[3] Thanks go to Jim Springfield for pointing this out.

```
error C2248: 'Release' : cannot access private member declared
   in class 'ATL::_NoAddRefReleaseOnCComPtr<T>'
```

The CopyTo Method

The CopyTo method makes an AddRef'ed copy of the interface pointer and places it in the specified location. Therefore, the CopyTo method produces an interface pointer that has a lifetime that is separate from the lifetime of the smart pointer that it copies.

```
HRESULT CopyTo(T** ppT) {
    ATLASSERT(ppT != NULL);
    if (ppT == NULL) return E_POINTER;
    *ppT = p;
    if (p) p->AddRef();
    return S_OK;
}
```

Often, you use the CopyTo method to copy a smart pointer to an [out] parameter. An [out] interface pointer must be AddRef'ed by the code returning the pointer:

```
STDMETHODIMP SomeClass::get_Object(
/* [out] */ IExpected** ppExpected) {
    // Interface saved in member m_object
    // of type CComPtr<IExpected>

    // Correctly AddRefs pointer
    return m_object.CopyTo (ppExpected) ;
}
```

Watch out for the following code—it probably doesn't do what you expect, and it isn't correct:

```
STDMETHODIMP SomeClass::get_Object (
/* [out] */ IExpected** ppExpected) {
    // Interface saved in member m_object
    // of type CComPtr<IExpected>
    *ppExpected = m_object ;  // Wrong! Does not AddRef pointer!
}
```

The Type-Cast Operator

When you assign a smart pointer to a raw pointer, you implicitly invoke the operator T() method. In other words, you cast the smart pointer to its underlying type. Notice that operator T() doesn't AddRef the pointer it returns:

```
operator T*() const { return (T*) p; }
```

That's because you don't want the AddRef in the following case:

```
STDMETHODIMP SomeClass::put_Object (
    /* [in] */ IExpected* pExpected);

// Interface saved in member m_object of type CComPtr<IExpected>
// Correctly does not AddRef pointer!
pObj->put_Object (m_object) ;
```

The Detach and Attach Methods

When you want to transfer ownership of the interface pointer in a CComPtr instance from the instance to an equivalent raw pointer, use the Detach method. It returns the underlying interface pointer and sets the smart pointer to NULL, ensuring that the destructor doesn't release the interface. The client calling Detach becomes responsible for releasing the interface.

```
T* Detach() { T* pt = p; p = NULL; return pt; }
```

You often use Detach when you need to return to a caller an interface pointer that you no longer need. Instead of providing the caller an AddRef'ed copy of the interface and then immediately releasing your held interface pointer, you can simply transfer the reference to the caller, thus avoiding extraneous AddRef/Release calls. Yes, it's a minor optimization, but it's also simple:

```
STDMETHODIMP SomeClass::get_Object (
/* [out] */ IExpected** ppExpected) {
  CComPtr<IExpected> pobj = /* Initialize the smart pointer */ ;
  *ppExpected = pobj->Detach(); // Destructor no longer Releases
  return S_OK;
}
```

When you want to transfer ownership of a raw interface pointer to a smart pointer, use the Attach method. It releases the interface pointer that the smart pointer holds and then sets the smart pointer to use the raw pointer. Note that, again, this technique avoids extraneous AddRef/Release calls and is a useful minor optimization:

```
void Attach(T* p2) { if (p) p->Release(); p = p2; }
```

Client code can use the `Attach` method to assume ownership of a raw interface pointer that it receives as an `[out]` parameter. The function that provides an `[out]` parameter is transferring ownership of the interface pointer to the caller.

```
STDMETHODIMP SomeClass::get_Object (
  /* [out] */ IExpected** ppObject);

void VerboseGetOption () {
  IExpected* p;
  pObj->get_Object (&p) ;

  CComPtr<IExpected> pE;
  pE.Attach (p); // Destructor now releases the interface pointer
  // Let the exceptions fall where they may now!!!
  CallSomeFunctionWhichThrowsExceptions();
}
```

Miscellaneous Smart Pointer Methods

The smart pointer classes also provide useful shorthand syntax for querying for a new interface: the `QueryInterface` method. It takes one parameter: the address of a variable that is of the type of the desired interface.

```
template <class Q>
HRESULT QueryInterface(Q** pp) const {
    ATLASSERT(pp != NULL && *pp == NULL);
    return p->QueryInterface(__uuidof(Q), (void**)pp);
}
```

This method reduces the chance of making the common mistake of querying for one interface (for example, `IID_IBar`), but specifying a different type of pointer for the returned value (for example, `IFoo*`).

```
CComPtr<IFoo> pfoo = /* Initialize to some IFoo */
IBar* pbar;

// We specify an IBar variable so the method queries for IID_IBar
HRESULT hr = pfoo.QueryInterface(&pBar);
```

Use the `IsEqualObject` method to determine whether two interface pointers refer to the same object:

```
bool IsEqualObject(IUnknown* pOther);
```

This method performs the test for COM identity: Query each interface for IID_IUnknown and compare the results. A COM object must always return the same pointer value when asked for its IUnknown interface. The IsEqualObject method expands a little on the COM identity test. It considers two NULL interface pointers to be equal objects.

```
bool SameObjects(IUnknown* punk1, IUnknown* punk2) {
    CComPtr<IUnknown> p (punk1);
    return p.IsEqualObject (punk2);
}

IUnknown* punk1 = NULL;
IUnknown* punk2 = NULL;
ATLASSERT (SameObjects(punk1, punk2); // true
```

The SetSite method associates a site object (specified by the punkParent parameter) with the object referenced by the internal pointer. The smart pointer must point to an object that implements the IObjectWithSite interface.

```
HRESULT SetSite(IUnknown* punkParent);
```

The Advise method associates a connection point sink object with the object the smart interface pointer references (which is the event source object). The first parameter is the sink interface. You specify the sink interface ID as the second parameter. The third parameter is an output parameter. The Advise method returns a token through this parameter that uniquely identifies this connection.

```
HRESULT Advise(IUnknown* pUnk, const IID& iid, LPDWORD pdw);
```

```
CComPtr<ISource> ps /* Initialized via some mechanism */ ;
ISomeSink* psink = /* Initialized via some mechanism */ ;
DWORD dwCookie;

ps->Advise (psink, __uuidof(ISomeSink), &dwCookie);
```

There is no Unadvise smart pointer method to end the connection because the pointer is not needed for the Unadvise. To break the connection, you need only the cookie, the sink interface identifier (IID), and an event source reference.

CComPtr Comparison Operators

Three operators provide comparison operations on a smart pointer. The operator!() method returns true when the interface pointer is NULL. The operator==()

method returns true when the comparison operand is equal to the interface pointer. The operator<() method is rather useless because it compares two interface pointers using their binary values. However, a class needs these comparison operators so that STL collections of class instances work properly.

```
bool operator!() const       { return (p == NULL); }
bool operator< (T* pT) const { return p <  pT; }
bool operator==(T* pT) const { return p == pT; }
bool operator!=(T* pT) const { return !operator==(pT); }
```

Using these comparison operators, all the following styles of code work:

```
CComPtr<IFoo> pFoo;
// Tests for pFoo.p == NULL using operator!
if (!pFoo)        {...}
// Tests for pFoo.p == NULL using operator==
if (pFoo == NULL) {...}
// Converts pFoo to T*, then compares to NULL
if (NULL == pFoo) {...}
```

The CComPtr Specialization for IDispatch

It's a royal pain to call an object's methods and properties using the IDispatch::Invoke method. You have to package all the arguments into VARIANT structures, build an array of those VARIANTs, and translate the name of the method to a DISPID. It's not only extremely difficult, but it's all tedious and error-prone coding. Here's an example of what it takes to make a simple call to the following ICalc::Add method:

```
// component IDL file
[
    object,
    uuid(2F6C88D7-C2BF-4933-81FA-3FBAFC3FC34B),
    dual,
]
interface ICalc : IDispatch {
    [id(1)] HRESULT Add([in] DOUBLE Op1,
        [in] DOUBLE Op2, [out,retval] DOUBLE* Result);
};

// client.cpp
HRESULT CallAdd(IDispatch* pdisp) {
```

```
        // Get the DISPID
        LPOLESTR pszMethod = OLESTR("Add");
        DISPID dispid;
        hr = pdisp->GetIDsOfNames(IID_NULL,
                                  &pszMethod,
                                  1,
                                  LOCALE_SYSTEM_DEFAULT,
                                  &dispid);

        if (FAILED(hr))
            return hr;

        // Set up the parameters
        DISPPARAMS dispparms;
        memset(&dispparms, 0 , sizeof(DISPPARAMS));
        dispparms.cArgs = 2;

        // Parameters are passed right to left
        VARIANTARG rgvarg[2];
        rgvarg[0].vt = VT_R8;
        rgvarg[0].dblVal = 6;
        rgvarg[1].vt = VT_R8;
        rgvarg[1].dblVal = 7;

        dispparms.rgvarg = &rgvarg[0];

        // Set up variable to hold method return value
        VARIANTARG vaResult;
        ::VariantInit(&vaResult);

        // Invoke the method
        hr = pdisp->Invoke(dispid,
                           IID_NULL,
                           LOCALE_SYSTEM_DEFAULT,
                           DISPATCH_METHOD,
                           &dispparms,
                           &vaResult,
                           NULL,
                           NULL);

        // vaResult now holds sum of 6 and 7
    }
```

Ouch! That's pretty painful for such a simple method call. The code to call a property on an IDispatch interface is very similar. Fortunately, ATL provides relief from writing code like this.

CComPtr provides a specialization for dealing with the IDispatch interface:

```
//specialization for IDispatch
template <>
class CComPtr<IDispatch> : public CComPtrBase<IDispatch> {
public:
    CComPtr()  {}
    CComPtr(IDispatch* lp)  :
        CComPtrBase<IDispatch>(lp) {}
    CComPtr(const CComPtr<IDispatch>& lp)  :
        CComPtrBase<IDispatch>(lp.p) {}
};
```

Because this class derives from CComPtrBase, it inherits the typical smart pointer methods. I examine only the ones that differ significantly from those discussed for the CComPtr and CComQIPtr classes.

Property Accessor and Mutator Methods

A few of the methods make it much easier to get and set properties on an object using the object's IDispatch interface. First, you can get the DISPID for a property, given its string name, by calling the GetIDOfName method:

```
HRESULT GetIDOfName(LPCOLESTR lpsz, DISPID* pdispid);
```

When you have the DISPID for a property, you can get and set the property's value using the GetProperty and PutProperty methods. You specify the DISPID of the property to get or set and send or receive the new value in a VARIANT structure:

```
HRESULT GetProperty(DISPID dwDispID, VARIANT* pVar);
HRESULT PutProperty(DISPID dwDispID, VARIANT* pVar);
```

You can skip the initial step and get and set a property given only its name using the well-named GetPropertyByName and PutPropertyByName methods:

```
HRESULT GetPropertyByName(LPCOLESTR lpsz, VARIANT* pVar);
HRESULT PutPropertyByName(LPCOLESTR lpsz, VARIANT* pVar);
```

Method Invocation Helper Functions

The CComPtr<IDispatch> specialization has a number of methods that are customized for the frequent cases of calling an object's method(s) using IDispatch. Four basic variations exist:

- Call a method by DISPID or name, passing zero parameters.
- Call a method by DISPID or name, passing one parameter.
- Call a method by DISPID or name, passing two parameters.
- Call a method by DISPID or name, passing an array of *N* parameters.

Each variation expects the DISPID or name of the method to invoke, the arguments, and an optional return value.

```
HRESULT Invoke0(DISPID dispid, VARIANT* pvarRet = NULL);
HRESULT Invoke0(LPCOLESTR lpszName, VARIANT* pvarRet = NULL);
HRESULT Invoke1(DISPID dispid, VARIANT* pvarParam1,
    VARIANT* pvarRet = NULL);
HRESULT Invoke1(LPCOLESTR lpszName,
        VARIANT* pvarParam1, VARIANT* pvarRet = NULL);
HRESULT Invoke2(DISPID dispid,
        VARIANT* pvarParam1, VARIANT* pvarParam2,
        VARIANT* pvarRet = NULL);
HRESULT Invoke2(LPCOLESTR lpszName,
        VARIANT* pvarParam1, VARIANT* pvarParam2,
        VARIANT* pvarRet = NULL);
HRESULT InvokeN(DISPID dispid,
        VARIANT* pvarParams, int nParams,
        VARIANT* pvarRet = NULL);
HRESULT InvokeN(LPCOLESTR lpszName,
        VARIANT* pvarParams, int nParams,
        VARIANT* pvarRet = NULL);
```

Note that when you are creating the parameter arrays, the parameters must be in reverse order: The last parameter should be at element 0, the next-to-last at element 1, and so on.

Using these helper functions, calling the Add method gets much simpler:

```
HRESULT TheEasyWay( IDispatch *spCalcDisp ) {
  CComPtr< IDispatch > spCalcDisp( pCalcDisp );

  CComVariant varOp1( 6.0 );
  CComVariant varOp2( 7.0 );
  CComVariant varResult;
```

```
    HRESULT hr = spCalcDisp.Invoke2( OLESTR( "Add" ),
      &varOp1, &varOp2, &varResult );
    // varResult now holds sum of 6 and 7
}
```

Finally, two static member functions exist: GetProperty and SetProperty. You can use these methods to get and set a property using its DISPID , even if you haven't encapsulated the IDispatch pointer in a CComPtr<IDispatch>.

```
static HRESULT GetProperty(IDispatch* pDisp, DISPID dwDispID,
    VARIANT* pVar);
static HRESULT PutProperty(IDispatch* pDisp, DISPID dwDispID,
    VARIANT* pVar);
```

Here's an example:

```
HRESULT GetCount(IDispatch* pdisp, long* pCount) {
    *pCount = 0;
    const int DISPID_COUNT = 1;

    CComVariant v;
    CComPtr<IDispatch>::GetProperty (pdisp, DISPID_COUNT, &v);

    HRESULT hr = v.ChangeType (VT_I4);
    If (SUCCEEDED (hr))
        *pCount = V_I4(&v) ;
    return hr;
}
```

The CComGITPtr Class

The Global Interface Table (GIT) provides a per-process cache for storing COM interfaces that you can efficiently unmarshal and access from any apartment in a process. COM objects that aggregate the free-threaded marshaler typically use the GIT to unmarshal interfaces that they hold as state because the object never knows which apartment it might be called from. The GIT provides a convenient place where objects that export an interface from their apartment can register interfaces, and where objects that import interfaces into their apartment can unmarshal and use the interface.

Typically, several steps are involved in using the GIT. First, the exporting apartment must use CoCreateInstance to create an instance of the GIT and obtain an IGlobalInterfaceTable pointer. The exporting apartment then calls IGlobalInterfaceTable::RegisterInterfaceInGlobal to register the interface in the GIT. As a result of the call to `RegisterInterfaceInGlobal`, the exporting apartment receives an apartment-neutral cookie that can safely be passed to other apartments (but *not* other processes) for unmarshaling. Any number of objects in any importing apartment can then use this cookie to retrieve an interface reference that is properly unmarshaled for use in their own apartment.

The code in the exporting apartment might typically look like the following:

```
HRESULT RegisterMyInterface(IMyInterface* pmi, DWORD* pdwCookie) {
    // this is usually a global
    IGlobalInterfaceTable* g_pGIT = NULL;
    HRESULT hr = ::CoCreateInstance(CLSID_StdGlobalInterfaceTable,
                                    NULL,
                                    CLSCTX_INPROC_SERVER,
                                    IID_IGlobalInterfaceTable,
                                    (void**)&g_pGIT);
    ATLASSERT(SUCCEEDED(hr));
    hr = g_pGIT->RegisterInterfaceInGlobal(pmi,
        __uuidof(pmi), pdwCookie);
    return hr;
}
```

The `pdwCookie` returned to the exporting apartment then is passed to another apartment. By using that cookie, any code in that apartment can retrieve the interface pointer registered in the GIT.

```
HRESULT ReadMyInterface(DWORD dwCookie) {
    // ... GIT pointer obtained elsewhere
    IMyInterface* pmi = NULL;
    hr = g_pGIT->GetInterfaceFromGlobal(dwCookie,
    __uuidof(pmi), (void**)&pmi);
    // use pmi as usual
    return hr;
}
```

The exporting apartment removes the interface from the GIT by calling `IGlobalInterfaceTable::RevokeInterfaceFromGlobal` and passing in the cookie it originally received.

ATL simplifies the coding required to perform the following steps by encapsulating the GIT functions in the `CComGITPtr` smart pointer class. This class is defined in `atlbase.h` as follows:

```
template <class T>
class CComGITPtr
{
```

```
    // ...
    DWORD m_dwCookie;
};
```

This class accepts an interface type as its template parameter and holds as its only state the cookie for the interface that will be registered in the GIT. The previously described operations that the exporting apartment performed are encapsulated by CComGITPtr. Under the covers, CComGITPtr simply manipulates the same GIT functions that would otherwise be invoked manually. Even the creation and caching of the GIT itself is managed for you. CComGITPtr retrieves a reference to the GIT from CAtlModule, which instantiates the GIT automatically the first time it is accessed and caches the resulting interface pointer for subsequent accesses. This class holds all sorts of information that is global to a COM server; this is discussed in detail in Chapter 5, "COM Servers."

CComGITPtr instances can be instantiated with four different constructors:

```
CComGITPtr() ;
CComGITPtr(T* p);
CComGITPtr(const CComGITPtr& git);
explicit CComGITPtr(DWORD dwCookie) ;
```

The first constructor simply initializes the m_dwCookie member variable to zero. The second constructor accepts an interface pointer. This constructor retrieves an IGlobalInterfaceTable pointer to a global instance of the GIT and calls RegisterInterfaceInGlobal. The resulting cookie is cached in m_dwCookie. The third constructor accepts a reference to an existing instance of CComGITPtr. This overload retrieves the interface associated with the passed-in git parameter, reregisters it in the GIT to get a second cookie, and stores the new cookie in its own m_dwCookie member variable. This leaves the two CComGITPtrs with separate registered copies of the same interface pointer. The fourth constructor accepts a cookie directly and caches the value. One nice thing about this constructor is that, in debug builds, the implementation tries to validate the cookie by retrieving an interface from the GIT using the cookie. The constructor asserts if this fails.

The three assignment operators CComGITPtr supplies perform operations identical to those of the corresponding constructors:

```
CComGITPtr<T>& operator=(T* p)
CComGITPtr<T>& operator=(const CComGITPtr<T>& git)
CComGITPtr<T>& operator=(DWORD dwCookie)
```

What's particularly nice about CComGITPtr is that the destructor takes care of the required GIT cleanup when the instance goes out of scope. Beware, though—this can get you into a bit of trouble if you're not careful, as you'll learn at the end of this section.

```
~CComGITPtr()  { Revoke(); }
```

As you can see, the destructor simply delegates its work to the Revoke method, which takes care of retrieving an IGlobalInterfaceTable pointer and using it to call RevokeInterfaceFromGlobal.

```
HRESULT Revoke()  {
    HRESULT hr = S_OK;
    if (m_dwCookie != 0) {
        CComPtr<IGlobalInterfaceTable> spGIT;
        HRESULT hr = E_FAIL;
        hr = AtlGetGITPtr(&spGIT);

        ATLASSERT(spGIT != NULL);
        ATLASSERT(SUCCEEDED(hr));
        if (FAILED(hr))
            return hr;

        hr = spGIT->RevokeInterfaceFromGlobal(m_dwCookie);
        if (SUCCEEDED(hr))
        m_dwCookie = 0;
    }
    return hr;
}
```

If you are working with a CComGITPtr instance that has already been initialized, you can use one of the Attach methods to associate a different interface with the instance:

```
HRESULT Attach(T* p) ;
HRESULT Attach(DWORD dwCookie) ;
```

The first version of Attach calls RevokeInterfaceFromGlobal if m_dwCookie is nonzero—that is, if this CComGITPtr is already managing an interface registered in the GIT. It then calls RegisterInterfaceInGlobal using the new interface p passed in and stores the resulting cookie. The second overload also removes the interface it managed from the GIT (if necessary) and then simply caches the cookie provided.

Correspondingly, the Detach method can be used to disassociate the interface from the CComGITPtr instance.

```
DWORD Detach() ;
```

This method simply returns the stored cookie value and sets `m_dwCookie` to zero. This means that the caller has now taken ownership of the registered interface pointer and must eventually call `RevokeInterfaceFromGlobal`.

These methods greatly simplify the code needed to register an interface pointer in the GIT and manage that registration. In fact, the code required in the exporting apartment reduces to a single line.

```
HRESULT RegisterMyInterface(IMyInterface* pmi) {
  CComGITPtr<IMyInterface> git(pmi);
  // creates GIT or gets ref to existing GIT
  // registers interface in GIT
  // retrieves cookie and caches it

    // ... interface removed from GIT when git goes out of scope
}
```

In the importing apartment, clients that want to use the registered interface pointer simply use the `CopyTo` method `CComGITPtr` provides:

```
HRESULT CopyTo(T** pp) const
```

This can be used in code like this:

```
HRESULT ReadMyInterface(const CComGITPtr<IMyInterface>& git) {
    IMyInterface* pmi = NULL;
    HRESULT hr = git.CopyTo(&pmi);
    ATLASSERT(SUCCEEDED(hr));

    //... use pmi as usual
}
```

A potentially dangerous race condition occurs if you're not careful using `CComGITPtr`. Remember that the entire reason for having a GIT is to make an interface accessible from multiple threads. This means that you will be passing GIT cookies from an exporting apartment that is not synchronized with code in the importing apartment that will be using the associated registered interface. If the lifetime of the `CComGITPtr` is not carefully managed, the importing apartment could easily end up with an invalid cookie. Here's the scenario:

```
void ThreadProc(void*);    // forward declaration
HRESULT RegisterInterfaceAndFork(IMyInterface* pmi) {
    CComGITPtr<IMyInterface>  git(pmi); // interface registered
```

```
        // create worker thread and pass CComGITPtr instance
        ::_beginthread(ThreadProc, 0, &git);
}
void ThreadProc(void* pv)
{
    CComGITPtr<IMyInterface>* pgit =
        (CComGITPtr<IMyInterface>*)pv;
    IMyInterface* pmi = NULL;
    HRESULT hr = pgit->CopyTo(&pmi);
    // ... do some work with pmi
}
```

The trouble with this code is that the RegisterInterfaceAndFork method could finish before the ThreadProc retrieves the interface pointer using CopyTo. This means that the git variable will go out of scope and unregister the IMyInterface pointer from the GIT too early. You must employ some manner of synchronization, such as WaitForSingleObject, to guard against problems like these.

In general, CComGITPtr shouldn't be used as a local variable. Its intended use is as a member variable or global. In those cases, the lifetime of the CComGITPtr object is automatically controlled by the lifetime of the object that contains it, or the lifetime of the process.

The CAutoPtr and CAutoVectorPtr Smart Pointer Classes

CComPtr was presented as a smart pointer class for managing a COM interface pointer. ATL 8 provides a related set of classes for managing pointers to instances of C++ classes, as opposed to CComPtr's management of interface pointers to COM coclasses. These classes provide a useful encapsulation of the operations required to properly manage the memory resources associated with a C++ object. CAutoPtr, CAutoVectorPtr, CAutoPtrArray, and CAutoPtrList are all defined in atlbase.h.

The CAutoPtr and CAutoVectorPtr Classes

The CAutoPtr template class wraps a C++ object created with the new operator. The class holds a pointer to the encapsulated object as its only state, and exposes convenient methods and operators for controlling the ownership, lifetime, and state of the internal C++ object. CAutoPtr is used in code like this:

```
STDMETHODIMP CMyClass::SomeFunc() {
    CFoo* pFoo = new Foo();          // instantiate C++ class
    CAutoPtr<CFoo> spFoo(pFoo);      // take ownership of pFoo
    spFoo->DoSomeFoo();
```

```
       // ... do other things with spFoo
}      // CAutoPtr deletes pFoo instance
       // when spFoo goes out of scope
```

This simple example demonstrates the basic usage pattern of CAutoPtr: Create an instance of a C++ class, transfer ownership of the pointer to CAutoPtr, operate on the CAutoPtr object as if it were the original C++ class, and let CAutoPtr destroy the encapsulated object or reclaim ownership of the pointer. Although this behavior is similar to that of the Standard C++ class auto_ptr, that class throws exceptions, whereas ATL's CAutoPtr does not. ATL developers sometimes do not link with the CRT, so the exception support required by auto_ptr would not be available.

CAutoVectorPtr enables you to manage a pointer to an array of C++ objects. It operates almost identically to CAutoPtr; the principal difference is that vector new[] and vector delete[] are used to allocate and free memory for the encapsulated objects. The comments in the sections that follow are written in terms of CAutoPtr, although most apply equally well to both CAutoPtr and CAutoVectorPtr.

Constructors and Destructor

CAutoPtr provides four constructors to initialize new instances. The first constructor simply creates a CAutoPtr instance with a NULL-encapsulated pointer.

```
CAutoPtr()  : m_p( NULL ) { }


template< typename TSrc >
CAutoPtr( CAutoPtr< TSrc >& p ) {
    m_p = p.Detach();  // Transfer ownership
}


CAutoPtr( CAutoPtr< T >& p ) {
    m_p = p.Detach();  // Transfer ownership
}


explicit CAutoPtr( T* p )  : m_p( p ) { }
```

To use this class to do any meaningful work, you have to associate a pointer with the instance using either the Attach method or one of the assignment operators (these are discussed shortly). The third constructor enables you to initialize with another CAutoPtr instance. This simply uses the Detach method to transfer ownership of the object encapsulated from the CAutoPtr instance passed in to the instance being constructed. The fourth constructor also transfers ownership of an object pointer, but using the object pointer directly as the constructor parameter. The second constructor is an interesting one. It defines a templatized constructor with a second type parameter, TSrc. This second template parameter represents a second type from which the CAutoPtr instance can be initialized. The type of the encapsulated pointer within CAutoPtr instance was established at declaration by the CAutoPtr class's template parameter T, as in this declaration:

```
CAutoPtr<CAnimal> spAnimal(pAnimal);
```

Here, CAnimal is the declared type of the encapsulate m_p object pointer. So, how is it that we have a constructor that enables us to initialize this pointer to a pointer of a different type? The answer is quite simple. Just as C++ allows pointers to instances of base types to be initialized with pointers to instances of derived types, the fourth CAutoPtr constructor allows instances of CAutoPtr<Base> to be initialized with instances of CAutoPtr<Derived>, as in the following:

```
class CAnimal { ... };
class CDog : public CAnimal { ... };
// ...
CDog* pDog = new CDog();
CAutoPtr<CAnimal> spAnimal(pDog);
```

The CAutoPtr destructor is invoked whenever the instance goes out of scope. It leverages the Free method to release the memory associated with the internal C++ class object.

```
~CAutoPtr() {
    Free();
}
void Free() {
    delete m_p;
    m_p = NULL;
}
```

CAutoPtr Operators

CAutoPtr defines two assignment operators:

```
template< typename TSrc >
CAutoPtr< T >& operator=( CAutoPtr< TSrc >& p ) {
    if(m_p==p.m_p) {
        ATLASSERT(FALSE);
    } else {
        Free();
```

```
            Attach( p.Detach() );  // Transfer ownership
        }
        return( *this );
    }

    CAutoPtr< T >& operator=( CAutoPtr< T >& p )  {
        if(*this==p) {
            if(this!=&p) {
                ATLASSERT(FALSE);
                p.Detach();
            } else {
            }
        } else {
            Free();
            Attach( p.Detach() );   // Transfer ownership
        }
        return( *this );
    }
}
```

Both of these operators behave the same. The difference is that the first version is templatized to a second type TSrc. As with the templatized constructor just discussed that accepts a TSrc template parameter, this assignment operator allows for assignment of pointers to instances of base types to be assigned to pointers to instances of derived types. You can take advantage of this flexibility in code such as the following:

```
class CAnimal { ... };
class CDog : public CAnimal { ... };
// ...

// instantiate a CAnimal
CAutoPtr<CAnimal> spAnimal(new CAnimal());

// instantiate a CDog
CAutoPtr<CDog> spDog(new CDog());
// CAnimal instance freed here
spAnimal = spDog;

// ... CDog instance will be freed when spAnimal
// goes out of scope
```

Regardless of whether you assign a CAutoPtr instance to the same type or to a derived type, the assignment operator first checks for some important misuses (such as multiple CAutoPtr objects pointing to the same underlying C++ object) and then calls the Free method to delete the encapsulated instance before taking ownership of the new instance. The call to p.Detach ensures that the instance on the right side of the assignment does not also try to delete the same object.

CAutoPtr also defines a cast operator and overloads the member access operator (->):

```
operator T*() const {
    return( m_p );
}
T* operator->() const {
    ATLASSERT( m_p != NULL );
    return( m_p );
}
```

Both operators simply return the value of the encapsulated pointer. The member access operator exposes the public member functions and variables of the encapsulated object, so you can use instances of CAutoPtr more like the encapsulated type:

```
class CDog {
public:
    void Bark() {}
    int m_nAge;
};
CAutoPtr<CDog> spDog(new Dog);
spDog->Bark();
spDog->m_nAge += 5;
```

Finally, CAutoPtr defines operator== and operator!= to do comparisons between two CAutoPtr objects.

```
bool operator!=(CAutoPtr<T>& p) const { return !operator==(p); }
bool operator==(CAutoPtr<T>& p) const { return m_p==p.m_p; }
```

CAutoVectorPtr

CAutoVectorPtr differs from CAutoPtr in only a few ways. First, CAutoVectorPtr does not define a constructor that allows the initialization of an instance using a derived type. Second, CAutoVectorPtr defines an Allocate function to facilitate construction of a collection of encapsulated instances.

```
bool Allocate( size_t nElements ) {
    ATLASSERT( m_p == NULL );
    ATLTRY( m_p = new T[nElements] );
```

```
    if( m_p == NULL ) {
        return( false );
    }

    return( true );
}
```

This method simply uses the vector `new[]` to allocate and initialize the number of instances specified with the `nElements` parameter. Here's how you might apply this capability:

```
class CAnimal { public: void Growl() {} };
// each instance is of type CAnimal
CAutoVectorPtr<CAnimal> spZoo;
// allocate and initialize 100 CAnimal's
spZoo.Allocate(100);
```

Note that `CAutoVectorPtr` does not overload the member access operator (->), as did `CAutoPtr`. So, you cannot write code like this:

```
spZoo->Growl();    // wrong!  can't do this => doesn't make sense
```

Of course, such an operation doesn't even make sense because you're not specifying which `CAnimal` instance should growl. You can operate on the encapsulated instances only after retrieving a specific one from the encapsulated collection. It's not clear why the ATL team didn't overload `operator[]` to provide a convenient arraylike syntax for accessing individual instances contained in a `CAutoVectorPtr` instance. So, you have to write code such as the following to get at members of a particular encapsulated instance:

```
((CAnimal*)spZoo)[5].Growl();
```

I find myself underwhelmed that the ATL team didn't simply overload `operator[]` to provide a more convenient arraylike syntax for accessing individual members of the collection. But, hey, it's their world—I'm just livin' in it.

`CAutoVectorPtr` has another limitation, but, unfortunately, I can't point the finger at Microsoft for this one. A consequence of `CAutoVectorPtr` using the vector `new[]` to allocate the collection of encapsulated objects is that only the default constructor of the encapsulated type is invoked. If the class you want `CAutoVectorPtr` to manage defines nondefault constructors and performs special initialization in them, the `Allocate` function has no way to call these constructors. This also means that your class must define a default (parameterless) constructor, or you won't even be able to use your class with `CAutoVectorPtr`. So, if we change our `CAnimal`, this code won't compile:

```
class CAnimal {
public:
CAnimal(int nAge) : m_nAge(nAge) {}
        void Growl() {}
private:
int m_nAge;
}

CAutoVectorPtr<CAnimal> spZoo;
spZoo.Allocate(100); // won't compile => no default constructor
```

The final difference `CAutoVectorPtr` has with `CAutoPtr` is in the implementation of the destructor. `Allocate` used the vector `new[]` to create and initialize the collection of encapsulated instances, so the destructor must match this with a vector `delete[]` operation. In C++, you must always match the vector allocation functions this way; otherwise, bad things happen. This ensures that the destructor for each object in the collection is run and that all the associated memory for the entire collection is properly released. Exactly what happens if this regimen isn't followed is compiler specific (and also compiler setting specific). Some implementations corrupt the heap immediately if `delete[]` is not used; others invoke the destructor of only the first object in the collection. `CAutoVectorPtr` does the right thing for you if you have let it handle the allocation via the `Allocate` member function. However, you can get yourself into trouble by improperly using `Attach`, with code such as the following:

```
class CAnimal {};
// allocate only a single instance
CAnimal* pAnimal = new Animal;
CAutoVectorPtr<CAnimal> spZoo;
// wrong, wrong!!! pAnimal is not a collection
spZoo.Attach(pAnimal)
```

In this code, the original pointer to the C++ instance was allocated using `new` instead of vector `new[]`. So, when `spZoo` goes out of scope and the destructor runs, it will eventually call vector `delete[]`. That will be bad. In fact, it will throw an exception, so be careful.

ATL Memory Managers

A Review of Windows Memory Management

Applications use memory for almost everything they do. In Windows, memory can be allocated from three principle places: the thread's stack, memory-mapped files, and heaps. Memory-mapped files are more specialized, so we don't discuss them further here. The stack is used to allocate local variables because their size is known at compile time and their allocation must be as efficient as possible. Allocating and deallocating storage from the stack involves merely incrementing and decrementing the stack pointer by the appropriate amount. Dynamic memory, however, is allocated and freed as the program runs, based on changing characteristics within the application. Instead of being allocated from the thread's stack, dynamic memory comes from pools of storage known as *heaps*. A heap is an independently managed block of memory that services dynamic memory allocation requests and reclaims memory that an application no longer uses. Typically, heaps expose APIs for creating the heap, destroying the heap, allocating a block of memory within the heap, and returning a block of memory to the heap. The precise algorithms employed in coordinating these tasks constitute what is commonly termed the *heap manager*. In general, heap managers implement various schemes for managing resources for specialized circumstances. The heap manager functions exposed for applications often reflect some of the differences that make one particular type of heap suitable over another for a particular circumstance.

In Windows, each process creates a *default heap* at initialization. Applications use Win32 functions such as `HeapCreate`, `HeapAlloc`, and `HeapFree` to manage the heap and blocks of data within the default heap. Because many Windows functions that can be called from multiple applications use this heap, the default heap is implemented to be thread safe. Access to the default heap is serialized so that multiple simultaneous threads accessing the heap will not corrupt it. Older versions of Windows used functions such as `LocalAlloc` and `GlobalAlloc` to manipulate the heap, but these functions are now deprecated. They run slower and offer fewer features than the `HeapXXX` suite.

Applications that link to the C-runtime library (which ATL projects now do by default) have access to another heap simply known as the CRT heap. The memory-management functions the CRT heap manager exposes are likely the most recognizable to the general C/C++ community because they are part of the C standard. With the CRT heap, functions such as `malloc` are used to obtain storage from the heap; `free` is used to return storage to the heap.

An application might need to use different heaps for various reasons, such as with specialized management requirements. For instance, COM introduces an additional set of complexities to the general problem of memory management. Memory addresses are allocated on a per-process basis, so a process cannot directly access data stored in another process. Yet COM allows data to be marshaled between processes. If a method call is remoted so that a client expects an [out] parameter from the object, the memory for that [out] parameter will be allocated in one process (the object's), and used and freed in another process (the client's). Clearly, a conventional heap has no way to straddle process boundaries to associate allocations in one process with free operations in another. The COM task allocator lives to provide this very service. Part of the COM programming conventions is that when allocating memory blocks that will be shared across a COM interface, that memory must be allocated by calling CoTaskMemAlloc and must be freed by the corresponding CoTaskMemFree. By agreeing on these standardized functions, the automatically generated proxy-stub code can properly allocate and free memory across COM boundaries. COM's remoting infrastructure does all the dirty work needed to create the illusion of a single heap that spans processes.

Several other reasons exist for managing memory with different heaps. Components that are allocated from separate heaps are better isolated from one another, which could make the heaps less susceptible to corruption. If objects will be accessed close together in time—say, within the same function—it is desirable for those objects to live close together in memory, which can result in fewer page faults and a marked improvement in overall performance. Some applications choose to implement custom, specialized memory managers that are tuned to specific requirements. Using separate heaps also could allow the application to avoid the overhead associated with synchronizing access to a single heap. As previously mentioned, a Win32 process's default heap is thread safe because it expects to be accessed simultaneously from multiple threads. This leads to thread contention because each heap access must pass through thread-safe interlocked operations. Applications can devote one heap to each thread and eliminate the synchronization logic and thread contention.

ATL simplifies the use of heaps through a series of concrete heap implementations that wrap Windows API functions and through an abstract interface that allows these implementations to be used polymorphically in other ATL classes that use memory resources.

The IAtlMemMgr Interface

The atlmem.h header file expresses the generic memory-management pattern through the definition of the IAtlMemMgr interface.

```
__interface IAtlMemMgr {
public:
    void* Allocate( size_t nBytes ) ;
    void Free( void* p ) ;
    void* Reallocate( void* p, size_t nBytes ) ;
    size_t GetSize( void* p ) ;
};
```

The four simple functions defined on this interface provide most of the dynamic memory functionality required in typical applications. Allocate reserves a contiguous region of space nBytes in size within the heap. Free takes a pointer to a memory block retrieved from Allocate and returns it to the heap so that it will be available for future allocation requests. The Reallocate method is useful when an allocated block is not large enough to accommodate additional data and it is more practical and/or efficient to grow the existing block than to allocate a new, larger one and copy the contents. Finally, GetSize accepts a pointer to a block obtained from Allocate and returns the current size of the block in bytes.

Many ATL classes are designed to support pluggable heap implementations by performing all their memory-management functions through an IAtlMemMgr reference. Developers can provide custom implementations of IAtlMemMgr and use them with ATL. This provides a great deal of flexibility in optimizing the performance of these classes to suit specific application requirements. ATL Server makes heavy use of IAtlMemMgr in processing SOAP requests and in stencil processing. Additionally, we've already seen how CStringT allows developers to supply an IAtlMemMgr implementation to optimize string-handling performance.

The Memory Manager Classes

Although it is useful to abstract memory management behind an interface to facilitate custom heap implementations, most applications don't need a high degree of sophistication in these implementations to build efficient components. Indeed, you can realize many of the benefits of multiple heaps with simple heap implementations. To that end, ATL provides five concrete implementations of IAtlMemMgr that you can use as is in many circumstances.

CComHeap is defined in atlcommem.h as follows:

```
class CComHeap :
    public IAtlMemMgr {
// IAtlMemMgr
public:
    virtual void* Allocate( size_t nBytes )  {
#ifdef _WIN64
        if( nBytes > INT_MAX ) { return( NULL ); }
#endif
        return( ::CoTaskMemAlloc( ULONG( nBytes ) ) );
    }
    virtual void Free( void* p ) {
        ::CoTaskMemFree( p );
    }
    virtual void* Reallocate( void* p, size_t nBytes )  {
```

```
#ifdef _WIN64
        if( nBytes > INT_MAX ) { return( NULL ); }
#endif
        return( ::CoTaskMemRealloc( p, ULONG( nBytes ) ) );
    }
    virtual size_t GetSize( void* p )  {
        CComPtr< IMalloc > pMalloc;
        ::CoGetMalloc( 1, &pMalloc );
        return( pMalloc->GetSize( p ) );
    }
};
```

As you can see, this class is merely a very thin wrapper on top of the COM task allocator API functions. `Allocate` simply delegates to `CoTaskMemAlloc`, and `Free` delegates to `CoTaskMemFree`. In fact, all five of the stock memory managers implement `IAtlMemMgr` in a similar manner; the prime difference is the underlying functions to which the managers delegate. Table 3.2 summarizes which heap-management functions are used for each of the ATL memory managers.

Table 3.2.   Heap Functions Used in ATL Memory Managers

Memory Manager Class	Heap Functions Used
CComHeap	CoTaskMemAlloc, CoTaskMemFree, CoTaskMemRealloc, IMalloc::GetSize
CCRTHeap	malloc, free, realloc, _msize
CLocalHeap	LocalAlloc, LocalFree, LocalReAlloc, LocalSize
CGlobalHeap	GlobalAlloc, GlobalFree, GlobalReAlloc, GlobalSize
CWin32Heap	HeapAlloc, HeapFree, HeapReAlloc, HeapSize

The `CCRTHeap` uses memory from the CRT heap, whereas `CLocalHeap` and `CGlobalHeap` both allocate memory from the process heap. The `LocalXXX` and `GlobalXXX` functions in the Win32 API exist now mostly for backward compatibility. You shouldn't really use them in new code anymore, so we don't discuss them further.

The `CWin32Heap` class is a bit different from the other heap classes in a couple important respects. Whereas the other memory managers allocate storage from the process heap, `CWin32Heap` requires that a valid `HANDLE` to a heap be created before using its `IAtlMemMgr` implementation. This gives the developer a bit more control over the details of the underlying heap that will be used, albeit with a bit more complexity. `CWin32Heap` supplies three constructors for initializing an instance:

```
CWin32Heap()  :    m_hHeap( NULL ), m_bOwnHeap( false ) { }
CWin32Heap( HANDLE hHeap )  :
    m_hHeap( hHeap ),
    m_bOwnHeap( false ) {
    ATLASSERT( hHeap != NULL );
}
CWin32Heap( DWORD dwFlags, size_t nInitialSize,
    size_t nMaxSize = 0 ) :
    m_hHeap( NULL ),
    m_bOwnHeap( true ) {
    ATLASSERT( !(dwFlags&HEAP_GENERATE_EXCEPTIONS) );
    m_hHeap = ::HeapCreate( dwFlags, nInitialSize, nMaxSize );
    if( m_hHeap == NULL ) { AtlThrowLastWin32(); }
}
```

The first constructor initializes a CWin32Heap instance with no associated heap. The second constructor initializes the instance with a handle to an existing heap obtained from a previous call to the Win32 HeapCreate API. Note that the m_bOwn-Heap member is set to false in this case. This member tracks whether the CWin32Heap instance owns the underlying heap. Thus, when the second constructor is used, the caller is still responsible for ultimately calling HeapDestroy to get rid of the heap later. The third constructor is arguably the simplest to use because it directly accepts the parameters required to create a heap and invokes HeapCreate automatically. The dwFlags parameter is a bit field that allows two different flags to be set. One of the two flags, HEAP_GENERATE_EXCEPTIONS, can be given to the underlying HeapCreate call to indicate that the system should raise an exception upon function failure. However, the code asserts if this flag is specified because the ATL code base isn't prepared for system exceptions to be thrown if an allocation fails. The other flag, HEAP_NO_SERIALIZE, relates to the synchronization options with heaps, discussed a bit earlier in this section. If this flag is specified, the heap is *not* thread safe. This can improve performance considerably because interlocked operations are no longer used to gain access to the heap. *However, it is the programmer's responsibility to ensure that multiple threads will not access a heap created with this flag set. Otherwise, heap corruption is likely to occur.* The nInitialSize parameter indicates how much storage should be reserved when the heap is created. You can use the nMaxSize parameter to specify how large the heap should be allowed to grow.

CWin32Heap also defines Attach and Detach operations to associate an existing heap with a CWin32Heap instance:

```
void Attach( HANDLE hHeap, bool bTakeOwnership ) {
    ATLASSERT( hHeap != NULL );
    ATLASSERT( m_hHeap == NULL );
    m_hHeap = hHeap;
    m_bOwnHeap = bTakeOwnership;
}
HANDLE Detach() {
    HANDLE hHeap;

    hHeap = m_hHeap;
    m_hHeap = NULL;
    m_bOwnHeap = false;

    return( hHeap );
}
```

Attach accepts a handle to a heap and a Boolean flag indicating whether the caller is transferring ownership of the heap to the CWin32Heap instance. This governs whether the destructor will destroy the heap. Detach simply surrenders ownership of the encapsulated heap by flipping the m_bOwnHeap member to FALSE and returning the handle to the caller. Note that Attach simply overwrites the existing heap handle stored in the CWin32Heap. If the class already held a non-NULL HANDLE, there would be no way to free that heap after the Attach is performed. As a result, you have a memory leak—and a really big one, at that. If you thought leaking memory from an object was bad, trying leaking entire heaps at a time! You might wonder at first why the Attach method doesn't simply destroy the existing heap before overwriting the internal handle. After all, CComVariant::Attach and CComSafe Array::Attach were shown earlier clearing their encapsulated data before attaching to a new instance. The difference here is that even if the CWin32Heap instance owns the heap (m_bOwnHeap is TRUE), it has no knowledge of what live objects out there have been allocated from that heap. Blindly destroying the existing heap would yank memory from any number of objects, which could be disastrous. You simply have to be careful. Here's the kind of code *you want to avoid*:

```
// create an instance and allocate a heap
CWin32Heap heap(0,       // no exceptions, use thread-safe access
                4000,    // initial size
                0);      // no max size => heap grows as needed

// manually create a second heap
HANDLE hHeap = ::HeapCreate(0, 5000, 0);

// this is gonna get you in a "heap" of trouble!
heap.Attach(hHeap, false /* same result if true */ );
```

Custom memory management commonly is used in string processing. Applications that allocate, free, and resize strings frequently can often tax memory managers and negatively impact performance. Multithreaded applications that do a lot of string processing can exhibit reduced performance because of thread contention for heap allocation requests. Moreover, heaps that service multithreaded applications can provide slower access because synchronization locks of some sort must be employed to ensure thread safety. One tactic to combat this is to provide a per-thread heap so that no synchronization logic is needed and thread contention does not occur.

We show an example of a specialized heap for string allocations using CWin32Heap and ATL's new CStencil class. This class is discussed in detail in later chapters when we cover building web applications with ATL Server. For now, recall from the discussion of web application development in Chapter 1, "Hello, ATL," that ATL produces web pages by processing stencil response files and rendering HTML-based text responses. This involves a great deal of string parsing and processing, and CStencil bears a lot of this burden. Its constructor enables you to pass in a custom memory manager to be used in all its string parsing. The following code demonstrates how to create a per-thread heap manager to be used for stencil processing:

```
DWORD g_dwTlsIndex;     // holds thread-local storage slot index
// g_dwTlsIndex = ::TlsAlloc() performed in other
// initialization code

// Create a private heap for use on this thread
// only => no synchronized access
CWin32Heap* pHeap = new CWin32Heap(HEAP_NO_SERIALIZE, 50000);

// Store the heap pointer in this thread's TLS slot
::TlsSetValue(g_dwTlsIndex, reinterpret_cast<void*>(
static_cast<IAtlMemMgr*>(pHeap)));

// ...

// Retrieve the heap pointer from TLS
pHeap = (IAtlMemMgr*)::TlsGetValue(g_dwTlsIndex);

// Create a new CStencil instance that uses the private heap
CStencil* pStencil = new CStencil(pHeap);
```

Notice the extra layer of casting when storing the heap pointer in the TLS slot. You need to hold on to the original CWin32Heap pointer with the concrete type because IAtlMemMgr doesn't have a virtual destructor. If you just had an IAtlMemMgr* to call delete on, the actual CWin32Heap destructor would not get called. That extra layer of casting is to make sure that you get the correct interface pointer converted to void* before storing it in the TLS. It's probably not strictly necessary in the current version of ATL, but if the heap implementation has multiple base classes, the cast to void* could cause some serious trouble.

Summary

ATL provides a rich set of classes for manipulating the data types COM programmers frequently use. The CComVariant class provides practically the same benefits as the CComBSTR class, but for VARIANT structures. If you use a VARIANT structure—and you will need to use one sooner or later—you should instead use the ATL CComVariant smart VARIANT class. You'll have far fewer problems with resource leaks.

SAFEARRAYs have a number of specialized semantics as well. CComSafeArray was shown to be a useful template class for managing both single- and multidimensional SAFEARRAYs. As with other managed resources, however, take care when dealing with CComSafeArray because the compiler cannot always tell you if you've written code that will result in a memory leak.

The CComPtr, CComQIPtr, and CComGITPtr smart pointer classes ease, but do not totally alleviate, the resource management needed for interface pointers. These classes have numerous useful methods that let you write more application code and deal less with the low-level resource-management details. You'll find smart pointers most useful when you're using interface pointers with exception handling.

Finally, you can control memory management in ATL with IAtlMemMgr and five concrete implementations that are supplied: CWin32Heap, CComHeap, CCRTHeap, CLocalHeap, and CGlobalHeap. You can program ATL classes such as CString to use memory from these heaps or even from a custom implementation of IAtlMemMgr, to provide a high degree of control and facilitate any number of performance optimizations.

CHAPTER

4

Objects in ATL

ATL's fundamental support for COM can be split into two pieces: objects and servers. This chapter covers classes and concentrates on how IUnknown is implemented as related to threading and various COM identity issues, such as standalone versus aggregated objects. The next chapter focuses on how to expose classes from COM servers.

Implementing IUnknown

A COM object has one responsibility: to implement the methods of IUnknown. Those methods perform two services, lifetime management and runtime type discovery, as follows:

```
interface IUnknown {
  // runtime type discovery
  HRESULT QueryInterface([in] REFIID riid,
                         [out, iid_is(riid)] void **ppv);

  // lifetime management
  ULONG AddRef();
  ULONG Release();
}
```

COM allows every object to implement these methods as it chooses (within certain restrictions, as described in Chapter 5, "COM Servers"). The canonical implementation is as follows:

```
// Server lifetime management
extern void ServerLock();
extern void ServerUnlock();

class CPenguin : public IBird, public ISnappyDresser {
public:
  CPenguin() : m_cRef(0) { ServerLock(); }
  virtual ~CPenguin()    { ServerUnlock(); }
```

```
    // IUnknown methods
    STDMETHODIMP QueryInterface(REFIID riid, void **ppv) {
        if( riid == IID_IBird || riid == IID_IUnknown )
            *ppv = static_cast<IBird*>(this);
        else if( riid == IID_ISnappyDresser )
            *ppv = static_cast<ISnappyDresser*>(this);
        else *ppv = 0;

        if( *ppv ) {
            reinterpret_cast<IUnknown*>(*ppv)->AddRef();
            return S_OK;
        }

        return E_NOINTERFACE;
    }

    ULONG AddRef()
    { return InterlockedIncrement(&m_cRef); }

    ULONG Release() {
        ULONG l = InterlockedDecrement(&m_cRef);
        if( l == 0 ) delete this;
        return l;
    }

    // IBird and ISnappyDresser methods...
private:
    ULONG m_cRef;
};
```

This implementation of IUnknown is based on several assumptions:

1. The object is heap-based because it removes itself using the delete operator. Furthermore, the object's outstanding references completely govern its lifetime. When it has no more references, it deletes itself.

2. The object is capable of living in a multithread apartment because it manipulates the reference count in a thread-safe manner. Of course, the other methods must be implemented in a thread-safe manner as well for the object to be fully thread safe.

3. The object is standalone and cannot be aggregated because it does not cache a reference to a controlling outer, nor does it forward the methods of IUnknown to a controlling outer.

4. The object exposes its interfaces using multiple inheritance.

5. The existence of the object keeps the server running. The constructor and the destructor are used to lock and unlock the server, respectively.

These common assumptions are not the only possibilities. Common variations include the following:

1. An object can be global and live for the life of the server. Such objects do not need a reference count because they never delete themselves.

2. An object might not need to be thread safe because it might be meant to live only in a single-threaded apartment.

3. An object can choose to allow itself to be aggregated as well as, or instead of, supporting standalone activation.

4. An object can expose interfaces using other techniques besides multiple inheritance, including nested composition, tear-offs, and aggregation.

5. You might not want the existence of an object to force the server to keep running. This is common for global objects because their mere existence prohibits the server from unloading.

Changing any of these assumptions results in a different implementation of IUnknown, although the rest of the object's implementation is unlikely to change much (with the notable exception of thread safety). These implementation details of IUnknown tend to take a very regular form and can be encapsulated into C++ classes. Frankly, we'd really like to use someone else's tested code and be able to change our minds later without a great deal of effort. We'd also like this boilerplate code to be easily separated from the actual behavior of our objects so that we can focus on our domain-specific implementation. ATL was designed from the ground up to provide just this kind of functionality and flexibility.

The Layers of ATL

ATL's support for building COM objects is separated into several layers, as shown in Figure 4.1.

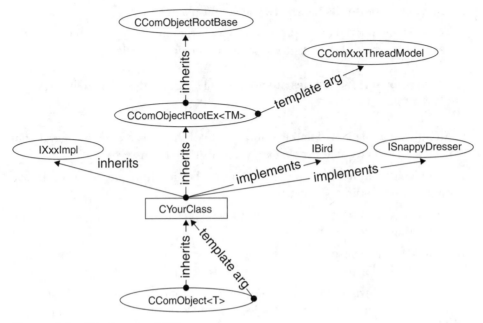

Figure 4.1   The layers of ATL

These layers break down into services exposed by ATL for building objects:

1. `CComObjectRootEx` uses a `CComXxxThreadModel` to provide "just thread-safe enough" object lifetime management and object locking.

2. `CComObjectRootBase` and `CComObjectRootEx` provide helper functions used in implementing `IUnknown`.

3. Your class, which derives from `CComObjectRootEx`, also derives from any interfaces it wants to implement, as well as providing the method implementations. You or one of the ATL `IXxxImpl` classes can provide method implementations.

4. `CComObject` et al, provides the actual implementation of the methods of `IUnknown` in a way consistent with your desires for object and server lifetime management requirements. This final layer actually derives from your class.

Your choice of base classes and the most derived class determines the way the methods of `IUnknown` are implemented. If your choices change, using different classes at compile time (or runtime) will change how ATL implements `IUnknown`, independently of the rest of the behavior of your object. The following sections explore each layer of ATL.

Threading Model Support

Just Enough Thread Safety

The thread-safe implementation of `AddRef` and `Release` shown previously might be overkill for your COM objects. For example, if instances of a specific class will live in only a single-threaded apartment, there's no reason to use the thread-safe Win32 functions `InterlockedIncrement` and `InterlockedDecrement`. For single-threaded objects, the following implementation of `AddRef` and `Release` is more efficient:

```
class Penquin {
...
  ULONG AddRef()
  { return ++m_cRef; }

  ULONG Release() {
      ULONG l = -m_cRef;
      if( l == 0 ) delete this;
      return l;
  }
...
};
```

Using the thread-safe Win32 functions also works for single-threaded objects, but unnecessary thread safety requires extra overhead. For this reason, ATL provides three classes, `CComSingleThreadModel`, `CComMultiThreadModel`, and `CComMulti-ThreadModelNoCS`. These classes provide two static member functions, `Increment` and `Decrement`, for abstracting away the differences between managing an object's lifetime count in a multithreaded manner versus a single-threaded one. The two versions of these functions are as follows (notice that both `CComMultiThreadModel` and `CComMultiThreadModelNoCS` have identical implementations of these functions):

```
class CComSingleThreadModel {
  static ULONG WINAPI Increment(LPLONG p) { return ++(*p); }
  static ULONG WINAPI Decrement(LPLONG p) { return -(*p); }
  ...
};

class CComMultiThreadModel {
  static ULONG WINAPI Increment(LPLONG p) { return InterlockedIncrement(p); }
  static ULONG WINAPI Decrement(LPLONG p) { return InterlockedDecrement(p); }
  ...
};
```

```
class CComMultiThreadModelNoCS {
    static ULONG WINAPI Increment(LPLONG p) { return InterlockedIncrement(p); }
    static ULONG WINAPI Decrement(LPLONG p) { return InterlockedDecrement(p); }
    ...
};
```

Using these classes, you can parameterize[1] the class to give a "just thread-safe enough" AddRef and Release implementation:

```
template <typename ThreadModel>
class Penguin {
...
    ULONG AddRef()
    { return ThreadModel::Increment(&m_cRef); }

    ULONG Release() {
        ULONG l = ThreadModel::Decrement(&m_cRef);
        if( l == 0 ) delete this;
        return l;
    }
...
};
```

Now, based on our requirements for the CPenguin class, we can make it just thread-safe enough by supplying the threading model class as a template parameter:

```
// Let's make a thread-safe CPenguin
CPenguin* pobj = new CPenguin<CComMultiThreadModel>( );
```

Instance Data Synchronization

When you create a thread-safe object, protecting the object's reference count isn't enough. You also have to protect the member data from multithreaded access. One popular method for protecting data that multiple threads can access is to use a Win32 critical section object, as shown here:

```
template <typename ThreadModel>
class CPenguin {
public:
```

---

[1] For an introduction to C++ templates and how they're used in ATL, see Appendix A, "C++ Templates by Example.

```
CPenguin()  {
  ServerLock();
  InitializeCriticalSection(&m_cs);
}

~CPenguin() { ServerUnlock(); DeleteCriticalSection(&m_cs); }

// IBird
STDMETHODIMP get_Wingspan(long* pnWingspan) {
  Lock(); // Lock out other threads during data read
  *pnWingSpan = m_nWingspan;
  Unlock();
  return S_OK;
}

STDMETHODIMP put_Wingspan(long nWingspan) {
  Lock(); // Lock out other threads during data write
  m_nWingspan = nWingspan;
  Unlock();
  return S_OK;
}
  ...
private:
  CRITICALSECTION m_cs;

  void Lock() { EnterCriticalSection(&m_cs); }
  void Unlock() { LeaveCriticalSection(&m_cs); }
};
```

Notice that before reading or writing any member data, the CPenguin object enters the critical section, locking out access by other threads. This coarse-grained, object-level locking keeps the scheduler from swapping in another thread that could corrupt the data members during a read or a write on the original thread. However, object-level locking doesn't give you as much concurrency as you might like. If you have only one critical section per object, one thread might be blocked trying to increment the reference count while another is updating an unrelated member variable. A greater degree of concurrency requires more critical sections, allowing one thread to access one data member while a second thread accesses another. Be careful using this kind of finer-grained synchronization—it often leads to deadlock:

```
class CZax : public IZax {
public:
  ...
```

```
// IZax
STDMETHODIMP GoNorth() {
    EnterCriticalSection(&m_cs1); // Enter cs1...
    EnterCriticalSection(&m_cs2); // ...then enter cs2
    // Go north...
    LeaveCriticalSection(&m_cs2);
    LeaveCriticalSection(&m_cs1);
}

STDMETHODIMP GoSouth() {
    EnterCriticalSection(&m_cs2); // Enter cs2...
    EnterCriticalSection(&m_cs1); // ...then enter cs1
    // Go south...
    LeaveCriticalSection(&m_cs1);
    LeaveCriticalSection(&m_cs2);
}
...
private:
    CRITICAL_SECTION  m_cs1;
    CRITICAL_SECTION  m_cs2;
};
```

Imagine that the scheduler let the northbound Zax[2] thread enter the first critical section and then swapped in the southbound Zax thread to enter the second critical section. If this happened, neither Zax could enter the other critical section; therefore, neither Zax thread would be able to proceed. This would leave them deadlocked while the world went on without them. Try to avoid this.[3]

Whether you decide to use object-level locking or finer-grained locking, critical sections are handy. ATL provides four class wrappers that simplify their use: CComCriticalSection, CComAutoCriticalSection, CComSafeDeleteCriticalSection, and CComAutoDeleteCriticalSection.

```
class CComCriticalSection {
public:
    CComCriticalSection()  {
        memset(&m_sec, 0, sizeof(CRITICAL_SECTION));
    }
    ~CComCriticalSection() { }
    HRESULT Lock()  {
```

---

[2] *The Sneeches and Other Stories*, by Theodor Geisel (aka Dr. Seuss).

[3] For more guidance on what to do about deadlocks, read *Win32 Multithreaded Programming* (O'Reilly and Associates, 1997), by Mike Woodring and Aaron Cohen.

```
        EnterCriticalSection(&m_sec);
        return S_OK;
    }

    HRESULT Unlock() {
        LeaveCriticalSection(&m_sec);
        return S_OK;
    }

    HRESULT Init() {
        HRESULT hRes = E_FAIL;
        __try {
            InitializeCriticalSection(&m_sec);
            hRes = S_OK;
        }
        // structured exception may be raised in
        // low memory situations
        __except(STATUS_NO_MEMORY == GetExceptionCode()) {
            hRes = E_OUTOFMEMORY;
        }

        return hRes;
    }

    HRESULT Term() {
        DeleteCriticalSection(&m_sec);
        return S_OK;
    }
    CRITICAL_SECTION m_sec;
};

class CComAutoCriticalSection : public CComCriticalSection {
public:
    CComAutoCriticalSection() {
        HRESULT hr = CComCriticalSection::Init();
        if (FAILED(hr))
            AtlThrow(hr);
    }
    ~CComAutoCriticalSection() {
        CComCriticalSection::Term();
    }
private :
    // Not implemented. CComAutoCriticalSection::Init
    // should never be called
    HRESULT Init();
    // Not implemented. CComAutoCriticalSection::Term
    // should never be called
```

```cpp
    HRESULT Term();
};

class CComSafeDeleteCriticalSection
    : public CComCriticalSection {
public:
    CComSafeDeleteCriticalSection(): m_bInitialized(false) { }

    ~CComSafeDeleteCriticalSection()  {
        if (!m_bInitialized) { return; }
        m_bInitialized = false;
        CComCriticalSection::Term();
    }

    HRESULT Init()  {
        ATLASSERT( !m_bInitialized );
        HRESULT hr = CComCriticalSection::Init();
        if (SUCCEEDED(hr)) {
            m_bInitialized = true;
        }
        return hr;
    }

    HRESULT Term()  {
        if (!m_bInitialized) { return S_OK; }
        m_bInitialized = false;
        return CComCriticalSection::Term();
    }

    HRESULT Lock() {
        ATLASSUME(m_bInitialized);
        return CComCriticalSection::Lock();
    }

private:
    bool m_bInitialized;
};

class CComAutoDeleteCriticalSection : public CComSafeDeleteCriticalSection {
private:
    // CComAutoDeleteCriticalSection::Term should never be called
    HRESULT Term() ;
};
```

Notice that CComCriticalSection does not use its constructor or destructor to initialize and delete the contained critical section. Instead, it contains Init and Term functions for this purpose. CComAutoCriticalSection, on the other hand, is easier to use because it automatically creates the critical section in its constructor and destroys it in the destructor.

CComSafeDeleteCriticalSection does half that job; it doesn't create the critical section until the Init method is called, but it always deletes the critical section (if it exists) in the destructor. You also have the option of manually calling Term if you want to explicitly delete the critical section ahead of the object's destruction. CComAutoDeleteCriticalSection, on the other hand, blocks the Term method by simply declaring it but never defining it; calling CComAutoDeleteCriticalSection::Term gives you a linker error. These classes were useful before ATL was consistent about supporting construction for global and static variables, but these classes are largely around for historical reasons at this point; you should prefer CComAutoCriticalSection.

Using a CComAutoCriticalSection in our CPenguin class simplifies the code a bit:

```
template <typename ThreadModel>
class CPenguin {
public:
  // IBird methods Lock() and Unlock() as before...
  ...
private:
  CComAutoCriticalSection m_cs;

  void Lock() { m_cs.Lock(); }
  void Unlock() { m_cs.Unlock(); }
};
```

Note that with both CComAutoCriticalSection and CComCriticalSection, the user must take care to explicitly call Unlock before leaving a section of code that has been protected by a call to Lock. In the presence of code that might throw exceptions (which a great deal of ATL framework code now does), this can be difficult to do because each piece of code that can throw an exception represents a possible exit point from the function. CComCritSecLock addresses this issue by automatically locking and unlocking in its constructor and destructor. CComCritSecLock is parameterized by the lock type so that it can serve as a wrapper for CComCriticalSection or CComAutoCriticalSection.

```
template< class TLock >
class CComCritSecLock {
public:
```

```cpp
    CComCritSecLock( TLock& cs, bool bInitialLock = true );
    ~CComCritSecLock() ;

    HRESULT Lock() ;
    void Unlock() ;

// Implementation
private:
    TLock& m_cs;
    bool m_bLocked;
...
};

template< class TLock >
inline CComCritSecLock< TLock >::CComCritSecLock(
    TLock& cs,bool bInitialLock )
    : m_cs( cs ), m_bLocked( false ) {
    if( bInitialLock ) {
        HRESULT hr;
        hr = Lock();
        if( FAILED( hr ) ) { AtlThrow( hr ); }
    }
}

template< class TLock >
inline CComCritSecLock< TLock >::~CComCritSecLock()  {
    if( m_bLocked ) { Unlock(); }
}

template< class TLock >
inline HRESULT CComCritSecLock< TLock >::Lock()  {
    HRESULT hr;
    ATLASSERT( !m_bLocked );
    hr = m_cs.Lock();
    if( FAILED( hr ) ) { return( hr ); }
    m_bLocked = true;
    return( S_OK );
}

template< class TLock >
inline void CComCritSecLock< TLock >::Unlock()  {
    ATLASSERT( m_bLocked );
    m_cs.Unlock();
    m_bLocked = false;
}
```

If the `bInitialLock` parameter to the constructor is true, the contained critical section is locked upon construction. In normal use on the stack, this is exactly what you want, which is why `true` is the default. However, as usual with constructors, if something goes wrong, you don't have an easy way to return the failure code. If you need to know whether the lock failed, you can pass `false` instead and then call `Lock` explicitly. `Lock` returns the `HRESULT` from the lock operation. This class ensures that the contained critical section is unlocked whenever an instance of this class leaves scope because the destructor automatically attempts to call `Unlock` if it detects that the instance is currently locked.

Notice that our `CPenguin` class is still parameterized by the threading model. There's no sense in protecting our member variables in the single-threaded case. Instead, it would be handy to have another critical section class that could be used in place of `CComCriticalSection` or `CComAutoCriticalSection`. ATL provides the `CComFakeCriticalSection` class for this purpose:

```
class CComFakeCriticalSection {
public:
    HRESULT Lock()    { return S_OK; }
    HRESULT Unlock()  { return S_OK; }
    HRESULT Init()    { return S_OK; }
    HRESULT Term()    { return S_OK; }
};
```

Given `CComFakeCriticalSection`, we could further parameterize the `CPenguin` class by adding another template parameter, but this is unnecessary. The ATL threading model classes already contain type definitions that map to a real or fake critical section, based on whether you're doing single or multithreading:

```
class CcomSingleThreadModel {
public:
    static ULONG WINAPI Increment(LPLONG p) {return ++(*p);}
    static ULONG WINAPI Decrement(LPLONG p) {return -(*p);}
    typedef CComFakeCriticalSection AutoCriticalSection;
    typedef CComFakeCriticalSection AutoDeleteCriticalSection;
    typedef CComFakeCriticalSection CriticalSection;
    typedef CComSingleThreadModel ThreadModelNoCS;
};

class CcomMultiThreadModel {
public:
    static ULONG WINAPI Increment(LPLONG p) {return InterlockedIncrement(p);}
    static ULONG WINAPI Decrement(LPLONG p) {return InterlockedDecrement(p);}
```

```
    typedef CComAutoCriticalSection AutoCriticalSection;
    typedef CComAutoDeleteCriticalSection
        AutoDeleteCriticalSection;
    typedef CComCriticalSection CriticalSection;
    typedef CComMultiThreadModelNoCS ThreadModelNoCS;
};

class CcomMultiThreadModelNoCS {
public:
    static ULONG WINAPI Increment(LPLONG p) {return InterlockedIncrement(p);}
    static ULONG WINAPI Decrement(LPLONG p) {return InterlockedDecrement(p);}
    typedef CComFakeCriticalSection AutoCriticalSection;
    typedef CComFakeCriticalSection AutoDeleteCriticalSection;
    typedef CComFakeCriticalSection CriticalSection;
    typedef CComMultiThreadModelNoCS ThreadModelNoCS;
};
```

These type definitions enable us to make the CPenguin class just thread safe enough for both the object's reference count and course-grained object synchronization:

```
template <typename ThreadingModel>
class CPenguin {
public:
    // IBird methods as before...
...
private:
    ThreadingModel::AutoCriticalSection m_cs;

    void Lock() { m_cs.Lock(); }
    void Unlock() { m_cs.Unlock(); }
};
```

This technique enables you to provide the compiler with operations that are just thread safe enough. If the threading model is CComSingleThreadModel, the calls to Increment and Decrement resolve to operator++ and operator–, and the Lock and Unlock calls resolve to empty inline functions.

If the threading model is CComMultiThreadModel, the calls to Increment and Decrement resolve to calls to InterlockedIncrement and InterlockedDecrement. The Lock and Unlock calls resolve to calls to EnterCriticalSection and LeaveCriticalSection.

Finally, if the model is CComMultiThreadModelNoCS, the calls to Increment and Decrement are thread safe, but the critical section is fake, just as with

CComSingleThreadModel. CComMultiThreadModelNoCS is designed for multithreaded objects that eschew object-level locking in favor of a more fine-grained scheme. Table 4.1 shows how the code is expanded based on the threading model class you use:

Table 4.1. Expanded Code Based on Threading Model Class

	CcomSingleThread-Model	CComMultiThread-Model	CComMultiThread-ModelNoCS
TM::Increment	++	Interlocked-Increment	Interlocked-Increment
TM::Decrement	–	Interlocked-Decrement	Interlocked-Decrement
TM::AutoCritical-Section::Lock	(Nothing)	EnterCritical-Section	(Nothing)
TM::AutoCritical-Section::Unlock	(Nothing)	LeaveCritical-Section	(Nothing)

The Server's Default Threading Model

ATL-based servers have a concept of a "default" threading model for things that you don't specify directly. To set the server's default threading model, you define one of the following symbols: _ATL_SINGLE_THREADED, _ATL_APARTMENT_THREADED, or _ATL_FREE_THREADED. If you don't specify one of these symbols, ATL assumes _ATL_FREE_THREADED. However, the ATL Project Wizard defines _ATL_APARTMENT_THREADED in the generated stdafx.h file. ATL uses these symbols to define two type definitions:

```
#if defined(_ATL_SINGLE_THREADED)
...
    typedef CComSingleThreadModel CComObjectThreadModel;
    typedef CComSingleThreadModel CComGlobalsThreadModel;

#elif defined(_ATL_APARTMENT_THREADED)
...
    typedef CComSingleThreadModel CComObjectThreadModel;
    typedef CComMultiThreadModel CComGlobalsThreadModel;

#elif defined(_ATL_FREE_THREADED)
...
```

```
    typedef CComMultiThreadModel CComObjectThreadModel;
    typedef CComMultiThreadModel CComGlobalsThreadModel;
...
#endif
```

Internally, ATL uses `CComObjectThreadModel` to protect instance data and `CComGlobalsThreadModel` to protect global and static data. Because the usage is difficult to override in some cases, you should make sure that ATL is compiled using the most protective threading model of any of the classes in your server. In practice, this means you should change the wizard-generated `_ATL_APARTMENT_THREADED` symbol to `_ATL_FREE_THREADED` if you have even one multithreaded class in your server.

The Core of IUnknown

Standalone Reference Counting

To encapsulate the `Lock` and `Unlock` methods as well as the "just thread-safe enough" reference counting, ATL provides the `CComObjectRootEx` base class, parameterized by the desired threading model[4]:

```
template <class ThreadModel>
class CComObjectRootEx : public CComObjectRootBase {
public:
    typedef ThreadModel _ThreadModel;
    typedef typename _ThreadModel::AutoCriticalSection _CritSec;
    typedef typename _ThreadModel::AutoDeleteCriticalSection _AutoDelCritSec;
    typedef CComObjectLockT<_ThreadModel> ObjectLock;

    ~CComObjectRootEx() {}

    ULONG InternalAddRef() {
        ATLASSERT(m_dwRef != -1L);
        return _ThreadModel::Increment(&m_dwRef);
    }
    ULONG InternalRelease() {
#ifdef _DEBUG
        LONG nRef = _ThreadModel::Decrement(&m_dwRef);
        if (nRef < -(LONG_MAX / 2)) {
```

---

[4] As an optimization, ATL provides a specialization of `CComObjectRootEx<CComSingleThreadModel>` that does not have a `_CritSec` object, side-stepping minimum object size requirements imposed by the compiler.

```
                ATLASSERT(0 &&
                _T("Release called on a pointer that has"
                    " already been released"));
        }
        return nRef;
#else
        return _ThreadModel::Decrement(&m_dwRef);
#endif
    }

    HRESULT _AtlInitialConstruct() { return m_critsec.Init(); }
    void Lock() {m_critsec.Lock();}
    void Unlock() {m_critsec.Unlock();}
private:
    _AutoDelCritSec m_critsec;
};


template <>
class CComObjectRootEx<CComSingleThreadModel>
    : public CComObjectRootBase {
public:
    typedef CComSingleThreadModel _ThreadModel;
    typedef _ThreadModel::AutoCriticalSection _CritSec;
    typedef _ThreadModel::AutoDeleteCriticalSection
        _AutoDelCritSec;
    typedef CComObjectLockT<_ThreadModel> ObjectLock;

    ~CComObjectRootEx() {}

    ULONG InternalAddRef() {
        ATLASSERT(m_dwRef != -1L);
        return _ThreadModel::Increment(&m_dwRef);
    }
    ULONG InternalRelease() {
#ifdef _DEBUG
        long nRef = _ThreadModel::Decrement(&m_dwRef);
        if (nRef < -(LONG_MAX / 2)) {
            ATLASSERT(0 && _T("Release called on a pointer "
                    "that has already been released"));
        }
        return nRef;
#else
        return _ThreadModel::Decrement(&m_dwRef);
#endif
```

```
      }

      HRESULT _AtlInitialConstruct() { return S_OK; }

      void Lock() {}
      void Unlock() {}
};
```

ATL classes derive from CComObjectRootEx and forward AddRef and Release calls to the InternalAddRef and InternalRelease methods when the object is created standalone (that is, not aggregated). Note that InternalRelease checks the decremented reference count against the somewhat odd-looking value -(LONG_MAX / 2). The destructor of CComObject (or one of its alternatives, discussed a bit later) sets the reference count to this value. The ATL designers could have used a different value here, but basing the value on LONG_MAX makes it unlikely that such a reference count could be reached under normal circumstances. Dividing LONG_MAX by 2 ensures that the resulting value can't mistakenly be reached by wrapping around from 0. InternalRelease simply checks the reference count against this value to see if you're trying to call Release on an object that has already been destroyed. If so, an assert is issued in debug builds.

The template specialization for CComSingleThreadModel demonstrates the "just safe enough" multithreading. When used in a single-threaded object, the Lock and Unlock methods do nothing, and no critical section object is created.

With the Lock and Unlock methods so readily available in the base class, you might be tempted to write the following *incorrect* code:

```
class CPenguin
    : public CComObjectRootEx<CComMultiThreadModel>, ... {
    STDMETHODIMP get_Wingspan(long* pnWingspan) {
      Lock();
      if( !pnWingspan ) return E_POINTER; // Forgot to Unlock
      *pnWingSpan = m_nWingspan;
      Unlock();
      return S_OK;
    }
    ...
};
```

To help you avoid this kind of mistake, CComObjectRootEx provides a type definition for a class called ObjectLock, based on CComObjectLockT parameterized by the threading model:

```
template <class ThreadModel>
class CcomObjectLockT {
public:
    CComObjectLockT(CComObjectRootEx<ThreadModel>* p) {
        if (p)
            p->Lock();
        m_p = p;
    }

    ~CComObjectLockT() {
        if (m_p)
            m_p->Unlock();
    }
    CComObjectRootEx<ThreadModel>* m_p;
};

template <>
class CComObjectLockT<CComSingleThreadModel> {
public:
    CComObjectLockT(CComObjectRootEx<CComSingleThreadModel>*) {}
    ~CComObjectLockT() {}
};
```

Instances of `CComObjectLockT` Lock the object passed to the constructor and `Unlock` it upon destruction. The `ObjectLock` type definition provides a convenient way to write code that will properly release the lock regardless of the return path:

```
class CPenguin
    : public CComObjectRootEx<CComMultiThreadModel>, ... {
    STDMETHODIMP get_Wingspan(long* pnWingspan) {
        ObjectLock lock(this);
        if( !pnWingspan ) return E_POINTER; // Unlock happens as
                                            //  stack unwinds
        *pnWingSpan = m_nWingspan;
         return S_OK;
    }
    ...
};
```

Of course, the specialization for `CComSingleThreadModel` ensures that in the single-threaded object, no locking is done. This is useful when you've changed your threading model; you don't pay a performance penalty for using an `ObjectLock` if you don't actually need one.

Table-Driven QueryInterface

In addition to "just thread-safe enough" implementations of `AddRef` and `Release` for standalone COM objects, `CComObjectRootEx` (via its base class, `CComObjectRootBase`) provides a static, table-driven implementation of `QueryInterface` called `InternalQueryInterface`:

```
static HRESULT WINAPI
CComObjectRootBase::InternalQueryInterface(
    void*                    pThis,
    const _ATL_INTMAP_ENTRY* pEntries,
    REFIID                   iid,
    void**                   ppvObject);
```

This function's job is to use the `this` pointer of the object, provided as the `pThis` parameter, and the requested interface to fill the `ppvObject` parameter with a pointer to the appropriate virtual function table pointer (`vptr`). It does this using the `pEntries` parameter, a zero-terminated array of `_ATL_INTMAP_ENTRY` structures:

```
struct _ATL_INTMAP_ENTRY {
    const IID*          piid;
    DWORD               dw;
    _ATL_CREATORARGFUNC* pFunc;
};
```

Each interface exposed from a COM object is one entry in the interface map, which is a class static array of `_ATL_INTMAP_ENTRY` structures. Each entry consists of an interface identifier, a function pointer, and an argument for the function represented as a `DWORD`. This provides a flexible, extensible mechanism for implementing `QueryInterface` that supports multiple inheritance, aggregation, tear-offs, nested composition, debugging, chaining, and just about any other wacky COM identity tricks C++ programmers currently use.[5] However, because most interfaces are implemented using multiple inheritance, you don't often need this much flexibility. For example, consider one possible object layout for instances of the `CPenguin` class, shown in Figure 4.2.

```
class CPenguin : public IBird, public ISnappyDresser {...};
```

---

[5] Chapter 5, "COM Servers," describes all these uses of the interface map.

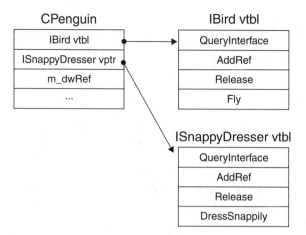

Figure 4.2   CPenguin object layout, including `vptrs` to `vtbls`

The typical implementation of `QueryInterface` for a class using multiple inheritance consists of a series of `if` statements and `static_cast` operations; the purpose is to adjust the `this` pointer by some fixed offset to point to the appropriate `vptr`. Because the offsets are known at compile time, a table matching interface identifiers to offsets would provide an appropriate data structure for adjusting the `this` pointer at runtime. To support this common case, `InternalQueryInterface` function treats the `_ATL_INTMAP_ENTRY` as a simple IID/offset pair if the `pFunc` member has the special value `_ATL_SIMPLEMAPENTRY`:

```
#define _ATL_SIMPLEMAPENTRY ((ATL::_ATL_CREATORARGFUNC*)1)
```

To be able to use the `InternalQueryInterface` function, each implementation populates a static interface map. To facilitate populating this data structure, and to provide some other methods used internally, ATL provides the following macros (as well as others described in Chapter 6, "Interface Maps"):

```
#define BEGIN_COM_MAP(class) ...
#define COM_INTERFACE_ENTRY(itf) ...
#define END_COM_MAP() ...
```

For example, our `CPenguin` class would declare its interface map like this:

```
class CPenguin :
    public CComObjectRootEx<CComMultiThreadModel>,
    public IBird,
    public ISnappyDresser {
...
```

```
public:
BEGIN_COM_MAP(CPenguin)
    COM_INTERFACE_ENTRY(IBird)
    COM_INTERFACE_ENTRY(ISnappyDresser)
END_COM_MAP()
...
};
```

In an abbreviated form, this would expand to the following:

```
class CPenguin :
    public CComObjectRootEx<CComMultiThreadModel>,
    public IBird,
    public ISnappyDresser {
...
public:
  IUnknown* GetUnknown() {
      ATLASSERT(_GetEntries()[0].pFunc == _ATL_SIMPLEMAPENTRY);
      return (IUnknown*)((int)this+_GetEntries()->dw); }
  }
  HRESULT _InternalQueryInterface(REFIID iid, void** ppvObject) {
      return InternalQueryInterface(this, _GetEntries(), iid, ppvObject);
  }
  const static _ATL_INTMAP_ENTRY* WINAPI _GetEntries() {
    static const _ATL_INTMAP_ENTRY _entries[] = {
        { &_ATL_IIDOF(IBird),           0, _ATL_SIMPLEMAPENTRY },
        { &_ATL_IIDOF(ISnappyDresser), 4, _ATL_SIMPLEMAPENTRY },
        { 0, 0, 0 }
    };
    return _entries;
  }
...
};
```

The `_ATL_IIDOF` macro expands as follows:

```
#ifndef _ATL_NO_UUIDOF
#define _ATL_IIDOF(x) __uuidof(x)
#else
#define _ATL_IIDOF(x) IID_##x
#endif
```

This macro lets you choose to use `__uuidof` operator or the standard naming convention to specify the IID for the interface in question for the entire project.

Figure 4.3 shows how this interface map relates to an instance of a `CPenguin` object in memory.

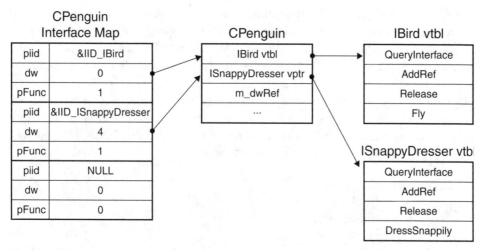

Figure 4.3   CPenguin interface map, CPenguin object, and vtbls

Something else worth mentioning is the GetUnknown member function that the BEGIN_COM_MAP provides. Although ATL uses this internally, it's also useful when passing your this pointer to a function that requires an IUnknown*. Because your class derives from potentially more than one interface, each of which derives from IUnknown, the compiler considers passing your own this pointer as an IUnknown* to be ambiguous.

```
HRESULT FlyInAnAirplane(IUnknown* punkPassenger);

// Penguin.cpp
STDMETHODIMP CPenguin::Fly() {
    return FlyInAnAirplane(this); // ambiguous
}
```

For these situations, GetUnknown is your friend, e.g.
```
STDMETHODIMP CPenguin::Fly() {
    return FlyInAnAirplane(this->GetUnknown()); // unambiguous
}
```

As you'll see later, GetUnknown is implemented by handing out the first entry in the interface map.

Support for Aggregation: The Controlled Inner

So far, we've discussed the implementation of IUnknown for standalone COM objects. However, if our object is to participate in aggregation as a controlled inner, our job is not to think for ourselves, but rather to be subsumed by the thoughts and prayers of another. A controlled inner does this by blindly forwarding all calls on the publicly available implementation of `IUnknown` to the controlling outer's implementation. The controlling outer's implementation is provided as the `pUnkOuter` argument to the `CreateInstance` method of `IClassFactory`. If our ATL-based COM object is used as a controlled inner, it simply forwards all calls to `IUnknown` methods to the `OuterQueryInterface`, `OuterAddRef`, and `OuterRelease` functions provided in `CComObjectRootBase`; these, in turn, forward to the controlling outer. The relevant functions of `CComObjectRootBase` are shown here:

```
class CComObjectRootBase {
public:
    CComObjectRootBase() { m_dwRef = 0L; }
    ...
    ULONG OuterAddRef() {
        return m_pOuterUnknown->AddRef();
    }
    ULONG OuterRelease() {
        return m_pOuterUnknown->Release();
    }
    HRESULT OuterQueryInterface(REFIID iid, void ** ppvObject) {
        return m_pOuterUnknown->QueryInterface(iid, ppvObject);
    }
    ...
    union {
        long       m_dwRef;
        IUnknown*  m_pOuterUnknown;
    };
};
```

Notice that `CComObjectRootBase` keeps the object's reference count and a pointer to a controlling unknown as a union. This implies that an object can either maintain its own reference count *or* be aggregated, but not both at the same time. This implication is not true. If the object is being aggregated, it must maintain a reference count *and* a pointer to a controlling unknown. In this case, discussed more later, ATL keeps the `m_pUnkOuter` in one instance of the `CComObjectBase` and derives from `CComObjectBase` again to keep the object's reference count.

More to Come

Although it's possible to implement the methods of `IUnknown` directly in your class using the methods of the base class `CComObjectRootEx`, most ATL classes don't. Instead, the actual implementations of the `IUnknown` methods are left to a class that derives from your class, as in `CComObject`. We discuss this after we talk about the responsibilities of your class.

Your Class

Because ATL provides the behavior for `IUnknown` in the `CComObjectRootEx` class and provides the actual implementation in the `CComObject` (and friends) classes, the job your class performs is pretty simple: derive from interfaces and implement their methods. Besides making sure that the interface map lists all the interfaces you're implementing, you can pretty much leave implementing `IUnknown` to ATL and concentrate on your custom functionality. This is, after all, the whole point of ATL in the first place.

ATL's Implementation Classes

Many standard interfaces have common implementations. ATL provides implementation classes of many standard interfaces. For example, `IPersistImpl`, `IConnectionPointContainerImpl`, and `IViewObjectExImpl` implement `IPersist`, `IConnectionPointContainer`, and `IViewObjectEx`, respectively. Some of these interfaces are common enough that many objects can implement them—for example, persistence, eventing, and enumeration. Some are more special purpose and related only to a particular framework, as with controls, Internet-enabled components, and Microsoft Management Console extensions. Most of the general-purpose interface implementations are discussed in Chapters 7, "Persistence in ATL"; 8, "Collections and Enumerators"; and 9, "Connection Points." The interface implementations related to the controls framework are discussed in Chapters 10, "Windowing," and 11, "ActiveX Controls." One implementation is general purpose enough to discuss right here: `IDispatchImpl`.

Scripting Support

For a scripting environment to access functionality from a COM object, the COM object must implement `IDispatch`:

```
interface IDispatch : IUnknown {
    HRESULT GetTypeInfoCount([out] UINT * pctinfo);

    HRESULT GetTypeInfo([in] UINT iTInfo,
        [in] LCID lcid,
        [out] ITypeInfo ** ppTInfo);

    HRESULT GetIDsOfNames([in] REFIID riid,
```

```
         [in, size_is(cNames)] LPOLESTR * rgszNames,
         [in] UINT cNames,
         [in] LCID lcid,
         [out, size_is(cNames)] DISPID * rgDispId);

    HRESULT Invoke([in] DISPID dispIdMember,
         [in] REFIID riid,
         [in] LCID lcid,
         [in] WORD wFlags,
         [in, out] DISPPARAMS * pDispParams,
         [out] VARIANT * pVarResult,
         [out] EXCEPINFO * pExcepInfo,
         [out] UINT * puArgErr);
}
```

The most important methods of IDispatch are GetIDsOfNames and Invoke. Imagine the following line of scripting code:

```
penguin.wingspan = 102
```

This translates into two calls on IDispatch. The first is GetIDsOfNames, which asks the object if it supports the wingspan property. If the answer is yes, the second call to IDispatch is to Invoke. This call includes an identifier (called a DISPID) that uniquely identifies the name of the property or method the client is interested in (as retrieved from GetIDsOfNames), the type of operation to perform (calling a method, or getting or setting a property), a list of arguments, and a place to put the result (if any). The object's implementation of Invoke is then required to interpret the request the scripting client made. This typically involves unpacking the list of arguments (which is passed as an array of VARIANT structures), converting them to the appropriate types (if possible), pushing them onto the stack, and calling some other method implemented that deals in real data types, not VARIANTs. In theory, the object's implementation could take any number of interesting, dynamic steps to parse and interpret the client's request. In practice, most objects forward the request to a helper, whose job it is to build a stack and call a method on an interface implemented by the object to do the real work. The helper makes use of type information held in a type library typically bundled with the server. COM type libraries hold just enough information to allow an instance of a TypeInfo object—that is, an object that implements ITypeInfo—to perform this service. The TypeInfo object used to implement IDispatch is usually based on a dual interface, defined in IDL like this:

```
[ object, dual, uuid(44EBF74E-116D-11D2-9828-00600823CFFB) ]
interface IPenguin : IDispatch {
```

```
            [propput] HRESULT Wingspan([in] long nWingspan);
            [propget] HRESULT Wingspan([out, retval] long* pnWingspan);
                      HRESULT Fly();
    }
```

Using a TypeInfo object as a helper allows an object to implement IDispatch like this (code in bold indicates differences between one implementation and another):

```
class CPenguin :
    public CComObectRootEx<CComSingleThreadModel>,
    public IBird,
    public ISnappyDresser,
    public IPenguin {
public:
    CPenguin() : m_pTypeInfo(0) {
        IID*       pIID   = &IID_IPenguin;
        GUID*      pLIBID = &LIBID_BIRDSERVERLib;
        WORD       wMajor = 1;
        WORD       wMinor = 0;
        ITypeLib* ptl = 0;
        HRESULT hr = LoadRegTypeLib(*pLIBID, wMajor, wMinor,
            0, &ptl);
        if( SUCCEEDED(hr) ) {
            hr = ptl->GetTypeInfoOfGuid(*pIID, &m_pTypeInfo);
            ptl->Release();
        }
    }

    virtual ~Penguin() {
        if( m_pTypeInfo ) m_pTypeInfo->Release();
    }

BEGIN_COM_MAP(CPenguin)
    COM_INTERFACE_ENTRY(IBird)
    COM_INTERFACE_ENTRY(ISnappyDresser)
    COM_INTERFACE_ENTRY(IDispatch)
    COM_INTERFACE_ENTRY(IPenguin)
END_COM_MAP()

    // IDispatch methods
    STDMETHODIMP GetTypeInfoCount(UINT *pctinfo) {
        return (*pctinfo = 1), S_OK;
    }
```

```
    STDMETHODIMP GetTypeInfo(UINT ctinfo, LCID lcid,
    ITypeInfo **ppti) {
        if( ctinfo != 0 ) return (*ppti = 0), DISP_E_BADINDEX;
        return (*ppti = m_pTypeInfo)->AddRef(), S_OK;
    }


    STDMETHODIMP GetIDsOfNames(REFIID riid, OLECHAR **rgszNames,
        UINT cNames, LCID lcid, DISPID *rgdispid) {
        return m_pTypeInfo->GetIDsOfNames(rgszNames, cNames,
            rgdispid);
    }


    STDMETHODIMP Invoke(DISPID dispidMember,
                        REFIID riid,
                        LCID lcid,
                        WORD wFlags,
                        DISPPARAMS *pdispparams,
                        VARIANT *pvarResult,
                        EXCEPINFO *pexcepinfo,
                        UINT *puArgErr) {
        return m_pTypeInfo->Invoke(static_cast<IPenguin*>(this),
                            dispidMember, wFlags,
                            pdispparams, pvarResult,
                            pexcepinfo, puArgErr);
    }
    // IBird, ISnappyDresser and IPenguin methods...
private:
    ITypeInfo*  m_pTypeInfo;
};
```

Because this implementation is so boilerplate (it varies only by the dual interface type, the interface identifier, the type library identifier, and the major and
minor version numbers), it can be easily implemented in a template base class.
ATL's parameterized implementation of IDispatch is IDispatchImpl:

```
template <class T,
        const IID* piid = &__uuidof(T),
        const GUID* plibid = &CAtlModule::m_libid,
        WORD wMajor = 1,
        WORD wMinor = 0,
        class tihclass = CComTypeInfoHolder>
class ATL_NO_VTABLE IDispatchImpl : public T {...};
```

Given `IDispatchImpl`, our `IPenguin` implementation gets quite a bit simpler:

```
class CPenguin :
    public CComObjectRootEx<CComMultiThreadModel>,
    public IBird,
    public ISnappyDresser,
    public IDispatchImpl<IPenguin, &IID_IPenguin> {
public:
BEGIN_COM_MAP(CPenguin)
    COM_INTERFACE_ENTRY(IBird)
    COM_INTERFACE_ENTRY(ISnappyDresser)
    COM_INTERFACE_ENTRY(IDispatch)
    COM_INTERFACE_ENTRY(IPenguin)
END_COM_MAP()
    // IBird, ISnappyDresser and IPenguin methods...
};
```

Supporting Multiple Dual Interfaces

I wish it wouldn't, but this question always comes up: "How do I support multiple dual interfaces in my COM objects?" My answer is always, "Why would you want to?"

The problem is, of the scripting environments I'm familiar with that require an object to implement `IDispatch`, not one supports `QueryInterface`. So although it's possible to use ATL to implement multiple dual interfaces, you have to choose which implementation to hand out as the "default"—that is, the one the client gets when asking for `IDispatch`. For example, let's say that instead of having a special `IPenguin` interface that represents the full functionality of my object to scripting clients, I decided to make all the interfaces dual interfaces.

```
[ dual, uuid(...) ] interface IBird : IDispatch {...}
[ dual, uuid(...) ] interface ISnappyDresser : IDispatch { ... };
```

You can implement both of these dual interfaces using ATL's `IDispatchImpl`:

```
class CPenguin :
    public CComObjectRootEx<CComSingleThreadModel>,
    public IDispatchImpl<IBird, &IID_IBird>,
    public IDispatchImpl<ISnappyDresser, &IID_ISnappyDresser> {
public:
BEGIN_COM_MAP(CPenguin)
    COM_INTERFACE_ENTRY(IBird)
    COM_INTERFACE_ENTRY(ISnappyDresser)
```

```
    COM_INTERFACE_ENTRY(IDispatch) // ambiguous
END_COM_MAP()
...
};
```

However, when you fill in the interface map in this way, the compiler gets upset. Remember that the COM_INTERFACE_ENTRY macro essentially boils down to a static_cast to the interface in question. Because two different interfaces derive from IDispatch, the compiler cannot resolve the one to which you're trying to cast. To resolve this difficulty, ATL provides another macro:

```
#define COM_INTERFACE_ENTRY2(itf, branch)
```

This macro enables you to tell the compiler which branch to follow up the inheritance hierarchy to the IDispatch base. Using this macro allows you to choose the default IDispatch interface:

```
class CPenguin :
    public CComObjectRootEx<CComSingleThreadModel>,
    public IDispatchImpl<IBird, &IID_IBird>,
    public IDispatchImpl<ISnappyDresser, &IID_ISnappyDresser> {
public:
BEGIN_COM_MAP(CPenguin)
    COM_INTERFACE_ENTRY(IBird)
    COM_INTERFACE_ENTRY(ISnappyDresser)
    COM_INTERFACE_ENTRY2(IDispatch, IBird) // Compiles
                                           // (unfortunately)
END_COM_MAP()
...
};
```

That brings me to my objection. Just because ATL and the compiler conspire to allow this usage doesn't mean that it's a good one. There is no good reason to support multiple dual interfaces on a single implementation. Any client that supports QueryInterface will not need to use GetIDsOfNames or Invoke. These kinds of clients are perfectly happy using a custom interface, as long as it matches their argument type requirements. On the other hand, scripting clients that don't support QueryInterface can get to methods and properties on only the default dual interface. For example, the following will not work:

```
// Since IBird is the default, its operations are available
penguin.fly
```

```
// Since ISnappyDresser is not the default, its operations
// aren't available
penguin.straightenTie // runtime error
```

So, here's my advice: Don't design your reusable, polymorphic COM interfaces as dual interfaces. Instead, if you're going to support scripting clients, define a single dual interface that exposes the entire functionality of the class, as I did when defining IPenguin in the first place. As an added benefit, this means that you have to define only one interface that supports scripting clients instead of mandating that all of them do.

Having said that, sometimes you don't have a choice. For example, when building Visual Studio add-ins, you need to implement two interfaces: _IDTExtensibility2 and IDTCommandTarget. Both of these are defined as dual interfaces, so the environment forces you to deal with this problem.[6] You'll need to look at the documentation and do some experimentation to figure out which of your IDispatch implementations should be the default.

CComObject Et Al

Consider the following C++ class:

```
class CPenguin :
  public CComObjectRootEx<CComMultiThreadModel>,
  public IBird,
  public ISnappyDresser {
public:
BEGIN_COM_MAP(CPenguin)
    COM_INTERFACE_ENTRY(IBird)
    COM_INTERFACE_ENTRY(ISnappyDresser)
END_COM_MAP()
    // IBird and ISnappyDresser methods...
    // IUnknown methods not implemented here
};
```

Because this class doesn't implement the methods of IUnknown, the following will fail at compile time:

---

[6] The annoying thing here is that Visual Studio *never even calls* the IDispatch side of these dual interfaces, so making them dual interfaces was completely unnecessary.

```
STDMETHODIMP
CPenguinCO::CreateInstance(IUnknown* pUnkOuter,
    REFIID riid, void** ppv) {
    ...
    CPenguin* pobj = new CPenguin; // IUnknown not implemented
    ...
}
```

Given `CComObjectRootBase`, you can easily implement the methods of `IUnknown`:

```
// Server lifetime management
extern void ServerLock();
extern void ServerUnlock();

class CPenguin :
  public CComObjectRootEx<CComMultiThreadModel>,
  public IBird,
  public ISnappyDresser {
public:
    CPengin()   { ServerLock(); }
    ~CPenguin() { ServerUnlock(); }
BEGIN_COM_MAP(CPenguin)
    COM_INTERFACE_ENTRY(IBird)
    COM_INTERFACE_ENTRY(ISnappyDresser)
END_COM_MAP()
    // IBird and ISnappyDresser methods...
    // IUnknown methods for standalone, heap-based objects
    STDMETHODIMP QueryInterface(REFIID riid, void** ppv)
    { return _InternalQueryInterface(riid, ppv); }

    STDMETHODIMP_(ULONG) AddRef()
    { return InternalAddRef(); }

    STDMETHODIMP_(ULONG) Release() {
        ULONG l = InternalRelease();
        if( l == 0 ) delete this;
        return l;
    }
};
```

Unfortunately, although this implementation does leverage the base class behavior, it has hard-coded assumptions about the lifetime and identity of our objects. For example, instances of this class can't be created as an aggregate. Just as we're able to encapsulate decisions about thread safety into the base class, we would like to encapsulate decisions about lifetime and identity. However, unlike thread-safety decisions, which are made on a per-class basis and are, therefore, safe to encode into a base class, lifetime and identity decisions can be made on a per-instance basis. Therefore, we'll want to encapsulate lifetime and identity behavior into classes meant to derive from our class.

Standalone Activation

To encapsulate the standalone, heap-based object implementation of IUnknown I just showed you, ATL provides CComObject, shown in a slightly abbreviated form here:

```
template <class Base>
class CComObject : public Base {
public:
    typedef Base _BaseClass;
    CComObject(void* = NULL)
    { _pAtlModule->Lock(); }     // Keeps server loaded

    // Set refcount to -(LONG_MAX/2) to protect destruction and
    // also catch mismatched Release in debug builds
    ~CComObject()  {
        m_dwRef = -(LONG_MAX/2);
        FinalRelease();
#ifdef _ATL_DEBUG_INTERFACES
        _AtlDebugInterfacesModule.DeleteNonAddRefThunk(
            _GetRawUnknown());
#endif
        _pAtlModule->Unlock();    // Allows server to unload
    }
    STDMETHOD_(ULONG, AddRef)()  {return InternalAddRef();}
    STDMETHOD_(ULONG, Release)()  {
        ULONG l = InternalRelease();
        if (l == 0) delete this;
        return l;
    }

    STDMETHOD(QueryInterface)(REFIID iid, void ** ppvObject)
    {return _InternalQueryInterface(iid, ppvObject);}

    template <class Q>
    HRESULT STDMETHODCALLTYPE QueryInterface(Q** pp)
    { return QueryInterface(__uuidof(Q), (void**)pp); }

    static HRESULT WINAPI CreateInstance(CComObject<Base>** pp) ;
};
```

Notice that CComObject takes a template parameter called Base. This is the base class from which CComObject derives to obtain the functionality of CComObjectRootEx, as well as whatever custom functionality we'd like to include in our objects. Given the implementation of CPenguin that did not include the implementation of the IUnknown methods, the compiler would be happy with CComObject used as follows (although I describe later why new shouldn't be used directly when creating ATL-based COM objects):

```
STDMETHODIMP
CPenguinCO::CreateInstance(IUnknown* pUnkOuter, REFIID riid,
    void** ppv) {
    *ppv = 0;
    if( pUnkOuter ) return CLASS_E_NOAGGREGATION;
    // Read on for why not to use new like this!
    CComObject<CPenguin>* pobj = new CComObject<CPenguin>;
    if( pobj ) {
        pobj->AddRef();
        HRESULT hr = pobj->QueryInterface(riid, ppv);
        pobj->Release();
        return hr;
    }
    return E_OUTOFMEMORY;
}
```

Besides the call to FinalRelease and the static member function CreateInstance (which are both described in the "Creators" section of this chapter), CComObject provides one additional item of note, the QueryInterface member function template[7]:

```
template <class Q>
HRESULT STDMETHODCALLTYPE QueryInterface(Q** pp)
{ return QueryInterface(__uuidof(Q), (void**)pp); }
```

This member function template uses the capability of the VC++ compiler to tag a type with a universally unique identifier (UUID). This capability has been available since VC++ 5.0 and takes the form of a declarative specifier (declspecs):

```
struct __declspec(uuid("00000000-0000-0000-C000-000000000046") IUnknown
{...};
```

---

[7] For a brief description of member function templates, see Appendix A, "C++ Templates by Example."

These `declspec` specifiers are output by the Microsoft IDL compiler and are available for both standard and custom interfaces. You can retrieve the UUID of a type using the `__uuidof` operator, allowing the following syntax:

```
void TryToFly(IUnknown* punk) {
    IBird* pbird = 0;
    if( SUCCEEDED(punk->QueryInterface(__uuidof(pbird),
        (void**)&pbird) ) {
        pbird->Fly();
        pbird->Release();
    }
}
```

Using the `QueryInterface` member function template provided in `CComObject` offers a bit more syntactic convenience, given a `CComObject`-based object reference:

```
void TryToFly(CComObject<CPenguin>* pPenguin) {
    IBird* pbird = 0;
    if( SUCCEEDED(pPenguin->QueryInterface(&pbird) ) {
        pbird->Fly();
        pbird->Release();
    }
}
```

Aggregated Activation

Notice that the `CPenguin` class object implementation shown previously disallowed aggregation by checking for a nonzero `pUnkOuter` and returning `CLASS_E_NOAGGRE-GATION`. If we want to support aggregation as well as—or instead of—standalone activation, we need another class to implement the forwarding behavior of aggregated instances. For this, ATL provides `CComAggObject`.

`CComAggObject` performs the chief service of being a controlled inner—that is, providing two implementations of `IUnknown`. One implementation forwards calls to the controlling outer, subsumed by its lifetime and identity. The other implementation is for private use of the controlling outer for actually maintaining the lifetime of and querying interfaces from the inner. To obtain the two implementations of `IUnknown`, `CComAggObject` derives from `CComObjectRootEx` twice, once directly and once indirectly via a contained instance of your class derived from `CComContained-Object`, as shown here:

```cpp
template <class contained>
class CComAggObject :
    public IUnknown,
    public CComObjectRootEx<
        contained::_ThreadModel::ThreadModelNoCS> {
public:
    typedef contained _BaseClass;
    CComAggObject(void* pv) : m_contained(pv)
    { _pAtlModule->Lock(); }

    ~CComAggObject() {
        m_dwRef = -(LONG_MAX/2);
        FinalRelease();
        _pAtlModule->Unlock();
    }

    STDMETHOD(QueryInterface)(REFIID iid, void ** ppvObject) {
        ATLASSERT(ppvObject != NULL);
        if (ppvObject == NULL)
            return E_POINTER;
        *ppvObject = NULL;

        HRESULT hRes = S_OK;
        if (InlineIsEqualUnknown(iid)) {
            *ppvObject = (void*)(IUnknown*)this;
            AddRef();
        }
        else
            hRes = m_contained._InternalQueryInterface(iid,
                ppvObject);
        return hRes;
    }

    STDMETHOD_(ULONG, AddRef)()
    { return InternalAddRef(); }

    STDMETHOD_(ULONG, Release)() {
        ULONG l = InternalRelease();
        if (l == 0) delete this;
        return l;
    }

    template <class Q>
    HRESULT STDMETHODCALLTYPE QueryInterface(Q** pp)
    { return QueryInterface(__uuidof(Q), (void**)pp); }
```

```
    static HRESULT WINAPI CreateInstance(LPUNKNOWN pUnkOuter,
        CComAggObject<contained>** pp);


    CComContainedObject<contained> m_contained;
};
```

You can see that instead of deriving from your class (passed as the template argument), CComAggObject derives directly from CComObjectRootEx. Its implementation of QueryInterface relies on the interface map you've built in your class, but its implementation of AddRef and Release access relies on the second instance of CComObjectRootBase it gets by deriving from CComObjectRootEx. This second instance of CComObjectRootBase uses the m_dwRef member of the union.

The first instance of CComObjectRootBase, the one that manages the m_pOuterUnknown member of the union, is the one CComAggObject gets by creating an instance of your class derived from CComContainedObject as the m_contained data member. CComContainedObject implements QueryInterface, AddRef, and Release by delegating to the m_pOuterUnknown passed to the constructor:

```
template <class Base>
class CComContainedObject : public Base {
public:
    typedef Base _BaseClass;
    CComContainedObject(void* pv) {
        m_pOuterUnknown = (IUnknown*)pv;
    }

    STDMETHOD(QueryInterface)(REFIID iid, void ** ppvObject) {
      return OuterQueryInterface(iid, ppvObject);
    }

    STDMETHOD_(ULONG, AddRef)()
    { return OuterAddRef(); }

    STDMETHOD_(ULONG, Release)()
    { return OuterRelease(); }

    template <class Q>
    HRESULT STDMETHODCALLTYPE QueryInterface(Q** pp)
    { return QueryInterface(__uuidof(Q), (void**)pp); }

    IUnknown* GetControllingUnknown()
    { return m_pOuterUnknown; }
};
```

Being the Controlled Inner

Using `CComAggObject` and its two implementations of `IUnknown`, our `CPenguin` class object implementation can support either standalone or aggregated activation without touching the `CPenguin` source:

```
STDMETHODIMP
CPenguinCO::CreateInstance(IUnknown* pUnkOuter, REFIID riid,
    void** ppv) {
    *ppv = 0;
    if( pUnkOuter ) {
        CComAggObject<CPenguin>* pobj =
                    new CComAggObject<CPenguin>(pUnkOuter);
        ...
    }
    else {
        CComObject<CPenguin>* pobj = new CComObject<CPenguin>;
        ...
    }
}
```

This usage provides the most efficient runtime decision making. If the object is standalone, it pays the price of one reference count and one implementation of `IUn-known`. If it is aggregated, it pays the price of one reference count, one pointer to the controlling outer, and two implementations of `IUnknown`. However, one additional price we're paying is one extra set of `vtbls`. By using both `CComAggObject<CPenguin>` and `CComObject<CPenguin>`, we've created two classes and, therefore, two sets of `vtbls`. If you've got a small number of instances or nearly all your instances are aggregated, you might want a single class that can handle both aggregated and standalone activation, thereby eliminating one set of `vtbls`. You do this by using `CComPolyObject` in place of both `CComObject` and `CComAggObject`:

```
STDMETHODIMP
CPenguinCO::CreateInstance(IUnknown* pUnkOuter, REFIID riid,
    void** ppv) {
    *ppv = 0;
    CComPolyObject<CPenguin>* pobj =
        new CComPolyObject<CPenguin>(pUnkOuter);
    ...
}
```

`CComPolyObject` is nearly identical to `CComAggObject`, except that, in its constructor, if the `pUnkOuter` is zero, it uses its second implementation of `IUnknown` as the outer for the first to forward to, as shown:

```
class CComPolyObject :
    public IUnknown,
    public CComObjectRootEx<
        contained::_ThreadModel::ThreadModelNoCS> {
public:
    ...
    CComPolyObject(void* pv) : m_contained(pv ? pv : this) {...}
    ...
};
```

The use of CComPolyObject saves a set of vtbls, so the module size is smaller, but the price you pay for standalone objects is getting an extra implementation of IUnknown as well as an extra pointer to that implementation.

Alternative Activation Techniques

Besides standalone operation, CComObject makes certain assumptions about where the object's memory has been allocated from (the heap) and whether the existence of the object should keep the server loaded (it does). For other needs, ATL provides five more classes meant to be the most derived class in your implementation hierarchy: CComObjectCached, CComObjectNoLock, CComObjectGlobal, CComObject-Stack, and CComObjectStackEx.

CComObjectCached

CComObjectCached objects implement reference counting, assuming that you're going to create an instance and then hold it for the life of the server, handing out references to it as requested. To avoid keeping the server running forever after the cached instance is created, the boundary for keeping the server running is a reference count of one, although the lifetime of the object is still managed on a boundary of zero:

```
template <class Base>
class CComObjectCached : public Base {
public:
    ...
    STDMETHOD_(ULONG, AddRef)()  {
        ULONG l = InternalAddRef();
        if (l == 2)
            _pAtlModule->Lock();
        return l;
    }
    STDMETHOD_(ULONG, Release)()  {
```

```
        ULONG 1 = InternalRelease();
        if (1 == 0)
            delete this;
        else if (1 == 1)
            _pAtlModule->Unlock();
        return 1;
    }
    ...
};
```

Cached objects are useful for in-process class objects:

```
static CComObjectCached<CPenguinCO>* g_pPenguinCO = 0;

BOOL WINAPI DllMain(HINSTANCE, DWORD dwReason, void*) {
  switch( dwReason ) {
  case DLL_PROCESS_ATTACH:
      g_pPenguinCO = new CComObjectCached<CPenguinCO>();

      // 1st ref. doesn't keep server alive
      if( g_pPenguinCO ) g_pPenguinCO->AddRef();
  break;

  case DLL_PROCESS_DETACH:
      if( g_pPenguinCO ) g_pPenguinCO->Release();
  break;
  }
  return TRUE;
}

STDAPI DllGetClassObject(REFCLSID clsid, REFIID riid,
    void** ppv) {
    // Subsequent references do keep server alive
    if( clsid == CLSID_Penguin && g_pPenguinCO )
      return g_pPenguinCO->QueryInterface(riid, ppv);
    return CLASS_E_CLASSNOTAVAILABLE;
}
```

CComObjectNoLock

Sometimes you don't want outstanding references on your object to keep the server alive. For example, class objects in an out-of-process server are cached in a table maintained by ole32.dll *some number of times* (it might not be one). For this reason, COM itself manages how the lifetime of a class object affects the lifetime of its out-of-process server using the LockServer method of the IClassFactory interface. For this use, ATL provides CComObjectNoLock, whose implementation does not affect the lifetime of the server:

```
template <class Base>
class CComObjectNoLock : public Base {
public:
    ...
    STDMETHOD_(ULONG, AddRef)()
    { return InternalAddRef(); }

    STDMETHOD_(ULONG, Release)() {
        ULONG l = InternalRelease();
        if (l == 0) delete this;
        return l;
    }
    ...
};
```

No-lock objects are useful for out-of-process class objects:

```
int WINAPI WinMain(HINSTANCE, HINSTANCE, LPSTR, int) {
    CoInitialize(0);

    CComObjectNoLock<CPenguinCO>* pPenguinCO =
        new CComObjectNoLock<CPenguinCO>();
    if( !pPenguinCO ) return E_OUTOFMEMORY;
        pPenguinCO->AddRef();

    DWORD   dwReg;
    HRESULT hr;

    // Reference(s) cached by ole32.dll won't keep server
    // from shutting down
    hr = CoRegisterClassObject(CLSID_Penguin, pPenguinCO, ...,
        &dwReg);
    if( SUCCEEDED(hr) ) {
        MSG msg; while( GetMessage(&msg, 0, 0, 0) ) DispatchMessage(&msg);
        CoRevokeClassObject(dwReg);
        pPenguinCO->Release();
    }

    CoUninitialize();
    return hr;
}
```

CComObjectGlobal

Just as it's handy to have an object whose existence or outstanding references don't keep the server alive, sometimes it's handy to have an object whose lifetime matches that of the server. For example, a global or static object is constructed once when the server is loaded and is not destroyed until after WinMain or DllMain has completed. Clearly, the mere existence of a global object cannot keep the server running, or the server could never be shut down. On the other hand, we'd like to be able to keep the server running if there are outstanding references to a global object. For this, we have CComObjectGlobal:

```
template <class Base>
class CComObjectGlobal : public Base {
public:

  ...
  STDMETHOD_(ULONG, AddRef)()  { return _pAtlModule->Lock(); }
  STDMETHOD_(ULONG, Release)() { return _pAtlModule->Unlock(); }
  ...
};
```

Global objects can be used instead of cached objects for implementing in-process class objects, but they're useful for any global or static object:

```
// No references yet, so server not forced to stay alive
static CComObjectGlobal<CPenguinCO> g_penguinCO;

STDAPI DllGetClassObject(REFCLSID clsid, REFIID riid,
    void** ppv) {
    // All references keep the server alive
    if( clsid == CLSID_Penguin )
        return g_penguinCO.QueryInterface(riid, ppv);
    return CLASS_E_CLASSNOTAVAILABLE;
}
```

CComObjectStack and CComObjectStackEx

Instead of using a global or static object, you might find yourself with the urge to allocate a COM object on the stack. ATL supports this technique with CComObject-Stack:

```
template <class Base>
class CComObjectStack : public Base {
public:
    ...
```

```
        STDMETHOD_(ULONG, AddRef)()
        { ATLASSERT(FALSE); return 0; }

        STDMETHOD_(ULONG, Release)()
        { ATLASSERT(FALSE); return 0; }

        STDMETHOD(QueryInterface)(REFIID iid, void** ppvObject)
        { ATLASSERT(FALSE); return E_NOINTERFACE; }
        ...
};
```

Based on the implementation, it should be clear that you're no longer doing COM. CComObjectStack shuts up the compiler, but you still cannot use any methods of IUnknown, which means that you cannot pass out an interface reference from an object on the stack. This is good because, as with a reference to anything on the stack, as soon as the stack goes away, the reference points at garbage. The nice thing about ATL's implementation of CComObjectStack is that it warns you at runtime that you're doing something bad:

```
void DoABadThing(IBird** ppbird) {
    CComObjectStack<CPenguin> penguin;
    penguin.Fly();             // Using IBird method is OK
    penguin.StraightenTie();   // Using ISnappyDresser method
                               // also OK

    // This will trigger an assert at runtime
    penguin.QueryInterface(IID_IBird, (void**)ppbird);
}
```

CComObjectStackEx addresses the limitations of CComObjectStack by providing a more useful implementation of IUnknown:

```
template <class Base>
class CComObjectStackEx : public Base {
public:
    typedef Base _BaseClass;

    CComObjectStackEx(void* = NULL) {
#ifdef _DEBUG
        m_dwRef = 0;
#endif
        m_hResFinalConstruct = _AtlInitialConstruct();
        if (SUCCEEDED(m_hResFinalConstruct))
            m_hResFinalConstruct = FinalConstruct();
```

```
    }

    virtual ~CComObjectStackEx() {
        // This assert indicates mismatched ref counts.
        //
        // The ref count has no control over the
        // lifetime of this object, so you must ensure
        // by some other means that the object remains
        // alive while clients have references to its interfaces.
        ATLASSUME(m_dwRef == 0);
        FinalRelease();
#ifdef _ATL_DEBUG_INTERFACES
        _AtlDebugInterfacesModule.DeleteNonAddRefThunk(
            _GetRawUnknown());
#endif
    }

    STDMETHOD_(ULONG, AddRef)() {
#ifdef _DEBUG
        return InternalAddRef();
#else
        return 0;
#endif
    }

    STDMETHOD_(ULONG, Release)() {
#ifdef _DEBUG
        return InternalRelease();
#else
        return 0;
#endif
    }

    STDMETHOD(QueryInterface)(REFIID iid, void ** ppvObject) {
        return _InternalQueryInterface(iid, ppvObject);
    }

    HRESULT m_hResFinalConstruct;
};
```

As you can see, CComObjectStackEx permits the use of the IUnknown methods, as long as they are called within the scope of the CComObjectStackEx instance. This allows methods called from within the instance scope to treat the object as if it were a typical heap-based COM object, as in the following:

```
void PlayWithBird() {
    CComObjectStackEx<CPenguin> penguin;
    IBird* pBird = NULL;
    penguin.QueryInterface(IID_IBird,
        (void**)&pBird);               // OK -> no assert
    DoBirdTricks(pBird);
}

void DoBirdTricks(IBird* pBird) {
    pBird->Fly();                      // IBird methods OK
    ISnappyDresser* pPenguin = NULL;
    pBird->QueryInterface(IID_ISnappyDresser,
        (void**)&pPenguin);            // OK
    pPenguin->StraightenTie();         // ISnappyDresser methods OK
    pPenguin->Release();               // OK -> no assert
}
```

One from Column A, Two from Column B. . .

Table 4.2 shows the various identity and lifetime options ATL provides.

Table 4.2. ATL's Identity and Lifetime Options

Class	Standalone or Aggregated	Heap or Stack	Existence Keeps Server Alive	Extent Refs Keep Server Alive	Useful IUnkown Methods
CcomObject	Standalone	Heap	Yes	Yes	Yes
CComAggObject	Aggregated	Heap	Yes	Yes	Yes
CComPolyObject	Standalone or aggregated	Heap	Yes	Yes	Yes
CComObjectCached	Standalone	Heap	No	Second Reference	Yes
CComObjectNoLock	Standalone	Heap	No	No	Yes
CComObjectGlobal	Standalone	Data seg.	No	Yes	Yes
CComObjectStack	Standalone	Stack	No	No	No
CComObjectStackEx	Standalone	Stack	No	No	Yes

ATL Creators

Multiphase Construction

As I've mentioned, ATL servers might not necessarily link with the CRT. However, living without the CRT can be a pain. Among other things, if you don't have the CRT, you also don't get C++ exceptions. That doesn't leave you much to do in the following scenario:

```
// CPenguin constructor
CPenguin::CPenguin() {
  HRESULT hr = CoCreateInstance(CLSID_EarthAtmosphere, 0,
    CLSCTX_ALL, IID_IAir, (void**)&m_pAir);
  if( FAILED(hr) ) {
    // Can't return an error from a ctor
    return hr;
    // Can't throw an error without the CRT
    throw hr;
    // This won't help
    OutputDebugString(__T("Help! Can't bre...\n"));
  }
}
```

The `OutputDebugString` isn't going to notify the client that the object it just created doesn't have the resources it needs to survive; there's no way to return the failure result back to the client. This hardly seems fair because the `IClassFactory` method `CreateInstance` that's creating our objects certainly can return an `HRESULT`. The problem is having a way to hand a failure from the instance to the class object so that it can be returned to the client. By convention, ATL classes provide a public member function called `FinalConstruct` for objects to participate in multiphase construction:

```
HRESULT FinalConstruct();
```

An empty implementation of the `FinalConstruct` member function is provided in `CComObjectRootBase`, so all ATL objects have one. Because `FinalConstruct` returns an `HRESULT`, now you have a clean way to obtain the result of any nontrivial construction:

```
HRESULT CPenguin::FinalConstruct() {
    return CoCreateInstance(CLSID_EarthAtmosphere, 0, CLSCTX_ALL,
                            IID_IAir, (void**)&m_pAir);
}
```

```
STDMETHODIMP
CPenguinCO::CreateInstance(IUnknown* pUnkOuter, REFIID riid,
    void** ppv) {
    *ppv = 0;
    if( !pUnkOuter ) {
        CComObject<CPenguin>* pobj = new CComObject<CPenguin>;
        if( !pobj ) return E_OUTOFMEMORY;
        HRESULT hr = pobj->FinalConstruct();
        if( SUCCEEDED(hr) ) ...
        return hr;
    }
    ...
}
```

You do have something else to consider, though. Notice that when `CreateIn-stance` calls `FinalConstruct`, it has not yet increased the reference count of the object. This causes a problem if, during the `FinalConstruct` implementation, the object handed a reference to itself to another object. If you think this is uncommon, remember the `pUnkOuter` parameter to the `IClassFactory` method `CreateInstance`. However, even without aggregation, it's possible to run into this problem. Imagine the following somewhat contrived but perfectly legal code:

```
// CPenguin implementation
HRESULT CPenguin::FinalConstruct() {
    HRESULT hr;
    hr = CoCreateInstance(CLSID_EarthAtmosphere, 0, CLSCTX_ALL,
                          IID_IAir, (void**)&m_pAir);
    if( SUCCEEDED(hr) ) {
        // Pass reference to object with reference count of 0
        hr = m_pAir->CheckSuitability(GetUnknown());
    }
    return hr;
}

// CEarthAtmosphere implementation in separate server
STDMETHODIMP CEarthAtmosphere::CheckSuitability(IUnknown* punk) {
    IBreatheO2* pbo2 = 0;
    HRESULT    hr = E_FAIL;

    // CPenguin's lifetime increased to 1 via QI
    hr = punk->QueryInterface(IID_IBreatheO2, (void**)&pbo2);
    if( SUCCEEDED(hr) ) {
        pbo2->Release(); // During this call, lifetime decreases
                         // to 0 and destruction sequence begins...
```

```
        }

        return (SUCCEEDED(hr) ? S_OK : E_FAIL);
    }
```

To avoid the problem of premature destruction, you need to artificially increase the object's reference count before `FinalConstruct` is called and then decrease its reference count afterward:

```
STDMETHODIMP
CPenguinCO::CreateInstance(IUnknown* pUnkOuter, REFIID riid,
    void** ppv) {
    *ppv = 0;
    if( !pUnkOuter ) {
        CComObject<CPenguin>* pobj = new CComObject<CPenguin>;
        if( FAILED(hr) ) return E_OUTOFMEMORY;

        // Protect object from pre-mature destruction
        pobj->InternalAddRef();
        hr = pobj->FinalConstruct();
        pobj->InternalRelease();

        if( SUCCEEDED(hr) ) ...
        return hr;
    }
    ...
}
```

Just Enough Reference Count Safety

Arguably, not all objects need their reference count artificially managed in the way just described. In fact, for multithreaded objects that don't require this kind of protection, extra calls to `InterlockedIncrement` and `InterlockedDecrement` represent unnecessary overhead. Toward that end, `CComObjectRootBase` provides a pair of functions just for bracketing the call to `FinalConstruct` in a "just reference count safe enough" way:

```
STDMETHODIMP
CPenguinCO::CreateInstance(IUnknown* pUnkOuter, REFIID riid,
    void** ppv) {
    *ppv = 0;
    if( !pUnkOuter ) {
        CComObject<CPenguin>* pobj = new CComObject<CPenguin>;
```

```
        if( FAILED(hr) ) return E_OUTOFMEMORY;

        // Protect object from pre-mature destruction (maybe)
        pobj->InternalFinalConstructAddRef();
        hr = pobj->FinalConstruct();
        pobj->InternalFinalConstructRelease();

        if( SUCCEEDED(hr) ) ...
        return hr;
    }
    ...
}
```

By default, `InternalFinalConstructAddRef` and `InternalFinalConstructRe-lease` incur no release build runtime overhead:

```
class CComObjectRootBase {
public:
  ...
  void InternalFinalConstructAddRef() {}
  void InternalFinalConstructRelease() {
    ATLASSERT(m_dwRef == 0);
  }
  ...
};
```

To change the implementation of `InternalFinalConstructAddRef` and `Inter-nalFinalConstructRelease` to provide reference count safety, ATL provides the following macro:

```
#define DECLARE_PROTECT_FINAL_CONSTRUCT() \
    void InternalFinalConstructAddRef()  { InternalAddRef(); } \
    void InternalFinalConstructRelease() { InternalRelease(); }
```

The `DECLARE_PROTECT_FINAL_CONSTRUCT` macro is used on a per-class basis to turn on reference count safety as required. Our `CPenguin` would use it like this:

```
class CPenguin : ... {
public:
  HRESULT FinalConstruct();
  DECLARE_PROTECT_FINAL_CONSTRUCT()
  ...
};
```

In my opinion, DECLARE_PROTECT_FINAL_CONSTRUCT is one ATL optimization too many. Using it requires not only a great deal of knowledge of COM and ATL internals, but also a great deal of knowledge of how to implement the objects you create in FinalConstruct methods. Because you often don't have that knowledge, the only safe thing to do is to always use DECLARE_PROTECT_FINAL_CONSTRUCT if you're handing out references to your instances in your FinalConstruct calls. And because that rule is too complicated, most folks will probably forget it. So here's a simpler one:

Every class that implements the FinalConstruct *member function should also have a* DECLARE_PROTECT_FINAL_CONSTRUCT *macro instantiation.*

Luckily, the wizard generates DECLARE_PROTECT_FINAL_CONSTRUCT when it generates a new class, so your FinalConstruct code will be safe by default. If you decide you don't want it, you can remove it.[8]

Another Reason for Multiphase Construction

Imagine a plain-vanilla C++ class that wants to call a virtual member function during its construction, and another C++ class that overrides that function:

```
class Base {
public:
    Base() { Init(); }
    virtual void Init() {}
};

class Derived : public Base {
public:
    virtual void Init() {}
};
```

Because it's fairly uncommon to call virtual member functions as part of the construction sequence, it's not widely known that the Init function during the constructor for Base will not be Derived::Init, but Base::Init. This might seem counterintuitive, but the reason it works this way is a good one: It doesn't make sense to call a virtual member function in a derived class until the derived class has been properly constructed. However, the derived class isn't properly constructed until after the base class has been constructed. To make sure that only functions of properly constructed classes are called during construction, the C++ compiler lays out two vtbls, one for Base and one for Derived. The C++ runtime then adjusts the vptr to point to the appropriate vtbl during the construction sequence.

---

[8] As my friend Tim Ewald always says, "Subtractive coding is easier than additive coding."

Although this is all part of the official C++ standard, it's not exactly intuitive, especially because it is so rarely used (or maybe it's so rarely used because it's unintuitive). Because it's rarely used, beginning with Visual C++ 5.0, Microsoft introduced `__declspec(novtable)` to turn off the adjustment of `vptrs` during construction. If the base class is an abstract base class, this often results in `vtbls` that are generated by the compiler but not used, so the linker can remove them from the final image.

This optimization is used in ATL whenever a class is declared using the `ATL_NO_VTABLE` macro:

```
#ifdef _ATL_DISABLE_NO_VTABLE
#define ATL_NO_VTABLE
#else
#define ATL_NO_VTABLE __declspec(novtable)
#endif
```

Unless the `_ATL_DISABLE_NO_VTABLE` is defined, a class defined using `_ATL_NO_VTABLE` has its constructor behavior adjusted with `__declspec(novtable)`:

```
class ATL_NO_VTABLE CPenguin ... {};
```

This is a good and true optimization, but classes that use it must not call virtual member functions in their constructors.[9] If virtual member functions need to be called during construction, leave them until the call to `FinalConstruct`, which is called after the most derived class's constructor and after the `vptrs` are adjusted to the correct values.

One last thing should be mentioned about `__declspec(novatble)`. Just as it turns off the adjustment of `vptrs` during construction, it turns off the adjustment of `vptrs` during destruction. Therefore, avoid calling virtual functions in the destructor as well; instead, call them in the object's `FinalRelease` member function.

FinalRelease

ATL calls the object's `FinalRelease` function after the object's final interface reference is released and before your ATL-based object's destructor is called:

```
void FinalRelease();
```

---

[9] Strictly speaking, the compiler will statically bind to virtual calls made in the constructor or the destructor. But if a statically bound function calls a dynamically bound function, you're still in big trouble.

The `FinalRelease` member function is useful for calling virtual member functions and releasing interfaces to other objects that also have pointers back to you. Because those other objects might want to query for an interface during its shutdown sequence, it's just as important to protect the object against double destruction as it was to protect it against premature destruction in `FinalConstruct`. Even though the `FinalRelease` member function is called when the object's reference count has been decreased to zero (which is why the object is being destroyed), the caller of `FinalRelease` artificially sets the reference count to `-(LONG_MAX/2)` to avoid double deletion. The caller of `FinalRelease` is the destructor of the most derived class:

```
CComObject::~CComObject()  {
    m_dwRef = -(LONG_MAX/2);
    FinalRelease();
    _AtlModule->Unlock();
}
```

Under the Hood

Just as two-phase construction applies to code you need to call to set up your objects, the ATL framework itself often needs to do operations at construction time that might fail. For example, creation of a lock object could fail for some reason. To handle this, ATL and `CComObjectRootBase` define a couple other entry points:

```
class CComObjectRootBase {
public:

    ...
    // For library initialization only
    HRESULT _AtlFinalConstruct() {
        return S_OK;
    }
    ...
    void _AtlFinalRelease() {}        // temp
};
```

These methods exist so that ATL has a place to put framework-initialization functions that aren't affected by your work in `FinalConstruct`. In addition to these methods, `CComObjectRootEx` defines this setup method:

```
template <class ThreadModel>
class CComObjectRootEx : public CComObjectRootBase {
public:
    ...
```

```
    HRESULT _AtlInitialConstruct() {
        return m_critsec.Init();
    }
};
```

CComAggObject, CComPolyObject, etc. all define their own implementation of _AtlInitialConstruct. At this time, nothing in the framework overrides _AtlFinal-Construct or _AtlFinalRelease. However, _AtlInitialConstruct *is* used; when you're creating objects, make sure that it gets called or your objects won't get initialized properly.

Creators

Because the extra steps to manage the multiphase construction process are easy to forget, ATL encapsulates this algorithm into several C++ classes called Creators. Each performs the appropriate multiphase construction. Each Creator class is actually just a way to wrap a scope around a single static member function called CreateInstance:

```
static HRESULT WINAPI CreateInstance(void* pv, REFIID riid, LPVOID* ppv);
```

The name of the Creator class is used in a type definition associated with the class; this is discussed in the next section.

CComCreator

CComCreator is a Creator class that creates either standalone or aggregated instances. It is parameterized by the C++ class being created—for example, CCom-Object<CPenguin>. CComCreator is declared like this:

```
template <class T1>
class CComCreator {
public:
    static HRESULT WINAPI CreateInstance(void* pv, REFIID riid,
        LPVOID* ppv) {
        ATLASSERT(ppv != NULL);
        if (ppv == NULL)
            return E_POINTER;
        *ppv = NULL;

        HRESULT hRes = E_OUTOFMEMORY;
        T1* p = NULL;
        ATLTRY(p = new T1(pv))
        if (p != NULL) {
```

```
            p->SetVoid(pv);
            p->InternalFinalConstructAddRef();
            hRes = p->_AtlInitialConstruct();
            if (SUCCEEDED(hRes))
                hRes = p->FinalConstruct();
            if (SUCCEEDED(hRes))
                hRes = p->_AtlFinalConstruct();
            p->InternalFinalConstructRelease();
            if (hRes == S_OK)
                hRes = p->QueryInterface(riid, ppv);
            if (hRes != S_OK)
                delete p;
        }
        return hRes;
    }
};
```

Using CComCreator simplifies our class object implementation quite a bit:

```
STDMETHODIMP
CPenguinCO::CreateInstance(IUnknown* pUnkOuter, REFIID riid,
    void** ppv) {
    typedef CComCreator<
        CComPolyObject<CPenguin> > PenguinPolyCreator;
    return PenguinPolyCreator::CreateInstance(pUnkOuter,
        riid, ppv);
}
```

Notice the use of the type definition to define a new Creator type. If we were to create penguins other places in our server, we would have to rebuild the type definition:

```
STDMETHODIMP CAviary::CreatePenguin(IBird** ppbird) {
    typedef CComCreator< CComObject<CPenguin> > PenguinCreator;
    return PenguinCreator::CreateInstance(0, IID_IBird, (void**)ppbird);
}
```

Defining a Creator like this outside the class being created has two problems. First, it duplicates the type-definition code. Second, and more important, we've taken away the right of the CPenguin class to decide for itself whether it wants to support aggregation; the type definition is making this decision now. To reduce code and let the class designer make the decision about standalone versus aggregate activation, by convention in ATL, you place the type definition inside the class declaration and give it the well-known name _CreatorClass:

```
class CPenguin : ... {
public:
    ...

    typedef CComCreator<
        CComPolyObject<CPenguin> > _CreatorClass;
};
```

Using the Creator type definition, creating an instance and obtaining an initial interface actually involves fewer lines of code than operator new and QueryInterface:

```
STDMETHODIMP CAviary::CreatePenguin(IBird** ppbird) {
    return CPenguin::_CreatorClass::CreateInstance(0,
        IID_IBird,
        (void**)ppbird);
}
```

Chapter 5, "COM Servers," discusses one other base class that your class will often derive from, CComCoClass.

```
class CPenguin : ...,
public CComCoClass<CPenguin, &CLSID_Penguin>, ... {...};
```

CComCoClass provides two static member functions, each called CreateInstance, that make use of the class's creators:

```
template <class T, const CLSID* pclsid = &CLSID_NULL>
class CComCoClass {
public:
    ...
    template <class Q>
    static HRESULT CreateInstance(IUnknown* punkOuter, Q** pp) {
        return T::_CreatorClass::CreateInstance(punkOuter,
            __uuidof(Q), (void**) pp);
    }
    template <class Q>
    static HRESULT CreateInstance(Q** pp) {
        return T::_CreatorClass::CreateInstance(NULL,
            __uuidof(Q), (void**) pp);
    }
};
```

This simplifies the creation code still further:

```
STDMETHODIMP CAviary::CreatePenguin(IBird** ppbird) {
    return CPenguin::CreateInstance(ppbird);
}
```

CComCreator2

You might like to support both standalone and aggregate activation using CComObject and CComAggObject instead of CComPolyObject because of the overhead associated with CComPolyObject in the standalone case. The decision can be made with a simple if statement, but then you lose the predefined CreateInstance code in CComCoClass. ATL provides CComCreator2 to make this logic fit within the existing Creator machinery:

```
template <class T1, class T2> class CComCreator2 {
public:
    static HRESULT WINAPI CreateInstance(void* pv, REFIID riid,
        LPVOID* ppv) {
        ATLASSERT(*ppv == NULL);
        return (pv == NULL) ? T1::CreateInstance(NULL, riid, ppv)
                            : T2::CreateInstance(pv, riid, ppv);
    }
};
```

Notice that CComCreator2 is parameterized by the types of two other Creators. All CComCreator2 does is check for a NULL pUnkOuter and forward the call to one of two other Creators. So, if you'd like to use CComObject and CComAggObject instead of CComPolyObject, you can do so like this:

```
class CPenguin : ... {
public:
    ...
    typedef CComCreator2< CComCreator< CComObject<CPenguin> >,
        CComCreator< CComAggObject<CPenguin> > >
        _CreatorClass;
};
```

Of course, the beauty of this scheme is that all the Creators have the same function, CreateInstance, and are exposed via a type definition of the same name, _CreatorClass. Thus, none of the server code that creates penguins needs to change if the designer of the class changes his mind about how penguins should be created.

CComFailCreator

One of the changes you might want to make to your creation scheme is to support either standalone or aggregate activation only, not both. To make this happen, you need a special Creator to return an error code to use in place of one of the Creators passed as template arguments to CComCreator2. That's what CComFailCreator is for:

```
template <HRESULT hr> class CComFailCreator {
public:
    static HRESULT WINAPI CreateInstance(void*, REFIID, LPVOID*)
    { return hr; }
};
```

If you'd like standalone activation only, you can use CComFailCreator as the aggregation creator template parameter:

```
class CPenguin : ... {
public:
    ...
    typedef CComCreator2< CComCreator< CComObject<CPenguin> >,
        CComFailCreator<CLASS_E_NOAGGREGATION> >
        _CreatorClass;
};
```

If you'd like aggregate activation only, you can use CComFailCreator as the standalone creator parameter:

```
class CPenguin : ... {
public:
    ...
    typedef CComCreator2< CComFailCreator<E_FAIL>,
        CComCreator< CComAggObject<CPenguin> > >
        _CreatorClass;
};
```

Convenience Macros

As a convenience, ATL provides the following macros in place of manually specifying the _CreatorClass type definition for each class:

```
#define DECLARE_POLY_AGGREGATABLE(x) public:\
    typedef ATL::CComCreator< \
    ATL::CComPolyObject< x > > _CreatorClass;
```

```
#define DECLARE_AGGREGATABLE(x) public: \
  typedef ATL::CComCreator2< \
    ATL::CComCreator< ATL::CComObject< x > >, \
    ATL::CComCreator< ATL::CComAggObject< x > > > \
    _CreatorClass;

#define DECLARE_NOT_AGGREGATABLE(x) public:\
  typedef ATL::CComCreator2< \
    ATL::CComCreator< ATL::CComObject< x > >, \
    ATL::CComFailCreator<CLASS_E_NOAGGREGATION> > \
    _CreatorClass;

#define DECLARE_ONLY_AGGREGATABLE(x) public:\
  typedef ATL::CComCreator2< \
    ATL::CComFailCreator<E_FAIL>, \
    ATL::CComCreator< ATL::CComAggObject< x > > > \
    _CreatorClass;
```

Using these macros, you can declare that CPenguin can be activated both stand-alone and aggregated like this:

```
class CPenguin : ... {
public:
    ...
    DECLARE_AGGREGATABLE(CPenguin)
};
```

Table 4.3 summarizes the classes the Creators use to derive from your class.

Table 4.3.   Creator Type-Definition Macros

Macro	Standalone	Aggregation
DECLARE_AGGREGATABLE	CComObject	CComAggObject
DECLARE_NOT_AGGREGATABLE	CComObject	—
DECLARE_ONLY_AGGREGATABLE	—	CComAggObject
DECLARE_POLY_AGGREGATABLE	CComPolyObject	CComPolyObject

Private Initialization

Creators are handy because they follow the multiphase construction sequence ATL-based objects use. However, Creators return only an interface pointer, not a pointer to the implementing class (as in `IBird*` instead of `CPenguin*`). This can be a problem if the class exposes public member functions or if member data is not available via a COM interface. Your first instinct as a former C programmer might be to simply cast the resultant interface pointer to the type you'd like:

```
STDMETHODIMP
CAviary::CreatePenguin(BSTR bstrName, long nWingspan,
    IBird** ppbird) {
    HRESULT hr;
    hr = CPenguin::_CreatorClass::CreateInstance(0,
        IID_IBird, (void**)ppbird);
    if( SUCCEEDED(hr) ) {
        // Resist this instinct!
        CPenguin* pPenguin = (CPenguin*)(*ppbird);
        pPenguin->Init(bstrName, nWingspan);
    }
    return hr;
}
```

Unfortunately, because `QueryInterface` allows interfaces of a single COM identity to be implemented on multiple C++ objects or even multiple COM objects, in many cases a cast won't work. Instead, you should use the `CreateInstance` static member functions of `CComObject`, `CComAggObject`, and `CComPolyObject`:

```
static HRESULT WINAPI
CComObject::CreateInstance(CComObject<Base>** pp);

static HRESULT WINAPI
CComAggObject::CreateInstance(IUnknown* puo,
    CComAggObject<contained>** pp);

static HRESULT WINAPI
CComPolyObject::CreateInstance(IUnknown* puo,
    CComPolyObject<contained>** pp);
```

These static member functions do not make Creators out of `CComObject`, `CComAggObject`, or `CComPolyObject`, but they each perform the additional work required to call the object's `FinalConstruct` (and `_AtlInitialConstruct`, and so on) member functions. The reason to use them, however, is that each of them returns a pointer to the most derived class:

```
STDMETHODIMP
CAviary::CreatePenguin(BSTR bstrName, long nWingspan,
    IBird** ppbird) {
```

```
    HRESULT hr;
    CComObject<CPenguin>* pPenguin = 0;
    hr = CComObject<CPenguin>::CreateInstance(&pPenguin);
    if( SUCCEEDED(hr) ) {
        pPenguin->AddRef();
        pPenguin->Init(bstrName, nWingspan);
        hr = pPenguin->QueryInterface(IID_IBird, (void**)ppbird);
        pPenguin->Release();
    }
    return hr;
}
```

The class you use for creation in this manner depends on the kind of activation you want. For standalone activation, use `CComObject::CreateInstance`. For aggregated activation, use `CComAggObject::CreateInstance`. For either standalone or aggregated activation that saves a set of `vtbls` at the expense of per-instance overhead, use `CComPolyObject::CreateInstance`.

Multiphase Construction on the Stack

When creating an instance of an ATL-based COM object, you should always use a Creator (or the static `CreateInstance` member function of `CComObject`, et al) instead of the C++ operator `new`. However, if you've got a global or a static object, or an object that's allocated on the stack, you can't use a Creator because you're not calling `new`. As discussed earlier, ATL provides two classes for creating instances that aren't on the heap: `CComObjectGlobal` and `CComObjectStack`. However, instead of requiring you to call `FinalConstruct` (and `FinalRelease`) manually, both of these classes perform the proper initialization and shutdown in their constructors and destructors, as shown here in `CComObjectGlobal`:

```
template <class Base>
class CComObjectGlobal : public Base {
public:
    typedef Base _BaseClass;
    CComObjectGlobal(void* = NULL) {
        m_hResFinalConstruct = S_OK;
        __if_exists(FinalConstruct) {
            __if_exists(InternalFinalConstructAddRef) {
                InternalFinalConstructAddRef();
            }
            m_hResFinalConstruct = _AtlInitialConstruct();
            if (SUCCEEDED(m_hResFinalConstruct))
                m_hResFinalConstruct = FinalConstruct();
            __if_exists(InternalFinalConstructRelease) {
```

```
                      InternalFinalConstructRelease();
            }
        }
    }
    ~CComObjectGlobal() {
        __if_exists(FinalRelease) {
            FinalRelease();
        }
    }
    ...
    HRESULT m_hResFinalConstruct;
};
```

Because there is no return code from a constructor, if you're interested in the result from `FinalConstruct`, you must check the cached result in the public member variable `m_hResFinalConstruct`.

Note in the previous code the use of the new `__if_exists` C++ keyword. This keyword allows for conditional compilation based on the presence of a symbol or member function. Derived classes, for instance, can check for the existence of particular members of a base class. Alternatively, the `__if_not_exists` keyword can be used to conditionally compile code based on the absence of specific symbol. These keywords are analogous to the `#ifdef` and `#ifndef` preprocessor directives, except that they operate on symbols that are not removed during the preprocessing stage.

Debugging

ATL provides a number of helpful debugging facilities, including both a normal and a categorized wrapper for producing debug output, a macro for making assertions, and debug output for tracing calls to `QueryInterface`, `AddRef`, and `Release` on an interface-by-interface basis. Of course, during a release build, all these debugging facilities fall away to produce the smallest, fastest binary image possible.

Making Assertions

Potentially the best debugging technique is to use assertions, which enable you to make assumptions in your code and, if those assumptions are invalidated, to be notified immediately. Although ATL doesn't exactly support assertions, it does provide the `ATLASSERT` macro. However, it's actually just another name for the Microsoft CRT macro `_ASSERTE`:

```
#ifndef ATLASSERT
#define ATLASSERT(expr) _ASSERTE(expr)
#endif
```

Flexible Debug Output

OutputDebugString is handy as the Win32 equivalent of printf, but it takes only a single string argument. We want a printf that outputs to debug output instead of standard output. ATL provides the AtlTrace function to do exactly that:

```
inline void _cdecl AtlTrace(LPCSTR pszFormat, ...)
inline void _cdecl AtlTrace(LPCWSTR pszFormat, ...)
```

Instead of calling the function directly, use the macro ATLTRACE. The macro calls the underlying function, but also adds file and line number information to the trace output. The macro expands to either a call to AtlTrace or nothing, depending on whether the _DEBUG symbol is defined. Typical usage is as follows:

```
HRESULT CPenguin::FinalConstruct() {
  ATLTRACE(__TEXT("%d+%d= %d\n"), 2, 2, 2+2);
}
```

ATLTRACE always generates output to the debug window. If you'd like to be even more selective about what makes it to debug output, ATL provides a second trace function, AtlTrace2, also with its own macro, ATLTRACE2:

```
void AtlTrace2(DWORD_PTR dwCategory, UINT nLevel,
    LPCSTR pszFormat, ...)
void AtlTrace2(DWORD_PTR dwCategory, UINT nLevel,
    LPCWSTR pszFormat, ...)
```

In addition to the format string and the variable arguments, AtlTrace2 takes a trace category and a trace level. The trace category is defined as an instance of the CTraceCategory class. ATL includes the following trace categories, already defined:

```
#ifdef _DEBUG
#define DECLARE_TRACE_CATEGORY( name ) \
    extern ATL::CTraceCategory name;
#else
#define DECLARE_TRACE_CATEGORY( name ) const DWORD_PTR name = 0;
#endif

DECLARE_TRACE_CATEGORY( atlTraceGeneral )
DECLARE_TRACE_CATEGORY( atlTraceCOM )
DECLARE_TRACE_CATEGORY( atlTraceQI )
DECLARE_TRACE_CATEGORY( atlTraceRegistrar )
DECLARE_TRACE_CATEGORY( atlTraceRefcount )
```

```
DECLARE_TRACE_CATEGORY( atlTraceWindowing )
DECLARE_TRACE_CATEGORY( atlTraceControls )
DECLARE_TRACE_CATEGORY( atlTraceHosting )
DECLARE_TRACE_CATEGORY( atlTraceDBClient )
DECLARE_TRACE_CATEGORY( atlTraceDBProvider )
DECLARE_TRACE_CATEGORY( atlTraceSnapin )
DECLARE_TRACE_CATEGORY( atlTraceNotImpl )
DECLARE_TRACE_CATEGORY( atlTraceAllocation )
DECLARE_TRACE_CATEGORY( atlTraceException )
DECLARE_TRACE_CATEGORY( atlTraceTime )
DECLARE_TRACE_CATEGORY( atlTraceCache )
DECLARE_TRACE_CATEGORY( atlTraceStencil )
DECLARE_TRACE_CATEGORY( atlTraceString )
DECLARE_TRACE_CATEGORY( atlTraceMap )
DECLARE_TRACE_CATEGORY( atlTraceUtil )
DECLARE_TRACE_CATEGORY( atlTraceSecurity )
DECLARE_TRACE_CATEGORY( atlTraceSync )
DECLARE_TRACE_CATEGORY( atlTraceISAPI )

// atlTraceUser categories are no longer needed.
// Just declare your own trace category using CTraceCategory.
DECLARE_TRACE_CATEGORY( atlTraceUser )
DECLARE_TRACE_CATEGORY( atlTraceUser2 )
DECLARE_TRACE_CATEGORY( atlTraceUser3 )
DECLARE_TRACE_CATEGORY( atlTraceUser4 )

#pragma deprecated( atlTraceUser )
#pragma deprecated( atlTraceUser2 )
#pragma deprecated( atlTraceUser3 )
#pragma deprecated( atlTraceUser4 )
```

The CTraceCategory class associates the category name with the underlying value so that it appears in the trace listing. The four atlTraceUserX categories exist for backward-compatibility; ATL versions 7 and earlier had no means of defining custom trace categories. For new code, you simply need to create a global instance of CTraceCategory like this:

```
CTraceCategory PenguinTraces( "CPenguin trace", 1 );
...
STDMETHODIMP CPenguin::Fly() {
    ATLTRACE2(PenguinTraces,    2,
        _T("IBird::Fly\n"));
    ATLTRACE2(PenguinTraces,    42,
```

```
        _T("Hmmm... Penguins can't fly...\n"));
    ATLTRACE2(atlTraceNotImpl, 0,
        _T("IBird::Fly not implemented!\n"));
    return E_NOTIMPL;
}
```

The trace level is a measure of severity, with 0 the most severe. ATL itself uses only levels 0 and 2. The documentation recommends that you stay between 0 and 4, but you can use any level up to 4,294,967,295 (although that might be a little too fine grained to be useful).

Also, because ATL uses `atlTraceNotImpl` so often, there's even a special macro for it:

```
#define ATLTRACENOTIMPL(funcname) \
  ATLTRACE2(atlTraceNotImpl, 2, \
  _T("ATL: %s not implemented.\n"), funcname); \
  return E_NOTIMPL
```

This macro is used a lot in the implementations of the OLE interfaces:

```
STDMETHOD(SetMoniker)(DWORD, IMoniker*) {
    ATLTRACENOTIMPL(_T("IOleObjectImpl::SetMoniker"));
}
```

Tracing Calls to QueryInterface

ATL's implementation of `QueryInterface` is especially well instrumented for debugging. If you define the `_ATL_DEBUG_QI` symbol before compiling, your objects will output their class name, the interface being queried for (by name[10], if available), and whether the query succeeded or failed. This is extremely useful for reverse engineering clients' interface requirements. For example, here's a sample of the `_ATL_DEBUG_QI` output when hosting a control in IE6:

```
CComClassFactory - IUnknown
CComClassFactory - IClassFactory
CComClassFactory - IClassFactory
CComClassFactory -  - failed
CPenguin - IUnknown
CPenguin -  - failed
```

---

[10] Interface names for remotable interfaces are available in the Registry as the default value of the `HKEY_CLASSES_ROOT\{IID}` key.

```
CPenguin - IOleControl
CPenguin - IClientSecurity - failed
CPenguin - IQuickActivate
CPenguin - IOleObject
CPenguin - IViewObjectEx
CPenguin - IPointerInactive - failed
CPenguin - IProvideClassInfo2
CPenguin - IConnectionPointContainer - failed
CPenguin - IPersistPropertyBag2 - failed
CPenguin - IPersistPropertyBag - failed
CPenguin - IPersistStreamInit
CPenguin - IViewObjectEx
CPenguin - IActiveScript - failed
CPenguin -  - failed
CPenguin - IOleControl
CPenguin - IOleCommandTarget - failed
CPenguin - IDispatchEx - failed
CPenguin - IDispatch
CPenguin - IOleControl
CPenguin - IOleObject
CPenguin - IOleObject
CPenguin - IRunnableObject - failed
CPenguin - IOleObject
CPenguin - IOleInPlaceObject
CPenguin - IOleInPlaceObjectWindowless
CPenguin - IOleInPlaceActiveObject
CPenguin - IOleControl
CPenguin - IClientSecurity - failed
```

Tracing Calls to AddRef and Release

The only calls more heavily instrumented for debugging than QueryInterface are AddRef and Release. ATL provides an elaborate scheme for tracking calls to AddRef and Release on individual interfaces. It is elaborate because each ATL-based C++ class has a single implementation of AddRef and Release, implemented in the most derived class—for example, CComObject. To overcome this limitation, when _ATL_DEBUG_INTERFACES is defined, ATL wraps each new interface[11] handed out via QueryInterface in another C++ object that implements a single interface. Each of these "thunk objects" keeps track of the real interface pointer, as well as the name

---

[11] ATL makes sure to always hand out the same thunk for each object's IUnknown* to observe the rules of COM identity as discussed in Chapter 5, "COM Servers."

of the interface and the name of the class that has implemented the interface. The thunk objects also keep track of an interface pointer–specific reference count that is managed, along with the object's reference count, in the thunk object's implementation of AddRef and Release. As calls to AddRef and Release are made, each thunk object knows exactly which interface is being used and dumps reference count information to debug output. For example, here's the same interaction between a control and IE6, but using _ATL_DEBUG_INTERFACES instead of _ATL_DEBUG_QI:

```
QIThunk-1    AddRef:   Object=0x021c2c88   Refcount=1   CComClassFactory-IUnknown
IThunk-2     AddRef:   Object=0x021c2c88   Refcount=1   CComClassFactory-IClassFactory
QIThunk-2    AddRef:   Object=0x021c2c88   Refcount=2   CComClassFactory-IClassFactory
QIThunk-2    Release:  Object=0x021c2c88   Refcount=1   CComClassFactory-IClassFactory
QIThunk-3    AddRef:   Object=0x021c2c88   Refcount=1   CComClassFactory-IClassFactory
QIThunk-2    Release:  Object=0x021c2c88   Refcount=0   CComClassFactory-IClassFactory
QIThunk-4    AddRef:   Object=0x021c2e38   Refcount=1   CPenguin-IUnknown
QIThunk-5    AddRef:   Object=0x021c2e40   Refcount=1   CPenguin-IOleControl
QIThunk-5    Release:  Object=0x021c2e40   Refcount=0   CPenguin-IOleControl
QIThunk-6    AddRef:   Object=0x021c2e60   Refcount=1   CPenguin-IQuickActivate
QIThunk-7    AddRef:   Object=0x021c2e44   Refcount=1   CPenguin-IOleObject
QIThunk-8    AddRef:   Object=0x021c2e4c   Refcount=1   CPenguin-IViewObjectEx
QIThunk-9    AddRef:   Object=0x021c2e68   Refcount=1   CPenguin-IProvideClassInfo2
QIThunk-9    Release:  Object=0x021c2e68   Refcount=0   CPenguin-IProvideClassInfo2
QIThunk-8    Release:  Object=0x021c2e4c   Refcount=0   CPenguin-IViewObjectEx
QIThunk-7    Release:  Object=0x021c2e44   Refcount=0   CPenguin-IOleObject
QIThunk-6    Release:  Object=0x021c2e60   Refcount=0   CPenguin-IQuickActivate
QIThunk-10   AddRef:   Object=0x021c2e3c   Refcount=1   CPenguin-IPersistStreamInit
QIThunk-10   Release:  Object=0x021c2e3c   Refcount=0   CPenguin-IPersistStreamInit
QIThunk-11   AddRef:   Object=0x021c2e4c   Refcount=1   CPenguin-IViewObjectEx
QIThunk-12   AddRef:   Object=0x021c2e40   Refcount=1   CPenguin-IOleControl
QIThunk-12   Release:  Object=0x021c2e40   Refcount=0   CPenguin-IOleControl
QIThunk-13   AddRef:   Object=0x021c2e38   Refcount=1   CPenguin-IDispatch
QIThunk-14   AddRef:   Object=0x021c2e40   Refcount=1   CPenguin-IOleControl
QIThunk-14   Release:  Object=0x021c2e40   Refcount=0   CPenguin-IOleControl
QIThunk-3    Release:  Object=0x021c2c88   Refcount=0   CComClassFactory-IClassFactory
QIThunk-15   AddRef:   Object=0x021c2e44   Refcount=1   CPenguin-IOleObject
QIThunk-16   AddRef:   Object=0x021c2e44   Refcount=1   CPenguin-IOleObject
QIThunk-16   Release:  Object=0x021c2e44   Refcount=0   CPenguin-IOleObject
QIThunk-15   Release:  Object=0x021c2e44   Refcount=0   CPenguin-IOleObject
QIThunk-17   AddRef:   Object=0x021c2e44   Refcount=1   CPenguin-IOleObject
QIThunk-18   AddRef:   Object=0x021c2e50   Refcount=1   CPenguin-IOleInPlaceObject
QIThunk-19   AddRef:   Object=0x021c2e50   Refcount=1   CPenguin-IOleInPlaceObjectWindowless
QIThunk-20   AddRef:   Object=0x021c2e48   Refcount=1   CPenguin-IOleInPlaceActiveObject
```

```
QIThunk-20  Release:  Object=0x021c2e48  Refcount=0  CPenguin-IOleInPlaceActiveObject
QIThunk-18  Release:  Object=0x021c2e50  Refcount=0  CPenguin-IOleInPlaceObject
QIThunk-19  AddRef:   Object=0x021c2e50  Refcount=2  CPenguin-IOleInPlaceObjectWindowless
QIThunk-17  Release:  Object=0x021c2e44  Refcount=0  CPenguin-IOleObject
QIThunk-19  Release:  Object=0x021c2e50  Refcount=1  CPenguin-IOleInPlaceObjectWindowless
QIThunk-21  AddRef:   Object=0x021c2e40  Refcount=1  CPenguin-IOleControl
QIThunk-21  Release:  Object=0x021c2e40  Refcount=0  CPenguin-IOleControl
QIThunk-22  AddRef:   Object=0x021c2e44  Refcount=1  CPenguin-IOleObject
QIThunk-23  AddRef:   Object=0x021c2e50  Refcount=1  CPenguin-IOleInPlaceObject
QIThunk-19  Release:  Object=0x021c2e50  Refcount=0  CPenguin-IOleInPlaceObjectWindowless
QIThunk-23  Release:  Object=0x021c2e50  Refcount=0  CPenguin-IOleInPlaceObject
QIThunk-22  Release:  Object=0x021c2e44  Refcount=0  CPenguin-IOleObject
QIThunk-24  AddRef:   Object=0x021c2e44  Refcount=1  CPenguin-IOleObject
QIThunk-25  AddRef:   Object=0x021c2e50  Refcount=1  CPenguin-IOleInPlaceObject
QIThunk-25  Release:  Object=0x021c2e50  Refcount=0  CPenguin-IOleInPlaceObject
QIThunk-24  Release:  Object=0x021c2e44  Refcount=0  CPenguin-IOleObject
QIThunk-13  Release:  Object=0x021c2e38  Refcount=0  CPenguin-IDispatch
QIThunk-11  Release:  Object=0x021c2e4c  Refcount=0  CPenguin-IViewObjectEx
QIThunk-26  AddRef:   Object=0x021c2e44  Refcount=1  CPenguin-IOleObject
QIThunk-26  Release:  Object=0x021c2e44  Refcount=0  CPenguin-IOleObject
QIThunk-4   Release:  Object=0x021c2e38  Refcount=0  CPenguin-IUnknown
QIThunk-1   Release:  Object=0x021c2c88  Refcount=0  CComClassFactory-IUnknown
```

ATL maintains a list of outstanding thunk objects. This list is used at server shutdown to detect any leaks—that is, any interfaces that the client has not released. When using _ATL_DEBUG_INTERFACES, watch your debug output for the string LEAK, which is an indication that someone has mismanaged an interface reference:

```
ATL: QIThunk - 4   LEAK: Object = 0x00962920   Refcount = 4
  MaxRefCount = 4   CCalc - ICalc
```

The most useful part of this notification is the index of QI thunk object. You can use this to track when the leaked interface is acquired by using the CAtlDebugInterfacesModule class. This is the class that manages the thunk objects during debug builds, and a global instance of this class called _AtlDebugInterfacesModule is automatically included in your class when the _ATL_DEBUG_INTERFACES symbol is defined. You can instruct the debugger to break at the appropriate time by setting the m_nIndexBreakAt member of the CAtlDebugInterfacesModule at server start-up time.

```
extern "C"
BOOL WINAPI DllMain(HINSTANCE hInstance, DWORD dwReason,
    LPVOID lpReserved) {
    hInstance;
    BOOL b = _AtlModule.DllMain(dwReason, lpReserved);
```

```
    // Trace down interface leaks
#ifdef _ATL_DEBUG_INTERFACES
    _AtlDebugInterfacesModule.m_nIndexBreakAt = 4;
#endif
    return b;
}
```

When that interface thunk is allocated, _AtlDebugInterfacesModule calls DebugBreak, handing control over to the debugger and allowing you to examine the call stack and plug the leak.

_ATL_DEBUG_REFCOUNT

Versions of ATL earlier than version 3 used the _ATL_DEBUG_REFCOUNT symbol to track interface reference counts for ATL IXxxImpl classes only. Because _ATL_DEBUG_INTERFACES is much more general, it has replaced _ATL_DEBUG_REF-COUNT, although _ATL_DEBUG_REFCOUNT is still supported for backward compatibility.

```
#ifdef _ATL_DEBUG_REFCOUNT
#ifndef _ATL_DEBUG_INTERFACES
#define _ATL_DEBUG_INTERFACES
#endif
#endif
```

Summary

ATL provides a layered approach to implementing IUnknown. The top layer, represented by the CComXxxThreadModel classes, provides helper functions and type definitions for synchronization required of both STAs and MTAs. The second level, CComObjectRootEx, uses the threading model classes to support "just thread-safe enough" AddRef and Release implementations and object-level locking. CComObjectRootEx also provides a table-driven implementation of QueryInterface, using an interface map provided by your class. Your class derives from CComObjectRootEx and any number of interfaces, providing the interface member function implementations. The final level is provided by CComObject and friends, which provide the implementation of QueryInterface, AddRef, and Release based on the lifetime and identity requirements of the object.

To allow each class to define its one lifetime and identity requirements, each class defines its own _CreatorClass, which defines the appropriate Creator. The Creator is responsible for properly creating an instance of your ATL-base class and should be used in place of the C++ operator new.

Finally, to debug your objects, ATL provides a number of debugging facilities, including tracing and interface usage and leak tracking.

5 | COM Servers

A Review of COM Servers

After you create one or more COM classes, you need to package the classes and install them on a system. The package is called a COM *Server*, which is a dynamically activated collection of the implementations of one or more COM classes. Modern Win32 versions of COM enable you to create a COM server as an in-process (inproc) server (a dynamic link library), an out-of-process server (an executable), or, on the Windows NT/2000/XP/2003 operating system, a system service executable.[1]

A COM server has three jobs, in addition to hosting the implementations of its classes:

- Register and unregister all classes in the server and, potentially, the server itself.

- Provide the COM Service Control Manager (SCM) access to all COM *class objects* implemented by the server (often called *exposing* the class objects). Class objects are frequently called *class factory objects* because they generally implement the IClassFactory interface.

- Manage the server's lifetime. This typically means allowing the SCM to unload an inproc server from memory when it's no longer used. A local server often terminates when there are no more references to objects managed by the server.

Technically, the first and third items are optional, but all COM servers should implement this functionality. Exactly how a server does this depends on the type of server.

---

[1] Here "Modern Win32 versions of COM" refers to Windows NT 4.0 and greater, Windows 98 and greater, and Windows 95 with the DCOM95 upgrade.

Inproc Servers

An inproc server is a dynamic link library (DLL) that contains five well-known entry points, one for the Win32 operating systems and the other four for COM:

```
BOOL WINAPI DllMain(HINSTANCE hInstance, DWORD dwReason,
    LPVOID lpReserved);

STDAPI DllRegisterServer(void);
STDAPI DllUnregisterServer(void);
STDAPI DllGetClassObject(REFCLSID rclsid, REFIID riid,
    LPVOID* ppv);
STDAPI DllCanUnloadNow(void);
```

Each of the Win32 operating systems calls a DLL's `DllMain` function when it loads a DLL into a process and removes a DLL from a process. The operating system also calls `DllMain` each time the current process creates a new thread and when a thread terminates cleanly. This function is optional but present in all ATL inproc servers.

The `DllRegisterServer` and `DllUnregisterServer` functions create and remove, respectively, in the Windows Registry all entries necessary for the correct operation of the server and its classes. When you use the REGSVR32 utility to register or unregister an inproc server, the utility loads the DLL and calls the appropriate one of these function in the DLL. Technically, both of these functions are optional, but, in practice, you want to have them in your server.

The COM SCM calls a server's `DllGetClassObject` function when it requires a class object exposed by the server. The server should return the requested interface, `riid`, on the specified class object, `rclsid`.

When you call the `CoFreeUnusedLibraries` API, COM asks each inproc server in your process whether COM should unload the DLL by calling the `DllCanUnloadNow` function. An `S_OK` return value means that the server permits COM to unload the server. An `S_FALSE` return value indicates that the server is busy and COM cannot unload it.

Local Servers and Service-Based Servers

A local server or Windows service is an executable image (EXE) server that contains one well-known entry point:

```
extern "C"
int WINAPI _tWinMain(HINSTANCE hInstance,
    HINSTANCE hPrevInstance, LPTSTR lpCmdLine, int nShowCmd);
```

Executables cannot provide multiple specialized entry points as DLLs can, so a local server must use a different technique to implement the three requirements of a COM server: registration, exposed class objects, and lifetime management.

A local server registers and unregisters itself, and then immediately terminates when the server parses its command line and finds the well-known (noncase-sensitive) command-line switches `Regserver` and `UnregServer`, respectively.

A local server exposes its class objects by calling the `CoRegisterClassObject` API and handing an `IUnknown` interface pointer to each of the server's class objects to the SCM. A local server must call this API after the SCM starts the server process.[2] When the server is ready to shut down, it must first call `CoRevokeClassObject` to notify the SCM that each of the server's class objects is no longer available for use.

A local server manages its own lifetime. When a server detects that there are no references to any of the objects managed by the server, the server can shut down—or not, as desired. As you'll see later in this chapter, detecting that there are no references is a little trickier than you might think.

COM Createable and Noncreateable Classes

A *COM createable class* is a COM object class that supports using the `CoCreateInstance` API to create instances. This implies that the class must provide a class object and that the class object implements the `IClassFactory` interface.

A noncreateable class typically provides no class object, so calling `CoCreateInstance` using the class's CLSID fails. In many designs, far more noncreateable classes exist than createable ones. For example, one version of Microsoft Excel had approximately 130 classes, only 3 of which were createable. You typically access interfaces on noncreateable classes through properties or methods on createable classes or on classes that have already been created by other means.

The Object Map and the CAtlModule Class

ATL uses two constructs to support the functionality all types of servers require: the *object map* and one of three `CAtlModule`-derived classes. As you'll see shortly, the behavior of a COM server differs considerably depending upon whether that server is an inproc server, a local server, or a Windows service. ATL has factored server functionality into `CAtlDllModuleT`, `CAtlExeModuleT`, and `CAtlServiceModuleT`,

---

[2] As of this writing, a local server must register its class objects within 120 seconds. The time was shorter in previous software releases. It might change again in the future, so simply register your class objects as quickly as possible.

each of which extends the CAtlModule base class. The discussion that follows refers to CAtlModule directly, but you should realize that one of the derived classes actually does most of the work. The object map (more properly entitled a class map) is a table of all classes implemented in the server.

Various methods of the CAtlModule class use the object map to do the following:

- Find each class and ask it to register and unregister itself
- Create the class object, if any, for each createable class
- Register and unregister the class objects with the SCM
- Find a table of implemented and required component categories for a class
- Call the static initialization and termination member functions for each class

The basic idea is that you describe the classes that you are implementing in a server using the object map. Whenever you need basic server functionality, there is probably a method of the CAtlModule class that implements much, if not all, of the required functionality.

Many methods in the CAtlModule class iterate over the entries in the object map and either ask each class to perform the required function or ask each class to provide the information needed to allow the method to do it.

The Object Map

ATL manages the object map by allocating a custom data segment within the PE file itself. Each coclass adds an entry to the object map by allocating the _ATL_OBJMAP_ENTRY structure (discussed in detail shortly) within that same data segment. This produces a series of _ATL_OBJMAP_ENTRY structures that are contiguous in memory and, thus, can easily be iterated over by CAtlModule when it needs to perform registration, class object creation, and other class-management services. Each class inserts an item into the object map via the OBJECT_ENTRY_AUTO macro declared in the class header file outside the class declaration itself, as in the following:

```
class CMyClass : public CComCoClass< ... >, ...
{
public:

   ...
};

OBJECT_ENTRY_AUTO(__uuidof(MyClass), CMyClass)
```

Here the coclass name declared in the IDL file is `MyClass`, so the `__uuidof` keyword returns the CLSID.

Readers familiar with previous versions of ATL will recall that the object map was implemented as a global C++ object declared in the server's `.cpp` file with macros such as `BEGIN_OBJECT_MAP` and `END_OBJECT_MAP`. This required each class to add information (namely, an `OBJECT_ENTRY` macro) to a separate header file not associated with the class, which complicates maintenance and causes every class in the server to be compiled twice. The nice thing about the new approach is that the file in which the `OBJECT_ENTRY_AUTO` macro appears doesn't matter; all classes that declare one contribute entries that are contiguous in memory. This means that information about each class can be located next to the class definition, where it logically belongs. The discussion of the `OBJECT_ENTRY_AUTO` macro later in this chapter reveals how ATL accomplishes this nifty trick.

The Object Map Macros

_ATL_OBJMAP_ENTRY Structure

The object map is an array of `_ATL_OBJMAP_ENTRY` structures that look like this:

```
struct _ATL_OBJMAP_ENTRY30 {
    const CLSID* pclsid;
    HRESULT (WINAPI *pfnUpdateRegistry)(BOOL bRegister);
    _ATL_CREATORFUNC* pfnGetClassObject;
    _ATL_CREATORFUNC* pfnCreateInstance;
    IUnknown* pCF;
    DWORD dwRegister;
    _ATL_DESCRIPTIONFUNC* pfnGetObjectDescription;
    _ATL_CATMAPFUNC* pfnGetCategoryMap;
    void (WINAPI *pfnObjectMain)(bool bStarting);
};

typedef _ATL_OBJMAP_ENTRY30 _ATL_OBJMAP_ENTRY;
```

The structure contains the following fields, many of which are pointers to functions:

Field	Description
pclsid	Pointer to CLSID for this class entry
pfnUpdateRegistry	The function that registers and unregisters the class
pfnGetClassObject	The Creator function that creates an instance of the class object
pfnCreateInstance	The Creator function that creates an instance of the class
pCF	Pointer to the class object instance—NULL if not yet created
dwRegister	Registration cookie CoRegisterClassObject returns
pfnGetObjectDescription	The function that returns the object description for the class
pfnGetCategoryMap	The function that returns the component category map
pfnObjectMain	The class initialization/termination function

OBJECT_ENTRY_AUTO Macro

You use the OBJECT_ENTRY_AUTO macro to specify a COM-createable class. Typically, this means the specified class derives from the CComCoClass base class. Often these are top-level objects in an object model. Clients typically create such top-level objects using CoCreateInstance.

```
#define OBJECT_ENTRY_AUTO(clsid, class) \
    __declspec(selectany) ATL::_ATL_OBJMAP_ENTRY \
    __objMap_##class = \
    {&clsid, class::UpdateRegistry, \
    class::_ClassFactoryCreatorClass::CreateInstance, \
    class::_CreatorClass::CreateInstance, NULL, 0, \
    class::GetObjectDescription, class::GetCategoryMap, \
    class::ObjectMain }; \
    extern "C" __declspec(allocate("ATL$__m"))\
```

```
    __declspec(selectany) \
    ATL::_ATL_OBJMAP_ENTRY* const __pobjMap_##class = \
    &__objMap_##class; \
    OBJECT_ENTRY_PRAGMA(class)
```

A key part of the previous `OBJECT_ENTRY_AUTO` macro definition is the `__declspec(allocate)` modifier used to allocate an item of type `_ATL_OBJMAP_ENTRY` in a data segment named `ATL$__m`. All classes in the server use this same macro (or the `NON_CREATEABLE` version discussed shortly), so they all add items to the same contiguous `ATL$__m` data segment, which lays out the `_ATL_OBJMAP_ENTRY` structures contiguously in memory. The `OBJECT_ENTRY_PRAGMA` is the bit that actually forces the linker to include a symbol pointing to the `_ATL_OBJMAP_ENTRY`. `OBJECT_ENTRY_PRAGMA` is defined as follows:

```
#if defined(_M_IX86)
#define OBJECT_ENTRY_PRAGMA(class)
    __pragma(comment(linker, "/include:___pobjMap_" #class));
...
#endif
```

The `pragma` shown in the macro definition has the same effect as passing the `/include` option to the command line of the linker. You might have noticed the `__declspec(selectany)` attribute adorning the `__objMap_##class` and `__pobj-Map_##class` variables in the `OBJECT_ENTRY_AUTO` macro. This construct appears in many places in ATL, and it's convenient because it instructs the linker to ignore multiple definitions of a global data item that it finds in a single object file. For instance, if more than one `.cpp` file included a class definition that contained the `OBJECT_ENTRY_AUTO` macro, both expansions of the `__objMap_##class` and `__pobj-Map_##class` globals would be defined multiple times and would produce linker errors.

Having each `_ATL_OBJMAP_ENTRY` from every class aligned contiguously in memory is part of what's needed to build an object map that `CAtlModule` can iterate over. The remaining parts are pointers that mark where in memory the map starts and where it ends. ATL is clever here as well. It creates two additional data segments named `ATL$__a` and `ATL$__z` and allocates a single `NULL _ATL_OBJMAP_ENTRY` pointer within each. The linker then arranges the three data segments alphabetically so that the `ATL$__m` segment containing all the server's `_ATL_OBJMAP_ENTRY` structures is sandwiched between two `NULL`s. The code in `atlbase.h` that does this is shown here:

```
#pragma section("ATL$__a", read, shared)
#pragma section("ATL$__z", read, shared)
#pragma section("ATL$__m", read, shared)
extern "C" {
__declspec(selectany) __declspec(allocate("ATL$__a"))
    _ATL_OBJMAP_ENTRY* __pobjMapEntryFirst = NULL;
__declspec(selectany) __declspec(allocate("ATL$__z"))
    _ATL_OBJMAP_ENTRY* __pobjMapEntryLast = NULL;
}

#if !defined(_M_IA64)
#pragma comment(linker, "/merge:ATL=.rdata")
#endif
```

The alphabetical order of sections in the resulting file is guaranteed through a special naming rule enforced by the linker. If a section name has a $ character in it, the linker goes through some odd but, in this case, useful gyrations. First, it arranges the segments in order alphabetically. Then, it strips the $ character and all characters after the $ in the section name and merges the sections. This way, you're guaranteed that the data in the ATL$__a segment comes first, then the ATL$__m segment comes next, and finally the ATL$__z segment. The actual linked PE format file then would have a single ATL segment instead of three separate ones.[3]

The final step is the /merge switch added by the final #pragma directive. This causes everything in the ATL segment to be merged into the standard .rdata section (which explains why you won't find the ATL section if you go looking with dumpbin).

Take a look at the following three class definitions:

```
class CDog : public CComCoClass< ... >, ...
{ };
OBJECT_ENTRY_AUTO(__uuidof(Dog), CDog)

class CCat: public CComCoClass< ... >, ...
{ };
OBJECT_ENTRY_AUTO(__uuidof(Cat), CCat)

class CMouse: public CComCoClass< ... >, ...
{ };
OBJECT_ENTRY_AUTO(__uuidof(Mouse), CMouse)
```

The actual layout of the object map in memory looks something like Figure 5.1.

---

[3] This also explains why the ATL team used ATL$__a, ATL$__m, and ATL$__z. It gives them future flexibility to add sections and make sure they show up in the right places.

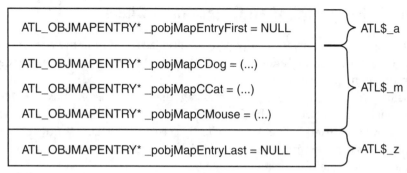

Figure 5.1 The ATL object map

The beginning of the map is marked by _pobjMapEntryFirst and its value is set to NULL. It's not possible to set _pobjMapEntryFirst to one of the first "real" entries in the map because each is a global object, and the order of global object construction in C++ is not guaranteed. As you'll see later when we peer into the CAtlModule-derived classes, all these classes must do to walk the object map is start at __pobjMapEntryFirst and increment a pointer until that pointer is NULL.

OBJECT_ENTRY_NON_CREATEABLE_EX_AUTO macro

You use the OBJECT_ENTRY_NON_CREATEABLE_EX_AUTO macro to specify a class that does not have an associated class object. Often these are non-top-level objects in an object model. Clients typically must call a method on a higher-level object in the object hierarchy to obtain an instance of this class. Because the specified class does not have an associated class object, clients cannot create an instance by calling CoCreateInstance.

```
#define OBJECT_ENTRY_NON_CREATEABLE_EX_AUTO(clsid, class) \
    __declspec(selectany) ATL::_ATL_OBJMAP_ENTRY \
    __objMap_##class = \
    {&clsid, class::UpdateRegistry, NULL, NULL, NULL, 0, NULL, \
    class::GetCategoryMap, class::ObjectMain }; \
    extern "C" __declspec(allocate("ATL$__m")) \
    __declspec(selectany) \
    ATL::_ATL_OBJMAP_ENTRY* const __pobjMap_##class = \
    &__objMap_##class; \
    OBJECT_ENTRY_PRAGMA(class)
```

You use the OBJECT_ENTRY_NON_CREATEABLE_EX_AUTO macro primarily for non-createable classes that need class-level initialization and uninitialization. Occasionally, you might want to have a noncreateable class maintain Registry entries, possibly persistent class configuration information and component categories.

Methods Required of an Object Map Class

The CAtlModule class registers, unregisters, initializes, and uninitializes noncreateable object map entries. In addition, it creates class objects and class instances for regular object map entries.

A class listed in the object map using the OBJECT_ENTRY_NON_CREATEABLE_EX_AUTO macro must provide the first three well-known static methods listed in Table 5.1. A class listed in the object map that uses the OBJECT_ENTRY_AUTO macro must provide the same three methods as a noncreateable class, plus the additional well-known static methods listed in Table 5.1.

Table 5.1. Object Map Support Functions

Static Member Function	Description
UpdateRegistry	Registers and unregisters the class. The DECLARE_REGISTRY_RESOURCE macros provide various implementations of this method for nonattributed projects. Attributed projects have an implementation injected by the attribute provider.
ObjectMain	Initializes and uninitializes the class. CComObjectRootBase provides a default implementation of this method.
GetCategoryMap	Returns a pointer to a component category map. The BEGIN_CATEGORY_MAP macro provides an implementation. CComObjectRootBase provides a default implementation of this method.
CreatorClass::CreateInstance	_The DECLARE_AGGREGATABLE macros set the _CreatorClass typedef to the name of the class that creates instances. CComCoClass provides a default definition of this typedef.
_ClassFactoryCreatorClass:: CreateInstance	The DECLARE_CLASSFACTORY macros set the _ClassFactoryCreatorClass typedef to the name of the class that creates class objects. CComCoClass provides a default definition of this typedef.
GetObjectDescription	Returns the object description text string. CComCoClass provides a default implementation of this method.

All classes listed in the object map must define an `UpdateRegistry` method, which is the only method not provided by any base class. As you'll see soon, ATL contains various macros that expand to different implementations of this method, so the method is not difficult to provide.

All ATL objects derive from `CComObjectRootBase`, so they already have a default implementation of the `ObjectMain` method.

Most createable ATL classes also derive from `CComCoClass`, which provides the implementation of all four remaining methods that an object map entry requires, as well as both of the required typedefs. ATL also contains a set of macros that define and implement `GetCategoryMap`.

Class Registration Support Methods

When a server registers all the COM classes it contains, ATL iterates over the object map. The `pfnUpdateRegistry` field in the object map contains a pointer to the class's `UpdateRegistry` method. For each entry, ATL calls the `UpdateRegistry` method to register or unregister the class. Then, it registers or unregisters the component categories for the class using the table of required and implemented categories that the `GetCategoryMap` method provides.

The GetObjectDescription Method

The `GetObjectDescription` static method retrieves the text description for your class object. As shown previously, the default implementation returns `NULL`. You can override this method with the `DECLARE_OBJECT_DESCRIPTION` macro. For example:

```
class CMyClass : public CComCoClass< ... >, ... {
public:
   DECLARE_OBJECT_DESCRIPTION("MyClass Object Description")


   ...
};
```

The UpdateRegistry Method

Every class that you list in the object map, whether createable or noncreateable, must provide an `UpdateRegistry` static member function. The ATL server implementation calls this method to ask the class to register and unregister itself, depending on the value of `bRegister`.

```
static HRESULT WINAPI UpdateRegistry(BOOL bRegister) ;
```

When you ask a COM server to register its classes, it registers all of them. You can't ask a server to register just one class or some subset of its classes. To register or unregister a subset of the classes in a server, you need to provide a Component Registrar object. This is a COM-createable class that implements the `IComponent-Registrar` interface. At one time, Microsoft Transaction Server was going to use the Component Registrar object to register and unregister individual classes in a server. However, I can find no references describing if, when, or how MTS/COM+ uses the Component Registrar object. Basically, as of this writing, the Component Registrar object and class object descriptions seem to be an unused feature, and you shouldn't use them.

The DECLARE_REGISTRY Macros

You can provide a custom implementation of `UpdateRegistry` (a.k.a. write it yourself) or use an ATL-provided implementation. ATL provides an implementation of this method when you use one of the following macros in your class declaration:

```
#define DECLARE_NO_REGISTRY()\
    static HRESULT WINAPI UpdateRegistry(BOOL /*bRegister*/) \
    {return S_OK;}

#define DECLARE_REGISTRY(class, pid, vpid, nid, flags)\
    static HRESULT WINAPI UpdateRegistry(BOOL bRegister) {\
        return _Module.UpdateRegistryClass(GetObjectCLSID(), \
            pid, vpid, nid,\
            flags, bRegister);\
    }

#define DECLARE_REGISTRY_RESOURCE(x)\
    static HRESULT WINAPI UpdateRegistry(BOOL bRegister) {\
    ...
    return ATL::_pAtlModule->UpdateRegistryFromResource(_T(#x), \
        bRegister); \
    ...
    }

#define DECLARE_REGISTRY_RESOURCEID(x)\
    static HRESULT WINAPI UpdateRegistry(BOOL bRegister) {\
    ...
    return ATL::_pAtlModule->UpdateRegistryFromResource(x, \
        bRegister); \
    ...
    }
```

In most circumstances, you shouldn't use two of these Registry macros. The `DECLARE_REGISTRY` macro relies upon the old ATL 3 `CComModule` class to do its work. `CComModule` is no longer used as of ATL 7; if you try to use `DECLARE_REGISTRY` in an ATL 7 or 8 project, you'll see compile errors resulting from references to the deprecated `CComModule` class. Unless you're porting an ATL 3 project to ATL 7+, you should not use `DECLARE_REGISTRY`.

The second Registry macro to steer clear of is the `DECLARE_NO_REGISTRY` macro. This macro simply returns `S_OK` from the `UpdateRegistry` method, so no class information is entered in the Registry. The intent was that noncreateable classes can't be created, so you shouldn't put their CLSID information in the Registry. The problem is that any class that wants to throw COM exceptions still needs the CLSID-ProgId association in the Registry. ATL's support code for populating COM exception objects relies upon the `ProgIdFromCLSID` function, which fails for any class that uses `DECLARE_NO_REGISTRY`.

The most flexible registration technique for ATL servers is to use Registry scripts. When asked to register or unregister, a server using Registry scripts uses an interpreter object to parse the script and make the appropriate Registry changes. The interpreter object implements the `IRegistrar` interface. ATL provides such an object, which can be either statically linked to reduce dependencies or dynamically loaded for the smallest code size. The choice is made via the `_ATL_STATIC_REGISTRY` macro, which is discussed later in this chapter.

The `DECLARE_REGISTRY_RESOURCE` and `DECLARE_REGISTRY_RESOURCEID` macros provide an implementation of `UpdateRegistry` that delegates the call to the `CAtlModule::UpdateRegistryFromResource` method. You specify a string resource name when you use the first macro. The second macro expects an integer resource identifier. The `UpdateRegistryFromResource` runs the script contained in the specified resource. When `bRegister` is `TRUE`, this method adds the script entries to the system Registry; otherwise, it removes the entries.

Registry Script Files

Registry scripts are text files that specify what Registry changes must be made for a given CLSID. Wizard-generated code uses an **RGS** extension by default for Registry script files. Your server contains the script file as a custom resource of type **REGISTRY** in your executable or DLL.

Registry script syntax isn't complicated; it can be summarized as follows:

```
[NoRemove | ForceRemove | val] Name [ = s | d | m | b 'Value']
{
  ... optional script entries for subkeys
}
```

The NoRemove prefix specifies that the parser should not remove the key when unregistering. The ForceRemove prefix specifies that the parser should remove the current key and any subkeys before writing the key.[4] The val prefix specifies that the entry is a named value, not a key. The s and d value prefixes indicate REG_SZ and REG_DWORD, respectively. The m value prefix indicates a multistring (REG_MULTI_SZ), and the b value prefix denotes a binary value (REG_BINARY). The Name token is the string for the named value or key. It must be surrounded by apostrophes when the string contains spaces; otherwise, the apostrophes are optional. ATL's parser recognizes the standard Registry keys—for example, HKEY_CLASSES_ROOT—as well as their four character abbreviations (HKCR).

Here's a REGEDIT4 sample for the nontrivial class registration for a sample class named Demagogue. Watch out: A few lines are too long to list on the page and have wrapped.

```
REGEDIT4
[HKEY_CLASSES_ROOT\ATLInternals.Demagogue.1]
@="Demagogue Class"
[HKEY_CLASSES_ROOT\ATLInternals.Demagogue.1\CLSID]
@="{95CD3731-FC5C-11D1-8CC3-00A0C9C8E50D}"
[HKEY_CLASSES_ROOT\ATLInternals.Demagogue]
@="Demagogue Class"
[HKEY_CLASSES_ROOT\ATLInternals.Demagogue\CLSID]
@="{95CD3731-FC5C-11D1-8CC3-00A0C9C8E50D}"
[HKEY_CLASSES_ROOT\ATLInternals.Demagogue\CurVer]
@="ATLInternals.Demagogue.1"
[HKEY_CLASSES_ROOT\CLSID\{95CD3731-FC5C-11D1-8CC3-00A0C9C8E50D}]
@="Demagogue Class"
[HKEY_CLASSES_ROOT\CLSID\{95CD3731-FC5C-11D1-8CC3-00A0C9C8E50D}\ProgID]
@="ATLInternals.Demagogue.1"
[HKEY_CLASSES_ROOT\CLSID\{95CD3731-FC5C-11D1-8CC3-
00A0C9C8E50D}\VersionIndependentProgID]
@="ATLInternals.Demagogue"
[HKEY_CLASSES_ROOT\CLSID\{95CD3731-FC5C-11D1-8CC3-
00A0C9C8E50D}\Programmable]
[HKEY_CLASSES_ROOT\CLSID\{95CD3731-FC5C-11D1-8CC3-
00A0C9C8E50D}\InprocServer32]
@="C:\\ATLINT~1\\Debug\\ATLINT~1.DLL"
"ThreadingModel"="Apartment"
[HKEY_CLASSES_ROOT\CLSID\{95CD3731-FC5C-11D1-8CC3-00A0C9C8E50D}\TypeLib]
```

---

[4] Be careful when writing Registry scripts by hand. For example, don't put the ForceRemove prefix on the node for HKEY_CLASSES_ROOT\CLSID. More than one developer machine has had to be repaved because a Registry script removed a lot more than was intended.

```
@="{95CD3721-FC5C-11D1-8CC3-00A0C9C8E50D}"
[HKEY_CLASSES_ROOT\CLSID\{95CD3731-FC5C-11D1-8CC3-00A0C9C8E50D}\Implemented
Categories]
[HKEY_CLASSES_ROOT\CLSID\{95CD3731-FC5C-11D1-8CC3-00A0C9C8E50D}\Implemented
Categories\{0D22FF22-28CC-11D2-ABDD-00A0C9C8E50D}]
```

The corresponding Registry script looks like this:

```
HKCR
{
  ATLInternals.Demagogue.1 = s 'Demagogue Class'
  {
    CLSID = s '{95CD3731-FC5C-11D1-8CC3-00A0C9C8E50D}'
  }
  ATLInternals.Demagogue = s 'Demagogue Class'
  {
    CLSID = s '{95CD3731-FC5C-11D1-8CC3-00A0C9C8E50D}'
    CurVer = s 'ATLInternals.Demagogue.1'
  }
  NoRemove CLSID
  {
    ForceRemove {95CD3731-FC5C-11D1-8CC3-00A0C9C8E50D} = s 'Demagogue
      Class'
    {
      ProgID = s 'ATLInternals.Demagogue.1'
      VersionIndependentProgID = s 'ATLInternals.Demagogue'
      ForceRemove 'Programmable'
      InprocServer32 = s '%MODULE%'
      {
        val ThreadingModel = s 'Apartment'
      }
      'TypeLib' = s '{95CD3721-FC5C-11D1-8CC3-00A0C9C8E50D}'
      'Implemented Categories'
      {
        {0D22FF22-28CC-11D2-ABDD-00A0C9C8E50D}
      }
    }
  }
}
```

When you have the resource script file, you reference the file in your server's resource (.rc) file. You can reference it using either an integer identifier or a string identifier. In a typical ATL project, each class can have a Registry script file, and the server as a whole typically has its own unique Registry script file.

In the following examples, the Demagogue script file uses the integer identifier IDR_DEMAGOGUE. The EarPolitic script file uses EARPOLITIC as its string identifier. ATL wizard-created classes use the DECLARE_REGISTRY_RESOURCEID macro to specify a resource by its integer identifier. You can use the DECLARE_REGISTRY_RESOURCE macro to identify a resource by its name.

```
// resource.h file
#define IDR_DEMAGOGUE                   102


// Server.rc file
IDR_DEMAGOGUE          REGISTRY DISCARDABLE     "Demagogue.rgs"
EARPOLITIC             REGISTRY DISCARDABLE     "EarPolitic.rgs"

// Demagogue.h file
class ATL_NO_VTABLE CDemagogue :
    public CComObjectRootEx<CComSingleThreadModel>,
    public CComCoClass<CDemagogue, &CLSID_Demagogue>,
...
public:
DECLARE_REGISTRY_RESOURCEID(IDR_DEMAGOGUE)
...
};


// EarPolitic.h file
class ATL_NO_VTABLE CEarPolitic :
    public CComObjectRootEx<CComSingleThreadModel>,
    public CComCoClass<CEarPolitic, &CLSID_EarPolitic>,
...
{
public:
DECLARE_REGISTRY_RESOURCE(EARPOLITIC)
...
};
```

Registry Script Variables

Note that in the Registry script, one of the lines references a symbol called %MODULE%.

```
InprocServer32 = s '%MODULE%'
```

When the parser evaluates the script, it replaces all occurrences of the Registry script variable %MODULE% with the actual results of a call to GetModuleFileName. So what the parser actually registered looked like this:

```
InprocServer32 = s 'C:\ATLInternals\Debug\ATLInternals.dll'
```

You can use additional, custom Registry script variables in your scripts. Your server must provide the Registry script parser with a table that maps variable names to replacement values when you ask the parser to parse the script. The parser substitutes the replacement values for the variable names before registration.

To use custom Registry script variables, first select the Registry script variable name, using percent signs to delimit the name. Here is a sample line from a Registry script:

```
DateInstalled = s '%INSTALLDATE%'
```

You now have two choices. If your script variables are global, you can provide an override of the AddCommonRGSReplacements method in your derived module class. An example implementation looks like this:

```
HRESULT AddCommonRGSReplacements(IRegistrarBase *pRegistrar) {
    BaseModule::AddCommonRGSReplacements( pRegistrar );
    OLECHAR wszDate [16]; SYSTEMTIME st;
    GetLocalTime(&st);
    wsprintfW(wszDate, L"%.4d/%.2d/%.2d", st.wYear,
        st.wMonth, st.wDay);
    pRegistrar->AddReplacement( OLESTR("INSTALLDATE"), wszDate );
}
```

You must call the base class's version of AddCommonRGSReplacements to make sure the APPID variable gets added as well.

If you don't want to have all of your replacements added in one place, you can define a custom UpdateRegistry method instead of using the DECLARE_REG-ISTRY_RESOURCEID macro in your class. In the method, build a table of replacement name-value pairs. Finally, call the CAtlModule::UpdateRegistryFromResource method, specifying the resource identifier, a register/unregister flag, and a pointer to the replacement name-value table. Note that ATL uses the provided table entries *in addition to* the default replacement map (which, as of this writing, contains only %MODULE% and %APPID%).

Here is an example from the Demagogue class that substitutes the variable %INSTALLDATE% with a string that contains the current date:

```
static HRESULT WINAPI UpdateRegistry(BOOL b) {
    OLECHAR wszDate [16]; SYSTEMTIME st;
    GetLocalTime(&st);
    wsprintfW(wszDate, L"%.4d/%.2d/%.2d", st.wYear,
        st.wMonth, st.wDay);
    _ATL_REGMAP_ENTRY rm[] = {
```

```
        { OLESTR("INSTALLDATE"), wszDate},
        { 0, 0 } };
    return _pAtlModule->UpdateRegistryFromResource(
        IDR_DEMAGOGUE, b, rm);
}
```

After registration of the class, the Registry key `DateInstalled` contains the year, month, and day, in the form yyyy/mm/dd, at the time of install.

The GetCategoryMap Method

The last step in the registration process for each class in the object map is to register the component categories for the class. The ATL server registration code calls each class's `GetCategoryMap` method to ask the class for its list of required and implemented component categories. The method looks like this:

```
static const struct _ATL_CATMAP_ENTRY* GetCategoryMap() { return NULL; }
```

The ATL server registration code uses the standard component category manager object (`CLSID_StdComponentCategoriesMgr`) to register your class's required and implemented categories. Older versions of Win32 operating systems do not have this component installed. When the category manager is not installed, your class's registration of its component categories silently fails. Typically, this is not good. However, Microsoft permits you to redistribute the standard component category manager (`comcat.dll`) with your application.

The Component Category Map

Typically, you use ATL-provided category map macros for the implementation of this method. Here's a typical category map:

```
// {0D22FF22-28CC-11d2-ABDD-00A0C9C8E50D}
static const GUID CATID_ATLINTERNALS_SAMPLES =
{0xd22ff22, 0x28cc, 0x11d2, {0xab, 0xdd, 0x0, 0xa0, 0xc9, 0xc8,
    0xe5, 0xd}};

BEGIN_CATEGORY_MAP(CDemagogue)
IMPLEMENTED_CATEGORY(CATID_ATLINTERNALS_SAMPLES)
END_CATEGORY_MAP()
```

This example defines a component category called CATID_ATLINTERNALS_SAMPLES. All examples in this book register themselves as a member of this category.

The Category Map Macros

The `BEGIN_CATEGORY_MAP` macro declares the `GetCategoryMap` static member function. This returns a pointer to an array of `_ATL_CATMAP_ENTRY` entries, each of which describes one component category that your class either requires or implements.

```
#define BEGIN_CATEGORY_MAP(x)\
  static const struct ATL::_ATL_CATMAP_ENTRY* GetCategoryMap() {\
  static const struct ATL::_ATL_CATMAP_ENTRY pMap[] = {
```

The `IMPLEMENTED_CATEGORY` and `REQUIRED_CATEGORY` macros populate the table with the appropriate entries:

```
#define IMPLEMENTED_CATEGORY(catid) { \
    _ATL_CATMAP_ENTRY_IMPLEMENTED, &catid },
#define REQUIRED_CATEGORY(catid) { \
    _ATL_CATMAP_ENTRY_REQUIRED, &catid },
```

The `END_CATEGORY_MAP` adds a delimiting entry to the table and completes the `GetCategoryMap` function:

```
#define END_CATEGORY_MAP()\
    { _ATL_CATMAP_ENTRY_END, NULL } };\
    return( pMap ); }
```

Each table entry contains a flag (indicating whether the entry describes a required category, an implemented category, and the end of table entry) and a pointer to the CATID.

```
struct _ATL_CATMAP_ENTRY {
    int iType;
    const CATID* pcatid;
};

#define _ATL_CATMAP_ENTRY_END         0
#define _ATL_CATMAP_ENTRY_IMPLEMENTED 1
#define _ATL_CATMAP_ENTRY_REQUIRED    2
```

The ATL helper function `AtlRegisterClassCategoriesHelper` iterates through the table and uses COM's standard component category manager to register each CATID as a required or implemented category for your class. The ATL server registration code uses this helper function to register the component categories for each class in the object map.

Unfortunately, the category map logic does not add a category to a system before trying to enroll a class as a member of the (nonexistent) category. If you want to add categories that don't already exist, you must enhance the registration of the server itself so that it registers any custom component categories your classes use. For example, the following Registry script registers the `AppID` for an inproc server and also adds a component category to the list of component categories on the system:

```
HKCR
{
    NoRemove AppID
    {
        {A11552A2-28DF-11d2-ABDD-00A0C9C8E50D} = s 'ATLInternals'
        'ATLInternals.DLL'
        {
            val AppID = s {A11552A2-28DF-11d2-ABDD-00A0C9C8E50D}

        }
    }
    NoRemove 'Component Categories'
    {
        {0D22FF22-28CC-11d2-ABDD-00A0C9C8E50D}
        {
            val 409 = s 'ATL Internals Example Components'
        }
    }
}
```

This technique defines all categories (just one in the previous example) that the classes implemented in this server in the System registry use. Separately, each class registers itself as a member of one or more of these categories.

Server, Not Class, Registration

Often, you need Registry entries for the server (inproc, local, or service) as a whole. For example, the `HKCR/AppID` Registry entries for a server apply to the entire DLL or EXE, and not to a specific class implemented in the DLL or EXE. As mentioned previously, you must register a new component category with the system before you can enroll a class as a member of the category. Until now, you've only seen support for registration of class-specific information.

This is simple enough. Write a Registry script that adds the entries the server requires, such as its `AppID` and component categories that the server's classes use. Then, register the server's script before registering all the classes implemented in the server. The wizard-generated code for all three server types does precisely this for you.

The ATL wizard-generated code for a server creates a Registry script file for your *server* registration in addition to any Registry script files for your classes. By default, the server Registry script defines only an AppID for the server. Here are the entries for an ATL project called MathServer:

```
// In the resource.h file
#define IDR_MATHSERVER          100

// In the MathServer.rc file
IDR_MATHSERVER REGISTRY "MathServer.rgs"

// MathServer.rgs file
HKCR
{
    NoRemove AppID
    {
        '%APPID%' = s 'MathServer'
        'MathServer.DLL'
        {
            val AppID = s '%APPID%'
        }
    }
}
```

The RGS files are similar for all three server types—inproc, local server, and Windows service. The mechanics used to invoke the registration code that executes the script differ among the three server types.

Inproc Server Registration

Inproc server registration for classes and for the server itself occurs in the call to the DllRegisterServer entry point. This method delegates the work to a specialization of CAtlModule that is used only for inproc servers; this class is called CAtlDllModuleT.

```
template <class T>
class ATL_NO_VTABLE CAtlDllModuleT : public CAtlModuleT<T> {
public :
  ...
  HRESULT DllRegisterServer(BOOL bRegTypeLib = TRUE) {
    ...
```

```
    T* pT = static_cast<T*>(this);
    HRESULT hr = pT->RegisterAppId();  // execute server script
    ...
    return hr;
  }
  ...
};
```

The `RegisterAppId` function ultimately calls the `UpdateRegistryFromResource` function through the `UpdateRegistryAppId` helper generated by the `DECLARE_REGISTRY_APPID_RESOURCEID` macro in our `project.cpp` file. This macro is discussed in more detail later in this chapter.

Local Server and Windows Service Registration

A local server specializes `CAtlModule` with a class called `CAtlExeModuleT`. A Windows service further extends `CAtlExeModuleT` with a derived class called `CAtlServiceModuleT`. Both classes supply `WinMain` code that registers the server's resource script entries and then calls the `_AtlModule` object's `RegisterServer` method to do the same for each class in the object map. These classes unregister each object in the server before running the server's unregistration script.

```
template <class T>
class CAtlExeModuleT : public CAtlModuleT<T> {
public :

  int WinMain(int nShowCmd) throw() {
    ...
    HRESULT hr = S_OK;

    LPTSTR lpCmdLine = GetCommandLine();
    if (pT->ParseCommandLine(lpCmdLine, &hr) == true)
      hr = pT->Run(nShowCmd);

    ...
  }

  bool ParseCommandLine(LPCTSTR lpCmdLine, HRESULT* pnRetCode) {
    *pnRetCode = S_OK;

    TCHAR szTokens[] = _T("-/");

    T* pT = static_cast<T*>(this);
    LPCTSTR lpszToken = FindOneOf(lpCmdLine, szTokens);
```

```
    while (lpszToken != NULL) {
      if (WordCmpI(lpszToken, _T("UnregServer"))==0) {
        *pnRetCode = pT->UnregisterServer(TRUE); // server script
        if (SUCCEEDED(*pnRetCode))
          *pnRetCode = pT->UnregisterAppId(); // all class scripts
        return false;
      }


      // Register as Local Server
      if (WordCmpI(lpszToken, _T("RegServer"))==0) {
        *pnRetCode = pT->RegisterAppId(); // server script
        if (SUCCEEDED(*pnRetCode))
          *pnRetCode = pT->RegisterServer(TRUE); // all class scripts
        return false;
      }


      lpszToken = FindOneOf(lpszToken, szTokens);
    }

    return true;
  }
};
```

Class Initialization and Uninitialization

The ObjectMain Method

In C++, constructors and destructors are used to provide instance-level initialization and cleanup—that is, code that runs each time an instance of a class is either created or destroyed. Often, it is useful to provide class-level initialization and cleanup code—code that runs only once per class, regardless of the number of class instances that are ultimately created. Some languages support such behavior directly through static constructors. Unfortunately, C++ is not one of those languages. So, ATL supports class-level initialization for all classes listed in the object map, createable and noncreateable, through the ObjectMain method. In fact, you'll frequently add a noncreateable class entry to the object map solely because the noncreateable class needs class-level initialization. (A createable class must always be in the object map and thus always receives class-level initialization.)

When an ATL server initializes, it iterates over the object map and calls the ObjectMain static member function (with the bStarting parameter set to true) of each class in the map. When an ATL server terminates, it calls the ObjectMain function (with the bStarting parameter set to false) of each class in the map. You always have a default implementation, provided by `CComObjectRootBase`, that does nothing and looks like this:

```
static void WINAPI  ObjectMain(bool /* bStarting */ ) {};
```

When you have class initialization and termination logic (compared to instance initialization and termination logic), define an `ObjectMain` static member function in your class and place the logic there.[5]

```
class ATL_NO_VTABLE CSoapBox :
    public CComObjectRootEx<CComSingleThreadModel>,
    ...
{
public:
    DECLARE_NO_REGISTRY()
    ...
    static void WINAPI ObjectMain(bool bStarting) ;
};
```

Instantiation Requests

Having class initialization logic run may be useful, but if clients can't create an instance, an initialized class is no help. Next, let's look at how ATL supports creating COM class factories to bring your COM objects to life.

Class Object Registration

ATL creates the class objects for an inproc server slightly differently than it does the class objects for a local server or service. For an inproc server, ATL defers creating each class object until the SCM actually requests the class object via `DllGetClassObject`. For a local server or service, ATL creates all class objects during server initialization and then registers the objects with the SCM.

For an inproc server, ATL uses the `AtlComModuleGetClassObject` helper function to scan the object map; create the class object, if necessary; and return the requested interface on the class object.

```
ATLINLINE ATLAPI AtlComModuleGetClassObject(
    _ATL_COM_MODULE* pComModule, REFCLSID rclsid, REFIID riid,
    LPVOID* ppv) {
```

---

[5] Instance initialization and termination logic should go in the `FinalConstruct` and `FinalRelease` methods, as Chapter 4, "Objects in ATL," describes.)

```
...
for (_ATL_OBJMAP_ENTRY** ppEntry =
    pComModule->m_ppAutoObjMapFirst;
    ppEntry < pComModule->m_ppAutoObjMapLast; ppEntry++) {
    if (*ppEntry != NULL) {
        _ATL_OBJMAP_ENTRY* pEntry = *ppEntry;
        if ((pEntry->pfnGetClassObject != NULL) &&
            InlineIsEqualGUID(rclsid, *pEntry->pclsid)) {
            if (pEntry->pCF == NULL) {
                CComCritSecLock<CComCriticalSection>
                    lock(pComModule->m_csObjMap, false);
                hr = lock.Lock();
                ...
                if (pEntry->pCF == NULL)
                    hr = pEntry->pfnGetClassObject(
                    pEntry->pfnCreateInstance,
                    __uuidof(IUnknown),
                    (LPVOID*)&pEntry->pCF);
            }
            if (pEntry->pCF != NULL)
                hr = pEntry->pCF->QueryInterface(riid,
                    ppv);
            break;
        }
    }
}

if (*ppv == NULL && hr == S_OK)
    hr = CLASS_E_CLASSNOTAVAILABLE;
return hr;
}
```

Notice how the logic checks to see if the class object has not already been created (pEntry->pCF == NULL), acquires the critical section that guards access to the object map, and then checks once more that pCF is still NULL. What might not be obvious is why ATL checks twice. This is to maximize concurrency by avoiding grabbing the critical section in the normal case (when the class factory has already been created).

Also notice that ATL caches the IUnknown interface for the class object in the object map entry's pCF member variable. Because the SCM can make subsequent requests for the same class object, ATL caches the IUnknown pointer to the object in the pCF field of the object map entry for the class. Subsequent requests for the same class object reuse the cached interface pointer.

You can use the helper method, called `GetClassObject`, in your `CAtlModuleT` global object (discussed in detail later in the chapter) to retrieve a previously registered class object. However, this works only for inproc servers; the `CAtlExeModuleT` and `CAtlServiceModuleT` classes, used for local servers and services, respectively, don't include this member function.

```
// Obtain a Class Factory (DLL only)
HRESULT GetClassObject(REFCLSID rclsid, REFIID riid,
    LPVOID* ppv);
```

You use it like this:

```
IClassFactory* pFactory;
HRESULT hr = _pAtlModule->GetClassObject (
 CLSID_Demagogue, IID_IClassFactory,
 reinterpret_cast< void** >(&pFactory));
```

A local server must register all its class objects during the server's initialization. ATL uses the `AtlComModuleRegisterClassObjects` helper function to register all the class objects in a local server. This helper function iterates over the object map calling `RegisterClassObject` for each object map entry.

```
ATLINLINE ATLAPI AtlComModuleRegisterClassObjects(
  _ATL_COM_MODULE* pComModule,
  DWORD dwClsContext, DWORD dwFlags) {
  ...
  HRESULT hr = S_FALSE;
  for (_ATL_OBJMAP_ENTRY** ppEntry =
    pComModule->m_ppAutoObjMapFirst;
    ppEntry < pComModule->m_ppAutoObjMapLast && SUCCEEDED(hr);
    ppEntry++) {
    if (*ppEntry != NULL)
      hr = (*ppEntry)->RegisterClassObject(dwClsContext,
        dwFlags);
    }
    return hr;
}
```

`RegisterClassObject` is a method of the `_ATL_OBJMAP_ENTRY` structure. It basically encapsulates the process of creating and then registering a class object from an object map entry. First, it ignores entries with a `NULL` `pfnGetClassObject` function pointer. This skips the noncreateable class entries in the map. Then, `RegisterClassObject` creates the instance of the class object and registers it:

```
struct _ATL_OBJMAP_ENTRY {
  HRESULT WINAPI RegisterClassObject(DWORD dwClsContext,
    DWORD dwFlags) {
    IUnknown* p = NULL;
    if (pfnGetClassObject == NULL) return S_OK;
    HRESULT hRes = pfnGetClassObject(pfnCreateInstance,
        __uuidof(IUnknown), (LPVOID*) &p);
    if (SUCCEEDED(hRes))
        hRes = CoRegisterClassObject(*pclsid, p,
            dwClsContext, dwFlags, &dwRegister);
    if (p != NULL) p->Release();
    return hRes;
  }
};
```

Notice that the function does not cache the IUnknown interface pointer to the class object that it creates: It hands the interface to the SCM (which caches the pointer), stores the registration code in the object map, and releases the interface pointer. Because ATL does not cache class object interface pointers in an out-of-process server, the simplest method to obtain your own class object from within the server is to ask the SCM for it by calling CoGetClassObject.

The _ClassFactoryCreatorClass and _CreatorClass Typedefs

When ATL created a class object in the previous examples, it asked your class to instantiate the class object by calling indirectly through the function pointer pfnGetClassObject, which ATL stores in the object map entry for the class.

```
struct _ATL_OBJMAP_ENTRY30 {
  ...
  _ATL_CREATORFUNC* pfnGetClassObject; // Creates a class object
  _ATL_CREATORFUNC* pfnCreateInstance; // Create a class instance
  ...
};
```

This member variable is of type _ATL_CREATORFUNC* and is a creator function.[6] Notice that the pfnCreateInstance member variable is also a creator function pointer.

---

[6] Although two types of creator functions logically exist (instance-creator functions and class-creator functions), all creator functions that the object map uses have a static member function with the example function signature. Chapter 4 discusses the various types of instance-creator functions in depth. This chapter discusses the various class-creator classes.

```
typedef HRESULT (WINAPI _ATL_CREATORFUNC)(void* pv, REFIID riid, LPVOID* ppv);
```

These function pointers are non-NULL only when you describe a COM-create-able class using the OBJECT_ENTRY_AUTO macro.

```
#define OBJECT_ENTRY_AUTO(clsid, class) \
    __declspec(selectany) ATL::_ATL_OBJMAP_ENTRY \
    __objMap_##class = \
    {&clsid, class::UpdateRegistry, \
    class::_ClassFactoryCreatorClass::CreateInstance, \
    class::_CreatorClass::CreateInstance, NULL, 0, \
    class::GetObjectDescription, class::GetCategoryMap, \
    class::ObjectMain }; \
    extern "C" __declspec(allocate("ATL$__m"))\
    __declspec(selectany) \
    ATL::_ATL_OBJMAP_ENTRY* const __pobjMap_##class = \
    &__objMap_##class; \
    OBJECT_ENTRY_PRAGMA(class)
```

A createable class must define a typedef called _ClassFactoryCreatorClass, which ATL uses as the name of the *class object's creator class*. The OBJECT_ENTRY_AUTO macro expects this creator class to have a static member function called CreateInstance, and it stores the address of this static member function in the pfnGetClassObject object map entry.

A createable class also must define a typedef called _CreatorClass, which ATL uses as the name of the *class instance's creator class*. The OBJECT_ENTRY_AUTO macro expects this creator class to have a static member function called CreateInstance, and it stores the address of this static member function in the pfnCreateInstance object map entry.

DECLARE_CLASSFACTORY

Typically, your createable class inherits a definition of the _ClassFactoryCreatorClass typedef from its CComCoClass base class. CComCoClass uses the DECLARE_CLASSFACTORY macro to define an appropriate default class object creator class, based on the type of server.

```
template <class T, const CLSID* pclsid = &CLSID_NULL>
class CComCoClass {
public:
    DECLARE_CLASSFACTORY()
    DECLARE_AGGREGATABLE(T)
    ...
};
```

The _ClassFactoryCreatorClass Typedef

The DECLARE_CLASSFACTORY macro evaluates to the DECLARE_CLASSFACTORY_EX macro with CComClassFactory as the cf argument. The DECLARE_CLASSFACTORY_EX macro produces a typedef for the symbol _ClassFactoryCreatorClass. This typedef is the name of a creator class that ATL uses to create the class object for a class.

```
#define DECLARE_CLASSFACTORY() DECLARE_CLASSFACTORY_EX(ATL::CComClassFactory)

#if defined(_WINDLL) | defined(_USRDLL)
#define DECLARE_CLASSFACTORY_EX(cf) \
    typedef ATL::CComCreator< \
      ATL::CComObjectCached< cf > > _ClassFactoryCreatorClass;
#else
// don't let class factory refcount influence lock count
#define DECLARE_CLASSFACTORY_EX(cf) \
    typedef ATL::CComCreator< \
      ATL::CComObjectNoLock< cf > > _ClassFactoryCreatorClass;
#endif
```

When you build an inproc server, ATL standard build options define the _USRDLL preprocessor symbol. This causes the _ClassFactoryCreatorClass typedef to evaluate to a CComCreator class that creates a CComObjectCached<cf> version of your class object class cf. Out-of-process servers evaluate the typedef as a CComCreator class that creates a CComObjectNoLock<cf> version of the class object class cf.

Class Object Usage of CComObjectCached and CComObjectNoLock

As described in Chapter 4, "Objects in ATL," the CComObjectCached::AddRef method does not increment the server's lock count until the cached object's reference count changes from 1 to 2. Similarly, Release doesn't decrement the server's lock count until the cached object's reference count changes from 2 to 1.

ATL caches the IUnknown interface pointer to an inproc server's class object in the object map. This cached interface pointer represents a reference. If this cached reference affects the server's lock count, the DLL cannot unload until the server releases the interface pointer. However, the server doesn't release the interface pointer until the server is unloading. In other words, the server would never unload in this case. By waiting to adjust the server's reference count until there is a second reference to the class object, the reference in the object map isn't sufficient to keep the DLL loaded.

Also described in Chapter 4, CComObjectNoLock never adjusts the server's lock count. This means that an instance of CComObjectNoLock does not keep a server loaded. This is exactly what you need for a class object in a local server.

When ATL creates a class object for an out-of-process server, it registers the class object with the SCM; then ATL releases its reference. However, the SCM keeps an unknown number of references to the class object, where "unknown" means one or more. Therefore, the CComObjectCached class doesn't work correctly for an out-of-process class object. ATL uses the CComObjectNoLock class for out-of-process class objects because references to such objects don't affect the server's lifetime in any way. However, in modern versions of COM, the marshaling stub calls the class object's LockServer method when it marshals an interface pointer to a remote client (where "remote" is any other apartment or context). This keeps the server loaded when out-of-apartment clients have a reference to the class object.

Class Object Instantiation: CComCreator::CreateInstance Revisited

Earlier in this chapter, you saw the ATL class object registration helper functions AtlComModuleGetClassObject and RegisterClassObject. When they create a class object, they call the class object's creator class's CreateInstance method, like this:

```
// Inproc server class object instantiation
ATLINLINE ATLAPI AtlComModuleGetClassObject(_ATL_COM_MODULE* pM,
                                REFCLSID rclsid,
                                REFIID riid, LPVOID* ppv) {
    ...
    hr = pEntry->pfnGetClassObject(pEntry->pfnCreateInstance,
                            __uuidof(IUnknown),
                            (LPVOID*)&pEntry->pCF);
    ...
} ;

// Out of process server class object instantiation
struct _ATL_OBJMAP_ENTRY {
  HRESULT WINAPI RegisterClassObject(DWORD dwClsContext,
  DWORD dwFlags) {
    ...
    HRESULT hRes = pfnGetClassObject(pfnCreateInstance,
      _uuidof(IUnknown), (LPVOID*) &p);
    ...
  }
};
```

Recall that the pfnGetClassObject member variable is set by the OBJECT_ENTRY_AUTO macro and contains a pointer to the CreateInstance method of _ClassFactoryCreatorClass:

```
class::_ClassFactoryCreatorClass::CreateInstance
```

For an inproc server, this evaluates to the following (assuming that you're using the default class factory class, which is `CComClassFactory`):

```
class::ATL::CComCreator<
    ATL::CComObjectCached< ATL::CComClassFactory >
>::CreateInstance
```

For an out-of-process server, this evaluates to:

```
class::ATL::CComCreator<
    ATL::CComObjectNoLock< ATL::CComClassFactory >
>::CreateInstance
```

This means that the `pfnGetClassObject` member points to the `CreateInstance` method of the appropriate parameterized `CComCreator` class. When ATL calls this `CreateInstance` method, the creator class creates the appropriate type of the `CComClassFactory` instance (cached or no lock) for the server. You learned the definition of the `CComCreator` class in Chapter 4, "Objects in ATL," but let's examine part of the code in depth:

```
template <class T1>
class CComCreator {
public:
    static HRESULT WINAPI CreateInstance(void* pv, REFIID riid,
        LPVOID* ppv) {
        ...
        ATLTRY(p = new T1(pv))
        if (p != NULL) {
            p->SetVoid(pv);
            ...
        }
        return hRes;
    }
};
```

After the creator class's `CreateInstance` method creates the appropriate class object, the method calls the class object's `SetVoid` method and passes it the `pv` parameter of the `CreateInstance` call.

Note that ATL uses a creator class to create both instances of class objects (sometimes called class factories) and instances of a class (often called COM objects). For regular COM objects, ATL defines the `SetVoid` method in `CComObjectRootBase` as a do-nothing method, so this creator class call to `SetVoid` has no effect on an instance of a class:

```
class CComObjectRootBase {
    ...
    void SetVoid(void*) {}
};
```

However, when a creator class creates an instance of a class factory, it typically creates a CComClassFactory instance. CComClassFactory overrides the SetVoid method. When a creator class calls the SetVoid method while creating a class factory instance, the method saves the pv parameter in its m_pfnCreateInstance member variable:

```
class CComClassFactory :
    public IClassFactory,
    public CComObjectRootEx<CComGlobalsThreadModel> {
public:
    ...
    void SetVoid(void* pv) { m_pfnCreateInstance = (_ATL_CREATORFUNC*)pv;}
    _ATL_CREATORFUNC* m_pfnCreateInstance;
};
```

Let's look at the class object–creation code in the ATL helper function again:

```
HRESULT hRes = pfnGetClassObject( pfnCreateInstance,
    __uuidof(IUnknown), (LPVOID*) &p);
```

The pfnGetClassObject variable points to the CreateInstance creator function that creates the appropriate instance of the *class object* for the server. The pfnCreateInstance variable points to the CreateInstance creator function that creates an instance of the *class*.

When ATL calls the pfnGetClassObject function, it passes the pfnCreateInstance object map entry member variable as the pv parameter to the CComClassFactory::CreateInstance method. The class object saves this pointer in its m_pfnCreateInstance member variable and calls the m_pfnCreateInstance function whenever a client requests the class object to create an instance of the class.

Whew! You must be wondering why ATL goes to all this trouble. Holding a function pointer to an instance-creation function increases the size of every class object by 4 bytes (the size of the m_pfnCreateInstance variable). Nearly everywhere else, ATL uses templates for this kind of feature. For example, we could define the CComClassFactory class to accept a template parameter that is the instance class to create. Then, each instance of the class object wouldn't need the extra 4-byte function pointer. The code would look something like this:

```
template <class T>
class CComClassFactory : ... {
  ...
  STDMETHOD(CreateInstance)(LPUNKNOWN pUnkOuter, REFIID riid,
      void** ppvObj) {
      ...
      ATLTRY(p = new T ());
      ...
  }
};
```

The problem with this alternative approach is that it actually takes more memory to implement. For example, let's assume that you have a server that implements three classes: A, B, and C.

On Win32, ATL's current approach takes 12 bytes per class object (4-byte vptr, 4-byte unused reference count, and 4-byte function pointer) times three class objects (A, B, and C), plus 20 bytes for a single CComClassFactory vtable (five entries of 4 bytes each). (All three classes objects are actually unique instances of the same CComClassFactory class, so all three share a single vtable. Each instance maintains a unique state—a function pointer—which creates different instance classes when called.) This is a total of 56 bytes for the three class objects. (Recall that ATL never creates more than one instance of a class object.)

The template approach takes 8 bytes per class object (4-byte vptr and 4-byte unused reference count) times three class objects (A, B, and C), plus 20 bytes each for three CComClassFactory vtables (one for CComClassFactory<A>, one for CComClassFactory<B>, and one for CComClassFactory<C>). In this case, the class object doesn't maintain state to tell it what instance class to create. Therefore, each class must have its own unique vtable that points to a unique CreateInstance method that calls new on the appropriate class. This is a total of 84 bytes.

This is mostly a theoretical calculation, though. Most heap managers round allocations up to a multiple of 16 bytes, which makes the instance sizes the same. This more or less makes moot the issue that class objects carry around a reference count member variable that they never use.

However, the memory savings are real, mainly because of the single required vtable. The function pointer implementation requires only a single copy of the IClassFactory methods and, therefore, only one vtable, regardless of the number of classes implemented by a server. The template approach requires one copy of the IClassFactory methods per class and, therefore, one vtable per class. The memory savings increase as you have more classes in a server.

I know, that's more detail than you wanted to know. Think of all the character and moral fiber you're building. That's why I'm here. Now, let's look at how CComClassFactory and related classes actually work.

CComClassFactory and Friends

DECLARE_CLASSFACTORY and CComClassFactory

Typically, ATL objects acquire a class factory by deriving from CComCoClass. This class includes the macro DECLARE_CLASSFACTORY, which declares CComClassFactory as the default class factory.

The CComClassFactory class is the most frequently used of the ATL-supplied class object implementations. It implements the IClassFactory interface and also explicitly specifies that the class object needs the same level of thread safety, CCom-GlobalsThreadModel, that globally available objects require. This is because multiple threads can access a class object when the server's threading model is apartment, free or both. Only when the server's threading model is single does the class object not need to be thread safe.

```
class CComClassFactory :
    public IClassFactory,
    public CComObjectRootEx<CComGlobalsThreadModel> {
public:
    BEGIN_COM_MAP(CComClassFactory)
        COM_INTERFACE_ENTRY(IClassFactory)
    END_COM_MAP()

    // IClassFactory
    STDMETHOD(CreateInstance)(LPUNKNOWN pUnkOuter, REFIID riid,
      void** ppvObj);
    STDMETHOD(LockServer)(BOOL fLock);

    // helper
    void SetVoid(void* pv);

    _ATL_CREATORFUNC* m_pfnCreateInstance;
};
```

Your class object must implement a CreateInstance method that creates an instance of your class. The CComClassFactory implementation of this method does some error checking and then calls the m_pfnCreateInstance function pointer to create the appropriate instance.

```
STDMETHOD(CreateInstance)(LPUNKNOWN pUnkOuter, REFIID riid,
    void** ppvObj) {
    ...
        else hRes = m_pfnCreateInstance(pUnkOuter, riid, ppvObj);
    }
    return hRes;
}
```

As described earlier, the object map entry for your class contains the original value for this function pointer. It points to an instance-creator class, as described in Chapter 4, "Objects in ATL," and is set by the following part of the OBJECT_ENTRY_AUTO macro:

```
class::_CreatorClass::CreateInstance, NULL, 0, \
```

When your class derives from CComCoClass, you inherit a typedef for _Creator-Class, which is be used unless you override it with a new definition.

```
template <class T, const CLSID* pclsid = &CLSID_NULL>
class CComCoClass {
public:
    DECLARE_AGGREGATABLE(T)
    ...
};
```

The default DECLARE_AGGREGATABLE macro defines a creator class, of type CCom-Creator2, that it uses to create instances of your class. This creator class creates instances using one of two other creator classes, depending on whether the instance is aggregated. It uses a CComCreator to create instances of CComObject<YourClass> when asked to create a nonaggregated instance; it creates instances of CComAggObject<YourClass> when you want your class to be aggregatable. When your class derives from CComCoClass, you inherit a typedef for _CreatorClass that is used unless you override it with a new definition.

```
#define DECLARE_AGGREGATABLE(x) public:\
    typedef ATL::CComCreator2< \
        ATL::CComCreator< \
            ATL::CComObject< x > >, \
        ATL::CComCreator< \
            ATL::CComAggObject< x > > \
        > _CreatorClass;
```

DECLARE_CLASSFACTORY_EX

You can specify a custom class factory class for ATL to use when creating instances of your object class. To override the default specification of CComClassFactory, add the DECLARE_CLASSFACTORY_EX macro to your object class and, as the macro parameter, specify the name of your custom class factory class. This class must derive from CComClassFactory and override the CreateInstance method. For example

```
class CMyClass : ..., public CComCoClass< ... > {
public:
  DECLARE_CLASSFACTORY_EX(CMyClassFactory)

  ...
};

class CMyClassFactory : public CComClassFactory {
  ...
  STDMETHOD(CreateInstance)(LPUNKNOWN pUnkOuter, REFIID riid,
    void** ppvObj);
};
```

ATL also provides three other macros that declare a class factory:

- DECLARE_CLASSFACTORY2. Uses CComClassFactory2 to control creation through a license.

```
#define DECLARE_CLASSFACTORY2(lic) \
    DECLARE_CLASSFACTORY_EX(CComClassFactory2<lic>)
```

- DECLARE_CLASSFACTORY_SINGLETON. Uses CComClassFactorySingleton to construct a single CComObjectCached object and return the object in response to all instantiation requests.

```
#define DECLARE_CLASSFACTORY_SINGLETON(obj) \
    DECLARE_CLASSFACTORY_EX(CComClassFactorySingleton<obj>)
```

- DECLARE_CLASSFACTORY_AUTO_THREAD. Uses CComClassFactoryAutoThread to create new instances in a round-robin manner in multiple apartments.

```
#define DECLARE_CLASSFACTORY_AUTO_THREAD() \
    DECLARE_CLASSFACTORY_EX(CComClassFactoryAutoThread)
```

DECLARE_CLASSFACTORY2 and CComClassFactory2<lic>

The DECLARE_CLASSFACTORY2 macro defines CComClassFactory2 as your object's class factory implementation. CComClassFactory2 implements the IClassFactory2 interface, which controls object instantiation using a license. A CComClassFactory2 class object running on a licensed system can provide a runtime license key that a client can save. Later, when the client runs on a nonlicensed system, it can use the class object only by providing the previously saved license key.

```
template <class license>
class CComClassFactory2 :
    public IClassFactory2,
    public CComObjectRootEx<CComGlobalsThreadModel>,
    public license {
public:
    ...

    STDMETHOD(CreateInstance)(LPUNKNOWN pUnkOuter, REFIID riid,
        void** ppvObj) {
        ...
        if (!IsLicenseValid()) return CLASS_E_NOTLICENSED;
        ...
            return m_pfnCreateInstance(pUnkOuter, riid, ppvObj);
    }

    STDMETHOD(CreateInstanceLic)(IUnknown* pUnkOuter,
        IUnknown* pUnkReserved, REFIID riid, BSTR bstrKey,
        void** ppvObject);
    STDMETHOD(RequestLicKey)(DWORD dwReserved, BSTR* pbstrKey);
    STDMETHOD(GetLicInfo)(LICINFO* pLicInfo);
    ...
};
```

Note that the main difference between CComClassFactory and CComClassFactory2 is that the latter class's CreateInstance method creates the instance only on a licensed system—that is, IsLicenseValid returns TRUE. The additional CreateInstanceLic method always creates an instance on a licensed system but creates an instance on an unlicensed system only when the caller provides the correct license key.

The template parameter to CComClassFactory2<license> must implement the following static functions:

VerifyLicenseKey	Returns TRUE if the argument is a valid license key.
GetLicenseKey	Returns a license key as a BSTR.
IsLicenseValid	Returns TRUE if the current system is licensed.

The following is an example of a simple license class:

```
const OLECHAR rlk[] = OLESTR("Some run-time license key") ;

class CMyLicense
```

```
{

protected:

  static BOOL VerifyLicenseKey(BSTR bstr) {
    return wcscmp (bstr, rlk) == 0;
  }

  static BOOL GetLicenseKey(DWORD dwReserved, BSTR* pBstr) {
    *pBstr = SysAllocString(rlk);
    return TRUE;
  }

  static BOOL IsLicenseValid() {
    // Validate that the current system is licensed...
    // May check for the presence of a specific license file, or
    // may check for a particular hardware device
    if (...) return TRUE;
  }
};
```

You specify this license class as the parameter to the DECLARE_CLASSFACTORY2 macro in your object class. It overrides the _ClassFactoryCreatorClass typedef inherited from CComCoClass.

```
class ATL_NO_VTABLE CEarPolitic :
    public CComObjectRootEx<CComSingleThreadModel>,
    public CComCoClass<CEarPolitic, &CLSID_EarPolitic>,
    ...
{
public:
    DECLARE_CLASSFACTORY2 (CMyLicense)
    ...
};
```

The client code required for creating instances of this licensed class depends upon whether the client machine is licensed or is an unlicensed machine that instead provides a runtime license key. Typically, development is performed on a licensed machine where CoCreateInstance is used as usual. Then a call to RequestLicenseKey is used on the licensed machine to obtain a runtime license key that is persisted to file (or some other medium). CComClassFactory2 invokes IsLicenseValid to ensure that the calling code is running on a licensed machine before it hands out a runtime license key via RequestLicenseKey. Clients on nonlicensed machines then use this runtime license key to create instances using `IClassFactory2::CreateInstanceLic`.

Here's what the client code might look like for creating an instance of our licensed `CEarPolitic` class and obtaining a runtime license key:

```
// Obtain pointer to IClassFactory2 interface
CComPtr<IClassFactory2> pcf;
::CoGetClassObject(__uuidof(CEarPolitic), CLSCTX_ALL, NULL,
    __uuidof(pcf), (void**)&pcf);

// Request a run-time license key -
// only succeeds on licensed machine
CComBSTR bstrKey;
pcf->RequestLicKey(NULL, &bstrKey);

// Save license key to a file for distribution
// to run-time clients
FILE* f = fopen("license.txt", "w+");
fwrite(bstrKey, sizeof(wchar_t), bstrKey.Length(), f);
fclose(f);
```

A user operating on a nonlicensed machine with a runtime license uses that license to create instances, like this:

```
// Obtain a pointer to the IClassFactory2 interface
CComPtr<IClassFactory2> pcf;
::CoGetClassObject(__uuidof(CEarPolitic), CLSCTX_ALL, NULL,
    __uuidof(pcf), (void**)&pcf);

// Read in the run-time license key from disk
WCHAR szKey[1025];
FILE* f = fopen("license.txt", "r");
int n = fread((void**)&szKey, sizeof(wchar_t), 1024, f);
szKey[n] = '\0';
fclose(f);

// Create an instance of the licensed object w/ the license key
CComBSTR bstrKey(szKey);
CComPtr<IEarPolitic> p;
hr = pcf->CreateInstanceLic(NULL, NULL, __uuidof(p), bstrKey,
    (void**)&p);
```

DECLARE_CLASSFACTORY_SINGLETON and CComClassFactorySingleton

The DECLARE_CLASSFACTORY_SINGLETON macro defines CComClassFactorySingleton as your object's class factory implementation. This class factory creates only a single instance of your class. All instantiation requests return the requested interface pointer on this one (singleton) instance.

The template parameter specifies the class of the singleton. The class factory creates this singleton object as a member variable, m_spObj, of the class factory.

```
template <class T>
class CComClassFactorySingleton : public CComClassFactory {
public:
  // IClassFactory
  STDMETHOD(CreateInstance)(LPUNKNOWN pUnkOuter, REFIID riid,
    void** ppvObj) {
    ...
    hRes = m_spObj->QueryInterface(riid, ppvObj);
    ...
    return hRes;
  }
  CComPtr<IUnknown> m_spObj;
};
```

The following is an example of a simple singleton class:

```
class CMyClass : ..., public CComCoClass< ... > {
public:
    DECLARE_CLASSFACTORY_SINGLETON(CMyClass)

    ...
};
```

Singletons Are Evil—Or, at the Very Least, Leaning Toward the Dark Side

You should avoid using singletons, if possible. A singleton in a DLL is unique only per process. A singleton in an out-of-process server is unique only per system, at best—and often not even then because of security and multiuse settings. Typically, most uses of a singleton are better modeled as multiple instances that share state instead of one shared instance.

In the current ATL implementation, the singleton class object does not marshal the interface pointer it produces to the calling apartment. This has subtle and potentially disastrous consequences. For example, imagine that you create an inproc singleton that resides in an STA. Every client from a different STA that "creates" the singleton receives a direct pointer to the singleton object, not to a proxy to the object, as you might expect. This has the following implications:

- An inproc singleton can be concurrently accessed by multiple threads, regardless of the apartment in which it lives.

- Therefore, the singleton must protect its state against such concurrent access.

- In addition, the singleton must be apartment neutral because, conceptually, it lives in all apartments.

- Therefore, an inproc singleton must not hold apartment-specific state, such as interface pointers, but instead should keep such pointers in the Global Interface Table (GIT).

- Finally, a singleton cannot be aggregated.

A preferable approach to using singletons is to use nonsingleton "accessor" objects to access some piece of shared state. These accessor objects operate on the shared state through a lock or synchronization primitive so that the data is protected from concurrent access by multiple instances of the accessor objects. In the next example, the shared state is modeled as a simple static variable that stores a bank account object. Instances of the CTeller class access the bank account only after successfully acquiring the account lock.

```
class CAccount {
public:
    void Audit() { ... }
    void Open() { ... }
    void Close() { ... }
    double Deposit(double dAmount) { ... }
    double Withdraw(double dAmount) { ... }
};

static CAccount s_account;              // shared state
static CComAutoCriticalSection s_lock; // lock for serializing
                                       // account access

class CTeller {
public:
    void Deposit(double dAmount) {
        s_lock.Lock();
        s_account.Deposit(dAmount);
        s_lock.Unlock();
    }
};
```

This technique of factoring out the shared state of the object still provides the semantics that most people seek when they turn to singletons, but it avoids the previous problems associated with singletons because the CTeller object itself is not a singleton. Each client that wants to manipulate the CAccount shared state creates a unique instance of the CTeller class. Consequently, a CTeller COM object can live in any apartment, can hold interface pointers, and need prevent only simultaneous access to the CAccount shared state instance.

DECLARE_CLASSFACTORY_AUTO_THREAD and CComClassFactoryAutoThread

The DECLARE_CLASSFACTORY_AUTO_THREAD macro defines CComClassFactoryAutoThread as your object's class factory implementation. This class factory creates each instance in one of a number of apartments. You can use this class only in an out-of-process server. Essentially, this class factory passes every instantiation request to your server's global instance of CAtlAutoThreadModuleT (discussed shortly), which does all the real work:

```
class CComClassFactoryAutoThread :
  ...
  STDMETHODIMP CreateInstance(LPUNKNOWN pUnkOuter, REFIID riid,
    void** ppvObj) {
    ...
    hRes = _pAtlAutoThreadModule.CreateInstance(
      m_pfnCreateInstance, riid, ppvObj);
    ...
  }
  ...
  _ATL_CREATORFUNC* m_pfnCreateInstance;
};
```

Whenever a server contains any classes using the DECLARE_CLASSFACTORY_AUTO_THREAD macro, the server's project.cpp file must declare a global instance of CAtlAutoThreadModule. (The name of the global variable used is immaterial.) The _pAtlAutoThreadModule variable shown earlier in the implementation of CreateInstance points to the global instance of CAtlAutoThreadModule that you declare in your project.cpp file. CAtlAutoThreadModule implements a pool of single-thread apartments (STAs) in an out-of-process server. By default, the server creates four STAs per processor on the system. The class factory forwards each instantiation request, in a round-robin order, to one of the STAs. This allocates the class instances in multiple apartments, which, in certain situations, can provide greater concurrent execution without the complexity of writing a thread-safe object.

The following is an example of a class that uses this class factory:

```
class CMyClass : ..., public CComCoClass< ... > {
public:
    DECLARE_CLASSFACTORY_AUTO_THREAD()

    ...
};
```

`CAtlAutoThreadModuleT` implements the `IAtlAutoThreadModule` interface, which ATL uses to create instances within `CComClassFactoryAutoThread`. You can name the global variable anything you want,[7] so the following declaration works just fine.

```
// project.cpp
CAtlAutoThreadModule g_AtlAutoModule;       // any name will do
```

ATL declares a global variable of type `IAtlAutoThreadModule` in `atlbase.h`.

```
__declspec(selectany)
IAtlAutoThreadModule* _pAtlAutoThreadModule;
```

This global variable is set in the constructor of `CAtlAutoThreadModuleT`, which is the template base class for `CAtlAutoThreadModule`:

```
template <class T,
    class ThreadAllocator = CComSimpleThreadAllocator,
    DWORD dwWait = INFINITE>
class ATL_NO_VTABLE CAtlAutoThreadModuleT
    : public IAtlAutoThreadModule {
public:
    CAtlAutoThreadModuleT(
        int nThreads = T::GetDefaultThreads()) {
        // only one per server
        ATLASSERT(_pAtlAutoThreadModule == NULL);
        _pAtlAutoThreadModule = this;
        m_pApartments = NULL;
        m_nThreads= 0;
    }
    ...
};
```

`CComClassFactoryAutoThread` checks that this `_pAtlAutoThreadModule` global is non-`NULL` before delegating instantiation requests to it. Debug builds issues an

---

[7] However, names with leading underscores are reserved to the compiler and library vendor, so you should avoid using them so you don't run into conflicts with your libraries.

assertion indicating that you have not declared an instance of CAtlAutoThreadModule. Release builds simply return E_FAIL from the CreateInstance call.

CAtlAutoThreadModule uses CComApartment to manage an apartment for each thread in the module. The template parameter defaults to CComSimpleThreadAllocator, which manages thread selection for CComAutoThreadModule.

```
class CComSimpleThreadAllocator {
public:
    CComSimpleThreadAllocator() { m_nThread = 0; }
    int GetThread(CComApartment* /*pApt*/, int nThreads) {
        if (++m_nThread == nThreads) m_nThread = 0;
        return m_nThread;
    }
    int m_nThread;
};
```

CComSimpleThreadAllocator provides one method, GetThread, which selects the thread on which CAtlAutoThreadModuleT creates the next object instance. You can write your own apartment selection algorithm by creating a thread allocator class and specify it as the parameter to CAtlAutoThreadModuleT.

For example, the following code selects the thread (apartment) for the next object instantiation randomly (though it has the downside that I'm using a C runtime library function to get the random number).

```
class CRandomThreadAllocator {
public:
    int GetThread(CComApartment* /*pApt*/, int nThreads) {
        return rand () % nThreads;
    }
};
```

Instead of selecting the default thread allocator by using CAtlAutoThreadModule, you create a new class that derives from CAtlAutoThreadModuleT and specify your new thread-selection class as the template parameter.

```
// project.cpp
class CRandomThreadModule :
public CAtlAutoThreadModuleT< CRandomThreadModule,
    CRandomThreadAllocator>
{
...
};

CRandomThreadModule g_RandomThreadModule; // name doesn't matter
```

Finally! You've seen the object map, which is a fundamental data structure in an ATL server. You've seen the various requirements and options for classes, both createable and noncreateable, for the classes to be listed in the object map. Now let's look at the part of ATL that actually uses the object map: the CAtlModule class, its derived classes, and the global variable of that type called _AtlModule.

The CAtlModule Class

All COM servers need to support registration, class objects, and lifetime management. Each type of server provides its registration, class objects, and lifetime management slightly differently, but the basic required functionality is the same for all types of servers.

ATL defines the CAtlModule base class and three derived classes, along with numerous helper methods that support server registration, class objects, and lifetime management. Each of the three derived classes provides support for a specific COM server type. CAtlDllModuleT provides inproc server functionality; CAtlExeModuleT and CAtlServiceModuleT support local servers and Windows service applications, respectively. Many of the methods in these classes simply iterate over the entries in the object map and ask each class in the map to perform the real work.

When you create an ATL COM server project using the Visual C++ ATL project wizard, it generates relatively boilerplate code that uses functionality in one of the CAtlModule-derived classes to implement the server.

An ATL server contains one global instance of the CAtlModule class, which the ATL project wizard names _AtlModule. The _AtlModule instance also holds state global to the entire server. You can access this via the global pointer _pAtlModule.

The _AtlModule Global Variable

An ATL inproc server uses the CAtlDllModuleT class directly by declaring a global instance of a project-specific module class derived from the CAtlDllModuleT server's project.cpp file. Here's what the module class definition and global variable declaration look like in the wizard-generated code for an inproc server called Math:

```
class CMathModule : public CAtlDllModuleT< CMathModule > {
public:
    DECLARE_LIBID(LIBID_Math)
    DECLARE_REGISTRY_APPID_RESOURCEID(IDR_MATH,
        "{9CB95B71-536A-476a-9244-61363F5C60CA}")
};

CMathModule _AtlModule;
```

The DECLARE_LIBID macro simply sets the m_libid member variable of the CAtlModule base class to the GUID value supplied as the macro parameter. The DECLARE_REGISTRY_APPID_RESOURCEID macro declares an UpdateRegistryAppId method and helper functions for registering the AppId for the server.

The custom module class that the wizard generates provides a place for you to customize the functionality of ATL's module classes. In many places, CAtlDllModuleT (as well as CExeModuleT and CServiceModuleT) downcasts to your custom module class so that a custom method is invoked if one is supplied. For instance, look at the implementation of DllRegisterServer that CAtlDllModuleT provides:

```
HRESULT DllRegisterServer(BOOL bRegTypeLib = TRUE) {
    T* pT = static_cast<T*>(this);
    HRESULT hr = pT->RegisterAppId();
    if (SUCCEEDED(hr))
        hr = pT->RegisterServer(bRegTypeLib);
    return hr;
}
```

Here, if your CMathModule had defined a custom version of RegisterAppId or RegisterServer, those custom versions would be invoked in lieu of the default implementation provided in CAtlDllModuleT.

A local server defines a specialized version of CAtlModule, called CAtlExeModuleT, in the server's project.cpp file:

```
class CMathModule : public CAtlExeModuleT< CMathModule > {
public:
    DECLARE_LIBID(LIBID_Math)
    DECLARE_REGISTRY_APPID_RESOURCEID(IDR_MATH,
        "{9CB95B71-536A-476a-9244-61363F5C60CA}")
};

CMathModule _AtlModule;
```

A service-based server also defines a specialized version of CAtlModule, called CAtlServiceModuleT, in the server's project.cpp file:

```
class CMathModule :
    public CAtlServiceModuleT< CMathModule, IDS_SERVICENAME >
{
public:
    DECLARE_LIBID(LIBID_Math)
    DECLARE_REGISTRY_APPID_RESOURCEID(IDR_MATH,
```

```
        "{9CB95B71-536A-476a-9244-61363F5C60CA}")
};
```

```
CMathModule _AtlModule;
```

The CAtlModule Registration Support

The CAtlModuleT class has extensive support for registration and unregistration of
COM objects and servers.

The RegisterServer and UnregisterServer Methods

The RegisterServer and UnregisterServer methods add or remove standard class
registration information (ProgID, version-independent ProgID, class description,
and threading model) into or from the system Registry. These methods call upon a
global instance of CAtlComModule, which, in turn, uses the AtlComModuleRegis-
terServer and AtlComModuleUnregisterServer helper functions to perform the
actual task.

```
HRESULT RegisterServer(BOOL bRegTypeLib = FALSE,
    const CLSID* pCLSID = NULL);
HRESULT UnregisterServer(BOOL bUnRegTypeLib = FALSE,
    const CLSID* pCLSID= NULL);
```

The RegisterServer method updates the system Registry for a single class
object when the pCLSID parameter is non-NULL. When the parameter is NULL, the
method calls the UpdateRegistry method for all classes listed in the object map.
When the bRegTypeLib parameter is TRUE, the method also registers the type library.

The UnregisterServer method removes the Registry entries for a single class
when the pCLSID parameter is non-NULL. When the parameter is NULL, the method
calls the UpdateRegistry method for all classes listed in the object map. The overloaded method that accepts a bUnRegTypeLib parameter also unregisters the type
library when the parameter is TRUE.

Inproc servers call upon this support from their DllRegisterServer and DllUnregisterServer functions:

```
STDAPI DllRegisterServer(void) {
    return _AtlModule.DllRegisterServer();
}
```

```
STDAPI DllUnregisterServer(void) {
    return _AtlModule.DllUnregisterServer();
```

```
}
```

The calls to CAtlDllModuleT's DllRegisterServer and DllUnregisterServer functions invoke RegisterServer and UnregisterServer on the CAtlModule base class. The calls to RegisterAppId and UnRegisterAppId execute the server's registration script. The DECLARE_REGISTRY_APPID_AND_RESOURCEID macro we supplied in our CAtlModule-derived class defined an UpdateRegistryAppId function that runs the server's registration script.

```cpp
template <class T>
class ATL_NO_VTABLE CAtlDllModuleT : public CAtlModuleT<T> {
public :
    ...
    HRESULT DllRegisterServer(BOOL bRegTypeLib = TRUE) {
        T* pT = static_cast<T*>(this);
        // server script
        HRESULT hr = pT->RegisterAppId();
         if (SUCCEEDED(hr))
            // all class scripts
            hr = pT->RegisterServer(bRegTypeLib);
        return hr;
    }
    HRESULT DllUnregisterServer(BOOL bUnRegTypeLib = TRUE) {
        T* pT = static_cast<T*>(this);
        // all class scripts
        HRESULT hr = pT->UnregisterServer(bUnRegTypeLib);
         if (SUCCEEDED(hr))
             // server script
            hr = pT->UnregisterAppId();
        return hr;
    }
    ...
};
```

With a local server, the ATL wizard generates a WinMain that simply delegates to CAtlExeModuleT::WinMain. This code parses the command line to determine which action (register or unregister) to take and then delegates the work to CAtlModule.

```cpp
bool CAtlExeModuleT< T >::ParseCommandLine(LPCTSTR lpCmdLine,
  HRESULT* pnRetCode) {
  ...

  if (WordCmpI(lpszToken, _T("UnregServer"))==0) {
    *pnRetCode = pT->UnregisterServer(TRUE);
```

```
  if (SUCCEEDED(*pnRetCode))
    *pnRetCode = pT->UnregisterAppId();
  return false;
}

// Register as Local Server
if (WordCmpI(lpszToken, _T("RegServer"))==0) {
  *pnRetCode = pT->RegisterAppId();
  if (SUCCEEDED(*pnRetCode))
    *pnRetCode = pT->RegisterServer(TRUE);
  return false;
}

...

return true;
}
```

The UpdateRegistryFromResource Methods

Notice that a COM server first calls the `RegisterAppId` to register the server-specific entries before registering the class-specific entries. This method calls the `UpdateRegistryAppId` method that our `DECLARE_REGISTRY_APPID_RESOURCEID` macro generates. Ultimately, the real work is delegated to the `UpdateRegistryFromResource` member function.

When you define the preprocessor symbol `_ATL_STATIC_REGISTRY`, the `UpdateRegistryFromResource` method maps to `UpdateRegistryFromResourceS`. When you do not define this preprocessor symbol, the method maps to `UpdateRegistryFromResourceD`. (The S or D stands for Static or Dynamic.) The difference between the two functions is simple: `UpdateRegistryFromResourceS` eventually calls code in `atlbase.h` that updates the Registry. The implementation of `UpdateRegistryFromResourceD`, on the other hand, calls out to the ATL Registrar component in `atl80.dll`[8] to do the registration. As a result, if you don't define `_ATL_STATIC_REG-ISTRY`, you need to distribute `atl80.dll` along with your COM server.[9]

---

[8] Actually, this can be `atl7.dll`, `atl71.dll`, or `atl80.dll`, depending on the version of ATL you're compiling against.

[9] `atl80.dll` is about 93KB in size. Separate versions of the registrar DLL used to exist for Win9x and WinNT, but they appear to have merged in this version of the library. Personally, I recommend using static linking just to avoid the need to distribute another DLL because the size cost is fairly minor.

```
#ifdef _ATL_STATIC_REGISTRY
#define UpdateRegistryFromResource UpdateRegistryFromResourceS
#else
#define UpdateRegistryFromResource UpdateRegistryFromResourceD
#endif


    // Resource-based Registration
#ifdef _ATL_STATIC_REGISTRY
    // Statically linking to Registry Component
    HRESULT WINAPI UpdateRegistryFromResourceS(LPCTSTR lpszRes,
        BOOL bRegister,
        struct _ATL_REGMAP_ENTRY* pMapEntries = NULL);
    HRESULT WINAPI UpdateRegistryFromResourceS(UINT nResID,
        BOOL bRegister,
        struct _ATL_REGMAP_ENTRY* pMapEntries = NULL);
#else
    HRESULT WINAPI UpdateRegistryFromResourceD(LPCTSTR lpszRes,
    BOOL bRegister,
    struct _ATL_REGMAP_ENTRY* pMapEntries = NULL) {
        USES_CONVERSION;
        return UpdateRegistryFromResourceDHelper(T2COLE(lpszRes),
                        bRegister, pMapEntries);
    }
    HRESULT WINAPI UpdateRegistryFromResourceD(UINT nResID,
        BOOL bRegister,
        struct _ATL_REGMAP_ENTRY* pMapEntries = NULL) {
        return UpdateRegistryFromResourceDHelper(
                    (LPCOLESTR)MAKEINTRESOURCE(nResID),
                    bRegister, pMapEntries);
    }
#endif
```

The Type Library Registration Methods

ATL provides a few other registration helper methods:

```
// Registry support (helpers)
HRESULT RegisterTypeLib();
HRESULT RegisterTypeLib(LPCTSTR lpszIndex);
HRESULT UnRegisterTypeLib();
HRESULT UnRegisterTypeLib(LPCTSTR lpszIndex);
```

As you might expect, `RegisterTypeLib` registers the type library contained in your server's resources. `UnRegisterTypeLib` unregisters it, of course. These two methods expect the type library to be present in your server's resources as a custom resource of type `TYPELIB` with integer resource identifier 1. You create such a resource by adding the following line to your server's .rc file.

```
1 TYPELIB "ATLInternals.tlb"
```

You can embed multiple type libraries in a server, although it's an unusual thing to do. You simply need to give them unique integer resource identifiers.

```
1 TYPELIB "ATLInternals.tlb"
2 TYPELIB "ATLInternalsEx.tlb"
```

To register and unregister the second type library, you must call the `Register-TypeLib` or `UnRegisterTypeLib` methods, respectively, and specify a string in the form `"\\N"`, where `N` is the integer index of the `TYPELIB` resource. The following lines register both type libraries from the previous resource script example:

```
_AtlModule.RegisterTypeLib ();
_AtlModule.RegisterTypeLib (_T ("\\2"));
```

CComCoClass Revisited

Earlier in this chapter, you saw how deriving from `CComCoClass` provided your class with a default implementation of a class factory, as well as default support for aggregation.

`CComCoClass` provides aggregation support via inheritance of the `DECLARE_AGGREGATABLE` macro's typedef of `_CreatorClass`. It also provides the default implementation of a class factory via inheritance of the `DECLARE_CLASS_FACTORY` macro's `_ClassFactoryCreatorClass` typedef.

The Error Methods

`CComCoClass` also provides a number of other useful static methods. Six of the methods are overloaded and call `Error`. They set up the COM `Error` object using its `IErrorInfo` interface to provide rich error information to the client. To call `Error`, your object must implement the `ISupportErrorInfo` interface.

When the `hRes` parameter is nonzero, `Error` returns the value of `hRes`. When `hRes` is zero, the first four versions of `Error` return `DISP_E_EXCEPTION`. The remaining two functions return the result of the macro MAKE_HRESULT(3, FACIL-ITY_ITF, nID), creating a custom failure HRESULT.

```
static HRESULT WINAPI
Error(LPCOLESTR lpszDesc, const IID& iid = GUID_NULL,
    HRESULT hRes = 0);

static HRESULT WINAPI
Error(LPCOLESTR lpszDesc, DWORD dwHelpID, LPCOLESTR lpszHelpFile,
    const IID& iid = GUID_NULL, HRESULT hRes = 0);

static HRESULT WINAPI
Error(LPCSTR lpszDesc, const IID& iid = GUID_NULL,
    HRESULT hRes = 0);

static HRESULT WINAPI
Error(LPCSTR lpszDesc, DWORD dwHelpID, LPCSTR lpszHelpFile,
    const IID& iid = GUID_NULL, HRESULT hRes = 0);

static HRESULT WINAPI
Error(UINT nID, const IID& iid = GUID_NULL, HRESULT hRes = 0,
    HINSTANCE hInst = _AtlBaseModule.GetResourceInstance());

static HRESULT WINAPI
Error(UINT nID, DWORD dwHelpID, LPCOLESTR lpszHelpFile,
    const IID& iid = GUID_NULL, HRESULT hRes = 0,
    HINSTANCE hInst = _AtlBaseModule.GetResourceInstance());
```

It might seem odd that ATL includes the Error functionality in CComCoClass instead of in a more widely applicable place, such as CComObjectRootEx. The reason for this placement is that COM error reporting needs a CLSID, and the CLSID is stored in CComCoClass. If you need to generate rich error information when your class isn't derived from CComCoClass, you can always call the ATL helper function AtlReportError. The CComCoClass::Error methods all use this helper function.

```
inline HRESULT WINAPI AtlReportError(const CLSID& clsid,
    UINT nID,
    const IID& iid = GUID_NULL,
    HRESULT hRes = 0,
    HINSTANCE hInst = _AtlBaseModule.GetResourceInstance());

inline HRESULT WINAPI AtlReportError(const CLSID& clsid,
    UINT nID, DWORD dwHelpID, LPCOLESTR lpszHelpFile,
    const IID& iid = GUID_NULL,
```

```
   HRESULT hRes = 0,
   HINSTANCE hInst = _AtlBaseModule.GetResourceInstance());

inline HRESULT WINAPI AtlReportError(const CLSID& clsid,
   LPCSTR lpszDesc,
   DWORD dwHelpID, LPCSTR lpszHelpFile,
   const IID& iid = GUID_NULL,
   HRESULT hRes = 0);

inline HRESULT WINAPI AtlReportError(const CLSID& clsid,
   LPCSTR lpszDesc,
   const IID& iid = GUID_NULL, HRESULT hRes = 0);

inline HRESULT WINAPI AtlReportError(const CLSID& clsid,
   LPCOLESTR lpszDesc,
   const IID& iid = GUID_NULL, HRESULT hRes = 0);

inline HRESULT WINAPI AtlReportError(const CLSID& clsid,
   LPCOLESTR lpszDesc, DWORD dwHelpID, LPCOLESTR lpszHelpFile,
   const IID& iid = GUID_NULL, HRESULT hRes = 0);
```

The Instantiation Methods

CComCoClass also provides two useful overloaded CreateInstance methods that create an instance of your class, one for creating an aggregated instance of your class and one that creates a nonaggregated instance:

```
template <class Q>
static HRESULT CreateInstance(IUnknown* punkOuter, Q** pp) {
  return T::_CreatorClass::CreateInstance(punkOuter, __uuidof(Q),
    (void**) pp);
}

template <class Q>
static HRESULT CreateInstance(Q** pp) {
  return T::_CreatorClass::CreateInstance(NULL, __uuidof(Q),
    (void**) pp);
}
```

You use these two methods like this.

```
ISpeaker* pSpeaker;
// Creates non-aggregated instance
HRESULT hr = CDemagogue::CreateInstance (&pSpeaker);
```

```
// Creates aggregated instance (assuming the class supports aggregation
HRESULT hr = CDemagogue::CreateInstance (punkOuter, &pSpeaker);
```

Note that the use of the __uuidof operator in the template functions means that you do not have to specify the interface ID for the interface that you want on the newly instantiated object. The compiler gets the ID from the type of the interface pointer variable you pass as an argument to the CreateInstance method.

ATL and the C Runtime Library

By default, ATL projects link with the C runtime library (CRT) in both debug and release configurations. Although linking with the CRT increases the size of each ATL server, the CRT provides useful functionality for memory management, string manipulation, and exception handling. Additionally, the CRT is responsible for calling the constructors of global objects when an executable is loaded. As a result, constructing anything but the most simplistic of projects without such important CRT functionality is impractical.

In the spirit of allowing developers to minimize the memory footprint of their COM servers, ATL provides a subset of CRT functionality that can be used in place of the CRT itself. By defining the preprocessor symbol _ATL_MIN_CRT, ATL projects will not link with the CRT. You can define this symbol from the project properties, as shown in Figure 5.2.

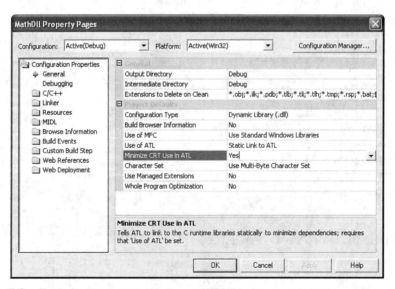

Figure 5.2 Defining _ATL_MIN_CRT in an ATL server

Setting Minimize CRT Use in ATL causes _ATL_MIN_CRT to be defined and keeps your server from linking with the CRT. It's important to realize that ATL does not make available all the functions that the CRT provides when this option is in use. If you happen to use a function that requires the CRT when _ATL_MIN_CRT is defined, you'll get the following somewhat cryptic linker error:

```
LIBCMT.LIB(crt0.obj) : error LNK2001:
unresolved external symbol _main
```

In ATL 3 and earlier, using _ATL_MIN_CRT left out one very important feature of the CRT: static and global object initialization. Global and static objects would *not* have their constructors or destructors called. Thankfully, ATL 7 and later provide an implementation of this feature even without CRT support. Inproc ATL servers include an implementation of _DllMainCRTStartup that invokes global constructors and destructors. ATL itself relies upon global constructors and destructors in many key places throughout the framework. For instance, in the discussion of ObjectMain presented earlier in this chapter, I told you that ATL invokes Object-Main when a server initializes without explaining precisely how this was done. With global constructors available both with and without _ATL_MIN_CRT defined, ATL is perfectly safe to invoke the ObjectMain methods of each class in the object map by using the constructor of the global CAtlModule instance:

```cpp
template <class T>
class ATL_NO_VTABLE CAtlDllModuleT : public CAtlModuleT<T> {
public :
    CAtlDllModuleT() {
        _AtlComModule.ExecuteObjectMain(true);
    }

    ~CAtlDllModuleT() {
        _AtlComModule.ExecuteObjectMain(false);
    }
    ...
}
```

Summary

The object map is the primary data table that the CAtlModule-derived _AtlModule object uses to register and unregister the classes in the server. CAtlModule provides numerous helper methods you can use to register and unregister your server, the classes in the server, and the component categories in the classes.

An ATL server creates a class factory for a class, as needed, using the class-creator function entry in the object map. This class factory then creates instances of the class using the instance-creator function entry in the object map. Typically, you inherit a default specification for the implementation of these two creator classes when you derive your class from CComCoClass. However, with the appropriate macro entries in your class, you can override these defaults and provide a custom class factory and custom instance creator function.

CComCoClass has some useful utility functions for reporting rich errors to a client using the COM ErrorInfo protocol. The class also has convenient instantiation methods that create an instance and query for the proper interface based on the type of the provided interface pointer variable.

CHAPTER
6 | Interface Maps

Chapter 4, "Objects in ATL," discussed how ATL implements IUnknown, but it covered only AddRef and Release completely. This chapter takes a look first at the requirements that COM makes on an object's implementation of QueryInterface and then at how ATL supports those requirements while still providing flexibility and extensibility.

Recall: COM Identity

From a client perspective, the rules of AddRef and Release are fairly stringent. Unless the client is careful about their use, objects can go away before expected or can stay around too long. However, the object is allowed to implement AddRef and Release in any number of ways, depending on how it wants to manage its own lifetime—for example, as a heap-based, stack-based, or cached object.

On the other hand, QueryInterface is easy to get right on the client side. Any client can ask an object if it supports any other functionality with a simple call. However, clients expect certain relationships between the interfaces on a COM object. These expectations form the laws of COM identity.

The Laws of COM Identity

The laws of COM identity say the following things about how an object must expose its interfaces via QueryInterface:

- A client must be capable of getting directly to any interface implemented by the object via QueryInterface.
- An object's interfaces must be static throughout its lifetime.
- QueryInterface for IUnknown must always succeed and must always return the same pointer value.

Direct Access to All Interfaces

The COM Specification states that an implementation of QueryInterface must be "reflexive, symmetric, and transitive." This means that, given an interface, a client must be capable of using an interface to get directly to any interface implemented on the object, including the interface the client is using to perform the query. These relationships are mandated to maintain an object's identity in the face of multiple references to the same object. If these relationships are not upheld, a client could find itself with some code that doesn't work just because it asked for the interfaces in the wrong order. With a properly implemented `QueryInterface`, query order does not matter.

Static Types

Each object can decide for itself whether it wants to expose an interface via `Query-Interface`, regardless of the class to which it belongs. However, after it has been asked and has answered either "Yes, I support that interface" or "No, I don't support that interface," it must stick to that answer. The reason for this is simple: After an object answers the query, it may never be asked again. For example, a client can pass a resultant interface pointer to another client, which never has to ask the object at all.

The potential for clients "talking among themselves" means that an object cannot use `QueryInterface` to make client-specific decisions—for example, those based on security constraints. The object also cannot use `QueryInterface` to make context decisions that could change during the life of an object, such as time of day. If a client caches an interface pointer returned when the context is favorable, it might not ask again when the context has changed.

An Object's Apartment-Specific Identifier

The remoting layer of COM uses the pointer returned when querying for `IUnknown` as an object's unique identifier in that apartment. Clients can also compare `IUnknown*`s as an identity test:

```
bool AreEqualObjects(IUnknown* punk1, IUnknown* punk2) {
  if( punk1 == null && punk2 == null ) return true;
  if( !punk1 || !punk2 ) return false;
  IUnknown* punka = 0; punk1->QueryInterface(IID_IUnknown,
    (void**)&punka);
  IUnknown* punkb = 0; punk2->QueryInterface(IID_IUnknown,
    (void**)&punkb);
  bool b = (punka == punkb);
  punka->Release(); punkb->Release();
  return b;
}
```

In fact, the ATL smart pointer classes have a method called `IsEqualObject` for performing just this comparison:

```
STDMETHODIMP CBall::SetPlaySurface(IRollSurface* prsNew) {
  if( m_sprs.IsEqualObject(prsNew) ) return S_OK;
  ...
}
```

However, although COM dictates that the pointer value of IUnknown must always be the same, it places no such restrictions on any other interface. This particular loophole leads to such techniques as tear-off interfaces, discussed further in this chapter.

Nothing Else

As long as these three laws are upheld, an implementation of QueryInterface can be developed using scenes from your most vivid fever dreams. Frankly, I doubt you'll be able to come up with any techniques wackier than those already known, as I present during the rest of this chapter. However, if you do, ATL's implementation of QueryInterface is fully extensible, as you'll see.

Table-Driven QueryInterface

The Raw Interface Map

ATL's implementation of QueryInterface is called InternalQueryInterface and is provided as a static member function of CComObjectRootBase (shown here with debugging extensions removed):

```
static HRESULT WINAPI
CComObjectRootBase::InternalQueryInterface(
  void*                 pThis,
  const _ATL_INTMAP_ENTRY* pEntries,
  REFIID                iid,
  void**                ppvObject)
{
    // First entry in the com map should be a simple map entry
    ATLASSERT(pEntries->pFunc == _ATL_SIMPLEMAPENTRY);
    HRESULT hRes = AtlInternalQueryInterface(pThis, pEntries,
        iid, ppvObject);
    return hRes;
}
```

I show you the implementation of the internal function, AtlInternalQueryInterface, later. First, let's discuss the ATL_INTMAP_ENTRY structure, an array of which is passed to InternalQueryInterface:

```
struct _ATL_INTMAP_ENTRY {
    const IID* piid;        // the interface id (IID)
    DWORD_PTR dw;
    _ATL_CREATORARGFUNC* pFunc; //NULL:end, 1:offset, n:ptr
};
```

Each entry provides a pointer to an interface identifier, a pointer to a function to retrieve the requested interface, and a user-defined parameter to pass to the function. Functions that fit into this table must have signatures defined by the _ATL_CREATORARGFUNC typedef:

```
typedef HRESULT (WINAPI _ATL_CREATORARGFUNC)(
    void* pv,           // Object's this pointer
    REFIID riid,        // IID of requested interface
    LPVOID* ppv,        // Storage for returned interface pointer
    DWORD_PTR dw);      // dw from the interface map entry
```

The job of the interface map function is to take the object's this pointer, the interface that the client is requesting, and the dw argument, and to return the appropriate interface pointer in the ppv argument. The function is free to do whatever it likes, within the laws of COM identity, to perform this magic. For example, the following function assumes that the dw member is the offset of the vptr from the this pointer—that is, this function assumes that we're using multiple inheritance (MI) to implement the interface:

```
HRESULT WINAPI _MI(void* pvThis, REFIID riid, LPVOID* ppv,
    DWORD dw) {
    *ppv = (BYTE*)pvThis + dw;
    reinterpret_cast<IUnknown*>(*ppv)->AddRef();
    return S_OK;
}
```

To fill in the _ATL_INTMAP_ENTRY for use with this function, we need to be able to calculate the offset of a vptr from the base, preferably at compile time. To help with this chore, ATL provides an interesting macro:

```
#define _ATL_PACKING 8
#define offsetofclass(base, derived) \
    ((DWORD_PTR)(static_cast<base*>((derived*)_ATL_PACKING))- \
    _ATL_PACKING)
```

The offsetofclass macro makes it look like we're asking the compiler to dereference a pointer with the value 8, which is not such a great value for a pointer.[1] Instead, we're asking the compiler to imagine a pointer to an object and to calculate the difference between that and a member inside that object, such as a vptr associated with a specific base class. The offsetofclass macro performs the same offset calculation the compiler does whenever it needs to perform a static_cast to a base class. Using offsetofclass enables us to fill an entry in an interface map like this:

```
class CBeachBall :
  public CComObjectRootEx<CComSingleThreadModel>,
  public ISphere,
  public IRollableObject,
  public IPlaything {
public:
const static _ATL_INTMAP_ENTRY* WINAPI
_GetEntries() {
  static const _ATL_INTMAP_ENTRY _entries[] = {
  { &IID_IUnknown, offsetofclass(ISphere, CBeachBall),
    _ATL_SIMPLEMAPENTRY },
  { &IID_ISphere, offsetofclass(ISphere, CBeachBall), _MI },
  { &IID_IRollableObject,  offsetofclass(IRollableObject,
    CBeachBall), _MI },
  { &IID_IPlaything, offsetofclass(IPlaything, CBeachBall),
    _MI },
  };
return _entries;
};

HRESULT _InternalQueryInterface(REFIID iid, void** ppvObject) {
  return InternalQueryInterface(this, _GetEntries(), iid,
    ppvObject);
}
...
};
```

Besides the population of the interface map, you can see a couple interesting things in this code snippet. First, the _InternalQueryInterface function calls _GetEntries to retrieve the static interface map and forwards it to the Internal-QueryInterface static member function in CComObjectRootBase. CComObject et al requires the _InternalQueryInterface function to implement QueryInterface.

---

[1] Microsoft didn't invent this particular oddity. The Standard C Runtime comes with a macro very much like offsetofclass, called offsetof.

Second, notice that `IUnknown` is the initial entry in the list and uses `_ATL_SIM-PLEMAPENTRY` instead of `_MI`. As discussed in Chapter 4, "Objects in ATL," the first entry is the one used for `IUnknown` and is required to be a *simple entry*. A simple entry is a special case that indicates that the interface is being exposed using multiple inheritance and that an offset is all that is needed to calculate the requested interface pointer. `_ATL_SIMPLEMAPENTRY` is a special value used in the `pFunc` field of the `_ATL_INTMAP_ENTRY` structure to indicate this case:

```
#define _ATL_SIMPLEMAPENTRY ((ATL::_ATL_CREATORARGFUNC*)1)
```

When `AtlInternalQueryInterface` encounters this special value, it knows how to perform the offset calculation just like the example function, `_MI`. Because `_ATL_SIMPLEMAPENTRY` completely replaces the need for a function that performs the offset calculation, ATL provides no interface map functions like `_MI`, although it provides others, as I discuss later.

Convenience Macros

You might enjoy writing the required `_InternalQueryInterface` and `_GetEntries` methods, as well as the `GetUnknown` method discussed in Chapter 4, but I do not. To write these functions and begin the static definition of the interface map, ATL provides `BEGIN_COM_MAP`:

```
#define BEGIN_COM_MAP(x) public: \
    typedef x _ComMapClass; \
    ...
    IUnknown* _GetRawUnknown()  { \
        ATLASSERT(_GetEntries()[0].pFunc == \
            _ATL_SIMPLEMAPENTRY); \
        return (IUnknown*)((INT_PTR)this+_GetEntries()->dw); \
    } \
    _ATL_DECLARE_GET_UNKNOWN(x) \
    HRESULT _InternalQueryInterface(REFIID iid, \
        void** ppvObject) { \
        return InternalQueryInterface(this, _GetEntries(), \
        iid, ppvObject); } \
    const static ATL::_ATL_INTMAP_ENTRY* WINAPI _GetEntries() { \
    static const ATL::_ATL_INTMAP_ENTRY _entries[] = { \
        DEBUG_QI_ENTRY(x)
```

To zero-terminate the interface map and round out the `_GetEntries` implementation, ATL provides `END_COM_MAP`:

```
#define END_COM_MAP() \
    __if_exists(_GetAttrEntries) {{NULL, \
        (DWORD_PTR)_GetAttrEntries, _ChainAttr }, }\
    {NULL, 0, 0}}; return _entries;} \
    virtual ULONG STDMETHODCALLTYPE AddRef( void) = 0; \
    virtual ULONG STDMETHODCALLTYPE Release( void) = 0; \
    STDMETHOD(QueryInterface)(REFIID, void**) = 0;
```

END_COM_MAP also provides another set of pure virtual member function definitions for QueryInterface, AddRef, and Release. This makes calls to IUnknown member functions unambiguous while calling them in the member functions of your ATL-based classes. We discuss the _GetAttrEntries function later in this chapter when we examine how ATL attributes can be used to declare an object's supported interfaces.

To populate each entry in the interface map, ATL provides a set of macros that begin with the COM_INTERFACE_ENTRY prefix. The simplest and most useful is COM_INTERFACE_ENTRY itself:

```
#define COM_INTERFACE_ENTRY(x)\
    {&_ATL_IIDOF(x), \
    offsetofclass(x, _ComMapClass), \
    _ATL_SIMPLEMAPENTRY},
```

Notice the use of _ComMapClass as the name of the class associated with the static interface map. BEGIN_COM_MAP provides this type. The _ATL_IIDOF macro, on the other hand, is ATL's way of turning an interface type name into the corresponding GUID. Based on the presence or absence of the _ATL_NO_UUIDOF symbol, ATL either uses the VC++-specific __uuidof operator[2] or uses the C preprocessor's token-pasting operator:

```
#ifndef _ATL_NO_UUIDOF
#define _ATL_IIDOF(x) __uuidof(x)
#else
#define _ATL_IIDOF(x) IID_##x
#endif
```

Using these macros, the interface map can be defined much more simply than in the previous example:

---

[2] The __declspec(uuid()) and __uuidof operators are discussed in Chapter 4, "Objects in ATL."

```
class CBeachBall :
  public CComObjectRootEx<CBeachBall>,
  public ISphere,
  public IRollableObject,
  public IPlaything {
public:
BEGIN_COM_MAP(CBeachBall)
  COM_INTERFACE_ENTRY(ISphere)
  COM_INTERFACE_ENTRY(IRollableObject)
  COM_INTERFACE_ENTRY(IPlaything)
END_COM_MAP()
  ...
};
```

AtlInternalQueryInterface

Checking for IUnknown

`InternalQueryInterface` delegates to a global function, `AtlInternalQueryInter-face`, to provide its implementation. Before walking the table of interface entries, `AtlInternalQueryInterface` checks the IID of the request. If `IUnknown` is requested, it pulls the first entry from the table and hands it back immediately, without walking the rest of the table. This is a welcome optimization, but it's more than that: It's absolutely necessary that `IUnknown` not be calculated by calling a function. Functions can fail and functions can return different values for the same interface identifier, both of which violate the laws of COM identity. The practical meaning for your classes is that the first entry must always be a simple one. Luckily, ATL is laden with assertions to this affect, so as long as you test your implementations at least once in debug mode before you ship them to your customers, you should be safe (on this note, anyway).

Walking the Table

At each entry in the table, a decision is made based on whether the `piid` member, a pointer to the interface identifier for that entry, is `NULL`. If it is not `NULL`, the IID of the entry is compared with the IID of the request. If a match is found, the function `pFunc` references are called and the result is returned to the client. If there is no match, the search advances to the next entry in the table.

On the other hand, if the `piid` member is `NULL`, no matter what the IID of the request is, the `pFunc` is called. If the result is `S_OK`, the result is returned to the client. Otherwise, the search continues with the next entry. This behavior is used for any of the `COM_INTERFACE_ENTRY_XXX_BLIND` macros, such as `COM_INTERFACE_ENTRY_AGGRE-GATE_BLIND`.

Implementation

The following is the implementation of `AtlInternalQueryInterface`:

```
ATLINLINE ATLAPI AtlInternalQueryInterface(
    void* pThis,
    const _ATL_INTMAP_ENTRY* pEntries,
    REFIID iid,
    void** ppvObject)
{
    ATLASSERT(pThis != NULL);
    ATLASSERT(pEntries!= NULL);

    if(pThis == NULL || pEntries == NULL)
        return E_INVALIDARG ;

    // First entry in the com map should be a simple map entry
    ATLASSERT(pEntries->pFunc == _ATL_SIMPLEMAPENTRY);
    if (ppvObject == NULL)
        return E_POINTER;
    *ppvObject = NULL;
    if (InlineIsEqualUnknown(iid)) { // use first interface
        IUnknown* pUnk=(IUnknown*)((INT_PTR)pThis+pEntries->dw);
        pUnk->AddRef();
        *ppvObject = pUnk;
        return S_OK;
    }
    while (pEntries->pFunc != NULL) {
        BOOL bBlind = (pEntries->piid == NULL);
        if (bBlind || InlineIsEqualGUID(*(pEntries->piid), iid)) {
            if (pEntries->pFunc == _ATL_SIMPLEMAPENTRY) { //offset
                ATLASSERT(!bBlind);
                IUnknown* pUnk = (IUnknown*)((INT_PTR)
                    pThis+pEntries->dw);
                pUnk->AddRef();
                *ppvObject = pUnk;
                return S_OK;
            }
            else { //actual function call
                HRESULT hRes = pEntries->pFunc(pThis,
                    iid, ppvObject, pEntries->dw);
                if (hRes == S_OK || (!bBlind && FAILED(hRes)))
                    return hRes;
            }
```

```
            }
        pEntries++;
        }
    return E_NOINTERFACE;
}
```

Multiple Inheritance

To support multiple inheritance (MI) of interfaces, ATL provides four separate interface entry macros. Two are for *straight casts* and two are for *branching casts*. A straight cast is a `static_cast` that the compiler needs no extra information to perform—that is, there are no ambiguities. On the other hand, a branching cast is used when a class has several base classes that all derive from the same base class themselves. Because a straight cast to the common base class would be ambiguous, the compiler needs the inheritance branch to follow to resolve the ambiguity.

Straight Casting

COM_INTERFACE_ENTRY and COM_INTERFACE_ENTRY_IID

As I mentioned, `COM_INTERFACE_ENTRY` is the one you'll use most of the time. Its close cousin is `COM_INTERFACE_ENTRY_IID`:

```
#define COM_INTERFACE_ENTRY_IID(iid, x) \
    { &iid, offsetofclass(x, _ComMapClass), _ATL_SIMPLEMAPENTRY},
```

This macro enables you to specify the IID separately from the name of the interface. The classic use of this macro is to avoid ambiguity. Imagine that you've got two interfaces that derive from the same base interface:

```
interface IGlobe : ISphere {};
interface IPlanet : ISphere {};
```

If you've got a class that derives from both of these interfaces, the compiler won't know which base class to cast to if you use `COM_INTERFACE_ENTRY` for `ISphere`:

```
class CDesktopGlobe :
    public CComObjectRootEx<CDesktopGlobe>,
    public IGlobe,
    public IPlanet {
public:
    ...
```

```
BEGIN_COM_MAP(CDesktopGlobe)
  COM_INTERFACE_ENTRY(ISphere) // ambiguous
  COM_INTERFACE_ENTRY(IGlobe)
  COM_INTERFACE_ENTRY(IPlanet)
END_COM_MAP()
  // ISphere methods
  ...
  // IGlobe methods
  ...
  // IPlanet methods
  ...
};
```

The problem is more easily seen when you look at the inheritance hierarchy in Figure 6.1.

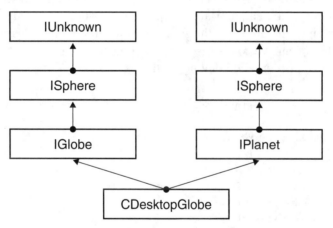

Figure 6.1.   CDesktopGlobe inheritance hierarchy

Figure 6.1 shows two interfaces that CDesktopGlobe has inherited from more than once, IUnknown and ISphere. IUnknown is not a problem because ATL handles it specially by choosing the first entry in the interface map (as discussed earlier). ISphere is a problem, though, because there are two of them, IGlobe and IPlanet. Each base interface has a separate vptr that points to a separate vtbl. Even though we've got a shared implementation of all the methods of ISphere and, therefore, duplicate entries in both the IGlobe and the IPlanet vtbls, the compiler needs us to pick one. COM_INTERFACE_ENTRY_IID enables us to resolve this ambiguity:

```
class CDesktopGlobe :
  public CComObjectRootEx<CDesktopGlobe>,
  public IGlobe,
```

```
  public IPlanet {
public:
...
BEGIN_COM_MAP(CDesktopGlobe)
  COM_INTERFACE_ENTRY_IID(IID_ISphere, IGlobe) // unambiguous
  COM_INTERFACE_ENTRY(IGlobe)
  COM_INTERFACE_ENTRY(IPlanet)
END_COM_MAP()
...
};
```

In this case, because we have shared implementations of the ISphere methods
in our implementation of IGlobe and IPlanet, it doesn't really matter which one we
hand out. Sometimes it matters very much. COM_INTERFACE_ENTRY_IID is often used
when exposing multiple dual interfaces, each of which derives from IDispatch.
Using IDispatchImpl, we provide base class implementations of IDispatch that are
different based on the dual interface we're implementing. In fact, any time you've
got multiple implementations of the same interface in the base classes, you must
decide which implementation is the "default." Imagine another example of a base
class interface implementation that has nothing to do with scripting:

```
template <typename Base> class ISphereImpl : public Base {...};
```

Using ISphereImpl looks like this:

```
class CDesktopGlobe :
  public CComObjectRootEx<CDesktopGlobe>,
  public ISphereImpl<IGlobe>,
  public ISphereImpl<IPlanet> {
public:
...
BEGIN_COM_MAP(CDesktopGlobe)
  COM_INTERFACE_ENTRY_IID(IID_ISphere, IGlobe) // Default ISphere
  COM_INTERFACE_ENTRY(IGlobe)
  COM_INTERFACE_ENTRY(IPlanet)
END_COM_MAP()
...
};
```

Here's the problem: If the client queries for IGlobe (or ISphere) and calls
ISphere methods, it gets different behavior than if it were to query for IPlanet and
call ISphere methods. Now the client has just the kind of order-of-query problem
that the laws of COM identity were built to prohibit. Multiple implementations of

the same base interface clearly violate the spirit, if not the letter, of the laws of COM identity.

Branch Casting

COM_INTERFACE_ENTRY2 and COM_INTERFACE_ENTRY2_IID

Both `COM_INTERFACE_ENTRY2` and `COM_INTERFACE_ENTRY2_IID` are simple entries meant for use with MI:

```
#define COM_INTERFACE_ENTRY2(x, x2)\
  { &_ATL_IIDOF(x),\
    reinterpret_cast<DWORD_PTR>( \
      static_cast<x*>( \
        static_cast<x2*>( \
          reinterpret_cast<_ComMapClass*>(8))))-8, \
    _ATL_SIMPLEMAPENTRY},

#define COM_INTERFACE_ENTRY2_IID(iid, x, x2)\
  { &iid,\
    reinterpret_cast<DWORD_PTR>( \
      static_cast<x*>( \
        static_cast<x2*>( \
          reinterpret_cast<_ComMapClass*>(8))))-8, \
    _ATL_SIMPLEMAPENTRY},
```

`COM_INTERFACE_ENTRY2` is much like `COM_INTERFACE_ENTRY_IID` because it enables you to resolve the problem of multiple bases:

```
class CDesktopGlobe :
  public CComObjectRootEx<CDesktopGlobe>,
  public IGlobe,
  public IPlanet {
public:
...
BEGIN_COM_MAP(CDesktopGlobe)
  COM_INTERFACE_ENTRY2(ISphere, IGlobe) // Use the IGlobal branch
  COM_INTERFACE_ENTRY(IGlobe)
  COM_INTERFACE_ENTRY(IPlanet)
END_COM_MAP()
...
};
```

This macro performs its magic by enabling you to specify two things, the interface to expose (such as `ISphere`) and the branch of the inheritance hierarchy to follow to get to the implementation of that interface (such as IGlobe). This macro is slightly different from COM_INTERFACE_ENTRY_IID, in that the interface is specified by name instead of by IID. If you want to be very explicit about both, use COM_INTERFACE_ENTRY2_IID:

```
class CDesktopGlobe :
  public CComObjectRootEx<CDesktopGlobe>,
  public IGlobe,
  public IPlanet {
public:
...
BEGIN_COM_MAP(CDesktopGlobe)
  COM_INTERFACE_ENTRY2_IID(&IID_ISphere, ISphere, IGlobe)
  COM_INTERFACE_ENTRY(IGlobe)
  COM_INTERFACE_ENTRY(IPlanet)
END_COM_MAP()
...
};
```

COM_INTERFACE_ENTRY2[_IID] provides no extra functionality beyond what COM_INTERFACE_ENTRY[_IID] provides, so I tend to always use the latter.

Handling Name Conflicts

One of the problems with MI is name collisions. Imagine the following interfaces:

```
interface ICowboy : IUnknown {
    HRESULT Draw();
};

interface IArtist : IUnknown {
    HRESULT Draw();
};
```

Because both Draw methods have the same signature, using straight MI requires a single shared implementation:

```
// Ace Powell was a cowboy/artist who lived in the western US
// from 1912 to his death in 1978. I'd like to thank Tim Ewald
// for this fabulous example, which I have used to death
// for years.
class CAcePowell :
    public CComObjectRootEx<CComSingleThreadModel>,
    public ICowboy,
    public IArtist
```

```
{
public:
BEGIN_COM_MAP(CAcePowell)
  COM_INTERFACE_ENTRY(ICowboy)
  COM_INTERFACE_ENTRY(IArtist)
END_COM_MAP()
...
  STDMETHODIMP Draw() { /* Act as a cowboy or an artist? */ }
};
```

The implied meaning of Draw is very different for an artist than it is for a cowboy, so we'd like to be able to provide two Draw implementations. We can deal with this predicament in a couple ways. The first solution uses a Microsoft-specific extension to the C++ language that allows a very intuitive syntax for disambiguating the Draw implementation. It's employed as follows:

```
class CAcePowell :
    public CComObjectRootEx<CComSingleThreadModel>,
    public ICowboy,
    public IArtist {
public:
BEGIN_COM_MAP(CAcePowell)
  COM_INTERFACE_ENTRY(ICowboy)
  COM_INTERFACE_ENTRY(IArtist)
END_COM_MAP()
...
  STDMETHODIMP IArtist::Draw() {
    /* Draw like an artist */
    return S_OK;
  }

  STDMETHODIMP ICowboy::Draw() {
    /* Draw like a cowboy */
    return S_OK;
  }
};
```

By decorating the method with the name of the interface, the compiler can figure out which Draw method you are implementing. However, there is an important limitation with this technique imposed by what I consider a bug in the compiler: You must place the body of these methods in the class declaration in the header file. If you try to just put a declaration in the header file and put the body in the CPP file, it won't compile.

This syntax is not Standard C++, so don't expect to use this with non-Microsoft compilers (not that much of the rest of this book would be useful on non-Microsoft compilers anyway). If you're implementing clashing methods from multiple interfaces, you might want to turn to alternative technique to address the problem of name collision. I call this technique, long known to the C++ community, *forwarding shims*.[3]

Forwarding shims rely upon the fact that although we can't distinguish methods in the most derived class, we can certainly distinguish the methods in individual base classes:

```
struct _IArtist : public IArtist {
  STDMETHODIMP Draw() { return ArtistDraw(); }
  STDMETHOD(ArtistDraw)() =0;
};

struct _ICowboy : public ICowboy {
  STDMETHODIMP Draw() { return CowboyDraw(); }
  STDMETHOD(CowboyDraw)() =0;
};
```

Both _IArtist and _ICowboy are shim classes that implement the method with the conflicting name and forward to another pure virtual member function with a unique name. Because both shims derive from the interface in question, the interfaces IArtist and ICowboy can still appear in the interface map without difficulty:

```
class CAcePowell :
    public CComObjectRootEx<CComSingleThreadModel>,
    public _ICowboy,
    public _IArtist {
public:
BEGIN_COM_MAP(CAcePowell)
  COM_INTERFACE_ENTRY(ICowboy)
  COM_INTERFACE_ENTRY(IArtist)
END_COM_MAP()
...
  STDMETHODIMP ArtistDraw();
  STDMETHODIMP CowboyDraw();
};
```

This trick fills the vtbls for IArtist and ICowboy with _IArtist::Draw and _ICowboy::Draw. These functions, in turn, forward to the more derived class's

---

[3] Tim Ewald showed me this technique originally, and Jim Springfield made me see its relevance to ATL.

implementation of ArtistDraw and CowboyDraw. The forwarding shims remove the name conflict at the cost of an extra vtable per shim class, an extra entry per method per vtable, and an extra virtual function invocation per call. If this extra cost bothers you, remove it using the standard ATL tricks[4]:

```
template <typename Deriving>
struct ATL_NO_VTABLE _IArtist : public IArtist {
  STDMETHODIMP Draw() {
    return static_cast<Deriving*>(this)->ArtistDraw();
  }
};

template <typename Deriving>
struct ATL_NO_VTABLE _ICowboy : public ICowboy {
  STDMETHODIMP Draw() {
    return static_cast<Deriving*>(this)->CowboyDraw();
  }
};

class ATL_NO_VTABLE CAcePowell :
    public CComObjectRootEx<CComSingleThreadModel>,
    public _ICowboy<CAcePowell>,
    public _IArtist<CAcePowell> {
public:
BEGIN_COM_MAP(CAcePowell)
  COM_INTERFACE_ENTRY(ICowboy)
  COM_INTERFACE_ENTRY(IArtist)
END_COM_MAP()
...
  HRESULT ArtistDraw();
  HRESULT CowboyDraw();
};
```

Don't Go Off Half-Cocked. . .

You might think it would be enough to change one of the names by using only one forwarding shim:

```
template <typename Deriving>
struct ATL_NO_VTABLE _ICowboy : public ICowboy {
```

---

[4] Don Box suggested the final efficiency trick, the use of ATL_NO_VTABLE.

```
    STDMETHODIMP Draw() {
      return static_cast<Deriving*>(this)->CowboyDraw();
    }
};

class ATL_NO_VTABLE CAcePowell :
    public CComObjectRootEx<CComSingleThreadModel>,
    public _ICowboy<CAcePowell>,
    public IArtist {
public:
BEGIN_COM_MAP(CAcePowell)
  COM_INTERFACE_ENTRY(ICowboy)
  COM_INTERFACE_ENTRY(IArtist)
END_COM_MAP()
...
    HRESULT Draw();        // Use for both IArtist::Draw and
                           // ICowboy::Draw
    HRESULT CowboyDraw(); // Never called!
};
```

Don't be tempted to try this. Remember that forwarding shims depend on over-riding the behavior for the same member function name in the base classes. If you provide an implementation of the function in question with the same name as the function you're implementing in the forwarding shim in the base, the forwarding shim function will never be called. By implementing one of the functions in the deriving class, you've effectively provided an implementation of both, putting you right back where you were in the first place.

Interface Coloring

In the same "sneaky C++ trick" way that forwarding shims let you fill the appropriate vtbl entries even if the compiler won't cooperate, ATL supports another technique called *interface coloring*. Interface coloring is based on the idea that two classes can be *layout compatible* but not *type compatible*. Two classes are layout compatible if they have the same vtbl structure: The functions must be in exactly the same order, and the parameters must be exactly the same. The names, however, may be different. For example, the following two classes are layout compatible because they each result in a vtbl with the same number of methods, and every method at the same offset has the same signature:

```
struct ISphere : IUnknown {
  STDMETHOD(Rotate)(long nDegrees, long* pnOrientation) =0;
  STDMETHOD(Twirl)(long nVelocity) =0;
```

```
};

struct IRedSphere {
  // Colored IUnknown methods
  STDMETHOD(RedQueryInterface)( REFIID riid, void** ppv) =0;
  STDMETHOD_(ULONG, RedAddRef)() =0;
  STDMETHOD_(ULONG, RedRelease)() =0;

  // Uncolored ISphere methods
  STDMETHOD(Rotate)(long nDegrees, long* pnOrientation) =0;
  STDMETHOD(Twirl)(long nVelocity) =0;
};
```

However, because `IRedSphere` does not derive from `ISphere`, `IRedSphere` is not type compatible: The compiler won't let you pass `IRedSphere` where `ISphere` is expected (without coercion). Cloning the layout of an interface is known as *interface coloring*. The layout-compatible interface is said to be *colored* because it is identical to the original, except for the names; that feature is not important to the runtime behavior of your object, just as a color is unimportant to the runtime behavior of your car. The names are used at compile time, though, and enable you to implement multiple versions of the same interface:

```
class CDesktopGlobe :
  public CComObjectRootEx<CComSingleThreadModel>,
  public IRedSphere,
  public IGlobe,
  public IPlanet {
public:
  ...
BEGIN_COM_MAP(CDesktopGlobe)
  // Expose IRedShere when ISphere is requested
  COM_INTERFACE_ENTRY_IID(IID_ISphere, IRedSphere)
  COM_INTERFACE_ENTRY(IGlobe)
  COM_INTERFACE_ENTRY(IPlanet)
END_COM_MAP()
  ...
  // Colored method implementations
  STDMETHODIMP RedQueryInterface(REFIID riid, void** ppv)
  { return GetUnknown()->QueryInterface(riid, ppv); }

  STDMETHODIMP_(ULONG) RedAddRef() {
    _ThreadModel::Increment(&m_cRefSphere);
    return GetUnknown()->AddRef();
  }
```

```
      STDMETHODIMP_(ULONG) RedRelease() {
        _ThreadModel::Decrement(&m_cRefSphere);
        return GetUnknown()->Release();
      }

  private:
    long  m_cRefSphere;
  };
```

By deriving from IRedSphere, we can provide an implementation of all the colored methods separately from the uncolored ones. By coloring the IUnknown methods of IRedSphere, we can handle IUnknown calls on ISphere separately from the other implementations of IUnknown by the other interfaces. In this case, we're using RedAddRef and RedRelease to keep track of an ISphere-specific reference count. And even though we expose IRedSphere to the client when it asks for ISphere, as far as the client is concerned, it has just an ISphere interface pointer. Because IRedSphere and ISphere are layout compatible, as far as COM is concerned, the client is right.

```
  void TryRotate(IUnknown* punk) {
    ISphere* ps = 0;

    // Implicit AddRef really a call to RedAddRef
    if(SUCCEEDED(punk->QueryInterface(IID_ISphere, (void**)&ps))) {
      // ps actually points to an IRedSphere*

      ps->Rotate();
      ps->Release();  // Really a call to RedRelease
    }
  }
```

COM_INTERFACE_ENTRY_IMPL and COM_INTERFACE_ENTRY_IMPL_IID

Interface coloring is somewhat interesting in the same way that a car wreck on the side of the road is interesting: It can be disconcerting as well and can slow traffic. Beginning with ATL 3.0, the vast majority of IXxxImpl classes no longer use interface coloring. In ATL 2.x, interface coloring was used for some, but not all, of the IXxxImpl classes to perform interface-specific reference counting. These implementation classes took the following form:

```
  template <typename Deriving> class IXxxImpl {...};
```

Instead of deriving from the interface the class implemented, the implementation class used interface coloring to make itself layout compatible with the implemented interface. This enabled each class to implement its own reference counting but prohibited the use of the simple COM_INTERFACE_ENTRY macro. Additional macros were provided to make the necessary entries in the interface map:

```
#define COM_INTERFACE_ENTRY_IMPL(x) \
    COM_INTERFACE_ENTRY_IID(_ATL_IIDOF(x), x##Impl<_ComMapClass>)

#define COM_INTERFACE_ENTRY_IMPL_IID(iid, x) \
    COM_INTERFACE_ENTRY_IID(iid, x##Impl<_ComMapClass>)
```

The interface coloring technique was useful only if you wanted to track some of the ATL-implemented interfaces. Beginning with ATL 3.0, ATL uses a more generic mechanism[5] that tracks reference counts on all interfaces. Toward that end, all the ATL-implementation classes actually derive from the interface in question, making the use of COM_INTERFACE_ENTRY_IMPL and COM_INTERFACE_ENTRY_IMPL_IID macros unnecessary. All new and ported code should use COM_INTERFACE_ENTRY or COM_INTERFACE_ENTRY_IID instead. Old code that used the IMPL forms of the macros still compiles under the new ATL and acts appropriately.

Tear-Off Interfaces

Although multiple inheritance is preferred when implementing multiple interfaces, it's not perfect. One of the problems is something called *vptr-bloat*. For each interface a class derives from, that's another vptr per instance of that class. Beefing up our beach ball implementation can lead to some significant overhead:

```
class CBeachBall :
  public CComObjectRootEx<CBeachBall>,
  public ISphere,
  public IRollableObject,
  public IPlaything,
  public ILethalObject,
  public ITakeUpSpace,
  public IWishIWereMoreUseful,
  public ITryToBeHelpful,
  public IAmDepressed {...};
```

---

[5] The _ALT_DEBUG_INTERFACES macro provides this service and is discussed in Chapter 4, "Objects in ATL."

Because each beach ball implements eight interfaces, each instance has 32 bytes of overhead on Win32 systems before the reference count or any useful state. If clients actually made heavy use of these interfaces, that wouldn't be too high of a price to pay. However, my guess is that most clients will use beach balls for their rollable and play-thing abilities. Because the other interfaces will be used infrequently, we'd rather not pay the overhead until they are used. For this, Crispin Goswell invented the tear-off interface, which he described in the article "The *COM Programmer's Cookbook*."[6]

Standard Tear-Offs

A tear-off interface is an interface that'd you want to expose on demand but not actually inherit from in the main class. Instead, an auxiliary class inherits from the interface to be torn off, and instances of that class are created any time a client queries for that interface. For example, assuming that few clients will think to turn a beach ball into a lethal weapon, ILethalObject would make an excellent tear-off interface for the CBeachBall class. Instead of using CComObjectRootEx as the base class, ATL classes implementing tear-off interfaces use the CComTearOffObjectBase as their base class:

```
template <class Owner, class ThreadModel = CComObjectThreadModel>
class CComTearOffObjectBase
    : public CComObjectRootEx<ThreadModel> {
public:
    typedef Owner _OwnerClass;
    Owner* m_pOwner;
    CComTearOffObjectBase() { m_pOwner = NULL; }
};
```

CComTearOffObjectBase provides one additional service, which is the caching of the *owner* of the tear-off interface. Each tear-off belongs to an owner object that has torn it off to satisfy a client's request. The owner is useful so that the tear-off instance can access member data or member functions of the owner class:

```
class CBeachBallLethalness :
  public CComTearOffObjectBase<CBeachBall,
    CComSingleThreadModel>,
  public ILethalObject {
public:
BEGIN_COM_MAP(CBeachBallLethalness)
```

---

[6] As of this writing, Crispin's article is available online at http://msdn.com/library/en-us/dncomg/html/msdn_com_co.asp (http://tinysells.com/50).

```
      COM_INTERFACE_ENTRY(ILethalObject)
END_COM_MAP()

  // ILethalObject methods
  STDMETHODIMP Kill() {
    m_pOwner->m_gasFill = GAS_HYDROGEN;
    m_pOwner->HoldNearOpenFlame();
    return S_OK;
  }
};
```

COM_INTERFACE_ENTRY_TEAR_OFF

To use this tear-off implementation, the owner class uses the COM_
INTERFACE_ENTRY_TEAR_OFF macro:

```
#define COM_INTERFACE_ENTRY_TEAR_OFF(iid, x) \
  { &iid, \
    (DWORD_PTR)&ATL::_CComCreatorData< \
        ATL::CComInternalCreator< ATL::CComTearOffObject< x > > \
        >::data, \
  _Creator },
```

_CComCreatorData is just a sneaky trick to fill in the dw entry of the interface entry with a function pointer to the appropriate creator function. The creator function is provided by CComInternalCreator, which is identical to CComCreator except that it calls _InternalQueryInterface to get the initial interface instead of QueryInterface. This is necessary because, as I show you soon, QueryInterface on a tear-off instance forwards to the owner, but we want the initial interface on a new tear-off to come from the tear-off itself. That is, after all, why we're creating the tear-off: to expose that interface.

The pFunc entry COM_INTERFACE_ENTRY_TEAR_OFF makes is the first instance of a nonsimple entry so far in this chapter and, thus, the first macro we've seen that cannot be used as the first entry in the interface map. The _Creator function is a static member of the CComObjectRootBase class that simply calls the Creator function pointer held in the dw parameter:

```
static HRESULT WINAPI
CComObjectRootBase::_Creator(void* pv, REFIID iid,
  void** ppv, DWORD_PTR dw) {
  _ATL_CREATORDATA* pcd = (_ATL_CREATORDATA*)dw;
  return pcd->pFunc(pv, iid, ppv);
}
```

The most derived class of a tear-off implementation is not `CComObject`, but rather `CComTearOffObject`. `CComTearOffObject` knows about the `m_pOwner` member of the base and fills it during construction. Because each tear-off instance is a separate C++ object, each maintains its own lifetime. However, to live up to the laws of COM identity, each tear-off forwards requests for new interfaces to the owner:

```
template <class Base>
class CComTearOffObject : public Base {
public:
    CComTearOffObject(void* pv) {
        ATLASSERT(m_pOwner == NULL);
        m_pOwner = reinterpret_cast<Base::_OwnerClass*>(pv);
        m_pOwner->AddRef();
    }

    ~CComTearOffObject() {
        m_dwRef = -(LONG_MAX/2);
        FinalRelease();
#ifdef _ATL_DEBUG_INTERFACES
        _AtlDebugInterfacesModule.DeleteNonAddRefThunk(
            _GetRawUnknown());
#endif
        m_pOwner->Release();
    }

    STDMETHOD_(ULONG, AddRef)() {
        return InternalAddRef();
    }

    STDMETHOD_(ULONG, Release)() {
        ULONG l = InternalRelease();
        if (l == 0)
            delete this;
        return l;
    }

    STDMETHOD(QueryInterface)(REFIID iid, void ** ppvObject) {
        return m_pOwner->QueryInterface(iid, ppvObject);
    }
};
```

To use a tear-off, the owner class adds an entry to its interface map:

```
class CBeachBall :
  public CComObjectRootEx<CBeachBall>,
  public ISphere,
  public IRollableObject,
  public IPlaything,
  //public ILethalObject, // Implemented by the tear-off
  public ITakeUpSpace,
  public IWishIWereMoreUseful,
  public ITryToBeHelpful,
  public IAmDepressed {
public:
BEGIN_COM_MAP(CBeachBall)
  COM_INTERFACE_ENTRY(ISphere)
  COM_INTERFACE_ENTRY(IRollableObject)
  COM_INTERFACE_ENTRY(IPlaything)
  COM_INTERFACE_ENTRY_TEAR_OFF(IID_ILethalObject,
    CBeachBallLethalness)
  COM_INTERFACE_ENTRY(ITakeUpSpace)
  COM_INTERFACE_ENTRY(IWishIWereMoreUseful)
  COM_INTERFACE_ENTRY(ITryToBeHelpful)
  COM_INTERFACE_ENTRY(IAmDepressed)
END_COM_MAP()
...
private:
  GAS_TYPE m_gasFill;
  void     HoldNearOpenFlame();
  // Tear-offs are generally friends
  friend class CBeachBallLethalness;
};
```

Because the owner class is no longer deriving from ILethalObject, each instance is 4 bytes lighter. However, when the client queries for ILethalObject, we're spending 4 bytes for the ILethalObject vptr in CBeachBallLethalness, 4 bytes for the CBeachBallLethalness reference count, and 4 bytes for the m_pOwner back pointer. You might wonder how spending 12 bytes to save 4 bytes actually results in a savings. I'll tell you: volume! Or rather, the lack thereof. Because we're paying only the 12 bytes during the lifetime of the tear-off instance and we've used extensive profiling to determine ILethalObject is rarely used, the overall object footprint should be smaller.

Tear-Off Caveats

Before wrapping yourself in the perceived efficiency of tear-offs, you should be aware of these cautions:

- **Tear-offs are only for rarely used interfaces.** Tear-off interfaces are an implementation trick to be used to reduce `vptr` bloat when extensive proto-typing has revealed this to be a problem. If you don't have this problem, save yourself the trouble and avoid tear-offs.

- **Tear-offs are for intra-apartment use only.** The stub caches a tear-off inter-face for the life of an object. In fact, the current implementation of the stub manager caches each interface twice, sending the overhead of that particular interface from 12 bytes to 24 bytes.

- **Tear-offs should contain no state of their own.** If a tear-off contains its own state, there will be one copy of that state per tear-off instance, breaking the spirit, if not the laws, of COM identity. If you have per-interface state, espe-cially large state that you want to be released when no client is using the inter-face, use a cached tear-off.

Cached Tear-Offs

You might have noticed that every query for `ILethalObject` results in a new tear-off instance, even if the client already holds an `ILethalObject` interface pointer. This might be fine for a single interface tear-off, but what about a related group of inter-faces that will be used together?[7] For example, imagine moving the other rarely used interfaces of `CBeachBall` to a single tear-off implementation:

```
class CBeachBallAttitude :
  public CComTearOffObjectBase<CBeachBall,
    CComSingleThreadModel>,
  public ITakeUpSpace,
  public IWishIWereMoreUseful,
  public ITryToBeHelpful,
  public IAmDepressed {
public:
BEGIN_COM_MAP(CBeachBallAttitude)
  COM_INTERFACE_ENTRY(ITakeUpSpace)
  COM_INTERFACE_ENTRY(IWishIWereMoreUseful)
  COM_INTERFACE_ENTRY(ITryToBeHelpful)
  COM_INTERFACE_ENTRY(IAmDepressed)
END_COM_MAP()
...
};
```

---

[7] The `Control` interfaces fit into this category for objects that also support nonvisual use.

The following use of this tear-off implementation compiles and exhibits the appropriate behavior, but the overhead of even a single tear-off is exorbitant:

```
class CBeachBall :
  public CComObjectRootEx<CBeachBall>,
  public ISphere,
  public IRollableObject,
  public IPlaything
  // No tearoff interfaces in base class list
{
public:
BEGIN_COM_MAP(CBeachBall)
  COM_INTERFACE_ENTRY(ISphere)
  COM_INTERFACE_ENTRY(IRollableObject)
  COM_INTERFACE_ENTRY(IPlaything)
  // tearoffs are listed in the interface map
  COM_INTERFACE_ENTRY_TEAR_OFF(IID_ILethalObject,
    CBeachBallLethalness)
  COM_INTERFACE_ENTRY_TEAR_OFF(IID_ITakeUpSpace,
    CBeachBallAttitude)
  COM_INTERFACE_ENTRY_TEAR_OFF(IID_IWishIWereMoreUseful,
    CBeachBallAttitude)
  COM_INTERFACE_ENTRY_TEAR_OFF(IID_ITryToBeHelpful,
    CBeachBallAttitude)
  COM_INTERFACE_ENTRY_TEAR_OFF(IID_IAmDepressed,
    CBeachBallAttitude)
END_COM_MAP()
...
};
```

Because we've grouped the "attitude" interfaces together into a single tear-off implementation, every time the client queries for any of them, it pays the overhead of all of them. To allow this kind of grouping but avoid the overhead of creating a new instance for every query, ATL provides an implementation of a *cached tear-off*. The owner holds a cached tear-off if there is even one outstanding interface to the tear-off. The initial query creates and caches the tear-off. Subsequent queries use the cached tear-off. The final release deletes the tear-off instance.

COM_INTERFACE_ENTRY_CACHED_TEAR_OFF

To support caching tear-offs, ATL provides another interface macro:

```
#define COM_INTERFACE_ENTRY_CACHED_TEAR_OFF(iid, x, punk) \
  { &iid, \
    (DWORD_PTR)&ATL::_CComCacheData< \
```

```
ATL::CComCreator< ATL::CComCachedTearOffObject< x > >, \
(DWORD_PTR)offsetof(_ComMapClass, punk) >::data, \
_Cache },
```

The _CComCacheData class is used to stuff a pointer into an _ATL_CACHEDATA structure:

```
struct _ATL_CACHEDATA {
  DWORD            dwOffsetVar;
  _ATL_CREATORFUNC* pFunc;
};
```

The use of this structure allows the dw to point to a Creator function pointer as well as another member, an offset. The offset is from the base of the owner class to the member data that is used to cache the pointer to the tear-off. The _Cache function, another static member function of CComObjectRootBase, uses the offset to calculate the address of the pointer and checks the pointer to determine whether to create a new instance of the cached tear-off:

```
static HRESULT WINAPI
CComObjectRootBase::_Cache(
    void* pv,
    REFIID iid,
    void** ppvObject,
    DWORD_PTR dw)
{
  HRESULT hRes = E_NOINTERFACE;
  _ATL_CACHEDATA* pcd = (_ATL_CACHEDATA*)dw;
  IUnknown** pp = (IUnknown**)((DWORD_PTR)pv + pcd->dwOffsetVar);
  if (*pp == NULL) hRes = pcd->pFunc(pv, __uuidof(IUnknown),
   (void**)pp);
  if (*pp != NULL) hRes = (*pp)->QueryInterface(iid, ppvObject);
  return hRes;
}
```

Just as an instance of a tear-off uses CComTearOffObject instead of CComObject to provide the implementation of IUnknown, cached tear-offs use CComCachedTearOffObject. CComCachedTearOffObject is nearly identical to CComAggObject[8] because of the way that the lifetime and identity of the tear-off are subsumed by that of the owner. The only difference is that the cached tear-off, like the tear-off, initializes the m_pOwner member.

---

[8] Discussed in Chapter 4, "Objects in ATL."

Replacing the inefficient use of COM_INTERFACE_ENTRY_TEAR_OFF with COM_INTERFACE_ENTRY_CACHED_TEAR_OFF looks like this:

```
class CBeachBall :
  public CComObjectRootEx<CBeachBall>,
  public ISphere,
  public IRollableObject,
  public IPlaything {
public:
BEGIN_COM_MAP(CBeachBall)
  COM_INTERFACE_ENTRY(ISphere)
  COM_INTERFACE_ENTRY(IRollableObject)
  COM_INTERFACE_ENTRY(IPlaything)
  COM_INTERFACE_ENTRY_TEAR_OFF(IID_ILethalObject,
    CBeachBallLethalness)
  COM_INTERFACE_ENTRY_CACHED_TEAR_OFF(IID_ITakeUpSpace,
    CBeachBallAttitude, m_spunkAttitude.p)
  COM_INTERFACE_ENTRY_CACHED_TEAR_OFF(IID_IWishIWereMoreUseful,
    CBeachBallAttitude, m_spunkAttitude.p)
  COM_INTERFACE_ENTRY_CACHED_TEAR_OFF(IID_ITryToBeHelpful,
    CBeachBallAttitude, m_spunkAttitude.p)
  COM_INTERFACE_ENTRY_CACHED_TEAR_OFF(IID_IAmDepressed,
    CBeachBallAttitude, m_spunkAttitude.p)
END_COM_MAP()
DECLARE_GET_CONTROLLING_UNKNOWN() // See the Aggregation section
...
public:
  CComPtr<IUnknown> m_spunkAttitude;
};
```

Another Use for Cached Tear-Offs

Cached tear-offs have another use that is in direct opposition to standard tear-offs: caching per-interface resources. For example, imagine a dictionary object that implements a rarely used IHyphenation interface:

```
interface IHyphenation : public IUnknown {
  HRESULT Hyphenate([in] BSTR bstrUnhyphed,
    [out, retval] BSTR* pbstrHyphed);
};
```

Performing hyphenation is a matter of consulting a giant look-up table. If a CDictionary object were to implement the IHyphenation interface, it would likely do so as a cached tear-off to manage the resources associated with the look-up table. When the hyphenation cached tear-off is first created, it acquires the look-up table. Because the tear-off is cached, subsequent queries use the same look-up table. After all references to the IHyphenation interface are released, the look-up table can be released. If we had used a standard tear-off for this same functionality, a naïve implementation would have acquired the resources for the look-up table for each tear-off.

Aggregation: The Controlling Outer

As with tear-offs, aggregation enables you to separate the code for a single identity into multiple objects. However, whereas using tear-offs require shared source between the owner and the tear-off class, aggregation does not. The controlling outer and the controlling inner do not have to share the same server or even the same implementation language (although they do have to share the same apartment). If you like, you can consider an aggregated object a kind of "binary cached tear-off." As with a cached tear-off, an aggregated instance's lifetime and identity are subsumed by that of the controlling outer. Just like a cached tear-off, an aggregated instance must have a way to obtain the interface pointer of the controlling outer. In a tear-off, we pass the owner as a constructor argument. In aggregation, we do the same thing, but using the COM constructor that accepts a single, optional constructor argument—that is, the pUnkOuter parameter of IClassFactory::CreateInstance and its wrapper, CoCreateInstance:

```
interface IClassFactory : IUnknown {
  HRESULT CreateInstance([in, unique] IUnknown* pUnkOuter,
                              [in] REFIID riid,
                 [out, iid_is(riid)] void **ppvObject);
  HRESULT LockServer([in] BOOL fLock);
};


WINOLEAPI CoCreateInstance([in] REFCLSID rclsid,
                [in, unique] LPUNKNOWN pUnkOuter,
                       [in] DWORD dwClsContext,
                       [in] REFIID riid,
            [out, iid_is(riid)] LPVOID FAR* ppv);
```

In Chapter 4, "Objects in ATL," I discussed how ATL supports aggregation as a controlled inner using CComAggObject (or CComPolyObject). In this chapter, I show you the four macros that ATL provides for the controlling outer in the aggregation relationship.

Planned Versus Blind Aggregation

After an aggregate is created, the controlling outer has two choices of how to exposed the interface(s) of the aggregate as its own. The first choice is *planned aggregation.* In planned aggregation, the controlling outer wants the inner to expose one of a set of interfaces known by the outer. Figure 6.2 illustrates planned aggregation.

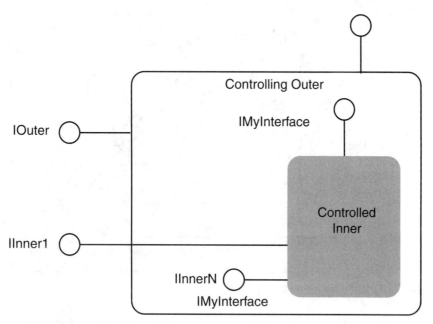

Figure 6.2.   Planned aggregation

The downside to this technique is that if the inner's functionality grows, clients using the outer cannot gain access to the additional functionality. The upside is that this could be exactly what the outer had in mind. For example, consider the standard interface `IPersist`:

```
interface IPersist : IUnknown {
  HRESULT GetClassID([out] CLSID *pClassID);
}
```

If the outer were to blindly expose the inner's implementation of `IPersist`, when the client called `GetClassID`, it would get the CLSID of the inner, not the outer. Because the client wants the outer object's class identifier, we have again broken the spirit of the COM identity laws. Planned aggregation helps prevent this breach.

Blind aggregation, on the other hand, allows the outer's functionality to grow with the inner's, but it provides the potential for exposing identity information from the inner. For this reason, blind aggregation should be avoided. Figure 6.3 shows blind aggregation.

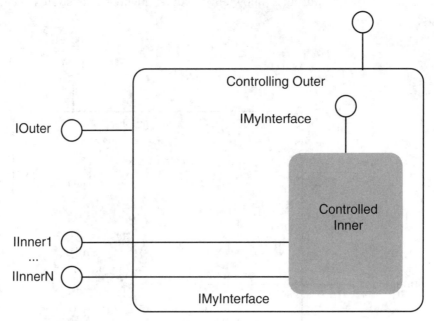

Figure 6.3. Blind aggregation

Manual Versus Automatic Creation

COM_INTERFACE_ENTRY_AGGREGATE and COM_INTERFACE_ENTRY_AGGREGATE_BLIND

ATL provides support for both planned and blind aggregation via the following two macros:

```
#define COM_INTERFACE_ENTRY_AGGREGATE(iid, punk) \
  { &iid, (DWORD_PTR)offsetof(_ComMapClass, punk), _Delegate },

#define COM_INTERFACE_ENTRY_AGGREGATE_BLIND(punk) \
  { NULL, (DWORD_PTR)offsetof(_ComMapClass, punk), _Delegate},
```

These macros assume that the aggregate has already been created manually and that the interface pointer is stored in the `punk` parameter to the macro. The `_Delegate` function forwards the `QueryInterface` request to that pointer:

```
static HRESULT WINAPI
CComObjectRootBase::_Delegate(
  void* pv,
  REFIID iid,
  void** ppvObject,
  DWORD dw)
{
  HRESULT hRes = E_NOINTERFACE;
  IUnknown* p = *(IUnknown**)((DWORD_PTR)pv + dw);
  if (p != NULL) hRes = p->QueryInterface(iid, ppvObject);
  return hRes;
}
```

To use aggregation of an inner that has been manually created, the classes use COM_INTERFACE_ENTRY_AGGREGATE or COM_INTERFACE_ENTRY_AGGREGATE_BLIND in the interface map:

```
class CBeachBall :
  public CComObjectRootEx<CBeachBall>,
  public ISphere,
  public IRollableObject,
  public IPlaything {
public:
BEGIN_COM_MAP(CBeachBall)
  COM_INTERFACE_ENTRY(ISphere)
  COM_INTERFACE_ENTRY(IRollableObject)
  COM_INTERFACE_ENTRY(IPlaything)
  COM_INTERFACE_ENTRY_AGGREGATE(IID_ILethalObject,
    m_spunkLethalness)
  COM_INTERFACE_ENTRY_AGGREGATE_BLIND(m_spunkAttitude)
END_COM_MAP()

DECLARE_GET_CONTROLLING_UNKNOWN()
DECLARE_PROTECT_FINAL_CONSTRUCT()

  HRESULT FinalConstruct() {
    HESULT hr;
    hr = CoCreateInstance(CLSID_Lethalness,
                          GetControllingUnknown(),
                          CLSCTX_INPROC_SERVER,
                          IID_IUnknown,
                          (void**)&m_spunkLethalness);
    if( SUCCEEDED(hr) ) {
```

```
        hr = CoCreateInstance(CLSID_Attitude,
                              GetControllingUnknown(),
                              CLSCTX_INPROC_SERVER,
                              IID_IUnknown,
                              (void**)&m_spunkAttitude);
    }

    return hr;
  }

  void FinalRelease() {
    m_spunkLethalness.Release();
    m_spunkAttitude.Release();
  }
...
public:
  CComPtr<IUnknown> m_spunkLethalness;
  CComPtr<IUnknown> m_spunkAttitude;
};
```

Notice that I have used the FinalConstruct method to create the aggregates so that failure stops the creation process. Notice also that because I've got a Final-Construct that hands out interface pointers to the object being created, I'm using DECLARE_PROTECT_FINAL_CONSTRUCT to protect against premature destruction. I've also got a FinalRelease method to manually release the aggregate interface pointers to protect against double destruction. Aggregation was one of the chief motivations behind the multiphase construction of ATL-based COM objects, so it's not surprising to see all the pieces used in this example.

However, one thing I've not yet mentioned is the DECLARE_GET_CONTROLLING_UNKNOWN macro. The controlling unknown is a pointer to the most controlling outer. Because aggregation can go arbitrarily deep, when aggregating, the outer needs to pass the pUnkOuter of the outermost object. To support this, ATL provides the GET_CONTROLLING_UNKNOWN macro to give an object the definition of a GetControllingUnknown function:

```
#define DECLARE_GET_CONTROLLING_UNKNOWN() public: \
  virtual IUnknown* GetControllingUnknown() { \
    return GetUnknown(); }
```

You might question the value of this function because it simply forwards to GetUnknown, but notice that it's virtual. If the object is actually being created as an aggregate while it is aggregating, GetControllingUnknown is overridden in CComContainedObject:

```
template <class Base> class CComContainedObject : public Base {
...
  IUnknown* GetControllingUnknown()
  { return m_pOuterUnknown; }
...
};
```

So, if the object is standalone, `GetControllingUnknown` returns the `IUnknown*` of the object, but if the object is itself being aggregated, `GetControllingUnknown` returns the `IUnknown*` of the outermost outer.

COM_INTERFACE_ENTRY_AUTOAGGREGATE and COM_INTERFACE_ENTRY_AUTOAGGREGATE_BLIND

If you're not doing any initialization of the aggregates, sometimes it seems a waste to create them until (or unless) they're needed. For automatic creation of aggregates on demand, ATL provides the following two macros:

```
#define COM_INTERFACE_ENTRY_AUTOAGGREGATE(iid, punk, clsid) \
  { &iid, \
    (DWORD_PTR)&ATL::_CComCacheData< \
    ATL::CComAggregateCreator<_ComMapClass, &clsid>, \
    (DWORD_PTR)offsetof(_ComMapClass, punk)>::data, \
    _Cache },

#define COM_INTERFACE_ENTRY_AUTOAGGREGATE_BLIND(punk, clsid) \
  { NULL, \
    (DWORD_PTR)&ATL::_CComCacheData< \
    ATL::CComAggregateCreator<_ComMapClass, &clsid>, \
    (DWORD_PTR)offsetof(_ComMapClass, punk)>::data, \
    _Cache },
```

The only new thing in these macros is the `CComAggregateCreator`, which simply performs the `CoCreateInstance` the first time the interface is requested:

```
template <class T, const CLSID* pclsid>
class CComAggregateCreator {
public:
  static HRESULT WINAPI CreateInstance(void* pv, REFIID,
    LPVOID* ppv) {
    T* p = (T*)pv;
    return CoCreateInstance(*pclsid, p->GetControllingUnknown(),
      CLSCTX_INPROC, __uuidof(IUnknown), ppv);
  }
};
```

Using automatic creation simplifies the outer's code somewhat:

```
class CBeachBall :
  public CComObjectRootEx<CBeachBall>,
  public ISphere,
  public IRollableObject,
  public IPlaything {
public:
BEGIN_COM_MAP(CBeachBall)
  COM_INTERFACE_ENTRY(ISphere)
  COM_INTERFACE_ENTRY(IRollableObject)
  COM_INTERFACE_ENTRY(IPlaything)
  COM_INTERFACE_ENTRY_AUTOAGGREGATE(IID_ILethalObject,
    m_spunkLethalness, CLSID_Lethalness)
  COM_INTERFACE_ENTRY_AUTOAGGREGATE_BLIND(m_spunkAttitude,
    CLSID_Attitude)
END_COM_MAP()

DECLARE_GET_CONTROLLING_UNKNOWN()

  void FinalRelease() {
    m_spunkLethalness.Release();
    m_spunkAttitude.Release();
  }
...
public:
  CComPtr<IUnknown> m_spunkLethalness;
  CComPtr<IUnknown> m_spunkAttitude;
};
```

Although we no longer need to perform the creation in `FinalConstruct`, we're still required to use `DECLARE_GET_CONTROLLING_UNKNOWN` and to provide storage for the aggregated interfaces. We still release the interfaces manually in `FinalRelease`, as well, to avoid double destruction.

Aggregating the Free Threaded Marshaler

The ATL Object Wizard directly supports one particularly interesting use of aggregation: aggregating the implementation of `IMarshal` provided by the Free Threaded Marshaler (FTM). Any object that aggregates the FTM is said to be an *apartment-neutral* object. Normally, passing an interface pointer between apartments, even in the same process, results in a proxy-stub pair. The proxy-stub pair maintains the concurrency and synchronization requirements of both the object and the client, but it also adds overhead. In-process objects that provide their own synchronization and prefer to snuggle up to the client without the overhead of the proxy-stub can aggregate the FTM. By aggregating the FTM, an object short-circuits the creation of the proxy-stub for in-process objects. Therefore, the object can be passed between apartments in the same address space without the overhead of a proxy-stub.

The wizard generates the following code when the Free Threaded Marshaler option is checked in the ATL Object Wizard:

```
class ATL_NO_VTABLE CBowlingBall :
  public CComObjectRootEx<CComMultiThreadModel>,
  public CComCoClass<CBowlingBall, &CLSID_BowlingBall>,
  public IBowlingBall
{
public:
  CBowlingBall() { m_pUnkMarshaler = NULL; }

DECLARE_REGISTRY_RESOURCEID(IDR_BOWLINGBALL)
DECLARE_GET_CONTROLLING_UNKNOWN()
DECLARE_PROTECT_FINAL_CONSTRUCT()

BEGIN_COM_MAP(CBowlingBall)
  COM_INTERFACE_ENTRY(IBowlingBall)
  COM_INTERFACE_ENTRY_AGGREGATE(IID_IMarshal, m_pUnkMarshaler.p)
END_COM_MAP()

  HRESULT FinalConstruct() {
    return CoCreateFreeThreadedMarshaler(GetControllingUnknown(),
                                         &m_pUnkMarshaler.p);
  }
  void FinalRelease() {
    m_pUnkMarshaler.Release();
  }

  CComPtr<IUnknown> m_pUnkMarshaler;
  ...
};
```

Because the CLSID of the FTM is not available, instead of using auto-creation, ATL uses CoCreateFreeThreadMarshaler to create an instance of the FTM in the FinalConstruct method.

FTM Danger, Will Robinson! Danger! Danger!

Aggregating the FTM is easy, so I should mention a couple of big responsibilities that you, the developer, accept by aggregating the FTM:

- **Apartment-neutral objects must be thread safe.** You can mark your class ThreadingModel=Apartment all day long, but because your object can be passed freely between apartments in the same process and, therefore, can used simultaneously by multiple threads, you'd better use CComMultiThreadModel and at least object-level locking. Fortunately, the ATL Object Wizard makes the FTM option available for selection only if you choose a threading model of Both or Neutral.

- **Apartment-neutral objects are not aggregatable.** Aggregating the FTM depends on being able to implement IMarshal. If the outer decides to implement IMarshal and doesn't ask the inner object, the inner can no longer be apartment neutral.

- **Apartment-neutral objects cannot cache interface pointers.** An apartment-neutral object is said to be *apartment neutral* because it doesn't care which apartment it is accessed from. However, other objects that an apartment-neutral object uses might or might not also be apartment-neutral. Interface pointers to objects that aren't apartment neutral can be used only in the apartment to which they belong. If you're lucky, the apartment-neutral object attempting to cache and use an interface pointer from another apartment will have a pointer to a proxy. Proxies know when they are being accessed outside their apartments and return RPC_E_WRONG_THREAD for all such method calls. If you're not so lucky, the apartment-neutral object obtains a raw interface pointer. Imagine the poor single-threaded object accessed simultaneously from multiple apartments as part of its duty to the apartment-neutral object. It will most likely work just fine until you need to give a demo to your biggest client.

The only safe way to cache interface pointers in an apartment-neutral object is as cookies obtained from the Global Interface Table (GIT). The GIT is a process-global object provided to map apartment-specific interface pointers to apartment-neutral cookies and back. The GIT was invented after the FTM and is provided in the third service pack to NT 4.0, the DCOM patch for Windows 95, and out of the box with Windows 98/2000/XP. If you're aggregating the FTM and caching interface pointers, you must use the GIT. ATL provides the CComGITPtr class, discussed in Chapter 3, "ATL Smart Types," to make dealing with the GIT easier.

For an in-depth discussion of the FTM, the GIT, and their use, read *Essential COM* (Addison-Wesley, 1997), by Don Box.

Interface Map Chaining

C++ programmers are accustomed to using inheritance of implementation for reuse. For example, we reuse the implementation provided in `CComObjectRootEx` as well as the various ATL implementation classes (such as `IDispatchImpl`) through inheritance. For each implementation class used, one or more corresponding entries must be made in the interface map. However, what about deriving from a class that already provides an interface map? For example

```
class CBigBeachBall :
  public CBeachBall,
  public IBigObject {
public:
BEGIN_COM_MAP(CBigBeachBall)
  COM_INTERFACE_ENTRY(IBigObject)
  // All entries from CBeachBall base?
END_COM_MAP()
...
};
```

COM_INTERFACE_ENTRY_CHAIN

When inheriting from a base class that provides its own interface map, we want to avoid duplicating all the entries in the deriving class's interface map. The reason is maintenance. If the base class decides to change how it supports an interface or wants to add or remove support for an interface, we've got to change the deriving classes, too. It would be much nicer to "inherit" the interface map along with the interface implementations. That's what `COM_INTERFACE_ENTRY_CHAIN` does:

```
#define COM_INTERFACE_ENTRY_CHAIN(classname) \
  { NULL, (DWORD_PTR)&ATL::_CComChainData<classname, \
    _ComMapClass>::data, _Chain },
```

The `_CComChainData` template simply fills the `dw` member of the interface entry with a pointer to the base class's interface map so that the `_Chain` function can walk that list when evaluating a query request:

```
static HRESULT WINAPI
CComObjectRootBase::_Chain(void* pv, REFIID iid,
  void** ppvObject, DWORD dw) {
  _ATL_CHAINDATA* pcd = (_ATL_CHAINDATA*)dw;
  void* p = (void*)((DWORD_PTR)pv + pcd->dwOffset);
  return InternalQueryInterface(p, pcd->pFunc(), iid, ppvObject);
}
```

If the _Chain function returns a failure—for example, if the base class doesn't support the requested interface—the search continues with the next entry in the table:

```
class CBigBadBeachBall :
  public CBeachBall,
  public IBigObject,
  public IBadObject {
public:
BEGIN_COM_MAP(CBigBadBeachBall)
  COM_INTERFACE_ENTRY(IBigObject)
  COM_INTERFACE_ENTRY_CHAIN(CBeachBall)
  COM_INTERFACE_ENTRY(IBadObject)
END_COM_MAP()
...
};
```

It might seem natural to put the chaining entries first in the interface map. However, remember that the first entry must be a simple entry, so you must put at least one of the derived class's interfaces first. If the derived class has no additional interfaces, use IUnknown as the first entry:

```
class CBetterBeachBall :
  public CBeachBall {
public:
BEGIN_COM_MAP(CBetterBeachBall)
  COM_INTERFACE_ENTRY(IUnknown)
  COM_INTERFACE_ENTRY_CHAIN(CBeachBall)
END_COM_MAP()
...
};
```

Just Say "No"

COM_INTERFACE_ENTRY_NOINTERFACE

Sometimes, you want to short-circuit the interface request by explicitly returning E_NOINTERFACE when a specific interface is requested. For this, ATL provides COM_INTERFACE_ENTRY_NOINTERFACE:

```
#define COM_INTERFACE_ENTRY_NOINTERFACE(x) \
  { &_ATL_IIDOF(x), NULL, _NoInterface },
```

The _NoInterface function does pretty much what you'd expect:

```
static HRESULT WINAPI
CComObjectRootBase::_NoInterface(void*, REFIID, void**,
  DWORD_PTR)
{ return E_NOINTERFACE; }
```

This interface map macro is handy when you've got blind entries in the interface map, as in blind aggregation or chaining, and you want to remove functionality that the inner object or the base class provides. For example

```
class CBigNiceBeachBall :
  public CBeachBall,
  public IBigObject {
public:
BEGIN_COM_MAP(CBigNiceBeachBall)
  COM_INTERFACE_ENTRY(IBigObject)
  COM_INTERFACE_ENTRY_NOINTERFACE(ILethalObject)
  COM_INTERFACE_ENTRY_CHAIN(CBeachBall)
END_COM_MAP()
...
};
```

Debugging

COM_INTERFACE_ENTRY_BREAK

Sometimes you need to debug your QueryInterface implementation. Maybe you're building a custom COM_MAP macro. Maybe you're seeing weird behavior on some interfaces. Sometimes the easiest way to track down a problem is in the debugger. This is where COM_INTERFACE_ENTRY_BREAK comes in:

```
#define COM_INTERFACE_ENTRY_BREAK(x) \
  { &_ATL_IIDOF(x), NULL, _Break },
```

The _Break function outputs some helpful debugging information and calls DebugBreak:

```
static HRESULT WINAPI
CComObjectRootbase::_Break(void*, REFIID iid, void**, DWORD) {
  (iid);
  _ATLDUMPIID(iid, _T("Break due to QI for interface "), S_OK);
```

```
    DebugBreak();
    return S_FALSE;
}
```

The call to DebugBreak is just like a breakpoint set in your debugger. It gives the active debugger the chance to take control of the process. When you're debugging, you can set other breakpoints and continue executing.

Extensibility

COM_INTERFACE_ENTRY_FUNC and COM_INTERFACE_ENTRY_FUNC_BLIND

ATL provides two macros for putting raw entries into the interface map:

```
#define COM_INTERFACE_ENTRY_FUNC(iid, dw, func) \
  { &iid, dw, func },

#define COM_INTERFACE_ENTRY_FUNC_BLIND(dw, func) \
  { NULL, dw, func },
```

These macros are the universal back door to ATL's implementation of QueryInterface. If you come up with another way of exposing COM interfaces, you can use these macros to achieve them, as long as it lives up to the laws of COM identity.

Direct Access to the this Pointer

One identity trick you can perform using COM_INTERFACE_ENTRY_FUNC was kicked around the ATL Mailing List for quite a while but was ultimately perfected by Don Box. (A slightly modified version of his solution is provided next.) In Chapter 4, "Objects in ATL," I presented the CreateInstance static member functions of CComObject, CComAgg-Object, and CComPolyObject when using private initialization. The CreateInstance method performed the same job as a Creator would but returned a pointer to the this pointer of the object instead of to only one of the interfaces. This was useful for calling member functions or setting member data that was not exposed via interfaces. We used this technique because it was unsafe to perform a cast. However, why not make QueryInterface perform the cast safely? In other words, why not add an entry to the interface map that returns the object's this pointer? Imagine a global function with the following implementation:

```
inline
HRESULT WINAPI _This(void* pv, REFIID iid,
  void** ppvObject, DWORD) {
```

```
    ATLASSERT(iid == IID_NULL);
    *ppvObject = pv;
    return S_OK;
}
```

This function takes the first parameter, pv, which points to the object's this pointer and hands it out directly in ppvObject. Notice also that this function does not AddRef the resultant interface pointer. Because it's returning an object pointer, not an interface pointer, it's not subject to the laws of COM. Remember, the this pointer is useful only within the server. To make sure that any out-of-apartment calls to QueryInterface fail, be sure to pick an interface ID without a proxy-stub, such as IID_NULL.

For example, imagine implementations of the following interfaces, creating a simple object model:

```
interface IBalloonMan : IUnknown {
    HRESULT CreateBalloon(long rgbColor, IBalloon** ppBalloon);
    HRESULT SwitchColor(IBalloon* pBalloon, long rgbColor);
};

interface IBalloon : IUnknown {
    [propget] HRESULT Color([out, retval] long *pVal);
};
```

Notice that the balloon's color can't be changed via IBalloon, but the implementation of IBalloonMan can give you a balloon of the color you want. If the implementations of IBalloonMan and IBalloon share the same server, the implementation of IBalloon can expose its this pointer via the _This function like this:

```
class ATL_NO_VTABLE CBalloon :
  public CComObjectRootEx<CComSingleThreadModel>,
  public CComCoClass<CBalloon>,
  public IBalloon {
public:
DECLARE_REGISTRY_RESOURCEID(IDR_BALLOON)
DECLARE_NOT_AGGREGATABLE(CBalloon)

DECLARE_PROTECT_FINAL_CONSTRUCT()

BEGIN_COM_MAP(CBalloon)
  COM_INTERFACE_ENTRY(IBalloon)
  COM_INTERFACE_ENTRY_FUNC(IID_NULL, 0, _This)
END_COM_MAP()
```

```
    // IBalloon
public:
  STDMETHOD(get_Color)(/*[out, retval]*/ long *pVal);

private:
  COLORREF  m_rgbColor;
  friend class CBalloonMan;
};
```

Because CBalloonMan is a friend of CBalloon, CBalloonMan can set the private color data member of CBalloon, assuming that it can obtain the object's this pointer. CBalloon's special entry for IID_NULL lets CBalloonMan do just that:

```
STDMETHODIMP CBalloonMan::CreateBalloon(long rgbColor,
  IBalloon** ppBalloon) {
  // Create balloon
  *ppBalloon = 0;
  HRESULT    hr = CBalloon::CreateInstance(0, ppBalloon);

  if( SUCCEEDED(hr) ) {
    // Use backdoor to acquire CBalloon's this pointer
    CBalloon*   pBalloonThis = 0;
    hr = (*ppBalloon)->QueryInterface(IID_NULL,
      (void**)&pBalloonThis);
    if( SUCCEEDED(hr) ) {
      // Use CBalloon's this pointer for private initialization
      pBalloonThis->m_rgbColor = rgbColor;
    }
  }
  return hr;
}
```

The benefit to this technique over the private initialization technique that the CreateInstance member function of CComObject et al exposes is that the this pointer can be obtained after creation:

```
STDMETHODIMP CBalloonMan::SwitchColor(IBalloon* pBalloon,
  long rgbColor) {
  // Use backdoor to acquire CBalloon's this pointer
  CBalloon*   pBalloonThis = 0;
  HRESULT hr = pBalloon->QueryInterface(IID_NULL, (void**)&pBalloonThis);
  if (SUCCEEDED(hr)) {
    hr = pBalloonThis->m_rgbColor = rgbColor;
  }
```

```
    return hr;
}
```

Clearly, this technique is a back-door hack with limited usefulness; it should not be used to subvert the binary boundary between client and object. However, it does have its own special charm. For objects that share the same apartment in the same server, it's a valid way to discover just who is who. If you find yourself using this technique, you might find the following macro to be a useful shortcut:

```
#define COM_INTERFACE_ENTRY_THIS() \
        COM_INTERFACE_ENTRY_FUNC(IID_NULL, 0, _This)
```

Per-Object Interfaces

Sometimes it's useful to handle interfaces on a per-object basis instead of a per-class basis. Another friend of mine, Martin Gudgin, provided the following example. If you want to implement something known as a "smart proxy," you have to keep track of the list of interfaces each object supports, and you might not know what those are until runtime. Each smart proxy object has its own list of interfaces, which can easily be managed by a member function. Unfortunately, interface maps can't hold member functions (believe me, I tried). However, you can use a combination of COM_INTERFACE_ENTRY_FUNC_BLIND and a static member function to perform the forwarding to a member function:

```
class ATL_NO_VTABLE CSmartProxy :
  public CComObjectRootEx<CComSingleThreadModel>,
  public CComCoClass<CSmartProxy, &CLSID_SmartProxy>,
  public IUnknown
{
public:
DECLARE_REGISTRY_RESOURCEID(IDR_SMARTPROXY)
DECLARE_PROTECT_FINAL_CONSTRUCT()

BEGIN_COM_MAP(CSmartProxy)
  COM_INTERFACE_ENTRY(IUnknown)
  COM_INTERFACE_ENTRY_FUNC_BLIND(0, _QI)
END_COM_MAP()

public:
  static HRESULT WINAPI _QI(void* pv, REFIID iid,
    void** ppvObject, DWORD) {
    // Forward to QI member function
```

```
    return ((CSmartProxy*)pv)->QI(iid, ppvObject);
  }

  // Per-object implementation of QI
  HRESULT QI(REFIID riid, void** ppv);
};
```

Of course, you might wonder why you'd go to all this trouble to get back to the per-object implementation of `QueryInterface` that you've come to know and love, but that's ATL.

Summary

Even when you understand and commit to the laws of COM identity, you'll find that they aren't very restrictive. Prefer multiple inheritance, but do not feel that ATL limits you to that technique. You can extend the interface map to support any identity trick that ATL doesn't support directly.

7 | **Persistence in ATL**

A Review of COM Persistence

Objects that have a persistent state should implement at least one persistence interface—and, preferably multiple interfaces—to provide the container with the most flexible choice of how it wants to save the object's state. Persistent state refers to data (typically properties and instance variables) that an object needs to have preserved before a container destroys the object. The container provides the saved state to the object after it re-creates the object so that the object can reinitialize itself to its previous state.

COM itself doesn't require an object to support persistence, nor does COM use such support if it's present in an object. COM simply documents a protocol by which clients can use any persistence support that an object provides. Often we refer to this persistence model as client-managed persistence because, in this model, the client determines where to save the persistent data (the medium) and when the save occurs.

COM defines some interfaces that model a persistence medium and, for some media, an implementation of the interfaces. Such interfaces typically use the naming convention IMedium, where the medium is Stream, Storage, PropertyBag, and so on. The medium interface has methods such as Read and Write that an object uses when loading and saving its state.

COM also documents interfaces that an object implements when it wants to support persistence into various media. Such interfaces typically use the naming convention IPersistMedium. The persistence interfaces have methods such as Load and Save that the client calls to request the object to restore or save its state. The client provides the appropriate medium interface to the object as an argument to the Load or Save requests. Figure 7.1 illustrates this model.

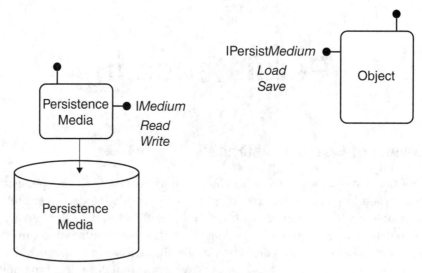

Figure 7.1. The client-managed persistence model

All `IPersistMedium` interfaces derive from the `IPersist` interface, which looks like this:

```
interface IPersist : IUnknown
{ HRESULT GetClassID([out] CLSID* pclsid); }
```

A client uses the `GetClassID` method when it wants to save the state of an object. Typically, the client queries for `IPersistMedium`, calls the `GetClassID` method to obtain the CLSID for the object the client wants to save, and then writes the CLSID to the persistence medium. The client then requests the object to save its state into the medium. Restoring the object is the inverse operation: The client reads the CLSID from the medium, creates an instance of the class, queries for the `IPersistMedium` interface on that object, and requests the object to load its state from the medium.

A client might ask an object to save its state in two basic forms: a self-describing set of named properties or an opaque binary stream of bytes.

When an object provides its state as a self-describing set of named properties, it provides each property as a name-type-value tuple to its client. The client then stores the properties in the form most convenient to the client, such as text on HTML pages. The benefit of self-describing data, such as <param> tags and XML, is that one entity can write it and another can read it without tight coupling between the two.

It is more efficient for an object to provide its state as a binary stream of bytes because the object doesn't need to provide a property name or translate each property into the name-type-value tuple. In addition, the client doesn't need to translate the property to and from text. However, opaque streams contain machine dependencies, such as byte order and floating point/character set representations, unless specifically addressed by the object writing the stream.

ATL provides support for both forms of persistence. Before we explore ATL's persistence implementation, let's look at how you might implement COM persistence directly.

IPropertyBag and IPersistPropertyBag

ActiveX control containers that implement a "save as text" mechanism typically use IPropertyBag and IPersistPropertyBag. A container implements IPropertyBag, and a control implements IPersistPropertyBag to indicate that it can persist its state as a self-describing set of named properties:

```
interface IPropertyBag : public IUnknown {
  HRESULT Read([in] LPCOLESTR  pszPropName,
    [in, out] VARIANT* pVar, [in] IErrorLog* pErrorLog);

  HRESULT Write([in] LPCOLESTR pszPropName, [in] VARIANT*  pVar);
};

interface IPersistPropertyBag : public IPersist {
  HRESULT InitNew ();
  HRESULT Load([in] IPropertyBag* pPropBag,
    [in] IErrorLog* pErrorLog);
  HRESULT Save([in] IPropertyBag* pPropBag,
    [in] BOOL fClearDirty,
    [in] BOOL fSaveAllProperties);
};
```

When a client (container) wants to have exact control over how individually named properties of an object are saved, it attempts to use an object's IPersist-PropertyBag interface as the persistence mechanism. The client supplies a property bag to the object in the form of an IPropertyBag interface.

When the object wants to read a property in IPersistPropertyBag::Load, it calls IPropertyBag::Read. When the object saves properties in IPersistProperty-Bag::Save, it calls IPropertyBag::Write. Each property is described with a name in pszPropName whose value is exchanged in a VARIANT. For read operations, the property bag provides the named property from the bag in the form specified by the input VARIANT, unless the type is VT_EMPTY; in that case, the property bag provides the property in any form that is convenient to the bag.

The information that the object provides for each property (name-type-value) during a save operation allows a client to save the property values as text, for instance. This is the primary reason a client might choose to support IPersist-PropertyBag. The client records errors that occur during reading into the supplied error log.

IPropertyBag2 and IPersistPropertyBag2

The IPropertyBag interface doesn't give an object much information about the properties contained in the bag. Therefore, the newer interface IPropertyBag2 gives an object much greater access to information about the properties in a bag. Objects that support persistence using IPropertyBag2 naturally implement the IPersistPropertyBag2 interface.

```
interface IPropertyBag2 : public IUnknown {
  HRESULT Read([in] ULONG cProperties, [in] PROPBAG2* pPropBag,
    [in]  IErrorLog* pErrLog, [out] VARIANT* pvarValue,
    [out] HRESULT*   phrError);
  HRESULT Write([in] ULONG cProperties, [in] PROPBAG2* pPropBag,
    [in]  VARIANT*   pvarValue);
  HRESULT CountProperties ([out] ULONG* pcProperties);
  HRESULT GetPropertyInfo([in] ULONG iProperty,
    [in] ULONG cProperties,
    [out] PROPBAG2* pPropBag, [out] ULONG* pcProperties);
  HRESULT LoadObject([in] LPCOLESTR pstrName, [in] DWORD dwHint,
    [in] IUnknown* pUnkObject, [in] IErrorLog* pErrLog);
};

interface IPersistPropertyBag2 : public IPersist {
  HRESULT InitNew ();
  HRESULT Load ([in] IPropertyBag2* pPropBag,
    [in] IErrorLog* pErrLog);
  HRESULT Save ([in] IPropertyBag2* pPropBag,
    [in] BOOL fClearDirty,
    [in] BOOL fSaveAllProperties);
  HRESULT IsDirty();
};
```

IPropertyBag2 is an enhancement of the IPropertyBag interface. IPropertyBag2 allows the object to obtain the number of properties in the bag and the type information for each property through the CountProperties and GetPropertyInfo methods. A property bag that implements IPropertyBag2 must also support IProp-ertyBag so that objects that support only IPropertyBag can access their properties.

Likewise, an object that supports IPersistPropertyBag2 must also support IPersistPropertyBag so that it can communicate with property bags that support only IPropertyBag.

When the object wants to read a property in IPersistPropertyBag2::Load, it calls IPropertyBag2::Read. When the object saves properties in IPersistPropertyBag2::Save, it calls IPropertyBag2::Write. The client records errors that occur during Read with the supplied IErrorLog interface.

Implementing IPersistPropertyBag

Clients ask an object to initialize itself only once. When the client has no initial values to give the object, the client calls the object's IPersistPropertyBag::InitNew method. In this case, the object should initialize itself to default values. When the client has initial values to give the object, it loads the properties into a property bag and calls the object's IPersistPropertyBag::Load method. When the client wants to save the state of an object, it creates a property bag and calls the object's IPersistPropertyBag::Save method.

This is pretty straightforward to implement in an object. For example, the Demagogue object has three properties: its name, speech, and volume. Here's an example of an implementation to save and restore the following three properties from a property bag:

```
class ATL_NO_VTABLE CDemagogue
    : public IPersistPropertyBag, ... {
    BEGIN_COM_MAP(CDemagogue)
      ...
      COM_INTERFACE_ENTRY(IPersistPropertyBag)
      COM_INTERFACE_ENTRY2(IPersist, IPersistPropertyBag)
    END_COM_MAP()
    ...
    CComBSTR m_name;
    long     m_volume;
    CComBSTR m_speech;

    STDMETHODIMP Load(IPropertyBag *pBag, IErrorLog *pLog) {
      // Initialize the VARIANT to VT_BSTR
      CComVariant v ((BSTR) NULL);
      HRESULT hr = pBag->Read(OLESTR("Name"), &v, pLog);
      if (FAILED(hr)) return hr;
      m_name = v.bstrVal;

      // Initialize the VARIANT to VT_I4
      v = 0L;
```

```
        hr = pBag->Read(OLESTR("Volume"), &v, pLog);
        if (FAILED(hr)) return hr;
        m_volume = v.lVal;

        // Initialize the VARIANT to VT_BSTR
        v = (BSTR) NULL;
        hr = pBag->Read(OLESTR("Speech"), &v, pLog);
        if (FAILED (hr)) return hr;
        m_speech = v.bstrVal;

        return S_OK;
    }

    STDMETHODIMP Save(IPropertyBag *pBag,
        BOOL fClearDirty, BOOL /* fSaveAllProperties */) {
        CComVariant v = m_name;
        HRESULT hr = pBag->Write(OLESTR("Name"), &v);
        if (FAILED(hr)) return hr;

        v = m_volume;
        hr = pBag->Write(OLESTR("Volume"), &v);
        if (FAILED(hr)) return hr;

        v = m_speech;
        hr = pBag->Write(OLESTR("Speech"), &v);
        if (FAILED(hr)) return hr;

        if (fClearDirty) m_fDirty = FALSE;
        return hr;
    }
};
```

The IStream, IpersistStreamInit, and IPersistStream Interfaces

COM objects that want to save their state efficiently as a binary stream of bytes typically implement IPersistStream or IPersistStreamInit. An *ActiveX control* that has persistent state must, at a minimum, implement either IPersistStream or IPersistStreamInit. The two interfaces are mutually exclusive and generally shouldn't be implemented together. A control implements IPersistStreamInit when it wants to know when it is newly created, as opposed to when it has been created and reinitialized from its existing persistent state. The IPersistStream interface does not provide a means to inform the control that it is newly created. The existence of either interface indicates that the control can save and load its persistent state into a stream—that is, an implementation of IStream.

The IStream interface closely models the Win32 file API, and you can easily implement the interface on any byte-oriented media. COM provides two implementations of IStream, one that maps to an OLE Structured Storage file and another that maps to a memory buffer.

```
interface ISequentialStream : IUnknown {
    HRESULT Read([out] void *pv, [in] ULONG cb,
        [out] ULONG *pcbRead);

    HRESULT Write( [in] void const *pv, [in] ULONG cb,
        [out] ULONG *pcbWritten);

}

interface IStream : ISequentialStream {
  HRESULT Seek([in] LARGE_INTEGER dlibMove,
            [in] DWORD dwOrigin,
            [out] ULARGE_INTEGER *plibNewPosition);
  //...
}

interface IPersistStreamInit : public IPersist {
        HRESULT IsDirty();
        HRESULT Load([in] LPSTREAM pStm);
        HRESULT Save([in] LPSTREAM pStm, [in] BOOL fClearDirty);
        HRESULT GetSizeMax([out] ULARGE_INTEGER*pCbSize);
        HRESULT InitNew();
};

interface IPersistStream : public IPersist {
        HRESULT IsDirty();
        HRESULT Load([in] LPSTREAM pStm);
        HRESULT Save([in] LPSTREAM pStm, [in] BOOL fClearDirty);
        HRESULT GetSizeMax([out] ULARGE_INTEGER*pCbSize);
};
```

When a client wants an object to save its state as an opaque stream of bytes, it typically attempts to use the object's IPersistStreamInit interface as the persistence mechanism. The client supplies the stream into which the object saves in the form of an IStream interface.

When the client calls IPersistStreamInit::Load, the object reads its properties from the stream by calling IStream::Read. When the client calls IPersistStreamInit::Save, the object writes its properties by calling IStream::Write. Note that unless the object goes to the extra effort of handling the situation, the stream contains values in an architecture-specific byte order.

Most recent clients prefer to use an object's IPersistStreamInit interface; if it's not present, they fall back and try to use IPersistStream. However, older client code might attempt to use only an object's IPersistStream implementation. To be compatible with both types of clients, your object must implement IPersistStream. However, other containers ask for only IPersistStreamInit, so to be compatible with them, you need to implement that interface.

However, you're not supposed to implement both interfaces because then it's unclear to the container whether the object needs to be informed when it's newly created. Pragmatically, the best solution to this dilemma is to support both interfaces when your object doesn't care to be notified when it's newly created, even though this violates the specification for controls.

Although IPersistStreamInit doesn't derive from IPersistStream (it can't because of the mutual exclusion aspect of the interfaces), they have identical v-tables for all methods except the last: the InitNew method. Because of COM's binary compatibility, when your object doesn't need an InitNew call, your object can hand out an IPersistStreamInit interface when asked for an IPersistStream interface. So with a single implementation of IPersistStreamInit and an extra COM interface map entry, your object becomes compatible with a larger number of clients.

```
class ATL_NO_VTABLE CDemagogue : public IPersistStreamInit, ... {
...
BEGIN_COM_MAP(CDemagogue)
  ...
  COM_INTERFACE_ENTRY(IPersistStreamInit)
  COM_INTERFACE_ENTRY_IID(IID_IPersistStream, IPersistStreamInit)
  COM_INTERFACE_ENTRY2(IPersist, IPersistStreamInit)
END_COM_MAP()
  ...
};
```

Implementing IPersistStreamInit

Clients ask an object to initialize itself only once. When the client has no initial values to give the object, the client calls the object's IPersistSteamInit::InitNew method. In this case, the object should initialize itself to default values. When the client has initial values to give the object, the client opens the stream and calls the object's IPersistStreamInit::Load method. When the client wants to save the state of an object, it creates a stream and calls the object's `IPersistStreamInit::Save` method.

As in the property bag implementation, this is quite straightforward to implement in an object. Here's an example of an implementation for the Demagogue object to save and restore its three properties to and from a stream:

```
class CDemagogue : public IPersistStreamInit, ... {
    CComBSTR m_name;
    long     m_volume;
    CComBSTR m_speech;
    BOOL     m_fDirty;

    STDMETHODIMP IsDirty() { return m_fDirty ? s_OK : S_FALSE; }

    STDMETHODIMP Load(IStream* pStream) {
        HRESULT hr = m_name.ReadFromStream(pStream);
        if (FAILED (hr)) return hr;

        ULONG cb;
        hr = pStream->Read (&m_volume, sizeof (m_volume), &cb);
        if (FAILED (hr)) return hr;
        hr = m_speech.ReadFromStream(pStream);
        if (FAILED (hr)) return hr;
        m_fDirty = FALSE ;
        return S_OK;
    }


    STDMETHODIMP Save (IStream* pStream) {
        HRESULT hr = m_name.WriteToStream (pStream);
        if (FAILED(hr)) return hr;

        ULONG cb;
        hr = pStream->Write(&m_volume, sizeof (m_volume), &cb);
        if (FAILED(hr)) return hr;

        hr = m_speech.WriteToStream (pStream);
        return hr;
    }

    STDMETHODIMP GetSizeMax(ULARGE_INTEGER* pcbSize) {
        if (NULL == pcbSize) return E_POINTER;
        // Length of m_name
        pcbSize->QuadPart = CComBSTR::GetStreamSize(m_name);
        pcbSize->QuadPart += sizeof (m_volume);
        // Length of m_speech
```

```
            pcbSize->QuadPart += CComBSTR::GetStreamSize(m_speech);
            return S_OK;
        }

    STDMETHODIMP InitNew() { return S_OK; }
};
```

IStorage and IPersistStorage

An embeddable object—an object that you can store in an OLE linking and embedding container such as Microsoft Word and Microsoft Excel—must implement IPersistStorage. The container provides the object with an IStorage interface pointer. The IStorage references a structured storage medium. The storage object (the object implementing the IStorage interface) acts much like a directory object in a traditional file system. An object can use the IStorage interface to create new and open existing substorages and streams within the storage medium that the container provides.

```
interface IStorage : public IUnknown {
  HRESULT CreateStream([string,in] const OLECHAR* pwcsName,
    [in] DWORD grfMode, [in] DWORD reserved1,
    [in] DWORD reserved2,
    [out] IStream** ppstm);

  HRESULT OpenStream([string,in] const OLECHAR* pwcsName,
    [unique][in] void* reserved1, [in] DWORD grfMode,
    [in] DWORD reserved2, [out] IStream** ppstm);

  HRESULT CreateStorage([string,in] const OLECHAR* pwcsName,
    [in] DWORD grfMode, [in] DWORD reserved1,
    [in] DWORD reserved2,
    [out] IStorage** ppstg);

  HRESULT OpenStorage(
    [string,unique,in] const OLECHAR* pwcsName,
    [unique,in] IStorage* pstgPriority,
    [in] DWORD grfMode, [unique,in] SNB snbExclude,
    [in] DWORD reserved, [out] IStorage** ppstg);

  // Following methods abbreviated for clarity...
  HRESULT CopyTo( ... );
  HRESULT MoveElementTo( ... )
  HRESULT Commit( ... )
  HRESULT Revert(void);
  HRESULT EnumElements( ... );
```

```
    HRESULT DestroyElement( . . , );
    HRESULT RenameElement( ... );
    HRESULT SetElementTimes( ... );
    HRESULT SetClass( ... );
    HRESULT SetStateBits( ... );
    HRESULT Stat( ... );
};

interface IPersistStorage : public IPersist {
  HRESULT IsDirty ();
  HRESULT InitNew ([unique,in] IStorage* pStg);
  HRESULT Load ([unique,in] IStorage* pStg);
  HRESULT Save ([unique,in] IStorage* pStgSave,
    [in] BOOL fSameAsLoad);
  HRESULT SaveCompleted ([unique,in] IStorage* pStgNew);
  HRESULT HandsOffStorage ();
};
```

The IsDirty, InitNew, Load, and Save methods work much as the similarly named methods in the persistence interfaces you've seen previously. However, unlike streams, when a container hands an object an IStorage during the InitNew or Load calls, the object can hold on to the interface pointer (after AddRef-ing it, of course). This permits the object to read and write its state incrementally instead of all at once, as do the other persistence mechanisms. A container uses the HandsOff-Storage and SaveCompleted methods to instruct the object to release the held interface and to give the object a new IStorage interface, respectively.

Typically, a container of embedded objects creates a storage to hold the objects. In this storage, the container creates one or more streams to hold the container's own state. In addition, for each embedded object, the container creates a substorage in which the container asks the embedded object to save its state.

This is a pretty heavy-weight persistence technique for many objects. Simple objects, such as in the Demagogue example used so far, don't really need this flexibility. Often, such objects simply create a stream in their given storage and save their state into the stream using an implementation of IPersistStreamInit. This is exactly what the ATL implementation of IPersistStorage does, so I defer creating a custom example here; you'll see the ATL implementation shortly.

ATL Persistence Implementation Classes

ATL provides implementations of the IPersistPropertyBag. IPersistStreamInit and IPersistStorage interfaces called IPersistPropertyBagImpl, IPersist-StreamInitImpl, and IPersistStorageImpl, respectively. Each template class takes one parameter, the name of the deriving class. You add support for these three persistence interfaces to your object like this:

```
class ATL_NO_VTABLE CDemagogue :
    public IPersistPropertyBagImpl<CDemagogue>,
    public IPersistStreamInitImpl<CDemagogue>,
    public IPersistStorageImpl<CDemagogue> {
...
BEGIN_COM_MAP(CDemagogue)
    ...
    COM_INTERFACE_ENTRY2(IPersist, IPersistPropertyBag)
    COM_INTERFACE_ENTRY(IPersistPropertyBag)
    COM_INTERFACE_ENTRY(IPersistStreamInit)
    COM_INTERFACE_ENTRY(IPersistStream)
    COM_INTERFACE_ENTRY(IPersistStorage)
END_COM_MAP()
    ...
};
```

Don't forget to add the COM MAP entry for IPersist. All three persistence interfaces derive from IPersist, not IUnknown, so you need to respond affirmatively to queries for IPersist. Note also that you need to use the COM_INTERFACE_ENTRY2 (or COM_INTERFACE_ENTRY_IID) macro because multiple base classes derive from IPersist.

The Property Map

The ATL implementation of these three persistence interfaces requires that your object provide a table that describes all the properties that should be saved and loaded during a persistence operation. This table is called the *property map*. ATL uses the property map of a class for two independent purposes: persistence support and control property page support (discussed in Chapter 11, "ActiveX Controls").

The various property map entries enable you to do the following:

- Define the properties of the COM object that the ATL persistence-implementation classes save and restore during a persistence request
- Define the member variables of the C++ class that the ATL persistence-implementation classes save and restore during a persistence request
- Define the property pages that a class uses
- Associate a property with its property page

The CDemagogue class's property map looks like this:

```
BEGIN_PROP_MAP(CDemagogue)
  PROP_ENTRY_EX("Speech", DISPID_SPEECH,
    CLSID_NULL, IID_ISpeaker)
  PROP_ENTRY_EX("Volume", DISPID_VOLUME,
    CLSID_NULL, IID_ISpeaker)
  PROP_ENTRY_EX("Name",   DISPID_NAME,
    CLSID_NULL, IID_INamedObject)
END_PROP_MAP()
```

The `BEGIN_PROP_MAP` and `END_PROP_MAP` macros define a class's property map. You list the persistent properties of an object in the property map using the `PROP_ENTRY` and `PROP_ENTRY_EX` macros. The `PROP_ENTRY` macro describes a property that the persistence implementation can access via the default dispatch interface—in other words, the interface retrieved when you query for `IID_IDispatch`. You use the `PROP_ENTRY_EX` macro to describe a property that the persistence implementation must access using some other specified dispatch interface. Both macros require the name of the property, the property's DISPID, and the CLSID of the property's associated property page (discussed in Chapter 11). The `PROP_ENTRY_EX` macro also requires the IID of the dispatch interface that supports the specified property; the `PROP_ENTRY` macro uses `IID_IDispatch`.

```
PROP_ENTRY (szDesc, dispid, clsid)
PROP_ENTRY_EX (szDesc, dispid, clsid, iidDispatch)
PROP_DATA_ENTRY (szDesc, member, vt)
```

You might also want to load and save member variables of your object that are not accessible via a dispatch interface. The `PROP_DATA_ENTRY` macro enables you to specify the name of a property, the member variable containing the value, and the VARIANT type of the variable, like so:

```
BEGIN_PROP_MAP(CBullsEye)
  PROP_DATA_ENTRY("_cx", m_sizeExtent.cx, VT_UI4)
  PROP_DATA_ENTRY("_cy", m_sizeExtent.cy, VT_UI4)
  ...
END_PROP_MAP()
```

Effectively, the `PROP_DATA_ENTRY` macro causes the persistence implementation to reach into your object, access the specified member variable for the length implied by the VARIANT type, place the data into a VARIANT, and write the VARIANT to the persistent medium. This is quite handy when you have a member variable that is a VARIANT-compatible type. However, it doesn't work for noncompatible types such as indexed properties. Note that a `PROP_PAGE` macro also is used to associate a property to a property page; I discuss its use in Chapter 11, "ActiveX Controls." The persistence implementations skip entries in the property map made with the PROP_PAGE macro.

One caution: Don't add a PROP_ENTRY, PROP_ENTRY_EX, or PROP_DATA_ENTRY macro that has a property name with an embedded space character. Some relatively popular containers, such as Visual Basic 6, provide an implementation of IPropertyBag that cannot handle names with embedded spaces.

When you have a member variable that you want to load and save during a persistence operation, and that variable is not a VARIANT-compatible type (for example, an indexed or array variable), the property map mechanism doesn't help. You have to override the appropriate member functions of the persistence implementation classes, and read and write the variable explicitly. To do this, you need to know the basic structure of the ATL persistence implementation.

The Persistence Implementations

Let's look at how the persistence implementations work, using the property bag persistence implementation as the example. All persistence implementations are similar.

The Property Map

The property map macros basically add a static member function called GetPropertyMap to your class. GetPropertyMap returns a pointer to an array of ATL_PROPMAP_ENTRY structures. The structure looks like this:

```
struct ATL_PROPMAP_ENTRY {
    LPCOLESTR szDesc;
    DISPID dispid;
    const CLSID* pclsidPropPage;
    const IID* piidDispatch;
    DWORD dwOffsetData;
    DWORD dwSizeData;
    VARTYPE vt;
};
```

For example, here's a property map and the resulting macro expansion:

```
BEGIN_PROP_MAP(CDemagogue)
    PROP_ENTRY("Speech", DISPID_SPEECH, CLSID_NULL)
    PROP_ENTRY_EX("Name", DISPID_NAME, CLSID_NULL,
      IID_INamedObject)
    PROP_DATA_ENTRY("_cx", m_sizeExtent.cx, VT_UI4)
END_PROP_MAP()
```

This property map expands to this:

```
__if_not_exists(__ATL_PROP_NOTIFY_EVENT_CLASS) {
    typedef ATL::_ATL_PROP_NOTIFY_EVENT_CLASS
        __ATL_PROP_NOTIFY_EVENT_CLASS;
}
static ATL::ATL_PROPMAP_ENTRY* GetPropertyMap() {
  static ATL::ATL_PROPMAP_ENTRY pPropMap[] = {
  {OLESTR(("Speech"), DISPID_SPEECH, &CLSID_NULL,
      __uudiof(IID_IDispatch), 0, 0, 0},
  {OLESTR("Name"),     DISPID_ NAME,  &CLSID_NULL,
      &IID_INamedObject, 0, 0, 0},
  {OLESTR("_cx"),      0,             &CLSID_NULL, NULL,
      offsetof(_PropMapClass, m_sizeExtent.cx),
      sizeof(((_PropMapClass*)0)-> m_sizeExtent.cx), VT_UI4},
  {NULL, 0, NULL, &IID_NULL, 0, 0, 0}
  };
  return pPropMap;
}
```

The szDesc field of the structure holds the name of the property. It's used only by the property bag persistence implementation.

The dispid field contains the property's dispatch identifier. All the persistence implementations need this so they can access the property via one of the object's IDispatch implementations by calling the Invoke method.

The pclsidPropPage field contains a pointer to the CLSID for the property page associated with the object. It's not used during persistence.

The piidDispatch field contains a pointer to the IID of the dispatch interface that supports this property. The specified dispid is unique to this interface.

Only PROP_DATA_ENTRY macros use the last three fields. The dwOffsetData field contains the offset of the specified member variable from the beginning of a class instance. The dwSizeData field contains the size of the variable in bytes, and the vt field contains the variable's VARTYPE (VARIANT type enumeration code).

The various persistence implementations basically iterate over this map and load or save the properties listed. For properties listed using PROP_ENTRY and PROP_ENTRY_EX, the implementations call IDispatch::Invoke with the specified dispid to get or put the property.

Invoke transfers each property via a VARIANT. The stream persistence implementation simply wraps the variant in a CComVARIANT instance and uses its Read-FromStream and WriteToStream methods to do all the hard work. Therefore, stream persistence supports all VARIANT types that the CComVARIANT persistence implementation supports (discussed in Chapter 3, "ATL Smart Types"). The property bag implementation has it even easier because property bags deal directly in VARIANTs.

For properties listed using the PROP_DATA_ENTRY macro, things aren't quite so simple. The IPersistStreamInit implementation directly accesses the object instance at the specified offset for the specified length. This reads or writes the specified number of bytes directly to or from the object.

However, the IPersistPropertyBag implementation must read and write properties held in a VARIANT. Therefore, this implementation copies the member variable of the object to a VARIANT before writing the property to the bag, and copies a VARIANT to the member variable after reading the property from the bag. The current implementation of IPersistPropertyBag persistence supports only a limited set of VARIANT types; worse, it silently fails to load and save properties with any VARTYPEs other than these:

- VT_UI1, VT_I1: Read and write the variable as a BYTE.
- VT_BOOL: Reads and writes the variable as a VARIANT_BOOL.
- VT_UI2, VT_I2: Read and write the variable as a short.
- VT_UI4, VT_I4, VT_INT, VT_UINT: Read and write the variable as a long.
- VT_BSTR: Reads and writes the variable as a BSTR.
- Any other VT_*: Silently fail.

IPersistPropertyBagImpl

The IPersistPropertyBagImpl<T> class implements the IPersistPropertyBag interface methods. IPersistPropertyBag, like all the persistence interfaces, derives from IPersist, which has one method: GetClassID.

```
interface IPersist : IUnknown
{ HRESULT GetClassID([out] CLSID* pclsid); }
```

All the persistence-implementation classes have the same implementation of GetClassID. They call a static member function named GetObjectCLSID method to retrieve the CLSID. This method must be in the deriving class (your object's class) or one of its base classes.

```
template <class T>
class ATL_NO_VTABLE IPersistPropertyBagImpl
    : public IPersistPropertyBag {
public:
    ...
    STDMETHOD(GetClassID)(CLSID *pClassID) {
        ATLTRACE(atlTraceCOM, 2, _T("IPersistPropertyBagImpl::GetClassID\n"));
        if (pClassID == NULL)
            return E_POINTER;
```

```
        *pClassID = T::GetObjectCLSID();
        return S_OK;
    }};
```

Normally, your class obtains its `GetObjectCLSID` static member function from `CComCoClass`:

```
template <class T, const CLSID* pclsid = &CLSID_NULL>
class CComCoClass {
public:
    ...
    static const CLSID& WINAPI GetObjectCLSID() {return *pclsid;}
};
```

This implies that a class must be createable for it to use the persistence classes. This is reasonable because it doesn't do much good to save a class to some persistent medium and then be unable to create a new instance when loading the object from that medium.

The `IPersistPropertyBagImpl<T>` class also implements the remaining `IPersistPropertyBag` methods, including, for example, the `Load` method. `IPersistPropertyBagImpl<T>::Load` calls `T::IPersistPropertyBag_Load` to do most of the work. This allows your class to provide this method when it needs a custom implementation of `Load`. Normally, your object (`class T`) doesn't provide an `IPersistPropertyBag_Load` method, so this call vectors to a default implementation provided by the base class `IPersistPropertyBagImpl<T>::IPersistPropertyBag_Load` method. The default implementation calls the global function `AtlIPersistPropertyBag_Load`. This global function iterates over the property map and, for each entry in the map, loads the property from the property bag:

```
template <class T>
class ATL_NO_VTABLE IPersistPropertyBagImpl
    : public IPersistPropertyBag {
public:
    ...
    // IPersistPropertyBag
    //
    STDMETHOD(Load)(LPPROPERTYBAG pPropBag,
        LPERRORLOG pErrorLog) {
        ATLTRACE(atlTraceCOM, 2, _T("IPersistPropertyBagImpl::Load\n"));
        T* pT = static_cast<T*>(this);
        ATL_PROPMAP_ENTRY* pMap = T::GetPropertyMap();
        ATLASSERT(pMap != NULL);
```

```
        return pT->IPersistPropertyBag_Load(pPropBag,
            pErrorLog, pMap);
    }
    HRESULT IPersistPropertyBag_Load(LPPROPERTYBAG pPropBag,
        LPERRORLOG pErrorLog, ATL_PROPMAP_ENTRY* pMap) {
        T* pT = static_cast<T*>(this);
        HRESULT hr = AtlIPersistPropertyBag_Load(pPropBag,
            pErrorLog, pMap, pT, pT->GetUnknown());
        if (SUCCEEDED(hr))
            pT->m_bRequiresSave = FALSE;
        return hr;
    }
    ...
};
```

This implementation structure provides three places where we can override methods and provide custom persistence support for a non-VARIANT-compatible property. We can override the Load method itself, in effect directly implementing the IPersistPropertyBag method. Alternatively, we can let ATL implement Load while our object implements IPersistPropertyBag_Load. Finally, we can let ATL implement Load and IPersistPropertyBag_Load while we provide a replacement global function called AtlIPersistPropertyBag_Load and play some linker tricks so that our object uses our global function instead of the ATL-provided one.

The most natural method is to implement Load. Normally, in this implementation, you call the base class Load method to read all properties described in the property map, and then read any custom, non-VARIANT-compatible properties:

```
HRESULT CMyObject::Load(LPPROPERTYBAG pPropBag,
    LPERRORLOG pErrorLog) {
    HRESULT hr =
IPersistPropertyBagImpl<CMyObject>::Load(pPropBag,pErrorLog);
    if (FAILED (hr)) return hr;

    // Read an array of VT_I4
    // This requires us to create a "name" for each array element
    // Read each element as a VARIANT, then re-create the array
    ...
}
```

This approach has a few disadvantages. It's a minor point, but the object now requires four methods for its persistence implementation: its Load, the base class Load, the base class IPersistPropertyBag_Load, and the AtlIPersistPropertyBag_Load. We could copy the base class Load implementation into the object's Load method, but that makes the object more fragile because future versions of ATL might change its persistence-implementation technique.

Another slight disadvantage to this approach is that it is clear from the ATL implementation that the ATL designers intended for your object to override IPersistPropertyBag_Load. Note the following code fragment from the default implementation of Load:

```
STDMETHOD(Load)(LPPROPERTYBAG pPropBag, LPERRORLOG pErrorLog) {
  ...
  T* pT = static_cast<T*>(this);
  ...
  return pT->IPersistPropertyBag_Load(pPropBag, pErrorLog, pMap);
}
```

Instead of directly calling IPersistPropertyBag_Load, which is present in the same class as the Load method, the code calls the method using a pointer to the deriving class—your object's class. This provides the same functionality as making the method virtual, without the overhead of a virtual function.

Generally, the best solution is to let the object provide its own implementation of the IPersistPropertyBag_Load method. In this implementation, the object can call the global function AtlIPersistProperyBag_Load and save any non-VARIANT-compatible properties it possessed. Here's an example from the BullsEye control described in Chapter 11, "ActiveX Controls." It contains a property that is an array of long integers. This can't be described as a VARIANT-compatible type because it's not a SAFEARRAY, so I can't list the property in the property map.

```
HRESULT CBullsEye::IPersistPropertyBag_Load(
    LPPROPERTYBAG pPropBag, LPERRORLOG pErrorLog,
    ATL_PROPMAP_ENTRY* pMap) {
    if (NULL == pPropBag) return E_POINTER;

    // Load the properties described in the PROP_MAP
    HRESULT hr = AtlIPersistPropertyBag_Load(pPropBag, pErrorLog,
        pMap, this, GetUnknown());
    if (SUCCEEDED(hr)) m_bRequiresSave = FALSE;

    if (FAILED (hr)) return hr;

    // Load the indexed property - RingValues
    // Get the number of rings
    short sRingCount;
    get_RingCount (&sRingCount);
```

```
        // For each ring, read its value
        for (short nIndex = 1; nIndex <= sRingCount; nIndex++) {

            // Create the base property name
            CComBSTR bstrName = OLESTR("RingValue");

            // Create ring number as a string
            CComVariant vRingNumber = nIndex;
            hr = vRingNumber.ChangeType (VT_BSTR);
            ATLASSERT (SUCCEEDED (hr));

            // Concatenate the two strings to form property name
            bstrName += vRingNumber.bstrVal;

            // Read ring value from the property bag
            CComVariant vValue = 0L;
            hr = pPropBag->Read(bstrName, &vValue, pErrorLog);
            ATLASSERT (SUCCEEDED (hr));
            ATLASSERT (VT_I4 == vValue.vt);

            if (FAILED (hr)) {
                hr = E_UNEXPECTED;
                break;
            }

            // Set the ring value
            put_RingValue (nIndex, vValue.lVal);
        }

        if (SUCCEEDED(hr)) m_bRequiresSave = FALSE;
        return hr;
    }
```

The Save method works symmetrically. The IPersistPropertyBagImpl<T> class
implements the Save method. IPersistPropertyBagImpl<T>::Save calls T::IPer-
sistPropertyBag_Save to do the work. Again, your object (class T) doesn't normally provide an IPersistPropertyBag_Save method, so this call vectors to a
default implementation that the base class IPersistPropertyBagImpl<T>::IPer-
sistPropertyBag_Save method provides. The default implementation calls the
global function AtlIPersistPropertyBag_Save. This global function iterates over
the property map and, for each entry in the map, saves the property to the property bag.

```
template <class T>
class ATL_NO_VTABLE IPersistPropertyBagImpl
    : public IPersistPropertyBag {
public:
    ...
    // IPersistPropertyBag
    //
    STDMETHOD(Save)(LPPROPERTYBAG pPropBag, BOOL fClearDirty,
        BOOL fSaveAllProperties) {
        ATLTRACE(atlTraceCOM, 2, _T("IPersistPropertyBagImpl::Save\n"));
        T* pT = static_cast<T*>(this);
        ATL_PROPMAP_ENTRY* pMap = T::GetPropertyMap();
        ATLASSERT(pMap != NULL);
        return pT->IPersistPropertyBag_Save(pPropBag,
            fClearDirty, fSaveAllProperties, pMap);
    }

    HRESULT IPersistPropertyBag_Save(LPPROPERTYBAG pPropBag,
        BOOL fClearDirty, BOOL fSaveAllProperties,
        ATL_PROPMAP_ENTRY* pMap) {
        T* pT = static_cast<T*>(this);
        HRESULT hr;
        hr = AtlIPersistPropertyBag_Save(pPropBag, fClearDirty,
            fSaveAllProperties, pMap, pT, pT->GetUnknown());
        if (fClearDirty && SUCCEEDED(hr)) {
            pT->m_bRequiresSave=FALSE;
        }
        return hr;
    }
};
```

Finally, `IPersistPropertyBagImpl` implements the `InitNew` method this way:

```
STDMETHOD(InitNew)() {
    ATLTRACE(atlTraceCOM, 2,
        _T("IPersistPropertyBagImpl::InitNew\n"));
    T* pT = static_cast<T*>(this);
    pT->m_bRequiresSave = TRUE;
    return S_OK;
}
```

Therefore, you need to override `InitNew` directly when you have any initialization to perform when there are no properties to load.

IPersistStreamInitImpl

The implementation contained in IPersistStreamInitImpl is quite similar to the one just described. The Load and Save methods call the IPersistStreamInit_Load and IPersistStreamInit_Save methods, which are potentially provided by the deriving object but typically provided by the default implementation in IPersist-StreamInitImpl. These implementations call the global helper functions AtlIPersistStreamInit_Load and AtlIPersistStreamInit_Save.

```
template <class T>
class ATL_NO_VTABLE IPersistStreamInitImpl
  : public IPersistStreamInit {
public:
  ...
  // IPersistStream
  STDMETHOD(Load)(LPSTREAM pStm) {
    ATLTRACE(atlTraceCOM, 2,
      _T("IPersistStreamInitImpl::Load\n"));
    T* pT = static_cast<T*>(this);
    return pT->IPersistStreamInit_Load(pStm,
      T::GetPropertyMap());
  }

  HRESULT IPersistStreamInit_Load(LPSTREAM pStm,
    ATL_PROPMAP_ENTRY* pMap) {
    T* pT = static_cast<T*>(this);
    HRESULT hr =
      AtlIPersistStreamInit_Load(pStm, pMap, pT,
        pT->GetUnknown());
    if (SUCCEEDED(hr)) pT->m_bRequiresSave = FALSE;
    return hr;
  }

  STDMETHOD(Save)(LPSTREAM pStm, BOOL fClearDirty) {
    T* pT = static_cast<T*>(this);
    ATLTRACE(atlTraceCOM, 2,
      _T("IPersistStreamInitImpl::Save\n"));
    return pT->IPersistStreamInit_Save(pStm, fClearDirty,
      T::GetPropertyMap());
  }

  HRESULT IPersistStreamInit_Save(LPSTREAM pStm,
    BOOL fClearDirty, ATL_PROPMAP_ENTRY* pMap) {
    T* pT = static_cast<T*>(this);
    return AtlIPersistStreamInit_Save(pStm, fClearDirty,
      pMap, pT, pT->GetUnknown());
  }
};
```

`IPersistStreamInitImpl` also implements the `InitNew` method this way:

```
STDMETHOD(InitNew)() {
    ATLTRACE(atlTraceCOM, 2,
      _T("IPersistStreamInitImpl::InitNew\n"));
    T* pT = static_cast<T*>(this);
    pT->m_bRequiresSave = TRUE;
  return S_OK;
}
```

Therefore, as with property bags, you need to override `InitNew` directly when you have any initialization to perform when there are no properties to load.

The implementation of the `IsDirty` method assumes the presence of a member variable named `m_bRequiresSave` somewhere in your class hierarchy.

```
STDMETHOD(IsDirty)() {
    ATLTRACE(atlTraceCOM, 2,
      _T("IPersistStreamInitImpl::IsDirty\n"));
    T* pT = static_cast<T*>(this);
    return (pT->m_bRequiresSave) ? S_OK : S_FALSE;
}
```

The persistence implementations originally assumed that only ActiveX controls would use them, as if controls were the only objects that needed a persistence implementation. Although ATL has greatly reduced the coupling between the control classes and the persistence implementation, the `CComControlBase` class normally provides the `m_bRequiresSave` variable and the `SetDirty` and `GetDirty` helper functions usually used to access the variable.

```
class ATL_NO_VTABLE CComControlBase {
public:
    void SetDirty(BOOL bDirty) { m_bRequiresSave = bDirty; }

    // Obtain the dirty state for the control
    BOOL GetDirty() { return m_bRequiresSave; }
    ...
    unsigned m_bRequiresSave:1;
};
```

To use the persistence-implementation classes in an object that doesn't derive from `CComControlBase`, you need to define the `m_bRequiresSave` variable in your class hierarchy somewhere. Typically, for convenience, you also define the `Set-Dirty` and `GetDirty` helper methods. Noncontrols can use this class to provide this persistence support:

```
class ATL_NO_VTABLE CSupportDirtyBit {
public:
  CSupportDirtyBit() : m_bRequiresSave(FALSE) {}
  void SetDirty(BOOL bDirty) {
    m_bRequiresSave = bDirty ? TRUE : FALSE;
  }
  BOOL GetDirty() { return m_bRequiresSave ? TRUE : FALSE; }
  BOOL m_bRequiresSave;
};
```

Finally, the IPersistStreamInitImpl class provides the following implementation of GetSizeMax:

```
STDMETHOD(GetSizeMax)(ULARGE_INTEGER* pcbSize) {
  HRESULT hr = S_OK;
  T* pT = static_cast<T*>(this);

  if (pcbSize == NULL)
    return E_POINTER;

  ATL_PROPMAP_ENTRY* pMap = T::GetPropertyMap();
  ATLENSURE(pMap != NULL);

  // Start the size with the size of the ATL version
  // we write out.
  ULARGE_INTEGER nSize;
  nSize.HighPart = 0;
  nSize.LowPart = sizeof(DWORD);

  CComPtr<IDispatch> pDispatch;
  const IID* piidOld = NULL;
  for (int i = 0; pMap[i].pclsidPropPage != NULL; i++) {
    if (pMap[i].szDesc == NULL)
      continue;

    // check if raw data entry
    if (pMap[i].dwSizeData != 0) {
      ULONG ulSize=0;
      //Calculate stream size for BSTRs special case
      if (pMap[i].vt == VT_BSTR) {
        void* pData = (void*)(pMap[i].dwOffsetData +
          (DWORD_PTR)pT);
        ATLENSURE(
          pData >= (void*)(DWORD_PTR)pMap[i].dwOffsetData
```

```
            && pData >= (void*)(DWORD_PTR)pT );
        BSTR bstr=*reinterpret_cast<BSTR*>(pData);
        ulSize=CComBSTR::GetStreamSize(bstr);
      } else {
        ulSize = pMap[i].dwSizeData;
      }
      nSize.QuadPart += ulSize;
      continue;
    }

    CComVariant var;
    if (pMap[i].piidDispatch != piidOld) {
      pDispatch.Release();
      if (FAILED(pT->GetUnknown()->
        QueryInterface(*pMap[i].piidDispatch,
        (void**)&pDispatch))) {
        ATLTRACE(atlTraceCOM, 0,
          _T("Failed to get a dispatch pointer for "
            "property #%i\n"), i);
        hr = E_FAIL;
        break;
      }
      piidOld = pMap[i].piidDispatch;
    }

    if (FAILED(pDispatch.GetProperty(pMap[i].dispid, &var))) {
      ATLTRACE(atlTraceCOM, 0,
        _T("Invoked failed on DISPID %x\n"),
        pMap[i].dispid);
      hr = E_FAIL;
      break;
    }
    nSize.QuadPart += var.GetSize();
  }
  *pcbSize = nSize;
  return hr;
}
```

Previous versions of ATL simply returned E_NOTIMPL from the GetSizeMax function. As of this writing, the MSDN documentation claims that ATL still does not implement this function. In any event, the implementation that ATL 8 actually provides is fairly straightforward. GetSizeMax loops through all the entries in the property map and accumulates the total size each entry requires in the nSize variable. If it finds a "raw" PROP_DATA_ENTRY, it simply increments the total nSize by the size of the member specified in the PROP_DATA_ENTRY macro. Alternatively, if it finds a PROP_ENTRY or PROP_ENTRY_EX in the map, it queries the object for the specified IDispatch interface and wraps the resulting interface pointer in a CComPtr. Recall from Chapter 3, "ATL Smart Types," that the CComPtr smart pointer template class provides a convenient specialization for IDispatch that exposes property "getters" and "setters." GetSizeMax uses CComPtr<IDispatch>::GetProperty to retrieve a VARIANT value for the property specified in the property map entry. The function wraps the returned VARIANT in a CComVariant and uses that class's GetSize function to increment the nSize total for the object.

IPersistStorageImpl

The ATL implementation of IPersistStorage is very simplistic. The Save method creates a stream called "Contents" within the provided storage and depends on an IPersistStreamInit implementation to write the contents of the stream.

```
template <class T>
class ATL_NO_VTABLE IPersistStorageImpl
    : public IPersistStorage {
public:
    STDMETHOD(Save)(IStorage* pStorage, BOOL fSameAsLoad) {
        ATLTRACE(atlTraceCOM, 2,
          _T("IPersistStorageImpl::Save\n"));
        CComPtr<IPersistStreamInit> p;
        p.p = IPSI_GetIPersistStreamInit();
        HRESULT hr = E_FAIL;
        if (p != NULL) {
            CComPtr<IStream> spStream;
            static LPCOLESTR vszContents = OLESTR("Contents");
            hr = pStorage->CreateStream(vszContents,
              STGM_READWRITE | STGM_SHARE_EXCLUSIVE | STGM_CREATE,
              0, 0, &spStream);
            if (SUCCEEDED(hr)) hr = p->Save(spStream, fSameAsLoad);
        }
        return hr;
    }
    ...
};
```

Similarly, the Load method opens the "Contents" stream and uses the IPersistStreamInit implementation to read the contents of the stream.

```
STDMETHOD(Load)(IStorage* pStorage) {
    ATLTRACE(atlTraceCOM, 2, _T("IPersistStorageImpl::Load\n"));
    CComPtr<IPersistStreamInit> p;
    p.p = IPSI_GetIPersistStreamInit();
    HRESULT hr = E_FAIL;
    if (p != NULL) {
        CComPtr<IStream> spStream;
        hr = pStorage->OpenStream(OLESTR("Contents"), NULL,
            STGM_DIRECT | STGM_SHARE_EXCLUSIVE, 0, &spStream);
    if (SUCCEEDED(hr)) hr = p->Load(spStream);
    }
    return hr;
}
```

The `InitNew` and `IsDirty` implementations retrieve the object's `IPersist-StreamInit` interface pointer (using a helper function to get the interface) and delegate to the same named method in that interface:

```
STDMETHOD(IsDirty)(void) {
    ATLTRACE(atlTraceCOM, 2,
      _T("IPersistStorageImpl::IsDirty\n"));
    CComPtr<IPersistStreamInit> p;
    p.p = IPSI_GetIPersistStreamInit();
    return (p != NULL) ? p->IsDirty() : E_FAIL;
}

STDMETHOD(InitNew)(IStorage*) {
    ATLTRACE(atlTraceCOM, 2,
      _T("IPersistStorageImpl::InitNew\n"));
    CComPtr<IPersistStreamInit> p;
    p.p = IPSI_GetIPersistStreamInit();
    return (p != NULL) ? p->InitNew() : E_FAIL;
}
```

One of the main reasons an object supports `IPersistStorage` is so the object can incrementally read and write its state. Unfortunately, the ATL implementation doesn't support this. The implementation does not cache the provided `IStorage` interface provided during the `Load` and `Save` calls, so it's not available for later incremental reads and writes. Not caching the `IStorage` interface makes implementing the last two methods trivial, however:

```
STDMETHOD(SaveCompleted)(IStorage* /* pStorage */) {
  ATLTRACE(atlTraceCOM, 2,
    _T("IPersistStorageImpl::SaveCompleted\n"));
```

```
    return S_OK;
}

STDMETHOD(HandsOffStorage)(void) {
    ATLTRACE(atlTraceCOM, 2, _T("IPersistStorageImpl::HandsOffStorage\n"));
    return S_OK;
}
```

Generally, most objects that need the functionality IPersistStorage provides can't use the implementation ATL provides. They must derive directly from IPersistStorage and implement all the methods explicitly.

Additional Persistence Implementations

Given what you've already seen, you might find it interesting to demonstrate an additional persistence implementation built using functionality we've already covered.

IPersistMemory

Let's look at implementing the IPersistMemory interface:

```
interface IPersistMemory : IPersist {
    HRESULT IsDirty();
    HRESULT Load([in, size_is(cbSize)] LPVOID pvMem,
        [in] ULONG cbSize);
    HRESULT Save([out, size_is(cbSize)] LPVOID pvMem,
        [in] BOOL fClearDirty, [in] ULONG cbSize);
    HRESULT GetSizeMax([out] ULONG* pCbSize);
    HRESULT InitNew();
};
```

The IPersistMemory interface allows a client to request that the object save its state to a fixed-size memory block (identified with a void*). The interface is very similar to IPersistStreamInit, except that it uses a memory block instead of an expandable IStream. The cbSize argument to the Load and Save methods indicates the amount of memory accessible through pvMem. The IsDirty, GetSizeMax, and InitNew methods are semantically identical to those in IPersistStreamInit.

Implementing the IPersistMemory interface

You've seen that ATL provides the IPersistStreamInitImpl class that saves and restores the state of an object to a stream. The COM API CreateStreamOnHGlobal returns an IStream implementation that reads and writes to a global memory block.

We can use the two together and easily implement IPersistMemory using the functionality IPersistStreamInitImpl provides.

With the exception of the Load and Save methods, all methods in our IPersistMemory implementation simply delegate to the same named method in ATL's IPersistStreamInit implementation.

```cpp
template <class T, class S = IPersistStreamInit>
class ATL_NO_VTABLE IPersistMemoryImpl : public IPersistMemory {
public:
    // IPersist
    STDMETHODIMP GetClassID(CLSID *pClassID) {
        ATLTRACE(atlTraceCOM, 2, _T("IPersistMemoryImpl::GetClassID\n"));
        T* pT = static_cast<T*>(this);
        S* psi = static_cast <S*> (pT);
        return psi->GetClassID(pClassID);
    }

    // IPersistMemory
    STDMETHODIMP IsDirty() {
        ATLTRACE(atlTraceCOM, 2,
            _T("IPersistMemoryImpl::IsDirty\n"));
        T* pT = static_cast<T*>(this);
        S* psi = static_cast <S*> (pT);
        return psi->IsDirty();
    }

    STDMETHODIMP Load(void* pvMem, ULONG cbSize) {
        ATLTRACE(atlTraceCOM, 2,
            _T("IPersistMemoryImpl::Load\n"));
        T* pT = static_cast<T*>(this);

        // Get memory handle. We need an actual HGLOBAL
        // here because it's required for CreateStreamOnHGlobal
        HGLOBAL h = GlobalAlloc(GMEM_MOVEABLE, cbSize);
        if (h == NULL) return E_OUTOFMEMORY;
        LPVOID pv = GlobalLock(h);
        if (!pv) return E_OUTOFMEMORY;

        // Copy to memory block
        CopyMemory (pv, pvMem, cbSize);
        CComPtr<IStream> spStrm;
        // Create stream on memory
        HRESULT hr = CreateStreamOnHGlobal (h, TRUE, &spStrm);
        if (FAILED (hr)) {
            GlobalUnlock (h);
```

```
            GlobalFree (h);
            return hr;
        }
        // Stream now owns the memory

        // Load from stream
        S* psi = static_cast <S*> (pT);
        hr = psi->Load (spStrm);

        GlobalUnlock (h);
        return hr;
    }

STDMETHODIMP Save(void* pvMem, BOOL fClearDirty,
    ULONG cbSize) {
    ATLTRACE(atlTraceCOM, 2,
        _T("IPersistMemoryImpl::Save\n"));
    T* pT = static_cast<T*>(this);

    // Get memory handle
    HGLOBAL h = GlobalAlloc (GMEM_MOVEABLE, cbSize);
    if (NULL == h) return E_OUTOFMEMORY;

    // Create stream on memory
    CComPtr<IStream> spStrm;
    HRESULT hr = CreateStreamOnHGlobal (h, TRUE, &spStrm);
    if (FAILED (hr)) {
        GlobalFree (h);
        return hr;
    }
    // Stream now owns the memory

    // Set logical size of stream to physical size of memory
    // (Global memory block allocation rounding causes
    // differences)
    ULARGE_INTEGER uli;
    uli.QuadPart = cbSize ;
    spStrm->SetSize (uli);

    S* psi = static_cast <S*> (pT);
    hr = psi->Save (spStrm, fClearDirty);
    if (FAILED (hr)) return hr;

    LPVOID pv = GlobalLock (h);
    if (!pv) return E_OUTOFMEMORY;
```

```
        // Copy to memory block
        CopyMemory (pvMem, pv, cbSize);

        return hr;
    }

    STDMETHODIMP GetSizeMax(ULONG* pcbSize) {
        if (pcbSize == NULL) return E_POINTER;
        *pcbSize = 0;

        T* pT = static_cast<T*>(this);
        S* psi = static_cast <S*> (pT);
        ULARGE_INTEGER uli ;
        uli.QuadPart = 0;
        HRESULT hr = psi->GetSizeMax (&uli);
        if (SUCCEEDED (hr)) *pcbSize = uli.LowPart;

        return hr;
    }

    STDMETHODIMP InitNew() {
        ATLTRACE(atlTraceCOM, 2,
            _T("IPersistMemoryImpl::InitNew\n"));
        T* pT = static_cast<T*>(this);
        S* psi = static_cast <S*> (pT);
        return psi->InitNew();
    }
};
```

Notice the use of static_cast to downcast the this pointer to the deriving class and then up-cast the resulting pointer to an IPersistStreamInit*. We do this so that we get a compile-time error when the class deriving from IPersistMemory-Impl doesn't also derive from IPersistStreamInit. This approach does require the deriving class to not implement IPersistStreamInit in an "unusual" way, such as on a tear-off interface or via aggregation.

Alternatively, we could have retrieved the IPersistStreamInit interface using QueryInterface:

```
        T* pT = static_cast<T*>(this);
        CComQIPtr<S> psi = pT->GetUnknown() ;
```

However, then we might find out at runtime that no IPersistStreamInit implementation is available, which means the object then ends up saying that it implements IPersistMemory without the capability to do so. I prefer compile-time errors whenever possible, so I chose the former approach accepting its limitations.

Using the IPersistMemoryImpl Template Class

An object uses this IPersistMemory implementation this way:

```
class ATL_NO_VTABLE CDemagogue :
    ...
    public IPersistStreamInitImpl<CDemagogue>,
    public IPersistMemoryImpl<CDemagogue>,
    public CSupportDirtyBit {
    ...
BEGIN_COM_MAP(CDemagogue)
    ...
    COM_INTERFACE_ENTRY2(IPersist, IPersistStreamInit)
    COM_INTERFACE_ENTRY(IPersistStreamInit)
    COM_INTERFACE_ENTRY(IPersistMemory)
END_COM_MAP()
```

Adding Marshal-by-Value Semantics Using Persistence

When you pass an interface pointer as a parameter to a remote (out-of-apartment) method call, the default in COM is to pass by reference. In other words, the object stays where it is, and only a reference to the object is given to the recipient of the call. This typically means that references to the object involve round-trips back to the object, which can be quite expensive. An object can override this pass-by-reference default by implementing the IMarshal interface.

The primary reason most developers implement IMarshal on an object is to give it pass-by-value semantics. In other words, when you pass an interface pointer to a remote method call, you prefer that COM pass a *copy* of the object to the method. All references to the object are then local and do not involve round-trips back to the "original" object. When an object implements IMarshal in such a way that it has pass-by-value semantics, we typically say that the object *marshals by value*.

```
interface IMarshal : public IUnknown {
  STDMETHOD GetUnmarshalClass([in] REFIID riid,
    [unique,in] void* pv,
    [in] DWORD dwDestContext,
    [unique,in] void* pvDestContext,
    [in] DWORD mshlflags, [out] CLSID* pCid);

  STDMETHOD GetMarshalSizeMax([in] REFIID riid,
    [unique,in] void* pv,
```

```
   [in] DWORD dwDestContext,
   [unique,in] void* pvDestContext,
   [in] DWORD mshlflags,
   [out] DWORD* pSize) ;

STDMETHOD MarshalInterface([unique,in] IStream* pStm,
   [in] REFIID riid, [unique][in] void* pv,
   [in] DWORD dwDestContext,
   [unique,in] void* pvDestContext,
   [in] DWORD mshlflags);

STDMETHOD UnmarshalInterface([unique,in] IStream* pStm,
   [in] REFIID riid, [out] void** ppv);

STDMETHOD ReleaseMarshalData([unique,in] IStream* pStm);

STDMETHOD DisconnectObject([in] DWORD dwReserved);
};
```

Given a complete implementation of `IPersistStream` or `IPersistStreamInit`, it's quite easy to build a marshal-by-value implementation of `IMarshal`.

A class typically implements marshal-by-value by returning its own CLSID as the result of the `GetUnmarshalClass` method. The `IPersistStream::GetClassID` method produces the needed CLSID.

The `GetMarshalSizeMax` method must return the number of bytes needed to save the persistent state of the object into a stream. The `IPersistStream::GetSize-Max` method produces the needed size.

The `MarshalInterface` and `UnmarshalInterface` methods need to write and read, respectively, the persistent state of the object into the provided stream. Therefore, we can use the `Save` and `Load` methods of `IPersistStream` for this functionality.

`ReleaseMarshalData` and `DisconnectObject` method can simply return S_OK.

Here's a template class that uses an object's `IPersistStreamInit` interface to provide a marshal-by-value implementation.[1] Once again, I decided to down-cast and up-cast using `static_cast` to obtain the `IPersistStreamInit` interface, so I receive an error at compile time when the deriving class doesn't implement `IPersistStreamInit`.

---

[1] This technique has a history, as does most software development. Jonathon Bordan wrote the first `IMarshalByValueImpl` after being inspired by a *Microsoft System Journal* article by Don Box. Brent Rector then modified Jonathon's example to the present form.

```
template <class T>
class ATL_NO_VTABLE IMarshalByValueImpl : public IMarshal {

  STDMETHODIMP GetUnmarshalClass(REFIID /* riid */,
    void* /* pv */,
    DWORD /* dwDestContext */,
    void* /* pvDestContext */,
    DWORD /* mshlflags */, CLSID *pCid) {
    T* pT = static_cast<T*>(this);
    IPersistStreamInit* psi =
      static_cast<IPersistStreamInit*>(pT);
    return psi->GetClassID (pCid);
  }

  STDMETHODIMP GetMarshalSizeMax(REFIID /* riid */,
    void* /* pv */,
    DWORD /* dwDestContext */,
    void* /* pvDestContext */,
    DWORD /* mshlflags */, DWORD* pSize) {
    T* pT = static_cast<T*>(this);
    IPersistStreamInit* psi =
      static_cast <IPersistStreamInit*> (pT);

    ULARGE_INTEGER uli = { 0 };

    HRESULT hr = psi->GetSizeMax(&uli);
    if (SUCCEEDED (hr)) *pSize = uli.LowPart;
    return hr;
  }

  STDMETHODIMP MarshalInterface(IStream *pStm, REFIID /* riid */,
    void* /* pv */, DWORD /* dwDestContext */,
    void* /* pvDestCtx */, DWORD /* mshlflags */) {
    T* pT = static_cast<T*>(this);
    IPersistStreamInit* psi = static_cast <IPersistStreamInit*> (pT);
    return psi->Save(pStm, FALSE);
  }

  STDMETHODIMP UnmarshalInterface(IStream *pStm, REFIID riid,
    void **ppv) {
    T* pT = static_cast<T*>(this);
    IPersistStreamInit* psi =
      static_cast <IPersistStreamInit*> (pT);
    HRESULT hr = psi->Load(pStm);
    if (SUCCEEDED (hr)) hr = pT->QueryInterface (riid, ppv);
    return hr;
  }
```

```
    STDMETHODIMP ReleaseMarshalData(IStream* /* pStm */) {
      return S_OK;
    }

    STDMETHODIMP DisconnectObject(DWORD /* dwReserved */) {
      return S_OK;
    }
};
```

You can use this template class to provide a marshal-by-value implementation for your object. You need to derive your class from the previous `IMarshalByVal-ueImpl` class (to get the `IMarshal` method implementations) and the `IPersist-StreamInitImpl` class. You must also add a `COM_INTERFACE_ENTRY` for `IMarshal` to the class's interface map. Here's an example:

```
class ATL_NO_VTABLE CDemagogue :
    ...
    public IPersistStreamInitImpl<CDemagogue>,
    public CSupportDirtyBit,
    public IMarshalByValueImpl<CDemagogue> {
    ...
  BEGIN_COM_MAP(CDemagogue)
      COM_INTERFACE_ENTRY2(IPersist, IPersistStreamInit)
      COM_INTERFACE_ENTRY(IPersistStreamInit)
      COM_INTERFACE_ENTRY(IMarshal)
  END_COM_MAP()
    ...
};
```

Note that adding marshal-by-value support to your class this way means that all instances of the class use pass-by-value semantics. It is not possible to pass one object instance by reference and another instance by value (assuming that both instances have the same marshaling context: in-proc, local, or different machine).

Summary

Many objects need some support for persistence, and ATL provides an easily extensible, table-driven implementation of the `IPersistStream[Init]` and the `IPersist-PropertyBag` interfaces. These implementations save and load the properties described by the class's property map entries. By overriding the appropriate methods, you can extend this persistence support for data types that property map entries do not support. The ATL implementation of `IPersistStorage` allows the object to be embedded into an OLE container but doesn't take advantage of many of the capabilities of the `IStorage` medium.

Using and extending the stream persistence support that ATL provides allows an object to offer additional functionality to its clients. For example, you've seen how to implement `IPersistMemory` support to your object (which MFC-based containers prefer). In addition, you can easily add marshal-by-value semantics to your class by reusing the stream persistence functionality.

8 | Collections and Enumerators

Many COM libraries are exposed as sets of objects known as *object models*. A COM object model is a parent object that holds a set of child objects. COM collections and enumerators are the glue that holds the parent and the children together. This chapter examines COM collections and enumerators and how they work together to build object models.

COM Collection and Enumeration Interfaces

Standard C++ Containers and Iterators

C++ programmers long ago learned to separate their collections into three pieces: the data itself, the container of the data, and an iterator for accessing the data. This separation is useful for building pieces separately from each other. The container's job is to enable the user to affect the contents of the collection. The iterator's job is to enable the user to access the contents of the container. And although the iterator implementation depends on how the container stores the data, the implementation details are hidden from the client of the container and the iterator. For example, imagine the following code for populating a container and then accessing it via an iterator:

```
void main() {
  // Populate the collection
  vector<long>  rgPrimes;
  for (long n = 0; n != 1000; ++n) {
    if (IsPrime(n)) rgPrimes.push_back(n);
  }

  // Count the number of items in the collection
  cout << "Primes: " << rgPrimes.size() << endl;

  // Iterate over the collection using sequential access
  vector<long>::iterator begin = rgPrimes.begin();
  vector<long>::iterator end   = rgPrimes.end();
```

```
   for (vector<long>::iterator it = begin; it != end; ++it) {
     cout << *it << " ";
   }
   cout << endl;
}
```

Because the container provides a well-known C++ interface, the client does not need to know the implementation details. In fact, C++ container classes are so uniform that this simple example would work just as well with a list or a deque as it does with a vector. Likewise, because the iterators that the container provides are uniform, the client doesn't need to know the implementation details of the iterator.

For the client to enjoy these benefits, the container and the iterator have certain responsibilities. The responsibilities of the container include the following:

- Can allow the user to manipulate the data. Most containers are of variable size and are populated by the client. However, some containers represent a fixed data set or a set of data that is calculated instead of stored.

- Can allow the user to obtain the count of items. Containers have a `size` method for this purpose.

- Can allow random access. The `std::vector` class allows this using `operator[]`, whereas the `std::list` class does not.

- Must allow the user to access the data at least sequentially, if not randomly. C++ containers provide this facility by exposing iterators.

Likewise, the responsibilities of the iterator entail the following:

- Must be capable of accessing the container's data. That data might be in some shared spot (such as memory, file, or database) where the collection and iterator can both access the data. Alternatively, the iterator might have its own copy of the data. This would allow one client to access a snapshot of the data while another client modified the data using the container. Finally, the iterator could generate the data on demand—for example, by generating the next prime number.

- The iterator must keep track of its current position in the collection of data. Every call to the iterator's `operator++` means to advance that position. Every call to the iterator's `operator*` means to hand out the data at the current position.

- The iterator must be capable of indicating the end of the data to the client.

Although C++ containers and iterators are handy in your C++ code, neither is useful as a way of communicating data via a COM interface. Instead, we turn to the COM equivalent of containers and iterators: COM collections and enumerators.

COM Collections and Enumerators

A *COM collection* is a COM object that holds a set of data and allows the client to manipulate its contents via a COM interface. In many ways, a COM collection is similar to a C++ container. Unfortunately, IDL doesn't support templates, so it's impossible to define a generic ICollection interface. Instead, COM defines collections through coding conventions.

By convention, a COM collection interface takes a minimum form. This form is shown here, pretending that IDL supported templates:

```
[ object, dual ]
template <typename T>
interface ICollection : IDispatch {
  [propget]
  HRESULT Count([out, retval] long* pnCount);

  [id(DISPID_VALUE), propget]
  HRESULT Item([in] long n, [out, retval] T* pnItem);

  [id(DISPID_NEWENUM), propget]
  HRESULT _NewEnum([out, retval] IUnknown** ppEnum);
};
```

Several features about this interface are worth noting:

- Although this minimal collection interface doesn't show any methods for adding or removing elements from the collection, most collections include such methods.

- Most collection interfaces are dual interfaces. An IDispatch-based interface is required for some convenient language-mapping features that I discuss later.

- Most collection interfaces have a read-only Count property that provides a count of the current elements in the collection. Not all collections can calculate a reliable count, however. Examples include a collection of all prime numbers and a collection of rows from a database query that hasn't yet been completed.

- Most collection interfaces have a read-only Item property for random access to a specific element. The first parameter is the index of the element to access, which I've shown as a long. It's also common for this to be a VARIANT so that a number index or a string name can be used. If the index is a number, it is often 1-based, but the creator of the container can choose any indexing scheme desired. Furthermore, the Item property should be given the standard DISPID DISPID_VALUE. This marks the property as the "default" property, which certain language mappings use to provide more convenient access. I show you how this works later.

■ An interface is a collection interface when it exposes an enumerator via the read-only property _NewEnum, which must be assigned the standard DISPID DISPID_NEWENUM. Visual Basic uses this DISPID to implement its For-Each syntax, as I show you soon.

None of the methods specified earlier is actually required; you need to add only the methods you expect to support. However, it's highly recommended to have all three. Without them, you've got a container with inaccessible contents, and you can't even tell how many things are trapped in there.

A *COM enumerator* is to a COM collection as an iterator is to a container. The collection holds the data and allows the client to manipulate it, and the enumerator allows the client sequential access. However, instead of providing sequential access one element at a time, as with an iterator, an enumerator allows the client to decide how many elements it wants. This enables the client to balance the cost of round-trips with the memory requirements to handle more elements at once. A COM enumerator interface takes the following form (again, pretending that IDL supported templates):

```
template <typename T>
interface IEnum : IUnknown {
  [local]
  HRESULT Next([in] ULONG celt,
               [out] T* rgelt,
               [out] ULONG *pceltFetched);

  [call_as(Next)] // Discussed later...
  HRESULT RemoteNext([in] ULONG celt,
                     [out, size_is(celt),
                      length_is(*pceltFetched)] T* rgelt,
                     [out] ULONG *pceltFetched);

  HRESULT Skip([in] ULONG celt);
  HRESULT Reset();
  HRESULT Clone([out] IEnum<T> **ppenum);
}
```

A COM enumerator interface has the following properties:

- The enumerator must be capable of accessing the data of the collection and maintaining a logical pointer to the next element to retrieve. All operations on an enumerator manage this logical pointer in some manner.

- The Next method allows the client to decide how many elements to retrieve in a single round-trip. A result of S_OK indicates that the exact number of elements requested by the celt parameter has been returned in the rgelt array. A result of S_FALSE indicates that the end of the collection has been reached and that the pceltFetched argument holds the number of elements actually retrieved. In addition to retrieving the elements, the Next method implementation must advance the logical pointer internally so that subsequent calls to Next retrieve additional data.

- The Skip method moves the logical pointer but retrieves no data. Notice that celt is an unsigned long, so there is no skipping backward. You can think of an enumerator as modeling a single-linked list, although, of course, it can be implemented any number of ways.

- The Reset method moves the logical pointer back to the beginning of the collection.

- The Clone method returns a copy of the enumerator object. The copy refers to the same data (although it can have its own copy) and points to the same logical position in the collection. The combination of Skip, Reset, and Clone makes up for the lack of a Back method.

Custom Collection and Enumerator Example

For example, let's model a collection of prime numbers as a COM collection:

```
[dual]
interface IPrimeNumbers : IDispatch {
  HRESULT CalcPrimes([in] long min, [in] long max);

  [propget]
  HRESULT Count([out, retval] long* pnCount);

  [propget, id(DISPID_VALUE)]
  HRESULT Item([in] long n, [out, retval] long* pnPrime);

  [propget, id(DISPID_NEWENUM)] // Not quite right...
  HRESULT _NewEnum([out, retval] IEnumPrimes** ppEnumPrimes);
};
```

The corresponding enumerator looks like this:

```
interface IEnumPrimes : IUnknown {
  [local]
  HRESULT Next([in] ULONG celt,
               [out] long* rgelt,
               [out] ULONG *pceltFetched);

  [call_as(Next)]
  HRESULT RemoteNext([in] ULONG celt,
                     [out, size_is(celt),
                        length_is(*pceltFetched)] long* rgelt,
                     [out] ULONG *pceltFetched);

  HRESULT Skip([in] ULONG celt);
  HRESULT Reset();
  HRESULT Clone([out] IEnumPrimes **ppenum);
};
```

Porting the previous C++ client to use the collection and enumerator looks like this:

```
void main() {
  CoInitialize(0);

  CComPtr<IPrimeNumbers>  spPrimes;
  if (SUCCEEDED(spPrimes.CoCreateInstance(CLSID_PrimeNumbers))) {
    // Populate the collection
    HRESULT hr = spPrimes->CalcPrimes(0, 1000);

    // Count the number of items in the collection
    long  nPrimes;
    hr = spPrimes->get_Count(&nPrimes);
    cout << "Primes: " << nPrimes << endl;

    // Enumerate over the collection using sequential access
    CComPtr<IEnumPrimes>  spEnum;
    hr = spPrimes->get__NewEnum(&spEnum);

    const size_t  PRIMES_CHUNK = 64;
    long          rgnPrimes[PRIMES_CHUNK];

    do {
      ULONG celtFetched;
```

```
    hr = spEnum->Next(PRIMES_CHUNK, rgnPrimes, &celtFetched);
    if (SUCCEEDED(hr)) {
      if (hr == S_OK) celtFetched = PRIMES_CHUNK;
      for (long* pn = &rgnPrimes[0];
        pn != &rgnPrimes[celtFetched]; ++pn) {
        cout << *pn << " ";
      }
    }
  }
  while (hr == S_OK);
  cout << endl;

  spPrimes.Release();
}

CoUninitialize();
}
```

This client code asks the collection object to populate itself via the CalcPrimes method instead of adding each prime number one at a time. Of course, this procedure reduces round-trips. The client further reduces round-trips when retrieving the data in chunks of 64 elements. A chunk size of any number greater than 1 reduces round-trips but increases the data requirement of the client. Only profiling can tell you the right number for each client/enumerator pair, but larger numbers are preferred to reduce round-trips.

Dealing with the Enumerator local/call_as Oddity

One thing that's rather odd about the client side of enumeration is the pceltFetched parameter filled by the Next method. The COM documentation is ambiguous, but it boils down to this: When only a single element is requested, the client doesn't have to provide storage for the number of elements fetched—that is, pceltFetched is allowed to be NULL. Normally, however, MIDL doesn't allow an [out] parameter to be NULL. So, to support the documented behavior for enumeration interfaces, all of them are defined with two versions of the Next method. The [local] Next method is for use by the client and allows the pceltFetched parameter to be NULL. The [call_as] RemoteNext method doesn't allow the pceltFetched parameter to be NULL and is the method that performs the marshaling. Although the MIDL compiler implements the RemoteNext method, we have to implement Next manually because we've marked the Next method as [local]. In fact, we're responsible for implementing two versions of the Next method. One version is called by the client and, in turn, calls the RemoteNext method implemented by the proxy. The other version is called by the stub and calls the Next method implemented by the object. Figure 8.1

shows the progression of calls from client to object through the proxy, the stub, and our custom code. The canonical implementation is as follows:

```
static HRESULT STDMETHODCALLTYPE
IEnumPrimes_Next_Proxy(
  IEnumPrimes* This, ULONG celt, long* rgelt,
  ULONG* pceltFetched) {
  ULONG cFetched;
  if (!pceltFetched && celt != 1) return E_INVALIDARG;
  return IEnumPrimes_RemoteNext_Proxy(This, celt, rgelt,
    pceltFetched ? pceltFetched : &cFetched);
}

static HRESULT STDMETHODCALLTYPE
IEnumPrimes_Next_Stub(
  IEnumPrimes* This, ULONG celt, long* rgelt,
  ULONG* pceltFetched) {
  HRESULT hr = This->lpVtbl->Next(This, celt, rgelt,
    pceltFetched);
  if (hr == S_OK && celt == 1) *pceltFetched = 1;
  return hr;
}
```

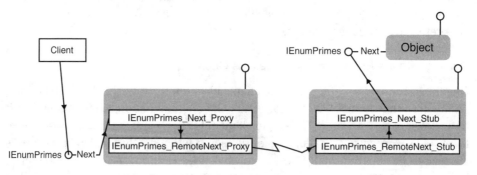

Figure 8.1   Call progression from client, through proxy and stub, to implementation of IEnumPrimes

Every enumeration interface includes this code in the proxy/stub implementation, including all the standard ones, such as IEnumUnknown, IEnumString, and IEnumVARIANT. The only difference in implementation is the name of the interface and the type of data being enumerated over (as shown in the IEnumPrimes example in bold).

When you're building the proxy/stub for your project using the <project>PS project generated by the ATL project template, and you have a custom enumeration interface, it's your job to inject that code into your proxy/stub. One way is to edit the <project>_p.c file, but if you were to recompile the IDL, the implementation would be lost. Another way is to add another .c file to the proxy/stub project. This is rather unpleasant and requires that you remember to update this code every time you edit the IDL file. The technique I prefer relies on macro definitions used during the proxy-/stub-building process and makes heavy use of the cpp_quote statement in IDL.[1] Whenever you have a custom enumeration interface, insert code like this at the bottom of the IDL file, and all will be right with the world (the bold code changes based on the enumeration interface):

```
cpp_quote("#ifdef __midl_proxy")
cpp_quote("static HRESULT STDMETHODCALLTYPE")
cpp_quote("IEnumPrimes_Next_Proxy")
cpp_quote("(IEnumPrimes* This, ULONG celt, long* rgelt,
  ULONG* pceltFetched)")
cpp_quote("{")
cpp_quote("  ULONG cFetched;")
cpp_quote("  if( !pceltFetched && celt != 1 )
  return E_INVALIDARG;")
cpp_quote("  return IEnumPrimes_RemoteNext_Proxy(This, celt,
  rgelt,")
cpp_quote("                      pceltFetched ?
  pceltFetched : &cFetched);")
cpp_quote("}")
cpp_quote("")
cpp_quote("static HRESULT STDMETHODCALLTYPE")
cpp_quote("IEnumPrimes_Next_Stub")
cpp_quote("(IEnumPrimes* This, ULONG celt, long* rgelt,
  ULONG* pceltFetched)")
cpp_quote("{")
cpp_quote("  HRESULT hr = This->lpVtbl->Next(This, celt, rgelt,")
cpp_quote("                           pceltFetched);")
cpp_quote("  if( hr == S_OK && celt == 1 ) *pceltFetched = 1;")
cpp_quote("  return hr;")
cpp_quote("}")
cpp_quote("#endif // __midl_proxy")
```

All the code within the cpp_quote statements is deposited into the <project>.h file, but because the __midl_proxy symbol is used, the code is compiled only when building the proxy/stub.

---

[1] I learned these tricks from Don Box and his enumeration-generation macros. These are available at www.sellsbrothers.com/links/dbox/enumgen.zip (http://tinysells.com/51).

An Enumeration Iterator

One other niggling problem with COM enumerators is their ease of use—or, rather, the lack thereof. It's good that a client has control of the number of elements to retrieve in a single round-trip, but logically the client is still processing the data one element at a time. This is obfuscated by the fact that we're using two loops instead of one. Of course, C++ being C++, there's no reason that a wrapper can't be built to remove this obfuscation.[2] Such a wrapper is included with the source code examples for this book. It's called the `enum_iterator` and is declared like this:

```
#ifndef ENUM_CHUNK
#define ENUM_CHUNK 64
#endif

template <typename EnumItf, const IID* pIIDEnumItf,
  typename EnumType, typename CopyClass = _Copy<EnumType> >
class enum_iterator {
public:
  enum_iterator(IUnknown* punkEnum = 0,
    ULONG nChunk = ENUM_CHUNK);
  enum_iterator(const enum_iterator& i);
  ~enum_iterator();

  enum_iterator& operator=(const enum_iterator& rhs);
  bool operator!=(const enum_iterator& rhs);
  bool operator==(const enum_iterator& rhs);

  enum_iterator& operator++();
  enum_iterator operator++(int);
  EnumType& operator*();

private:
  ...
};
```

The `enum_iterator` class provides a standard C++-like forward iterator that wraps a COM enumerator. The type of the enumeration interface and the type of data that it enumerates are specified as template parameters. The buffer size is passed, along with the pointer to the enumeration interface, as a constructor argument. The first constructor allows for the common use of forward iterators. Instead

---

[2] Or replace one obfuscation for another, depending on your point of view.

of asking a container for the beginning and ending iterators, the beginning iterator is created by passing a non-NULL enumeration interface pointer. The end iterator is created by passing NULL. The copy constructor is used when forming a looping statement. This iterator simplifies the client enumeration code considerably:

```
...
// Enumerate over the collection using sequential access
CComPtr<IEnumPrimes>  spEnum;
hr = spPrimes->get__NewEnum(&spEnum);

// Using an C++-like forward iterator
typedef enum_iterator<IEnumPrimes, &IID_IEnumPrimes, long>
  primes_iterator;
primes_iterator begin(spEnum, 64);
primes_iterator end;
for (primes_iterator it = begin; it != end; ++it) {
  cout << *it << " ";
 }
cout << endl;
...
```

Or if you'd like to get a little more fancy, you can use the enum_iterator with a function object and a standard C++ algorithm, which helps you avoid writing the looping code altogether:

```
struct OutputPrime {
  void operator()(const long& nPrime) {
    cout << nPrime << " ";
  }
};
```

```
    ...
    // Using a standard C++ algorithm
    typedef enum_iterator<IEnumPrimes, &IID_IEnumPrimes, long>
      primes_iterator;
    for_each(primes_iterator(spEnum, 64), primes_iterator(),
      OutputPrime());
    ...
```

This example might not be as clear to you as the looping example, but it warms the cockles of my C++ heart.

Enumeration and Visual Basic 6.0

In the discussion that follows and in all references to Visual Basic in this chapter, we talk specifically about Visual Basic 6.0, not the latest version, VB .NET. COM collections and enumerations evolved with VB6 in mind, so it's insightful to examine client-side programming with VB6 and collections. VB .NET, of course, is an entirely different subject and squarely outside the scope of this book.

The C++ `for_each` algorithm might seem a lot like the Visual Basic 6.0 (VB) `For-Each` statement, and it is. The `For-Each` statement allows a VB programmer to access each element in a collection, whether it's an intrinsic collection built into VB or a custom collection developed using COM. Just as the `for_each` algorithm is implemented using iterators, the `For-Each` syntax is implemented using a COM enumerator—specifically, `IEnumVARIANT`. To support the `For-Each` syntax, the collection interface must be based on `IDispatch` and must have the `_NewEnum` property marked with the special DISPID value `DISPID_NEWENUM`. Because our prime number collection object exposes such a method, you might be tempted to write the following code to exercise the `For-Each` statement:

```
Private Sub Command1_Click()
    Dim primes As IPrimeNumbers
    Set primes = New PrimeNumbers
    primes.CalcPrimes 0, 1000

    MsgBox "Primes: " & primes.Count

    Dim sPrimes As String
    Dim prime As Variant

    For Each prime In primes ' Calls Invoke(DISPID_NEWENUM)
        sPrimes = sPrimes & prime & " "
    Next prime

    MsgBox sPrimes
End Sub
```

When VB sees the `For-Each` statement, it invokes the `_NewEnum` property, looking for an enumerator that implements `IEnumVARIANT`. To support this use, our prime number collection interface must change from exposing `IEnumPrimes` to exposing `IEnumVARIANT`. Here's the twist: The signature of the method is actually `_NewEnum(IUnknown**)`, not `_NewEnum(IEnumVARIANT**)`. VB takes the `IUnknown*` returned from `_NewEnum` and queries for `IEnumVARIANT`. It would've been nice for VB to avoid an extra round-trip, but perhaps at one point, the VB team expected to support other enumeration types.

Modifying `IPrimeNumbers` to support the VB `For-Each` syntax looks like this:

```
[dual]
interface IPrimeNumbers : IDispatch {
  HRESULT CalcPrimes([in] long min, [in] long max);

  [propget]
  HRESULT Count([out, retval] long* pnCount);

  [propget, id(DISPID_VALUE)]
  HRESULT Item([in] long n, [out, retval] long* pnPrime);

  [propget, id(DISPID_NEWENUM)]
  HRESULT _NewEnum([out, retval] IUnknown** ppunkEnum);
};
```

This brings the `IPrimeNumbers` interface into line with the `ICollection` template form we showed you earlier. In fact, it's fair to say that the `ICollection` template form was defined to work with VB.

Note one important thing about VB's `For-Each` statement. If your container contains objects (your returned variants contain `VT_UNKNOWN` or `VT_DISPATCH`), the contained objects *must* implement the `IDispatch` interface. If they don't, you'll get an "item not an object" error at runtime from VB 6.

The VB Subscript Operator

Using the `Item` method, a VB client can access each individual item in the collection one at a time:

```
...
Dim i As Long
For i = 1 To primes.Count
    sPrimes = sPrimes & primes.Item(i) & " "
Next i
...
```

Because I marked the `Item` method with `DISPID_VALUE`, VB allows the following abbreviated syntax that makes a collection seem like an array (if only for a second):

```
...
Dim i As Long
For i = 1 To primes.Count
    sPrimes = sPrimes & primes(i) & " " ' Invoke(DISPID_VALUE)
Next i
...
```

Assigning a property the DISPID_VALUE dispatch identifier makes it the default property, as far as VB is concerned. Using this syntax results in VB getting the default property—that is, calling Invoke with DISPID_VALUE. However, because we're dealing with array syntax in VB, we have two problems. The first is knowing where to start the index—1 or 0? A majority of existing code suggests making collections 1-based, but only a slight majority. As a collection implementer, you get to choose. As a collection user, you get to guess. In general, if you anticipate a larger number of VB clients for your collection, choose 1-based—and whatever you do, *please* document the decision.

The other concern with using array-style access is round-trips. Using the Item property puts us smack dab in the middle of what we're trying to avoid by using enumerators: one round-trip per data element. If you think that using the For-Each statement and, therefore, enumerators under VB solves both these problems, you're half right. Unfortunately, Visual Basic 6.0 continues to access elements one at a time, even though it's using IEnumVARIANT::Next and is perfectly capable of providing a larger buffer. However, using the ForEach syntax does allow you to disregard whether the Item method is 1-based or 0-based.

The Server Side of Enumeration

Because the semantics of enumeration interfaces are loose, you are free to implement them however you like. The data can be pulled from an array, a file, a database result set, or wherever it is stored. Even better, you might want to calculate the data on demand, saving yourself calculations and storage for elements in which the client isn't interested. Either way, if you're doing it by hand, you have some COM grunge code to write. Or, if you like, ATL is there to help write that grunge code.

Enumerating Arrays

CComEnum

Because enumeration interfaces are all the same except for the actual data being enumerated, their implementation can be standardized, given a couple assumptions. Depending on how you've stored your data, you can use one of two ATL enumeration interface classes. The most flexible implementation class enables you to provide your data in a standard C++-like collection. This is called CComEnum-OnSTL (discussed later). The simplest implementation assumes that you've stored your data as an array. It's called CComEnum, and the complete implementation is as follows:

```
template <class Base, const IID* piid, class T, class Copy,
    class ThreadModel = CComObjectThreadModel>
class ATL_NO_VTABLE CComEnum :
    public CComEnumImpl<Base, piid, T, Copy>,
    public CComObjectRootEx< ThreadModel > {
public:
    typedef CComEnum<Base, piid, T, Copy > _CComEnum;
    typedef CComEnumImpl<Base, piid, T, Copy > _CComEnumBase;
    BEGIN_COM_MAP(_CComEnum)
        COM_INTERFACE_ENTRY_IID(*piid, _CComEnumBase)
    END_COM_MAP()
};
```

Although this implementation consists of only a few lines of code, there's quite a lot going on here. The template arguments are as follows:

- `Base` is the enumeration interface to be implemented—for example, `IEnumPrimes`.

- `piid` is a pointer to the interface being implemented—for example, `&IID_IEnumPrimes`.

- `piid` `T` is the type of data being enumerated—for example, `long`.

- `Copy` is the class responsible for copying the data into the client's buffer as part of the implementation of `Next`. It can also be used to cache a private copy of the data in the enumerator to guard against simultaneous access and manipulation.

- `ThreadModel` describes just how thread safe this enumerator needs to be. When you specify nothing, it uses the dominant threading model for objects, as described in Chapter 4, "Objects in ATL." Of course, because a COM enumerator is a COM object like any other, it requires an implementation of `IUnknown`. Toward that end, `CComEnum` derives from `CComObjectRootEx`. You'll see later that I further derive `CComObject` from `CComEnum` to fill in the `vtbl` properly.

Really, `CComEnum` is present simply to bring `CComObjectRootEx` together with `CComEnumImpl`, the base class that actually implements `Next`, `Skip`, `Reset`, and `Clone`. Figure 8.2 shows how these classes fit together.

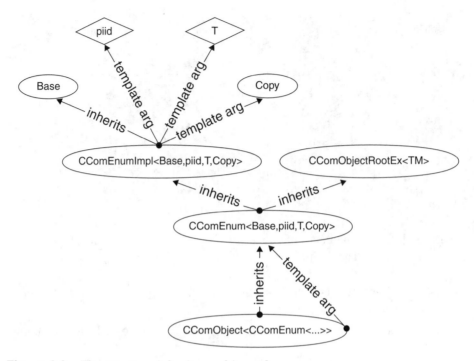

Figure 8.2 The CComEnum inheritance hierarchy

Copy Policy Classes

The fundamental job of the enumerator is to copy the collection's data into the buffer that the client provides. If the data being enumerated is a pointer or a structure that contains pointers, a simple memcpy or assignment will not do the trick. Instead, the client needs its own deep copy of each element, which it can release when it has finished with it. Toward that end, ATL enumerators use a class called a *copy policy class*, often just called a *copy policy*, to scope static methods for dealing with deep-copy semantics. The static methods of a copy policy are like the Increment and Decrement methods of the threading model classes, except that instead of incrementing and decrementing a long, copy policies know how to initialize, copy, and destroy data. For simple types, ATL provides a template copy policy class:

```
template <class T>
class _Copy {
public:
    static HRESULT copy(T* p1, const T* p2) {
        Checked::memcpy_s(p1, sizeof(T), p2, sizeof(T));
```

```
        return S_OK;
    }
    static void init(T*) {}
    static void destroy(T*) {}
};
```

Given an array of a simple type (such as long), this template works just fine:

```
HRESULT CopyRange(long* dest, long* src, size_t count) {
  for (size_t i = 0; i != count; ++i) {
    HRESULT hr = _Copy<long>::copy(&dest[i], &src[i]);
    if( FAILED(hr) ) {
      while( i > 0 ) _Copy<long>::destroy(&dest[-i]);
      return hr;
    }
  }
  return S_OK;
}
```

However, given something with trickier semantics, such as a VARIANT or an OLESTR, memcpy is too shallow. For the four most commonly enumerated data types, ATL provides specializations of the _Copy template:

```
template<> class _Copy<VARIANT>;
template<> class _Copy<LPOLESTR>;
template<> class _Copy<OLEVERB>
template<> class _Copy<CONNECTDATA>;
```

For example, the copy policy for VARIANTs looks like this:

```
template<> class _Copy<VARIANT> {
public:
    static HRESULT copy(VARIANT* p1, const VARIANT* p2) {
        p1->vt = VT_EMPTY;
        return VariantCopy(p1, const_cast<VARIANT*>(p2));
    }
    static void init(VARIANT* p) {p->vt = VT_EMPTY;}
    static void destroy(VARIANT* p) {VariantClear(p);}
};
```

If you're dealing with interface pointers, again, the _Copy template won't do, but building your own specialization for each interface you want to copy is a bit arduous. For interfaces, ATL provides the _CopyInterface copy policy class parameterized on the type of interface you're managing:

```
template <class T> class _CopyInterface {
public:
    static HRESULT copy(T** p1, T** p2) {
        ATLENSURE(p1 != NULL && p2 != NULL);
        *p1 = *p2;
        if (*p1)
            (*p1)->AddRef();
        return S_OK;
    }
    static void init(T** ) {}
    static void destroy(T** p) {if (*p) (*p)->Release();}
};
```

Using copy policies, we now have a generic way to initialize, copy, and delete any kind of data, making it easy to build a generic and safe duplication routine:

```
template <typename T, typename Copy>
HRESULT CopyRange(T* dest, T* src, size_t count) {
  for (size_t i = 0; i != count; ++i) {
    HRESULT hr = Copy::copy(&dest[i], &src[i]);
    if( FAILED(hr) ) {
      while( i > 0 ) Copy::destroy(&dest[-i]);
      return hr;
    }
  }
  return S_OK;
}
```

CComEnumImpl's implementation of the Next method uses the copy policy passed as the template parameter to initialize the client's buffer and fill it with data from the collection, much like our sample CopyRange routine. However, before we jump right into the Next method, let's see how CComEnumImpl does its job.

CComEnumImpl

To implement the methods of an enumeration interface, CComEnumImpl maintains five data members:

```
template <class Base, const IID* piid, class T, class Copy>
class ATL_NO_VTABLE CComEnumImpl : public Base {
public:
```

```
        CComEnumImpl();
        virtual ~CComEnumImpl();

        STDMETHOD(Next)(ULONG celt, T* rgelt, ULONG* pceltFetched);
        STDMETHOD(Skip)(ULONG celt);
        STDMETHOD(Reset)(void)
        STDMETHOD(Clone)(Base** ppEnum);

        HRESULT Init(T* begin, T* end, IUnknown* pUnk,
                     CComEnumFlags flags = AtlFlagNoCopy);

        CComPtr<IUnknown> m_spUnk;
        T* m_begin;
        T* m_end;
        T* m_iter;
        DWORD m_dwFlags;
        ...
};
```

The m_begin, m_end, and m_iter members are each pointers to the type of data being enumerated, as passed via the T template parameter. Each of these members keeps track of pointers into an array of the data being enumerated. In classic standard C++ style, m_begin points to the beginning of the array, m_end points to one past the end of the array, and m_iter points to the next element to hand out. The m_dwFlags member determines if and when to copy initialization data that the creator of the enumerator provides. The m_spUnk member refers to the owner of the data if the enumerator is sharing it instead of keeping its own copy. The implementations of Next, Skip, Reset, and Clone use these variables to provide their behavior. These variables are set in the Init method of CComEnumImpl.

Initializing CComEnumImpl

Calling the Init method requires the data to be arranged in an array. Maybe the collection is already maintaining the data as an array, or maybe it's not. Either way, the begin parameter to Init must be a pointer to the beginning of an array of the type being enumerated, and the end parameter must be one past the end of the same array. Where that array comes from and how the enumerator manages it depend on the last parameter to Init, the flags parameter. This parameter can take one of three values:

- AtlFlagNoCopy means that the collection already maintains its data in an array of the type being enumerated and is willing to share the data with the enumerator. This is more efficient because the enumerator doesn't keep its own copy;

it merely initializes m_begin, m_end, and m_iter to point at the collection's data. However, this can lead to unpredictable results if a client uses the collection to modify the data while it's being enumerated.

If you use the AtlFlagNoCopy flag, you should pass an interface pointer to the collection that owns the data as the pUnk parameter to Init. The enumerator caches this interface pointer, adding to the reference count of the collection. This is necessary to keep an enumerator from outliving the collection and, more important, the data that the collection is maintaining. For each of the other two flags, pUnk is NULL.

- AtlFlagCopy means that the collection already maintains the data in the appropriate format but would prefer the enumerator to have its own copy of the data. This is less efficient but ensures that no manipulation of the collection affects the data that the enumerator maintains.

- AtlFlagTakeOwnership means that the collection doesn't maintain its data in an array of a type appropriate for the enumerator to use. Instead, the collection has allocated an array of the data type being enumerated using operator new[] for sole use of the enumerator. When the enumerator is destroyed, it should destroy its copy of the data using operator delete[]. This is especially handy for the implementation of IEnumVARIANT because most developers prefer to keep data in types more specific than VARIANT but are willing to provide an array of VARIANTs when creating the enumerator.

CComEnumImpl Implementation

The most interesting part of the CComEnumImpl implementation is the Next method. Recall that Next's job is to copy the client-requested number of elements into the client-provided buffer. CComEnumImpl's implementation of the Next method is identical in concept to the CopyRange function I showed you earlier. Next uses the copy policy to copy the data provided by the collection at initialization into the client's buffer. If anything goes wrong, the copy policy is used to destroy the data already copied. The rest of the logic is argument validation and involves watching for the end of the data.

```
template <class Base, const IID* piid, class T, class Copy>
STDMETHODIMP CComEnumImpl<Base, piid, T, Copy>::Next(
    ULONG celt, T* rgelt,
    ULONG* pceltFetched) {
    if (pceltFetched != NULL)
        *pceltFetched = 0;
    if (celt == 0)
        return E_INVALIDARG;
    if (rgelt == NULL || (celt != 1 && pceltFetched == NULL))
        return E_POINTER;
```

```
    if (m_begin == NULL || m_end == NULL || m_iter == NULL)
        return E_FAIL;
    ULONG nRem = (ULONG)(m_end - m_iter);
    HRESULT hRes = S_OK;
    if (nRem < celt)
        hRes = S_FALSE;
    ULONG nMin = celt < nRem ? celt : nRem ;
    if (pceltFetched != NULL)
        *pceltFetched = nMin;
    T* pelt = rgelt;
    while(nMin-) {
        HRESULT hr = Copy::copy(pelt, m_iter);
        if (FAILED(hr)) {
            while (rgelt < pelt)
                Copy::destroy(rgelt++);
            if (pceltFetched != NULL)
                *pceltFetched = 0;
            return hr;
        }
        pelt++;
        m_iter++;
    }
    return hRes;
}
```

The implementations of Skip and Reset are trivial:

```
template <class Base, const IID* piid, class T, class Copy>
STDMETHODIMP CComEnumImpl<Base, piid, T, Copy>::Skip(ULONG celt) {
    if (celt == 0)
        return E_INVALIDARG;

    ULONG nRem = ULONG(m_end - m_iter);
    ULONG nSkip = (celt > nRem) ? nRem : celt;
    m_iter += nSkip;
    return (celt == nSkip) ? S_OK : S_FALSE;
}

template <class Base, const IID* piid, class T, class Copy>
STDMETHODIMP CComEnumImpl<Base, piid, T, Copy>::Reset()
{ m_iter = m_begin;return S_OK; }
```

The Clone method is responsible for duplicating the current enumerator. This means creating a new enumerator of the same type and initializing it using the Init method. However, the data is never copied again for subsequent enumerators. Instead, if the collection indicated that the data was to be shared, a new enumerator gets the IUnknown* of the original collection, giving the collection another reason to live. Otherwise, if the enumerator is keeping its own copy of the data, the new enumerator is given the IUnknown* of the original enumerator. Because enumerators are read-only, one copy of the data serves for all enumerators.

```cpp
template <class Base, const IID* piid, class T, class Copy>
STDMETHODIMP CComEnumImpl<Base, piid, T, Copy>::Clone(
  Base** ppEnum) {
  typedef CComObject<CComEnum<Base, piid, T, Copy> > _class;
  HRESULT hRes = E_POINTER;
  if (ppEnum != NULL) {
    *ppEnum = NULL;
    _class* p;
    hRes = _class::CreateInstance(&p);
    if (SUCCEEDED(hRes)) {
    // If this object has ownership of the data then we
    // need to keep it around
      hRes = p->Init(m_begin, m_end, (m_dwFlags & BitOwn) ?
        this : m_spUnk);
      if (SUCCEEDED(hRes)) {
        p->m_iter = m_iter;
        hRes = p->_InternalQueryInterface(*piid, (void**)ppEnum);
      }
      if (FAILED(hRes))
        delete p;
    }
  }
  return hRes;
}
```

CComEnum Use

As an example of a typical CComEnum use, let's implement the IPrimeNumbers collection interface:

```
[dual]
interface IPrimeNumbers : IDispatch {
  HRESULT CalcPrimes([in] long min, [in] long max);
```

```
  [propget]
  HRESULT Count([out, retval] long* pnCount);

  [propget, id(DISPID_VALUE)]
  HRESULT Item([in] long n, [out, retval] long* pnPrime);

  [propget, id(DISPID_NEWENUM)]
  HRESULT _NewEnum([out, retval] IUnknown** ppunkEnum);
};
```

The collection maintains a list of the prime numbers in a C++ vector. The Calc-Primes method populates the collection:

```
STDMETHODIMP CPrimeNumbers::CalcPrimes(long min, long max) {
  m_rgPrimes.clear();
  for (long n = min; n <= max; ++n ) {
    if (IsPrime(n)) m_rgPrimes.push_back(n);
  }
  return S_OK;
}
```

The get_Count and get_Item methods use the vector to perform their duties:

```
STDMETHODIMP CPrimeNumbers::get_Count(long* pnCount) {
  *pnCount = m_rgPrimes.size();
  return S_OK;
}
```

```
STDMETHODIMP CPrimeNumbers::get_Item(long n, long* pnPrime) {
  // Oh, let's be 1-based today...
  if (n < 1 || n > m_rgPrimes.size()) return E_INVALIDARG;
  *pnPrime = m_rgPrimes[n-1];
  return S_OK;
}
```

Because we're going out of our way to support VB with our collection interface, the get__NewEnum method returns an interface on an implementation of IEnum-VARIANT. Because the name of the parameterized enumerator is used more than once, it's often handy to use a type definition:

```
typedef CComEnum< IEnumVARIANT, &IID_IEnumVARIANT, VARIANT,
  _Copy<VARIANT> > CComEnumVariant;
```

Remember, the CComEnum template parameters are, in order, the interface we'd like the enumerator to implement, the IID of that interface, the type of data we'd like to enumerate, and, finally, a copy policy class for copying the data from the enumerator's copy to the client's buffer. To provide an implementation of IUnknown, the CComEnum class is further used as the base class for a new CComObject class. Using this type definition, the implementation of get__NewEnum entails creating an instance of an enumerator, initializing it with array data, and filling ppunkEnum with a pointer to the enumerator for use by the client. Because we're keeping the data as a vector, however, we have to allocate an array of VARIANTs manually, fill the data from the vector, and pass ownership to the enumeration using AtlFlagTakeOwnership. The following code illustrates this procedure:

```
STDMETHODIMP CPrimeNumbers::get__NewEnum(IUnknown** ppunkEnum) {
  *ppunkEnum = 0;

  // Create an instance of the enumerator
  CComObject<CComEnumVariant>*  pe = 0;
  HRESULT hr = CComObject<CComEnumVariant>::CreateInstance(&pe);
  if (SUCCEEDED(hr)) {
    pe->AddRef();

    // Copy data from vector<long> to VARIANT*
    size_t    nPrimes = m_rgPrimes.size();
    VARIANT*  rgvar = new VARIANT[nPrimes];
    if (rgvar) {
      ZeroMemory(rgvar, sizeof(VARIANT) * nPrimes);
      VARIANT*  pvar = &rgvar[0];
      for (vector<long>::iterator it = m_rgPrimes.begin();
           it != m_rgPrimes.end();
           ++pvar, ++it ) {
        pvar->vt = VT_I4;
        pvar->lVal = *it;
      }

      // Initialize enumerator
      hr = pe->Init(&rgvar[0], &rgvar[nPrimes], 0,
        AtlFlagTakeOwnership);
      if (SUCCEEDED(hr)) {
        // Fill outbound parameter
        hr = pe->QueryInterface(IID_IUnknown, (void**)ppunkEnum);
      }
    }
    else {
```

```
        hr = E_OUTOFMEMORY;
    }

    pe->Release();
  }

  return hr;
}
```

Unfortunately, this code leaves an unpleasant taste in one's mouth. Although it would have been considerably simpler if we'd already had an array of VARIANTs holding the data, frankly, that's rare. C++ programmers tend to use containers other than the error-prone C++ array. Because of this tendency, we were forced to translate the data from our preferred format to the preferred format of the ATL enumerator implementation. Given the regularity of a container's C++ interface, this seems like a waste. In an ideal world, we'd have an enumeration implementation that could handle a standard C++ container instead of an array. In an ideal world, we'd have CComEnumOnSTL. Welcome to my ideal world.

Enumerating Standard C++ Collections

CComEnumOnSTL[3]

The declaration of CComEnumOnSTL is similar to that of CComEnum:

```
template <class Base, const IID* piid, class T, class Copy,
    class CollType, class ThreadModel = CComObjectThreadModel>
class ATL_NO_VTABLE CComEnumOnSTL :
    public IEnumOnSTLImpl<Base, piid, T, Copy, CollType>,
    public CComObjectRootEx< ThreadModel > {
public:
    typedef CComEnumOnSTL<Base, piid, T, Copy, CollType,
        ThreadModel > _CComEnum;
    typedef IEnumOnSTLImpl<Base, piid, T, Copy, CollType >
        _CComEnumBase;
    BEGIN_COM_MAP(_CComEnum)
        COM_INTERFACE_ENTRY_IID(*piid, _CComEnumBase)
    END_COM_MAP()
};
```

---

[3] Technically, there's no such thing as the "STL"; there's just the standard C++ library. The ATL classes were named before the C++ standard was finalized, so they still use the old "STL" name.

The chief difference between CComEnumOnSTL and CComEnum is the addition of the CollType template parameter. This parameter indicates the type of collection to iterate over. The base class, IEnumOnSTLImpl, uses the collection to implement the Next, Skip, Reset, and Clone methods of the enumeration interface. The type of collection passed as the CollType must expose at least the following C++ interface:

```
template <typename T> class CollType {
public:
  class const_iterator; // Forward declaration
  const_iterator begin() const;
  const_iterator end() const;

  class const_iterator {
  public:
    const_iterator(const const_iterator& it); // To support
                                              // postfix ++
    const_iterator& operator=(const const_iterator& it);
    bool operator!=(const const_iterator& rhs);
    const T& operator*();
    const_iterator operator++(int); // Postfix ++
  };
};
```

All existing standard C++ collections adhere to these minimum requirements. If you want to make your own collection, it must adhere to this interface as well. I'll show you later how defining your own collection type is useful for enumerating data calculated on demand.

IEnumOnSTLImpl

The base class of CComEnumOnSTL, IEnumOnSTLImpl, uses the standard C++-like collection passed as the CollType parameter to implement the Next, Skip, Reset, and Clone methods. The following is the declaration of IEnumOnSTLImpl:

```
template <class Base, const IID* piid, class T,
    class Copy, class CollType>
class ATL_NO_VTABLE IEnumOnSTLImpl : public Base {
public:
    HRESULT Init(IUnknown *pUnkForRelease, CollType& collection);

    STDMETHOD(Next)(ULONG celt, T* rgelt, ULONG* pceltFetched);
    STDMETHOD(Skip)(ULONG celt);
    STDMETHOD(Reset)(void);
```

```
    STDMETHOD(Clone)(Base** ppEnum);

// Data
    CComPtr<IUnknown> m_spUnk;
    CollType* m_pcollection;
    typename CollType::const_iterator m_iter;
};
```

As with `CComEnumImpl`, `IEnumOnSTLImpl` keeps an `m_spUnk` pointer. However, unlike `CComEnumImpl`, the `m_spUnk` pointer should never be `NULL` and, therefore, the `pUnkForRelease` parameter to `Init` should never be `NULL`. Notice that `IEnumOnSTLImpl` keeps no `m_dwFlags` member data. It has no option for copying the data from the collection. Instead, it needs to ensure that the collection holding the data outlives the enumerator. Every call to `Init` assumes the equivalent of the `CComEnum`'s `AtlFlagNoCopy` flag. Although this is more efficient than `AtlFlagCopy` or the manual copying required for `AtlFlagTakeOwnership`, if the collection changes while it's being enumerated, the behavior is undefined. If you need ATL's C++-based enumerator to have its own copy of the data, you must wrap a copy of the data in its own COM object, a technique I show you later.

CComEnumOnSTL Use

If our prime number collection object held a collection of VARIANTs, the implementation of `get__NewEnum` would look like this:

```
STDMETHODIMP CPrimeNumbers::get__NewEnum(IUnknown** ppunkEnum) {
  *ppunkEnum = 0;

  typedef CComEnumOnSTL<IEnumVARIANT, &IID_IEnumVARIANT, VARIANT,
                        _Copy<VARIANT>, vector<VARIANT> >
        CComEnumVariantOnVector;

  CComObject<CComEnumVariantOnVector>* pe = 0;
  HRESULT hr = CComObject<CComEnumVariantOnVector>::CreateInstance(&pe);
  if (SUCCEEDED(hr)) {
    pe->AddRef();

    hr = pe->Init(this->GetUnknown(), m_rgPrimes);
    if (SUCCEEDED(hr)) {
      hr = pe->QueryInterface(ppunkEnum);
    }

    pe->Release();
```

```
    }

    return hr;
}
```

Of course, we'd prefer not to keep a collection of VARIANTs. Instead, we'd like
to keep a collection of a type that matches our needs—in this case, longs. Fortunately, unlike CComEnumImpl, IEnumOnSTLImpl allows on-demand data conversion,
enabling us to keep our collection in a convenient type but still providing the data
in a format that the enumerator requires.

On-Demand Data Conversion

The implementations of the Next, Skip, Reset, and Clone methods using a standard
C++ collection are almost identical to those of the CComEnumImpl class. The single
significant difference is a nifty loophole in the IEnumOnSTLImpl's Next method. The
CComEnumImpl class ties the data type being enumerated to the data type held in the
array of the enumerator. However, IEnumOnSTLImpl has no such limitation. Look at
this snippet from IEnumOnSTLImpl's Next method:

```
template <class Base, const IID* piid, class T, class Copy,
  class CollType>
STDMETHODIMP
IEnumOnSTLImpl<Base, piid, T, Copy, CollType>::Next(
  ULONG celt, T* rgelt, ULONG* pceltFetched) {
  ...
  T* pelt = rgelt;
  while (SUCCEEDED(hr) && m_iter != m_pcollection->end() &&
    nActual < celt) {
    hr = Copy::copy(pelt, &*m_iter);
    ...
  }
  ...
    return hr;
}
```

The template parameters allow the type of the *pelt to be different from the
type of the &*m_iter. In other words, the type of data that the collection holds can
be different from the type of data that the client receives in the call to Next. This
means that the copy policy class must still be capable of initializing and destroying
the data of the type being enumerated, but the copy operation could actually be
hijacked to convert from one data type to another.

Imagine the following copy policy:

```
struct _CopyVariantFromLong {
    static HRESULT copy(VARIANT* p1, long* p2) {
    p1->vt = VT_I4;
    p1->lVal = *p2;
    return S_OK;
  }

  static void init(VARIANT* p)    { VariantInit(p); }
  static void destroy(VARIANT* p) { VariantClear(p); }
};
```

If the collection held longs but the enumerator exposed VARIANTs, the _Copy-VariantFromLong copy policy could be used to convert that data on demand. For example, if the prime number collection object was keeping a collection of longs, the following code would create an enumerator that could convert from long to VARIANT, as appropriate, during the client's Next call:

```
STDMETHODIMP CPrimeNumbers::get__NewEnum(IUnknown** ppunkEnum) {
    *ppunkEnum = 0;

    typedef CComEnumOnSTL<IEnumVARIANT, &IID_IEnumVARIANT, VARIANT,
                          _CopyVariantFromLong, vector<long> >
        CComEnumVariantOnVectorOfLongs;

    CComObject<CComEnumVariantOnVectorOfLongs>* pe = 0;
    ... // The rest is the same!
}
```

The only difference between this example and the previous one is the enumerator type definition. Instead of building it using a vector of VARIANTs, we build it using a vector of longs. Because the data type of the collection is different from the data type of the enumerator, we simply provide a copy policy class whose copy method converts appropriately. This is an especially useful technique for mapping between whatever is the most convenient type to hold in your collection object and VARIANTs to support the VB For-Each syntax.

Giving CComEnumOnSTL Its Own Copy

As I mentioned, unlike CComEnum, CComEnumOnSTL doesn't provide an option to copy the data the collection holds. Instead, it assumes that it will share the data with the collection. Sometimes, this can lead to undefined behavior if the collection is being modified while it is also being enumerated. All is not lost, however. It is possible to give a CComEnumOnSTL object its own copy of the data. The key is to build a COM object whose job it is to hold the original container for the life of the enumerator. Then, when `Init` is called, `pUnkForRelease` is the pointer to this container copy object. When the enumerator is done, it releases the container copy object, thus destroying the copy of the data. Unfortunately, ATL provides no such class. Fortunately, it's easy to build one. `CComContainerCopy` is a generic class for holding a copy of a standard C++ container. The complete implementation follows:

```
template <typename CollType, typename ThreadingModel =
  CComObjectThreadModel>
class CComContainerCopy :
  public CComObjectRootEx<ThreadingModel>,
  public IUnknown { // CComEnumOnSTL only needs an IUnknown*
public:
  HRESULT Copy(const CollType& coll) {
    try {
      m_coll = coll;
      return S_OK;
    }
    catch(...) {
      return E_OUTOFMEMORY;
    }
  }

BEGIN_COM_MAP(CComContainerCopy)
    COM_INTERFACE_ENTRY(IUnknown)
END_COM_MAP()

  CollType  m_coll;
};
```

Notice that the `CComContainerCopy` class is parameterized by the type of collection it is to hold. This class can be used to copy any standard C++-like container. The `Copy` method copies the collection using assignment. Because the `CComContainerCopy` class derives only from `IUnknown`, it is ideally suited for one purpose: as the first argument to `IEnumOnStlImpl`'s `Init` method. The second argument is the public `m_coll` member. Using the `Copy` method of the `CComContainerCopy` class mimics the use of the `CComEnum` class's `AtlFlagCopy`. The collection already has the data in the appropriate format, but the enumerator should have its own copy. Populating the `m_coll` member of the `CComContainerCopy` directly works like `AtlFlagTakeOwnership`. The collection doesn't already have the data in the appropriate format, but the container has converted the data for use by the enumerator. An example of `CComContainerCopy` using the `Copy` method follows:

```
STDMETHODIMP CPrimeNumbers::get__NewEnum(IUnknown** ppunkEnum) {
  *ppunkEnum = 0;

  typedef CComEnumOnSTL<IEnumVARIANT, &IID_IEnumVARIANT, VARIANT,
                        _Copy<VARIANT>, vector<VARIANT> >
      CComEnumVariantOnVector;

  CComObject<CComEnumVariantOnVector>* pe = NULL;
  HRESULT hr = CComObject<CComEnumVariantOnVector>::CreateInstance(&pe);
  if (SUCCEEDED(hr)) {
    pe->AddRef();

    // Create the container copy
    CComObject< CComContainerCopy< vector<VARIANT> > >*
      pCopy = NULL;
    // Use pCopy as a scoping mechanism to bind to the
    // static CreateInstance
    hr = pCopy->CreateInstance(&pCopy);
    if (SUCCEEDED(hr)) {
      pCopy->AddRef();

      // Copy the C++ container to the container copy
      hr = pCopy->Copy(m_rgPrimes);
      if (SUCCEEDED(hr)) {

        // Init the enumerator with the copy
        hr = pe->Init(pCopy->GetUnknown(), pCopy->m_coll);
        if (SUCCEEDED(hr)) {
          hr = pe->QueryInterface(ppunkEnum);
        }
      }
      pCopy->Release();
    }
    pe->Release();
  }

  return hr;
}
```

On-Demand Data Calculation

CComEnum requires initialization with an array of data that is already calculated. CComEnumOnSTL, on the other hand, accesses the data by calling member functions on objects that we provide. Therefore, calculating data on demand is a matter of providing implementations of the member functions that perform the calculations instead of accessing precalculated results.

For example, there's no reason the collection of prime numbers needs to precalculate all the results and store them. Instead, we need a standard C++-like container that looks like what CComEnumOnSTL needs (as I showed you before) but calculates the next prime number on demand. This container has two responsibilities. The first is to keep track of the range of values to iterate over. The second responsibility is to expose an iterator for both the beginning and one past the ending of the data. The beginning and ending iterator must be exposed via begin and end methods, and each must return a value of type const_iterator, a type nested inside the class. The PrimesContainer class lives up to both these responsibilities:

```cpp
class PrimesContainer {
public:
    class const_iterator; // Forward declaration

    PrimesContainer() : m_min(0), m_max(0) {}

    // For IPrimeNumbers::CalcPrimes
    void SetRange(long min, long max)
    { m_min = min; m_max = max; }

    // For IPrimeNumbers::get_Count
    size_t  size()
    { return CountPrimes(m_min, m_max); }

    // For IPrimeNumbers::get_Item
    long operator[](size_t i)
    { return NthPrime(i + 1, m_min, m_max); }

    // The rest is for CComEnumOnSTL
    const_iterator begin() const
    { return const_iterator(m_min, m_max); }

    const_iterator end() const
    { return const_iterator(); }

    class const_iterator {...};
private:
    long  m_min, m_max;
};
```

Notice that, in addition to supporting the minimum interface required by the implementation of CComEnumOnSTL, the PrimesContainer class provides a SetRange method for managing the range of prime numbers, a size method for counting the prime numbers in the range, and an operator[] method for extracting items in a random-access fashion. These methods make the PrimesContainer class suitable for implementing the IPrimeNumbers interface.

```
class ATL_NO_VTABLE CPrimeNumbers :
    public CComObjectRootEx<CComSingleThreadModel>,
    public CComCoClass<CPrimeNumbers, &CLSID_PrimeNumbers>,
    public IDispatchImpl<IPrimeNumbers, &IID_IPrimeNumbers> {
public:
...
// IPrimeNumbers
public:
  STDMETHODIMP CalcPrimes(long min, long max)
  { m_rgPrimes.SetRange(min, max); return S_OK; }

  STDMETHODIMP get_Count(long* pnCount)
  { *pnCount = m_rgPrimes.size(); return S_OK; }

  STDMETHODIMP get_Item(long n, long* pnPrime) {
    if (n < 1 || n > m_rgPrimes.size() ) return E_INVALIDARG;
    *pnPrime = m_rgPrimes[n-1];
    return S_OK;
  }

  STDMETHODIMP get__NewEnum(IUnknown** ppunkEnum) {
    *ppunkEnum = NULL;

    typedef CComEnumOnSTL<IEnumVARIANT, &IID_IEnumVARIANT,
      VARIANT, _CopyVariantFromLong, PrimesContainer >
      CComEnumVariantOnPrimesContainer;

    CComObject<CComEnumVariantOnPrimesContainer>* pe = NULL;
    HRESULT hr = pe->CreateInstance(&pe);
    if (SUCCEEDED(hr)) {
      pe->AddRef();

      hr = pe->Init(this->GetUnknown(), m_rgPrimes);
      if (SUCCEEDED(hr)) {
        hr = pe->QueryInterface(ppunkEnum);
      }
      pe->Release();
    }
```

```
    return hr;
  }

private:
  PrimesContainer m_rgPrimes;
};
```

In fact, this code is nearly identical to the code I've already shown you. The difference is that, instead of using a container that already has a precalculated set of values, we have one that knows how to calculate them on demand. Specifically, the iterator does the magic:

```
class PrimesContainer {
...
  const_iterator begin() const
  { return const_iterator(m_min, m_max); }

  const_iterator end() const
  { return iterator(); }

class const_iterator {
  public:
    const_iterator (long min = -1, long max = -1)
    : m_max(max), m_next(NthPrime(1, min, max))
    { if( m_next == -1 ) m_max = -1;   } // Match end()

    bool operator!=(const const_iterator& rhs)
    { return (m_next != rhs.m_next || m_max != rhs.m_max); }

    const long& operator*()
    { return m_next; }

    const_iterator operator++(int) {
      const_iterator it(m_next, m_max);
      m_next = NthPrime(1, m_next + 1, m_max);
      if( m_next == -1 ) m_max = -1; // Match end()
      return it;
    }

  private:
    long  m_next, m_max;
  };
...
};
```

The key to understanding the iterator is understanding how CComEnumOnSTL uses it. CComEnumOnSTL keeps a pointer to the collection, called m_pcollection, and an iterator, called m_iter, that marks the current position in the container. The m_iter data member is initialized when the enumerator is constructed or when Reset is called to the result of m_pcollection->begin(). The implementation of begin constructs an iterator that uses the range of possible prime numbers to cache the next prime number and the maximum number to check. As the container is iterated, the next prime number is calculated one ahead of the request. For every element in the container, the following sequence is performed:

1. m_pcollection->end() constructs an iterator that marks the end of the data. This, in turn, creates an iterator with –1 for each of m_min, m_max, and m_next. Special member data values are common for constructing an iterator that marks the end of the data.

2. operator!= compares the current iterator with the ending iterator.

3. operator* pulls out the prime number at the current location of the iterator.

4. The postfix operator++ calculates the next prime number. If there are no more prime numbers, m_min, m_max, and m_next are each set to –1 to indicate the end of the data. The next time through the loop, the comparison with the ending iterator succeeds and CComEnumOnSTL detects that it has reached the end of the collection.

You can see this behavior by looking at the main loop in the CComEnumOn-STLImpl::Next implementation:

```
template <class Base, const IID* piid, class T, class Copy,
  class CollType>
STDMETHODIMP
IEnumOnSTLImpl<Base, piid, T, Copy, CollType>::Next(
  ULONG celt, T* rgelt, ULONG* pceltFetched) {
  ...

  ULONG nActual = 0;
  HRESULT hr = S_OK;
  T* pelt = rgelt;
  while (SUCCEEDED(hr) &&
         m_iter != m_pcollection->end() && nActual < celt) {
    hr = Copy::copy(pelt, &*m_iter);
    if (FAILED(hr)) {
      while (rgelt < pelt) Copy::destroy(rgelt++);
      nActual = 0;
    }
```

```
   else {
      pelt++;
      m_iter++;
      nActual++;
   }
  }
  ...
  return hr;
}
```

If you find the occasion to calculate data on demand using a custom container and iterator pair, yours will be called in the same sequence. This gives you an opportunity to calculate data appropriately for your data set—for example, lines in a file, records in a database, bytes from a socket. Why go to all this trouble to calculate data on demand? Efficiency in both time and space. There are 9,592 prime numbers between 0 and 100,000. Precalculating and storing the primes as longs costs nearly 38 KB. Worse, the client must wait for all primes to be calculated in this range, even if it never gets around to enumerating them all. On the other hand, calculating them on demand requires the m_min and m_max members of the container and the m_next and m_max members of the current iterator. That's 16 bytes no matter how many prime numbers we'd like to calculate, and the cost of calculating them is realized only when the client requests the next chunk.[4]

Collections

ICollectionOnSTLImpl

In addition to parameterized implementations of enumeration interfaces, ATL provides parameterized implementations of collection interfaces, assuming that you're willing to keep your data in a standard C++-like container. The implementation is provided by the ICollectionOnSTLImpl class:

```
template <class T, class CollType, class ItemType,
          class CopyItem, class EnumType>
class ICollectionOnSTLImpl : public T {
public:
  STDMETHOD(get_Count)(long* pcount);
  STDMETHOD(get_Item)(long Index, ItemType* pvar);
```

---

[4] Of course, there are far more efficient ways to store and calculate prime numbers than what I have shown here. Even so, space versus time trade-offs make calculating on demand an attractive option.

```
   STDMETHOD(get__NewEnum)(IUnknown** ppUnk);


   CollType m_coll;
};
```

The `ICollectionOnSTLImpl` class provides an implementation of the three standard collection properties much like what I showed you earlier. The chief difference is that the container is managed for you in the `m_coll` member data of the `ICollectionOnSTLImpl` class. That means that you can't provide a copy of the data to the enumerators, but you can still use a collection that calculates on demand and you can still convert from a convenient type to the type required by the enumerator exposed from `get__NewEnum`. This is because, although you get to decide the type of the container in a template parameter, you're no longer implementing `get__NewEnum`.

The template parameters of `ICollectionOnSTLImpl` are as follows:

- The `T` parameter indicates the base class—For example, `IDispatchImpl-<IPrimeNumbers and &IID_IPrimeNumbers>`. `ICollectionOnSTLImpl` provides the implementation of the standard three properties of this base class, but the deriving class is responsible for the rest.

- The `CollType` parameter indicates the type of container to keep—for example, `vector<long>` or `PrimesContainer`.

- The `ItemType` parameter indicates the type of data exposed from the iterator of the collection—for example, `long`.

- The `CopyItem` parameter indicates the type of the copy policy class. This copy policy is used only in the implementation of the `get_Item` method. The copy policy should be capable of copying from a container that holds items of type `ItemType` to a single [out] parameter of type `ItemType`. If you were managing a container of `long numbers`, the `CopyItem` type would be `_Copy<long>`.

- The `EnumType` parameter indicates the type of the enumeration-implementation class. This enumeration must be capable of enumerating over a container just like `CComEnumOnSTL`. An example `EnumType` parameter is `CCom-Enum-OnSTLImpl<IEnumVARIANT, &IID_IEnumVARIANT, VARIANT, _Copy<VARIANT>, vector<VARIANT> >`.

ICollectionOnSTLImpl Usage

The best way to understand the `ICollectionOnSTLImpl` class is to see it in action. The first C++based implementation of the `IPrimesCollection` standard collection interface assumed that we wanted to manage a precalculated container of VARIANTs. This can be done using `ICollectionOnSTLImpl`:

```cpp
// Needed for implementation of get_Item.
// Converts the storage type (VARIANT) to the item type (long).
struct _CopyLongFromVariant {
  static HRESULT copy(long* p1, VARIANT* p2) {
    if (p2->vt == VT_I4) {
      *p1 = p2->lVal;
      return S_OK;
    }
    else {
      VARIANT var;
      HRESULT hr = VariantChangeType(&var, p2, 0, VT_I4);
      if (SUCCEEDED(hr)) *p1 = var.lVal;
      return hr;
    }
  }

  static void init(long* p)    { }
  static void destroy(long* p) { }
};

// Needed for implementation of IDispatch methods
typedef IDispatchImpl<IPrimeNumbers, &IID_IPrimeNumbers>
  IPrimeNumbersDualImpl;

// Needed for implementation of get__NewEnum method
typedef CComEnumOnSTL<IEnumVARIANT, &IID_IEnumVARIANT, VARIANT,
  _Copy<VARIANT>, vector<VARIANT> > ComEnumVariantOnVector;

// Needed for implementation of standard collection methods
typedef ICollectionOnSTLImpl<IPrimeNumbersDualImpl,
  vector<VARIANT>, long, _CopyLongFromVariant,
    CComEnumVariantOnVector>
      IPrimeNumbersCollImpl;

class ATL_NO_VTABLE CPrimeNumbers :
  public CComObjectRootEx<CComSingleThreadModel>,
  public CComCoClass<CPrimeNumbers, &CLSID_PrimeNumbers>,
  public IPrimeNumbersCollImpl
{
public:
...
// IPrimeNumbers
public:
  STDMETHODIMP CalcPrimes(long min, long max) {
```

```
    m_coll.clear();
    for (long n = min; n <= max; ++n) {
      if (IsPrime(n)) {
        VARIANT var = {VT_I4};
        var.lVal = n;
        m_coll.push_back(var);
      }
    }

    return S_OK;
  }
};
```

If we wanted to precalculate the prime numbers but keep them as a vector of long numbers, this is how we'd use ICollectionOnSTLImpl:

```
// Needed for implementation of get__NewEnum.
// Converts the storage type (long) to the
// enumeration type (VARIANT).
struct _CopyVariantFromLong {
    static HRESULT copy(VARIANT* p1, long* p2) {
    if (p1->vt == VT_I4) {
      *p2 = p1->lVal;
      return S_OK;
    }
    else {
      VARIANT var;
      HRESULT hr = VariantChangeType(&var, p1, 0, VT_I4);
      if( SUCCEEDED(hr) ) *p2 = var.lVal;
      return hr;
    }
  }

  static void init(VARAINT* p)    { ::VariantInit(p); }
  static void destroy(VARIANT* p) { ::VariantClear(p); }
};

// Needed for implementation of IDispatch methods
typedef IDispatchImpl<IPrimeNumbers, &IID_IPrimeNumbers>
  IPrimeNumbersDualImpl;

// Needed for implementation of get__NewEnum method
typedef CComEnumOnSTL<IEnumVARIANT, &IID_IEnumVARIANT, VARIANT,
  _CopyLongFromVariant, vector<VARIANT> >
```

```
  CComEnumVariantOnVectorOfLongs;

// Needed for implementation of standard collection methods
typedef ICollectionOnSTLImpl<IPrimeNumbersDualImpl,
  vector<long>, long, _Copy<long>,
  CComEnumVariantOnVectorOfLongs>
  IPrimeNumbersCollImpl;

class ATL_NO_VTABLE CPrimeNumbers :
  public CComObjectRootEx<CComSingleThreadModel>,
  public CComCoClass<CPrimeNumbers, &CLSID_PrimeNumbers>,
  public IPrimeNumbersCollImpl {
public:
...
// IPrimeNumbers
public:
  STDMETHODIMP CalcPrimes(long min, long max) {
    m_coll.clear();
    for (long n = min; n <= max; ++n) {
      if (IsPrime(n)) {
        m_coll.push_back(n);
      }
    }

    return S_OK;
  }
};
```

Finally, if we wanted to have the prime numbers calculated on demand and exposed as long numbers, we'd use ICollectionOnSTLImpl:

```
// Calculates prime numbers on demand
class PrimesContainer;

// Needed for implementation of get_Item.
// Converts the storage type (VARIANT) to the item type (long).
struct _CopyVariantFromLong;

// Needed for implementation of IDispatch methods
typedef IDispatchImpl<IPrimeNumbers, &IID_IPrimeNumbers>
  IPrimeNumbersDualImpl;

// Needed for implementation of get__NewEnum method
typedef CComEnumOnSTL<IEnumVARIANT, &IID_IEnumVARIANT, VARIANT,
```

```
  _CopyVariantFromLong, PrimesContainer >
  CComEnumVariantOnPrimesContainer;

// Needed for implementation of standard collection methods
typedef ICollectionOnSTLImpl<IPrimeNumbersDualImpl,
  PrimesContainer, long, _Copy<long>,
  CComEnumVariantOnPrimesContainer>
  IPrimeNumbersCollImpl;

class ATL_NO_VTABLE CPrimeNumbers :
  public CComObjectRootEx<CComSingleThreadModel>,
  public CComCoClass<CPrimeNumbers, &CLSID_PrimeNumbers>,
  public IPrimeNumbersCollImpl {
public:
...
// IPrimeNumbers
public:
  STDMETHODIMP CalcPrimes(long min, long max)
  { m_coll.SetRange(min, max); }
};
```

Jim Springfield, the father of ATL, says "ICollectionOnSTLImpl is not for the faint of heart." He's absolutely right. It provides a lot of flexibility, but at the expense of complexity. Still, when you've mastered the complexity, as with any good class library, you can get a lot done with very little code.

Standard C++ Collections of ATL Data Types

If you're a fan of the standard C++ library, you might find yourself wanting to keep some of ATL's smart types (such as CComBSTR, CComVariant, CComPtr, and CComQIPtr) in a standard C++ container. Many containers have a requirement concerning the elements they hold that makes this difficult for ATL smart types: operator& must return an address to an instance of the type being held. However, all the smart types except CComVariant overload operator& to return the address of the internal data:

```
BSTR* CComBSTR:operator&()   { return &m_str; }
T**   CComPtr::operator&()   { ATLASSERT(p==NULL); return &p; }
T**   CComQIPtr::operator&() { ATLASSERT(p==NULL); return &p; }
```

These overloads mean that CComBSTR, CComPtr, and CComQIPtr cannot be used in many C++ containers or with standard C++ algorithms with the same requirement.

The classic workaround for this problem is to maintain a container of a type that holds the ATL smart type but that doesn't overload `operator&`. ATL provides the `CAdapt` class for this purpose.

ATL Smart Type Adapter

The `CAdapt` class is provided for the sole purpose of wrapping ATL smart types for use in C++ containers. It's parameterized to accept any of the current or future such types:

```
template <class T> class CAdapt {
public:
    CAdapt() { }

    CAdapt(__in const T& rSrc) :
        m_T( rSrc )
    { }

    CAdapt(__in const CAdapt& rSrcCA) :
        m_T( rSrcCA.m_T )
    { }

    CAdapt& operator=(__in const T& rSrc)
    { m_T = rSrc; return *this; }

    bool operator<(__in const T& rSrc) const
    { return m_T < rSrc; }

    bool operator==(__in const T& rSrc) const
    { return m_T == rSrc; }

    operator T&()
    { return m_T; }

    operator const T&() const
    { return m_T; }

T m_T;
};
```

Notice that `CAdapt` does not have an `operator&`, so it works just fine for C++ containers and collections. Also notice that the real data is held in a public member variable called `m_T`. Typical usage requires using either this data member or a `static_cast` to obtain the underlying data.

CAdapt Usage

For example, imagine that you want to expose prime numbers as words instead of digits. Of course, you'd like the collection to support multiple languages, so you want to expose the strings in Unicode. Also, you'd like to support type-challenged COM mappings, so the strings have to be BSTRs. These requirements suggest the following interface:

```
[ object, dual]
interface IPrimeNumberWords : IDispatch {
  HRESULT CalcPrimes([in] long min, [in] long max);

  [propget]
  HRESULT Count([out, retval] long* pnCount);

  [propget, id(DISPID_VALUE)]
  HRESULT Item([in] long n,
    [out, retval] BSTR* pbstrPrimeWord);

  [propget, id(DISPID_NEWENUM)]
  HRESULT _NewEnum([out, retval] IUnknown** ppunkEnum);
};
```

Notice that the Item property exposes the prime number as a string, not a number. Also keep in mind that although the signature of _NewEnum is unchanged, we will be returning VARIANTs to the client that contain BSTRs, not long numbers.

Because we're dealing with one of the COM data types that's inconvenient for C++ programmers, BSTRs, we'd like to use the CComBSTR smart data type described in Chapter 3, "ATL Smart Types." The compiler doesn't complain if we use a data member like this to maintain the data:

```
vector<CComBSTR> m_rgPrimes;
```

Unfortunately, depending on what we do with the vector, some obscure runtime errors can result because of CComBSTR's overloaded operator&. Instead, we use CAdapt to hold the data:

```
vector< CAdapt<CComBSTR> > m_rgPrimes;
```

Of course, because we're using strings, our method implementations change. To calculate the data, we change the prime numbers to strings:

```
STDMETHODIMP CPrimeNumberWords::CalcPrimes(long min, long max) {
  while (min <= max) {
    if (IsPrime(min)) {
      char sz[64];
      CComBSTR bstr = NumWord(min, sz);
      m_rgPrimes.push_back(bstr);
    }
    ++min;
  }

  return S_OK;
}
```

Notice how we can simply push a CComBSTR onto the vector. The compiler uses the CAdapt<CComBSTR> constructor that takes a const CComBSTR& to construct the appropriate object for the vector to manage. The get_Count method doesn't change, but the get_Item method does:

```
STDMETHODIMP CPrimeNumberWords::get_Item(long n,
  BSTR* pbstrPrimeWord) {
  if (n < 1 || n > m_rgPrimes.size()) return E_INVALIDARG;

  CComBSTR& bstr = m_rgPrimes[n-1].m_T;
  return bstr.CopyTo(pbstrPrimeWord);
}
```

Notice that we're reaching into the vector and pulling out the appropriate element. Again, remember that the type of element we're holding is CAdapt<CComBSTR>, so I've used the m_T element to access the CComBSTR data inside. However, because the CAdapt<CComBSTR> class has an implicit cast operator to CComBSTR&, using the m_T member explicitly is not necessary.

Finally, the get__NewEnum method must also change. Remember that we're implementing IEnumVARIANT, but instead of holding long numbers, we're holding BSTRs. Therefore, the on-demand data conversion must convert between a CAdapt<CComBSTR> (the data type held in the container) to a VARIANT holding a BSTR. This can be accomplished with another custom copy policy class:

```
struct _CopyVariantFromAdaptBstr {
    static HRESULT copy(VARIANT* p1, CAdapt<CComBSTR>* p2) {
    p1->vt = VT_BSTR;
    p1->bstrVal = p2->m_T.Copy();
    return (p1->bstrVal ? S_OK : E_OUTOFMEMORY);
  }
```

```
static void init(VARIANT* p)    { VariantInit(p); }
static void destroy(VARIANT* p) { VariantClear(p); }
};
```

The corresponding enumeration type definition looks like this:

```
typedef CComEnumOnSTL<IEnumVARIANT, &IID_IEnumVARIANT, VARIANT,
                      _CopyVariantFromAdaptBstr,
                      vector< CAdapt<CComBSTR> > >
        CComEnumVariantOnVectorOfAdaptBstr;
```

Using these two type definitions, implementing get__NewEnum looks much like it always does:

```
STDMETHODIMP CPrimeNumberWords::get__NewEnum(
  IUnknown** ppunkEnum) {
  *ppunkEnum = 0;

  CComObject<CComEnumVariantOnVectorOfAdaptBstr>* pe = 0;
  HRESULT hr = pe->CreateInstance(&pe);
  if( SUCCEEDED(hr) ) {
    pe->AddRef();

    hr = pe->Init(this->GetUnknown(), m_rgPrimes);
    if (SUCCEEDED(hr)) {
      hr = pe->QueryInterface(ppunkEnum);
    }

    pe->Release();
  }

  return hr;
}
```

Using ICollectionOnSTLImpl with CAdapt

If you want to combine the use of ICollectionOnSTLImpl with CAdapt, you already have half the tools: the custom copy policy and the enumeration type definition. You still need another custom copy policy that copies from the vector of CAdapt<CComBSTR> to the BSTR* that the client provides to implement get_Item. This copy policy can be implemented like this:

```
struct _CopyBstrFromAdaptBstr {
    static HRESULT copy(BSTR* p1, CAdapt<CComBSTR>* p2) {
    *p1 = SysAllocString(p2->m_T);
    return (p1 ? S_OK : E_OUTOFMEMORY);
  }

  static void init(BSTR* p)    { }
  static void destroy(BSTR* p) { SysFreeString(*p); }
};
```

Finally, we can use CAdapt with ICollectionOnSTLImpl like this:

```
typedef IDispatchImpl<IPrimeNumberWords, &IID_IPrimeNumberWords>
        IPrimeNumberWordsDualImpl;

typedef ICollectionOnSTLImpl<IPrimeNumberWordsDualImpl,
                             vector< CAdapt<CComBSTR> >,
                             BSTR,
                             _CopyBstrFromAdaptBstr,
                             CComEnumVariantOnVectorOfAdaptBstr>
        IPrimeNumberWordsCollImpl;

class ATL_NO_VTABLE CPrimeNumberWords :
  public CComObjectRootEx<CComSingleThreadModel>,
  public CComCoClass<CPrimeNumberWords,
    &CLSID_PrimeNumberWords>,
  public IPrimeNumberWordsCollImpl {
public:
...
// IPrimeNumberWords
public:
  STDMETHODIMP CalcPrimes(long min, long max) {
    while (min <= max) {
      if (IsPrime(min)) {
        char      sz[64];
        CComBSTR  bstr = NumWord(min, sz);
        m_coll.push_back(bstr);
      }
      ++min;
    }

    return S_OK;
  }
};
```

ATL Collections

Using standard C++ puts one burden firmly on the shoulders of the developer: exception handing. Many calls into collections and algorithms can cause exceptions that must be caught before they leave the method boundary.[5] And because C++ exception handling requires the C runtime (CRT), the CRT libraries must be linked with any ATL project that uses the standard C++ library. Although ATL servers do link with the CRT by default, it remains the case that some ATL servers are built without the CRT; therefore, an alternative for the standard library is needed. ATL includes three classes that provide basic array, list, and map functionality that are not unlike the C++ vector, list, and map classes. In the spirit of ATL, none of these classes throws exceptions or requires the CRT. Arguably more compelling than freedom from the CRT, these classes are specialized to yield additional classes tailored for use with COM by automatically managing collections of types such as interfaces.

CAtlArray

This class is a dynamically sized array that grows on demand. It is a template class, so it can hold any kind of data. Its declaration is as follows:

```
template< typename E, class ETraits = CElementTraits< E > >
class CatlArray {

public:
    CAtlArray() ;
    ~CAtlArray() ;

    size_t GetCount() const ;
    bool IsEmpty() const ;
    bool SetCount( size_t nNewSize, int nGrowBy = -1 );

    void FreeExtra() ;
    void RemoveAll() ;

    const E& GetAt( size_t iElement ) const;
    E& GetAt( size_t iElement );

    const E* GetData() const ;
```

---

[5] Letting a C++ or Win32 structured exception escape a COM method is illegal. All such exceptions must be caught and turned into appropriate HRESULTs. For more information on this topic, see *Effective COM* (Addison-Wesley, 1998), by Don Box, Keith Brown, Tim Ewald, and Chris Sells.

```
    E* GetData() ;

    void SetAt( size_t iElement, INARGTYPE element );
    void SetAtGrow( size_t iElement, INARGTYPE element );

    size_t Add();
    size_t Add( INARGTYPE element );
    size_t Append( const CAtlArray< E, ETraits >& aSrc );

    void Copy( const CAtlArray< E, ETraits >& aSrc );

    const E& operator[]( size_t iElement ) const;
    E& operator[]( size_t iElement );

    void InsertAt( size_t iElement, INARGTYPE element,
        size_t nCount = 1 );
    void InsertArrayAt( size_t iStart,
        const CAtlArray< E, ETraits >* paNew );
    void RemoveAt( size_t iElement, size_t nCount = 1 );

#ifdef _DEBUG
    void AssertValid() const;
#endif  // _DEBUG

// Implementation
private:
    E* m_pData;
    size_t m_nSize;
    size_t m_nMaxSize;
    int m_nGrowBy;

    // Private to prevent use
    CAtlArray( const CAtlArray& ) ;
    CAtlArray& operator=( const CAtlArray& ) ;
};
```

The class members manage the memory associated with the m_pData member, a dynamically sized array of type E. The second template parameter (ETraits) to the CAtlArray class is the key to understanding how ATL supports collections of different element types. This class provides methods for copying elements, comparing elements, moving elements, and computing element hash values for building hash tables. By default, CAtlArray uses a template class called CElementTraits that supplies implementations of these element policies that are appropriate for simple data types. Storing more complex objects typically requires "overriding" these default policies by passing in an alternate class for the ETraits parameter. Indeed, you'll see in a moment that ATL does precisely this to provide more specialized collection classes for dealing with commonly used types such as interfaces.

Here are the five static member functions and two typedefs ATL expects you to provide for the class specified as the ETraits template parameter. In these method signatures, T represents the element type.

```
typedef const T& INARGTYPE;  // type to be used for
                             // adding elements
typedef T& OUTARGTYPE;       // type to be used for
                             // retrieving elements

static bool CompareElements( const T& element1,
  const T& element2 );

static int CompareElementsOrdered( const T& element1,
  const T& element2 );

static ULONG Hash( const T& element ) ;

static void CopyElements( T* pDest, const T* pSrc,
  size_t nElements );

static void RelocateElements( T* pDest, T* pSrc,
  size_t nElements );
```

The default CElementTraits class that AtlArray uses ultimately resolves to CDefaultElementTraits when primitive types such as int and bool are specified as the array element type. This class supplies the required static member functions through three base classes, one providing the comparison policy, one encapsulating the hashing algorithm, and another supplying the correct element copy semantics.

```
template< typename T >
class CDefaultElementTraits :
    public CElementTraitsBase< T >,
    public CDefaultHashTraits< T >,
    public CDefaultCompareTraits< T >
{ ... };
```

ATL provides template specializations of the CElementTraits class that automatically handle the unique comparison and copying semantics of the CComBSTR and CComVariant smart types. Additionally, a different hashing algorithm is used for these types to produce a better statistical distribution of hash keys than would result with the trivial algorithm used for primitive types.

For dealing with arrays of interfaces, ATL provides CInterfaceArray. Its definition simply derives from CAtlArray and uses CComQIPtr as the array element type and a special interface-savvy element traits class.

```
template< class I, const IID* piid = &__uuidof( I ) >
class CInterfaceArray :
  public CAtlArray< ATL::CComQIPtr< I, piid >,
    CComQIPtrElementTraits< I, piid > >
{ ... }
```

A special array type called CAutoPtrArray is also available for dealing with arrays of smart pointers. It is also defined in terms of CAtlArray.

```
template< typename E >
class CAutoPtrArray :
  public CAtlArray< ATL::CAutoPtr< E >,
    CAutoPtrElementTraits< E > >
{ ... }
```

Here's how you might use CInterfaceArray in code:

```
void GetPrimes(CInterfaceArray<IPrimeCalc>* prgCalc) {
  // Declare array of IPrimeCalc interface pointers
  CInterfaceArray<IPrimeCalc> rgCalc;

  // Populate array
  for (int i = 0; i < 50; i++) {
    IPrimeCalc* pCalc = NULL;
    ::CoCreateInstance(CLSID_CPrimeCalc, NULL, CLSCTX_ALL,
      __uuidof(pCalc), (void**)&pCalc);

    rgCalc[i] = pCalc;    // ERROR: operator[] doesn't grow array

    rgCalc.Add(pCalc);    // grows array, inserts, calls AddRef
    pCalc->Release();
  }

  *prgCalc = rgCalc; // ERROR: operator= marked private
                     // to prevent use

  prgCalc->InsertArrayAt(0, &rgCalc); // OK, prgCalc has
                                      // 50 AddRef'd itfs
```

```
} // CInterfaceArray destructor calls
  // Release on all elements in rgCalc
```

Unfortunately, CAtlArray isn't very useful for implementing an enumeration interface, even though it could be easily used with CComEnum, because you're not likely to want to hold data in the same type as is being enumerated. Because CComEnum doesn't support conversion on demand as CComEnumOnSTL does, you must manually convert your CAtlArray data into an array of data appropriate for enumerating.

CAtlList

The CAtlList collection class provides a convenient way to store objects in an ordered list. Compared to CAtlArray, inserting elements into CAtlList is quite fast because it occurs in constant time. However, you can't access the elements in a list by index as you can with an array. Like its array-based cousin, CAtlList is defined in terms of an element traits class that encapsulates the details of dealing with individual items in the list.

```
template< typename E, class ETraits = CElementTraits< E > >
class CAtlList {
public:
    typedef typename ETraits::INARGTYPE INARGTYPE;

private:
    class CNode : ... {
    ...
    public:
        CNode* m_pNext;
        CNode* m_pPrev;
        E m_element;
    };

public:
    CAtlList( UINT nBlockSize = 10 ) ;
    ~CAtlList() ;

    size_t GetCount() const ;
    bool IsEmpty() const ;

    E& GetHead() ;
    const E& GetHead() const ;
    E& GetTail() ;
    const E& GetTail() const ;
```

```
    E RemoveHead();
    E RemoveTail();
    void RemoveHeadNoReturn() ;
    void RemoveTailNoReturn() ;

    POSITION AddHead();
    POSITION AddHead( INARGTYPE element );
    void AddHeadList( const CAtlList< E, ETraits >* plNew );

    POSITION AddTail();
    POSITION AddTail( INARGTYPE element );
    void AddTailList( const CAtlList< E, ETraits >* plNew );

    void RemoveAll() ;

    POSITION GetHeadPosition() const ;
    POSITION GetTailPosition() const ;
    E& GetNext( POSITION& pos ) ;
    const E& GetNext( POSITION& pos ) const ;
    E& GetPrev( POSITION& pos ) ;
    const E& GetPrev( POSITION& pos ) const ;

    E& GetAt( POSITION pos ) ;
    const E& GetAt( POSITION pos ) const ;
    void SetAt( POSITION pos, INARGTYPE element );
    void RemoveAt( POSITION pos ) ;

    POSITION InsertBefore( POSITION pos, INARGTYPE element );
    POSITION InsertAfter( POSITION pos, INARGTYPE element );

    POSITION Find( INARGTYPE element,
        POSITION posStartAfter = NULL ) const ;
    POSITION FindIndex( size_t iElement ) const ;

    void MoveToHead( POSITION pos ) ;
    void MoveToTail( POSITION pos ) ;
    void SwapElements( POSITION pos1, POSITION pos2 ) ;

// Implementation
private:
    CNode* m_pHead;
    CNode* m_pTail;
    CNode* m_pFree;
    ...
};
```

This class manages a doubly linked list of CNode objects, each of which simply hold pointers to the data of the specified type (E), as well as pointers to the previous and next nodes in the list. Two list classes are also provided for dealing with smart pointers and interface pointers: CAutoPtrList and CInterfaceList. As with their array-based counterparts, these classes simply use CAtlList as their base class and specify type-specific element trait classes.

```
template< class I, const IID* piid = &__uuidof( I ) >
class CInterfaceList :
  public CAtlList< ATL::CComQIPtr< I, piid >,
    CComQIPtrElementTraits< I, piid > >
{ ... }

template< typename E >
class CAutoPtrList :
  public CAtlList< ATL::CAutoPtr< E >,
    CAutoPtrElementTraits< E > >
{ ... }
```

CAtlMap

If you want the functionality of the C++ map class , ATL provides CAtlMap:

```
template< typename K, typename V,
  class KTraits = CElementTraits< K >,
  class VTraits = CElementTraits< V > >
class CAtlMap {
public:
  typedef typename KTraits::INARGTYPE KINARGTYPE;
  typedef typename KTraits::OUTARGTYPE KOUTARGTYPE;
  typedef typename VTraits::INARGTYPE VINARGTYPE;
  typedef typename VTraits::OUTARGTYPE VOUTARGTYPE;

  class CPair : ... {
  public:
    const K m_key;
    V m_value;
  };

private:
  class CNode : public CPair    { ... }
  ...
  size_t GetCount() const ;
```

```
    bool IsEmpty() const ;

    bool Lookup( KINARGTYPE key, VOUTARGTYPE value ) const;
    const CPair* Lookup( KINARGTYPE key ) const ;
    CPair* Lookup( KINARGTYPE key ) ;
    V& operator[]( KINARGTYPE key ) ;

    POSITION SetAt( KINARGTYPE key, VINARGTYPE value );
    void SetValueAt( POSITION pos, VINARGTYPE value );

    bool RemoveKey( KINARGTYPE key ) ;
    void RemoveAll() ;
    void RemoveAtPos( POSITION pos ) ;

    POSITION GetStartPosition() const ;
    void GetNextAssoc( POSITION& pos, KOUTARGTYPE key,
      VOUTARGTYPE value ) const;
    const CPair* GetNext( POSITION& pos ) const ;
    CPair* GetNext( POSITION& pos ) ;
    const K& GetNextKey( POSITION& pos ) const ;
    const V& GetNextValue( POSITION& pos ) const ;
    V& GetNextValue( POSITION& pos ) ;
    void GetAt( POSITION pos, KOUTARGTYPE key,
      VOUTARGTYPE value ) const;
    CPair* GetAt( POSITION pos ) ;
    const CPair* GetAt( POSITION pos ) const ;
    const K& GetKeyAt( POSITION pos ) const ;
    const V& GetValueAt( POSITION pos ) const ;
    V& GetValueAt( POSITION pos ) ;

    UINT GetHashTableSize() const ;
    bool InitHashTable( UINT nBins, bool bAllocNow = true );
    void EnableAutoRehash() ;
    void DisableAutoRehash() ;
    void Rehash( UINT nBins = 0 );
    void SetOptimalLoad( float fOptimalLoad, float fLoThreshold,
      float fHiThreshold, bool bRehashNow = false );

// Implementation
private:
  CNode** m_ppBins;
  CNode* m_pFree;

  ...
};
```

CAtlMap maintains a list of nodes, each of which holds a key and a value. In this case, element trait classes must be provided for both the key type and the value type. The key is used to generate a hash for locating nodes in the list. CAtlMap would be useful for implementing collection item lookup by name instead of by index.

Be aware that CAtlMap does not have the same performance guarantees as the C++ std::map<> container. std::map<> uses a balanced binary tree that guarantees O(lg N) performance for inserts or lookups. CAtlMap, on the other hand, uses a hash table. Under good conditions, the hash table can give O(1) lookup performance, but a bad hash function can reduce the hash table to linear searches.

Object Models

A COM object model is a hierarchy of objects. Collections allow the subobjects to be manipulated. Enumerators allow these objects to be accessed. Most object models have one top-level object and several noncreateable subobjects. The following stylized IDL shows a minimal object model:

```
library OBJECTMODELLib {
    importlib("stdole32.tlb");
    importlib("stdole2.tlb");

    // Document sub-object ////////////////////////////////////////
    [ object, dual ] interface IDocument : IDispatch {
      [propget] HRESULT Data([out, retval] BSTR *pVal);
      [propput] HRESULT Data([in] BSTR newVal);
    };

    coclass Document {
        [default] interface IDocument;
    };

    // Documents collection ////////////////////////////////////////
    [ object, dual ] interface IDocuments : IDispatch {
      HRESULT AddDocument([out, retval] IDocument** ppDocument);
      [propget] HRESULT Count([out, retval] long* pnCount);
      [id(DISPID_VALUE), propget]
      HRESULT Item([in] long n, [out, retval] IDocument** ppdoc);
      [id(DISPID_NEWENUM), propget]
      HRESULT _NewEnum([out, retval] IUnknown** ppEnum);
    };

    coclass Documents {
        [default] interface IDocuments;
```

```
    };

    // Application top-level object /////////////////////////////
    [ object, dual ] interface IApplication : IDispatch {
      [propget] HRESULT Documents(
        [out, retval] IDocuments** pVal);
    };

    coclass Application {
        [default] interface IApplication;
    };
};
```

An instance hierarchy of this object model looks like Figure 8.3.

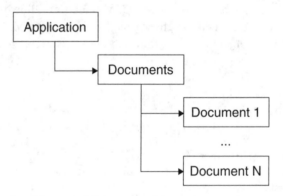

Figure 8.3   Simple object model instance hierarchy

Implementing the Top-Level Object

The top-level object of an object model is createable and exposes any number of
properties and any number of collection subobjects. The example implementation
looks like the following:

```
class ATL_NO_VTABLE CApplication :
    public CComObjectRootEx<CComSingleThreadModel>,
    public CComCoClass<CApplication, &CLSID_Application>,
    public IDispatchImpl<IApplication, &IID_IApplication> {
public:
DECLARE_REGISTRY_RESOURCEID(IDR_APPLICATION)
DECLARE_NOT_AGGREGATABLE(CApplication)
DECLARE_PROTECT_FINAL_CONSTRUCT()
```

```
BEGIN_COM_MAP(CApplication)
    COM_INTERFACE_ENTRY(IApplication)
    COM_INTERFACE_ENTRY(IDispatch)
END_COM_MAP()

  // Create instance of the Documents collection
  HRESULT CApplication::FinalConstruct()
  {  return CDocuments::CreateInstance(&m_spDocuments); }

// IApplication
public:
  // Hand out the Documents collection to interested parties
  STDMETHODIMP CApplication::get_Documents(IDocuments** pVal)
  { return m_spDocuments.CopyTo(pVal); }

private:
  CComPtr<IDocuments> m_spDocuments;
};
```

Implementing the Collection Object

The collection object is the most difficult of the three layers to implement, not because of any difficult code, but because of the maze of type definitions. The first set is required to implement the enumerator:

```
template <typename T>
struct _CopyVariantFromAdaptItf {
  static HRESULT copy(VARIANT* p1, CAdapt< CComPtr<T> >* p2) {
    HRESULT hr = p2->m_T->QueryInterface(IID_IDispatch,
      (void**)&p1->pdispVal);
    if (SUCCEEDED(hr)) {
      p1->vt = VT_DISPATCH;
    }
    else {
      hr = p2->m_T->QueryInterface(IID_IUnknown,
        (void**)&p1->punkVal);
      if( SUCCEEDED(hr) ) {
        p1->vt = VT_UNKNOWN;
      }
    }

    return hr;
  }

  static void init(VARIANT* p)     { VariantInit(p); }
```

```
    static void destroy(VARIANT* p) { VariantClear(p); }
};

typedef CComEnumOnSTL<IEnumVARIANT, &IID_IEnumVARIANT, VARIANT,
  _CopyVariantFromAdaptItf<IDocument>,
  list< CAdapt< CComPtr<IDocument> > > >
  CComEnumVariantOnListOfDocuments;
```

The _CopyVariantFromAdaptItf class is a reusable class that converts an interface into a VARIANT for use in enumerating a collection of interface pointers. The collection object is expected to hold a C++ container of elements of type CAdapt<CComPtr<T>>. Notice how the copy policy is used in the type definition of CComEnumVariantsOnListOfDocuments to obtain the implementation of IEnumVARIANT for the collection object.

The next set of type definitions is for the implementation of the collection methods:

```
template <typename T>
struct _CopyItfFromAdaptItf {
    static HRESULT copy(T** p1, CAdapt< CComPtr<T> >* p2) {
    if( *p1 = p2->m_T ) return (*p1)->AddRef(), S_OK;
    return E_POINTER;
  }

  static void init(T** p)    {}
  static void destroy(T** p) { if( *p ) (*p)->Release(); }
};

typedef ICollectionOnSTLImpl<
  IDispatchImpl<IDocuments, &IID_IDocuments>,
  list< CAdapt< CComPtr<IDocument> > >,
  IDocument*,
  _CopyItfFromAdaptItf<IDocument>,
  CComEnumVariantOnListOfDocuments>
  IDocumentsCollImpl;
```

The _CopyItfFromAdaptItf is used to implement the Item property, again assuming a C++ container holding elements of type CAdapt<CComPtr<T>>. The copy policy is then used to define the collection interface implementation, IDocumentsCollImpl.

Finally, IDocumentsCollImpl is used as the base class of the IDocuments implementation:

```
class ATL_NO_VTABLE CDocuments :
    public CComObjectRootEx<CComSingleThreadModel>,
    public CComCoClass<CDocuments>, // noncreateable
    public IDocumentsCollImpl
{
public:
DECLARE_NO_REGISTRY()
DECLARE_NOT_AGGREGATABLE(CDocuments)
DECLARE_PROTECT_FINAL_CONSTRUCT()

BEGIN_COM_MAP(CDocuments)
    COM_INTERFACE_ENTRY(IDocuments)
    COM_INTERFACE_ENTRY(IDispatch)
END_COM_MAP()

// IDocuments
public:
  STDMETHODIMP AddDocument(IDocument** ppDocument) {
    // Create a document to hand back to the client
    HRESULT hr = CDocument::CreateInstance(ppDocument);
    if( SUCCEEDED(hr) ) {
      // Put the document on the list
      CComPtr<IDocument>  spDoc = *ppDocument;
      m_coll.push_back(spDoc);
    }

    return hr;
  }
};
```

The benefit of all the type definitions is that the standard methods of the collection are implemented for us. We only have to implement the AddDocument method, which creates a new CDocument and adds it to the list that the ICollectionOnSTLImpl base class maintains.

Implementing the Subobjects

The subobjects can do whatever you want, including maintaining collections of objects further down the hierarchy. Our example maintains a BSTR, representing its data:

```
STDMETHODIMP CDocument::get_Data(BSTR *pVal) {
  return m_bstrData.CopyTo(pVal);
}
```

```
STDMETHODIMP CDocument::put_Data(BSTR newVal) {
  m_bstrData = newVal;
  return (m_bstrData || !newVal ? S_OK : E_OUTOFMEMORY);
}
```

Using the Object Model

You normally design an object model to be used by many language mappings, including scripting environments. Here's an example HTML page that uses this example object model:

```
<html>
<script language=vbscript>
    dim app
    set app = CreateObject("ObjectModel.Application")

    dim docs
    set docs = app.Documents

    dim doc
    set doc = docs.AddDocument
    doc.Data = "Document 1"

    set doc = docs.AddDocument
    doc.Data = "Document 2"

    for each doc in docs
        msgbox doc.data
    next
</script>
</html>
```

Summary

COM has abstractions much like those of the C++ standard library. Collections maintain lists of things, often objects. Enumerators enable navigation over the list of things maintained in a collection. To standardize access to collections and enumerators, they have a standard protocol. These standards aren't required, but if they are followed, they make an object model programmer's life easier because the usage is familiar. Implementing an object model is a matter of defining the higher-level object, the lower-level object, and the collection that joins the two. ATL implements both collection and enumeration interfaces, if you're not afraid of the type definitions required to make it all work.

9 | **Connection Points**

A Review of Connection Points

An object implements one or more interfaces to expose its functionality. The term *connection points* refers to a logically inverse mechanism that allows an object to expose its capability to *call* one or more specific interfaces.

Another perspective is that `QueryInterface` allows a client *to retrieve from* an object a pointer to an interface that the object implements. Connection points allow a client *to give* an object a pointer to an interface that the client implements. In the first case, the client uses the retrieved interface pointer to call methods provided by the object. In the second case, the object uses the provided interface pointer to call methods provided by the client.

A slightly closer inspection of the two mechanisms reveals that `QueryInterface` allows a client to retrieve from an object only interfaces that the client knows how to call. Connection points allow a client to provide to an object only interfaces that the object knows how to call.

A *connection* has two parts: the object making calls to the methods of a specific interface, called the *source* or, alternatively, the *connection point;* and the object implementing the interface (receiving the calls), called the *sink object* (see Figure 9.1) Using my terminology from earlier paragraphs, the object is the source and makes calls to the sink interface methods. The client is the sink and implements the sink interface. One additional complexity is that a particular source object can have connections to multiple sink objects.

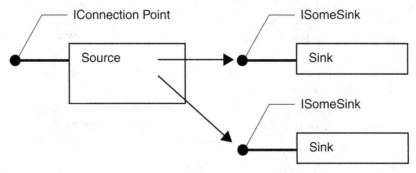

Figure 9.1 A connection to two sinks

The IConnectionPoint Interface

A client uses the source object's implementation of the IConnectionPoint interface to establish a connection. Here is the definition of the IConnectionPoint interface:

```
interface IConnectionPoint : IUnknown {
    HRESULT GetConnectionInterface ([out] IID* pIID);
    HRESULT GetConnectionPointContainer (
        [out] IConnectionPointContainer** ppCPC);
    HRESULT Advise ([in] IUnknown* pUnkSink,
        [out] DWORD* pdwCookie);
    HRESULT Unadvise ([in] DWORD dwCookie);
    HRESULT EnumConnections ([out] IEnumConnections** ppEnum);
}
```

The GetConnectionInterface method returns the interface identifier (IID) of the sink interface for which a connection point makes calls. Using the previous example, calling GetConnectionInterface returns IID_ISomeSink. A client calls the Advise method to establish a connection. The client provides the appropriate sink interface pointer for the connection point and receives a magic cookie (token) that represents the connection. A client can later call the Unadvise method, specifying the magic cookie to break the connection. The EnumConnections method returns a standard COM enumeration object that a client uses to enumerate all the current connections that a connection point holds. The last method is GetConnectionPoint-Container, which introduces a new complexity.

So far, this design allows a source object to make calls on only one specific interface. The source object maintains a list of clients that want to receive calls on that specific interface. When the source object determines that it should call one of the methods of its sink interface, the source iterates through its list of sink objects, calling that method for each sink object. What the design (again, as described so far) doesn't include is the capability for an object to originate calls on multiple different interfaces using this mechanism. Alternatively, to present the question directly, we have a design in which an object can support multiple connections to a single connection point, but how can an object support multiple different connection points?

The solution is to demote the source object to subobject status and have an encapsulating object, called the connectable object (see Figure 9.2), act as a container of these source subobjects. A client uses the source object's GetConnection-PointContainer method to retrieve a pointer to the connectable object. A connectable object implements the IConnectionPointContainer interface.

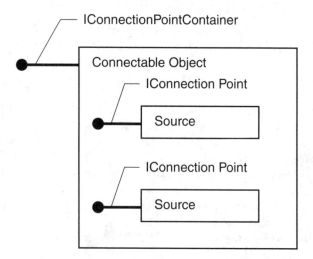

Figure 9.2 A connectable object

Implementing IConnectionPointContainer indicates that a COM object supports connection points and, more specifically, that it can provide a connection point (a source subobject) for each sink interface the connectable object knows how to call. Clients then use the connection point as described previously to establish the connection.

The IConnectionPointContainer Interface

Here is the definition of the IConnectionPointContainer interface:

```
interface IConnectionPointContainer : IUnknown {
  HRESULT EnumConnectionPoints (
    [out] IEnumConnectionPoints ** ppEnum);
  HRESULT FindConnectionPoint ([in] REFIID riid,
    [out] IConnectionPoint** ppCP);
}
```

You call the FindConnectionPoint method to retrieve an IConnectionPoint interface pointer to a source subobject that originates calls on the interface specified by the riid parameter. The EnumConnectionPoints method returns a standard COM enumerator subobject that implements the IEnumConnectionPoints interface. You can use this enumerator interface to retrieve an IConnectionPoint interface pointer for each connection point that the connectable object supports.

Most often, a client that wants to establish a connection to a connectable object does the following (with error checking removed for clarity):

```
CComPtr<IUnknown>
  spSource = /* Set to the source of the events */ ;
CComPtr<_ISpeakerEvents>
  spSink = /* Sink to receive the events */ ;
DWORD dwCookie ;

CComPtr<IConnectionPointContainer> spcpc;
HRESULT hr = spSource.QueryInterface (&spcpc);

CComPtr<IConnectionPoint> spcp ;
hr = spcpc->FindConnectionPoint(__uuidof(_ISpeakerEvents),
  &spcp);
hr = spcp->Advise (spSink, &dwCookie) ;// Establish connection
// Time goes by, callbacks occur...
hr = spcp->Unadvise (dwCookie) ;        // Break connection
```

In fact, ATL provides two useful functions that make and break the connection between a source and a sink object. The AtlAdvise function makes the connection between a connectable object's connection point (specified by the pUnkCP and iid parameters) and a sink interface implementation (specified by the pUnk parameter), and returns a registration code for the connection in the pdw location. The AtlUnadvise function requests the connectable object's connection point to break the connection identified by the dw parameter.

```
ATLAPI AtlAdvise(IUnknown* pUnkCP, IUnknown* pUnk,
                 const IID& iid, LPDWORD pdw);
ATLAPI AtlUnadvise(IUnknown* pUnkCP, const IID& iid, DWORD dw);
```

You use these functions like this:

```
DWORD dwCookie;
// Make a connection
hr = AtlAdvise(spSource, spSink, __uuidof(_ISpeakerEvents),
  &dwCookie);
// ... Receive callbacks ...
// Break the connection
hr = AtlUnadvise(spSource, __uuidof(_ISpeakerEvents), dwCookie);
```

In summary, to establish a connection, you need an interface pointer for the connectable object, an interface pointer to an object that implements the sink interface, and the sink interface ID.

You commonly find connection points used by ActiveX controls. An ActiveX control is often a source of events. An event source implements event callbacks as method calls on a specified event sink interface. Typically, an ActiveX control container implements an event sink interface so that it can receive specific events from its contained controls. Using the connection points protocol, the control container establishes a connection from the source of events in the control (the connection point) to the event sink in the container. When an event occurs, the connection point calls the appropriate method of the sink interface for each sink connected to the connection point.

I should point out that the connection points design is deliberately a very general mechanism, which means that using connection points isn't terribly efficient in some cases.[1] Connection points are most useful when an unknown number of clients might want to establish callbacks to a variety of different sink interfaces. In addition, the connection points protocol is well known; therefore, objects with no custom knowledge of each other can use it to establish connections. If you are writing both the source and sink objects, you might want to invent a custom protocol that is easier to use than the connection point protocol, to trade interface pointers.

Creating an ATL-Based Connectable Object

The Brilliant Example Problem That Produces Blinding Insight

Let's create a Demagogue COM object that represents a public speaker. The ATL-based CDemagogue class implements the ISpeaker interface. When asked to Speak, a speaker can whisper, talk, or yell his speech, depending on the value of Volume.

```
interface ISpeaker : IDispatch {
    [propget, id(1)] HRESULT Volume([out, retval] long *pVal);
    [propput, id(1)] HRESULT Volume([in] long newVal);
    [propget, id(2)] HRESULT Speech([out, retval] BSTR *pVal);
    [propput, id(2)] HRESULT Speech([in] BSTR newVal);
    [id(3)] HRESULT Speak();
};
```

Whispering, talking, and yelling generate event notifications on the _ISpeakerEvents source dispatch interface, and the recipients of the events hear the speech. Many client components can receive event notifications only when the source interface is a dispatch interface.

---

[1] For ActiveX controls and other in-process objects, connection points are acceptable, but when round-trips are a concern, they are horrid. Read *Effective COM* (Addison-Wesley, 1998), by Don Box, Keith Brown, Tim Ewald, and Chris Sells, for an in-depth discussion of these issues.

```
dispinterface _ISpeakerEvents {
properties:
methods:
    [id(1)] void OnWhisper(BSTR bstrSpeach);
    [id(2)] void OnTalk(BSTR bstrSpeach);
    [id(3)] void OnYell(BSTR bstrSpeach);
};
```

The underscore prefix is a naming convention that causes many type library browsers to not display the interface name. Because an event interface is an implementation detail, typically you don't want such interfaces displayed to the authors of scripting languages when they use your component.

Note that the Microsoft Interface Definition Language (MIDL) compiler prefixes DIID_ to the name of a dispinterface when it generates its named globally unique identifier (GUID). So DIID__ISpeakerEvents is the named GUID for this interface.

Therefore, the following coclass definition describes a Demagogue. I've added an interface that lets me name a particular Demagogue if I don't like the default (which is Demosthenes).

```
coclass Demagogue {
    [default]           interface        IUnknown;
                        interface        ISpeaker;
                        interface        INamedObject;
    [default, source] dispinterface _ISpeakerEvents;
};
```

I start with the CDemagogue class: an ATL-based, single-threaded-apartment-resident, COM-createable object to represent a Demagogue.

```
class ATL_NO_VTABLE CDemagogue :
    public CComObjectRootEx<CComSingleThreadModel>,
    public CComCoClass<CDemagogue, &CLSID_Demagogue>,
    public ISupportErrorInfo,
    public IDispatchImpl<ISpeaker, &IID_ISpeaker,
        &LIBID_ATLINTERNALSLib>,
    ...
{ ... };
```

Seven Steps to a Connectable Object

There are seven steps to creating a connectable object using ATL:

1. Implement the IConnectionPointContainer interface.

2. Implement QueryInterface so that it responds to requests for IID_IConnectionPointContainer.

3. Implement the IConnectionPoint interface for each source interface that the connectable object supports.

4. Provide a connection map that is a table that associates an IID with a connection point implementation.

5. Update the coclass definition for the connectable object class in your IDL file to specify each source interface. Each source interface must have the [source] attribute. The primary source interface should have the [default, source] attributes.

6. Typically, you implement helper methods that call the sink methods for all connected sinks.

7. You must call the helper methods at the appropriate times.

Adding Required Base Classes to Your Connectable Object

For an object to fire events using the connection points protocol, the object must be a connectable object. This means that the object must implement the IConnectionPointContainer interface. You can use an ATL-provided implementation of IConnectionPointContainer and IConnectionPoint by deriving the connectable object class from the appropriate base classes.

Step 1. Derive the CDemagogue connectable object class from the ATL template class IConnectionPointContainerImpl. This template class requires one parameter, the name of your derived class. This derivation provides the connectable object with an implementation of the IConnectionPointContainer interface.

```
class ATL_NO_VTABLE CDemagogue :
    ...
    public IConnectionPointContainerImpl<CDemagogue>,
    ...
```

Changes to the COM_MAP for a Connectable Object

Step 2. Any time you add a new interface implementation to a class, you should immediately add support for the interface to your QueryInterface method. ATL implements QueryInterface for an object by searching the object's COM_MAP for an entry matching the requested IID. To indicate that the object supports the IConnectionPointContainer interface, add a COM_INTERFACE_ENTRY macro for the interface:

```
BEGIN_COM_MAP(CDemagogue)
...
    COM_INTERFACE_ENTRY(IConnectionPointContainer)
...
END_COM_MAP ()
```

Adding Each Connection Point

A connection point container needs a collection of connection points to contain (otherwise, the container is somewhat boring as well as misleading). For each source interface that the connectable object supports, you need a connection point subobject. A connection point subobject is logically a separate object (that is, its COM object identity is unique) that implements the IConnectionPoint interface.

Step 3. To create connection point subobjects, you derive your connectable object class from the template class IConnectionPointImpl one or more times—once for each source interface supported by the connectable object. This derivation provides the connectable object with one or more implementations of the IConnectionPoint interface on separately reference-counted subobjects. The IConnectionPointImpl class requires three template parameters: the name of your connectable object class, the IID of the connection point's source interface, and, optionally, the name of a class that manages the connections.

```
class ATL_NO_VTABLE CDemagogue :
    ...
    public IConnectionPointContainerImpl<CDemagogue>,
    public IConnectionPointImpl<CDemagogue, &DIID__ISpeakerEvents>
    ...
```

Where, O Where Are the Connection Points? Where, O Where Can They Be?

Any implementation of IConnectionPointContainer needs some fundamental information: a list of connection point objects and the IID that each connection point object supports. The ATL implementation uses a table called a *connection point map* in which you provide the required information. You define a connection point map in your connectable object's class declaration using three ATL macros.

The BEGIN_CONNECTION_POINT_MAP macro specifies the beginning of the table. The only parameter is the class name of the connectable object. Each CONNECTION_POINT_ENTRY macro places an entry in the table and represents one connection point. The macro's only parameter is the IID of the interface that the connection point supports.

Note that the CONNECTION_POINT_ENTRY macro requires you to specify an IID, whereas the COM_INTERFACE_ENTRY macro needs an interface class name. Historically, you could always prepend an IID_ prefix to an interface class name to produce the name of the GUID for the interface. Earlier versions of ATL's COM_INTERFACE_ENTRY macro actually did this to produce the appropriate IID.

However, source interfaces have no such regular naming convention. Various versions of MFC, MKTYPLIB, and MIDL have generated different prefixes to a dispinterface. The CONNECTION_POINT_ENTRY macro couldn't assume a prefix, so you had to specify the IID explicitly. By default, ATL uses the __uuidof keyword to obtain the IID for a class.

The END_CONNECTION_MAP macro generates an end-of-table marker and code that returns the address of the connection map as well as its size.

Step 4. Here's the connection map for the CDemagogue class:

```
BEGIN_CONNECTION_POINT_MAP(CDemagogue)
    CONNECTION_POINT_ENTRY(__uuidof(_ISpeakerEvents))
END_CONNECTION_POINT_MAP()
```

Update the coclass to Support the Source Interface

Step 5. Clients often read the type library, which describes an object that is a source of events, to determine certain implementation details, such as the object's source interface(s). You need to ensure that the source object's coclass description is up-to-date by adding an entry to describe the source interface.

```
coclass Demagogue
{
    [default]            interface      IUnknown;
                         interface      ISpeaker;
                         interface      INamedObject;
    [default, source] dispinterface _ISpeakerEvents;
};
```

Where There Are Events, There Must Be Fire

So far, we have a Demagogue connectable object that is a container of connection points and one connection point. The implementation, as presented up to now, permits a client to register a callback interface with a connection point. All the enumerators will work. The client can even disconnect. However, the connectable object never issues any callbacks. This isn't terribly useful and has been a bit of work for no significant gain, so we'd better finish things. A connectable object needs to call the sink interface methods, otherwise known as *firing* the events.

To fire an event, you call the appropriate event method of the sink interface for each sink interface pointer registered with a connection point. This task is complex enough that you'll generally find it useful to add event-firing helper methods to your connectable object class. You have one helper method in your connectable object class for each method in each of your connection points' supported interfaces.

You fire an event by calling the associated event method of a particular sink interface. You do this for each sink interface registered with the connection point. This means you need to iterate through a connection point's list of sink interfaces and call the event method for each interface pointer. "How and where does a connection point maintain this list?" you ask. Good timing, I was about to get to that.

Each `IConnectionPointImpl` base class object (which means each connection point) contains a member variable `m_vec` that ATL declares as a vector of `IUnknown` pointers. However, you don't need to call `QueryInterface` to get the appropriate sink interfaces out of this collection; ATL's implementation of `IConnection-PointImpl::Advise` has already performed this query for you. For example, the vector in the connection point associated with `DIID_ISpeakerEvents` actually contains `_ISpeakerEvents` pointers.

By default, `m_vec` is a `CComDynamicUnkArray` object, which is a dynamically allocated array of `IUnknown` pointers, each a client sink interface pointer for the connection point. The `CComDynamicUnkArray` class grows the vector as required, so the default implementation provides an unlimited number of connections.

Alternatively, when you declare the `IConnectionPointImpl` base class, you can specify that `m_vec` is a `CComUnkArray` object that holds a fixed number of sink interface pointers. Use the `CComUnkArray` class when you want to support a fixed maximum number of connections. ATL also provides an explicit template, `CComUnkArray<1>`, that is specialized for a single connection

Step 6. To fire an event, you iterate through the array and, *for each non-*NULL *entry*, call the sink interface method associated with the event you want to fire. Here's a simple helper method that fires the `OnTalk` event of the `_ISpeakerEvents` interface.

Note that `m_vec` is unambiguous only when you have a single connection point.

```
HRESULT Fire_OnTalk(BSTR bstrSpeech)
{
    CComVariant arg, varResult;
    int nIndex, nConnections = m_vec.GetSize();

    for (nIndex = 0; nIndex < nConnections; nIndex++) {
        CComPtr<IUnknown> sp = m_vec.GetAt(nIndex);
        IDispatch* pDispatch =
            reinterpret_cast<IDispatch*>(sp.p);
        if (pDispatch != NULL) {
            VariantClear(&varResult);
            arg = bstrSpeech;
            DISPPARAMS disp = { &arg, NULL, 1, 0 };
            pDispatch->Invoke(0x2, IID_NULL, LOCALE_USER_DEFAULT,
                DISPATCH_METHOD, &disp, &varResult, NULL, NULL);
```

```
        }
    }
    return varResult.scode;
}
```

The ATL Connection Point Proxy Generator

Writing the helper methods that call a connection point interface method is tedious and prone to errors. An additional complexity is that a sink interface can be a custom COM interface or a `dispinterface`. Considerably more work is involved in making a `dispinterface` callback (that is, using `IDispatch::Invoke`) than making a `vtable` callback. Unfortunately, the `dispinterface` callback is the most frequent case because it's the only event mechanism that scripting languages, Internet Explorer, and most ActiveX control containers support.

The Visual Studio 2005 IDE, however, provides a source code–generation tool that generates a connection point class that contains all the necessary helper methods for making callbacks on a specific connection point interface. In the Visual Studio 2005 Class View pane, right-click on the C++ class that you want to be a source of events. Select the Add Connection Point menu item from the context menu. The Implement Connection Point Wizard appears (see Figure 9.3).

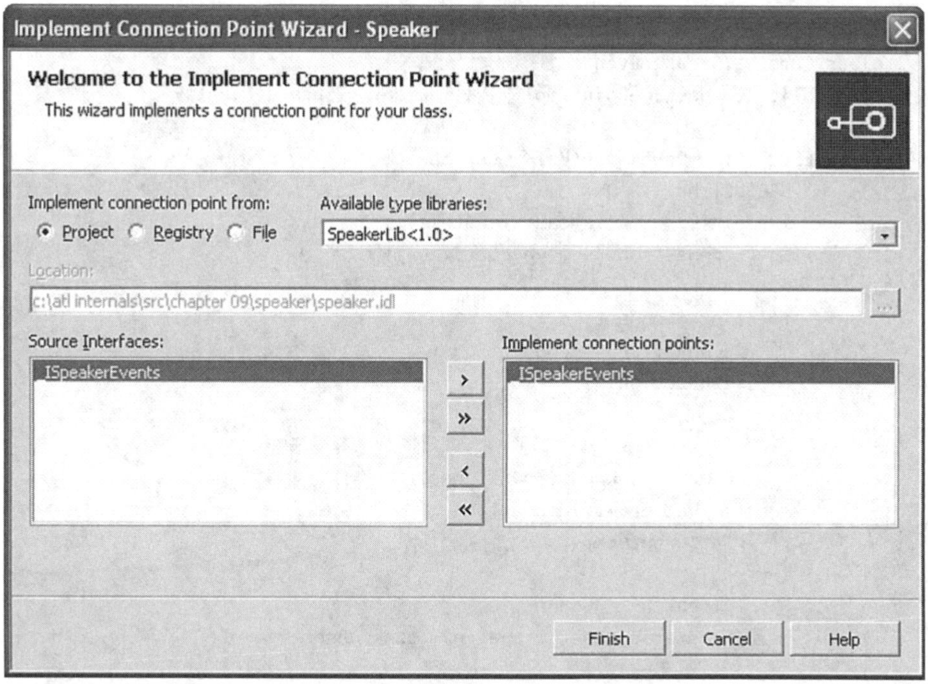

Figure 9.3   The Implement Connection Point dialog box

The Implement Connection Point Wizard creates one or more classes (declared and defined in the specified header file) that represent the specified interface(s) and their methods. To use the code generator, you must have a type library that describes the desired event interface. The code generator reads the type library description of an interface and generates a class, derived from IConnection-PointImpl, that contains an event-firing helper function for each interface method. You specify the generated class name as one of your connectable object's base classes. This base class implements a specific connection point and contains all necessary event-firing helper methods.

The Implement Connection Point Proxy-Generated Code

The proxy generator produces a template class with a name in the form CProxy_<SinkInterfaceName>. This proxy class requires one parameter: your connectable object's class name. The proxy class derives from an IConnection-PointImpl template instantiation that specifies your source interface.

Here is the code that the Implement Connection Point Wizard generates for the previously described _ISpeakerEvents interface:

```
#pragma once

template<class T>
class CProxy_ISpeakerEvents :
    public IConnectionPointImpl<T, &__uuidof(_ISpeakerEvents)> {
public:
    HRESULT Fire_OnWhisper(BSTR bstrSpeech) {
        HRESULT hr = S_OK;
        T * pThis = static_cast<T*>(this);
        int cConnections = m_vec.GetSize();

        for (int iConnection = 0;
             iConnection < cConnections;
             iConnection++)
        {
            pThis->Lock();
            CComPtr<IUnknown> punkConnection =
              m_vec.GetAt(iConnection);
            pThis->Unlock();

            IDispatch * pConnection =
                static_cast<IDispatch*>(punkConnection.p);

            if (pConnection) {
                CComVariant avarParams[1];
```

```
                avarParams[0] = bstrSpeech;
                DISPPARAMS params = { avarParams, NULL, 1, 0 };
                hr = pConnection->Invoke(DISPID_ONWHISPER,
                    IID_NULL,
                    LOCALE_USER_DEFAULT,
                    DISPATCH_METHOD,
                    &params, NULL, NULL, NULL);
            }
        }
        return hr;
    }


    // Other methods similar, deleted for clarity

    };
```

Using the Connection Point Proxy Code

Putting everything together so far, here are the pertinent parts of the CDemagogue connectable object declaration. The only change from previous examples is the use of the generated connection point proxy class, CProxy_ISpeakerEvents<CDemagogue>, as a base class for the connection point instead of the more generic IConnectionPointImpl class.

```
class ATL_NO_VTABLE CDemagogue :
...
    public IConnectionPointContainerImpl<CDemagogue>,
    public CProxy_ISpeakerEvents<CDemagogue>, ... {

BEGIN_COM_MAP(CDemagogue)
...
    COM_INTERFACE_ENTRY(IConnectionPointContainer)
...
END_COM_MAP()

BEGIN_CONNECTION_POINT_MAP(CDemagogue)
    CONNECTION_POINT_ENTRY(__uuidof(_ISpeakerEvents))
END_CONNECTION_POINT_MAP()
...
};
```

Firing the Events

Step 7. The final step to make everything work is to fire each event at the appropriate time. When to do this is application-specific, but here is one example.

The CDemagogue object makes its speech when a client calls the Speak method. The Speak method, based on the current volume property, either whispers, talks, or yells. It does this by calling the OnWhisper, OnTalk, or OnYell event methods, as appropriate, of all clients listening to the demagogue's _ISpeakerEvents interface.

```
STDMETHODIMP CDemagogue::Speak() {
    if (m_nVolume <= -100)
        return Fire_OnWhisper(m_bstrSpeech);

    if (m_nVolume >= 100)
        return Fire_OnYell(m_bstrSpeech);

    return Fire_OnTalk(m_bstrSpeech);
}
```

Going the Last Meter/Mile, Adding One Last Bell

The changes described so far provide a complete implementation of the connection point protocol. However, one last change makes your connectable object easier for clients to use. A connectable object should provide convenient client access to information about the interfaces that the object supports.

More specifically, many clients that want to receive events from a connectable object can ask the object for its IProvideClassInfo2 interface. Microsoft Internet Explorer, Visual Basic, and ATL-based ActiveX control containers do this, for example. The client calls the GetGUID method of this interface with the parameter GUID-KIND_DEFAULT_SOURCE_DISP_IID to retrieve the IID of the primary event dispinterface that the connectable object supports. This is the IID of the dispinterface listed in the connectable object's coclass description with the [default, source] attributes.

Supporting IProvideClassInfo2 gives arbitrary clients a convenient mechanism for determining the primary event source IID and then using the IID to establish a connection. Note that the IID returned by this call to GetGUID must be a dispinterface; it cannot be a standard IUnknown-derived (vtable) interface.

When a connectable object fails the query for IProvideClassInfo2, some clients ask for IProvideClassInfo. A client can use this interface to retrieve an ITypeInfo pointer about the connectable object's class. With a considerable bit of effort, a client can use this ITypeInfo pointer and determine the default source interface that the connectable object supports. The IProvideClassInfo2 interface derives from the IProvideClassInfo interface, so by implementing the first interface, you've already implemented the second one.

Because most connectable objects should implement the IProvideClassInfo2 interface, ATL provides a template class for the implementation, IProvideClass-Info2Impl, which provides a default implementation of all the IProvideClassInfo and IProvideClassInfo2 methods. The declaration of the class looks like this:

```
template <const CLSID* pcoclsid, const IID* psrcid,
    const GUID* plibid = &CAtlModule::m_libid,
    WORD wMajor = 1, WORD wMinor = 0,
    class tihclass = CComTypeInfoHolder>
class ATL_NO_VTABLE IProvideClassInfo2Impl
    : public IProvideClassInfo2
{ ... }
```

To use this implementation in your connectable object, you must derive the connectable object class from the `IProvideClassInfo2Impl` class. The last two template parameters in the following example are the major and minor version numbers of the component's type library. They default to 1 and 0, respectively, so I didn't need to list them. However, when you change the type library's version number, you also need to change the numbers in the template invocation. You won't get a compile error if you fail to make the change, but things won't work correctly.

By always listing the version number explicitly, I remember to make this change more often:

```
#define LIBRARY_MAJOR   1
#define LIBRARY_MINOR   0

class ATL_NO_VTABLE CDemagogue :
...
    public IConnectionPointContainerImpl<CDemagogue>,
    public CProxy_ISpeakerEvents<CDemagogue>,
    public IProvideClassInfo2Impl<&CLSID_Demagogue,
        &__uuidof(_ISpeakerEvents),
        &LIBID_ATLINTERNALSLib, LIBRARY_MAJOR, LIBRARY_MINOR>,
...
};
```

You also need to update the interface map so that `QueryInterface` responds to `IProvideClassInfo` and `IProvideClassInfo2`.

```
BEGIN_COM_MAP(CDemagogue)
...
  COM_INTERFACE_ENTRY(IProvideClassInfo2)
  COM_INTERFACE_ENTRY(IProvideClassInfo)
END_COM_MAP()
```

Finally, here are all connectable-object-related changes in one place:

```
#define LIBRARY_MAJOR   1
#define LIBRARY_MINOR   0

// Event dispinterface
dispinterface _ISpeakerEvents {
properties:
methods:
    [id(1)] void OnWhisper(BSTR bstrSpeech);
    [id(2)] void OnTalk(BSTR bstrSpeech);
    [id(3)] void OnYell(BSTR bstrSpeech);
};

// Connectable object class
coclass Demagogue {
    [default]             interface       IUnknown;
                          interface       ISpeaker;
                          interface       INamedObject;
    [default, source] dispinterface _ISpeakerEvents;
};

// Implementation class for coclass Demagogue
class ATL_NO_VTABLE CDemagogue :
...
    public IConnectionPointContainerImpl<CDemagogue>,
    public CProxy_ISpeakerEvents<CDemagogue>,
    public IProvideClassInfo2Impl<&CLSID_Demagogue,
        &__uuidof(_ISpeakerEvents),
        &LIBID_ATLINTERNALSLib, LIBRARY_MAJOR, LIBRARY_MINOR>,
    ... {
public:
BEGIN_COM_MAP(CDemagogue)
    COM_INTERFACE_ENTRY(IConnectionPointContainer)
    COM_INTERFACE_ENTRY(IProvideClassInfo2)
    COM_INTERFACE_ENTRY(IProvideClassInfo)
...
END_COM_MAP()

BEGIN_CONNECTION_POINT_MAP(CDemagogue)
    CONNECTION_POINT_ENTRY(__uuidof(_ISpeakerEvents))
END_CONNECTION_POINT_MAP()
...
};
```

Creating an Object That Is an Event Recipient

It is quite easy, in theory, to implement an object that receives events on a single interface. You define a class that implements the interface and connect the object to the event source. We have a Demagogue class that generates events on the _ISpeakerEvents dispatch interface. Let's define a CEarPolitic class (clearly one ear of the body politic) that implements _ISpeakerEvents.

```
coclass EarPolitic {
    [default] dispinterface _ISpeakerEvents;
};
```

Now, implement the class using ATL as the CEarPolitic class.

```
class ATL_NO_VTABLE CEarPolitic :
  ...
  public _ISpeakerEvents,
  ... {
public:
  ...
BEGIN_COM_MAP(CEarPolitic)
  COM_INTERFACE_ENTRY(IDispatch)
  COM_INTERFACE_ENTRY(_ISpeakerEvents)
...
END_COM_MAP()

// _ISpeakerEvents
  STDMETHOD(GetTypeInfoCount)(UINT* pctinfo);
  STDMETHOD(GetTypeInfo)(UINT itinfo, LCID lcid,
    ITypeInfo** pptinfo);
  STDMETHOD(GetIDsOfNames)(REFIID riid, LPOLESTR* rgszNames,
    UINT cNames, LCID lcid, DISPID* rgdispid);
  STDMETHOD(Invoke)(DISPID dispidMember, REFIID riid, LCID lcid,
    WORD wFlags, DISPPARAMS* pdispparams, VARIANT* pvarResult,
    EXCEPINFO* pexcepinfo, UINT* puArgErr);
};
```

Unfortunately, an event interface is typically a dispinterface, so the normal interface-implementation techniques don't work. When you run the MIDL compiler, all you get for the generated _ISpeakerEvents interface is this:

```
MIDL_INTERFACE("A924C9DE-797F-430d-913D-93158AD2D801")
_ISpeakerEvents : public IDispatch
{
};
```

Instead of being able to simply implement the methods of the interface as regular C++ member functions, we must implement the IDispatch interface and support, at a minimum, the Invoke method. Invoke is a tedious method to write for any nontrivial event interface.

Another alternative is to use the IDispatch interface implementation that the IDispatchImpl template class provides. Unfortunately, the template class requires parameters describing a dual interface, not a dispinterface. To use IDispatchImpl, you need to define a dummy dual interface that has the same dispatch methods, dispatch identifiers, and function signatures as the event dispinterface.

This has more implications than are usually apparent. A dispinterface is not immutable, unlike a regular COM interface. If you don't control the definition of the dispinterface, it might change from release to release. (It's not that likely to change, but it is possible.) This means your dual interface needs to change as well. This implies that you cannot document the dual interface because, after it is published, it is immutable because some client may implement it. Because you should not describe the dual interface in a type library (because that documents it), you cannot use the universal type library-driven-marshaler and need a remoting proxy/stub for the dual interface. These are all theoretical issues because the dual interface, in this case, is an implementation detail that is specific to the implementation class, but the issues give us motivation enough to look for another solution.

On a slightly different note, what if you want to receive the same events from more than one event source and you want to know which source fired the event? For example, let's say you want to implement an EarPolitic class that acts as a judge listening to _ISpeakerEvents from both a Defendant object and a Plaintiff object. Each object is a source of OnWhisper, OnTalk, and OnYell events, but the judge needs to keep track of who is saying what.

This requires you to implement the _ISpeakerEvents interface multiple times: once for each event source. Providing separate implementations of any interface multiple times in a class requires each implementation to be in a separate COM identity. Two typical solutions to this problem are member-wise composition (in which each implementation is in a nested class) and something similar to tear-off interfaces (in which each implementation is in a separate class).

The IDispEventImpl and IDispEventSimpleImpl Classes

To avoid these issues, ATL provides two template classes, IDispEventImpl and IDispEventSimpleImpl, that provide an implementation of the IDispatch interface for an ATL COM object. Typically, you use one of these classes in an object that wants to receive event callbacks. Both classes implement the dispatch interface on a nested class object that maintains a separate COM identity from the deriving class. This means that you can derive from these classes multiple times when you need to implement multiple source-dispatch interfaces.

The `IDispEventImpl` class requires a type library that describes the dispatch interface. The class uses the `typeinfo` at runtime to map the `VARIANT` parameters received in the `Invoke` method call to the appropriate types and stack frame layout necessary for calling the event-handler member function.

```
template <UINT nID, class T, const IID* pdiid = &IID_NULL,
         const GUID* plibid = &GUID_NULL,
         WORD wMajor = 0, WORD wMinor = 0,
         class tihclass = CComTypeInfoHolder>
class ATL_NO_VTABLE IDispEventImpl :
    public IDispEventSimpleImpl<nID, T, pdiid>
{ ... }
```

The `IDispEventSimpleImpl` class doesn't use a type library, so it's a more light-weight class. You use it when you don't have a type library or when you want to be more efficient at runtime.

```
template <UINT nID, class T, const IID* pdiid>
class ATL_NO_VTABLE IDispEventSimpleImpl :
    public _IDispEventLocator<nID, pdiid>
{ ... }
```

When using the `IDispEventSimpleImpl` class, you must provide an `_ATL_FUNC_INFO` structure containing information that describes the expected parameters for the event handler.

```
struct _ATL_FUNC_INFO {
    CALLCONV cc;              // Calling convention
    VARTYPE vtReturn;        // VARIANT type for return value
    SHORT nParams;            // Number of parameters
    VARTYPE pVarTypes[_ATL_MAX_VARTYPES]; // Array of parameter
                                          // VARIANT type
};
```

Notice that `IDispEventImpl` derives from the `IDispEventSimpleImpl` class. The `IDispEventSimpleImpl` class calls the event handler based on the information in an `_ATL_FUNC_INFO` structure. You can provide the structure statically (at compile time) by referencing the structure in the sink map (described later in this chapter).

When you provide no structure reference, the `IDispEventSimpleImpl` class calls the virtual method `GetFuncInfoFromId` to get an `_ATL_FUNC_INFO` structure for the event handler associated with the specified `DISPID`. You provide the structure dynamically by overriding `GetFuncInfoFromId` and returning the appropriate structure when called. You must use GetFuncInfoFromId when you want to call different event methods based on the locale provided by the event source.

Here's the default implementation provided by the IDispEventSimpleImpl class:

```
//Helper for finding the function index for a DISPID
virtual HRESULT GetFuncInfoFromId(const IID& iid,
  DISPID dispidMember,
  LCID lcid,
  _ATL_FUNC_INFO& info) {
  ATLTRACE(_T("TODO: Classes using IDispEventSimpleImpl "
    "should override this method\n"));
  ATLASSERT(0);
  ATLTRACENOTIMPL(_T("IDispEventSimpleImpl::GetFuncInfoFromId"));
}
```

The IDispEventImpl class overrides this virtual method to create the structure from the typeinfo in the specified type library.

Implementing an Event Sink

The *easiest* way to implement one or more event sinks in a nonattributed ATL object is to derive the object one or more times from IDispEventImpl—once for each unique event interface coming from each unique event source. Here's the template class specification once more:

```
template <UINT nID, class T, const IID* pdiid = &IID_NULL,
        const GUID* plibid = &GUID_NULL,
        WORD wMajor = 0, WORD wMinor = 0,
        class tihclass = CComTypeInfoHolder>
class ATL_NO_VTABLE IDispEventImpl :
    public IDispEventSimpleImpl<nID, T, pdiid>
{ ... }
```

The nID parameter specifies an identifier for the event source that is unique to the deriving class T. You'll see in Chapter 11, "ActiveX Controls," that when the event source is a contained control and the event recipient is a composite control, the identifier is the contained control's child window identifier.

A composite control can default all other IDispEventImpl template parameters, but an arbitrary COM object must specify all parameters except the last. The pdiid parameter specifies the GUID for the event dispinterface that this class implements. The dispinterface must be described in the type library specified by the plibid parameter and the type library major and minor version numbers, wMajor and wMinor. The tihclass parameter specifies the class to manage the type information for the deriving class T. The default CComTypeInfoHolder class is generally acceptable.

The more *efficient* way to implement one or more event sinks in an ATL object uses the IDispEventSimpleImpl class and needs no type library at runtime. However, you must provide the necessary _ATL_FUNC_INFO structure, as described previously. When using the IDispEventSimpleImpl class, you need to specify only the nID event source identifier, the deriving class T, and the pdiid GUID for the event dispinterface:

```
template <UINT nID, class T, const IID* pdiid>
class ATL_NO_VTABLE IDispEventSimpleImpl :
    public _IDispEventLocator<nID, pdiid>
{ ... }
```

Using the easier technique, let's redefine the CEarPolitic class to implement the _ISpeakerEvents dispatch interface twice: once for a Demagogue acting as a Defendant and once for a different Demagogue acting as a Plaintiff. We have a type library, so we use the IDispEventImpl class to implement the sink for the Defendant object's _ISpeakerEvents callbacks. We use the IDispEventSimpleImpl class for the Plaintiff object's _ISpeakerEvents callbacks to demonstrate the alternative implementation. We typically introduce a typedef for each event interface implementation, to minimize typing and mistakes.

```
static const int  DEFENDANT_SOURCE_ID = 0 ;
static const int  PLAINTIFF_SOURCE_ID = 1 ;

class CEarPolitic;

typedef IDispEventImpl<DEFENDANT_SOURCE_ID,
  CEarPolitic,
  &__uuidof(_ISpeakerEvents),
  &LIBID_ATLINTERNALSLib,
  LIBRARY_MAJOR, LIBRARY_MINOR> DefendantEventImpl;

typedef IDispEventSimpleImpl<PLAINTIFF_SOURCE_ID,
  CEarPolitic, &__uuidof(_ISpeakerEvents)> PlaintiffEventImpl;
```

In this example, we arbitrarily chose 0 and 1 for the event source identifiers. The identifiers could have been any numbers. Now, we need to derive the CEarPolitic class from the two event-implementation classes:

```
class ATL_NO_VTABLE CEarPolitic :
    ...
    public DefendantEventImpl,
    public PlaintiffEventImpl {

// Event sink map required in here

};
```

The Event Sink Map

The IDispEventSimpleImpl class's implementation of the Invoke method receives the event callbacks. When the event source calls the Invoke method, it specifies the event that has occurred using the DISPID parameter. The IDispEventSimpleImpl implementation searches an event sink table for the function to call when event DISPID occurs on dispatch interface DIID from event source identifier SOURCE.

You specify the beginning of the event sink map using the BEGIN_SINK_MAP macro within the declaration of the class that derives from IDispEventImpl or IDispEventSimpleImpl. You map each unique SOURCE/DIID/DISPID triple to the proper event-handling method using the SINK_ENTRY, SINK_ENTRY_EX, and SINK_ENTRY_INFO macros.

- SINK_ENTRY(SOURCE, DISPID, func). Use this macro in a composite control to name the handler for the specified event in the specified contained control's default source interface. This macro assumes the use of IDispEventImpl and assumes that you call the AtlAdviseSinkMap function to establish the connection. The AtlAdviseSinkMap function assumes that your class is derived from CWindow. All in all, the SINK_ENTRY macro isn't very useful for nonuser-interface (UI) objects that want to receive events.

- SINK_ENTRY_EX(SOURCE, DIID, DISPID, func). Use this macro to indicate the handler for the specified event in the specified object's specified source interface. This macro is most useful for non-UI objects that want to receive events and for composite controls that want to receive events from a contained control's nondefault source interface.

- SINK_ENTRY_INFO(SOURCE, DIID, DISPID, func, info). This macro is similar to the SINK_ENTRY_EX macro, with the addition that you can specify the _ATL_FUNC_INFO structure to be used when calling the event handler. You typically use this macro when using the IDispEventSimpleImpl class.

You end the event sink map using the END_SINK_MAP macro.

The general form of the table is as follows:

```
BEGIN_SINK_MAP(CEarPolitic)
   SINK_ENTRY_EX(SOURCE, DIID, DISPID, EventHandlerFunc)
   SINK_ENTRY_INFO(SOURCE, DIID, DISPID, EventHandlerFunc, &info)
...
END_SINK_MAP()
```

In the CEarPolitic example, there are three events, all from the same dispatch interface but coming from two different event sources. Therefore, we need six event sink map entries. We can use the SINK_ENTRY_EX macro to identify the event handlers for the Defendant event source. We don't need to specify the _ATL_FUNC_INFO structure because the IDispEventImpl base class uses the type library to provide the appropriate structure at runtime. We need to use the SINK_ENTRY_INFO macro for the Plaintiff object. Because we used the IDisp-EventSimpleImpl base class, we need to provide the function information structure describing each event method.

Each function information structure describes one event method. The structure contains the calling convention, the VARIANT type of the return value of the method, the number of parameters, and the VARIANT types of each of the parameters. The calling convention should be set to CC_STDCALL because that's what the IDispEventSimpleImpl class expects the event handlers to use.

Here are the function prototypes for the Plaintiff's three event methods and their information structures (all identical in this example). Event handlers typically do not return a value—that is, they are void functions. *Note:* The proper vtReturn value in the _ATL_FUNC_INFO structure to represent a void function return is VT_EMPTY, not VT_VOID.

```
void __stdcall OnHearPlaintiffWhisper(BSTR bstrText);
void __stdcall OnHearPlaintiffTalk(BSTR bstrText);
void __stdcall OnHearPlaintiffYell(BSTR bstrText);

static const int  DISPID_WHISPER = 1 ;
static const int  DISPID_TALK    = 2 ;
static const int  DISPID_YELL    = 3 ;

_ATL_FUNC_INFO OnHearWhisperInfo = {
  CC_STDCALL, VT_EMPTY, 1, { VT_BSTR }};
_ATL_FUNC_INFO OnHearTalkInfo    = {
  CC_STDCALL, VT_EMPTY, 1, { VT_BSTR }};
_ATL_FUNC_INFO OnHearYellInfo    = {
  CC_STDCALL, VT_EMPTY, 1, { VT_BSTR }};
```

Here's the event sink map for the `CEarPolitic` object:

```
BEGIN_SINK_MAP(CEarPolitic)
  SINK_ENTRY_EX(DEFENDANT_SOURCE_ID, __uuidof(_ISpeakerEvents),
    DISPID_WHISPER, OnHearDefendantWhisper)
  SINK_ENTRY_EX(DEFENDANT_SOURCE_ID, __uuidof(_ISpeakerEvents),
    DISPID_TALK, OnHearDefendantTalk)
  SINK_ENTRY_EX(DEFENDANT_SOURCE_ID, __uuidof(_ISpeakerEvents),
    DISPID_YELL, OnHearDefendantYell)
  SINK_ENTRY_INFO(PLAINTIFF_SOURCE_ID, __uuidof(_ISpeakerEvents),
    DISPID_WHISPER, OnHearPlaintiffWhisper, &OnHearWhisperInfo)
  SINK_ENTRY_INFO(PLAINTIFF_SOURCE_ID, __uuidof(_ISpeakerEvents),
    DISPID_TALK, OnHearPlaintiffTalk, &OnHearTalkInfo)
  SINK_ENTRY_INFO(PLAINTIFF_SOURCE_ID, __uuidof(_ISpeakerEvents),
    DISPID_YELL, OnHearPlaintiffYell, &OnHearYellInfo)
END_SINK_MAP()
```

One caution: The sink map contains a hard-coded `DISPID` for each event. This means that the sink map technically is specific to a particular `dispinterface` version. COM allows the `DISPID`s in a `dispinterface` to change from version to version. Now, this isn't something that often happens—and a control vendor that does such a thing is just asking for tech support calls and angry customers. But it is allowed.

The only absolutely correct way to obtain a `DISPID` is to ask the object implementing the dispinterface at startup for the `DISPID` corresponding to an event. For a source interface, this is impossible because when you build the sink, you're implementing the source interface, so there's no object to query. The only realistic option is to read the object's type library at runtime. ATL, Visual Basic, and MFC don't support this. They all assume that the `DISPID`s in a `dispinterface` will never change, as a questionable performance optimization.

The Callback Methods

The callback method specified by the sink entry macros must use the `__stdcall` calling convention. The parameters for each callback method specified in the sink map must agree in type and number with the corresponding event method as described in the type library. Here are the `Defendant`'s event methods; they are identical to the `Plaintiff`'s, as expected:

```
void __stdcall OnHearDefendantWhisper(BSTR bstrText);
void __stdcall OnHearDefendantTalk(BSTR bstrText);
void __stdcall OnHearDefendantYell(BSTR bstrText);
```

After two remaining steps, the `CEarPolitic` class will be complete: Implement the callback methods and establish the connection between a `CEarPolitic` instance and a Demagogue (which invokes the _ISpeakerEvents methods).

We use the following simple implementation for each of the event handlers:

```
void __stdcall CEarPolitic::OnHearDefendantTalk(BSTR bstrText) {
  CComBSTR title ;
  CreateText(title, OLESTR("defendant"),
    OLESTR("talking"), m_defendant);

  MessageBox(NULL, COLE2CT(bstrText), COLE2CT(title), MB_OK);
}

void CEarPolitic::CreateText(CComBSTR& bstrText,
  LPCOLESTR strRole,
  LPCOLESTR strAction,
  LPUNKNOWN punk) {
    bstrText = m_bstrName;
    bstrText += OLESTR(" hears the ");
    bstrText += strRole;
    bstrText += OLESTR(" (");

    CComQIPtr<INamedObject> spno = punk;
    CComBSTR bstrName;
    HRESULT hr = spno->get_Name (&bstrName) ;

    bstrText.AppendBSTR(bstrName);
    bstrText += OLESTR(") ");

    bstrText += strAction;
}
```

Connecting the Event Sink to an Event Source

When your class is a composite control, you should use the `AtlAdviseSinkMap` function to establish and remove the connections between all the source interfaces of the contained controls listed in the sink map and your `IDispEventImpl` implementation(s). This method uses the event source identifier as a child window identifier. Using the `CWindow::GetDlgItem` method, `AtlAdviseSinkMap` navigates to a child window handle and, from there, to the contained control's `IUnknown` interface. From the `IUnknown` interface, it gets the `IConnectionPointContainer` interface and the appropriate connection point, and calls its `Advise` method.

```
template <class T>
inline HRESULT AtlAdviseSinkMap(T* pT, bool bAdvise);
```

You *must* use the AtlAdviseSinkMap function to establish the connections any time you use the IDispEventImpl class and you specify only the first two template parameters, using default values for the rest. Not specifying the source interface implies using the default source interface for the event source. The AtlAdvise-SinkMap method determines the default source interface, if unspecified, for each event source and establishes the connection point to that interface.

When your class isn't a composite control, as in the ongoing example, you must explicitly call the DispEventAdvise method of each of your IDispEventSimpleImpl (or derived) base classes to connect each event source to each event sink implementation. The pUnk parameter to the DispEventAdvise method is any interface on the event source; the piid parameter is the desired source dispatch interface GUID. The DispEventUnadvise method breaks the connection.

```
template <UINT nID, class T, const IID* pdiid>
class ATL_NO_VTABLE IDispEventSimpleImpl : ... {
...
    HRESULT DispEventAdvise(IUnknown* pUnk, const IID* piid);
    HRESULT DispEventUnadvise(IUnknown* pUnk, const IID* piid);
...
}
```

Here is the IListener interface. We added it to the EarPolitic coclass to provide a means of determining whether a COM object can listen to a Defendant and a Plaintiff. It also provides the ListenTo and StopListening methods to establish and break the connection point between a Speaker event source and the Defendant or Plaintiff event sink.

```
interface IListener : IDispatch {
  typedef enum SpeakerRole { Defendant, Plaintiff } SpeakerRole;

  [id(1)] HRESULT ListenTo(SpeakerRole role, IUnknown* pSpeaker);
  [id(2)] HRESULT StopListening(SpeakerRole role);
};
```

The implementation of these methods is straightforward. ListenTo calls the DispEventAdvise method on the appropriate event sink to establish the connection:

```
STDMETHODIMP CEarPolitic::ListenTo(SpeakerRole role,
  IUnknown *pSpeaker) {
  HRESULT hr = StopListening(role) ; // Validates role
  if (FAILED(hr)) return hr ;

  switch (role) {
```

```
    case Defendant:
      hr = DefendantEventImpl::DispEventAdvise (pSpeaker,
        &DIID__ISpeakerEvents);
      if (SUCCEEDED(hr))
        m_defendant = pSpeaker;
      else
        Error(OLESTR("The defendant does not support listening"),
          __uuidof(IListener), hr);
      break;

    case Plaintiff:
      hr = PlaintiffEventImpl::DispEventAdvise (pSpeaker,
        &DIID__ISpeakerEvents);
      if (SUCCEEDED(hr))
        m_plaintiff = pSpeaker;
      else
        Error(OLESTR("The Plaintiff does not support listening"),
          __uuidof(IListener), hr);
      break;
  }
  return hr;
}
```

The StopListening method calls DispEventUnadvise to break the connection:

```
STDMETHODIMP CEarPolitic::StopListening(SpeakerRole role) {
  HRESULT hr = S_OK;
  switch (role) {
  case Defendant:
    if (m_defendant)
      hr = DefendantEventImpl::DispEventUnadvise (m_defendant,
        &DIID__ISpeakerEvents);

    if (FAILED(hr))
      Error (OLESTR("Unexpected error trying to stop listening "
        "to the defendant"), __uuidof(IListener), hr);

    m_defendant = NULL;
    break;

  case Plaintiff:
    if (m_plaintiff)
      hr = PlaintiffEventImpl::DispEventUnadvise(m_plaintiff,
        &DIID__ISpeakerEvents);
```

```
        if (FAILED(hr))
          Error(OLESTR("Unexpected error trying to stop listening "
            "to the Plaintiff"), __uuidof(IListener), hr);

        m_plaintiff = NULL;
        break;

    default:
      hr = E_INVALIDARG;
      break;
    }

    return hr;
  }
```

In summary, use the `IDispEventImpl` and `IDispEventSimpleImpl` classes to implement an event sink for a dispatch interface. Call the `DispEventAdvise` and `DispEventUnadvise` methods of each class to establish and break the connection.

Derive your class directly from the source interface when the source is a simple COM interface. Call the `AtlAdvise` and `AtlUnadvise` global functions to establish and break the connection. When you need to implement the same source interface multiple times, use one of the various standard techniques (nested composition, method coloring, separate classes, or intermediate base classes) to avoid name collisions.

How It All Works: The Messy Implementation Details

Classes Used by an Event Source

The IConnectionPointContainerImpl Class

Let's start by examining the `IConnectionPointContainerImpl` template class implementation of the `IConnectionPointContainer` interface.

First, the class needs to provide a `vtable` that is compatible with the `IConnectionPointContainer` interface. This `vtable` must contain five methods: the three `IUnknown` methods and the two `IConnectionPointContainer` methods.

```
template <class T>
class ATL_NO_VTABLE IConnectionPointContainerImpl
  : public IconnectionPointContainer {
  typedef CComEnum<IEnumConnectionPoints,
    &__uuidof(IEnumConnectionPoints), IConnectionPoint*,
    _CopyInterface<IConnectionPoint> >
  CComEnumConnectionPoints;
```

```
public:
  STDMETHOD(EnumConnectionPoints)(
    IEnumConnectionPoints** ppEnum) {
    if (ppEnum == NULL) return E_POINTER;

    *ppEnum = NULL;
    CComEnumConnectionPoints* pEnum = NULL;
    ATLTRY(pEnum = new CComObject<CComEnumConnectionPoints>)
    if (pEnum == NULL) return E_OUTOFMEMORY;

    int nCPCount;
    const _ATL_CONNMAP_ENTRY* pEntry = T::GetConnMap(&nCPCount);

    // allocate an initialize a vector of connection point
    // object pointers
    USES_ATL_SAFE_ALLOCA;
    if ((nCPCount < 0) || (nCPCount >
      (INT_MAX / sizeof(IConnectionPoint*))))
      return E_OUTOFMEMORY;
    size_t nBytes=0;
    HRESULT hr=S_OK;
    if( FAILED(hr=::ATL::AtlMultiply(&nBytes,
      sizeof(IConnectionPoint*),
      static_cast<size_t>(nCPCount)))) {
        return hr;
    }
    IConnectionPoint** ppCP =
      (IConnectionPoint**)_ATL_SAFE_ALLOCA(
      nBytes, _ATL_SAFE_ALLOCA_DEF_THRESHOLD);
    if (ppCP == NULL) {
      delete pEnum;
      return E_OUTOFMEMORY;
    }

    int i = 0;
    while (pEntry->dwOffset != (DWORD_PTR)-1) {
      if (pEntry->dwOffset == (DWORD_PTR)-2) {
        pEntry++;
        const _ATL_CONNMAP_ENTRY* (*pFunc)(int*) =
          (const _ATL_CONNMAP_ENTRY* (*)(int*))(
          pEntry->dwOffset);
        pEntry = pFunc(NULL);
        continue;
      }
```

```
      ppCP[i++] = (IConnectionPoint*)(
        (INT_PTR)this+pEntry->dwOffset);
      pEntry++;
    }


    // copy the pointers: they will AddRef this object
    HRESULT hRes = pEnum->Init(((IConnectionPoint**)&ppCP[0],
      (IConnectionPoint**)&ppCP[nCPCount],
      reinterpret_cast<IConnectionPointContainer*>(this),
      AtlFlagCopy);
    if (FAILED(hRes)) {
      delete pEnum;
      return hRes;
    }
    hRes = pEnum->QueryInterface(
      __uuidof(IEnumConnectionPoints),
      (void**)ppEnum);
    if (FAILED(hRes)) delete pEnum;
    return hRes;
  }

STDMETHOD(FindConnectionPoint)(REFIID riid,
    IConnectionPoint** ppCP) {
    if (ppCP == NULL) return E_POINTER;
    *ppCP = NULL;
    HRESULT hRes = CONNECT_E_NOCONNECTION;
    const _ATL_CONNMAP_ENTRY* pEntry = T::GetConnMap(NULL);
    IID iid;
    while (pEntry->dwOffset != (DWORD_PTR)-1) {
      if (pEntry->dwOffset == (DWORD_PTR)-2) {
        pEntry++;
        const _ATL_CONNMAP_ENTRY* (*pFunc)(int*) =
          (const _ATL_CONNMAP_ENTRY* (*)(int*))(
            pEntry->dwOffset);
        pEntry = pFunc(NULL);
        continue;
      }
      IConnectionPoint* pCP =
        (IConnectionPoint*)((INT_PTR)this+pEntry->dwOffset);
      if (SUCCEEDED(pCP->GetConnectionInterface(&iid)) &&
        InlineIsEqualGUID(riid, iid)) {
        *ppCP = pCP;
        pCP->AddRef();
        hRes = S_OK;
```

```
        break;
    }
    pEntry++;
    }
    return hRes;
  }
};
```

The `IUnknown` methods are easy: The class doesn't implement them. You bring in the proper implementation of these three methods when you define a `CComObject` class parameterized on your connectable object class—for example, `CComObject<CConnectableObject>`.

The `CComEnumConnectionPoints` typedef declares a class for a standard COM enumerator that implements the `IEnumConnectionPoints` interface. You use this class of enumerator to enumerate `IConnectionPoint` interface pointers. A template expansion of the ATL `CComEnum` class provides the implementation. The implementation of the `EnumConnectionPoints` method creates and returns an instance of this enumerator.

`EnumConnectionPoints` begins with some basic error checking and then creates a new instance of a `CComEnumConnectionPoints` enumerator on the heap. The ATL enumerator implementation requires an enumerator to be initialized after instantiation. ATL enumerators are rather inflexible: To initialize an enumerator, you must pass it an array of the items the enumerator enumerates. In this particular case, the enumerator provides `IConnectionPoint` pointers, so the initialization array must be an array of `IConnectionPoint` pointers.

A connectable object's connection map contains the information needed to produce the array of `IConnectionPoint` pointers. Each connection map entry contains the offset in the connectable object from the base of the `IConnectionPoint-ContainerImpl` instance (that is, the current `this` pointer value) to the base of an `IConnectionPointImpl` instance.

`EnumConnectionPoints` allocates space for the initialization array on the stack, using `_ATL_SAFE_ALLOCA`. It iterates through each entry of the connection map, calculates the `IConnectionPoint` interface pointer to each `IConnectionPointImpl` object, and stores the pointer in the array. Note that these pointers are not reference-counted because the lifetime of the pointers in a stack-based array is limited to the method lifetime.

The call to the enumerator `Init` method initializes the instance. It's critical here to use the `AtlFlagCopy` argument. This informs the enumerator to make a proper copy of the items in the initialization array. For interface pointers, this means to `AddRef` the pointers when making the copy. Refer to Chapter 8, "Collections and Enumerators," for details on COM enumerator initialization.

The `pEnum` pointer is a `CComEnumConnectionPoints` pointer, although it would be a bit better if it were declared as a `CComObject<CComEnumConnectionPoints>` pointer

because that's what it actually is. Regardless, EnumConnectionPoints must return an
IEnumConnectionPoints pointer, not pEnum itself, so it queries the enumerator (via
pEnum) for the appropriate interface pointer and returns the pointer.

The FindConnectionPoint method is quite straightforward. After the usual initial error checking, FindConnectionPoint uses the connection map to calculate an
IConnectionPoint interface pointer to each connection point in the connectable
object. Using the interface pointer, it asks each connection point for the IID of its
supported interface and compares it with the IID it's trying to find. A match causes
it to return the appropriate AddRef'ed interface pointer with status S_OK; otherwise,
failure returns the CONNECT_E_NOCONNECTION status code.

One minor oddity is the check to see if the offset is -2 when walking through
the connection point map. This is a value that appears only when using attributed
ATL (discussed in Appendix D, "Attributed ATL"). Attributed ATL inserts a second
connection point map into your class. The check for an offset of -2 is used to signal
that it's time to jump from the standard connection point map into the attributed
map. This is done by calling the function pointer in that slot to get the new starting
address of the next map to walk. This has the potential to be a general-purpose
chaining mechanism for connection point maps; however, the connection-point
macros don't support it, so it would take a good deal of hacking.

Most of the real work is left to the connection point implementation, so let's
look at it next.

The IConnectionPointImpl Class

The IConnectionPointImpl template class implements the IConnectionPoint interface. To do that, the class needs to provide a vtable that is compatible with the
IConnectionPoint interface. This vtable must contain eight methods: the three IUnknown methods and the five IConnectionPoint methods.

The first item of note is that the IConnectionPointImpl class derives from the
_ICPLocator class:

```
template <class T, const IID* piid,
  class CDV = CComDynamicUnkArray >
class ATL_NO_VTABLE IConnectionPointImpl
  : public _ICPLocator<piid>
{ ... }
```

The _ICPLocator Class

```
template <const IID* piid>
class ATL_NO_VTABLE _ICPLocator {
public:
```

```
        //this method needs a different name than QueryInterface
        STDMETHOD(_LocCPQueryInterface)(REFIID riid,
            void ** ppvObject) = 0;
        virtual ULONG STDMETHODCALLTYPE AddRef(void) = 0;
        virtual ULONG STDMETHODCALLTYPE Release(void) = 0;
};
```

The `_ICPLocator` class contains the declaration of the virtual method, `_LocCP-QueryInterface`. A virtual method occupies a slot in the `vtable`, so this declaration states that calls through the first entry in the `vtable`, the entry callers use to invoke `QueryInterface`, will be sent to the method `_LocCPQueryInterface`. The declaration is purely virtual, so a derived class needs to provide the implementation. This is important because each connection point needs to provide a unique implementation of `_LocCPQueryInterface`.

A connection point must maintain a COM object identity that is separate from its connection point container. Therefore, a connection point needs its own implementation of `QueryInterface`. If you named the first virtual method in the `_ICPLocator` class `QueryInterface`, C++ multiple inheritance rules would see the name as just another reference to a single implementation of `QueryInterface` for the connectable object. Normally, that's exactly what you want. For example, imagine that you have a class derived from three interfaces. All three interfaces mention the virtual method `QueryInterface`, but you want a single implementation of the method that all base classes share. Similarly, you want a shared implementation of `AddRef` and `Release` as well. But you don't want this for a connection point in a base class.

The idea here is that we want to expose two different COM identities (the connectable object and the connection point), which requires two separate implementations of `QueryInterface`. But we merge the remaining `IUnknown` implementation (`AddRef` and `Release`) because we don't want to keep a separate reference count for each connection point. ATL uses this "unique" approach to avoid having to delegate `AddRef` and `Release` calls from the connection point object to the connectable object.

The IConnectionPointImpl Class's Methods

The `IUnknown` methods are more complicated in `IConnectionPointImpl` than was the case in `IConnectionPointContainerImpl` so that a connection point can implement its own unique `QueryInterface` method. For a connection point, this is the `_LocCP-QueryInterface` virtual method.

```
template <class T, const IID* piid,
   class CDV = CComDynamicUnkArray >
class ATL_NO_VTABLE IConnectionPointImpl
```

```
  : public _ICPLocator<piid> {
  typedef CComEnum<IEnumConnections,
    &__uuidof(IEnumConnections), CONNECTDATA,
    _Copy<CONNECTDATA> > CComEnumConnections;
  typedef CDV _CDV;
public:
  ~IConnectionPointImpl();
  STDMETHOD(_LocCPQueryInterface)(REFIID riid, void ** ppvObject) {
#ifndef _ATL_OLEDB_CONFORMANCE_TESTS
    ATLASSERT(ppvObject != NULL);
#endif
    if (ppvObject == NULL)
      return E_POINTER;
    *ppvObject = NULL;

    if (InlineIsEqualGUID(riid, __uuidof(IConnectionPoint)) ||
      InlineIsEqualUnknown(riid)) {
      *ppvObject = this;
      AddRef();
#ifdef _ATL_DEBUG_INTERFACES
      _AtlDebugInterfacesModule.AddThunk((IUnknown**)ppvObject,
        _T("IConnectionPointImpl"), riid);
#endif // _ATL_DEBUG_INTERFACES
      return S_OK;
    }
    else
      return E_NOINTERFACE;
  }

  STDMETHOD(GetConnectionInterface)(IID* piid2) {
    if (piid2 == NULL)
      return E_POINTER;
    *piid2 = *piid;
    return S_OK;
  }
  STDMETHOD(GetConnectionPointContainer)(
    IConnectionPointContainer** ppCPC) {
    T* pT = static_cast<T*>(this);
    // No need to check ppCPC for NULL since
    // QI will do that for us
    return pT->QueryInterface(
      __uuidof(IConnectionPointContainer), (void**)ppCPC);
  }

  STDMETHOD(Advise)(IUnknown* pUnkSink, DWORD* pdwCookie);
  STDMETHOD(Unadvise)(DWORD dwCookie);
```

```
    STDMETHOD(EnumConnections)(IEnumConnections** ppEnum);
    CDV m_vec;
};
```

The _LocCPQueryInterface Method

The _LocCPQueryInterface method has the same function signature as the COM QueryInterface method, but it responds to only requests for IID_IUnknown and IID_IConnectionPoint by producing an AddRef'ed pointer to itself. This gives each base class instance of an IConnectionPointImpl object a unique COM identity.

The AddRef and Release Methods

As usual, you bring in the proper implementation of these two methods when you define a CComObject class parameterized on your connectable object class—for example, CComObject<CConnectableObject>.

The GetConnectionInterface and GetConnectionPointContainer Methods

The GetConnectionInterface interface method simply returns the source interface IID for the connection point, so the implementation is trivial. The GetConnection-PointContainer interface method is also simple, but some involved typecasting is required to request the correct interface pointer.

The issue is that the current class, this particular IConnectionPointImpl expansion, doesn't support the IConnectionPointContainer interface. But the design of the template classes requires your connectable object class, represented by class T in the template, to implement the IConnectionPointContainer interface:

```
T* pT = static_cast<T*>(this);
return pT->QueryInterface(IID_IConnectionPointContainer,
    (void**)ppCPC);
```

The typecast goes from the connection point subobject down the class hierarchy to the (deriving) connectable object class and calls that class's QueryInterface implementation to obtain the required IConnectionPointContainer interface pointer.

The Advise, Unadvise, and EnumConnections Methods

The Advise, Unadvise, and EnumConnections methods all need a list of active connections. Advise adds new entries to the list, Unadvise removes entries from the list, and EnumConnections returns an object that enumerates over the list.

This list is of template parameter type CDV. By default, this is type CComDynamic-UnkArray, which provides a dynamically growable array implementation of the list. As I described previously, ATL provides a fixed-size list implementation and a specialized single-entry list implementation. However, it is relatively easy to provide a custom list implementation because the Advise, Unadvise, and EnumConnections implementations always access the list through its well-defined methods: Add, Remove, begin, end, GetCookie, and GetUnknown.

The CComEnumConnections typedef declares a class for a standard COM enumerator that implements the IEnumConnections interface. You use this class of enumerator to enumerate CONNECTDATA structures, which contain a client sink interface pointer and its associated magic cookie-registration token. A template expansion of the ATL CComEnum class provides the implementation. The implementation of the EnumConnections interface method creates and returns an instance of this enumerator.

The Advise Method

```
template <class T, const IID* piid, class CDV>
STDMETHODIMP IConnectionPointImpl<T, piid, CDV>::Advise(
    IUnknown* pUnkSink,
    DWORD* pdwCookie) {
    T* pT = static_cast<T*>(this);
    IUnknown* p;
    HRESULT hRes = S_OK;
    if (pdwCookie != NULL)
        *pdwCookie = 0;
    if (pUnkSink == NULL || pdwCookie == NULL)
        return E_POINTER;
    IID iid;
    GetConnectionInterface(&iid);
    hRes = pUnkSink->QueryInterface(iid, (void**)&p);
    if (SUCCEEDED(hRes)) {
        pT->Lock();
        *pdwCookie = m_vec.Add(p);
        hRes = (*pdwCookie != NULL) ? S_OK :
            CONNECT_E_ADVISELIMIT;
        pT->Unlock();
        if (hRes != S_OK)
            p->Release();
    }
    else if (hRes == E_NOINTERFACE)
        hRes = CONNECT_E_CANNOTCONNECT;
    if (FAILED(hRes))
        *pdwCookie = 0;
    return hRes;
}
```

The `Advise` method retrieves the sink interface IID for this connection point and queries the `IUnknown` pointer that the client provides for the sink interface. This ensures that the client passes an interface pointer to an object that actually implements the expected sink interface. Failure to provide the correct interface pointer produces a `CONNECT_E_CANNOTCONNECT` error. You don't want to keep a connection to something that can't receive the callback. Plus, by obtaining the correct interface pointer here, the connection point doesn't have to query for it during each callback.

When the query succeeds, the connection point needs to add the connection to the list. So, it acquires a lock on the entire connectable object, adds the connection to the list if there's room, and releases the lock.

The Unadvise Method

```
template <class T, const IID* piid, class CDV>
STDMETHODIMP IConnectionPointImpl<T, piid, CDV>::Unadvise(
    DWORD dwCookie) {
    T* pT = static_cast<T*>(this);
    pT->Lock();
    IUnknown* p = m_vec.GetUnknown(dwCookie);
    HRESULT hRes = m_vec.Remove(dwCookie) ? S_OK :
        CONNECT_E_NOCONNECTION;
    pT->Unlock();
    if (hRes == S_OK && p != NULL)
        p->Release();
    return hRes;
}
```

The `Unadvise` method is relatively simple. It locks the connectable object, asks the list class to translate the provided magic cookie value into the corresponding `IUnknown` pointer, removes the connection identified by the cookie, unlocks the connectable object, and releases the held sink interface pointer.

The EnumConnections Method

`EnumConnection` begins with some basic error checking and then creates a new instance of a `CComObject<CComEnumConnections>` enumerator on the heap. As before, the ATL enumerator implementation requires that an enumerator be initialized from an array after instantiation—in this particular case, a contiguous array of `CONNECTDATA` structures.

```
template <class T, const IID* piid, class CDV>
STDMETHODIMP IConnectionPointImpl<T, piid, CDV>::EnumConnections(
    IEnumConnections** ppEnum) {
    if (ppEnum == NULL)
        return E_POINTER;
```

```
*ppEnum = NULL;
CComObject<CComEnumConnections>* pEnum = NULL;
ATLTRY(pEnum = new CComObject<CComEnumConnections>)
if (pEnum == NULL)
    return E_OUTOFMEMORY;
T* pT = static_cast<T*>(this);
pT->Lock();
CONNECTDATA* pcd = NULL;
ATLTRY(pcd = new CONNECTDATA[m_vec.end()-m_vec.begin()])
if (pcd == NULL) {
    delete pEnum;
    pT->Unlock();
    return E_OUTOFMEMORY;
}
CONNECTDATA* pend = pcd;
// Copy the valid CONNECTDATA's
for (IUnknown** pp = m_vec.begin();pp<m_vec.end();pp++) {
    if (*pp != NULL)
    {
        (*pp)->AddRef();
        pend->pUnk = *pp;
        pend->dwCookie = m_vec.GetCookie(pp);
        pend++;
    }
}
// don't copy the data, but transfer ownership to it
pEnum->Init(pcd, pend, NULL, AtlFlagTakeOwnership);
pT->Unlock();
HRESULT hRes = pEnum->_InternalQueryInterface(
    __uuidof(IEnumConnections), (void**)ppEnum);
if (FAILED(hRes))
    delete pEnum;
return hRes;
}
```

The connection list stores IUnknown pointers. The CONNECTDATA structure contains the interface pointer and its associated magic cookie. EnumConnections allocates space for the initialization array from the heap. It iterates through the connection list entries, copying the interface pointer and its associated cookie to the dynamically allocated CONNECTDATA array. It's important to note that any non-NULL interface pointers are AddRef'ed. This copy of the interface pointers has a lifetime greater than the EnumConnections method.

The call to the enumerator `Init` method initializes the instance. It's critical here to use the `AtlFlagTakeOwnership` argument. This informs the enumerator to use the provided array directly instead of making yet another copy of it. This also means that the enumerator is responsible for correctly releasing the elements in the array as well as the array itself.

The `EnumConnections` method now uses `_InternalQueryInterface` to return an `IEnumConnections` interface pointer on the enumerator object, which, at this point, is the only outstanding reference to the enumerator.[2]

Classes Used by an Event Sink

First, you need to understand the big picture about event sinks. Your object class might want to implement multiple event sink interfaces or the same event sink interface multiple times. All event sink interfaces need nearly identical functionality: `IUnknown`, `IDispatch`, `Invoke`, and the capability to look up the `DISPID` in a sink map and delegate the event method call to the appropriate event handler. But each implementation also needs some custom functionality—specifically, each implementation must be a unique COM identity.

ATL defines a class named `_IDispEvent` that implements the common functionality and, through template parameters and interface coloring, allows each derivation from this one C++ class to maintain a unique COM identity. This means that ATL implements all specialized event sink implementations using a single C++ class, `_IDispEvent`.

The _IDispEvent Class

Let's examine the `_IDispEvent` class. The first interesting aspect is that it is intended to be used as an abstract base class. The first three virtual methods are declared using the COM standard calling convention and are all purely virtual. The first method is `_LocDEQueryInterface`, and the following two are the `AddRef` and `Release` methods. This gives the `_IDispEvent` class the `vtable` of a COM object that supports the `IUnknown` interface. The `_IDispEvent` class cannot simply derive from `IUnknown` because it needs to provide a specialized version of `QueryInterface`. A derived class needs to supply the `_LocDEQueryInterface`, `AddRef`, and `Release` methods.

---

[2] `EnumConnections` uses `_InternalQueryInterface` instead of `IUnknown::QueryInterface` because the latter results in a virtual function call, whereas the former is a more efficient direct call.

```
class ATL_NO_VTABLE _IDispEvent {
...
public:
    //this method needs a different name than QueryInterface
    STDMETHOD(_LocDEQueryInterface)(REFIID riid,
        void ** ppvObject) = 0;
    virtual ULONG STDMETHODCALLTYPE AddRef(void) = 0;
    virtual ULONG STDMETHODCALLTYPE Release(void) = 0;
...
};
```

The class maintains five member variables, only one of which is always used, m_dwEventCookie. Each member variable is initialized by the constructor:

```
_IDispEvent() :
  m_libid(GUID_NULL),
  m_iid(IID_NULL),
  m_wMajorVerNum(0),
  m_wMinorVerNum(0),
  m_dwEventCookie(0xFEFEFEFE)
{ }
```

The m_dwEventCookie variable holds the connection point registration value returned from the source object's IConnectionPoint::Advise method until it's needed to break the connection. The class assumes that no event source will ever use the value 0xFEFEFEFE as the connection cookie because it uses that value as a flag to indicate that no connection is established.[3]

The m_libid, m_iid, m_wMajorVerNum, and m_wMinorVerNum variables hold the type library GUID, the source interface IID, and the type library major and minor version number, respectively.

```
GUID m_libid;
IID m_iid;
unsigned short m_wMajorVerNum;
unsigned short m_wMinorVerNum;
DWORD m_dwEventCookie;
```

---

[3] Note that this places a constraint on a connection list implementation (that is, the CDV template parameter class)—namely, that it never provides the value 0xFEFEFEFE as a connection cookie.

Of course, the _IDispEvent class could maintain a separate "connection established" flag, but that would increase the size of a class instance. Minimizing instance size doesn't seem to be a concern in the _IDispEvent class, though, because the class contains four other member variables that aren't always used. Typically, the approach in ATL is to factor out into a separate, derived class any member variables that aren't always needed in its base class.

This _IDispEvent class provides the DispEventAdvise and DispEventUnadvise methods, which establish and break, respectively, a connection between the specified source object's (pUnk) source interface (piid) and the _DispEvent sink object.

```
HRESULT DispEventAdvise(IUnknown* pUnk, const IID* piid) {
    ATLENSURE(m_dwEventCookie == 0xFEFEFEFE);
    return AtlAdvise(pUnk, (IUnknown*)this, *piid, &m_dwEventCookie);
}

HRESULT DispEventUnadvise(IUnknown* pUnk, const IID* piid) {
    HRESULT hr = AtlUnadvise(pUnk, *piid, m_dwEventCookie);
    m_dwEventCookie = 0xFEFEFEFE;
    return hr;
}
```

You can implement multiple event sinks in a single ATL COM object. In the most general case, this means that you need a unique event sink for each different source of events (source identifier). Furthermore, you need a unique event sink object for each separate connection (source interface) to a source of events.

The _IDispEventLocator Class

Implementing multiple event sinks requires the sink to derive indirectly from _IDispEvent multiple times. But we need to do so in a way that allows us to find a particular _IDispEvent base class instance, given a source object identifier and the source interface on that object.

ATL uses the template class _IDispEventLocator to do this. Each unique _IDispEventLocator template invocation produces a different, addressable _IDispEvent event sink instance.[4]

```
template <UINT nID, const IID* piid>
class ATL_NO_VTABLE _IDispEventLocator : public _IDispEvent {
public:
};
```

[4] Keith Brown pointed out that it would have been more appropriate to call these Locator classes COM-Identity classes—for example, _IDispEventCOMIdentity and IConnectionPointCOMIdentity. Their fundamental purpose is to provide a unique base class instance for each required COM identity. Yes, you need to locate the appropriate base class when needed, but the sole purpose in renaming the QueryInterface method is to implement a separate identity.

The IDispEventSimpleImpl Class

The `IDispEventSimpleImpl` class implements the `IDispatch` interface. It derives from the `_IDispEventLocator<nID, pdiid>` class to inherit the `IUnknown` vtable, the member variables, and the connection-point `Advise` and `Unadvise` support that the `_IDispEvent` base class provides.

```
template <UINT nID, class T, const IID* pdiid>
class ATL_NO_VTABLE IDispEventSimpleImpl :
    public _IDispEventLocator<nID, pdiid> {
// Abbreviated for clarity
    STDMETHOD(_LocDEQueryInterface)(REFIID riid,
        void ** ppvObject);
    virtual ULONG STDMETHODCALLTYPE AddRef();
    virtual ULONG STDMETHODCALLTYPE Release();
    STDMETHOD(GetTypeInfoCount)(UINT* pctinfo);
    STDMETHOD(GetTypeInfo)(UINT itinfo, LCID lcid,
        ITypeInfo** pptinfo);
    STDMETHOD(GetIDsOfNames)(REFIID riid, LPOLESTR* rgszNames,
        UINT cNames, LCID lcid, DISPID* rgdispid);
    STDMETHOD(Invoke)(DISPID dispidMember, REFIID riid,
        LCID lcid, WORD wFlags, DISPPARAMS* pdispparams,
        VARIANT* pvarResult, EXCEPINFO* pexcepinfo,
        UINT* puArgErr);
};
```

Notice that the `IDispEventSimpleImpl` class provides an implementation of the `_LocDEQueryInterface`, `AddRef`, and `Release` methods that it inherited from its `_IDispEvent` base class. Notice also that the next four virtual methods are the standard `IDispatch` interface methods. The `IDispEventSimpleImpl` class now has the proper vtable to support `IDispatch`. It cannot simply derive from `IDispatch` to obtain the vtable because the class needs to provide a specialized version of `QueryInterface`.

The `IDispEventSimpleImpl` class implements the `_LocDEQueryInterface` method so that each event sink is a separate COM identity from that of the deriving class. The event sink object is supposed to respond positively to requests for its source dispatch interface ID, the `IUnknown` interface, the `IDispatch` interface, and the GUID contained in the `m_iid` member variable.

```
STDMETHOD(_LocDEQueryInterface)(REFIID riid,
    void ** ppvObject) {
    ATLASSERT(ppvObject != NULL);
    if (ppvObject == NULL)
```

```
            return E_POINTER;
        *ppvObject = NULL;

        if (InlineIsEqualGUID(riid, IID_NULL))
            return E_NOINTERFACE;

        if (InlineIsEqualGUID(riid, *pdiid) ||
            InlineIsEqualUnknown(riid) ||
            InlineIsEqualGUID(riid, __uuidof(IDispatch)) ||
            InlineIsEqualGUID(riid, m_iid)) {

            *ppvObject = this;
            AddRef();
#ifdef _ATL_DEBUG_INTERFACES
            _AtlDebugInterfacesModule.AddThunk(
                (IUnknown**)ppvObject, _T("IDispEventImpl"),
                riid);
#endif // _ATL_DEBUG_INTERFACES
            return S_OK;
        }
        else
            return E_NOINTERFACE;
    }
```

The `IDispEventSimpleImpl` class also provides a simple implementation of the `AddRef` and `Release` methods. This permits the class to be used directly as a COM object.

```
template <UINT nID, class T, const IID* pdiid>
class ATL_NO_VTABLE IDispEventSimpleImpl : ... {
...
    virtual ULONG STDMETHODCALLTYPE AddRef()  { return 1; }
    virtual ULONG STDMETHODCALLTYPE Release() { return 1; }
...
};
```

However, when you compose the class into a more complex ATL-based COM object, the `AddRef` and `Release` methods in the deriving class are used. In other words, an `AddRef` to the event sink of a typical ATL COM object calls the deriving object's `CComObject::AddRef` method (or whatever your most-derived class is). Watch out for reference-counting cycles due to this. A client holds a reference to the event source, which holds a reference to (nominally) the event sink but is actually to the client itself.

The `IDispEventSimpleImpl` class implements the `GetTypeInfoCount`, `GetType-Info`, and `GetIDsOfNames` methods by returning the error `E_NOTIMPL`. An event-dispatch interface is required only to support the `IUnknown` methods and the `Invoke` method.

```
STDMETHOD(GetTypeInfoCount)(UINT*)
{ATLTRACENOTIMPL(_T("IDispEventSimpleImpl::GetTypeInfoCount"));}

STDMETHOD(GetTypeInfo)(UINT, LCID, ITypeInfo**)
{ATLTRACENOTIMPL(_T("IDispEventSimpleImpl::GetTypeInfo"));}

STDMETHOD(GetIDsOfNames)(REFIID, LPOLESTR*, UINT, LCID, DISPID*)
{ATLTRACENOTIMPL(_T("IDispEventSimpleImpl::GetIDsOfNames"));}

STDMETHOD(Invoke)(DISPID dispidMember, REFIID, LCID lcid, WORD /*wFlags*/,
                  DISPPARAMS* pdispparams, VARIANT* pvarResult,
                  EXCEPINFO* /*pexcepinfo*/, UINT* /*puArgErr*/);
```

The `Invoke` method searches the deriving class's event sink map for the appropriate event handler for the current event. It finds the appropriate sink map by calling `_GetSinkMap`, which is a static member function defined in the deriving class by the `BEGIN_SINK_MAP` macro (described later in this section). The proper event handler is the entry that has the matching event source ID (`nID`) as the template invocation, the same source interface IID (`pdiid`) as the template invocation, and the same `DISPID` as the argument to `Invoke`.

When the matching event sink entry specifies an `_ATL_FUNC_INFO` structure (meaning that the event sink entry was defined using the `SINK_ENTRY_INFO` macro), `Invoke` uses the structure to call the handler. Otherwise, `Invoke` calls the `GetFuncInfoFromId` virtual function to obtain the required structure. When the `GetFuncInfoFromId` function fails, `Invoke` silently returns `S_OK`. This is as it should be because an event handler must respond with `S_OK` to events the handler doesn't recognize.

You must override the `GetFuncInfoFromId` method when using the `SINK_ENTRY_EX` macro with the `IDispEventSimpleImpl` class. The default implementation silently fails:

```
virtual HRESULT GetFuncInfoFromId(const IID&, DISPID, LCID,
  _ATL_FUNC_INFO&) {
  ATLTRACE(_T("TODO: Classes using IDispEventSimpleImpl should "
    "override this method\n"));
  ATLASSERT(0);
  ATLTRACENOTIMPL(_T("IDispEventSimpleImpl::GetFuncInfoFromId"));
}
```

This means that if you use the `IDispEventSimpleImpl` class directly, and you specify an event hander using the `SINK_ENTRY_EX` macro, and you forget to override the `GetFuncInfoFromId` method or you implement it incorrectly, everything compiles cleanly but *your event handler will never be called.*

The `IDispEventSimpleImpl` class provides some overloaded helper methods for establishing and breaking a connection to an event source. The following two methods establish and break a connection between the current sink and the specified event interface (`piid`) on the specified event source (`pUnk`):

```
// Helpers for sinking events on random IUnknown*
   HRESULT DispEventAdvise(IUnknown* pUnk, const IID* piid) {
       ATLENSURE(m_dwEventCookie == 0xFEFEFEFE);
       return AtlAdvise(pUnk, (IUnknown*)this, *piid, &m_dwEventCookie);
   }

   HRESULT DispEventUnadvise(IUnknown* pUnk, const IID* piid) {
       HRESULT hr = AtlUnadvise(pUnk, *piid, m_dwEventCookie);
       m_dwEventCookie = 0xFEFEFEFE;
       return hr;
   }
```

The next two methods establish and break a connection between the current sink and the specified event source using the sink's dispatch interface:

```
HRESULT DispEventAdvise(IUnknown* pUnk) {
  return _IDispEvent::DispEventAdvise(pUnk, pdiid);
}

HRESULT DispEventUnadvise(IUnknown* pUnk) {
  return _IDispEvent::DispEventUnadvise(pUnk, pdiid);
}
```

The Sink Map: Associated Structure, Macros, and the _GetSinkMap Method

The sink map is an array of `_ATL_EVENT_ENTRY` structures. The structure contains the following fields:

`nControlID`	The event source identifier; control ID for contained controls
`piid`	The source dispatch interface IID
`nOffset`	The offset of the event sink implementation from the deriving class
`dispid`	The event callback dispatch ID
`pfn`	The member function pointer of the event handler to invoke[5]
`pInfo`	The _ATL_FUNC_INFO structure used for the event-handler call

---

[5] If you've been wondering why your event-handler functions have to use the `__stdcall` calling convention; the declaration of this pointer specifies it.

```
template <class T>
struct _ATL_EVENT_ENTRY {
    UINT nControlID; // ID identifying object instance
    const IID* piid; // dispinterface IID
    int nOffset;     // offset of dispinterface from this pointer
    DISPID dispid;   // DISPID of method/property
    void (__stdcall T::*pfn)();  // method to invoke
    _ATL_FUNC_INFO* pInfo; // pointer to info structure
};
```

When you use the BEGIN_SINK_MAP macro, you define a static member function in your class called _GetSinkMap. It returns the address of the array of _ATL_EVENT_ENTRY structures.

```
#define BEGIN_SINK_MAP(_class)\
    typedef _class _GetSinkMapFinder;\
    static const ATL::_ATL_EVENT_ENTRY<_class>* _GetSinkMap() {\
        PTM_WARNING_DISABLE \
        typedef _class _atl_event_classtype;\
        static const ATL::_ATL_EVENT_ENTRY<_class> map[] = {
```

Each SINK_ENTRY_INFO macro adds one _ATL_EVENT_ENTRY structure to the array.

```
#define SINK_ENTRY_INFO(id, iid, dispid, fn, info) {id, &iid,
  (int)(INT_PTR)(static_cast<ATL::_IDispEventLocator<
    id, &iid>*>((_atl_event_classtype*)8))-8,
  dispid, (void (__stdcall _atl_event_classtype::*)())fn, info},
```

Two aspects of the macro are a little unusual. The following expression computes the offset of the _IDispEventLocator<id, &iid> base class with respect to your deriving class (the class containing the sink map). This enables us to find the appropriate event sink referenced by the sink map entry.

```
(int)(INT_PTR)(static_cast<_IDispEventLocator<
    id, &iid>*>((_atl_event_classtype*)8))-8
```

The following cast saves the event-handler function address as a pointer to a member function:

```
(void (__stdcall _atl_event_classtype::*)()) fn
```

The SINK_ENTRY_EX macro is the same as the SINK_ENTRY_INFO macro with a NULL pointer for the function information structure. The SINK_ENTRY macro is the same as the SINK_ENTRY_INFO macro with IID_NULL for the dispatch interface and a NULL pointer for the function information structure.

```
#define SINK_ENTRY_EX(id, iid, dispid, fn) \
  SINK_ENTRY_INFO(id, iid, dispid, fn, NULL)
#define SINK_ENTRY(id, dispid, fn) \
  SINK_ENTRY_EX(id, IID_NULL, dispid, fn)
```

The END_SINK_MAP macro ends the array and completes the _GetSinkMap function implementation:

```
#define END_SINK_MAP() {0, NULL, 0, 0, NULL, NULL} }; \
  return map;\
```

The IDispEventImpl Class

Finally, we come to the IDispEventImpl class. This is the class that the code-generation wizards use. It derives from the IDispEventSimpleImpl class and, therefore, inherits all the functionality previously discussed. The additional template parameters specify a type library that describes the source dispatch interface for the event sink.

```
template <UINT nID, class T, const IID* pdiid = &IID_NULL,
  const GUID* plibid = &GUID_NULL,
  WORD wMajor = 0, WORD wMinor = 0,
  class tihclass = CComTypeInfoHolder>
class ATL_NO_VTABLE IDispEventImpl :
  public IDispEventSimpleImpl<nID, T, pdiid>
{ ... }
```

The main feature of the IDispEventImpl class is that it uses the type information to implement functionality that is missing in the base class. The class implements the GetTypeInfoCount, GetTypeInfo, and GetIDsOfNames methods using the type library via a CComTypeInfoHolder object:

```
STDMETHOD(GetTypeInfoCount)(UINT* pctinfo) {
  *pctinfo = 1; return S_OK; }
STDMETHOD(GetTypeInfo)(UINT itinfo, LCID lcid, ITypeInfo** pptinfo)
{ return _tih.GetTypeInfo(itinfo, lcid, pptinfo); }
STDMETHOD(GetIDsOfNames)(REFIID riid, LPOLESTR* rgszNames,
  UINT cNames, LCID lcid, DISPID* rgdispid) {
    return _tih.GetIDsOfNames(riid, rgszNames, cNames,
      lcid, rgdispid);
}
```

It also overrides the `GetFuncInfoFromId` method and initializes an `_ATL_FUNC_INFO` structure using the information provided in the type library:

```
HRESULT GetFuncInfoFromId(const IID& iid,
    DISPID dispidMember, LCID lcid,
    ATL_FUNC_INFO& info) {
    CComPtr<ITypeInfo> spTypeInfo;

    if (InlineIsEqualGUID(*_tih.m_plibid, GUID_NULL))
    {
        m_InnerLibid = m_libid;
        m_InnerIid = m_iid;
        _tih.m_plibid = &m_InnerLibid;
        _tih.m_pguid = &m_InnerIid;
        _tih.m_wMajor = m_wMajorVerNum;
        _tih.m_wMinor = m_wMinorVerNum;
    }
    HRESULT hr = _tih.GetTI(lcid, &spTypeInfo);
    if (FAILED(hr))
        return hr;
    return AtlGetFuncInfoFromId(spTypeInfo, iid,
        dispidMember, lcid, info);
}
```

Summary

The connection point protocol defines a mechanism for a client interested in receiving event callbacks to pass its event sink interface pointer to an event source. Neither the client nor the event source needs to be written with knowledge of each other. Objects hosted on a web page or, more generally, objects used by scripting languages must use the connection points protocol to fire events to the scripting engine. Also, ActiveX controls fire their events using the connection points protocol. Although this protocol is acceptable for intra-apartment use, it is inefficient (when considering round-trips) for use across an apartment boundary.

ATL provides the `IDispEvent` and `IDispEventSimple` classes for a client object to use to receive event callbacks. Additionally, ATL provides the Implement Connection Point Wizard so you can easily generate a class that manages a connection point and contains helper methods to fire the events to all connected clients.

10 | Windowing

ATL is not simply a set of wrapper classes for COM. In the same style, it also wraps the section of the Win32 API related to creating and manipulating windows, dialogs, and window controls. In addition to basic support to remove the grudge of Windows programming, the ATL windowing classes include such advanced features as subclassing and superclassing. Furthermore, this window support forms the basis for both COM controls and COM control containment, covered in following chapters.

The Structure of a Windows Application

A standard Windows application consists of several well-known elements:

- The entry point, _tWinMain, which provides the HINSTANCE of the application, the command-line arguments and the flag indicating how to show the main window

- A call to RegisterClass to register the main window class

- A call to CreateWindow(Ex) to create the main window

- A call to ShowWindow and UpdateWindow to show the main window

- A message loop to dispatch messages

- A procedure to handle the main window's messages

- A set of message handlers for messages that the main window is interested in handling

- A call to DefWindowProc to let Windows handle messages that the main window is not interested in

- A call to PostQuitMessage after the main window has been destroyed

A bare-bones example follows:

```
#include "stdafx.h" // Includes windows.h and tchar.h
LRESULT CALLBACK WndProc(HWND, UINT, WPARAM, LPARAM);
```

```
// Entry point
int APIENTRY _tWinMain(HINSTANCE hinst,
                       HINSTANCE /*hinstPrev*/,
                       LPTSTR    pszCmdLine,
                       int       nCmdShow) {
  // Register the main window class
  LPCTSTR     pszMainWndClass = __T("WindowsApp");
  WNDCLASSEX  wc = { sizeof(WNDCLASSEX) };
  wc.style          = CS_HREDRAW | CS_VREDRAW;
  wc.hInstance      = hinst;
  wc.hIcon          = LoadIcon(0, IDI_APPLICATION);
  wc.hCursor        = LoadCursor(0, IDC_ARROW);
  wc.hbrBackground  = (HBRUSH)(COLOR_WINDOW+1);
  wc.lpszClassName  = pszMainWndClass;
  wc.lpfnWndProc    = WndProc;
  if( !RegisterClassEx(&wc) ) return -1;

  // Create the main window
  HWND    hwnd = CreateWindowEx(WS_EX_CLIENTEDGE,
                                pszMainWndClass,
                                __T("Windows Application"),
                                WS_OVERLAPPEDWINDOW,
                                CW_USEDEFAULT, 0,
                                CW_USEDEFAULT, 0,
                                0, 0, hinst, 0);
  if( !hwnd ) return -1;

  // Show the main window
  ShowWindow(hwnd, nCmdShow);
  UpdateWindow(hwnd);

  // Main message loop
  MSG msg;
  while( GetMessage(&msg, 0, 0, 0) ) {
    TranslateMessage(&msg);
    DispatchMessage(&msg);
  }

  return msg.wParam;
}


// Windows procedure
LRESULT CALLBACK WndProc(HWND hwnd, UINT nMsg, WPARAM wparam,
  LPARAM lparam) {
```

```
switch( nMsg ) {
// Message handlers for messages we're interested in
case WM_PAINT: {
  PAINTSTRUCT ps;
  HDC         hdc = BeginPaint(hwnd, &ps);
  RECT        rect; GetClientRect(hwnd, &rect);
  DrawText(hdc, __T("Hello, Windows"), -1, &rect,
            DT_CENTER | DT_VCENTER | DT_SINGLELINE);
  EndPaint(hwnd, &ps);
}
break;

// Post the quit message when main window is destroyed
case WM_DESTROY:
  PostQuitMessage(0);
break;

// Let Windows handle messages we don't want
default:
  return DefWindowProc(hwnd, nMsg, wparam, lparam);
break;
}

return 0;
}
```

All Windows applications have similar requirements. These requirements can be expressed in procedural Win32 calls, as the example just showed. However, when procedural calls model an underlying object model, C++ programmers feel compelled to wrap those calls behind member functions. The Windowing part of the Win32 API (often called User32) is clearly implementing an underlying object model consisting of Window classes (represented by the WNDCLASSEX structure), Window objects (represented by the HWND), and member function invocation (represented by calls to the WndProc). For the C++ programmer adverse to the schism between a preferred object model and that of User32, ATL provides a small set of windowing classes, as shown in Figure 10.1.

The classes in bold, CWindow, CWindowImpl, CWinTraits, CWinTraitsOR, CDialogImpl, CSimpleDialog and, CContainedWindowT, are the most important. The others, CWindowImplRoot, CWindowImplBaseT, and CDialogImplBaseT, are helper classes to separate parameterized code from invariant code. This separation helps to reduce template-related code bloat, but these classes are not a fundamental part of the ATL windowing classes. The former classes form the discussion for the bulk of the rest of this chapter.

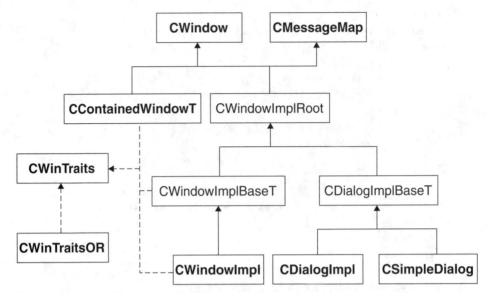

Figure 10.1   UML diagram of ATL window classes

CWindow

An HWND Wrapper

The most basic of the windowing classes in ATL is `CWindow`. Its chief job is to hold an `HWND`, which it can obtain via several member functions:

```
class CWindow {
public:
    CWindow(HWND hWnd = NULL)  :
        m_hWnd(hWnd)
    { }

    CWindow& operator=(HWND hWnd)
    { m_hWnd = hWnd; return *this; }

    void Attach(HWND hWndNew) {
        ATLASSERT(m_hWnd == NULL);
        ATLASSERT((hWndNew == NULL) || ::IsWindow(hWndNew));
        m_hWnd = hWndNew;
    }
```

```
    HWND Create(LPCTSTR lpstrWndClass, HWND hWndParent,
        _U_RECT rect = NULL,
        LPCTSTR szWindowName = NULL,
        DWORD dwStyle = 0, DWORD dwExStyle = 0,
        _U_MENUorID MenuOrID = 0U,
        LPVOID lpCreateParam = NULL) {
        // Calls ::CreateWindowEx and caches result in m_hWnd
        ...
        return m_hWnd;
    }
    ...
};
```

The HWND itself is available either as a public data member or via the HWND type-cast operator:

```
class CWindow {
public:
  HWND m_hWnd;
  operator HWND() const { return m_hWnd; }
  ...
};
```

If you want to clear the HWND, you can set m_hWnd manually or use the Detach member function:

```
inline HWND CWindow::Detach() {
    HWND hWnd = m_hWnd;
    m_hWnd = NULL;
    return hWnd;
}
```

A CWindow object represents a wrapper around the HWND, not the window itself. The CWindow destructor does not destroy the underlying window. Hence, there's really no need to ever call Detach.

HWND Wrapper Functions

When the CWindow object has an HWND, you can make use of the rest of the CWindow class member functions. The purpose of CWindow is to act as a wrapper for all the functions of the User32 API. For every function that takes an HWND as the first argument, the CWindow class has a corresponding member function that uses the cached m_hWnd. For example, instead of the calling SetWindowText:

```
void SayHello(HWND hwnd) {
  SetWindowText(hwnd, __T("Hello"));
}
```

you use the `SetWindowText` member function:

```
void SayHello(HWND hwnd) {
  CWindow wnd = hwnd;
  wnd.SetWindowText(__T("Hello"));
}
```

And when I said that all the User32 functions take an `HWND` as a first parameter, I meant *all*. As near as I can tell, with the exception of one function (`SetFore-groundWindow`), the entire Windowing API is represented as a member function of `CWindow`. The `CWindow` class declaration comments break the wrapped functions into several categories:

Alert functions	Attributes	Caret functions
Clipboard functions	Coordinate-mapping functions	Dialog box item functions
Font functions		Hot key functions
Icon functions	Help functions	Message functions
Miscellaneous operations	Menu functions	Timer functions
Update and painting functions	Scrolling functions	Window size and position functions
	Window-access functions	
Window state functions	Window text functions	Window tree access

HWND Helper Functions

The vast majority of the `CWindow` member functions are merely inline wrappers on the raw functions. This means that you get the syntactic convenience of member functions without any additional runtime overhead. In addition, several helper functions above and beyond straight wrappers encapsulate common functionality that we often end up writing repeatedly:

```
class CWindow {
...
  DWORD GetStyle() const;
  DWORD GetExStyle() const;
  BOOL  ModifyStyle(DWORD dwRemove, DWORD dwAdd,
    UINT nFlags = 0);
  BOOL  ModifyStyleEx(DWORD dwRemove, DWORD dwAdd,
```

```
    UINT nFlags = 0);
  BOOL  ResizeClient(int nWidth, int nHeight,
    BOOL bRedraw = TRUE);
  HWND  GetDescendantWindow(int nID) const;
  BOOL  CenterWindow(HWND hWndCenter = NULL);
  BOOL  GetWindowText(BSTR* pbstrText);
  BOOL  GetWindowText(BSTR& bstrText);
  HWND  GetTopLevelParent() const;
  HWND  GetTopLevelWindow() const;
...
};
```

Likewise, CWindow provides a number of type-safe wrappers for calling SendMessage for common messages, performing the error-prone casting chores for us:

```
class CWindow {
...
  void  SetFont(HFONT hFont, BOOL bRedraw = TRUE);
  HFONT GetFont() const;
  void  Print(HDC hDC, DWORD dwFlags) const;
  void  PrintClient(HDC hDC, DWORD dwFlags) const;
  void  SetRedraw(BOOL bRedraw = TRUE);
  HICON SetIcon(HICON hIcon, BOOL bBigIcon = TRUE);
  HICON GetIcon(BOOL bBigIcon = TRUE) const;
  int   SetHotKey(WORD wVirtualKeyCode, WORD wModifiers);
  DWORD GetHotKey() const;
  void  NextDlgCtrl() const;
  void  PrevDlgCtrl() const;
  void  GotoDlgCtrl(HWND hWndCtrl) const;
  void  SendMessageToDescendants(UINT message, WPARAM wParam = 0,
    LPARAM lParam = 0, BOOL bDeep = TRUE);
...
};
```

Using CWindow

Before we can put the CWindow class to use in our sample Windows application, we have to establish support for the ATL window classes in our Win32 application. If you run the Visual Studio 2005 Win32 Project Wizard, on the second page, you'll see a check box for Add Common Header Files for ATL, as shown in Figure 10.2.

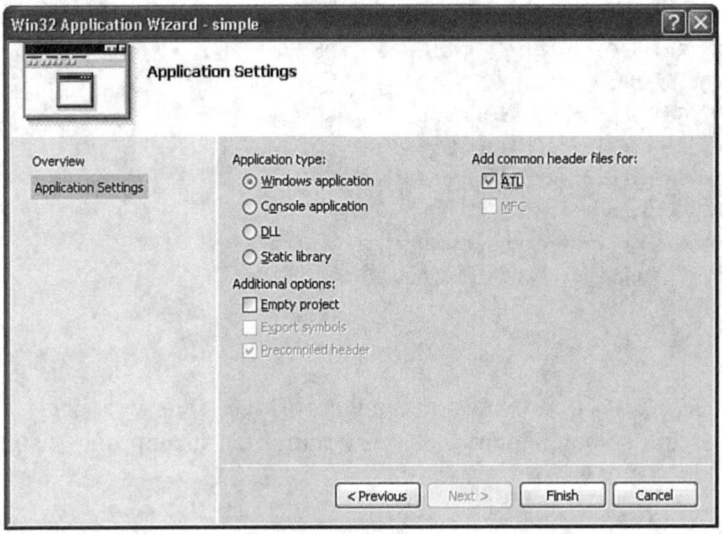

Figure 10.2 Options for Win32 projects

This check box adds the following lines to the precompiled header file stdafx.h:

```
#include <atlbase.h>
#include <atlstr.h>
```

The ATL windowing classes are defined in atlwin.h. The project template creates a skeleton application that doesn't use the ATL windowing classes, so we'll also need to include atlwin.h in the stdafx.h generated by the ATL project template:

```
// stdafx.h
...
#include <atlwin.h>
```

After we've included atlwin.h, we can start using CWindow instead of raw Win32 calls.

The Win32 Project Wizard creates an InitInstance function that uses the Win32 API to register the window class and create the main window. We can update it to use CWindow instead like this:

```
BOOL InitInstance(HINSTANCE hInstance, int nCmdShow) {
    // Store instance handle in our global variable
    hInst = hInstance;
```

```
CWindow wnd;
wnd.Create(szWindowClass, 0, CWindow::rcDefault,
    __T("Windows Application"), WS_OVERLAPPEDWINDOW,
    WS_EX_CLIENTEDGE );

if (!wnd) {
  return FALSE;
}

wnd.CenterWindow( );
wnd.ShowWindow( nCmdShow );
wnd.UpdateWindow( );
return TRUE;
}
```

Notice that the structure of the program remains the same. The only difference is that we're calling member functions instead of global functions. WndProc can be similarly updated:

```
LRESULT CALLBACK WndProc(HWND hWnd, UINT nMsg, WPARAM wParam,
    LPARAM lParam) {
    CWindow wnd( hWnd );

    switch (nMsg) {
    // ...
    case WM_PAINT: {
        PAINTSTRUCT ps;
        HDC hdc = wnd.BeginPaint(&ps);
        RECT rect; wnd.GetClientRect(&rect);

        DrawText(hdc, __T("Hello, Windows"), -1, &rect,
            DT_CENTER | DT_VCENTER | DT_SINGLELINE);
        wnd.EndPaint(&ps);
        break;
    }
    // ... the rest is the same
    return 0;
}
```

CWindow is a step in the right direction. Instead of calling global functions and passing a handle, we're now able to call member functions on an object. However, we're still registering a Windows class instead of creating a C++ class, and we're still handing callbacks via a WndProc instead of via member functions.

To completely fulfill our desires, we need the next most important class in the ATL windowing hierarchy, `CWindowImpl`.

CWindowImpl

The Window Class

The `CWindowImpl` class derives ultimately from `CWindow` and provides two additional features, window class registration and message handling. We discuss message handling after we explore how `CWindowImpl` manages the window class. First, notice that, unlike `CWindow`, the `CWindowImpl` member function `Create` doesn't take the name of a window class:

```
template <class T, class TBase = CWindow,
        class TWinTraits = CControlWinTraits>
class ATL_NO_VTABLE CWindowImpl
    : public CWindowImplBaseT< TBase, TWinTraits > {
public:
    DECLARE_WND_CLASS(NULL)

    HWND Create(HWND hWndParent, _U_RECT rect = NULL,
        LPCTSTR szWindowName = NULL,
        DWORD dwStyle = 0, DWORD dwExStyle = 0,
        _U_MENUorID MenuOrID = 0U, LPVOID lpCreateParam = NULL);
...
};
```

Instead of passing the name of the window class, the name of the window class is provided in the `DECLARE_WND_CLASS` macro. A value of `NULL` causes ATL to generate a window class of the form: `ATL<8-digit number>`. We could declare a `CWindowImpl`-based class using the same window class name we registered using `RegisterClass`. However, that's not necessary. It's far more convenient to let ATL register the window class the first time we call `Create` on an instance of our `CWindowImpl`-derived class. This initial window class registration is done in the implementation of `CWindowImpl::Create`:

```
HWND CWindowImpl::Create(HWND hWndParent, _U_RECT rect = NULL,
        LPCTSTR szWindowName = NULL,
        DWORD dwStyle = 0, DWORD dwExStyle = 0,
        _U_MENUorID MenuOrID = 0U, LPVOID lpCreateParam = NULL) {
    // Generate a class name if one is not provided
    if (T::GetWndClassInfo().m_lpszOrigName == NULL)
```

```
    T::GetWndClassInfo().m_lpszOrigName = GetWndClassName();

// Register the window class if it hasn't
// already been registered
ATOM atom = T::GetWndClassInfo().Register(
  &m_pfnSuperWindowProc);

...
}
```

Using a class derived from `CWindowImpl`, our program has gotten much smaller. We can eliminate the `InitInstance` function and place the main window creation directly in the `_tWinMain` function:

```
class CMainWindow : public CWindowImpl<CMainWindow> {...};

// Entry point
int APIENTRY _tWinMain(HINSTANCE hinst,
  HINSTANCE /*hinstPrev*/,
  LPTSTR    pszCmdLine,
  int       nCmdShow) {

  // Initialize global strings
  LoadString(hInstance, IDS_APP_TITLE, szTitle, MAX_LOADSTRING);

  CMainWindow wnd;

  wnd.Create( 0, CWindow::rcDefault, szTitle,
    WS_OVERLAPPEDWINDOW, WS_EX_CLIENTEDGE );
  if( !wnd ) {
    return FALSE;
  }
  wnd.CenterWindow( );
  wnd.ShowWindow( nCmdShow );
  wnd.UpdateWindow( );

  // Show the main window, run the message loop
  ...

  return msg.wParam;
}
```

We can also eliminate the generated `WndProc`; the `CWindowImpl` class provides message maps to handle message processing, as discussed later in the section "Handling Messages."

Modifying the Window Class

Each `CWindowImpl` class maintains a static data structure called a `CWndClassInfo`, which is a type definition for either an `_ATL_WNDCLASSINFOA` or an `_ATL_WNDCLASSIN-FOW` structure, depending on whether you're doing a Unicode build. The Unicode version is shown here:

```
struct _ATL_WNDCLASSINFOW {
    WNDCLASSEXW m_wc;
    LPCWSTR m_lpszOrigName;
    WNDPROC pWndProc;
    LPCWSTR m_lpszCursorID;
    BOOL m_bSystemCursor;
    ATOM m_atom;
    WCHAR m_szAutoName[5+sizeof(void)*CHAR_BIT];
    ATOM Register(WNDPROC* p)
    { return AtlModuleRegisterWndClassInfoW(&_AtlWinModule,
        &_AtlBaseModule, this, p); }
};
```

The most important members of this structure are `m_wc` and `m_atom`. The `m_wc` member represents the window class structure—that is, what you would use to register a class if you were doing it by hand. The `m_atom` is used to determine whether the class has already been registered. This is useful if you want to make changes to the `m_wc` before the class has been registered.

Each class derived from `CWindowImpl` gets an instance of `CWndClassInfo` in the base class from the use of the `DECLARE_WND_CLASS` macro, defined like so:

```
#define DECLARE_WND_CLASS(WndClassName) \
static CWndClassInfo& GetWndClassInfo() { \
  static CWndClassInfo wc = { \
    { sizeof(WNDCLASSEX), CS_HREDRAW | CS_VREDRAW | CS_DBLCLKS, \
      StartWindowProc, 0, 0, NULL, NULL, NULL, \
      (HBRUSH)(COLOR_WINDOW + 1), NULL, WndClassName, NULL \
    }, \
    NULL, NULL, IDC_ARROW, TRUE, 0, _T("") \
  }; \
  return wc; \
}
```

This macro defines a function called GetWndClassInfo and initializes the values to commonly used defaults. If you want to also specify the class style and the background color, you can use another macro, called DECLARE_WND_CLASS_EX:

```
#define DECLARE_WND_CLASS_EX(WndClassName, style, bkgnd) \
static CWndClassInfo& GetWndClassInfo() { \
  static CWndClassInfo wc = { \
    { sizeof(WNDCLASSEX), style, StartWindowProc, \
      0, 0, NULL, NULL, NULL, (HBRUSH)(bkgnd + 1), NULL, \
      WndClassName, NULL \
    }, \
    NULL, NULL, IDC_ARROW, TRUE, 0, _T("") \
  }; \
  return wc; \
}
```

However, neither macro provides enough flexibly to set all the window class information you want, such as large and small icons, the cursor, or the background brush. Although it's possible to define an entire set of macros in the same vein as DECLARE_WND_CLASS, the combinations of what you want to set and what you want to leave as a default value quickly get out of hand. Frankly, it's easier to modify the CWndClassInfo structure directly using the GetWndClassInfo function. The CWindow-Impl-derived class's constructor is a good place to do that, using the m_atom variable to determine whether the window class has already been registered:

```
CMainWindow( ) {
    CWndClassInfo& wci = GetWndClassInfo();

    if( !wci.m_atom ) {
        wci.m_wc.lpszMenuName = MAKEINTRESOURCE(IDC_ATLHELLOWIN);
        wci.m_wc.hIcon = LoadIcon(
            _AtlBaseModule.GetResourceInstance(),
            MAKEINTRESOURCE(IDI_ATLHELLOWIN));
        wci.m_wc.hIconSm = LoadIcon(
            _AtlBaseModule.GetResourceInstance(),
            MAKEINTRESOURCE(IDI_SMALL));
        wci.m_wc.hbrBackground = CreateHatchBrush(HS_DIAGCROSS,
            RGB(0, 0, 255));
    }
}
```

Setting the WNDCLASSEX member directly works for most of the members of the m_wc member of CWndClassInfo. However, the ATL team decided to treat cursors differently. For cursors, the CWndClassInfo structure has two members, m_lpszCursorID and m_bSystemCursor, which are used to override whatever is set in the hCursor member of m_wc. For example, to set a cursor from the available system cursors, you must do the following:

```
// Can't do this:
// wci.m_wc.hCursor = LoadCursor(0, MAKEINTRESOURCE(IDC_CROSS));

// Must do this:
wci.m_bSystemCursor = TRUE;
wci.m_lpszCursorID = IDC_CROSS;
```

Likewise, to load a custom cursor, the following is required:

```
// Can't do this:
// wci.m_wc.hCursor = LoadCursor(
//    _AtlBaseModule.GetResourceInstance(),
//    MAKEINTRESOURCE(IDC_BAREBONES));

// Must do this:
wci.m_bSystemCursor = FALSE;
wci.m_lpszCursorID = MAKEINTRESOURCE(IDC_BAREBONES);
```

Remember to keep this special treatment of cursors in mind when creating CWindowImpl-derived classes with custom cursors.

Window Traits

In the same way that an icon and a cursor are coupled with a window class, often it makes sense for the styles and the extended styles to be coupled as well. For example, frame windows have different styles than child windows. When we develop a window class, we typically know how it will be used; for example, our CMainWindow class will be used as a frame window, and WS_OVERLAPPEDWINDOW will be part of the styles for every instance of CMainWindow. Unfortunately, there is no way to set default styles for a window class in the Win32 API. Instead, the window styles must be specified in every call to CreateWindowEx. To allow default styles and extended styles to be coupled with a window class, ATL enables you to group styles and reuse them in an instance of the CWinTrait class:

```
template <DWORD t_dwStyle = 0, DWORD t_dwExStyle = 0>
class CWinTraits {
public:
  static DWORD GetWndStyle(DWORD dwStyle)
```

```
  { return dwStyle == 0 ? t_dwStyle : dwStyle; }
  static DWORD GetWndExStyle(DWORD dwExStyle)
  { return dwExStyle == 0 ? t_dwExStyle : dwExStyle; }
};
```

As you can see, the `CWinTrait` class holds a set of styles and extended styles. When combined with a style or an extended style `DWORD`, it hands out the passed `DWORD` if it is nonzero; otherwise, it hands out its own value. For example, to bundle my preferred styles into a Windows trait, I would do the following:

```
typedef CWinTraits<WS_OVERLAPPEDWINDOW, WS_EX_CLIENTEDGE>
  CMainWinTraits;
```

A Window traits class can be associated with a `CWindowImpl` by passing it as a template parameter:

```
class CMainWindow : public CWindowImpl<CMainWindow,
  CWindow, CMainWinTraits>
{...};
```

Now when creating instances of a `CWindowImpl`-derived class, I can be explicit about what parameters I want. Or, by passing zero for the style or the extended style, I can get the Window traits style associated with the class:

```
// Use the default value of 0 for the style and the
// extended style to get the window traits for this class.
wnd.Create(NULL, CWindow::rcDefault, __T("Windows Application"));
```

Because I've used a `CWinTrait` class to group related styles and extended styles, if I need to change a style in a trait, the change is propagated to all instances of any class that uses that trait. This saves me from finding the instances and manually changing them one at a time. For the three most common kinds of windows— frame windows, child windows, and MDI child windows—ATL comes with three built-in window traits classes:

```
typedef
CWinTraits<WS_CHILD | WS_VISIBLE | WS_CLIPCHILDREN |
  WS_CLIPSIBLINGS, 0>
CControlWinTraits;

typedef
CWinTraits<WS_OVERLAPPEDWINDOW | WS_CLIPCHILDREN |
```

```
   WS_CLIPSIBLINGS,
   WS_EX_APPWINDOW | WS_EX_WINDOWEDGE>
CFrameWinTraits;

typedef
CWinTraits<WS_OVERLAPPEDWINDOW | WS_CHILD |
  WS_VISIBLE | WS_CLIPCHILDREN |
  WS_CLIPSIBLINGS,
  WS_EX_MDICHILD>
CMDIChildWinTraits;
```

If you want to leverage the styles of an existing window traits class but add styles, you can use the CWindowTraitsOR class:

```
template <DWORD t_dwStyle = 0, DWORD t_dwExStyle = 0,
          class TWinTraits = CControlWinTraits>
class CWinTraitsOR {
public:
  static DWORD GetWndStyle(DWORD dwStyle) {
    return dwStyle | t_dwStyle |
      TWinTraits::GetWndStyle(dwStyle);
  }
  static DWORD GetWndExStyle(DWORD dwExStyle) {
  return dwExStyle | t_dwExStyle | TWinTraits::GetWndExStyle(dwExStyle);
  }
};
```

Using CWinTraitsOR, CMainWinTraits can be redefined like so:

```
// Leave CFrameWinTraits styles alone.
// Add the WS_EX_CLIENTEDGE bit to the extended styles.
typedef CWinTraitsOR<0, WS_EX_CLIENTEDGE, CFrameWinTraits>
  CMainWinTraits;
```

The Window Procedure

To handle window messages, every window needs a window procedure (WndProc). This WndProc is set in the lpfnWndProc member of the WNDCLASSEX structure used during window registration. You might have noticed that in the expansion of DECLARE_WND_CLASS and DECLARE_WND_CLASS_EX, the name of the windows procedure is StartWindowProc. StartWindowProc is a static member function of CWindowImplBase. Its job is to establish the mapping between the CWindowImpl-derived object's HWND and the object's this pointer. The goal is to handle calls made by Windows to a WndProc global function and map them to a member function on an object. The mapping between HWND and an object's this pointer is done by the StartWindowProc when handling the first window message.[1] After the new HWND is cached in the CWindowImpl-derived object's member data, the object's real window procedure is substituted for the StartWindowProc, as shown here:

```
template <class TBase, class TWinTraits>
LRESULT CALLBACK
CWindowImplBaseT< TBase, TWinTraits >::StartWindowProc(
    HWND hWnd,
    UINT uMsg,
    WPARAM wParam, LPARAM lParam)
{
    CWindowImplBaseT< TBase, TWinTraits >* pThis =
        (CWindowImplBaseT< TBase, TWinTraits >*)
        _AtlWinModule.ExtractCreateWndData();
    ATLASSERT(pThis != NULL);
    pThis->m_hWnd = hWnd;

    pThis->m_thunk.Init(pThis->GetWindowProc(), pThis);
    WNDPROC pProc = pThis->m_thunk.GetWNDPROC();
    WNDPROC pOldProc = (WNDPROC)::SetWindowLongPtr(hWnd,
        GWLP_WNDPROC, (LONG_PTR)pProc);
    return pProc(hWnd, uMsg, wParam, lParam);
}
```

The m_thunk member is the interesting part. The ATL team had several different options it could have used to map the HWND associated with each incoming window message to the object's this pointer responsible for handling the message. It could have kept a global table that mapped HWNDs to this pointers, but the look-up time would grow as the number of windows grew. It could have tucked the this pointer into the window data,[2] but then the application/component developer could unwittingly overwrite the data when doing work with window data. Plus, empirically, this look-up is not as fast as one might like when handling many messages per second.

---

[1] The first window message is the moment when Windows first communicates the new HWND to the application. This happens before CreateWindow[Ex] returns with the HWND.

[2] A window can maintain extra information via the cbWndExtra member of the WNDCLASS[EX] structure or via the GetWindowLong/SetWindowLong family of functions.

Instead, the ATL team used a technique based on a set of Assembly (ASM) instructions grouped together into a *thunk*, avoiding any look-up. The term *thunk* is overused in Windows, but in this case, the thunk is a group of ASM instructions that keeps track of a `CWindowImpl` object's `this` pointer and acts like a function—specifically, a `WndProc`. Each `CWindowImpl` object gets its own thunk—that is, each object has its own `WndProc`. A thunk is a set of machine instructions built on-the-fly and executed. For example, imagine two windows of the same class created like this:

```
class CMyWindow : public CWindowImpl<CMyWindow> {...};
CMyWindow wnd1; wnd1.Create(...);
CMyWindow wnd2; wnd2.Create(...);
```

Figure 10.3 shows the per-window class and per-`HWND` data maintained by Windows on the 32-bit Intel platform, the thunks, and the `CWindowImpl` objects that would result from this example code.

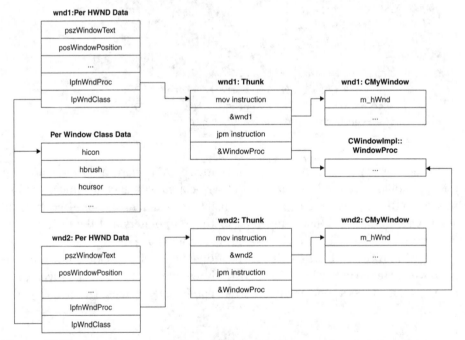

Figure 10.3   One thunk per CWindowImpl object

The thunk's job is to replace the `HWND` on the stack with the `CWindowImpl` object's `this` pointer before calling the `CWindowImpl` static member function `WindowProc` to further process the message. The ASM instructions that replace the HWND with the object's this pointer are kept in a data structure called the _stdcallthunk. Versions of this structure are defined for 32-bit x86, AMD64, ALPHA, MIPS, SH3, ARM, and IA64 (Itanium) processors. The 32-bit x86 definition follows:

```
#if defined(_M_IX86)
PVOID __stdcall __AllocStdCallThunk(VOID);
VOID  __stdcall __FreeStdCallThunk(PVOID);

#pragma pack(push,1)
struct _stdcallthunk {
    DWORD   m_mov;      // mov dword ptr [esp+0x4], pThis
                        // (esp+0x4 is hWnd)
    DWORD   m_this;     // Our CWindowImpl this pointer
    BYTE    m_jmp;      // jmp WndProc
    DWORD   m_relproc;  // relative jmp

    BOOL Init(DWORD_PTR proc, void* pThis) {
        m_mov = 0x042444C7;  //C7 44 24 0C
        m_this = PtrToUlong(pThis);
        m_jmp = 0xe9;
        m_relproc = DWORD((INT_PTR)proc -
            ((INT_PTR)this+sizeof(_stdcallthunk)));
        // write block from data cache and
        //  flush from instruction cache
        FlushInstructionCache(GetCurrentProcess(), this,
            sizeof(_stdcallthunk));
        return TRUE;
    }

    // some thunks will dynamically allocate the
    // memory for the code
    void* GetCodeAddress() {
        return this;
    }
    void* operator new(size_t) {
        return __AllocStdCallThunk();
    }

    void operator delete(void* pThunk) {
        __FreeStdCallThunk(pThunk);
    }
};
```

```
#pragma pack(pop)

#elif defined(_M_AMD64)
... // Other processors omitted for clarity
```

As you can see, this structure initializes itself with the appropriate machine code to implement the per-window code needed to feed the right this pointer into the window proc. The overload of operator new is needed to deal with the no-execute protection feature on newer processors. The call to __AllocStdCallThunk ensures that the thunk is allocated on a virtual memory page that has execute permissions instead of on the regular heap, which might not allow code execution.

This data structure is kept per CWindowImpl-derived object and is initialized by StartWindowProc with the object's this pointer and the address of the static member function used as the window procedure. The m_thunk member that StartWindowProc initializes and uses as the thunking window procedure as an instance of the CWndProcThunk class follows:

```
class CwndProcThunk {
public:
    _AtlCreateWndData cd;
    CStdCallThunk thunk;

    BOOL Init(WNDPROC proc, void* pThis) {
        return thunk.Init((DWORD_PTR)proc, pThis);
    }
    WNDPROC GetWNDPROC() {
        return (WNDPROC)thunk.GetCodeAddress();
    }
};
```

After the thunk has been set up in StartWindowProc, each window message is routed from the CWindowImpl object's thunk to a static member function of CWindow-Impl, to a member function of the CWindowImpl object itself, shown in Figure 10.4.

On each Window message, the thunk removes the HWND provided by Windows as the first argument and replaces it with the CWindowImpl-derived object's this pointer. The thunk then forwards the entire call stack to the actual window procedure. Unless the virtual GetWindowProc function is overridden, the default window procedure is the WindowProc static function shown here:

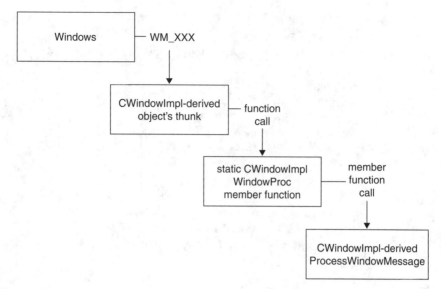

Figure 10.4 Each message is routed through a thunk to map the `HWND` to the `this` pointer.

```
template <class TBase, class TWinTraits>
LRESULT CALLBACK
CWindowImplBaseT< TBase, TWinTraits >::WindowProc(HWND hWnd,
    UINT uMsg, WPARAM wParam, LPARAM lParam) {

    CWindowImplBaseT< TBase, TWinTraits >* pThis =
        (CWindowImplBaseT< TBase, TWinTraits >*)hWnd;

    // set a ptr to this message and save the old value
    _ATL_MSG msg(pThis->m_hWnd, uMsg, wParam, lParam);
    const _ATL_MSG* pOldMsg = pThis->m_pCurrentMsg;
    pThis->m_pCurrentMsg = &msg;

    // pass to the message map to process
    LRESULT lRes;
    BOOL bRet = pThis->ProcessWindowMessage(pThis->m_hWnd,
        uMsg, wParam, lParam, lRes, 0);

    // restore saved value for the current message
    ATLASSERT(pThis->m_pCurrentMsg == &msg);

    // do the default processing if message was not handled
```

```
    if(!bRet) {
        if(uMsg != WM_NCDESTROY)
            lRes = pThis->DefWindowProc(uMsg, wParam, lParam);
        else {
            // unsubclass, if needed
            LONG_PTR pfnWndProc = ::GetWindowLongPtr(
                pThis->m_hWnd, GWLP_WNDPROC);
            lRes = pThis->DefWindowProc(uMsg, wParam, lParam);
            if(pThis->m_pfnSuperWindowProc != ::DefWindowProc &&
                ::GetWindowLongPtr(pThis->m_hWnd, GWLP_WNDPROC)
                == pfnWndProc)
                ::SetWindowLongPtr(pThis->m_hWnd, GWLP_WNDPROC,
                    (LONG_PTR)pThis->m_pfnSuperWindowProc);
            // mark window as destroyed
            pThis->m_dwState |= WINSTATE_DESTROYED;
        }
    }

    if((pThis->m_dwState & WINSTATE_DESTROYED) && pOldMsg== NULL) {
        // clear out window handle
        HWND hWndThis = pThis->m_hWnd;
        pThis->m_hWnd = NULL;
        pThis->m_dwState &= ~WINSTATE_DESTROYED;
        // clean up after window is destroyed
        pThis->m_pCurrentMsg = pOldMsg;
        pThis->OnFinalMessage(hWndThis);
    }
    else {
        pThis->m_pCurrentMsg = pOldMsg;
    }
    return lRes;
}
```

The first thing `WindowProc` does is extract the object's this pointer from the call stack by casting the `HWND` parameter. Because this `HWND` parameter has been cached in the object's `m_hWnd` member, no information is lost. However, if you override `GetWindowProc` and provide a custom `WndProc` for use by the window thunk, remember that the `HWND` is a `this` pointer, not an `HWND`.

After obtaining the object's `this` pointer, `WindowProc` caches the current message into the `m_pCurrentMsg` member of the `CWindowImpl`-derived object. This message is then passed along to the `CWindowImpl`-derived object's virtual member function `ProcessWindowMessage`, which must be provided by the deriving class with the following signature:

```
virtual BOOL
ProcessWindowMessage(HWND hWnd, UINT uMsg,
  WPARAM wParam, LPARAM lParam,
  LRESULT& lResult, DWORD dwMsgMapID);
```

This is where any message handling is to be done by the object. For example, our CMainWindow could handle Windows messages like this:

```
class CMainWindow : public CWindowImpl<CMainWindow> {
public:
  virtual BOOL
  ProcessWindowMessage(HWND hWnd, UINT uMsg,
    WPARAM wParam, LPARAM lParam,
    LRESULT& lResult, DWORD /*dwMsgMapID*/) {
    BOOL bHandled = TRUE;
    switch( uMsg ) {
    case WM_PAINT:   lResult = OnPaint(); break;
    case WM_DESTROY: lResult = OnDestroy(); break;
    default:         bHandled = FALSE; break;
    }
    return bHandled;
  }

private:
  LRESULT OnPaint(); {
    PAINTSTRUCT ps;
    HDC         hdc = BeginPaint(&ps);
    RECT        rect; GetClientRect(&rect);
    DrawText(hdc, __T("Hello, Windows"), -1, &rect,
             DT_CENTER | DT_VCENTER | DT_SINGLELINE);
    EndPaint(&ps);
    return 0;
  }

  LRESULT OnDestroy() {
    PostQuitMessage(0);
    return 0;
  }
};
```

Notice that the message handlers are now member functions instead of global functions. This makes programming a bit more convenient. For example, inside the

OnPaint handler, BeginPaint, GetClientRect, and EndPaint all resolve to member functions of the CMainWindow object to which the message has been sent. Also notice that returning FALSE from ProcessWindowMessage is all that is required if the window message is not handled. WindowProc handles calling DefWindowProc for unhandled messages.

As a further convenience, WindowProc calls OnFinalMessage after the window handles the last message and after the HWND has been zeroed out. This is handy for shutdown when used on the application's main window. For example, we can remove WM_DESTROY from our switch statement and replace the OnDestroy handler with OnFinalMessage:

```
virtual void CMainWindow::OnFinalMessage(HWND /*hwnd*/)
{ PostQuitMessage(0); }
```

As you might imagine, writing the ProcessWindowMessage function involves a lot of boilerplate coding, tediously mapping window messages to function names. I show you the message map that will handle this chore for us in the later section, "Handling Messages."

Window Superclassing

The Windows object model of declaring a window class and creating instances of that class is similar to that of the C++ object model. The WNDCLASSEX structure is to an HWND as a C++ class declaration is to a this pointer. Extending this analogy, Windows *superclassing*[3] is like C++ inheritance. Superclassing is a technique in which the WNDCLASSEX structure for an existing window class is duplicated and given its own name and its own WndProc. When a message is received for that window, it's routed to the new WndProc. If that WndProc decides not the handle that message fully, instead of being routed to DefWindowProc, the message is routed to the original WndProc. If you think of the original WndProc as a virtual function, the superclassing window overrides the WndProc and decides on a message-by-message basis whether to let the base class handle the message.

The reason to use superclassing is the same reason to use inheritance of implementation: The base class has some functionality that the deriving class wants to extend. ATL supports superclassing via the DECLARE_WND_SUPERCLASS macro:

```
#define DECLARE_WND_SUPERCLASS(WndClassName, OrigWndClassName) \
static ATL::CWndClassInfo& GetWndClassInfo() \
{ \
```

---

[3] The theory of Windows superclassing is beyond the scope of this book. For a more in-depth discussion, see *Win32 Programming* (Addison-Wesley, 1997), by Brent Rector and Joe Newcomer.

```
    static ATL::CWndClassInfo wc = \
    { \
        { sizeof(WNDCLASSEX), 0, StartWindowProc, \
            0, 0, NULL, NULL, NULL, NULL, NULL, \
            WndClassName, NULL }, \
        OrigWndClassName, NULL, NULL, TRUE, 0, _T("") \
    }; \
    return wc; \
}
```

The WndClassName is the name of the deriving class's window class. As with DECLARE_WND_CLASS[_EX], to have ATL generate a name, use NULL for this parameter. The OrigWndClassName parameter is the name of the existing window class you want to "inherit" from.

For example, the existing edit control provides the ES_NUMBER style to indicate that it should allow the input of only numbers. If you want to provide similar functionality but allow the input of only letters, you have two choices. First, you can build your own edit control from scratch. Second, you can superclass the existing edit control and handle WM_CHAR messages like this:

```
// Letters-only edit control
class CLetterBox : public CWindowImpl<CLetterBox> {
public:
    DECLARE_WND_SUPERCLASS(0, "EDIT")

    virtual BOOL
    ProcessWindowMessage(HWND hWnd, UINT uMsg,
        WPARAM wParam, LPARAM lParam,
        LRESULT& lResult, DWORD /*dwMsgMapID*/) {
        BOOL bHandled = TRUE;
        switch( uMsg ) {
        case WM_CHAR:
            lResult = OnChar((TCHAR)wParam, bHandled); break;
        default:
            bHandled = FALSE; break;
        }
        return bHandled;
    }

private:
    LRESULT OnChar(TCHAR c, BOOL& bHandled) {
        if( isalpha(c) ) bHandled = FALSE;
        else             MessageBeep(0xFFFFFFFF);
```

```
        return 0;
    }
};
```

When an instance of CLetterBox is created, it looks and acts just like a built-in Windows edit control, except that it accepts only letters, beeping otherwise.

Although superclassing is powerful, it turns out that it is rarely used. Superclassing is useful when you need to create more than one instance of a derived window type. More often in Win32 development, you instead want to customize a single window. A much more commonly used technique is known as subclassing, which I discuss later when I present CContainedWindow in the section titled (surprisingly enough) "CContainedWindow."

Handling Messages

Whether it's superclassing, subclassing, or neither, a major part of registering a Window class is providing the WndProc. The WndProc determines the behavior of the window by handling the appropriate messages. You've seen how the default WindowProc that ATL provides routes the messages to the ProcessWindowMessage function that your CWindowImpl-derived class provides. You've also seen how tedious it is to route messages from the ProcessWindowMessage function to the individual message-handler member functions. Toward that end, ATL provides a set of macros for building a message map that will generate an implementation of ProcessWindowMessage for you. Providing the skeleton of the message map are the BEGIN_MSG_MAP and END_MSG_MAP macros, defined like this:

```
#define BEGIN_MSG_MAP(theClass) \
public: \
    BOOL ProcessWindowMessage(HWND hWnd, UINT uMsg, \
        WPARAM wParam, LPARAM lParam, LRESULT& lResult, \
        DWORD dwMsgMapID = 0) \
    { \
        BOOL bHandled = TRUE; \
        (hWnd); (uMsg); (wParam); (lParam); \
        (lResult); (bHandled); \
        switch(dwMsgMapID) \
        { \
        case 0:


#define END_MSG_MAP() \
        break; \
        default: \
```

```
    ATLTRACE(ATL::atlTraceWindowing, 0, \
      _T("Invalid message map ID (%i)\n"), \
      dwMsgMapID); \
    ATLASSERT(FALSE); \
    break; \
  } \
  return FALSE; \
}
```

Notice that the message map is a giant switch statement. However, the switch is not on the message IDs themselves, but rather on the message map ID. A single set of message map macros can handle the messages of several windows, typically the parent and several children. The parent window, the window for which we're providing the message map, is identified with the message map ID of 0. Later I discuss segregating message handling into different sections of the same message map, resulting in nonzero message map IDs.

Handling General Messages

Each message that the window wants to handle corresponds to an entry in the message map. The simplest is the MESSAGE_HANDLER macro, which provides a handler for a single message:

```
#define MESSAGE_HANDLER(msg, func) \
  if(uMsg == msg) { \
    bHandled = TRUE; \
    lResult = func(uMsg, wParam, lParam, bHandled); \
    if(bHandled) return TRUE; \
  }
```

If you want to use a single message handler for a range of Windows messages, you can use the MESSAGE_RANGE_HANDLER macro:

```
#define MESSAGE_RANGE_HANDLER(msgFirst, msgLast, func) \
  if(uMsg >= msgFirst && uMsg <= msgLast) { \
    bHandled = TRUE; \
    lResult = func(uMsg, wParam, lParam, bHandled); \
    if(bHandled) return TRUE; \
  }
```

Using the message map macros, we can replace the sample implementation of ProcessWindowMessage with the following message map:

```
BEGIN_MSG_MAP(CMainWindow)
  MESSAGE_HANDLER(WM_PAINT, OnPaint)
END_MSG_MAP()
```

This expands roughly to the following implementation of `ProcessWindow-Message`:

```
// BEGIN_MSG_MAP(CMainWindow)
BOOL ProcessWindowMessage(HWND hWnd, UINT uMsg, WPARAM wParam,
                          LPARAM lParam, LRESULT& lResult,
                          DWORD dwMsgMapID = 0) {
    BOOL bHandled = TRUE;
    switch (dwMsgMapID) {
    case 0:

      // MESSAGE_HANDLER(WM_PAINT, OnPaint)
      if(uMsg == WM_PAINT) {
        bHandled = TRUE;
        lResult = OnPaint(uMsg, wParam, lParam, bHandled);
        if (bHandled) return TRUE;
      }

      // END_MSG_MAP()
      break;
    default:
      ATLTRACE2(atlTraceWindowing, 0,
        _T("Invalid message map ID (%i)\n"),
        dwMsgMapID);
      ATLASSERT(FALSE);
      break;
    }
    return FALSE;
  }
```

Note two points here. First, if there is an entry in the message map, that message is assumed to be handled—that is, the default window procedure is not called for that message. However, the `BOOL&` `bHandled` is provided to each message handler, so you can change it to `FALSE` in the message handler if you want ATL to keep looking for a handler for this message. If you are subclassing or superclassing, the original window procedure receives the message only when `bHandled` is set to `FALSE`. Also, it's possible that another message handler further down the map will receive the message. This is useful for message map chaining, which I discuss in the section "Message Chaining." Ultimately, if nobody is interested in the message, `DefWindowProc` gets it.

The second interesting note in this generated code is the member function signature required to handle a message map entry. All general messages are passed to a message handler with the following signature:

```
LRESULT
MessageHandler(UINT nMsg, WPARAM wparam, LPARAM lparam,
BOOL& bHandled);
```

You can either add the entry and the member function by hand, or, in Class view, you can right-click any class with a message map, choose Properties, and click the Messages button at the top of the property window. This gives you a list of the messages that you can handle, and, if you enter a function name in one of the slots, Visual Studio adds a MessageHandler macro to the map, a declaration to the .h file, and a stub to the .cpp file (as described in Chapter 1, ""Hello, ATL). Unfortunately, however you add the handler, you're still responsible for *cracking* your own messages. When you crack a message, you pull the data appropriate for the specific message from the wParam and lParam arguments passed to the message-handler method. For example, if you want to extract the coordinates of a mouse click, you must manually unpack the x and y positions from the lParam argument:

```
LRESULT CMainWindow::OnLButtonDown(UINT nMsg, WPARAM wParam,
    LPARAM lParam, BOOL &bHandled) {
    int xPos = GET_X_LPARAM(lParam);
    int yPos = GET_Y_LPARAM(lParam);
    ...
    return 0;
}
```

At last count, there were more than 300 standard messages, each with their own interpretation of WPARAM and LPARAM, so this can be quite a job. Luckily, the Windows Template Library (WTL)[4] add-on library to ATL, mentioned later in this chapter, provides this and more.

WM_COMMAND and WM_NOTIFY Messages

Of the hundreds of Windows messages, ATL provides a bit of message-cracking assistance for two of them, WM_COMMAND and WM_NOTIFY. These messages represent how a Windows control communicates with its parent. I should point out that Windows controls are not OLE or ActiveX controls. A standard Windows control is a child window whose class is defined by the Windows operating system. Some of these controls have been with us since Windows 1.0. Classic examples of Windows

---

[4] Available at http://wtl.sourceforge.net.

control include buttons, scrollbars, edit boxes, list boxes, and combo boxes. With the new Windows shell introduced with Windows 95, these controls were expanded to include toolbars, status bars, tree views, list views, rich-text edit boxes, and more. Furthermore, with the integration of Internet Explorer with the shell, more Windows controls were introduced to include rebars, the date picker, and the IP address control, for example.

Creating a Windows control is a matter of calling CreateWindow with the proper window class name—for example, EDIT—just like creating any other kind of window. Communicating from the parent to a child Windows controls is a matter of calling SendMessage with the appropriate parameters, as in EM_GETSEL to get the currently selected text in a child EDIT control. Communicating from a child window to its parent also works via SendMessage, most often using the WM_COMMAND or WM_NOTIFY messages. These messages provide enough information packed into WPARAM and LPARAM to describe the event of which the control is notifying the parent, as shown here:

```
WM_COMMAND
  wNotifyCode = HIWORD(wParam);  // notification code
  wID = LOWORD(wParam);          // item, control, or
                                 // accelerator identifier
  hwndCtl = (HWND)lParam;        // handle of control


WM_NOTIFY
  idCtrl = (int)wParam;          // control identifier
  pnmh = (LPNMHDR)lParam;        // address of NMHDR structure
```

Notice that the WM_NOTIFY message is accompanied by a pointer to a NMHDR, which is defined like this:

```
typedef struct tagNMHDR {
  HWND hwndFrom;  // handle of the control
  UINT idFrom;    // control identifier
  UINT code;      // notification code
} NMHDR;
```

For example, an edit box notifies the parent of a change in the text with a WM_COMMAND message using the EN_CHANGE notification code. The parent might or might not want to handle this particular message. If it does, it wants to avoid the responsibility of breaking out the individual parts of the command notification. ATL provides several macros for splitting the parts of WM_COMMAND and WM_NOTIFY messages. All these macros assume the following handler-function signatures:

```
LRESULT
CommandHandler(WORD wNotifyCode, WORD wID, HWND hWndCtl,
  BOOL& bHandled);

LRESULT
NotifyHandler(int idCtrl, LPNMHDR pnmh, BOOL& bHandled);
```

The most basic handler macros are COMMAND_HANDLER and NOTIFY_HANDLER:

```
#define COMMAND_HANDLER(id, code, func) \
  if(uMsg == WM_COMMAND && \
    id == LOWORD(wParam) && \
    code == HIWORD(wParam)) \
  { \
    bHandled = TRUE; \
    lResult = func(HIWORD(wParam), LOWORD(wParam), \
      (HWND)lParam, bHandled); \
    if(bHandled) return TRUE; \
  }

#define NOTIFY_HANDLER(id, code, func) \
  if(uMsg == WM_NOTIFY && \
    id == ((LPNMHDR)lParam)->idFrom && \
    code == ((LPNMHDR)lParam)->code) \
  { \
    bHandled = TRUE; \
    lResult = func((int)wParam, (LPNMHDR)lParam, bHandled); \
    if(bHandled) return TRUE; \
  }
```

These basic handler macros let you specify both the id of the control and the command/notification code that the control is sending. Using these macros, handling an EN_CHANGE notification from an edit control looks like this:

```
COMMAND_HANDLER(IDC_EDIT1, EN_CHANGE, OnEdit1Change)
```

Likewise, handling a TBN_BEGINDRAG notification from a toolbar control looks like this:

```
NOTIFY_HANDLER(IDC_TOOLBAR1, TBN_BEGINDRAG, OnToolbar1BeginDrag)
```

As an example, let's add a menu bar to the sample Windows application:

```
int APIENTRY _tWinMain(HINSTANCE hinst,
                       HINSTANCE /*hinstPrev*/,
                       LPTSTR    pszCmdLine,
                       int       nCmdShow) {
    // Initialize the ATL module
    ...

    // Create the main window
    CMainWindow wnd;

    // Load a menu
    HMENU hMenu = LoadMenu(_Module.GetResourceInstance(),
                           MAKEINTRESOURCE(IDR_MENU));

    // Use the value 0 for the style and the extended style
    // to get the window traits for this class.
    wnd.Create(0, CWindow::rcDefault, __T("Windows Application"),
        0, 0, (UINT)hMenu);
    if( !wnd ) return -1;

    ... // The rest is the same
}
```

Assuming standard File, Exit and Help, About items in our menu, handling the menu item selections looks like this:

```
class CMainWindow : public CWindowImpl<CMainWindow,
    CWindow, CMainWinTraits> {
public:
BEGIN_MSG_MAP(CMainWindow)
    MESSAGE_HANDLER(WM_PAINT, OnPaint)
    COMMAND_HANDLER(ID_FILE_EXIT, 0, OnFileExit)
    COMMAND_HANDLER(ID_HELP_ABOUT, 0, OnHelpAbout)
END_MSG_MAP()
...
    LRESULT OnFileExit(WORD wNotifyCode, WORD wID, HWND hWndCtl,
                       BOOL& bHandled);
    LRESULT OnHelpAbout(WORD wNotifyCode, WORD wID, HWND hWndCtl,
                        BOOL& bHandled);
};
```

You might notice that menus are a little different from most Windows controls. Instead of using the ID of a child window as the first parameter, such as for an edit control, we use the ID of the menu item; the command code itself is unused. In general, it's not uncommon for the ID or the code to be unimportant when routing a message to a handler. You've already seen one example: Handling a menu item doesn't require checking the code. Another example of when you don't need to worry about the code is if you want to route all events for one control to a single handler. Because the code is provided as an argument to the handler, further decisions can be made about how to handle a specific code for a control. To route events without regard for the specific code, ATL provides COMMAND_ID_HANDLER and NOTIFY_ID_HANDLER:

```
#define COMMAND_ID_HANDLER(id, func) \
  if(uMsg == WM_COMMAND && id == LOWORD(wParam)) \
  { \
        bHandled = TRUE; \
    lResult = func(HIWORD(wParam), LOWORD(wParam), \
      (HWND)lParam, bHandled); \
    if(bHandled) \
      return TRUE; \
  }

#define NOTIFY_ID_HANDLER(id, func) \
  if(uMsg == WM_NOTIFY && id == ((LPNMHDR)lParam)->idFrom) \
  { \
        bHandled = TRUE; \
    lResult = func((int)wParam, (LPNMHDR)lParam, bHandled); \
    if(bHandled) \
    return TRUE; \
  }
```

Using COMMAND_ID_HANDLER, our menu routing would more conventionally be written this way:

```
COMMAND_ID_HANDLER(ID_FILE_EXIT, OnFileExit)
COMMAND_ID_HANDLER(ID_HELP_ABOUT, OnHelpAbout)
```

Furthermore, if you want to route notifications for a range of controls, ATL provides COMMAND_RANGE_HANDLER and NOTIFY_RANGE_HANDLER:

```
#define COMMAND_RANGE_HANDLER(idFirst, idLast, func) \
  if(uMsg == WM_COMMAND && LOWORD(wParam) >= idFirst  && \
    LOWORD(wParam) <= idLast) \
  { \
        bHandled = TRUE; \
```

```
  lResult = func(HIWORD(wParam), LOWORD(wParam), \
    (HWND)lParam, bHandled); \
  if(bHandled) \
  return TRUE; \
}

#define NOTIFY_RANGE_HANDLER(idFirst, idLast, func) \
  if(uMsg == WM_NOTIFY && \
    ((LPNMHDR)lParam)->idFrom >= idFirst && \
    ((LPNMHDR)lParam)->idFrom <= idLast) \
  { \
      bHandled = TRUE; \
    lResult = func((int)wParam, (LPNMHDR)lParam, bHandled); \
    if(bHandled) \
    return TRUE; \
  }
```

It's also possible that you want to route messages without regard for their ID. This is useful if you want to use a single handler for multiple controls. ATL supports this use with COMMAND_CODE_HANDLER and NOTIFY_CODE_HANDLER:

```
#define COMMAND_CODE_HANDLER(code, func) \
  if(uMsg == WM_COMMAND && code == HIWORD(wParam)) \
  { \
    bHandled = TRUE; \
    lResult = func(HIWORD(wParam), LOWORD(wParam), \
      (HWND)lParam, bHandled); \
    if(bHandled) \
    return TRUE; \
  }

#define NOTIFY_CODE_HANDLER(cd, func) \
  if(uMsg == WM_NOTIFY && cd == ((LPNMHDR)lParam)->code) \
  { \
    bHandled = TRUE; \
    lResult = func((int)wParam, (LPNMHDR)lParam, bHandled); \
    if(bHandled) \
    return TRUE; \
  }
```

Again, because the ID of the control is available as a parameter to the handler, you can make further decisions based on which control is sending the notification code.

Why WM_NOTIFY?

As an aside, you might be wondering why we have both WM_COMMAND and WM_NOTIFY. After all, WM_COMMAND alone sufficed for Windows 1.0 through Windows 3.*x*. However, when the new shell team was building the new controls, team members really wanted to send along more information than just the ID of the control and the notification code. Unfortunately, all the bits of both WPARAM and LPARAM were already being used in WM_COMMAND, so the shell team invented a new message so that they could send a pointer to a structure as the LPARAM, keeping the ID of the control in the WPARAM (as in WM_NOTIFY). However, if you examine the definition of the NMHDR structure, you'll notice that there is no more information than was available in WM_COMMAND. Actually, there is a difference. Depending on the type of control that is sending the message, the LPARAM could point to something else that has the same layout as an NMHDR but that has extra information tacked onto the end. For example, if you receive a TBN_BEGIN_DRAG, the NMHDR pointer actually points to an NMTOOLBAR structure:

```
typedef struct tagNMTOOLBAR {
    NMHDR    hdr;
    int      iItem;
    TBBUTTON tbButton;
    int      cchText;
    LPTSTR   pszText;
} NMTOOLBAR, FAR* LPNMTOOLBAR;
```

Because the first member of the NMTOOLBAR structure is an NMDHR, it's safe to cast the LPARAM to an NMHDR, even though it actually points at an NMTOOLBAR. If you want, you can consider this "inheritance" for C programmers. . ..

Message Reflection and Forwarding

In many cases, Windows controls send messages to their parent windows: when a button is clicked, when a treeview item is expanded, or when a list-box item is selected, for example. These messages are usually the result of user action, and the parent window is often the best place to handle the user's request.

Other messages are also sent to the parent window. These messages are sent not as the result of a user's action, but as a way for the parent window to customize something about the control's operation. The classic example is the WM_CTLCOL-ORXXX set of messages, which are sent to the parent window to allow it to change the default colors when a control draws. Handling such messages is fairly easy. For example, imagine that I want to display a static window with red text on a green background:

```cpp
class CMainWindow : public CWindowImpl< CMainWindow, CWindow,
    CMainWinTraits >
{
public:
    CMainWindow( ) {
    }

    BEGIN_MSG_MAP(CMainWindow)
        MESSAGE_HANDLER(WM_CREATE, OnCreate)
        MESSAGE_HANDLER(WM_CTLCOLORSTATIC, OnControlColorStatic)
    END_MSG_MAP()

private:
    LRESULT OnCreate(UINT nMsg, WPARAM wParam, LPARAM lParam,
        BOOL& bHandled) {
        m_staticBackground = ::CreateSolidBrush(RGB(0, 255, 0));

        RECT rc;
        rc.left = 25;
        rc.right = 300;
        rc.top = 25;
        rc.bottom = 75;

        if( m_message.Create(_T("static"),
            m_hWnd, rc, _T("Static Message"),
            WS_VISIBLE | WS_CHILD ) ) {
            return 0;
        }
        return -1;
    }

    LRESULT OnControlColorStatic(UINT nMsg,
        WPARAM wParam, LPARAM lParam,
        BOOL& bHandled) {
        HDC hdc = reinterpret_cast< HDC >( wParam );
        ::SetTextColor(hdc, RGB(255, 0, 0) );
        ::SetBkColor( hdc, RGB(0, 255, 0 ) );
        return reinterpret_cast< LRESULT >(m_staticBackground);
    }

    void OnFinalMessage(HWND hWnd) {
        ::DeleteObject( m_staticBackground );
        PostQuitMessage(0);
    }
```

```
    CWindow m_message;
    HBRUSH m_staticBackground;
};
```

This code is fairly straightforward. At creation, we create a brush to hand to the static control when it paints. When we receive the WM_CTLCOLORSTATIC, we set up the provided HDC to draw in the proper colors. OnFinalMessage cleans up the brush we created so that we can be nice Windows citizens.

This implementation works well . . . until you add a second static control. Then, you need to figure out which control is drawing and set its colors appropriately in the OnControlColorStatic method. Or what if you want custom colors for a second window class? Now, we have to start copying and pasting. Ideally, we want to build a single CColoredStatic window class and let it handle all the details.

The only tricky part about writing that class is that the underlying static control is hard-wired to send the WM_CTLCOLORSTATIC message *only* to its parent window. Somehow in the implementation of CColoredStatic, we need to hook the message map of our parent window, preferably without having to warp the implementation of the parent window class to support our new child control.

The traditional Windows approach to this problem is to have your control subclass its parent window. This can be done, but it is a little tricky to get right. ATL has introduced a new feature called *notification reflection* that lets us easily get these parent notifications back to the original control.

In the parent message map, you need to add the REFLECT_NOTIFICATIONS() macro. This macro is defined as follows:

```
#define REFLECT_NOTIFICATIONS() \
    { \
        bHandled = TRUE; \
        lResult = ReflectNotifications(uMsg, \
            wParam, lParam, bHandled); \
        if(bHandled) \
            return TRUE; \
    }
```

This passes the message on to the ReflectNotifications method, which is defined in CWindowImplRoot:

```
template <class TBase>
LRESULT CWindowImplRoot< TBase >::ReflectNotifications(UINT uMsg,
    WPARAM wParam, LPARAM lParam, BOOL& bHandled)
{
    HWND hWndChild = NULL;
```

```
switch(uMsg) {
case WM_COMMAND:
    if(lParam != NULL)     // not from a menu
        hWndChild = (HWND)lParam;
    break;
case WM_NOTIFY:
    hWndChild = ((LPNMHDR)lParam)->hwndFrom;
    break;
case WM_PARENTNOTIFY:
    switch(LOWORD(wParam)) {
    case WM_CREATE:
    case WM_DESTROY:
        hWndChild = (HWND)lParam;
        break;
    default:
        hWndChild = GetDlgItem(HIWORD(wParam));
        break;
    }
    break;
case WM_DRAWITEM:
    if(wParam)     // not from a menu
        hWndChild = ((LPDRAWITEMSTRUCT)lParam)->hwndItem;
    break;
case WM_MEASUREITEM:
    if(wParam)     // not from a menu
        hWndChild = GetDlgItem(
            ((LPMEASUREITEMSTRUCT)lParam)->CtlID);
    break;
case WM_COMPAREITEM:
    if(wParam)     // not from a menu
        hWndChild = ((LPCOMPAREITEMSTRUCT)lParam)->hwndItem;
    break;
case WM_DELETEITEM:
    if(wParam)     // not from a menu
        hWndChild = ((LPDELETEITEMSTRUCT)lParam)->hwndItem;

    break;
case WM_VKEYTOITEM:
case WM_CHARTOITEM:
case WM_HSCROLL:
case WM_VSCROLL:
    hWndChild = (HWND)lParam;
    break;
case WM_CTLCOLORBTN:
```

```
        case WM_CTLCOLORDLG:
        case WM_CTLCOLOREDIT:
        case WM_CTLCOLORLISTBOX:
        case WM_CTLCOLORMSGBOX:
        case WM_CTLCOLORSCROLLBAR:
        case WM_CTLCOLORSTATIC:
            hWndChild = (HWND)lParam;
            break;
        default:
            break;
        }

        if(hWndChild == NULL) {
            bHandled = FALSE;
            return 1;
        }

        ATLASSERT(::IsWindow(hWndChild));
        return ::SendMessage(hWndChild, OCM__BASE + uMsg,
            wParam, lParam);
}
```

This function simply looks for all the standard parent notifications and, if found, forwards the message back to the control that sent it. One thing to notice is that the message ID is changed by adding OCM_BASE to the message code. A set of macros is defined for forwarded messages that begin with OCM_ instead of WM_. The message values are changed so that the child control can tell that the message is a reflection back from its parent instead of a notification from one of its own children.

For our self-colorizing static control, we need to handle OCM_CTLCOLORSTATIC as follows:

```
class CColoredStatic : public CWindowImpl< CColoredStatic > {
public:
    DECLARE_WND_SUPERCLASS(0, _T("STATIC"))

    CColoredStatic( COLORREF foreground, COLORREF background ) {
        m_foreground = foreground;
        m_background = background;
        m_backgroundBrush = ::CreateSolidBrush( m_background );
    }

    ~CColoredStatic( ) {
        ::DeleteObject( m_backgroundBrush );
    }
```

```
private:

    BEGIN_MSG_MAP(CColoredStatic)
        MESSAGE_HANDLER(OCM_CTLCOLORSTATIC, OnControlColorStatic)
    END_MSG_MAP()

    LRESULT OnControlColorStatic(UINT nMsg, WPARAM wParam,
        LPARAM lParam, BOOL& bHandled) {
        HDC hdc = reinterpret_cast< HDC >( wParam );
        ::SetTextColor(hdc, m_foreground );
        ::SetBkColor( hdc, m_background );
        return reinterpret_cast< LRESULT >(m_backgroundBrush);
    }

    COLORREF m_foreground;
    COLORREF m_background;
    HBRUSH m_backgroundBrush;
};
```

Our parent window class is simplified as well:

```
class CMainWindow :
    public CWindowImpl< CMainWindow, CWindow, CMainWinTraits >
{
public:
    CMainWindow( ) :
        m_message( RGB( 0, 0, 255 ), RGB(255, 255, 255) ) {
    }

    BEGIN_MSG_MAP(CMainWindow)
        MESSAGE_HANDLER(WM_CREATE, OnCreate)
        REFLECT_NOTIFICATIONS()
    END_MSG_MAP()
...
};
```

A set of macros for use in the child control message map corresponds to the regular ones that handle command and notification messages: REFLECTED_ COMMAND_HANDLER, REFLECTED_COMMAND_ID_HANDLER, REFLECTED_NOTIFY_HANDLER, and so on. In addition, DEFAULT_REFLECTION_HANDLER sends the reflected message down to DefWindowProc.

There's one minor nagging nit with the message-reflection setup: We still need to modify our parent window class. It sure would be nice to avoid this, especially when building reusable controls. Luckily, the ATL authors thought of this with the

`CWindowWithReflectorImpl` class. Using this class is quite easy: Simply replace your `CWindowImpl` base class with `CWindowWithReflectorImpl`:

```
class CColoredStatic :
    public CWindowWithReflectorImpl< CColoredStatic >
{
// ... the rest is exactly the same ...
};
```

You can now remove the `REFLECT_NOTIFICATIONS()` macro from the parent's message map, and messages will still be routed as before.

The implementation of `CWindowWithReflectorImpl` is quite small:

```
template <class T, class TBase , class TWinTraits >
class ATL_NO_VTABLE CWindowWithReflectorImpl :
    public CWindowImpl< T, TBase, TWinTraits > {
public:
    HWND Create(HWND hWndParent, _U_RECT rect = NULL,
        LPCTSTR szWindowName = NULL,
        DWORD dwStyle = 0, DWORD dwExStyle = 0,
        _U_MENUorID MenuOrID = 0U, LPVOID lpCreateParam = NULL) {
        m_wndReflector.Create(hWndParent, rect, NULL,
            WS_VISIBLE | WS_CHILD |
            WS_CLIPSIBLINGS | WS_CLIPCHILDREN, 0,
            Reflector::REFLECTOR_MAP_ID);
        RECT rcPos = { 0, 0, rect.m_lpRect->right,
            rect.m_lpRect->bottom };
        return CWindowImpl<
            T, TBase, TWinTraits >::Create(m_wndReflector,
            rcPos, szWindowName, dwStyle, dwExStyle,
            MenuOrID, lpCreateParam);
    }

    typedef CWindowWithReflectorImpl<
        T, TBase, TWinTraits > thisClass;
    BEGIN_MSG_MAP(thisClass)
        MESSAGE_HANDLER(WM_NCDESTROY, OnNcDestroy)
        MESSAGE_HANDLER(WM_WINDOWPOSCHANGING,
            OnWindowPosChanging)
    END_MSG_MAP()

    LRESULT OnNcDestroy(UINT, WPARAM, LPARAM, BOOL& bHandled) {
        m_wndReflector.DestroyWindow();
        bHandled = FALSE;
```

```
        return 1;
    }

    LRESULT OnWindowPosChanging(UINT uMsg,
        WPARAM wParam, LPARAM lParam,
        BOOL& ) {
        WINDOWPOS* pWP = (WINDOWPOS*)lParam;
        m_wndReflector.SetWindowPos(m_wndReflector.GetParent(),
            pWP->x, pWP->y, pWP->cx, pWP->cy, pWP->flags);
        pWP->flags |= SWP_NOMOVE;
        pWP->x = 0;
        pWP->y = 0;
        return DefWindowProc(uMsg, wParam, lParam);
    }

    // reflector window stuff
    class Reflector : public CWindowImpl<Reflector> {
    public:
        enum { REFLECTOR_MAP_ID = 69 };
        DECLARE_WND_CLASS_EX(_T("ATLReflectorWindow"), 0, -1)
        BEGIN_MSG_MAP(Reflector)
            REFLECT_NOTIFICATIONS()
        END_MSG_MAP()
    } m_wndReflector;
};
```

This class actually creates *two* windows. The inner window is your actual window. The outer window is an invisible parent window that does nothing but reflect parent notifications back to the control. This extra parent window includes the REFLECT_NOTIFICATIONS macro in its message maps so you don't have to.

The best thing about this implementation is the transparency. CWindowWithReflectorImpl::Create returns the HWND of the inner control, not the invisible outer window. The parent can send messages to the control directly and doesn't have to know anything about the outer invisible window.

Message Forwarding

Just as some messages are inconveniently hard-wired to go to a parent window, sometimes messages are hard-wired to go to a window, but we'd rather let the parent handle it. This can be especially useful if you're building a composite control: a single control that contains multiple child controls. The notifications will go up to the parent control, but we might want to pass them to the composite control's parent easily.

To do this, add the `FORWARD_NOTIFICATIONS()` macro to your control's message map.

```
#define FORWARD_NOTIFICATIONS() { \
        bHandled = TRUE; \
        lResult = ForwardNotifications(uMsg, \
            wParam, lParam, bHandled); \
        if(bHandled) \
            return TRUE; \
    }
```

This macro calls the `ForwardNotifications` function defined in `CWindowImpl-Root`:

```
template <class TBase>
LRESULT
CWindowImplRoot< TBase >::ForwardNotifications(UINT uMsg,
    WPARAM wParam, LPARAM lParam, BOOL& bHandled) {
    LRESULT lResult = 0;
    switch(uMsg) {
    case WM_COMMAND:
    case WM_NOTIFY:
    case WM_PARENTNOTIFY:
    case WM_DRAWITEM:
    case WM_MEASUREITEM:
    case WM_COMPAREITEM:
    case WM_DELETEITEM:
    case WM_VKEYTOITEM:
    case WM_CHARTOITEM:
    case WM_HSCROLL:
    case WM_VSCROLL:
    case WM_CTLCOLORBTN:
    case WM_CTLCOLORDLG:
    case WM_CTLCOLOREDIT:
    case WM_CTLCOLORLISTBOX:
    case WM_CTLCOLORMSGBOX:
    case WM_CTLCOLORSCROLLBAR:
    case WM_CTLCOLORSTATIC:
        lResult = GetParent().SendMessage(uMsg, wParam, lParam);
        break;
    default:
        bHandled = FALSE;
        break;
```

```
        }
        return lResult;
}
```

The implementation is very simple; it forwards the message straight up to the parent window. There is no change in the message ID, so the parent window can use a normal WM_ message ID in its message map.

Between message reflection and forwarding, it's quite easy to shuffle standard notifications up and down the windowing tree as needed.

Message Chaining

If you find yourself handling messages in the same way, you might want to reuse the message-handler implementations. If you're willing to populate the message map entries yourself, there's no reason you can't use normal C++ implementation techniques:

```cpp
template <typename Deriving>
class CFileHandler {
public:
  LRESULT OnFileNew(WORD, WORD, HWND, BOOL&);
  LRESULT OnFileOpen(WORD, WORD, HWND, BOOL&);
  LRESULT OnFileSave(WORD, WORD, HWND, BOOL&);
  LRESULT OnFileSaveAs(WORD, WORD, HWND, BOOL&);
  LRESULT OnFileExit(WORD, WORD, HWND, BOOL&);
};


class CMainWindow :
    public CWindowImpl<CMainWindow, CWindow, CMainWinTraits>,
    public CFileHandler<CMainWindow>
{
public:
BEGIN_MSG_MAP(CMainWindow)
  MESSAGE_HANDLER(WM_PAINT, OnPaint)
  // Route messages to base class
  COMMAND_ID_HANDLER(ID_FILE_NEW, OnFileNew)
  COMMAND_ID_HANDLER(ID_FILE_OPEN, OnFileOpen)
  COMMAND_ID_HANDLER(ID_FILE_SAVE, OnFileSave)
  COMMAND_ID_HANDLER(ID_FILE_SAVE_AS, OnFileSaveAs)
  COMMAND_ID_HANDLER(ID_FILE_EXIT, OnFileExit)
  COMMAND_ID_HANDLER(ID_HELP_ABOUT, OnHelpAbout)
END_MSG_MAP()
...
};
```

This technique is somewhat cumbersome, however. If the base class gained a new message handler, such as OnFileClose, each deriving class would have to manually add an entry to its message map. We'd really like the capability to "inherit" a base class's message map as well as a base class's functionality. For this, ATL provides *message chaining*.

Simple Message Chaining

Message chaining is the capability to extend a class's message map by including the message map of a base class or another object altogether. The simplest macro of the message chaining family is CHAIN_MSG_MAP:

```
#define CHAIN_MSG_MAP(theChainClass) { \
  if (theChainClass::ProcessWindowMessage(hWnd, uMsg, \
    wParam, lParam, lResult)) \
  return TRUE; \
}
```

This macro allows chaining to the message map of a base class:

```
template <typename Deriving>
class CFileHandler {
public:
// Message map in base class
BEGIN_MSG_MAP(CMainWindow)
  COMMAND_ID_HANDLER(ID_FILE_NEW, OnFileNew)
  COMMAND_ID_HANDLER(ID_FILE_OPEN, OnFileOpen)
  COMMAND_ID_HANDLER(ID_FILE_SAVE, OnFileSave)
  COMMAND_ID_HANDLER(ID_FILE_SAVE_AS, OnFileSaveAs)
  COMMAND_ID_HANDLER(ID_FILE_EXIT, OnFileExit)
END_MSG_MAP()

  LRESULT OnFileNew(WORD, WORD, HWND, BOOL&);
  LRESULT OnFileOpen(WORD, WORD, HWND, BOOL&);
  LRESULT OnFileSave(WORD, WORD, HWND, BOOL&);
  LRESULT OnFileSaveAs(WORD, WORD, HWND, BOOL&);
  LRESULT OnFileExit(WORD, WORD, HWND, BOOL&);
};

class CMainWindow :
    public CWindowImpl<CMainWindow, CWindow, CMainWinTraits>,
    public CFileHandler<CMainWindow>
{
public:
```

```
BEGIN_MSG_MAP(CMainWindow)
  MESSAGE_HANDLER(WM_PAINT, OnPaint)
  COMMAND_ID_HANDLER(ID_HELP_ABOUT, OnHelpAbout)
  // Chain to a base class
  CHAIN_MSG_MAP(CFileHandler<CMainWindow>)
END_MSG_MAP()
...
};
```

Any base class that provides its own implementation of Process-
WindowMessage—for example, with the message map macros—can be used as a
chainee. Also notice that CFileHandler is parameterized by the name of the deriving class. This is useful when used with static cast to obtain a pointer to the more
derived class. For example, when implementing OnFileExit, you need to destroy
the window represented by the deriving class:

```
template <typename Deriving>
LRESULT CFileHandler<Deriving>::OnFileExit(
    WORD, WORD, HWND, BOOL&) {
    static_cast<Deriving*>(this)->DestroyWindow();
    return 0;
}
```

Message chaining to a base class can be extended for any number of base
classes. For example, if you wanted to handle the File, Edit, and Help menus in separate base classes, you would have several chain entries:

```
class CMainWindow :
    public CWindowImpl<CMainWindow, CWindow, CMainWinTraits>,
    public CFileHandler<CMainWindow>,
    public CEditHandler<CMainWinow>,
    public CHelpHandler<CMainWindow>
{
public:
BEGIN_MSG_MAP(CMainWindow)
  MESSAGE_HANDLER(WM_PAINT, OnPaint)
  COMMAND_ID_HANDLER(ID_HELP_ABOUT, OnHelpAbout)
  // Chain to a base class
  CHAIN_MSG_MAP(CFileHandler<CMainWindow>)
  CHAIN_MSG_MAP(CEditHandler<CMainWindow>)
  CHAIN_MSG_MAP(CHelpHandler<CMainWindow>)
END_MSG_MAP()
...
};
```

If instead of chaining to a base class message map you want to chain to the message map of a data member, you can use the CHAIN_MSG_MAP_MEMBER macro:

```
#define CHAIN_MSG_MAP_MEMBER(theChainMember) { \
  if (theChainMember.ProcessWindowMessage(hWnd, uMsg, \
    wParam, lParam, lResult)) \
  return TRUE; \
}
```

If a handler will be a data member, it needs to access a pointer to the actual object differently; a static cast won't work. For example, an updated CFileHandler takes a pointer to the window for which it's handling messages in the constructor:

```
template <typename TWindow>
class CFileHandler {
public:
BEGIN_MSG_MAP(CFileHandler)
  COMMAND_ID_HANDLER(ID_FILE_NEW, OnFileNew)
  COMMAND_ID_HANDLER(ID_FILE_OPEN, OnFileOpen)
  COMMAND_ID_HANDLER(ID_FILE_SAVE, OnFileSave)
  COMMAND_ID_HANDLER(ID_FILE_SAVE_AS, OnFileSaveAs)
  COMMAND_ID_HANDLER(ID_FILE_EXIT, OnFileExit)
END_MSG_MAP()

  CFileHandler(TWindow* pwnd) : m_pwnd(pwnd) {}

  LRESULT OnFileNew(WORD, WORD, HWND, BOOL&);
  LRESULT OnFileOpen(WORD, WORD, HWND, BOOL&);
  LRESULT OnFileSave(WORD, WORD, HWND, BOOL&);
  LRESULT OnFileSaveAs(WORD, WORD, HWND, BOOL&);
  LRESULT OnFileExit(WORD, WORD, HWND, BOOL&);

private:
  TWindow* m_pwnd;
};
```

An updated implementation would use the cached pointer to access the window instead of a static cast:

```
template <typename TWindow>
LRESULT CFileHandler<TWindow>::OnFileExit(WORD, WORD wID,
    HWND, BOOL&) {
  m_pwnd->DestroyWindow();
  return 0;
}
```

When we have an updated handler class, using it looks like this:

```
class CMainWindow :
  public CWindowImpl<CMainWindow, CWindow, CMainWinTraits> {
public:
BEGIN_MSG_MAP(CMainWindow)
  MESSAGE_HANDLER(WM_PAINT, OnPaint)
  COMMAND_ID_HANDLER(ID_HELP_ABOUT, OnHelpAbout)
  // Chain to the CFileHandler member
  CHAIN_MSG_MAP_MEMBER(m_handlerFile)
END_MSG_MAP()
...
private:
  CFileHandler<CMainWindow> m_handlerFile;
};
```

Alternate Message Maps

It's possible to break a message map into multiple pieces. Each piece is called an *alternate message map*. Recall that the message map macros expand into a switch statement that switches on the dwMsgMapID parameter to ProcessWindowMessage. The main part of the message map is the first part and is identified with a zero message map ID. An alternate part of the message map, on the other hand, is distinguished with a nonzero message map ID. As each message comes in, it's routed first by message map ID and then by message. When a window receives its own messages and those messages chained from another window, an alternate part of the message map allows the window to distinguish where the messages are coming from. A message map is broken into multiple parts using the ALT_MSG_MAP macro:

```
#define ALT_MSG_MAP(msgMapID) \
  break; \
  case msgMapID:
```

For example, imagine a child window that is receiving messages routed to it from the main window:

```
class CView : public CWindowImpl<CView> {
public:
BEGIN_MSG_MAP(CView)
// Handle CView messages
  MESSAGE_HANDLER(WM_PAINT, OnPaint)

// Handle messages chained from the parent window
ALT_MSG_MAP(1)
```

```
    COMMAND_HANDLER(ID_EDIT_COPY, OnCopy)
  END_MSG_MAP()
  ...
};
```

Because the message map has been split, the child window (CView) receives only its own messages in the main part of the message map. However, if the main window were to chain messages using CHAIN_MSG_MAP_MEMBER, the child would receive the messages in the main part of the message map, not the alternate part. To chain messages to an alternate part of the message map, ATL provides two macros, CHAIN_MSG_MAP_ALT and CHAIN_MSG_MAP_ALT_MEMBER:

```
#define CHAIN_MSG_MAP_ALT(theChainClass, msgMapID) { \
  if (theChainClass::ProcessWindowMessage(hWnd, uMsg, \
    wParam, lParam, lResult, msgMapID)) \
  return TRUE; \
}
```

```
#define CHAIN_MSG_MAP_ALT_MEMBER(theChainMember, msgMapID) { \
  if (theChainMember.ProcessWindowMessage(hWnd, uMsg, \
    wParam, lParam, lResult, msgMapID)) \
  return TRUE; \
}
```

For example, for the parent window to route unhandled messages to the child, it can use CHAIN_MSG_ALT_MEMBER like this:

```
class CMainWindow : ... {
public:
BEGIN_MSG_MAP(CMainWindow)
  MESSAGE_HANDLER(WM_CREATE, OnCreate)
  ...
  // Route unhandled messages to the child window
  CHAIN_MSG_MAP_ALT_MEMBER(m_view, 1)
END_MSG_MAP()

  LRESULT OnCreate(UINT, WPARAM, LPARAM, BOOL&) {
    return m_view.Create(m_hWnd, CWindow::rcDefault) ? 0 : -1;
  }
  ...
private:
  CView m_view;
};
```

Dynamic Chaining

Message map chaining to a base class or a member variable is useful but not as flexible as you might like. What if you want a looser coupling between the window that sent the message and the handler of the message? For example, the MFC WM_COMMAND message routing depends on just such a loose coupling. The View receives all the WM_COMMAND messages initially, but the Document handles file-related command messages. If we want to construct such a relationship using ATL, we have one more chaining message map macro, CHAIN_MSG_MAP_DYNAMIC:

```
#define CHAIN_MSG_MAP_DYNAMIC(dynaChainID) { \
  if (CDynamicChain::CallChain(dynaChainID, hWnd, \
    uMsg, wParam, lParam, lResult)) \
  return TRUE; \
}
```

Chaining sets up a relationship between two objects that handle messages. If the object that first receives the message doesn't handle it, the second object in line can handle it. The relationship is established using a *dynamic chain ID*. A dynamic chain ID is a number that the primary message processor uses to identify the secondary message processor that wants to process unhandled messages. To establish the dynamic chaining relationship, two things must happen. First, the secondary message processor must derive from CMessageMap:

```
class ATL_NO_VTABLE CMessageMap {
public:
  virtual BOOL
  ProcessWindowMessage(HWND hWnd, UINT uMsg, WPARAM wParam,
    LPARAM lParam, LRESULT& lResult, DWORD dwMsgMapID) = 0;
};
```

CMessageMap is actually a poorly named class. A better name would be something like CMessageHandler or even CMessageProcessor. All that CMessageMap does is guarantee that every class that derives from it will implement ProcessWindowMessage. In fact, CWindowImpl derives from it as well, making an implementation of ProcessWindowMessage mandatory for CWindowImpl-derived classes. A secondary message processor must derive from CMessageMap so that it can be placed in the ATL_CHAIN_ENTRY structure managed by the primary message processor:

```
struct ATL_CHAIN_ENTRY {
  DWORD        m_dwChainID;
  CMessageMap* m_pObject;
```

```
    DWORD           m_dwMsgMapID;
};
```

A primary message processor that wants to chain messages dynamically derives from CDynamicChain, a base class that manages a dynamic array of ATL_CHAIN_ENTRY structures. CDynamicChain provides two important member functions. The first, SetChainEntry, is used to add an ATL_CHAIN_ENTRY structure to the list:

```
BOOL
CDynamicChain::SetChainEntry(DWORD dwChainID, CMessageMap* pObject,
  DWORD dwMsgMapID = 0);
```

The other important function, CallChain, is used by the CHAIN_MSG_MAP_DYNAMIC macro to chain messages to any interested parties:

```
BOOL
CDynamicChain::CallChain(DWORD dwChainID, HWND hWnd, UINT uMsg,
  WPARAM wParam, LPARAM lParam, LRESULT& lResult);
```

As an example of this technique, imagine an application built using a simplified Document/View architecture. The main window acts as the frame, holding the menu bar and two other objects, a document and a view. The view manages the client area of the main window and handles the painting of the data maintained by the document. The view is also responsible for handling view-related menu commands, such as Edit | Copy. The document is responsible for maintaining the current state as well as handling document-related menu commands, such as File | Save. To route command messages to the view, the main window uses an alternate message map, member function chaining (which we've already seen). However, to continue routing commands from the view to the document, after creating both the document and the view, the main window "hooks" them together using SetChainEntry. Any messages unhandled by the view automatically are routed to the document by the CHAIN_MSG_MAP_DYNAMIC entry in the view's message map. Finally, the document handles any messages it likes, leaving unhandled messages for DefWindowProc.

The main window creates the document and view, and hooks them together:

```
class CMainWindow :
  public CWindowImpl<CMainWindow, CWindow, CMainWinTraits> {
public:
BEGIN_MSG_MAP(CMainWindow)
  // Handle main window messages
```

```
   MESSAGE_HANDLER(WM_CREATE, OnCreate)
   ...
   // Route unhandled messages to the view
   CHAIN_MSG_MAP_ALT_MEMBER(m_view, 1)

   // Pick up messages the view hasn't handled
   COMMAND_ID_HANDLER(ID_HELP_ABOUT, OnHelpAbout)
END_MSG_MAP()

   CMainWindow() : m_doc(this), m_view(&m_doc) {
      // Hook up the document to receive messages from the view
      m_view.SetChainEntry(1, &m_doc, 1);
   }

private:
   // Create the view to handle the main window's client area
   LRESULT OnCreate(UINT, WPARAM, LPARAM, BOOL&)
   {
      return (m_view.Create(m_hWnd, CWindow::rcDefault) ? 0 : -1);
   }

   LRESULT OnHelpAbout(WORD, WORD, HWND, BOOL&);
   virtual void OnFinalMessage(HWND /*hwnd*/);
   ...
private:
   CDocument<CMainWindow>  m_doc;
   CView<CMainWindow>      m_view;
};
```

The view handles the messages it wants and chains the rest to the document:

```
template <typename TMainWindow>
class CView :
   public CWindowImpl<CView>,
   // Derive from CDynamicChain to support dynamic chaining
   public CDynamicChain {
public:
   CView(CDocument<TMainWindow>* pdoc) : m_pdoc(pdoc) {
      // Set the document-managed string
      m_pdoc->SetString(__T("ATL Doc/View"));
   }

BEGIN_MSG_MAP(CView)
   // Handle view messages
   MESSAGE_HANDLER(WM_PAINT, OnPaint)
```

```
ALT_MSG_MAP(1) // Handle messages from the main window
  CHAIN_MSG_MAP_DYNAMIC(1) // Route messages to the document
END_MSG_MAP()

private:
  LRESULT OnPaint(UINT, WPARAM, LPARAM, BOOL&);

private:
  // View caches its own document pointer
  CDocument<TMainWindow>* m_pdoc;
};
```

The document handles any messages it receives from the view:

```
template <typename TMainWindow>
class CDocument :
  // Derive from CMessageMap to receive dynamically
  // chained messages
  public CMessageMap {
public:
BEGIN_MSG_MAP(CDocument)

// Handle messages from the view and the main frame
ALT_MSG_MAP(1)
  COMMAND_ID_HANDLER(ID_FILE_NEW, OnFileNew)
  COMMAND_ID_HANDLER(ID_FILE_OPEN, OnFileOpen)
  COMMAND_ID_HANDLER(ID_FILE_SAVE, OnFileSave)
  COMMAND_ID_HANDLER(ID_FILE_SAVE_AS, OnFileSaveAs)
  COMMAND_ID_HANDLER(ID_FILE_EXIT, OnFileExit)
END_MSG_MAP()

  CDocument(TMainWindow* pwnd) : m_pwnd(pwnd) { *m_sz = 0; }

  void    SetString(LPCTSTR psz);
  LPCTSTR GetString();

// Message handlers
private:
  LRESULT OnFileNew(WORD, WORD, HWND, BOOL&);
  LRESULT OnFileOpen(WORD, WORD, HWND, BOOL&);
  LRESULT OnFileSave(WORD, WORD, HWND, BOOL&);
  LRESULT OnFileSaveAs(WORD, WORD, HWND, BOOL&);
  LRESULT OnFileExit(WORD, WORD, HWND, BOOL&);
```

```
private:
  TMainWindow* m_pwnd;
  TCHAR         m_sz[64];
};
```

Filtering Chained Messages

In many ways, ATL's `CMessageMap` is like MFC's `CCmdTarget`. However, MFC makes a distinction between command messages and noncommand messages. Although it's useful for the view and the document to participate in handling the main window's command messages, the rest—for example, WM_XXX—aren't nearly so useful. The view and the document manage to ignore the rest of the messages using alternate parts of their message maps, but still, it would be nice if every message weren't routed this way. Unfortunately, there's no built-in way to route only command messages using the message-chaining macros. However, a custom macro could do the trick:

```
#define CHAIN_COMMAND_DYNAMIC(dynaChainID) { \
  if ((uMsg == WM_COMMAND) && (HIWORD(wParam) == 0) && \
      CDynamicChain::CallChain(dynaChainID, hWnd, uMsg, \
        wParam, lParam, lResult)) \
  return TRUE; \
}
```

This macro would chain only WM_COMMAND messages with a code of 0—that is, menu commands, very much like MFC does. However, you'd still need corresponding equivalents for the nondynamic message-chaining macros.[5]

CDialogImpl

Dialogs represent a declarative style of user interface development. Whereas normal windows provide all kinds of flexibility (you can put anything you want in the client area of a window), dialogs are more static. Actually, dialogs are just windows whose layout has been predetermined. The built-in dialog box window class knows how to interpret dialog box resources to create and manage the child windows that make up a dialog box. To show a dialog box *modally*—that is, while the dialog

---

[5] This is left as an exercise to the very capable readers of this book.

is visible, the parent is inaccessible—Windows provides the `DialogBoxParam`[6] function:

```
int DialogBoxParam(
    HINSTANCE hInstance,      // handle to application instance
    LPCTSTR   lpTemplate,     // identifies dialog box template
    HWND      hWndParent,     // handle to owner window
    DLGPROC   lpDialogFunc,   // pointer to dialog box procedure
    LPARAM    dwInitParam);   // initialization value
```

The result of the `DialogBoxParam` function is the command that closed the dialog, such as `IDOK` or `IDCANCEL`. To show the dialog box *modelessly*—that is, the parent window is still accessible while the dialog is showing—the `CreateDialogParam`[7] function is used instead:

```
HWND CreateDialogParam(
    HINSTANCE hInstance,      // handle to application instance
    LPCTSTR   lpTemplate,     // identifies dialog box template
    HWND      hWndParent,     // handle to owner window
    DLGPROC   lpDialogFunc,   // pointer to dialog box procedure
    LPARAM    dwInitParam);   // initialization value
```

Notice that the parameters to `CreateDialogParam` are identical to those to `DialogBoxParam`, but the return value is different. The return value from `CreateDialogParam` represents the `HWND` of the new dialog box window, which will live until the dialog box window is destroyed.

Regardless of how a dialog is shown, however, developing a dialog is the same. First, you lay out a dialog resource using your favorite resource editor. Second, you develop a dialog box procedure (`DlgProc`). The `WndProc` of the dialog box class calls the `DlgProc` to give you an opportunity to handle each message (although you never have to call `DefWindowProc` in a `DlgProc`). Third, you call either `DialogBoxParam` or `CreateDialogParam` (or one of the variants) to show the dialog. This is the same kind of grunt work we had to do when we wanted to show a window (that is, register a window class, develop a `WndProc`, and create the window). And just as ATL lets us work with `CWindow`-derived objects instead of raw windows, ATL also lets us work with `CDialogImpl`-derived classes instead of raw dialogs.

---

[6] The `DialogBox` function is merely a wrapper around `DialogBoxParam`, passing 0 for the `dwInitParam` argument.

[7] Likewise, `CreateDialog` is a wrapper around the `CreateDialogParam` function.

Showing a Dialog

CDialogImpl provides a set of wrapper functions around common dialog operations (such as DialogBoxParam and CreateDialogParam):

```
template <class T, class TBase /* = CWindow */>
class ATL_NO_VTABLE CDialogImpl :
    public CDialogImplBaseT< TBase > {
public:
    // modal dialogs
    INT_PTR DoModal(HWND hWndParent = ::GetActiveWindow(),
        LPARAM dwInitParam = NULL) {
        BOOL result;

        result = m_thunk.Init(NULL,NULL);
        if (result == FALSE) {
            SetLastError(ERROR_OUTOFMEMORY);
            return -1;
        }

        _AtlWinModule.AddCreateWndData(&m_thunk.cd,
            (CDialogImplBaseT< TBase >*)this);

        return ::DialogBoxParam(
            _AtlBaseModule.GetResourceInstance(),
            MAKEINTRESOURCE(static_cast<T*>(this)->IDD),
            hWndParent, T::StartDialogProc, dwInitParam);
    }

    BOOL EndDialog(int nRetCode) {
        return ::EndDialog(m_hWnd, nRetCode);
    }

    // modeless dialogs
    HWND Create(HWND hWndParent, LPARAM dwInitParam = NULL) {
        BOOL result;

        result = m_thunk.Init(NULL,NULL);
        if (result == FALSE) {
            SetLastError(ERROR_OUTOFMEMORY);
            return NULL;
        }

        _AtlWinModule.AddCreateWndData(&m_thunk.cd,
```

```
                (CDialogImplBaseT< TBase >*)this);

        HWND hWnd = ::CreateDialogParam(_AtlBaseModule.
                    GetResourceInstance(),
            MAKEINTRESOURCE(static_cast<T*>(this)->IDD),
            hWndParent, T::StartDialogProc, dwInitParam);
        return hWnd;
    }

    // for CComControl
    HWND Create(HWND hWndParent, RECT&,
        LPARAM dwInitParam = NULL)
    {
        return Create(hWndParent, dwInitParam);
    }

    BOOL DestroyWindow()
    {
        return ::DestroyWindow(m_hWnd);
    }
};
```

A couple of interesting things are going on in this small class. First, notice the use of the thunk. ATL sets up a thunk between Windows and the ProcessWindowMessage member function of your CDialogImpl-based objects, just as it does for CWindowImpl-based objects. In addition to all the tricks that WindowProc performs (see the section "The Window Procedure," earlier in this chapter), the static member function CDialogImpl::DialogProc manages the weirdness of DWL_MSGRESULT. For some dialog messages, the DlgProc must return the result of the message. For others, the result is set by calling SetWindowLong with DWL_MSGRESULT. And although I can never remember which is which, ATL can. Our dialog message handlers need only return the value; if it needs to go into the DWL_MSGRESULT, ATL puts it there.

Something else interesting to notice is that CDialogImpl derives from CDialogImplBaseT, which provides some other helper functions:

```
template <class TBase>
class ATL_NO_VTABLE CDialogImplBaseT :
  public CWindowImplRoot<TBase> {
public:
  virtual WNDPROC GetDialogProc() { return DialogProc; }
  static LRESULT CALLBACK StartDialogProc(HWND, UINT,
    WPARAM, LPARAM);
  static LRESULT CALLBACK DialogProc(HWND, UINT, WPARAM, LPARAM);
  LRESULT DefWindowProc() { return 0; }
```

```
  BOOL MapDialogRect(LPRECT pRect) {
    return ::MapDialogRect(m_hWnd, pRect);
  }
  virtual void OnFinalMessage(HWND /*hWnd*/) {}
};
```

Again, notice the use of the StartDlgProc to bootstrap the thunk and the DialogProc function that actually does the mapping to the ProcessWindowMessage member function. Also notice the DefWindowProc member function. Remember, for DlgProcs, there's no need to pass an unhandled message to DefWindowProc. Because the message-handling infrastructure of ATL requires a DefWindowProc, the CDialogImplBaseT class provides an inline, do-nothing function that the compiler is free to toss away.

More useful to the dialog developer are the CDialogImplBaseT member functions MapDialogRect and OnFinalMessage. MapDialogRect is a wrapper around the Windows function MapDialogRect, which maps dialog-box units to pixels. Finally, OnFinalMessage is called after the last dialog message has been processed, just like the CWindowImpl::OnFinalMessage member function.

You might wonder how far the inheritance hierarchy goes for CDialogImpl. Refer again to Figure 10.1. Notice that CDialogImpl ultimately derives from CWindow, so all the wrappers and helpers that are available for windows are also available to dialogs.

Before we get too far away from CDialogImpl, notice where the dialog resource identifier comes from. The deriving class is required to provide a numeric symbol called IDD indicating the resource identifier. For example, assuming a resource ID of IDD_ABOUTBOX, a typical "about" box would be implemented like this:

```
class CAboutBox : public CDialogImpl<CAboutBox> {
public:
BEGIN_MSG_MAP(CAboutBox)
  MESSAGE_HANDLER(WM_INITDIALOG, OnInitDialog)
  COMMAND_ID_HANDLER(IDOK, OnOK);
END_MSG_MAP()

  enum { IDD = IDD_ABOUTBOX };

private:
  LRESULT OnInitDialog(UINT, WPARAM, LPARAM, BOOL&) {
    CenterWindow();
    return 1;
  }
```

```
    LRESULT OnOK(WORD, UINT, HWND, BOOL&) {
      EndDialog(IDOK);
      return 0;
    }
};
```

CAboutBox has all the elements. It derives from CDialogImpl, has a message map, and provides a value for IDD that indicates the resource ID. You can add an ATL dialog object from the Add Item option in Visual Studio, but it's not difficult to do by hand.

Using a CDialogImpl-derived class is a matter of creating an instance of the class and calling either DoModal or Create:

```
LRESULT CMainWindow::OnHelpAbout(WORD, WORD, HWND, BOOL&) {
  CAboutBox dlg;
  dlg.DoModal();
  return 0;
}
```

Simple Dialogs

For simple modal dialogs, such as "about" boxes, that don't have interaction requirements beyond the standard buttons (such as OK and Cancel), ATL provides CSimpleDialog:

```
template <WORD t_wDlgTemplateID, BOOL t_bCenter /* = TRUE */>
class CSimpleDialog : public CDialogImplBase {
public:
    INT_PTR DoModal(HWND hWndParent = ::GetActiveWindow()) {
        _AtlWinModule.AddCreateWndData(&m_thunk.cd,
            (CDialogImplBase*)this);

        INT_PTR nRet =
            ::DialogBox(_AtlBaseModule.GetResourceInstance(),
                MAKEINTRESOURCE(t_wDlgTemplateID), hWndParent,
                StartDialogProc);
        m_hWnd = NULL;
        return nRet;
    }

    typedef CSimpleDialog<t_wDlgTemplateID, t_bCenter> thisClass;
    BEGIN_MSG_MAP(thisClass)
        MESSAGE_HANDLER(WM_INITDIALOG, OnInitDialog)
```

```
        COMMAND_RANGE_HANDLER(IDOK, IDNO, OnCloseCmd)
    END_MSG_MAP()

    LRESULT OnInitDialog(UINT, WPARAM, LPARAM, BOOL&) {
        // initialize controls in dialog with
        // DLGINIT resource section
        ExecuteDlgInit(t_wDlgTemplateID);
        if(t_bCenter)
            CenterWindow(GetParent());
        return TRUE;
    }

    LRESULT OnCloseCmd(WORD, WORD wID, HWND, BOOL& ) {
        ::EndDialog(m_hWnd, wID);
        return 0;
    }
};
```

Notice that the resource ID is passed as a template parameter, as is a flag indicating whether the dialog should be centered. This reduces the definition of the CAboutBox class to the following type definition:

```
typedef CSimpleDialog<IDD_ABOUTBOX> CAboutBox;
```

However, the use of CAboutBox remains the same.

The call to ExecuteDlgInit in the OnInitDialog method is worth mentioning. When you build a dialog using the Visual Studio dialog editor and you add a combo box, the contents of that combo box are not stored in the regular Dialog resource. Instead, they're stored in a custom resource type named RT_DLGINIT. The normal dialog APIs completely ignore this initialization data. ExecuteDlgInit contains the code needed to read the RT_DLGINIT resource and properly initialize any combo boxes on the dialog.

Data Exchange and Validation

Unfortunately, most dialogs aren't simple. In fact, most are downright complicated. This complication is mostly due to two reasons: writing data to child controls managed by the dialog, and reading data from child controls managed by the dialog. Exchanging data with a modal dialog typically goes like this:

1. The application creates an instance of a CDialogImpl-derived class.

2. The application copies some data into the dialog object's data members.

3. The application calls DoModal.

4. The dialog handles WM_INITDIALOG by copying data members into child controls.

5. The dialog handles the OK button by validating that data held by child controls. If the data is not valid, the dialog complains to the users and makes them keep trying until either they get it right or they get frustrated and click the Cancel button.

6. If the data is valid, the data is copied back into the dialog's data members, and the dialog ends.

7. If the application gets IDOK from DoModal, it copies the data from the dialog data members over its own copy.

If the dialog is to be shown modelessly, the interaction between the application and the dialog is a little different, but the relationship between the dialog and its child controls is the same. A modeless dialog sequence goes like this (differences from the modal case are shown in italics):

1. The application creates an instance of a CDialogImpl-derived class.

2. The application copies some data into the dialog object's data members.

3. The applications calls *Create*.

4. The dialog handles WM_INITDIALOG by copying data members into child controls.

5. The dialog handles the *Apply* button by validating that data held by child controls. If the data is not valid, the dialog complains to the users and makes them keep trying until either they get it right or they get frustrated and click the Cancel button.

6. If the data is valid, the data is copied back into the dialog's data members and *the application is notified*[8] *to read the updated data from the dialog.*

7. *When the application is notified*, it copies the data from the dialog data members over its own copy.

Whether modal or modeless, the dialog's job is to exchange data between its data members and the child controls, and to validate it along the way. MFC has something called DDX/DDV (Dialog Data eXchange/Dialog Data Validation) for just this purpose. ATL has no such support, but it turns out to be quite easy to build yourself. For example, to beef up our standalone windows application sample, imagine a dialog that allows us to modify the display string, as shown in Figure 10.5.

---

[8] A custom window message sent to the dialog's parent is excellent for this duty.

Figure 10.5 A dialog that needs to manage data exchange and validation

The `CDialogImpl`-based class looks like this:

```
class CStringDlg : public CDialogImpl<CStringDlg> {
public:
  CStringDlg() { *m_sz = 0; }

BEGIN_MSG_MAP(CStringDlg)
  MESSAGE_HANDLER(WM_INITDIALOG, OnInitDialog)
  COMMAND_ID_HANDLER(IDOK, OnOK)
  COMMAND_ID_HANDLER(IDCANCEL, OnCancel)
END_MSG_MAP()

  enum { IDD = IDD_SET_STRING };
  TCHAR m_sz[64];

private:
  bool CheckValidString() {
    // Check the length of the string
    int cchString =
      ::GetWindowTextLength(GetDlgItem(IDC_STRING));
    return cchString ? true : false;
  }

  LRESULT OnInitDialog(UINT, WPARAM, LPARAM, BOOL&) {
    CenterWindow();

    // Copy the string from the data member
    // to the child control (DDX)
    SetDlgItemText(IDC_STRING, m_sz);

    return 1; // Let dialog manager set initial focus
  }

  LRESULT OnOK(WORD, UINT, HWND, BOOL&) {
    // Complain if the string is of zero length (DDV)
    if( !CheckValidString() ) {
      MessageBox("Please enter a string", "Hey!");
      return 0;
    }
```

```
    // Copy the string from the child control
    // to the data member (DDX)
    GetDlgItemText(IDC_STRING, m_sz, lengthof(m_sz));

    EndDialog(IDOK);
    return 0;
  }

  LRESULT OnCancel(WORD, UINT, HWND, BOOL&) {
    EndDialog(IDCANCEL);
    return 0;
  }
};
```

In this example, DDX-like functionality happens in OnInitDialog and OnOK. OnInitDialog copies the data from the data member into the child edit control. Likewise, OnOK copies the data from the child edit control back to the data member and ends the dialog if the data is valid. The validity of the data (DDV-like) is checked before the call to EndDialog in OnOK by calling the helper function Check-ValidString. I decided that a zero-length string would be too boring, so I made it invalid. In this case, OnOK puts up a message box and doesn't end the dialog. To be fair, MFC would have automated all this with a macro-based table, which makes handling a lot of DDX/DDV chores easier, but ATL certainly doesn't prohibit data exchange or validation. The WTL library mentioned earlier also has rich DDX/DDV support.

I can do even better in the data validation area with this example. This sample—and MFC-based DDX/DDV—validates only when the user presses the OK button, but sometimes it's handy to validate as the user enters the data. For example, by handling EN_CHANGE notifications from the edit control, I can check for a zero-length string as the user enters it. If the string ever gets to zero, disabling the OK button would make it impossible for the user to attempt to commit the data at all, making the complaint dialog unnecessary. The following updated sample shows this technique:

```
class CStringDlg : public CDialogImpl<CStringDlg> {
public:
  ...
BEGIN_MSG_MAP(CStringDlg)
  ...
  COMMAND_HANDLER(IDC_STRING, EN_CHANGE, OnStringChange)
END_MSG_MAP()
```

```
private:
  void CheckValidString() {
    // Check the length of the string
    int cchString =
      ::GetWindowTextLength(GetDlgItem(IDC_STRING));

    // Enable the OK button only if the string
    // is of non-zero length
    ::EnableWindow(GetDlgItem(IDOK), cchString ? TRUE : FALSE);
  }

  LRESULT OnInitDialog(UINT, WPARAM, LPARAM, BOOL&) {
    CenterWindow();

    // Copy the string from the data member
    // to the child control (DDX)
    SetDlgItemText(IDC_STRING, m_sz);

    // Check the string length (DDV)
    CheckValidString();

    return 1; // Let dialog manager set initial focus
  }

LRESULT OnOK(WORD, UINT, HWND, BOOL&) {
    // Copy the string from the child control to the data member (DDX)
    GetDlgItemText(IDC_STRING, m_sz, lengthof(m_sz));

    EndDialog(IDOK);
    return 0;
  }

  LRESULT OnStringChange(WORD, UINT, HWND, BOOL&) {
    // Check the string length each time it changes (DDV)
    CheckValidString();
    return 0;
  }

  ... // The rest is the same
};
```

In this case, notice that OnInitDialog takes on some DDV responsibilities and OnOK loses some. In OnInitDialog, if the string starts with a zero length, the OK button is immediately disabled. In the OnStringChange handler for EN_CHANGE, as the text in the edit control changes, we revalidate the data, enabling or disabling the OK button as necessary. Finally, we know that if we reach the OnOK handler, the OK button must be enabled and the DDV chores must already have been done. Neither ATL nor MFC can help us with this kind of DDV, but neither hinders us from providing a UI that handles both DDX and DDV in a friendly way.

Window Control Wrappers

Child Window Management

You might have noticed in the last two samples that whenever I needed to manipulate a child control—for example, when getting and setting the edit control's text, or enabling and disabling the OK button—I used a dialog item function. The ultimate base class of CDialogImpl, CWindow, provides a number of helper functions to manipulate child controls:

```
class CWindow {
public:
  ...
  // Dialog-Box Item Functions

  BOOL CheckDlgButton(int nIDButton, UINT nCheck);
  BOOL CheckRadioButton(int nIDFirstButton, int nIDLastButton,
                        int nIDCheckButton);

  int DlgDirList(LPTSTR lpPathSpec, int nIDListBox,
    int nIDStaticPath, UINT nFileType);
  int DlgDirListComboBox(LPTSTR lpPathSpec, int nIDComboBox,
    int nIDStaticPath, UINT nFileType);

  BOOL DlgDirSelect(LPTSTR lpString, int nCount,
    int nIDListBox);
  BOOL DlgDirSelectComboBox(LPTSTR lpString, int nCount,
    int nIDComboBox);

  UINT GetDlgItemInt(int nID, BOOL* lpTrans = NULL,
                     BOOL bSigned = TRUE) const;
  UINT GetDlgItemText(int nID, LPTSTR lpStr,
    int nMaxCount) const;
  BOOL GetDlgItemText(int nID, BSTR& bstrText) const;

  HWND GetNextDlgGroupItem(HWND hWndCtl,
    BOOL bPrevious = FALSE) const;
  HWND GetNextDlgTabItem(HWND hWndCtl,
    BOOL bPrevious = FALSE) const;

  UINT IsDlgButtonChecked(int nIDButton) const;
```

```
  LRESULT SendDlgItemMessage(int nID, UINT message,
    WPARAM wParam = 0, LPARAM lParam = 0);

  BOOL SetDlgItemInt(int nID, UINT nValue, BOOL bSigned = TRUE);
  BOOL SetDlgItemText(int nID, LPCTSTR lpszString);
};
```

ATL adds no overhead to these functions, but because they're just inline wrappers of Windows functions, you can feel that something's not quite as efficient as it could be when you use one of these functions. Every time we pass in a child control ID, the window probably does a lookup to figure out the HWND and then calls the actual function on the window. For example, if I ran the zoo, SetDlgItemText would be implemented like this:

```
BOOL SetDlgItemText(HWND hwndParent, int nID,
  LPCTSTR lpszString) {
  HWND hwndChild = GetDlgItem(hwndParent, nID);
  if( !hwndChild ) return FALSE;
  return SetWindowText(hwndChild, lpszString);
}
```

That implementation is fine for family, but when your friends come over, it's time to pull out the good dishes. I'd prefer to cache the HWND and use SetWindowText. Plus, if I want to refer to a dialog and or a main window with an HWND, why would I want to refer to my child windows with UINT? Instead, I find it convenient to wrap windows created by the dialog manager with CWindow objects in OnInitDialog:

```
LRESULT CStringDlg::OnInitDialog(UINT, WPARAM, LPARAM, BOOL&) {
  CenterWindow();

  // Cache HWNDs
  m_edit.Attach(GetDlgItem(IDC_STRING));
  m_ok.Attach(GetDlgItem(IDOK));

  // Copy the string from the data member
  // to the child control (DDX)
  m_edit.SetWindowText(m_sz);

  // Check the string length (DDV)
  CheckValidString();

  return 1; // Let dialog manager set initial focus
}
```

Now, the functions that used any of the dialog item family of functions can use CWindow member functions instead:

```
void CStringDlg::CheckValidString() {
  // Check the length of the string
  int cchString = m_edit.GetWindowTextLength();

  // Enable the OK button only if the string is
  // of non-zero length
  m_ok.EnableWindow(cchString ? TRUE : FALSE);
}

LRESULT CStringDlg::OnOK(WORD, UINT, HWND, BOOL&) {
  // Copy the string from the child control to
  // the data member (DDX)
  m_edit.GetWindowText(m_sz, lengthof(m_sz));

  EndDialog(IDOK);
  return 0;
}
```

A Better Class of Wrappers

Now, my examples have been purposefully simple. A dialog box with a single edit control is not much work, no matter how you build it. However, let's mix things up a little. What if we were to build a dialog with a single list box control instead, as shown in Figure 10.6?

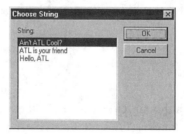

Figure 10.6 A dialog with a list box

This simple change makes the implementation more complicated. Instead of being able to use SetWindowText, as we could with an edit control, we must use special window messages to manipulate this list box control. For example, populating the list box and setting the initial selection involves the following code:

```
LRESULT
CStringListDlg::OnInitDialog(UINT, WPARAM, LPARAM, BOOL&) {
  CenterWindow();
```

```
// Cache list box HWND
m_lb.Attach(GetDlgItem(IDC_LIST));

// Populate the list box
m_lb.SendMessage(LB_ADDSTRING, 0,
  (LPARAM)__T("Hello, ATL"));
m_lb.SendMessage(LB_ADDSTRING, 0,
  (LPARAM)__T("Ain't ATL Cool?"));
m_lb.SendMessage(LB_ADDSTRING, 0,
  (LPARAM)__T("ATL is your friend"));

// Set initial selection
int n = m_lb.SendMessage(LB_FINDSTRING, 0, (LPARAM)m_sz);
if( n == LB_ERR ) n = 0;
m_lb.SendMessage(LB_SETCURSEL, n);

return 1; // Let dialog manager set initial focus
}
```

Likewise, pulling out the final selection in OnOK is just as much fun:

```
LRESULT CStringListDlg::OnOK(WORD, UINT, HWND, BOOL&) {
  // Copy the selected item
  int n = m_lb.SendMessage(LB_GETCURSEL);
  if( n == LB_ERR ) n = 0;
  m_lb.SendMessage(LB_GETTEXT, n, (LPARAM)(LPCTSTR)m_sz);

  EndDialog(IDOK);
  return 0;
}
```

The problem is that although CWindow provides countless wrapper functions that are common to all windows, it does not provide any wrappers for the built-in Windows controls (for example, list boxes). And although MFC provides such wrapper classes as CListBox, ATL doesn't. However, unofficially, buried deep in the atlcon[9] sample lives an undocumented and unsupported set of classes that fit the bill nicely. The atlcontrols.h file defines the following window control wrappers inside the ATLControls namespace:

---

[9] As of this writing, this sample is available online at http://msdn.microsoft.com/library/default.asp?url=/library/en-us/vcsample/html/_sample_atl_ATLCON.asp (http://tinysells.com/52).

CAnimateCtrl	CButton	CComboBox	CComboBoxEx
CDateTimePickerCtrl	CDragListBox	CEdit	CFlatScrollBar
CheaderCtrl	CHotKeyCtrl	CImageList	CIPAddressCtrl
ClistBox	CListViewCtrl	CMonthCalendarCtrl	CPagerCtrl
CProgressBarCtrl	CReBarCtrl	CRichEditCtrl	CScrollBar
CStatic	CStatusBarCtrl	CTabCtrl	CToolBarCtrl
CToolInfo	CToolTipCtrl	CTrackBarCtrl	CTreeItem
CTreeViewCtrl	CTreeViewCtrlEx	CupDownCtrl	

For example, the `CListBox` class provides a set of inline wrapper functions, one per `LB_XXX` message. The following shows the ones that would be useful for the sample:

```
template <class Base>
class CListBoxT : public Base {
public:
  ...
  // for single-selection listboxes
  int GetCurSel() const
  { return (int)::SendMessage(m_hWnd, LB_GETCURSEL, 0, 0L); }

  int SetCurSel(int nSelect)
  {
    return (int)::SendMessage(m_hWnd, LB_SETCURSEL, nSelect, 0L);
  }
  ...
  // Operations
  // manipulating listbox items
  int AddString(LPCTSTR lpszItem)
  { return (int)::SendMessage(m_hWnd, LB_ADDSTRING, 0, (LPARAM)lpszItem);
}
```

```
  ...
  // selection helpers
  int FindString(int nStartAfter, LPCTSTR lpszItem) const
  { return (int)::SendMessage(m_hWnd, LB_FINDSTRING, nStartAfter,
                         (LPARAM)lpszItem); }
  ...
};

typedef CListBoxT<CWindow>  CListBox;
```

Assuming a data member of type ATLControls::CListBox, the updated sample dialog code now looks much more pleasing:

```
LRESULT
CStringListDlg::OnInitDialog(UINT, WPARAM, LPARAM, BOOL&) {
    CenterWindow();

    // Cache listbox HWND
    m_lb.Attach(GetDlgItem(IDC_LIST));

    // Populate the listbox
    m_lb.AddString(__T("Hello, ATL"));
    m_lb.AddString(__T("Ain't ATL Cool?"));
    m_lb.AddString(__T("ATL is your friend"));

    // Set initial selection
    int n = m_lb.FindString(0, m_sz);
    if( n == LB_ERR ) n = 0;
    m_lb.SetCurSel(n);

    return 1; // Let dialog manager set initial focus
}

LRESULT CStringListDlg::OnOK(WORD, UINT, HWND, BOOL&) {
    // Copy the selected item
    int n = m_lb.GetCurSel();
    if( n == LB_ERR ) n = 0;
    m_lb.GetText(n, m_sz);

    EndDialog(IDOK);
    return 0;
}
```

Because the window control wrappers are merely a collection of inline functions that call SendMessage for you, the generated code is the same. The good news, of course, is that you don't have to pack the messages yourself.

The ATLCON sample itself hasn't been updated since 2001, but the atlcontrols.h header still works just fine. Unfortunately, a lot of new and updated common controls have been released since then, and, of course, the header doesn't reflect these updates. If you need updated control wrappers or want support for more sophisticated UI functions, check out the Windows Template Library (WTL).[10]

---

[10] Available at http://wtl.sourceforge.net.

WTL is a library that is written on top of and in the same style as ATL, but it provides much of the functionality that MFC does: message routing, idle time processing, convenient control wrappers, DDX/DDV support, and more.

CContainedWindow

The Parent Handling the Messages of the Child

A CWindow-based object lets an existing window class handle its messages. This is useful for wrapping child windows. A CWindowImpl-based object handles its own messages via a message map. This is handy for creating parent windows. Often, you want to let a parent window handle messages for a child window. Objects of another ATL window class, CContainedWindow, let the parent window handle the messages and let an existing window class handle the messages the parent doesn't. This centralizes message handling in a parent window. The parent window can either create an instance of the child window class or let someone else (such as the dialog manager) create it and then subclass it later (I discuss subclassing soon). Either way, the messages of the child window are routed through the message map of the parent window. How does the parent window discern its own messages from those of one or more children? You guessed it: alternate message maps. Each CContainedWindow gets a message map ID, and its messages are routed to that alternate part of the parent's message map.

To support the creation of both contained and subclassed windows, CContainedWindow is defined like this:

```
template <class TBase, class TWinTraits>
class CContainedWindowT : public Tbase {
public:
  CWndProcThunk m_thunk;
  LPCTSTR m_lpszClassName;
  WNDPROC m_pfnSuperWindowProc;
  CMessageMap* m_pObject;
  DWORD m_dwMsgMapID;
  const _ATL_MSG* m_pCurrentMsg;

  // If you use this constructor you must supply
  // the Window Class Name, Object* and Message Map ID
  // Later to the Create call
  CContainedWindowT();

  CContainedWindowT(LPTSTR lpszClassName, CMessageMap* pObject,
    DWORD dwMsgMapID = 0);
```

```
CContainedWindowT(CMessageMap* pObject, DWORD dwMsgMapID = 0);

void SwitchMessageMap(DWORD dwMsgMapID);

const _ATL_MSG* GetCurrentMessage() const;

LRESULT DefWindowProc();
LRESULT DefWindowProc(UINT uMsg, WPARAM wParam, LPARAM lParam);

static LRESULT CALLBACK
StartWindowProc(HWND hWnd, UINT uMsg,
  WPARAM wParam, LPARAM lParam);

static LRESULT CALLBACK
WindowProc(HWND hWnd, UINT uMsg,
  WPARAM wParam, LPARAM lParam);

ATOM RegisterWndSuperclass();

HWND Create(HWND hWndParent, _U_RECT rect,
  LPCTSTR szWindowName = NULL,
  DWORD dwStyle = 0, DWORD dwExStyle = 0,
  _U_MENUorID MenuOrID = 0U, LPVOID lpCreateParam = NULL);

HWND Create(CMessageMap* pObject, DWORD dwMsgMapID,
  HWND hWndParent,
  _U_RECT rect, LPCTSTR szWindowName = NULL,
  DWORD dwStyle = 0, DWORD dwExStyle = 0,
  _U_MENUorID MenuOrID = 0U, LPVOID lpCreateParam = NULL);

HWND Create(LPCTSTR lpszClassName, CMessageMap* pObject,
  DWORD dwMsgMapID, HWND hWndParent, _U_RECT rect,
  LPCTSTR szWindowName = NULL,
  DWORD dwStyle = 0, DWORD dwExStyle = 0,
  _U_MENUorID MenuOrID = 0U, LPVOID lpCreateParam = NULL);

BOOL SubclassWindow(HWND hWnd);

// Use only if you want to subclass before window
// is destroyed, WindowProc will automatically subclass
// when window goes away
HWND UnsubclassWindow(BOOL bForce = FALSE);

LRESULT ReflectNotifications(UINT uMsg, WPARAM wParam,
```

```
      LPARAM lParam, BOOL& bHandled);
};

typedef CContainedWindowT<CWindow> CContainedWindow;
```

Notice that CContainedWindow does not derive from CWindowImpl, nor does it derive from CMessageMap. CContainedWindow objects do not have their own message map. Instead, the WindowProc static member function of CContainedWindow routes messages to the parent window. The specific message map ID is provided either to the constructor or to the Create function.

Creating Contained Windows

Notice also the various constructors and Create functions: Some take the name of the window class, and some do not. If you want a parent window to handle a child window's messages, you have quite a bit of flexibility. For example, to morph the letter box example to create an edit control that accepts only letters, CContained-Window would be used like this:

```
class CMainWindow :
  public CWindowImpl<CMainWindow, CWindow, CMainWindowTraits> {
public:
...
BEGIN_MSG_MAP(CMainWindow)
  ...
// Handle the child edit control's messages
ALT_MSG_MAP(1)
  MESSAGE_HANDLER(WM_CHAR, OnEditChar)
END_MSG_MAP()

  LRESULT OnCreate(UINT, WPARAM, LPARAM, BOOL&) {
    // Create the contained window, routing its messages to us
    if( m_edit.Create("edit", this, 1, m_hWnd,
      &CWindow::rcDefault) ) {
      return 0;
    }
    return -1;
  }

  // Let the child edit control receive only letters
  LRESULT OnEditChar(UINT, WPARAM wparam, LPARAM,
    BOOL& bHandled) {
    if( isalpha((TCHAR)wparam) ) bHandled = FALSE;
```

```
    else                        MessageBeep(0xFFFFFFFF);
    return 0;
  }
...
private:
  CContainedWindow  m_edit;
};
```

When the main window is created, this code associates an HWND with the CContainedWindow object m_edit by creating a new edit control, identified because of the window class passed as the first parameter to Create. The second parameter is a CMessageMap pointer for where the contained windows messages will be routed. This parameter is most often the parent window, but it doesn't have to be.

To separate the parent's messages from the child's, the parent's message map is divided into two parts, the main part and one alternate part. The ID of the alternate part of the message map is passed as the third parameter to Create.

Finally, to filter all characters but the letters sent to the contained edit control, the WM_CHAR handler passes through only the WM_CHAR messages that contain letters. By setting bHandled to FALSE, the parent window indicates to the CContainedWindow WndProc that it should keep looking for a handler for this message. Eventually, after the message map has been exhausted (including any chaining that might be going on), the WindowProc passes the message onto the edit control's normal WndProc. For nonletters, the WM_CHAR handler leaves bHandled set to TRUE (the default), which stops the message from going anywhere else and stops the child edit control from seeing any WM_CHAR messages without letters in them. As far as the child edit control is concerned, the user entered only letters.

Subclassing Contained Windows

CContainedWindow, as previously described, works well if you are the one to call Create. However, in several important scenarios, you want to hook the message processing of a window that has already been created—for example, if the dialog manager has already created an edit control. In this case, to get hold of the window's messages, you must *subclass*[11] it. Previously in this chapter, I described superclassing as the Windows version of inheritance for window classes. Subclassing is a more modest and frequently used technique. Instead of creating a whole new window class, with subclassing, we merely hijack the messages of a single window. Subclassing is accomplished by creating a window of a certain class and

---

[11] For a more complete dissection of Windows subclassing, see *Win32 Programming* (Addison-Wesley, 1997), by Brent Rector and Joe Newcomer.

replacing its WndProc with our own using SetWindowLong(GWL_WNDPROC). The replacement WndProc gets all the messages first and can decide whether to let the original WndProc handle it as well. If you think of superclassing as specialization of a class, subclassing is specialization of a single instance. Subclassing is usually performed on child windows, such as an edit box that the dialog wants to restrict to letters only. The dialog would subclass the child edit control during WM_INITDIALOG and handle WM_CHAR messages, throwing out any that weren't suitable.

For example, subclassing an edit control in a dialog would look like this:

```
class CLettersDlg : public CDialogImpl<CLettersDlg> {
public:
  // Set the CMessageMap* and the message map id
  CLettersDlg() : m_edit(this, 1) {}

BEGIN_MSG_MAP(CLettersDlg)
  ...
ALT_MSG_MAP(1)
  MESSAGE_HANDLER(WM_CHAR, OnEditChar)
END_MSG_MAP()

  enum { IDD = IDD_LETTERS_ONLY };

  LRESULT OnInitDialog(UINT, WPARAM, LPARAM, BOOL&) {
    // Subclass the existing child edit control
    m_edit.SubclassWindow(GetDlgItem(IDC_EDIT));

    return 1; // Let the dialog manager set the initial focus
  }
  ...
private:
  CContainedWindow  m_edit;
};
```

In this case, because the sample doesn't call Create, it has to pass the CMessageMap pointer and the message map ID of the child edit control in the constructor using the member initialization list syntax. When the contained window knows who to route the messages to and which part of the message map to route to, it needs to know only the HWND of the window to subclass. It gets this in the SubclassWindow call in the WM_INITDIALOG handler. The CContainedWindow implementation of SubclassWindow shows how subclassing is performed:

```
template <class TBase, class TWinTraits>
BOOL CContainedWindowT<TBase, TWinTraits>::SubclassWindow(
    HWND hWnd) {
```

```
    BOOL result;

    result = m_thunk.Init(WindowProc, this);
    if (result == FALSE) {
        return result;
    }


    WNDPROC pProc = m_thunk.GetWNDPROC();
    WNDPROC pfnWndProc = (WNDPROC)::SetWindowLongPtr(hWnd,
        GWLP_WNDPROC, (LONG_PTR)pProc);
    if(pfnWndProc == NULL)
        return FALSE;
    m_pfnSuperWindowProc = pfnWndProc;
    m_hWnd = hWnd;
    return TRUE;
}
```

The important part is the call to SetWindowLong passing GWL_WNDPROC. This replaces the current window object's WndProc with an ATL thunking version that routes messages to the container. It also returns the existing WndProc, which CContainedWindow caches to call for any messages that the container doesn't handle.

Containing the Window Control Wrappers

After being introduced to the ATL Windows control wrapper classes, such as CEdit and CListBox, you might dread window containment. If CContainedWindow derives from CWindow, where do all the nifty inline wrappers functions come from? Never fear, ATL is here. As you've already seen, CContainedWindow is really just a type definition for the CContainedWindowT template class. One of the parameters is a windows traits class, which doesn't help you. The other, however, is the name of the base class. CContainedWindow uses CWindow as the base for CContaintedWindowT, but there's no reason you have to. By using one of the ATL Windows control wrapper classes instead, you can have a contained window that also has all the wrapper functions. For example, we can change the type of the m_edit variable like this:

```
CContainedWindowT<ATLControls::CEdit> m_edit;
```

This technique is especially handy when you're using Create instead of SubclassWindow. With Create, you have to provide the name of the window class. If you call Create without a window class, the CContainedWindow object attempts to acquire a window class by calling the base class function GetWndClassName, which CWindow implements like this:

```
static LPCTSTR CWindow::GetWndClassName()
{ return NULL; }
```

However, each of the ATL window control wrappers overrides this function to provide its window class name:

```
static LPCTSTR CEditT::GetWndClassName()
{ return _T("EDIT"); }
```

Now, when creating an instance of one of the contained window wrapper classes, you don't have to dig through the documentation to figure out the class name of your favorite intrinsic window class; you can simply call `Create`:

```
class CMainWindow : public CWindowImpl<...> {
...
  LRESULT OnCreate(UINT, WPARAM, LPARAM, BOOL&) {
    // Window class name provided by base class
    if( m_edit.Create(this, 1, m_hWnd, &CWindow::rcDefault) ) {
      // Now we can use methods of CEditT
      m_edit.InsertText( 0, _T("Here's some text") );
      return 0;
    }
    return -1;
  }
...
private:
  CContainedWindowT<ATLControls::CEdit> m_edit;
};
```

Summary

ATL applies the same principles of efficiency and flexibility that were originally developed for COM to another part of the Windows API: User32. This support takes the form of a small set of windowing classes. `CWindow`, which forms the root class of the windowing hierarchy, provides a large number of inline wrapper functions for manipulating an existing `HWND`. To create a new window class, or to superclass an existing one and handle messages from windows of that class, ATL provides `CWindowImpl`. `CDialogImpl` provides the same functionality for dialog boxes, both modal and modeless. To subclass child windows and manage messages in the parent, ATL provides `CContainedWindow`. These classes can be used in standalone applications or in COM servers. For COM servers that expose COM controls, the windowing classes form the core of how input and output are managed, as discussed in the following chapter.

ActiveX Controls

A Review of ActiveX Controls

A complete review of the COM interfaces and interactions between an ActiveX control and a control container is outside the scope of this book. If you are unfamiliar with the various interfaces and interactions described in this chapter, various other texts specifically address these topics. *Inside OLE* (Microsoft Press, 1995), by Kraig Brockschmidt, is the original COM text; it devotes hundreds of pages to in-place activation and visual interface components.

An ActiveX control is a superset of an in-place activated object, so you also need to read the *OLE Controls Specification* from Microsoft, which describes the requirements to be a control. In addition, the *OLE Controls 1996 Specification*, commonly referred to as the OC96 spec, documents optimizations for control activations (such as windowless controls and windowless control containment), two-pass rendering for nonrectangular windows, hit testing for nonrectangular windows, fast-activation protocols between controls and containers, and numerous other features.

Instead of rewording the material available in these references, I show you how to implement such an object. This chapter describes how to implement a feature-complete ActiveX control using ATL.

ActiveX Control Functionality

A control incorporates much of the functionality you saw in earlier chapters. For example, a control is a COM object. Therefore, an ATL control contains all the standard functionality of an ATL-based COM object. A control is a user-interface (UI) component; therefore, it has thread affinity and should live in a single-threaded apartment. A control thus derives from the `CComObjectRootEx<CComSingleThread-Model>` base class.

A control must be a createable class so its container can instantiate it. Therefore, the control class also derives from `CComCoClass`. Many controls use the `CCom-CoClass` default class object's implementation of the `IClassFactory` interface. Licensed controls override this default by specifying the `DECLARE_CLASSFACTORY2` macro, which declares a class object that implements the `IClassFactory2` interface.

In addition, most controls support one or more of the following features:

- Stock properties and methods such as `ForeColor` and `Refresh` that a container can access via the control's `IDispatch` implementation.

- Custom properties and methods that a container can access via the control's `IDispatch` implementation.

- Stock and custom event callback methods using the connection points protocol to a container's `dispinterface` implementation. This requires the control to implement the `IConnectionPointContainer` and `IProvideClassInfo2` interfaces, as well as a connection point that makes calls to the event `dispinterface`.

- Property change notifications to one or more clients using the connection points protocol to the clients' `IPropertyNotifySink` interface implementations. Control properties that send such change notifications should be marked in the control's type library using the `bindable` or `requestedit` attributes, as appropriate.

- On-demand rendering of a view of the object via the `IViewObject`, `IViewObject2`, and `IViewObjectEx` interfaces.

- Standard OLE control functionality, as provided by the `IOleControl` interface, and in-place activation using the `IOleObject` and `IOleInPlaceActiveObject` interfaces.

- Persistence support for various containers. At a minimum, a control typically provides support so that a container can save the object into a stream using the `IPersistStreamInit` interface. Many controls also support persistence to a property bag using `IPersistPropertyBag` because Visual Basic and Internet Explorer prefer this medium. Some controls additionally support `IPersistStorage` so that they can be embedded into OLE documents.

- Fast and efficient windowless activation, as provided by the `IOleInPlaceObjectWindowless` interface when the control's container supports this optimization.

- Fast and efficient exchange of multiple interfaces during activation between a control and its controls using the `IQuickActivate` interface.

- Object safety settings either through component category membership or via `IObjectSafety`.

- Drag-and-drop support, as provided by implementations of the `IDataObject`, `IDropSource`, and `IDropTarget` interfaces.

- A graphical user interface that provides a means to edit the control's properties. Typically, a control provides one or more COM objects, called *property pages*, each of which displays a user interface that can modify a logically related subset of the control's properties. A container requests the CLSIDs of the property page COM objects using the control's `ISpecifyPropertyPages` interface implementation.

- A container's capability to access information about the properties of a control that supports property pages by using the `IPerPropertyBrowsing` interface. For example, the container can obtain a text string describing a property, determine which property page contains the user interface to edit the property, and retrieve a list of strings describing the allowed values for the property.

- Support for arranging the control's properties by category in Visual Basic's property view. A control implements the `ICategorizeProperties` interface to provide the list of categories to Visual Basic and to map each property to a category.

- Default keyboard handling for an ActiveX control. This is commonly needed for tabbing, default button presses on Enter, arrow keys, and pop-up help.

- `MiscStatus` flags settings for a control. Special settings are necessary for some controls to operate properly.

Property Page Functionality

Because a control frequently provides one or more property pages, a complete control implementation also supplies one or more property page objects, which do the following:

- Implement (at least) the `IPropertyPage` interface, which provides the main features of a property page object.

- Optionally implement the `IPropertyPage2` interface to support selection of a specific property. Visual Basic uses this support to open the correct property page and set the input focus directly to the specified control when the user wants to edit a property.

- Receive property change notifications from one or more controls using the connection points protocol to the property page's `IPropertyNotifySink` interface implementation.

The BullsEye Control Requirements

 This chapter describes the ATL implementation of a feature-rich control called `BullsEye`. The `BullsEye` control implements all the previously described features. The `BullsEye` control draws a bull's eye. You can configure the number of rings in the bull's eye (from one to nine) and the color of the center ring, as well as the color of the ring adjacent to the center (called the alternate ring color). `BullsEye` draws additional rings by alternately using the center and alternate colors.

The area around the bull's eye can be transparent or opaque. When transparent, the background around the bull's eye shows through. When opaque, the bull's eye fills the area around the circle using the background color. By default, `BullsEye`

uses the container's ambient background color as the background color. BullsEye also uses the foreground color to draw a line separating each ring

You can assign score values to each ring. By default, the center ring is worth 512 points and each other ring is worth half the points of its adjacent inner ring. When a user clicks on a ring, the control fires an OnRingHit event and an OnScoreChanged event. The argument to the OnRingHit event method specifies the ring upon which the user clicked. Rings are numbered from 1 to N, where 1 is the centermost ring. The OnScoreChanged event specifies the point value of the clicked ring. For example, clicking on ring 2 with default scores fires an OnScoreChanged event with an argument of 256 points.

In addition, when you click on one of the bull's-eye rings, the control can provide feedback by playing a sound. By default, you hear the sound of an arrow striking the bull's eye. The Boolean Beep property, when set to TRUE, indicates that the control should play its sound on a ring hit.

BullsEye supports all standard control functionality. In addition to windowed activation, BullsEye can be activated as a windowless control when its container supports such functionality.

Many containers ask their controls to save their state using the IPersist-StreamInit interface and an IStream medium. When embedding a control in an OLE document, a container asks a control to save its state using the IPersistStorage interface and the IStorage medium. A container, such as Internet Explorer and Visual Basic, that prefers to save the state of a control as textual name/value pairs uses the control's IPersistPropertyBag interface and the IPropertyBag medium. BullsEye supports all three persistence protocols and media—streams, storages, and property bags.

BullsEye also provides two property pages. One property page is custom to the BullsEye control and enables you to set the Enabled, Beep (sound on ring hit), and BackStyle (transparent) properties (see Figure 11.1).

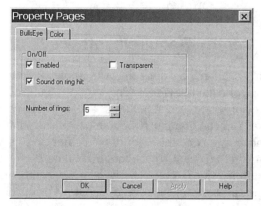

Figure 11.1 BullsEye custom property page

The other property page is the standard color-selection property page (see Figure 11.2). The BullsEye control has four color properties: the center ring color, the alternate ring color, the background color (used to fill the area around the bull's eye) and the foreground color (used to draw the separator line between rings).

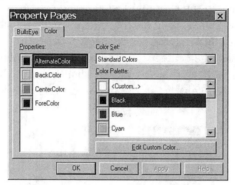

Figure 11.2 BullsEye color property page

The BullsEye control also categorizes its properties for Visual Basic 6. VB6 has a property-view window in which you can select a view that sorts the properties by standard and control-defined categories (see Figure 11.3).

Figure 11.3 Visual Basic 6 property view window for BullsEye

The BullsEye control lists its color properties and the RingCount property in the standard Appearance category. The control lists its Beep property in the standard Behavior category.

BullsEye also supports *per-property browsing*, which allows a control to specify a list of strings that a container should display as the available choices for a property's value. Notice in the example Visual Basic property view window that, in the Behavior category, Visual Basic displays the strings "Yes, make noise" and "No, be mute" as the selections available for the Beep property.

Also notice that the Misc category contains an entry called (About) that represents the AboutBox stock method. BullsEye displays the dialog box shown in Figure 11.4 when the user selects the About entry.

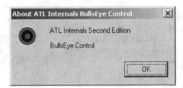

Figure 11.4   BullsEye About box

Requirements: The Properties and Methods

BullsEye supports the four stock properties shown in Table 11.1.

Table 11.1.   BullsEye Stock Properties

Property Name	Type	Stock DISPID	Description
BackColor	OLE_COLOR	DISPID_BACKCOLOR	Background color
BackStyle	Long	DISPID_BACKSTYLE	Background style, transparent or opaque
Enabled	VARIANT_BOOL	DISPID_ENABLED	Enabled status, TRUE or FALSE
ForeColor	OLE_COLOR	DISPID_FORECOLOR	Foreground color

In addition, BullsEye supports all three stock methods, as shown in Table 11.2.

Table 11.2.   BullsEye Stock Methods

Method Name	Stock DISPID	Description
AboutBox	DISPID_ABOUTBOX	Displays the control's Help About dialog box
DoClick	DISPID_DOCLICK	Simulates a mouse click on the control
Refresh	DISPID_REFRESH	Redraws the control

Finally, `BullsEye` supports the custom properties listed in Table 11.3.

Table 11.3. `BullsEye` Custom Properties

Property Name	Type	Custom DISPID	Description
Application	IDispatch*	DISPID_APPLICATION	Returns the IDispatch* for the hosting application
AlternateColor	OLE_COLOR	DISPID_ALTERNATECOLOR	Gets/sets the color of the alternate (even) rings
Beep	VARIANT_BOOL	DISPID_BEEP	Enables/disables sound effects for the control
CenterColor	OLE_COLOR	DISPID_CENTERCOLOR	Gets/sets the color of the center (odd) rings
Parent	IDispatch*	DISPID_PARENT	Returns the IDispatch* for the control's parent
RingCount	Short	DISPID_RINGCOUNT	Gets/sets the number of rings
RingValue	Long	DISPID_RINGVALUE	Gets/sets the value of each ring

Declaring the Properties and Methods in IDL

A control container accesses the properties and methods of a control using the control's `IDispatch` interface. A control must therefore provide an implementation of `IDispatch` when it has properties and methods.

ATL-based controls in general—and the `BullsEye` control, specifically—implement their properties and methods using a dual interface, not a dispatch interface, even though a dual interface is unnecessary because the `vtable` portion of the dual interface typically goes unused. A custom C++ control container can access the control's properties and methods using the `vtable`, but no other container currently does. Visual Basic 6 accesses properties and methods of a control using the control's `IDispatch` interface. Visual Basic uses the `vtable` portion of a dual interface only for noncontrol objects.

The `BullsEye` control provides access to its properties and methods on the default `IBullsEye` dual interface. When you generate a new ATL-based control class, the wizard generates the definition of the default dual interface, but you must populate the definition with the accessor methods for your control's properties and the control's methods. Listing 11.1 gives the definition of the IBullsEye interface.

Listing 11.1   The IBullsEye Interface

```
[ object,
  uuid(B4FBD008-B03D-4F48-9C5B-4A981EB6A515),
  dual, nonextensible, helpstring("IBullsEye Interface"),
  pointer_default(unique)
]
interface IBullsEye : IDispatch {
    const int DISPID_ALTERNATECOLOR = 1;
    const int DISPID_BEEP = 2;
    const int DISPID_CENTERCOLOR = 3;
    const int DISPID_RINGCOUNT = 4;
    const int DISPID_RINGVALUE = 5;
    const int DISPID_APPLICATION = 6;
    const int DISPID_PARENT = 7;

    // Stock Properties
    [propput, bindable, requestedit, id(DISPID_BACKCOLOR)]
    HRESULT BackColor([in]OLE_COLOR clr);
    [propget, bindable, requestedit, id(DISPID_BACKCOLOR)]
    HRESULT BackColor([out,retval]OLE_COLOR* pclr);
    [propput, bindable, requestedit, id(DISPID_BACKSTYLE)]
    HRESULT BackStyle([in]long style);
    [propget, bindable, requestedit, id(DISPID_BACKSTYLE)]
    HRESULT BackStyle([out,retval]long* pstyle);
    [propput, bindable, requestedit, id(DISPID_FORECOLOR)]
    HRESULT ForeColor([in]OLE_COLOR clr);
    [propget, bindable, requestedit, id(DISPID_FORECOLOR)]
    HRESULT ForeColor([out,retval]OLE_COLOR* pclr);
    [propput, bindable, requestedit, id(DISPID_ENABLED)]
    HRESULT Enabled([in]VARIANT_BOOL vbool);
    [propget, bindable, requestedit, id(DISPID_ENABLED)]
    HRESULT Enabled([out,retval]VARIANT_BOOL* pbool);

// Stock methods
    [id(DISPID_ABOUTBOX)] HRESULT AboutBox( );
    [id(DISPID_DOCLICK)] HRESULT DoClick( );
    [id(DISPID_REFRESH)] HRESULT Refresh( );
```

```
    // Custom properties
    [propget, bindable, requestedit, id(DISPID_APPLICATION)]
    HRESULT Application([out, retval] IDispatch** pVal);

    [propget, bindable, requestedit, id(DISPID_ALTERNATECOLOR)]
    HRESULT AlternateColor([out, retval] OLE_COLOR* pVal);
    [propput, bindable, requestedit, id(DISPID_ALTERNATECOLOR)]
    HRESULT AlternateColor([in] OLE_COLOR newVal);

    [propget, bindable, requestedit, id(DISPID_BEEP)]
    HRESULT Beep([out, retval] VARIANT_BOOL* pVal);
    [propput, bindable, requestedit, id(DISPID_BEEP)]
    HRESULT Beep([in] VARIANT_BOOL newVal);

    [propget, bindable, requestedit, id(DISPID_CENTERCOLOR)]
    HRESULT CenterColor([out, retval] OLE_COLOR* pVal);
    [propput, bindable, requestedit, id(DISPID_CENTERCOLOR)]
    HRESULT CenterColor([in] OLE_COLOR newVal);

    [propget, bindable, requestedit, id(DISPID_PARENT)]
    HRESULT Parent([out, retval] IDispatch** pVal);

    [propget, bindable, requestedit, id(DISPID_RINGCOUNT)]
    HRESULT RingCount([out, retval] SHORT* pVal);
    [propput, bindable, requestedit, id(DISPID_RINGCOUNT)]
    HRESULT RingCount([in] SHORT newVal);

    [propget, bindable, requestedit, id(DISPID_RINGVALUE)]
    HRESULT RingValue([in] SHORT sRingNumber,
        [out, retval] LONG* pVal);
    [propput, bindable, requestedit, id(DISPID_RINGVALUE)]
    HRESULT RingValue([in] SHORT sRingNumber, [in] LONG newVal);
};
```

Requirements: The Events

BullsEye Custom Events

The BullsEye control doesn't support any of the stock events. However, it has two custom events, as detailed in Table 11.4.

Table 11.4.   BullsEye Custom Events

Event	Event DISPID	Description
void OnRingHit (short sRingNumber)	DISPID_ONRINGHIT	The user clicked on one of the bull's-eye rings. The argument specifies the ring that the user clicked. Rings are numbers from 1 to *N* from the center outward.
void OnScoreChanged (long RingValue)	DISPID_ONSCORECHANGED	This event follows the OnRingHit event when the user clicks on a bull's-eye ring. The argument specifies the score value of the ring that the user clicked.

An event interface contains only methods and should be a dispatch interface for all containers to receive the event callbacks. Some containers, such as Visual Basic, can receive event callbacks on custom IUnknown-derived interfaces. An event interface should never be a dual interface.

Declaring the Event Dispatch Interface in IDL

Listing 11.2 gives the definition of the _IBullsEyeEvents dispatch interface. For the constants for the DISPIDs to appear in the MIDL-generated C/C++ header file, the definitions of the constants must appear in the IDL file outside of the library block. You must define the dispinterface itself inside the library block.

Listing 11.2   The _IBullsEyeEvents Dispatch Interface

```
const int DISPID_ONRINGHIT     = 1;
const int DISPID_ONSCORECHANGED = 2;

[ uuid(58D6D8CB-765D-4C59-A41F-BBA8C40F7A14),
  helpstring("Event interface for BullsEye Control")
]
dispinterface _IBullsEyeEvents {
    properties:
    methods:
    [id(DISPID_ONRINGHIT)]
    void OnRingHit(short ringNumber);
    [id(DISPID_ONSCORECHANGED)]
    void OnScoreChanged(long ringValue);
};
```

Requirements: The BullsEye and Property Page Coclasses

You must also define the `BullsEye` coclass in the library block of the IDL file (see Listing 11.3). At a minimum, you must specify the default `IDispatch` interface (`IBullsEye`) via which a container can access the control's properties and methods, and the default source interface (`_IBullsEyeEvents`) through which the `BullsEye` control fires events to its container.

Listing 11.3   The `BullsEye` Coclass

```
[    uuid(E9312AF5-1C11-4BA4-A0C6-CB660E949B78),
     control, helpstring("BullsEye Class")
]
coclass BullsEye {
    [default] interface IBullsEye;
    [default, source] dispinterface _IBullsEyeEvents;
};
```

Additionally, you should define all the custom property page classes implemented by your control in the library block of the IDL file. `BullsEye` has only one custom property page, called `BullsEyePropPage` (see Listing 11.4).

Listing 11.4   The `BullsEyePropPage` Coclass

```
[    uuid(47446235-8500-43a2-92A7-F0686FDAA69C),
     helpstring("BullsEye Property Page class")
]
coclass BullsEyePropPage {
    interface IUnknown;
};
```

Creating the Initial Control Using the ATL Wizard

Some people prefer to write all the code for a control by hand. They don't care for the wizard-generated code because they don't understand what it does. Occasionally, the wizard-generated code is incorrect as well. Even if you generate the initial code base using the wizard, you will change it greatly before the control is complete anyway, so you might as well save some time and effort initially by using the wizard.

Selecting Options for the CBullsEye Implementation Class

Using the requirements for the BullsEye control, I created an ATL project and used the Add Class dialog box to add an ATL control. First, I defined the name of my implementation class, (CBullsEye), its source filenames, the primary interface name (IBullsEye), and various COM object registration information (see Figure 11.5).

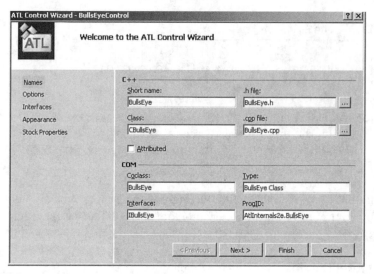

Figure 11.5   BullsEye Names dialog box

The Options screen (see Figure 11.6) looks much like the Options page you get when adding a simple object. In addition to letting you choose the interface type and threading model, it lets you choose what type of control you want.

In this case, I chose Standard Control because it matches the BullsEye requirements the best of the three choices.[1] The Options page in this wizard is slightly different than the Simple Object Wizard's Options page. Controls need thread affinity (because they are UI components and use window handles, which are associated with a thread). Therefore, the wizard correctly allows you to request only the Single or Apartment threading models for a control.

The Minimal Control check box[2] tells the wizard that you want to support only the minimum interfaces needed to be an ActiveX control. This means that when

---

[1] Composite and DHTML controls are discussed in Chapter 12, "Control Containment."

[2] ATL 3.0 used the term "Lite control" for what's now handled by the Minimal Control check box. Some documentation and names in the ATL source still use the "Lite" term.

you get to the Interfaces page in the wizard (see Figure 11.7), the Supported list will be empty by default instead of the standard set you normally get.

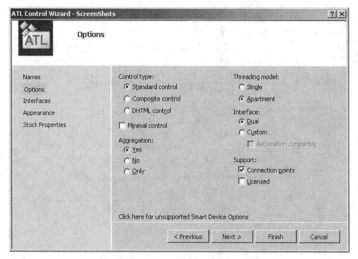

Figure 11.6   COM object options for the BullsEye control

Containers access a control's properties and methods using the control's IDispatch interface. The easiest way to get an IDispatch implementation in your control is to specify that the primary interface should be a dual interface. If you specify the Custom interface option, you must implement IDispatch separately on the control. Controls can be aggregated or not. I've requested that BullsEye support aggregation, even though it increases the size of each instance by 8 bytes.

Next, we get to choose from a set of stock interfaces (see Figure 11.7).

In addition to the standard list the wizard supplies, I added the IPropertyNotify-Sink interface, which is the standard interface for the control to tell its container that a property has changed.

The Appearance page, shown in Figure 11.8, enables you to select various control options that are not available elsewhere.

The options on the Appearance page specify various optimizations that ActiveX control containers can take advantage of. The Opaque option says that your control is completely opaque: None of the container's background will show through your control. Containers can use this to avoid having to paint the background under the control. Solid Background (which means anything only when Opaque is also specified) indicates that the background of your control is a solid color instead of a patterned brush. Later, I discuss how to implement the BullsEye rendering code so that it supports transparent areas around the bull's eye, but let's start with an opaque control. Your choices for these two options appear in the code as a DECLARE_VIEW_STATUS macro in your class declaration. This macro provides a method that returns the options you chose. The IViewObjectExImpl< > template uses this method to implement the IViewObjectEx interface.

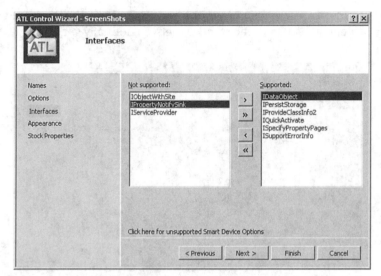

Figure 11.7   Interfaces for the `BullsEye` control

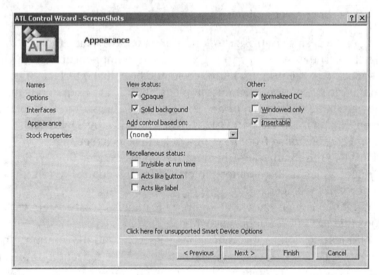

Figure 11.8   Miscellaneous control options for the `BullsEye` control

The Normalize DC (device context) option causes your control to override the `OnDraw` method for its rendering. When not selected, the control overrides the `OnDrawAdvanced` method. By default. `OnDrawAdvanced` saves the state of the device context, switches to `MM_TEXT` mapping mode, calls `OnDraw`, and then restores the saved device context. Therefore, when you ask for a normalized DC and don't override `OnDrawAdvanced`, you introduce a little more overhead. `BullsEye` uses this support, though.

Windowed Only states that the control does not support windowless activation; the control *must* have its own window. This is useful for drop targets, for example, that need to receive window messages, but the BullsEye control can handle windowless activation.

Insertable adds a Registry entry under the control's CLSID key that makes the control show up in the standard Insert Object dialog box used by OLE containers, as in the various Microsoft Office applications. Selecting this option also adds support for the IPersistStorage and IDataObject interfaces.

The Add Control Based On option enables you to create an ActiveX control that superclasses one of the standard Windows controls: Button, ComboBox, Edit, and more. A total of 16 options are available here, but the typical ActiveX control generally will be a new window class, so None is the default.

The Miscellaneous Status bits provide a couple extra pieces of information to the container: They result in Registry changes in the RGS file and the introduction of a DECLARE_OLEMISC_STATUS macro into your header file. Invisible at Runtime means that the control displays only at design time, not at runtime. The VB Timer control is the canonical example of this behavior. Acts Like Button controls can be set as the default OK or Cancel buttons on dialog boxes or on forms. Finally, Acts Like Label is used for a control that doesn't accept keyboard focus, but that can be an accelerator key to select the next control in the Tab order (surprisingly enough, this is exactly how a label behaves).

Figure 11.8 shows the options chosen for the BullsEye control.

Finally, you can have the wizard generate support for any stock properties that you want the control to support. BullsEye requires four stock properties, which I've selected in the dialog box in Figure 11.9. ATL provides the implementation of the property-accessor methods.

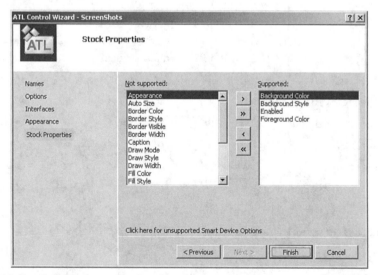

Figure 11.9 Stock properties for the BullsEye control

No wizard support exists for stock methods, so you have to implement them, as well as the `BullsEye` custom properties, by hand.

Base Classes Used by Wizard-Generated Classes

The ATL wizard generates the initial source code for a control. The control class derives from a number of different base classes, depending on the type of control you ask the wizard to generate. The wizard also adds support for various features based on selections you make from the ATL Object Wizard Properties dialog pages. Table 11.5 summarizes the base classes used by the different types of wizard-generated controls.

Table 11.5. Base Classes Used by Various Control Types

Base Classes Used	Standard Control	Minimal Standard Control	Composite Control	DHTML Control	Minimal Composite Control	Minimal DHTML Control
CComObjectRootEx<TM>	✔	✔	✔	✔	✔	✔
CComCoClass	✔	✔	✔	✔	✔	✔
CComControl	✔	✔		✔		✔
CComCompositeControl			✔		✔	
CStockPropImpl	SP	SP	SP	SP	SP	SP
IConnectionPointContainerImpl	CP	CP	CP	CP	CP	CP
IDataObjectImpl	✔		✔	✔		
IDispatchImpl	No SP and dual	No SP and dual	No SP and dual	✔	No SP and dual	✔
IOleControlImpl	✔	✔	✔	✔	✔	✔
IOleInPlaceActiveObjectImpl	✔	✔	✔	✔	✔	✔
IOleInPlaceObjectWindowlessImpl	✔	✔	✔	✔	✔	✔
IOleObjectImpl	✔	✔	✔	✔	✔	✔
IPersistStorageImpl	✔		✔	✔		
IPersistStreamInitImpl	✔	✔	✔	✔	✔	✔
IPropertyNotifySinkCP	CP		CP	CP		
IProvideClassInfo2Impl	✔		✔	✔		
IQuickActivateImpl	✔		✔	✔		

Base Classes Used	Standard Control	Minimal Standard Control	Composite Control	DHTML Control	Minimal Composite Control	Minimal DHTML Control
ISpecifyPropertyPagesImpl	✔		✔	✔		
ISupportErrorInfoImpl	SEI	SEI	SEI	SEI	SEI	SEI
IViewObjectExImpl	✔	✔	✔	✔	✔	✔
Control uses normalized DC	User	User	✔	User	✔	User
Control is windowed only	User	User	✔	✔	✔	✔

SP = Stock properties selected; CP = Connection points enabled; SEI = SupportErrorInfo enabled; User = User chosen option on Appearance wizard page when creating class

The Initial BullsEye Source Files

The Initial CBullsEye Class Declaration

Listing 11.5 shows the initial wizard-generated class declaration for the CBullsEye control class. We have to make a number of changes to the class before it meets all the requirements described at the beginning of the chapter. For example, we need to add a few more base classes to obtain all the required control functionality. Also, presently the control supports no properties except the stock properties I selected via the wizard dialog boxes. Plus, there is quite of bit of implementation code to write to make the control draw and behave as a bull's eye. I'll get to all that, but first let's look at the initial source code.

I've reformatted the source code slightly from the original wizard-generated source code to group related functionality and to add a few comments (see Listing 11.5).

Listing 11.5   The Initial Wizard-Generated CBullsEye Class

```
// CBullsEye
class ATL_NO_VTABLE CBullsEye :
    // COM object support
    public CComObjectRootEx<CComSingleThreadModel>,
    // Class object support
    public CComCoClass<CBullsEye, &CLSID_BullsEye>,
    // Default dual interface for control.
```

```
          // Requests for properties preprocessed by
          // stock property base class
          public CStockPropImpl<CBullsEye, IBullsEye>,
          // Error info support for default dual interface
          public ISupportErrorInfo,
          // Basic "lite" control implementation
          public CComControl<CBullsEye>
          public IOleControlImpl<CBullsEye>,
          public IOleObjectImpl<CBullsEye>,
          public IOleInPlaceActiveObjectImpl<CBullsEye>,
          public IOleInPlaceObjectWindowlessImpl<CBullsEye>,
          public IViewObjectExImpl<CBullsEye>,
          // "Lite" control persistence implementation
          public IPersistStreamInitImpl<CBullsEye>,
          // Full control additional implementation
#ifndef _WIN32_WCE
          // Support for OLE Embedding
          public IDataObjectImpl<CBullsEye>,
#endif
          public IPersistStorageImpl<CBullsEye>,
          // Support for property pages
          public ISpecifyPropertyPagesImpl<CBullsEye>,
          // Support for fast activation
          public IQuickActivateImpl<CBullsEye>,
          // Connection point implementation
          public IConnectionPointContainerImpl<CBullsEye>,
          public CProxy_IBullsEyeEvents<CBullsEye>,
          public IProvideClassInfo2Impl<&CLSID_BullsEye,
              &__uuidof(_IBullsEyeEvents), &LIBID_BullsEyeControlLib>,
          // Selection of IPropertyNotifySink adds additional
          // connection point for property change notifications
          public IPropertyNotifySinkCP<CBullsEye>,
#ifdef _WIN32_WCE
          // IObjectSafety is required on Windows CE for the
          // control to be loaded correctly
          public IObjectSafetyImpl<CBullsEye,
              INTERFACESAFE_FOR_UNTRUSTED_CALLER>,
#endif
{
public:
          CBullsEye()    { }


DECLARE_REGISTRY_RESOURCEID(IDR_BULLSEYE)
```

```
DECLARE_PROTECT_FINAL_CONSTRUCT()

    HRESULT FinalConstruct() { return S_OK; }

    void FinalRelease() { }

DECLARE_OLEMISC_STATUS(OLEMISC_RECOMPOSEONRESIZE |
    OLEMISC_CANTLINKINSIDE |
    OLEMISC_INSIDEOUT |
    OLEMISC_ACTIVATEWHENVISIBLE |
    OLEMISC_SETCLIENTSITEFIRST
)


BEGIN_COM_MAP(CBullsEye)
    // Default dual interface to control
    COM_INTERFACE_ENTRY(IBullsEye)
    COM_INTERFACE_ENTRY(IDispatch)
    // Error info support for default dual interface
    COM_INTERFACE_ENTRY(ISupportErrorInfo)
    // Basic "lite" control implementation
    COM_INTERFACE_ENTRY(IOleControl)
    COM_INTERFACE_ENTRY(IOleObject)
    COM_INTERFACE_ENTRY(IOleInPlaceActiveObject)
    COM_INTERFACE_ENTRY(IOleInPlaceObject)
    COM_INTERFACE_ENTRY(IOleInPlaceObjectWindowless)
    COM_INTERFACE_ENTRY2(IOleWindow, IOleInPlaceObjectWindowless)
    COM_INTERFACE_ENTRY(IViewObjectEx)
    COM_INTERFACE_ENTRY(IViewObject2)
    COM_INTERFACE_ENTRY(IViewObject)
    // "Lite" control persistence implementation
    COM_INTERFACE_ENTRY(IPersistStreamInit)
    COM_INTERFACE_ENTRY2(IPersist, IPersistStreamInit)
    // Full control additional implementation
    // Support for OLE Embedding
#ifndef _WIN32_WCE
    COM_INTERFACE_ENTRY(IDataObject)
#endif
    COM_INTERFACE_ENTRY(IPersistStorage)
    // Support for property pages
    COM_INTERFACE_ENTRY(ISpecifyPropertyPages)
    // Support for fast activation
    COM_INTERFACE_ENTRY(IQuickActivate)
    // Support for connection points
    COM_INTERFACE_ENTRY(IConnectionPointContainer)
```

```
        COM_INTERFACE_ENTRY(IProvideClassInfo)
        COM_INTERFACE_ENTRY(IProvideClassInfo2)
#ifdef _WIN32_WCE
        // IObjectSafety is required on Windows CE for the
        // control to be loaded correctly
        COM_INTERFACE_ENTRY_IID(IID_IObjectSafety, IObjectSafety)
#endif
END_COM_MAP()

// Initially, the control's stock properties are the only
// properties supported via persistence and property pages.
BEGIN_PROP_MAP(CBullsEye)
        PROP_DATA_ENTRY("_cx", m_sizeExtent.cx, VT_UI4)
        PROP_DATA_ENTRY("_cy", m_sizeExtent.cy, VT_UI4)
#ifndef _WIN32_WCE
        PROP_ENTRY("BackColor", DISPID_BACKCOLOR,
            CLSID_StockColorPage)
#endif
        PROP_ENTRY("BackStyle", DISPID_BACKSTYLE, CLSID_NULL)
        PROP_ENTRY("Enabled", DISPID_ENABLED, CLSID_NULL)
#ifndef _WIN32_WCE
        PROP_ENTRY("ForeColor", DISPID_FORECOLOR,
            CLSID_StockColorPage)
#endif
END_PROP_MAP()

BEGIN_CONNECTION_POINT_MAP(CBullsEye)
        // Property change notifications
        CONNECTION_POINT_ENTRY(IID_IPropertyNotifySink)
        // Our default connection point
        CONNECTION_POINT_ENTRY(__uuidof(_IBullsEyeEvents))
END_CONNECTION_POINT_MAP()

// Initially the control passes all Windows messages
// to the base class
BEGIN_MSG_MAP(CBullsEye)
        CHAIN_MSG_MAP(CComControl<CBullsEye>)
        DEFAULT_REFLECTION_HANDLER()
END_MSG_MAP()

// ISupportsErrorInfo
        STDMETHOD(InterfaceSupportsErrorInfo)(REFIID riid) {
            // Implementation deleted for clarity...
        }
```

```
    // IViewObjectEx
    DECLARE_VIEW_STATUS(VIEWSTATUS_SOLIDBKGND |
        VIEWSTATUS_OPAQUE)

// IBullsEye
public:
    HRESULT OnDraw(ATL_DRAWINFO& di) {
        // Sample drawing code omitted for clarity
    }

    // Storage for values of stock properties
    OLE_COLOR m_clrBackColor;
    LONG m_nBackStyle;
    BOOL m_bEnabled;
    OLE_COLOR m_clrForeColor;

    // Stock property change notification functions
    void OnBackColorChanged() {
        ATLTRACE(_T("OnBackColorChanged\n"));
    }
    void OnBackStyleChanged() {
        ATLTRACE(_T("OnBackStyleChanged\n"));
    }
    void OnEnabledChanged() {
        ATLTRACE(_T("OnEnabledChanged\n"));
    }
    void OnForeColorChanged() {
        ATLTRACE(_T("OnForeColorChanged\n"));
    }
};
```

The Initial IBullsEye Interface

Listing 11.6 is the initial wizard-generated IDL description for the IBullsEye interface. The wizard generates the interface containing any stock properties you've
specified. We need to add all the custom properties for the control, as well as any
stock and custom methods that the control supports.

Listing 11.6   The Initial Wizard-Generated IDL for the `IBullsEye` Interface

```
[
    object,
    uuid(B4FBD008-B03D-4F48-9C5B-4A981EB6A515),
    dual,
    nonextensible,
    helpstring("IBullsEye Interface"),
    pointer_default(unique)
]
interface IBullsEye : IDispatch{
    [propput, bindable, requestedit, id(DISPID_BACKCOLOR)]
    HRESULT BackColor([in]OLE_COLOR clr);
    [propget, bindable, requestedit, id(DISPID_BACKCOLOR)]
    HRESULT BackColor([out,retval]OLE_COLOR* pclr);
    [propput, bindable, requestedit, id(DISPID_BACKSTYLE)]
    HRESULT BackStyle([in]long style);
    [propget, bindable, requestedit, id(DISPID_BACKSTYLE)]
    HRESULT BackStyle([out,retval]long* pstyle);
    [propput, bindable, requestedit, id(DISPID_FORECOLOR)]
    HRESULT ForeColor([in]OLE_COLOR clr);
    [propget, bindable, requestedit, id(DISPID_FORECOLOR)]
    HRESULT ForeColor([out,retval]OLE_COLOR* pclr);
    [propput, bindable, requestedit, id(DISPID_ENABLED)]
    HRESULT Enabled([in]VARIANT_BOOL vbool);
    [propget, bindable, requestedit, id(DISPID_ENABLED)]
    HRESULT Enabled([out,retval]VARIANT_BOOL* pbool);
};
```

The Initial _IBullsEyeEvents Dispatch Interface

The initial `_IBullsEyeEvents` dispatch interface is empty (see Listing 11.7). We need to add the `BullsEye` custom events to the `dispinterface`. When a control supports any of the stock events, you add them to the event interface as well.

Listing 11.7   The Initial Wizard-Generated IDL for the `_IBullsEyeEvent` Dispatch Interface

```
[ uuid(58D6D8CB-765D-4C59-A41F-BBA8C40F7A14),
    helpstring("_IBullsEyeEvents Interface")
]
dispinterface _IBullsEyeEvents {
```

```
    properties:
    methods:
};
```

Developing the BullsEye Control Step by Step

Stock Properties and Methods

Updating Stock Properties and Methods in the IDL

Your IDL file describing the control's default dispatch interface must contain an entry for each stock property accessor method and all stock methods you support. The Add ATL Control Wizard generates the method definitions for those stock properties added using the wizard dialog boxes. Listing 11.6 shows the method definitions for the BullsEye properties.

The Add ATL Control Wizard has no support for stock methods. You must add any stock methods explicitly to the default dispatch interface definition in your IDL file. Only three stock methods (AboutBox, DoClick, and Refresh) are defined, and BullsEye supports them all. I've added the following lines to the IBullsEye interface definition:

```
interface IBullsEye : IDispatch {
    ...
    [id(DISPID_ABOUTBOX)] HRESULT AboutBox();
    [id(DISPID_DOCLICK)] HRESULT DoClick();
    [id(DISPID_REFRESH)] HRESULT Refresh();
};
```

Listing 11.1, shown earlier in this chapter, contains the complete definition of the IBullsEye interface with all these changes.

Implementing Stock Properties and Methods Using CStockPropImpl

The CStockPropImpl class contains an implementation of every stock property you can choose from the Stock Properties page in the ATL Object Wizard. A control derives from CStockPropImpl when it wants an implementation of any of the stock properties. The declaration of the template class looks like this:

```
template < class T, class InterfaceName,
    const IID* piid = &_ATL_IIDOF(InterfaceName),
    const GUID* plibid = &CAtlModule::m_libid,
    WORD wMajor = 1, WORD wMinor = 0,
    class tihclass = CComTypeInfoHolder>
```

```
class ATL_NO_VTABLE CStockPropImpl :
    public IDispatchImpl< InterfaceName, piid, plibid,
    wMajor, wMinor, tihclass >
```

The class T parameter is the name of your control class. The InterfaceName parameter is the name of the dual interface defining the stock property propget and propput methods. The CStockPropImpl class implements these accessor methods. The piid parameter is a pointer to the IID for the InterfaceName interface. The plibid parameter is a pointer to the GUID of the type library that contains a description of the InterfaceName interface.

The CBullsEye class implements its stock properties using CStockPropImpl like this:

```
class ATL_NO_VTABLE CBullsEye :
    public CStockPropImpl<CBullsEye, IBullsEye, &IID_IBullsEye,
                    &LIBID_ATLINTERNALSLib>,
    ...
```

The CStockPropImpl class contains an implementation of the property accessor (get and put) methods for all stock properties. These methods notify and synchronize with the control's container when any stock property changes.

Most controls don't need support for all the possible stock properties. However, the CStockPropImpl base class contains supporting code for all stock properties. This code needs a data member for each property. ATL expects your deriving class, the control class, to provide the data members for only the stock properties that your control supports. You must name these data members the same variable name as used by the CStockPropImpl class. Table 11.6 lists the appropriate name for each supported stock property.

Table 11.6.   Stock Properties Supported by CStockPropImpl

Stock Property	Data Member	Stock Property	Data Member
APPEARANCE	m_nAppearance	FILLCOLOR	m_clrFillColor
AUTOSIZE	m_bAutoSize	FILLSTYLE	m_nFillStyle
BACKCOLOR	m_clrBackColor	FONT	m_pFont
BACKSTYLE	m_nBackStyle	FORECOLOR	m_clrForeColor
BORDERCOLOR	m_clrBorderColor	HWND	m_hWnd
BORDERSTYLE	m_nBorderStyle	MOUSEICON	m_pMouseIcon
BORDERVISIBLE	m_bBorderVisible	MOUSEPOINTER	m_nMousePointer
BORDERWIDTH	m_nBorderWidth	PICTURE	m_pPicture

Stock Property	Data Member	Stock Property	Data Member
CAPTION	m_bstrCaption	READYSTATE	m_nReadyState
DRAWMODE	m_nDrawMode	TABSTOP	m_bTabStop
DRAWSTYLE	m_nDrawStyle	TEXT	m_bstrText
DRAWWIDTH	m_nDrawWidth	VALID	m_bValid
ENABLED	m_bEnabled		

The CStockPropImpl class contains property-accessor methods *for all these properties*. In theory, that means you must provide member variables for every single one of them in your class, to avoid getting an "Undefined variable" compile error. Luckily for us, the ATL authors took advantage of one of the new extensions to C++:

```
class CStockPropImpl {
  ...
  HRESULT STDMETHODCALLTYPE get_Picture(IPictureDisp** ppPicture) {
    __if_exists(T::m_pPicture) {
      ATLTRACE(atlTraceControls,2,
        _T("CStockPropImpl::get_Picture\n"));
      ATLASSERT(ppPicture != NULL);
      if (ppPicture == NULL)
        return E_POINTER;

      T* pT = (T*) this;
      *ppPicture = pT->m_pPicture;
      if (*ppPicture != NULL)
        (*ppPicture)->AddRef();
    }
    return S_OK;
  }
  ...
};
```

Notice the __if_exists block. You saw this back in Chapter 4, "Objects in ATL"; here it's used to make sure the property accessor logic is compiled in only if the underlying variable has been declared in your control. This way, you don't have to worry about size bloat to store stock properties you're not using. The downside of this space optimization is this: When you add a member variable to your control class to hold a stock property and you misspell the member variable name, you receive no compilation errors. The code in CStockPropImpl does nothing and returns S_OK.

The Add ATL Control Wizard generates the proper member variables in your control's class when you add a stock property initially. For example, here are the member variables generated for the stock properties in the CBullsEye class:

```
class CBullsEye : ... {
  ...
  OLE_COLOR m_clrBackColor;
  LONG      m_nBackStyle;
  BOOL      m_bEnabled;
  OLE_COLOR m_clrForeColor;
};
```

CStockPropImpl implements explicit put and get methods for the stock properties that are interface pointers, including FONT, MOUSEICON, and PICTURE. It also implements a get method for the HWND stock property. For each other stock property, CStockPropImpl invokes one of three macros that expand to a standard put and get method for the property: These macros are IMPLEMENT_STOCKPROP, IMPLEMENT_BOOL_STOCKPROP, and IMPLEMENT_BSTR_STOCKPROP.

The IMPLEMENT_STOCKPROP (type, frame, pname, dispid) macro's parameters are as follows:

- type. The data type for the stock property you want an implementation for.
- fname. The function name for the get and put methods. The get method will be named get_fname, and the put method will be named put_fname. For example, when fname is Enabled, the method names are put_Enabled and get_Enabled.
- pname. Specifies the name of the member variable that will hold the state of the stock property. For example, if pname is bEnabled, the macro-created get and put methods will reference m_bEnabled.
- dispid. The dispatch ID for the stock property.

The IMPLEMENT_BOOL_STOCKPROP(fname, pname, dispid) macro implements a stock Boolean property's accessor methods. It has the same attributes as listed for the IMPLEMENT_STOCKPROP macro, except that the get method tests the value of the data member containing the property and returns VARIANT_TRUE or VARIANT_FALSE instead of returning the value.

The IMPLEMENT_BSTR_STOCKPROP(fname, pname, dispid) macro implements a stock text property's accessor methods using a BSTR.

Let's look at the implementation of the IMPLEMENT_STOCKPROP macro. The ATL code illustrates a couple other issues that are worth noting and that apply to all stock properties.

```
#define IMPLEMENT_STOCKPROP(type, fname, pname, dispid) \
    HRESULT STDMETHODCALLTYPE put_##fname(type pname) { \
        __if_exists(T::m_##pname) { \
            ATLTRACE(ATL::atlTraceControls,2, \
                _T("CStockPropImpl::put_%s\n"), #fname); \
            T* pT = (T*) this; \
            if (pT->m_nFreezeEvents == 0 && \
                pT->FireOnRequestEdit(dispid) == S_FALSE) \
                return S_FALSE; \
            pT->m_##pname = pname; \
            pT->m_bRequiresSave = TRUE; \
            if (pT->m_nFreezeEvents == 0) \
                pT->FireOnChanged(dispid); \
            __if_exists(T::On##fname##Changed) { \
                pT->On##fname##Changed(); \
            } \
            pT->FireViewChange(); \
            pT->SendOnDataChange(NULL); \
        } \
        return S_OK; \
    } \
    HRESULT STDMETHODCALLTYPE get_##fname(type* p##pname) { \
        __if_exists(T::m_##pname) { \
            ATLTRACE(ATL::atlTraceControls,2, \
                _T("CStockPropImpl::get_%s\n"), #fname); \
            ATLASSERT(p##pname != NULL); \
            if (p##pname == NULL) \
                return E_POINTER; \
            T* pT = (T*) this; \
            *p##pname = pT->m_##pname; \
        } \
        return S_OK; \
    }
```

First, notice that the put method fires an `OnRequestEdit` and an `OnChanged` event notification to the control's container before and after, respectively, changing the value of a stock property. Second, the put method fires the `OnRequestEdit` and `OnChanged` events after checking a control's freeze event. When a control's freeze event count (maintained in `CComControlBase` in the `m_nFreezeEvents` member variable) is nonzero, a control should hold off firing events or discard them completely. If this rule isn't followed, some containers will break.

For example, the Test Container application shipped with Visual C++ 6.0 crashes when a control fires change notifications in its `FinalConstruct` method.

A control should be capable of calling `FreezeEvents(TRUE)` in `FinalConstruct` to disable change notifications, initialize its properties using the put methods, and then call `FreezeEvents (FALSE)` to enable change notifications if they were previously enabled

Occasionally, you'll decide to support additional stock properties after creating the initial source code. The wizard lacks support for adding features to your class after the initial code generation, so you'll have to make the previously described changes to your code manually.

Finally, often you'll want to do some work beyond what the stock property put functions perform. For example, the `CBullsEye` class needs to know whenever the background color changes so that it can delete the old background brush and schedule the rendering logic to create a new background brush. In the middle of the put method generated by the `IMPLEMENT_STOCKPROP` macro, there's this code:

```
#define IMPLEMENT_STOCKPROP(type, fname, pname, dispid) \
  ...
          __if_exists(T::On##fname##Changed) { \
             pT->On##fname##Changed(); \
          } \
```

When you added the stock properties to the control, the Add ATL Control Wizard also added methods called `On<propname>Changed`. If there is an appropriately named method in your class (`OnBackColorChanged` for the `BackColor` property, for example), the stock property put method calls that method when the property value changes. This is useful when you need to do things beyond just storing the value. For example, the `CBullsEye` control needs to know when the background color changes, so it can delete the old background brush and schedule the rendering logic to create a new background brush.

Custom Properties and Methods

Adding Custom Properties and Methods to the IDL

In addition to stock properties, your control's default dispatch interface must contain an entry for the property get and put methods for each custom control property, as well as all the stock and custom methods you support. The Add ATL Control Wizard doesn't currently support stock methods, so you add them to your class as if they were custom methods (which, in fact, they are, except that you don't get to choose the function signatures or the DISPID).

To add a custom property, you must edit the IDL file and then add the corresponding methods to your C++ class. You can use Class view to add the properties. Right-click the interface and select Add, Add Property. This adds the appropriate definitions to the IDL file. Unfortunately, unlike in previous versions of Visual Studio, this step *only* updates the IDL file; you have to manually add the property get/put methods to your C++ class. At least the compiler gives you the helpful "Cannot instantiate abstract class" error message if you forget or get the signature wrong.

The `BullsEye` control supports the stock methods and custom properties listed in Tables 11.2 and 11.3, respectively. Listing 11.1 contains the complete definition for the `IBullsEye` interface, but here's an excerpt showing the definition of the `CenterColor` custom property and the `AboutBox` stock method.

```
interface IBullsEye : IDispatch {
...
    [propput, bindable, requestedit, id(DISPID_CENTERCOLOR)]
    HRESULT CenterColor([in] OLE_COLOR newVal);

    [propget, bindable, requestedit, id(DISPID_CENTERCOLOR)]
    HRESULT CenterColor([out, retval] OLE_COLOR *pVal);

    [id(DISPID_ABOUTBOX)] HRESULT AboutBox();
...
};
```

Note that Class view does not let you define a symbol for the DISPID; it takes only integers in the dialog box. It's usually a good idea to go back into the IDL afterward and define a symbol, as we've already done in the IDL file for the `BullsEye` control.

Implementing Custom Properties and Stock and Custom Methods

You need to add a function prototype to your control class for each method added to the IDL in the previous step. For the previous custom property and stock method, I added the following function prototypes to the `CBullsEye` class:

```
class CBullsEye : ... {
  ...
  STDMETHODIMP get_CenterColor(/*[out, retval]*/OLE_COLOR *pVal);
  STDMETHODIMP put_CenterColor(/*[in]*/ OLE_COLOR newVal);
  STDMETHODIMP AboutBox();
  ...
};
```

Declaring the Function Prototypes

Note that you must declare each interface member function as using the STD-METHODIMP calling convention. A system header file defines this macro to be the appropriate calling convention for COM interface methods on a given operating system. This calling convention does change among various operating systems. Because you are using the macro instead of explicitly writing its expansion, your code is more portable across operating systems. On the Win32 operating systems, the macro expands to HRESULT __stdcall.

The code that the ATL wizards generate incorrectly uses the STDMETHOD macro. On Win32 operating systems, this macro expands as virtual HRESULT __stdcall, which just happens to work. It doesn't necessarily work on other operating systems that support COM.

Basically, STDMETHOD should be used only in the *original definition* of an interface; this is typically the MIDL-generated header. (However, MIDL doesn't use the macro; it simply generates its expansion instead.) When implementing an interface method in a class (which we are doing in CBullsEye), you should use the STDMETHODIMP macro.

You must manually make a couple changes to the method definitions. First, most properties should have the bindable and requestedit attributes. This is because the property put methods fire change notifications to a container before and after changing a property. Therefore, you need to change each method as shown in the following section.

Defining the Functions

The function implementations are all quite straightforward. The get_CenterColor method validates its argument and returns the value of the CenterColor property:

```
STDMETHODIMP CBullsEye::get_CenterColor(OLE_COLOR *pVal) {
    if (NULL == pVal) return E_POINTER;
    *pVal = m_clrCenterColor;
    return S_OK;
}
```

The put_CenterColor method, like all property change functions, is a bit more complicated:

```
STDMETHODIMP CBullsEye::put_CenterColor(OLE_COLOR newVal) {
    if (m_clrCenterColor == newVal) return S_OK;

    if (!m_nFreezeEvents)
      if (FireOnRequestEdit(DISPID_CENTERCOLOR) == S_FALSE)
        return S_FALSE;

    m_clrCenterColor = newVal;            // Save new color
    ::DeleteObject (m_centerBrush);       // Clear old brush color
    m_centerBrush = NULL;
```

```
    m_bRequiresSave = TRUE;              // Set dirty flag
    if (!m_nFreezeEvents)
      FireOnChanged(DISPID_CENTERCOLOR); // Notify container
    FireViewChange();                    // Request redraw
    SendOnDataChange(NULL);              // Notify advise sinks

    return S_OK;
}
```

First, the method checks to see if the new value is the same as the current value of the CenterColor property. If so, the value isn't changing, so we exit quickly. Then, as in the stock property code, it properly checks to see if the container presently doesn't want to receive events—that is, if the freeze events count is nonzero.

When the container has not frozen events, the put_CenterColor method fires the OnRequestEdit event to ask the container for permission to change the Center-Color property. When the container refuses the change, put_CenterColor returns S_FALSE.

When the container grants permission, put_CenterColor updates the member variable in the control that contains the color. It also changes some values that cause the control's rendering code to use the new color the next time the control redraws.

After the method changes the property, it sets the control's dirty flag (m_b-RequiresSave) to remember that the state of the control now needs to be saved. The various persistence implementations check this flag when executing their IsDirty method.

Next, the method fires the OnChanged event to notify the container of the property change, assuming that events are not frozen.

The CenterColor property affects the visual rendering (view) of the control. When a control changes such properties, the control should notify its container that the control's appearance has changed by calling the FireViewChange function. In response, eventually, the container asks the control to redraw itself. After that, the method notifies all advise sinks (which typically means the container) that the state (data) of the control has changed by calling SendOnDataChange.

Note that the state of a control changes independently of the control's view. Some control property changes, such as changes to CBullsEye's Beep property, have no effect on the appearance of the control, so the put_Beep method doesn't call FireViewChange.

At this point, the astute reader might have noticed the similarity between the code implementing the CenterColor property and the code generated by the IMPLE-MENT_STOCKPROP macro. If your property logic is almost identical to that for the stock properties, you can save yourself a lot of typing by using the macro instead:

```
class CBullsEye : ... {
    ...
    void OnCenterColorChanged() {
        ::DeleteObject(m_centerBrush);
        m_centerBrush = 0;
        }

IMPLEMENT_STOCKPROP(OLE_COLOR, CenterColor,
    clrCenterColor, DISPID_CENTERCOLOR);
    ...
private:
    // Storage for the property value
    OLE_COLOR m_clrCenterColor;
    ...
};
```

If you're using IMPLEMENT_STOCKPROP this way, you can simply leave out the declarations for the get and put methods; the macro adds them for you. To do any custom logic you need in the property setter, you can use the OnXXXChanged method (as I did in the OnCenterColorChanged method).

There's a fair bit of irony in this. In ATL 3, IMPLEMENT_STOCKPROP was the documented way to implement properties, and it didn't work. To get a fully functional property, you had to write code like the implementation of put_CenterColor shown previously. In ATL 8, IMPLEMENT_STOCKPROP is now undocumented but works just fine for defining custom properties.

Finally, our final custom method, the stock AboutBox method, simply displays the About dialog box.

```
STDMETHODIMP CBullsEye::AboutBox() {
    CAboutDlg dlg;
    dlg.DoModal();
    return S_OK;
}
```

Stock and Custom Events

Adding Stock and Custom Events to the IDL

Your IDL file describing the control's default source interface must contain an entry for each stock and custom event method you support. As described previously, for maximum compatibility with all control containers, you should implement the default source interface as a dispatch interface. No current support exists in the IDE for adding event methods to a dispinterface, despite what it might look like. For example, in my current Class View window, there's an entry for _IBullsEye-Events, as shown in Figure 11.10.

Figure 11.10 Class View— it lies!

Look closely at that window. Notice that it doesn't have the spoon interface icon; instead, it's the normal class icon. If you right-click there, it will allow you to add a method, but it's actually editing the generated header file that you get when you run MIDL on your .idl file. Any change you make will be overwritten the next time you run MIDL. In previous versions of Visual Studio, Class View was fairly smart about such things. In VS 2005, not so much.

The BullsEye control needs to support the two custom events described in Table 11.4. Here's the updated IDL describing the event dispatch interface. All dispatch interfaces must be defined within the library block of an IDL file.

```
[ uuid(58D6D8CB-765D-4C59-A41F-BBA8C40F7A14),
  helpstring("_IBullsEyeEvents Interface")
]
dispinterface _IBullsEyeEvents {
    properties:
    methods:
    [id(DISPID_ONRINGHIT)]
    void OnRingHit(short ringNum);
    [id(DISPID_ONSCORECHANGED)]
    void OnScoreChanged(long ringValue);
};
```

You'll also want to ensure that the IDL correctly describes the BullsEye class itself. The BullsEye coclass definition in the library block of the IDL file should define the IBullsEye interface as the default interface for the control and the _IBullsEyeEvents dispatch interface as the default source interface.

```
[ uuid(E9312AF5-1C11-4BA4-A0C6-CB660E949B78),
  control, helpstring("BullsEye Class")
]
coclass BullsEye {
    [default] interface IBullsEye;
    [default, source] dispinterface _IBullsEyeEvents;
};
```

This is what the wizard generates when you choose to implement connection points, but it never hurts to double-check.

Adding Connection Point Support for the Events

Many containers use the connection points protocol to hand the container's sink interface pointer to the event source (the control). Chapter 9, "Connection Points," discusses connection points in detail, so here I just summarize the steps needed for a control.

To support connection point events, a control must implement the IConnectionPointContainer interface as well as one IConnectionPoint interface for each outgoing (source) interface. Typically, most controls support two source interfaces: the control's default source dispatch interface (_IBullsEyeEvents for the BullsEye control) and the property change notification source interface (IPropertyNotifySink).

Implementing the IConnectionPointContainer Interface

When you initially create the source code for a control and select the Support Connection Points option, the ATL Object Wizard adds the IConnectionPointContainerImpl base class to your control class declaration. This is ATL's implementation of the IConnectionPointContainer interface. You need to add this base class explicitly if you decide to support connection points after creating the initial source code.

```
class ATL_NO_VTABLE CBullsEye :
    ...
    // Connection point container support
    public IConnectionPointContainerImpl<CBullsEye>,
    ...
```

You also need one connection point for each source interface that your control supports. ATL provides the IConnectionPointImpl class, which is described in depth in Chapter 9, as an implementation of the `IConnectionPoint` interface. Typically, you do not directly use this class; instead, you derive a new class from `IConnectionPointImpl` and customize the class by adding various event-firing methods. Your control will inherit from this derived class.

Supporting Property Change Notifications

ATL provides a specialization of `IConnectionPointImpl`, called `IPropertyNotifySinkCP`, that implements a connection point for the `IPropertyNotifySink` interface. The `IPropertyNotifySinkCP` class also defines the type definition `__ATL_PROP_NOTIFY_EVENT_CLASS` (note the double leading underscore) as an alias for the `CFirePropNotifyEvent` class.

```
template <class T, class CDV = CComDynamicUnkArray >
class ATL_NO_VTABLE IPropertyNotifySinkCP :
    public IConnectionPointImpl<T, &IID_IPropertyNotifySink, CDV> {
public:
    typedef CFirePropNotifyEvent __ATL_PROP_NOTIFY_EVENT_CLASS;
};
```

When you use the ATL Object Wizard to create a full control that supports connection points, the wizard adds the `IPropertyNotifySinkCP` base class to your control:

```
class ATL_NO_VTABLE CBullsEye :
    ...
    public IPropertyNotifySinkCP<CBullsEye>,
    ...
```

Recall that a control's property put methods, for both custom and stock properties, call the `FireOnRequestEdit` and `FireOnChanged` functions to send property-change notifications. These methods are defined in the `CComControl` class like this:

```
template <class T, class WinBase =  CWindowImpl< T > >
class ATL_NO_VTABLE CComControl :
  public CComControlBase, public WinBase {
public:
  HRESULT FireOnRequestEdit(DISPID dispID) {
    T* pT = static_cast<T*>(this);
    return T::__ATL_PROP_NOTIFY_EVENT_CLASS::FireOnRequestEdit
      (pT->GetUnknown(), dispID);
  }
```

```
HRESULT FireOnChanged(DISPID dispID) {
  T* pT = static_cast<T*>(this);
  return T::__ATL_PROP_NOTIFY_EVENT_CLASS::FireOnChanged
    (pT->GetUnknown(), dispID);
}
...
};
```

Therefore, the call to `FireOnChanged` in a property put method of a `CComControl`-derived class actually is a call to the `FireOnChanged` of the class `__ATL_PROP_NOTIFY_EVENT_CLASS` (note the double leading underscore) within your actual control class. When you derive your control class from `IPropertyNotifySinkCP`, your control class inherits a `typedef` for `_ATL_PROP_NOTIFY_EVENT_CLASS` (note the single leading underscore).

```
typedef CFirePropNotifyEvent _ATL_PROP_NOTIFY_EVENT_CLASS;
```

The two types come together in the property map in your control class. The `BEGIN_PROP_MAP` macro defines the type `__ATL_PROP_NOTIFY_EVENT_CLASS` (note the double leading underscore) as equivalent to the type `_ATL_PROP_NOTIFY_EVENT_CLASS` (note the single leading underscore).

```
#define BEGIN_PROP_MAP(theClass) \
    __if_not_exists(__ATL_PROP_NOTIFY_EVENT_CLASS) { \
        typedef ATL::_ATL_PROP_NOTIFY_EVENT_CLASS
        __ATL_PROP_NOTIFY_EVENT_CLASS; \
    } \
...
```

The `__if_not_exists` block in the `BEGIN_PROP_MAP` definition does the typedef only if the `__ATL_PROP_NOTIFY_EVENT_CLASS` isn't defined. This gives you the chance to override the event class by defining the typedef yourself, if you want.

In the `BullsEye` control, this means that when your property put method calls `FireOnChanged`, this is actually a call to your `CComControl::FireOnChanged` base class method.

- `FireOnChanged` calls `CBullsEye::__ATL_PROP_NOTIFY_EVENT_CLASS::FireOnChanged`.

- The property map aliases `__ATL_PROP_NOTIFY_EVENT_CLASS` (two leading underscores) to `_ATL_PROP_NOTIFY_EVENT_CLASS` (one leading underscore).

- `IPropertyNotifySinkCP` aliases `_ATL_PROP_NOTIFY_SINK_CLASS` to `CFirePropNotifyEvent`.

- Therefore, you actually call the `CBullsEye::CFirePropNotifyEvent::FireOn-Changed` function.

The `CFirePropNotifyEvent` class contains two static methods, `FireOnRequest-Edit` and `FireOnChanged`, that use your control's own connection point support to enumerate through all connections for the `IPropertyNotifySink` interface and call the `OnRequestEdit` and `OnChanged` methods, respectively, of each connection.

```
class CFirePropNotifyEvent {
public:
  // Ask any objects sinking the IPropertyNotifySink
  // notification if it is ok to edit a specified property
  static HRESULT FireOnRequestEdit(IUnknown* pUnk, DISPID dispID) {
    CComQIPtr<IConnectionPointContainer,
      &__uuidof(IConnectionPointContainer)> pCPC(pUnk);
    if (!pCPC) return S_OK;

    CComPtr<IConnectionPoint> pCP;
    pCPC->FindConnectionPoint(__uuidof(IPropertyNotifySink),
      &pCP);
    if (!pCP) return S_OK;

    CComPtr<IEnumConnections> pEnum;
    if (FAILED(pCP->EnumConnections(&pEnum)))
      return S_OK;

    CONNECTDATA cd;
    while (pEnum->Next(1, &cd, NULL) == S_OK) {
      if (cd.pUnk) {
        HRESULT hr = S_OK;
        CComQIPtr<IPropertyNotifySink,
          &__uuidof(IPropertyNotifySink)> pSink(cd.pUnk);

        if (pSink != NULL)
          hr = pSink->OnRequestEdit(dispID);

        cd.pUnk->Release();
        if (hr == S_FALSE) return S_FALSE;
      }
    }
    return S_OK;
  }
```

```
// Notify any objects sinking the IPropertyNotifySink
// notification that a property has changed
static HRESULT FireOnChanged(IUnknown* pUnk, DISPID dispID) {
  CComQIPtr<IConnectionPointContainer,
    &__uuidof(IConnectionPointContainer)> pCPC(pUnk);
  if (!pCPC) return S_OK;

  CComPtr<IConnectionPoint> pCP;
  pCPC->FindConnectionPoint(__uuidof(IPropertyNotifySink),
    &pCP);
  if (!pCP) return S_OK;
  CComPtr<IEnumConnections> pEnum;

  if (FAILED(pCP->EnumConnections(&pEnum)))
    return S_OK;

  CONNECTDATA cd;
  while (pEnum->Next(1, &cd, NULL) == S_OK) {
    if (cd.pUnk) {
      CComQIPtr<IPropertyNotifySink,
        &__uuidof(IPropertyNotifySink)> pSink(cd.pUnk);

      if (pSink != NULL)
        pSink->OnChanged(dispID);
      cd.pUnk->Release();
    }
  }
  return S_OK;
}
};
```

This means that you must derive your control class from IPropertyNoti-fySinkCP to get the typedef that maps the FireOnRequestEdit and FireOnChanged methods in CComControl to the actual firing functions in CFirePropNotifyEvent.

When you don't derive from IPropertyNotifySinkCP, you can still call the Fire-OnRequestEdit and FireOnChanged methods in CComControl. This is because ATL defines a typedef for the symbol _ATL_PROP_NOTIFY_EVENT_CLASS at global scope:

```
typedef CFakeFirePropNotifyEvent _ATL_PROP_NOTIFY_EVENT_CLASS;
```

When your control derives from IPropertyNotifySinkCP, you inherit a definition for _ATL_PROP_NOTIFY_EVENT_CLASS that hides the global definition. When you don't derive from IPropertyNotifySinkCP, the compiler uses the global definition just given. The CFakeFirePropNotifyEvent class looks like this:

```
class CFakeFirePropNotifyEvent {
public:
  static HRESULT FireOnRequestEdit(IUnknown* /*pUnk*/,
    DISPID /*dispID*/)
  { return S_OK; }

  static HRESULT FireOnChanged(IUnknown* /*pUnk*/,
    DISPID /*dispID*/)
  { return S_OK; }
};
```

In the BullsEye control, this means that when you don't derive from IPropertyNotifySinkCP and your property put method calls FireOnChanged:

- This is actually a call to your CComControl::FireOnChanged base class method.
- FireOnChanged calls CBullsEye::__ATL_PROP_NOTIFY_EVENT_CLASS::FireOnChanged.
- The property map aliases __ATL_PROP_NOTIFY_EVENT_CLASS (two leading underscores) to _ATL_PROP_NOTIFY_EVENT_CLASS (one leading underscore).
- The global typedef aliases _ATL_PROP_NOTOFY_SINK_CLASS to CFakeFirePropNotifyEvent.
- Therefore, you actually call the CBullsEye::CFakeFirePropNotifyEvent::FireOnChanged function, which simply returns S_OK.

Supporting the Control's Event Connection Point

A connection point (or more than one) is essential to most ActiveX controls. Without an outgoing interface, the host for your control has no way of knowing when it needs to react to a change in the control. Chapter 9 discussed the details on implementing connection points, so we won't repeat the details here.

You'll want to use a specialization of IConnectionPointImpl for each of your control's event interfaces. Typically, a control implements only one event interface because Visual Basic and scripting languages can hook up to only the default event interface. This is the interface you describe in your object's coclass definition with the [default, source] attributes. However, a custom C++ client to your control can connect to any of its source interfaces.

The specialized class derives from IConnectionPointImpl and adds the appropriate event-firing helper methods for your events. The easiest way to create a specialized connection point class is to use the Implement Connection Point menu item, described in Chapter 9.

Here's the specialized connection point class, CProxy_IBullsEyeEvents, generated by the wizard for the _IBullsEyeEvents dispatch interface:

```cpp
#pragma once

template<class T>
class CProxy_IBullsEyeEvents :
  public IConnectionPointImpl<T, &__uuidof(_IBullsEyeEvents)> {
public:
  HRESULT Fire_OnRingHit(short ringNum) {
    HRESULT hr = S_OK;
    T * pThis = static_cast<T *>(this);
    int cConnections = m_vec.GetSize();

    for (int iConnection = 0;
      iConnection < cConnections; iConnection++) {
      pThis->Lock();
      CComPtr<IUnknown> punkConnection =
        m_vec.GetAt(iConnection);
      pThis->Unlock();

      IDispatch * pConnection =
        static_cast<IDispatch *>(punkConnection.p);

      if (pConnection) {
        CComVariant avarParams[1];
        avarParams[0] = ringNum;
        avarParams[0].vt = VT_I2;
        DISPPARAMS params = { avarParams, NULL, 1, 0 };
        hr = pConnection->Invoke(DISPID_ONRINGHIT, IID_NULL,
          LOCALE_USER_DEFAULT, DISPATCH_METHOD, &params,
          NULL, NULL, NULL);
      }
    }
    return hr;
  }

  HRESULT Fire_OnScoreChanged(long ringValue)
  {
    // Code similar to above deleted for clarity
  }
};
```

You use this class by adding it to the base class list of the control. Therefore, BullsEye now has two connection points in its base class list:

```
class ATL_NO_VTABLE CBullsEye :
    // events and property change notifications
    public CProxy_IBullsEyeEvents<CBullsEye>,
    public IPropertyNotifySinkCP<CBullsEye>,
    ...
```

Updating the Connection Map

Finally, the IConnectionPointContainerImpl class needs a table that associates source interface IIDs with the base class IConnectionPointImpl specialization that implements the connection point. You define this table in your control class using the BEGIN_CONNECTION_POINT_MAP, CONNECTION_POINT_ENTRY, and END_CON-NECTION_POINT_MAP macros, described in Chapter 9.

Here's the table for the CBullsEye class:

```
BEGIN_CONNECTION_POINT_MAP(CBullsEye)
    CONNECTION_POINT_ENTRY(DIID__IBullsEyeEvents)
    CONNECTION_POINT_ENTRY(IID_IPropertyNotifySink)
END_CONNECTION_POINT_MAP()
```

Supporting IProvideClassInfo2

Many containers, such as Visual Basic and Internet Explorer, use a control's IProvideClassInfo2 interface to determine the control's event interface. When a control doesn't support IProvideClassInfo2, these containers assume that the control doesn't source events and never establish a connection point to your control. Other containers, such as test container, don't use a control's IProvideClassInfo2 interface and browse a control's type information to determine the default source interface.

ATL provides an implementation of this interface in IProvideClassInfo2Impl. To use it, derive your control class from IProvideClassInfo2Impl. The IProvideClass-Info2 interface itself derives from the IProvideClassInfo interface, so when you update your control's interface map, you need to provide entries for both interfaces.

```
class ATL_NO_VTABLE CBullsEye :
    public IProvideClassInfo2Impl<&CLSID_BullsEye,
                                  &DIID__IBullsEyeEvents,
                                  &LIBID_ATLInternalsLib>,
    ...
{
    ...
```

```
    BEGIN_COM_MAP(CBullsEye)
       ...
       // Support for connection points
       COM_INTERFACE_ENTRY(IConnectionPointContainer)
       COM_INTERFACE_ENTRY(IProvideClassInfo2)
       COM_INTERFACE_ENTRY(IProvideClassInfo)
    END_COM_MAP()
    ...
};
```

On-Demand Rendering of Your Control's View

The BullsEye control now has stock properties and custom properties, correctly responds to QueryInterface calls, and implements an outgoing connection point. There's just one thing: Aren't controls supposed to be visual? It's time to talk about how ActiveX controls actually draw their UI.

A control must be capable of rendering its image when requested by its container. A control receives a rendering request in basically three different situations:

1. The control has a window that receives a WM_PAINT message. A control handles this request in CComControlBase::OnPaint.

2. The control is windowless, and the container's window receives a WM_PAINT message encompassing the area that the control occupies. A control handles this request in CComControlBase::IViewObject_Draw.

3. The container requests that the control render its image into a metafile. A control handles this request in CComControlBase::IDataObject_GetData.

Although all three types of rendering requests arrive at the control via different mechanisms, the ATL control implementation classes eventually forward the requests to a control's OnDrawAdvanced method.

```
virtual HRESULT OnDrawAdvanced( ATL_DRAWINFO& di );
```

ATL bundles all parameters to the rendering requests into an ATL_DRAWINFO structure. You need to use the information in this structure when drawing your control. Most of the fields are simply copies of similar parameters to the IViewObject::Draw method:

```
struct ATL_DRAWINFO {
  UINT cbSize;          // Set to sizeof(ATL_DRAWINFO)
  DWORD dwDrawAspect;   // Drawing aspect - typically
```

```
                                  // DVASPECT_CONTENT
    LONG lindex;                  // Commonly -1, which specifies
                                  // all of the data
    DVTARGETDEVICE* ptd;  // Render to this target device
    HDC hicTargetDev;       // Information context for target device
    HDC hdcDraw;              // Draw on this device context
    LPCRECTL prcBounds;   // Rectangle in which to draw
    LPCRECTL prcWBounds;  // WindowOrg and Ext if metafile
    BOOL bOptimize;          // Can control use drawing optimizations?
    BOOL bZoomed;            // Object extent differs from
                                  // drawing rectangle?
    BOOL bRectInHimetric; // Rectangle in HiMetric?
    SIZEL ZoomNum;           // Rectangle size: ZoomX =
                                  // ZoomNum.cx/ZoomDen.cx
    SIZEL ZoomDen;           // Extent size: ZoomY =
                                  // ZoomNum.cy/ZoomDen.cy
};
```

ATL provides the following default implementation of the OnDrawAdvanced method in CComControl:

```
inline HRESULT
CComControlBase::OnDrawAdvanced(ATL_DRAWINFO& di) {
  BOOL bDeleteDC = FALSE;
  if (di.hicTargetDev == NULL) {
    di.hicTargetDev = AtlCreateTargetDC(di.hdcDraw, di.ptd);
    bDeleteDC = (di.hicTargetDev != di.hdcDraw);
  }
  RECTL rectBoundsDP = *di.prcBounds;
  BOOL bMetafile =
    GetDeviceCaps(di.hdcDraw, TECHNOLOGY) == DT_METAFILE;
  if (!bMetafile) {
    ::LPtoDP(di.hdcDraw, (LPPOINT)&rectBoundsDP, 2);
    SaveDC(di.hdcDraw);
    SetMapMode(di.hdcDraw, MM_TEXT);
    SetWindowOrgEx(di.hdcDraw, 0, 0, NULL);
    SetViewportOrgEx(di.hdcDraw, 0, 0, NULL);
    di.bOptimize = TRUE; //since we save the DC we can do this
  }
  di.prcBounds = &rectBoundsDP;
  GetZoomInfo(di);
```

```
HRESULT hRes = OnDraw(di);
if (bDeleteDC)
  ::DeleteDC(di.hicTargetDev);
if (!bMetafile)
  RestoreDC(di.hdcDraw, -1);
return hRes;
}
```

CComControl::OnDrawAdvanced prepares a normalized device context for drawing and then calls your control class's OnDraw method. A normalized device context is so called because the device context has (some of) the normal defaults for a device context—specifically, the mapping mode is MM_TEXT, the window origin is 0,0, and the viewport origin is 0,0. Override the OnDrawAdvanced method when you want to use the device context passed by the container as is, without normalizing it. For example, if you don't want these defaults values, you should override OnDrawAdvanced instead of OnDraw, for greater efficiency.

When a container asks a control to draw into a device context, the container specifies whether the control can use optimized drawing techniques. When the bOptimize flag in the ATL_DRAWINFO structure is TRUE, this means that the DC will have some[3] of its settings automatically restored after the call to OnDraw returns. Thus, in your drawing code, you don't have to worry about setting the DC to its original settings (brushes, pens, and so on). It's not really much of an optimization, but every little bit helps.

- When IDataObject_GetData calls OnDrawAdvanced to retrieve a rendering of the control in a metafile, IDataObject_GetData saves the device context state, calls OnDrawAdvanced, and then restores the device context state. Therefore, IDataObject_GetData sets the bOptimize flag to TRUE.

- When OnPaint calls OnDrawAdvanced to have the control render to its window, the bOptimize flag is set to FALSE.

- When IViewObject_Draw calls OnDrawAdvanced to have the control render to the container's window, the bOptimize flag is set to TRUE only if the container supports optimized drawing.

When you override OnDrawAdvanced, you should always check the value of the bOptimize flag and restore the state of the device context as necessary.

For a nonmetafile device context device, OnDrawAdvanced saves the state of the entire device context and restores it after calling your control's OnDraw method. Because of this, the default OnDrawAdvanced method sets the bOptimize flag to TRUE.

---

[3] More specifically, those settings that get saved and restored by the SaveDC/RestoreDC GDI calls.

When you override OnDraw in ATL's current implementation, the bOptimize flag is always TRUE. This doesn't mean that you shouldn't check the flag. It means that you should always go to the effort of supporting optimized drawing when overriding OnDraw because such support is always used.

Listing 11.8 gives excerpts of the drawing code for the BullsEye control. A few features in this code are noteworthy:

- BullsEye supports transparent drawing via the BackStyle stock property. When BackStyle is 1 (opaque), the control uses the background color to fill the area around the bull's eye. When BackStyle is 0 (transparent), the control doesn't draw to the area outside the circle of the bull's eye. This leaves the area around the circle transparent, and the underlying window contents show through.

- BullsEye draws differently into a metafile device context than into another device context. You cannot do some operations when drawing to a metafile. Therefore, BullsEye sets up the device context slightly differently in these two cases.

- BullsEye supports optimized drawing.

The OnDraw method handles the interface to ATL: receiving the ATL_DRAWINFO structure, and figuring out what mapping mode and coordinate system to use, depending on whether the DC is for a metafile. The DrawBullsEye method, on the other hand, actually does the drawing.

Listing 11.8 BullsEye OnDraw and DrawBullsEye Methods

```
#define ASSERT_SUCCESS( b ) ATLASSERT( ( b ) != 0 )
#define VERIFY_SUCCESS( c ) { BOOL bSuccess = ( c ); \
   ATLASSERT( bSuccess != 0 ); }

// Drawing code

static const int LOGWIDTH = 1000;

HRESULT CBullsEye::OnDraw(ATL_DRAWINFO &di) {
    CRect rc = *( ( RECT * )di.prcBounds );
    HDC hdc  = di.hdcDraw;

    // Create brushes as needed
    ...

    // First, fill in background color in invalid area when
```

```
    // BackStyle is Opaque
    if (m_nBackStyle == 1 /* Opaque*/ ) {
        VERIFY_SUCCESS( ::FillRect( hdc, &rc, m_backBrush ) );
    }

    int nPrevMapMode;
    POINT   ptWOOrig, ptVOOrig;
    SIZE szWEOrig, szVEOrig;

    BOOL bMetafile =
        GetDeviceCaps( di.hdcDraw, TECHNOLOGY ) == DT_METAFILE;
    if( !bMetafile ) {
        // OnDrawAdvanced normalized the device context
        // We are now using MM_TEXT and the coordinates
        // are in device coordinates.

        // Establish convenient coordinate system for on screen
        ...
    } else {
        // We will be played back in ANISOTROPIC mapping mode
        // Set up bounding rectangle and coordinate system
        // for metafile
        ...
    }

    // Draw the BullsEye
    DrawBullsEye( di );

    // Note on optimized drawing:
    // Even when using optimized drawing, a control cannot
    // leave a changed mapping mode, coordinate transformation
    // value, selected bitmap, clip region, or metafile in the
    // device context.

    if (!bMetafile) {
        ::SetMapMode (hdc, nPrevMapMode);

        ::SetViewportOrgEx (hdc, ptVOOrig.x,  ptVOOrig.y,  NULL);
        ::SetViewportExtEx (hdc, szVEOrig.cx, szVEOrig.cy, NULL);
    }

    ::SetWindowOrgEx (hdc, ptWOOrig.x,  ptWOOrig.y,  NULL);
    ::SetWindowExtEx (hdc, szWEOrig.cx, szWEOrig.cy, NULL);

    return S_OK;
}
```

```
void CBullsEye::DrawBullsEye(ATL_DRAWINFO &di) {
    HDC hdc  = di.hdcDraw;

    // Create brushes as needed
    ...

    // Compute the width of a ring
    short sRingCount;
    HRESULT hr = get_RingCount( &sRingCount );
    ATLASSERT( SUCCEEDED( hr ) );

    int ringWidth = LOGWIDTH / (sRingCount * 2 - 1);

    // Draw the border between rings using the border pen
    HPEN hOldPen = (HPEN)SelectObject( hdc, m_borderPen );

    HBRUSH hOldBrush = 0;

    for( short i = sRingCount - 1; i >= 0; --i ) {
        // Draw the current ring
        ...

        // Set the correct ring color
        HBRUSH hBrush = ( HBRUSH )::SelectObject( hdc, ringBrush );
        // First time through, save the original brush
        if( hOldBrush == 0 ) {
            hOldBrush = hBrush;
        }
        ...
    }

    // When optimized drawing not in effect,
    // restore the original pen and brush
    if( !di.bOptimize ) {
        ::SelectObject( hdc, hOldPen );
        ::SelectObject( hdc, hOldBrush );
    }
}
```

Property Persistence

A control typically needs to save its state upon its container's request. Various containers prefer different persistence techniques. For example, Internet Explorer and Visual Basic prefer to save a control's state using a property bag, which is an association (or dictionary) of text name/value pairs. The dialog editor in Visual C++ prefers to save a control's state in binary form using a stream. Containers of embedded objects save the objects in structured storage.

ATL provides three persistence interface implementations, as discussed in Chapter 7, "Persistence in ATL":

IPersistStreamInitImpl   Saves properties in binary form into a stream

IPersistStorageImpl   Saves properties in binary form in structured storage

IPersistPropertyBagImpl   Saves properties as name/value pairs

Most controls should derive from all three persistence-implementation classes so that they support the widest variety of containers. The BullsEye control does this:

```
class ATL_NO_VTABLE CBullsEye :
    ...
    // Persistence
    public IPersistStreamInitImpl<CBullsEye>,
    public IPersistStorageImpl<CBullsEye>,
    public IPersistPropertyBagImpl<CBullsEye>,
};
```

As always, you need to add entries to the COM map for each supported interface. The persistence interfaces all derive from IPersist, so you need to add it to the COM map as well.

```
BEGIN_COM_MAP(CBullsEye)
    ...
    // Persistence
    COM_INTERFACE_ENTRY(IPersistStreamInit)
    COM_INTERFACE_ENTRY2(IPersist, IPersistStreamInit)
    COM_INTERFACE_ENTRY(IPersistStorage)
    COM_INTERFACE_ENTRY(IPersistPropertyBag)
END_COM_MAP()
```

All three persistence implementations save the properties listed in the control's property map. You define the property map using the BEGIN_PROP_MAP and END_PROP_MAP macros. Here's the CBullsEye class's property map:

```
BEGIN_PROP_MAP(CBullsEye)
  PROP_DATA_ENTRY("_cx", m_sizeExtent.cx, VT_UI4)
  PROP_DATA_ENTRY("_cy", m_sizeExtent.cy, VT_UI4)
  PROP_ENTRY("BackStyle",       DISPID_BACKSTYLE,
    CLSID_BullsEyePropPage)
  PROP_ENTRY("Beep",            DISPID_BEEP,
    CLSID_BullsEyePropPage)
```

```
      PROP_ENTRY("Enabled",        DISPID_ENABLED,
         CLSID_BullsEyePropPage)
      PROP_ENTRY("RingCount",       DISPID_RINGCOUNT,
         CLSID_BullsEyePropPage)
      PROP_ENTRY("AlternateColor",  DISPID_ALTERNATECOLOR,
         CLSID_StockColorPage)
      PROP_ENTRY("BackColor",       DISPID_BACKCOLOR,
         CLSID_StockColorPage)
      PROP_ENTRY("CenterColor",     DISPID_CENTERCOLOR,
         CLSID_StockColorPage)
      PROP_ENTRY("ForeColor",       DISPID_FORECOLOR,
         CLSID_StockColorPage)
   END_PROP_MAP()
```

The ATL Object Wizard adds the first two `PROP_DATA_ENTRY` macros to a control's property map when it generates the initial source code. These entries cause ATL to save and restore the extent of the control. When you describe a persistent property using a `PROP_DATA_ENTRY` macro, ATL directly accesses the member variable in the control.

You must explicitly add entries for any additional properties that the control needs to persist. The `BullsEye` control lists all but one of its persistent properties using the `PROP_ENTRY` macro. This macro causes ATL to save and restore the specified property by accessing the property using the default dispatch interface for the control. Alternatively, you can use the `PROP_ENTRY_EX` macro to specify the IID, other than `IID_IDispatch`, of the dispatch interface that supports the property. You use the `PROP_ENTRY_EX` macro when your control supports multiple dispatch interfaces with various properties accessible via different dispatch interfaces. Supporting multiple dispatch interfaces is generally not a good thing to do.[4]

One caution: Don't add a `PROP_ENTRY` macro that has a property name that contains an embedded space character. Some relatively popular containers, such as Visual Basic, provide an implementation of `IPropertyBag::Write` that cannot handle names with embedded spaces.

For properties described with the `PROP_ENTRY` and `PROP_ENTRY_EX` macros, the various persistence implementations query for the appropriate interface and call `IDispatch::Invoke`, specifying the `DISPID` from the property map entry to get and put the property.

The ATL property map can handle most property types without custom code, but sometimes you need to customize how your properties are persisted. For example, the `BullsEye` control has one additional property—the `RingValues`

---

[4] For a discussion of why this is a bad thing, see Chapter 4.

indexed (array) property—and the ATL property map doesn't support indexed properties. To persist such properties, you must explicitly implement the IPersist-StreamInit_Save, IPersistStreamInit_Load, IPersistPropertyBag_Save, and IPersistPropertyBag_Load methods normally provided by the ATL persistence-implementation classes and read/write the indexed property. Here's an example from the BullsEye control that calls the ATL implementation of IPersistProperty-Bag_Load and then saves the indexed property:

```
HRESULT CBullsEye::IPersistPropertyBag_Load(
  LPPROPERTYBAG pPropBag,
  LPERRORLOG pErrorLog,
  ATL_PROPMAP_ENTRY* pMap) {
  if (NULL == pPropBag) return E_POINTER;

  // Load the properties described in the PROP_MAP
  HRESULT hr =
    IPersistPropertyBagImpl<CBullsEye>::IPersistPropertyBag_Load(
      pPropBag, pErrorLog, pMap);
  if (SUCCEEDED(hr))
    m_bRequiresSave = FALSE;

  if (FAILED (hr)) return hr;

  // Load the indexed property - RingValues

  // Get the number of rings
  short sRingCount;
  get_RingCount (&sRingCount);

  // For each ring, read its value
  for (short nIndex = 1; nIndex <= sRingCount; nIndex++) {

    // Create the base property name
    CComBSTR bstrName = OLESTR("RingValue");

    // Create ring number as a string
    CComVariant vRingNumber = nIndex;
    hr = vRingNumber.ChangeType (VT_BSTR);
    ATLASSERT (SUCCEEDED (hr));

    // Concatenate the two strings to form property name
    bstrName += vRingNumber.bstrVal;

    // Read ring value from the property bag
    CComVariant vValue = 0L;
    hr = pPropBag->Read(bstrName, &vValue, pErrorLog);
```

```
    ATLASSERT (SUCCEEDED (hr));
    ATLASSERT (VT_I4 == vValue.vt);

    if (FAILED (hr)) {
      hr = E_UNEXPECTED;
      break;
    }

    // Set the ring value
    put_RingValue (nIndex, vValue.lVal);
  }

  if (SUCCEEDED(hr)) m_bRequiresSave = TRUE;
  return hr;
}
```

IQuickActivate

Some control containers ask a control for its IQuickActivate interface and use it to quickly exchange a number of interfaces between the container and the control during the control's activation process—thus the interface name.

ATL provides an implementation of this interface, IQuickActivateImpl, which, by default, full, composite, and HTML controls use. However, a control container also gives a control a few ambient properties during this quick activation process that the ATL implementation doesn't save. If your control needs these ambient properties—BackColor, ForeColor, and Appearance—it's more efficient to save them during the quick activation process than to incur three more round-trips to the container to fetch them later.

The tricky aspect is that a container might not quick-activate your control. Therefore, the control should save the ambient properties when quick-activated or retrieve the ambient properties when the container provides the control's client site, but not both. Luckily, it's easy to add this functionality to your control.

When a container quick-activates your control, it calls the control's IQuickActivate::QuickActivate method, which is present in your control's IQuickActivateImpl base class. This method delegates the call to your control class's IQuickActivate_QuickActivate method. By default, a control class doesn't provide the method, so the call invokes a default implementation supplied by CComControlBase. You simply need to provide an implementation of the IQuickActivate_QuickActivate method that saves the ambient properties and forwards the call to the method in CComControlBase, like this:

```
HRESULT CBullsEye::IQuickActivate_QuickActivate(
    QACONTAINER *pQACont,
    QACONTROL *pQACtrl) {
```

```
    m_clrForeColor = pQACont->colorFore;
    m_clrBackColor = pQACont->colorBack;
    m_nAppearance  = (short) pQACont->dwAppearance;
    m_bAmbientsFetched = true;

    HRESULT hr = CComControlBase::IQuickActivate_QuickActivate(
        pQACont, pQACtrl);
    return hr;
}
```

Note that the function also sets a flag, m_bAmbientsFetched, to remember that it has already obtained the ambient properties and, therefore, shouldn't fetch them again when the control receives its client site. BullsEye initializes the flag to false in its constructor and checks the flag in its IOleObject_SetClientSite method like this:

```
HRESULT CBullsEye::IOleObject_SetClientSite(
    IOleClientSite *pClientSite) {
    HRESULT hr =
        CComControlBase::IOleObject_SetClientSite(pClientSite);
    if (!m_bAmbientsFetched) {
        GetAmbientBackColor (m_clrBackColor);
        GetAmbientForeColor (m_clrForeColor);
        GetAmbientAppearance (m_nAppearance);
    }
    return hr;
}
```

Component Categories

Frequently, you'll want your control to belong to one or more component categories. For example, the BullsEye control belongs to the ATL Internals Sample Components category. Additionally, BullsEye is a member of the Safe for Initialization and Safe for Scripting categories, so scripts on an HTML page can initialize and access it without security warnings. Adding the proper entries to the control's category map registers the class as a member of the specified component categories. BullsEye uses this category map:

```
BEGIN_CATEGORY_MAP(CBullsEye)
  IMPLEMENTED_CATEGORY(CATID_ATLINTERNALS_SAMPLES)
  IMPLEMENTED_CATEGORY(CATID_SafeForScripting)
  IMPLEMENTED_CATEGORY(CATID_SafeForInitializing)
END_CATEGORY_MAP()
```

Registering a control as a member of the Safe for Initialization or Safe for Scripting component categories is a static decision. In other words, you're deciding that the control is or is not always safe. A control might prefer to restrict its functionality at runtime when it needs to be safe for initialization or scripting, but then prefer to have its full, potentially unsafe functionality available at other times.

Such controls must implement the IObjectSafety interface. ATL provides a default implementation of this interface in the IObjectSafetyImpl class. As a template parameter, you specify the safety options that the control supports. A container can use a method of this interface to selectively enable and disable each supported option. A control can determine its current safety level, and potentially disable or enable unsafe functionality, by checking the m_dwCurrentSafety member variable.

You use this implementation class like most of the others, derive your control class from the appropriate template class, and add the proper interface entry to the COM interface map. BullsEye would do it like this:

```
class ATL_NO_VTABLE CBullsEye :
  ...
  // Object safety support
  public IObjectSafetyImpl<CBullsEye,
    INTERFACESAFE_FOR_UNTRUSTED_CALLER |
    INTERFACESAFE_FOR_UNTRUSTED_DATA>,
  ...

BEGIN_COM_MAP(CBullsEye)
  // Object safety support
  COM_INTERFACE_ENTRY(IObjectSafety)
  ...
END_COM_MAP()

STDMETHODIMP(FormatHardDrive)( ) {
  if( m_dwCurrentSafety == 0 ) {
    // Container isn't asking for safe behavior, perform mayhem
    ...
    return S_OK; // We just erased a hard drive,
                 // how could we not be ok?
  }
  else {
    // Container has asked we play nice, so don't
    // actually erase the drive
    ...
    return S_FALSE; // Ok, we succeeded, but we're
                    // being a little grumpy
  }
```

ICategorizeProperties

Visual Basic provides a property view that displays the properties of a control on a form. The property view can display the properties on a control alphabetically or grouped by arbitrary categories. Figure 11.3 shows the categorized list of the BullsEye control's properties when the control is contained on a Visual Basic form.

A control must implement the ICategorizeProperties interface so that Visual Basic can display the control's properties in the appropriate categories in its property view. Unfortunately, this interface isn't presently defined in any system IDL file or any system header file, and ATL provides no implementation class for the interface. So, here's what you need to do to support it.

First, here's the IDL for the interface:

```
[
    object, local,
    uuid(4D07FC10-F931-11CE-B001-00AA006884E5),
    helpstring("ICategorizeProperties Interface"),
    pointer_default(unique)
]
interface ICategorizeProperties : IUnknown {
    typedef [public] int PROPCAT;

    const int PROPCAT_Nil        = -1;
    const int PROPCAT_Misc       = -2;
    const int PROPCAT_Font       = -3;
    const int PROPCAT_Position   = -4;
    const int PROPCAT_Appearance = -5;
    const int PROPCAT_Behavior   = -6;
    const int PROPCAT_Data       = -7;
    const int PROPCAT_List       = -8;
    const int PROPCAT_Text       = -9;
    const int PROPCAT_Scale      = -10;
    const int PROPCAT_DDE        = -11;

    HRESULT MapPropertyToCategory([in] DISPID dispid,
        [out] PROPCAT* ppropcat);
    HRESULT GetCategoryName([in] PROPCAT propcat, [in] LCID lcid,
        [out] BSTR* pbstrName);
}
```

I keep this IDL in a separate file, CategorizeProperties.idl, and import the file into the BullsEye.idl file. At this point, it's highly unlikely that Microsoft will add this interface to a system IDL file, so having it in a separate IDL file makes it easier to reuse the definition in multiple projects.

You implement the interface like all interfaces in ATL: Derive your control class from ICategorizeProperties, add the interface entry to the control's interface map, and implement the two methods, MapPropertyToCategory and GetCategoryName. Note that there are 11 predefined property categories with negative values. You can define your own custom categories, but be sure to assign them positive values.

The MapPropertyToCategory method returns the appropriate property category value for the specified property.

```
const int PROPCAT_Scoring = 1;

STDMETHODIMP CBullsEye::MapPropertyToCategory(
    /*[in]*/ DISPID dispid, /*[out]*/ PROPCAT* ppropcat) {
    if (NULL == ppropcat) return E_POINTER;

    switch (dispid) {
    case DISPID_FORECOLOR:
    case DISPID_BACKCOLOR:
    case DISPID_CENTERCOLOR:
    case DISPID_ALTERNATECOLOR:
    case DISPID_RINGCOUNT:
    case DISPID_BACKSTYLE:
        *ppropcat = PROPCAT_Appearance;
        return S_OK;

    case DISPID_BEEP:
    case DISPID_ENABLED:
        *ppropcat = PROPCAT_Behavior;
        return S_OK;

    case DISPID_RINGVALUE:
        *ppropcat = PROPCAT_Scoring;
        return S_OK;

    default:
        return E_FAIL;
    }
}
```

The GetCategoryName method simply returns a BSTR containing the category name. You need to support only your custom category values because Visual Basic knows the names of the standard property category values.

```
STDMETHODIMP CBullsEye::GetCategoryName(/*[in]*/ PROPCAT propcat,
    /*[in]*/ LCID lcid,
    /*[out]*/ BSTR* pbstrName)
{
    if(PROPCAT_Scoring == propcat) {
        *pbstrName = ::SysAllocString(L"Scoring");
        return S_OK;
    }
    return E_FAIL;
}
```

BullsEye supports one custom category, Scoring, and associates its Ring-Value property with the category. Unfortunately, the RingValue property is an indexed property, and Visual Basic doesn't support indexed properties. Thus, the RingValue property doesn't appear in Visual Basic's property view, either in the alphabetic list or in the categorized list.

Per-Property Browsing

When Visual Basic and similar containers display a control's property in a property view, they can ask the control for a string that better describes the property's current value than the actual value of the property. For example, a particular property might have valid numerical values of 1, 2, and 3, which represent the colors red, blue, and green, respectively. When Visual Basic asks the control for a display string for the property when the property has the value 2, the control returns the string "blue".

A container uses the control's IPerPropertyBrowsing interface to retrieve the display strings for a control's properties. When the control doesn't provide a display string for a property, some containers, such as Visual Basic, provide default formatting, if possible.[5] Of course, the container can always simply display the actual property value.

Notice in Figure 11.3 that the Visual Basic property view displays Yes for the value of the Beep property (which was set to -1) and Transparent for the BackStyle property (which was set to 0). To provide custom display strings for a property's value, your control must implement IPerPropertyBrowsing and override the Get-DisplayString method. You return the appropriate string for the requested property based on the property's current value. Here's the GetDisplayString method for the CBullsEye class:

---

[5] Visual Basic first queries a control for IPerPropertyBrowsing to retrieve the display strings for a property. When that query fails, Visual Basic loads the type library and retrieves the enumerated values that were specified in the IDL for the property, if available. Failing that, Visual Basic displays the actual property value.

```
STDMETHODIMP CBullsEye::GetDisplayString(DISPID dispid,
    BSTR *pBstr) {
    ATLTRACE2(atlTraceControls,2,
        _T("CBullsEye::GetDisplayString\n"));
    switch (dispid) {
    case DISPID_BEEP:
        if (VARIANT_TRUE == m_beep)
            *pBstr = SysAllocString (OLESTR("Yes"));
        else
            *pBstr = SysAllocString (OLESTR("No"));

        return *pBstr ? S_OK : E_OUTOFMEMORY;

    case DISPID_BACKSTYLE:
        if (1 == m_nBackStyle)
            *pBstr = SysAllocString (OLESTR("Opaque"));
        else
            *pBstr = SysAllocString (OLESTR("Transparent"));

        return *pBstr ? S_OK : E_OUTOFMEMORY;

    case DISPID_ALTERNATECOLOR: // Make VB apply default
    case DISPID_BACKCOLOR:      // formatting for these
    case DISPID_CENTERCOLOR:    // color properties.
    case DISPID_FORECOLOR:      // Otherwise it displays color
                                // values in decimal and doesn't
                                // draw the color sample
                                // correctly
        return S_FALSE;  // This is an undocumented return
                         // value that works...
    }

    return
        IPerPropertyBrowsingImpl<CBullsEye>::GetDisplayString(
            dispid, pBstr);
}
```

The IPerPropertyBrowsingImpl<T>::GetDisplayString implementation fetches the value of the specified property and, if it's not already a BSTR, converts the value into a BSTR using VariantChangeType. This produces relatively uninteresting display strings for anything but simple numerical value properties.

Visual Basic provides default formatting for certain property types, such as OLE_COLOR and VARIANT_BOOL properties, but only if your GetDisplayString method doesn't provide a string for the property. The default implementation fails when the property doesn't exist, when the property exists but cannot be converted into a BSTR, or when the BSTR memory allocation fails. This basically means that the default implementation of GetDisplayString often provides less than useful strings for many properties.

BullsEye's GetDisplayString method lets Visual Basic provide default formatting for all its OLE_COLOR properties by returning S_FALSE when asked for those properties. This value isn't documented as a valid return value for GetDisplayString, but there are a couple of convincing reasons to use it: First, the default ATL implementation of GetDisplayString returns this value when it cannot provide a display string for a property. Second, it works.

When you let Visual Basic provide the display string for an OLE_COLOR property, it displays the color value in hexadecimal and displays a color sample. ATL's default implementation displays the color value in decimal, and the sample image is typically always black. When you let Visual Basic provide the display string for a VARI-ANT_BOOL property, Visual Basic displays True and False. ATL's default implementation displays –1 and 0, respectively.

Also notice in Figure 11.3 that when you click on a property in Visual Basic's property view to modify the property, a drop-down arrow appears to the right side of the property value. Clicking this arrow produces a drop-down list that contains strings representing the valid selections for the property. You provide this support via the IPerPropertyBrowsing interface, too. A container calls the interface's Get-PredefinedStrings method to retrieve the strings that the container displays in the drop-down list. For each string, the method also provides a DWORD value (cookie). When a user selects one of the strings from the drop-down list, the container calls the interface's GetPredefinedValue method and provides the cookie. The method returns the property value associated with the selected string. The container then typically performs a property put IDispatch call to change the property to the predefined value.

The BullsEye control supports predefined strings and values for the Beep and BackStyle properties, as shown in the following code:

```
/************************/
/* GetPredefinedStrings */
/************************/

#define DIM(a) (sizeof(a)/sizeof(a[0]))

static const LPCOLESTR    rszBeepStrings [] = {
  OLESTR("Yes, make noise"), OLESTR("No, be mute") };
static const DWORD        rdwBeepCookies [] = { 0, 1 };
static const VARIANT_BOOL rvbBeepValues  [] = {
    VARIANT_TRUE, VARIANT_FALSE };
```

```
static const UINT cBeepStrings = DIM(rszBeepStrings);
static const UINT cBeepCookies = DIM(rdwBeepCookies);
static const UINT cBeepValues  = DIM(rvbBeepValues);

static const LPCOLESTR    rszBackStyleStrings [] = {
  OLESTR("Opaque"), OLESTR("Transparent") };
static const DWORD        rdwBackStyleCookies [] = { 0, 1 };
static const long         rvbBackStyleValues  [] = { 1, 0 };

static const UINT cBackStyleStrings = DIM(rszBackStyleStrings);
static const UINT cBackStyleCookies = DIM(rdwBackStyleCookies);
static const UINT cBackStyleValues  = DIM(rvbBackStyleValues);

STDMETHODIMP CBullsEye::GetPredefinedStrings(
  /*[in]*/ DISPID dispid,
  /*[out]*/ CALPOLESTR *pcaStringsOut,
  /*[out]*/ CADWORD *pcaCookiesOut) {
   ATLTRACE2(atlTraceControls,2,
    _T("CBullsEye::GetPredefinedStrings\n"));
  if (NULL == pcaStringsOut || NULL == pcaCookiesOut)
    return E_POINTER;

  ATLASSERT (cBeepStrings == cBeepCookies);
  ATLASSERT (cBeepStrings == cBeepValues);

  ATLASSERT (cBackStyleStrings == cBackStyleCookies);
  ATLASSERT (cBackStyleStrings == cBackStyleValues);

  pcaStringsOut->cElems = 0;
  pcaStringsOut->pElems = NULL;
  pcaCookiesOut->cElems = 0;
  pcaCookiesOut->pElems = NULL;

  HRESULT hr = S_OK;
  switch (dispid) {
  case DISPID_BEEP:
    hr = SetStrings (cBeepValues, rszBeepStrings, pcaStringsOut);
    if (FAILED (hr)) return hr;
    return SetCookies (cBeepValues, rdwBeepCookies,
      pcaCookiesOut);

  case DISPID_BACKSTYLE:
    hr = SetStrings (cBackStyleValues, rszBackStyleStrings,
      pcaStringsOut);
    if (FAILED (hr)) return hr;
```

```
    return SetCookies (cBackStyleValues, rdwBackStyleCookies,
      pcaCookiesOut);
  }
  return
    IPerPropertyBrowsingImpl<CBullsEye>::GetPredefinedStrings(
      dispid, pcaStringsOut, pcaCookiesOut);
}


/*********************/
/* GetPredefinedValue */
/*********************/

STDMETHODIMP CBullsEye::GetPredefinedValue(
  DISPID dispid, DWORD dwCookie, VARIANT* pVarOut) {
  if (NULL == pVarOut) return E_POINTER;

  ULONG i;
  switch (dispid) {
  case DISPID_BEEP:
    // Walk through cookie array looking for matching value
    for (i = 0; i < cBeepCookies; i++) {
      if (rdwBeepCookies[i] == dwCookie) {
        pVarOut->vt = VT_BOOL;
        pVarOut->boolVal = rvbBeepValues [i];
        return S_OK;
      }
    }
    return E_INVALIDARG;

  case DISPID_BACKSTYLE:
    // Walk through cookie array looking for matching value
    for (i = 0; i < cBackStyleCookies; i++) {
      if (rdwBackStyleCookies[i] == dwCookie) {
        pVarOut->vt = VT_I4;
        pVarOut->lVal = rvbBackStyleValues [i];
        return S_OK;
      }
    }
    return E_INVALIDARG;
  }

  return
    IPerPropertyBrowsingImpl<CBullsEye>::GetPredefinedValue(
      dispid, dwCookie, pVarOut);
}
```

Some containers let you edit a control's property using the appropriate property page for the property. When you click on such a property in Visual Basic's property view, Visual Basic displays a small button containing . . . to the right of the property value. Clicking this button displays the control's property page for the property.

A container uses a control's `IPerPropertyBrowsing::MapPropertyToPage` method to find the property page for a property. ATL's implementation of this method uses the property map to determine which property page corresponds to a particular property. When a property doesn't have a property page, you specify `CLSID_NULL` as follows:

```
PROP_ENTRY("SomeProperty", DISPID_SOMEPROPERTY, CLSID_NULL)
```

`IPerPropertyBrowsingImpl` finds this entry in the property map and returns the error `PERPROP_E_NOPAGEAVAILABLE`. This prevents Visual Basic from displaying the property page ellipses button ("...").

Keyboard Handling for an ActiveX Control

When an ATL-based ActiveX control has the focus on a Visual Basic form, it does not give the focus to the default button on the form (the button with a `Default` property of `True`) when you press Enter. ATL provides implementations of the `IOleControl::GetControlInfo` and `IOleInPlaceActiveObject::TranslateAccelerator` methods. The `GetControlInfo` method returns `E_NOTIMPL`. A container calls a control's `GetControlInfo` method to get the control's keyboard mnemonics and keyboard behavior, and it calls the control's `TranslateAccelerator` method to process the key presses.

`BullsEye` overrides the default implementation of `GetControlInfo` provided by ATL with the following code:

```
STDMETHODIMP CBullsEye::GetControlInfo(CONTROLINFO *pci) {
    if(!pci) return E_POINTER;
    pci->hAccel   = NULL;
    pci->cAccel   = 0;
    pci->dwFlags  = 0;
    return S_OK;
}
```

The default implementation of `TranslateAccelerator` looks like this:

```
STDMETHOD(TranslateAccelerator)(LPMSG pMsg) {
  T* pT = static_cast<T*>(this);
  HRESULT hRet = S_OK;
```

```
  MSG msg = *pMsg;
  if (pT->PreTranslateAccelerator(&msg, hRet))
  return hRet;

  CComPtr<IOleControlSite> spCtlSite;
  hRet = pT->InternalGetSite(__uuidof(IOleControlSite),
    (void**)&spCtlSite);
  if (SUCCEEDED(hRet)) {
    if (spCtlSite != NULL) {
      DWORD dwKeyMod = 0;
      if (::GetKeyState(VK_SHIFT) < 0)
        dwKeyMod += 1;      // KEYMOD_SHIFT
      if (::GetKeyState(VK_CONTROL) < 0)
        dwKeyMod += 2;      // KEYMOD_CONTROL
      if (::GetKeyState(VK_MENU) < 0)
        dwKeyMod += 4;      // KEYMOD_ALT
      hRet = spCtlSite->TranslateAccelerator(&msg, dwKeyMod);
    }
    else
      hRet = S_FALSE;
  }
  return (hRet == S_OK) ? S_OK : S_FALSE;
}
```

When the BullsEye control has the input focus, these method implementations pass all Tab and Enter key presses to the container for processing. This implementation allows one to tab into and out of the BullsEye control. While the control has the input focus, pressing the Enter key activates the default pushbutton on a Visual Basic form, if any.

For the BullsEye control, it doesn't make much sense to allow a user to tab into the control. You can use the MiscStatus bits for a control to inform the control's container that the control doesn't want to be activated by tabbing. A container asks a control for its MiscStatus setting by calling the control's IOle-Object::GetMisc-Status method. ATL provides an implementation of this method in the IOleControlImpl class:

```
STDMETHOD(GetMiscStatus)(DWORD dwAspect, DWORD *pdwStatus) {
  ATLTRACE2(atlTraceControls,2,
    _T("IOleObjectImpl::GetMiscStatus\n"));
  return OleRegGetMiscStatus(T::GetObjectCLSID(),
    dwAspect, pdwStatus);
}
```

This code simply delegates the call to the OleRegGetMiscStatus function, which reads the value from the control's Registry entry. A control can have multiple Misc-Status values—one for each drawing aspect that the control supports. Most controls support the drawing aspect DVASPECT_CONTENT, which has the value of 1. You specify the drawing aspect as a subkey of MiscStatus. The value of the subkey is the string of decimal numbers comprising the sum of the desired OLEMISC enumeration values.

For example, BullsEye uses the following MiscStatus settings:

OLEMISC_SETCLIENTSITEFIRST	131072
OLEMISC_NOUIACTIVATE	16384
OLEMISC_ACTIVATEWHENVISIBLE	256
OLEMISC_INSIDEOUT	128
CANTLINKINSIDE	16
OLEMISC_RECOMPOSEONRESIZE	1

The sum of these values is 14,7857, so you specify that as the value of the subkey called 1 of your class.

```
ForceRemove {7DC59CC5-36C0-11D2-AC05-00A0C9C8E50D} =
s 'BullsEye Class' {
    ...
    'MiscStatus' = s '0'
    {
        '1' = s '147857'
    }
}
```

Alternatively, BullsEye can override the GetMiscStatus method and provide the desired value; the Registry entry then would not be needed:

```
STDMETHODIMP CBullsEye::GetMiscStatus (
    DWORD dwAspect, DWORD *pdwStatus) {
    if (NULL == pdwStatus) return E_POINTER;

    *pdwStatus =
            OLEMISC_SETCLIENTSITEFIRST |
            OLEMISC_ACTIVATEWHENVISIBLE |
            OLEMISC_INSIDEOUT |
            OLEMISC_CANTLINKINSIDE |
```

```
                OLEMISC_RECOMPOSEONRESIZE |
                OLEMISC_NOUIACTIVATE ;

        return S_OK;
    }
```

The OLEMISC_NOUIACTIVATE setting prevents Visual Basic from giving the Bulls-Eye control the input focus when a user attempts to tab into the control.

Summary

ActiveX controls use much of the functionality discussed so far. An ATL-based control typically supports properties and methods using ATL's IDispatchImpl support. In addition, a control typically fires events; therefore, it often derives from IConnectionPointContainerImpl and uses a connection point proxy-generated class (IconnectionPointImpl derived) for each connection point. A control generally requires persistence support, so it uses one or more of the persistence-implementation classes: IPersistSrteamInitImpl, IPersistPropertyBagImpl, and IPersistStorageImpl.

In addition, many controls should implement numerous other interfaces so that they integrate well with various control containers, such as Visual Basic. In the next chapter, you learn how ATL supports hosting ActiveX controls, and how to write a control container using ATL.

CHAPTER
12 | **Control Containment**

Containment of COM controls can take many forms. A window can contain any number of COM controls, as can a dialog or another control (called a composite control). All these containers share common characteristics, which is the subject of this chapter.

How Controls Are Contained

To contain a COM control,[1] a container must do two things:

1. Provide a window to act as the parent for the child COM control. The parent window can be used by a single child COM control or can be shared by many.

2. Implement a set of COM interfaces that the control uses to communicate with the container. The container must provide at least one object per control, called the site, to implement these interfaces. However, the interfaces can be spread between up to two other container-provided objects, called the document and the frame.

The window that the container provides can be a parent window of the control or, in the case of a windowless control, can be shared by the control. The control uses the window in its interaction with the user. The interfaces that the container implements are used for integration with the control and mirror those that the control implements. Figure 12.1 shows the major interfaces that the container implements and how they are mirrored by those that the control implements.

As mentioned in Chapter 11, "ActiveX Controls," full coverage of the interaction between controls and containers is beyond the scope of this book. Refer to the sources listed in Chapter 11 for more information.[2] However, this chapter presents those things you need to know to host controls both in standalone applications and

---

[1] This chapter doesn't distinguish between OLE controls and ActiveX controls.

[2] You might also want to refer to the MSDN article "Notes on Implementing an OLE Control Container" for control container–specific information at http://msdn.microsoft.com/library/default.asp?url=/library/en-us/dnaxctrl/html/msdn_contcntr.asp (http://tinysells.com/60).

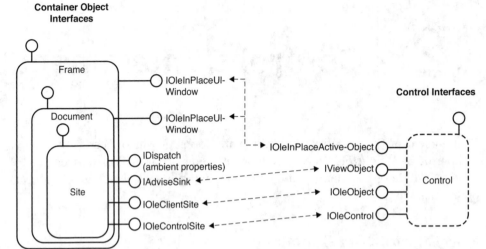

Figure 12.1   Container and control interfaces

inside COM servers. Your hosting options include windows, dialogs, and composite controls. Before diving into the details of dialogs or controls hosting other controls, let's start with the basics by examining control containment in a simple frame window.

Basic Control Containment

Control Creation

The control-creation process in ATL exposes the core of how ATL hosts controls. Figure 12.2 shows the overall process. What follows is a detailed look at the relevant bits of code involved.

ATL's implementation of the required container interfaces is called CAxHostWindow.[3]

```
// This class is not cocreateable
class ATL_NO_VTABLE CAxHostWindow :
  public CComCoClass<CAxHostWindow , &CLSID_NULL>,
  public CComObjectRootEx<CComSingleThreadModel>,
  public CWindowImpl<CAxHostWindow>,
  public IAxWinHostWindow,
  public IOleClientSite,
```

---

[3] This class is defined in atlhost.h.

```
    public IOleInPlaceSiteWindowless,
    public IOleControlSite,
    public IOleContainer,
    public IObjectWithSiteImpl<CAxHostWindow>,
    public IServiceProvider,
    public IAdviseSink,
#ifndef _ATL_NO_DOCHOSTUIHANDLER
    public IDocHostUIHandler,
#endif
    public IDispatchImpl<IAxWinAmbientDispatch,
        &IID_IAxWinAmbientDispatch,
        &LIBID_ATLLib>
    {...};
```

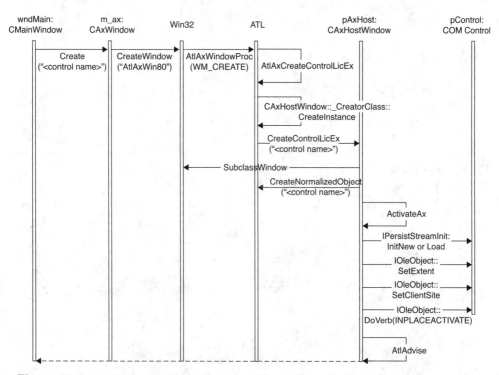

Figure 12.2 A UML sequence diagram of the ATL control-creation process

Notice that a `CAxHostWindow` is two things: a window (from `CWindowImpl`) and a COM implementation (from `CComObjectRootEx`). When the container wants to host a control, it creates an instance of `CAxHostWindow`, but not directly. Instead, it creates an instance of a window class defined by ATL, called `AtlAxWin80`. This window acts as the parent window for the control and eventually is subclassed by an instance of `CAxHostWindow`. Before an instance of this window class can be created, the window class must first be registered. ATL provides a function called `AtlAxWinInit` to register the `AtlAxWin80` window class.

```cpp
// This either registers a global class
// (if AtlAxWinInit is in ATL.DLL)
// or it registers a local class
ATLINLINE ATLAPI_(BOOL) AtlAxWinInit() {
  CComCritSecLock<CComCriticalSection> lock(
    _AtlWinModule.m_csWindowCreate, false);
  if (FAILED(lock.Lock())) {
    ATLTRACE(atlTraceHosting, 0,
      _T("ERROR : Unable to lock critical section "
        "in AtlAxWinInit\n"));
    ATLASSERT(0);
    return FALSE;
  }
  WM_ATLGETHOST = RegisterWindowMessage(_T("WM_ATLGETHOST"));
  WM_ATLGETCONTROL = RegisterWindowMessage(
    _T("WM_ATLGETCONTROL"));
  WNDCLASSEX wc;
  // first check if the class is already registered
  wc.cbSize = sizeof(WNDCLASSEX);
  BOOL bRet = ::GetClassInfoEx(
    _AtlBaseModule.GetModuleInstance(),
    CAxWindow::GetWndClassName(), &wc);

  // register class if not
  if(!bRet) {
    wc.cbSize = sizeof(WNDCLASSEX);
#ifdef _ATL_DLL_IMPL
    wc.style = CS_GLOBALCLASS | CS_DBLCLKS;
    bAtlAxWinInitialized = true;
#else
    wc.style = CS_DBLCLKS;
#endif
    wc.lpfnWndProc = AtlAxWindowProc;
    wc.cbClsExtra = 0;
    wc.cbWndExtra = 0;
    wc.hInstance = _AtlBaseModule.GetModuleInstance();
    wc.hIcon = NULL;
    wc.hCursor = ::LoadCursor(NULL, IDC_ARROW);
    wc.hbrBackground = (HBRUSH)(COLOR_WINDOW + 1);
    wc.lpszMenuName = NULL;
```

```
   wc.lpszClassName =
     CAxWindow::GetWndClassName(); // "AtlAxWin80"
   wc.hIconSm = NULL;

   ATOM atom= ::RegisterClassEx(&wc);
   if(atom) {
    _AtlWinModule.m_rgWindowClassAtoms.Add(atom);
    bRet=TRUE;
   } else {
     bRet=FALSE;
   }
 }

 if(bRet) {
   // first check if the class is already registered
   memset(&wc, 0, sizeof(WNDCLASSEX));
   wc.cbSize = sizeof(WNDCLASSEX);
   bRet = ::GetClassInfoEx(_AtlBaseModule.GetModuleInstance(),
     CAxWindow2::GetWndClassName(), &wc);
   // register class if not
   if(!bRet) {
     wc.cbSize = sizeof(WNDCLASSEX);
#ifdef _ATL_DLL_IMPL
     wc.style = CS_GLOBALCLASS | CS_DBLCLKS;
#else
     wc.style = CS_DBLCLKS;
#endif
     wc.lpfnWndProc = AtlAxWindowProc2;
     wc.cbClsExtra = 0;
     wc.cbWndExtra = 0;
     wc.hInstance = _AtlBaseModule.GetModuleInstance();
     wc.hIcon = NULL;
     wc.hCursor = ::LoadCursor(NULL, IDC_ARROW);
     wc.hbrBackground = (HBRUSH)(COLOR_WINDOW + 1);
     wc.lpszMenuName = NULL;
     wc.lpszClassName =
       CAxWindow2::GetWndClassName();//"AtlAxWinLic80"
     wc.hIconSm = NULL;
     ATOM atom= RegisterClassEx(&wc);

     if (atom) {
       _AtlWinModule.m_rgWindowClassAtoms.Add(atom);
       bRet=TRUE;
     } else {
```

```
        bRet=FALSE;
      }
    }
  }
  return bRet;
}
```

This function actually registers two window classes: AtlAxWin80 and AtlAxWin-Lic80. The difference, if you haven't guessed from the names, is that the latter supports embedding controls that require a runtime license.

You don't need to manually call AtlAxWinInit: It is called from the ATL code at the various places where these window classes are needed, as you'll see later. Multiple calls are fine: The function checks to make sure the window classes are registered first before doing anything.

After the AtlAxWin80 class has been registered, creating an instance of one also creates an instance of CAxHostWindow. The CAxHostWindow object uses the title of the window as the name of the control to create and to host. For example, the following code creates a CAxHostWindow and causes it to host a new instance of the BullsEye control developed in Chapter 10, "Windowing":

```
class CMainWindow : public CWindowImpl<CMainWindow, ...> {
...
  LRESULT OnCreate(UINT uMsg, WPARAM wParam, LPARAM lParam,
    BOOL& lResult) {
    // Create the host window, the CAxHostWindow object, and
    // the BullsEye control, and host the control
    RECT    rect; GetClientRect(&rect);
    LPCTSTR pszName = __T("ATLInternals.BullsEye");
    HWND    hwndContainer = m_ax.Create(__T("AtlAxWin80"),
      m_hWnd, rect, pszName, WS_CHILD | WS_VISIBLE);
    if( !hwndContainer ) return -1;
    return 0;
  }

private:
  CWindow m_ax;
};
```

The creation of the CAxHostWindow object and the corresponding control is initiated in the WM_CREATE handler of the AtlAxWin80 window procedure AtlAxWindowProc:

```
static LRESULT CALLBACK
AtlAxWindowProc(HWND hWnd, UINT uMsg, WPARAM wParam,
 LPARAM lParam) {
 switch(uMsg) {
 case WM_CREATE: {
   // create control from a PROGID in the title
   // This is to make sure drag drop works
   ::OleInitialize(NULL);

   CREATESTRUCT* lpCreate = (CREATESTRUCT*)lParam;
   int nLen = ::GetWindowTextLength(hWnd);
   CAutoStackPtr<TCHAR> spName(
     (TCHAR *)_malloca((nLen + 1) * sizeof(TCHAR)));
   if(!spName) {
     return -1;
   }
   // Extract window text to be used as name of control to host
   ::GetWindowText(hWnd, spName, nLen + 1);
   ::SetWindowText(hWnd, _T(""));
   IAxWinHostWindow* pAxWindow = NULL;
   ...


   USES_CONVERSION_EX;
   CComPtr<IUnknown> spUnk;
   // Create AxHostWindow instance and host the control
   HRESULT hRet = AtlAxCreateControlLic(T2COLE_EX_DEF(spName),
     hWnd, spStream, &spUnk, NULL);
   if(FAILED(hRet)) return -1; // abort window creation

   hRet = spUnk->QueryInterface(__uuidof(IAxWinHostWindow),
     (void**)&pAxWindow);
   if(FAILED(hRet)) return -1; // abort window creation
   // Keep a CAxHostWindow interface pointer in the window's
   // user data
   ::SetWindowLongPtr(hWnd, GWLP_USERDATA,
     (DWORD_PTR)pAxWindow);
   // continue with DefWindowProc
   }
 break;

 case WM_NCDESTROY: {
   IAxWinHostWindow* pAxWindow =
     (IAxWinHostWindow*)::GetWindowLongPtr(hWnd, GWLP_USERDATA);
   // When window goes away, release the host (and the control)
```

```
    if(pAxWindow != NULL) pAxWindow->Release();
    OleUninitialize();
  }
  break;

  case WM_PARENTNOTIFY: {
    if((UINT)wParam == WM_CREATE) {
      ATLASSERT(lParam);
      // Set the control parent style for the AxWindow
      DWORD dwExStyle = ::GetWindowLong((HWND)lParam,
        GWL_EXSTYLE);
      if(dwExStyle & WS_EX_CONTROLPARENT) {
        dwExStyle = ::GetWindowLong(hWnd, GWL_EXSTYLE);
        dwExStyle |= WS_EX_CONTROLPARENT;
        ::SetWindowLong(hWnd, GWL_EXSTYLE, dwExStyle);
      }
    }
  }
  break;

  default:
      break;
  }

  return ::DefWindowProc(hWnd, uMsg, wParam, lParam);
}
```

Notice that the window's text, as passed to the call to CWindow::Create, is used as the name of the control to create. The call to AtlAxCreateControlLic, passing the name of the control, forwards to AtlAxCreateControlLicEx, which furthers things by creating a CAxHostWindow object and asking it to create and host the control:

```
ATLINLINE ATLAPI AtlAxCreateControlLicEx(
  LPCOLESTR lpszName,
  HWND hWnd,
  IStream* pStream,
  IUnknown** ppUnkContainer,
  IUnknown** ppUnkControl,
  REFIID iidSink,
  IUnknown* punkSink,
  BSTR bstrLic) {
  AtlAxWinInit();
```

```
HRESULT hr;
CComPtr<IUnknown> spUnkContainer;
CComPtr<IUnknown> spUnkControl;

hr = CAxHostWindow::_CreatorClass::CreateInstance(NULL,
  __uuidof(IUnknown), (void**)&spUnkContainer);
if(SUCCEEDED(hr)) {
  CComPtr<IAxWinHostWindowLic> pAxWindow;
  spUnkContainer->QueryInterface(__uuidof(IAxWinHostWindow),
    (void**)&pAxWindow);
  CComBSTR bstrName(lpszName);
  hr = pAxWindow->CreateControlLicEx(bstrName, hWnd, pStream,
    &spUnkControl, iidSink, punkSink, bstrLic);
}
if(ppUnkContainer != NULL) {
  if (SUCCEEDED(hr)) {
    *ppUnkContainer = spUnkContainer.p;
    spUnkContainer.p = NULL;
  }
  else
    *ppUnkContainer = NULL;
}
if (ppUnkControl != NULL) {
  if (SUCCEEDED(hr)) {
    *ppUnkControl = SUCCEEDED(hr) ? spUnkControl.p : NULL;
    spUnkControl.p = NULL;
  }
  else
    *ppUnkControl = NULL;
}
return hr;
}
```

IAxWinHostWindow

AtlAxCreateControlEx uses the IAxWinHostWindow interface to create the control.
IAxWinHostWindow is one of the few interfaces that ATL defines and is one of the
interfaces that CAxHostWindow implements. Its job is to allow for management of the
control that it's hosting:

```
interface IAxWinHostWindow : IUnknown {
  HRESULT CreateControl([in] LPCOLESTR lpTricsData,
    [in] HWND hWnd, [in] IStream* pStream);
```

```
      HRESULT CreateControlEx([in] LPCOLESTR lpTricsData,
        [in] HWND hWnd, [in] IStream* pStream,
        [out] IUnknown** ppUnk,
        [in] REFIID riidAdvise, [in] IUnknown* punkAdvise);
      HRESULT AttachControl([in] IUnknown* pUnkControl,
        [in] HWND hWnd);
      HRESULT QueryControl([in] REFIID riid,
        [out, iid_is(riid)] void **ppvObject);
      HRESULT SetExternalDispatch([in] IDispatch* pDisp);
      HRESULT SetExternalUIHandler(
        [in] IDocHostUIHandlerDispatch* pDisp);
    };
```

A second interface, IAxWinHostWindowLic, derives from IAxWinHostWindow and supports creating licensed controls:

```
interface IAxWinHostWindowLic : IAxWinHostWindow {
  HRESULT CreateControlLic([in] LPCOLESTR lpTricsData,
    [in] HWND hWnd, [in] IStream* pStream, [in] BSTR bstrLic);
  HRESULT CreateControlLicEx([in] LPCOLESTR lpTricsData,
    [in] HWND hWnd, [in] IStream* pStream,
    [out]IUnknown** ppUnk, [in] REFIID riidAdvise,
    [in]IUnknown* punkAdvise, [in] BSTR bstrLic);
};
```

To create a new control in CAxHostWindow, IAxWinHostWindow provides Create-Control or CreateControlEx, which AtlAxCreateControlEx then uses after the CAx-HostWindow object is created. The parameters for CreateControl[Ex] are as follows:

- lpTricsData. The name of the control to create. It can take the form of a CLSID, a ProgID, a URL, a filename, or raw HTML. We discuss this more later.

- hWnd. Parent window in which to host the control. This window is subclassed by CAxHostWindow.

- pStream. Stream that holds object-initialization data. The control is initialized via IPersistStreamInit. If pStream is non-NULL, Load is called. Otherwise, Init-New is called.

- ppUnk. Filled with an interface to the newly created control.

- riidAdvise. If not IID_NULL, CAxHostWindow attempts to set up a connection-point connection between the control and the sink object represented by the punkAdvise parameter. CAxHostWindow manages the resultant cookie and tears down the connection when the control is destroyed.

- punkAdvise. An interface to the sink object that implements the sink interface specified by riidAdvise.

The CreateControlLicEx method adds one more parameter:
- bstrLic. This string contains the licensing key. If the string is empty, the control is created using the normal CoCreateInstance call. If there *is* a licensing key in the string, the control is created via the IClassFactory2 interface, which supports creating licensed controls.

The AttachControl method of the IAxWinHostWindow method attaches a control that has already been created and initialized to an existing CAxHostWindow object. The QueryControl method allows access to the control's interfaces being hosted by the CAxHostWindow object. Both SetExternalDispatch and SetExternalUIHandler are used when hosting the Internet Explorer HTML control and will be discussed at the end of the chapter in the HTML Controls section.

CreateControlLicEx

CAxHostWindow's implementation of CreateControlLicEx subclasses[4] the parent window for the new control, creates a new control, and then activates it. If an initial connection point is requested, AtlAdvise is used to establish that connection. If the newly created control is to be initialized from raw HTML or to be navigated to via a URL, CreateControlLicEx does that, too:

```
STDMETHODIMP CAxHostWindow::CreateControlLicEx(
  LPCOLESTR lpszTricsData,
  HWND hWnd,
  IStream* pStream,
  IUnknown** ppUnk,
  REFIID iidAdvise,
  IUnknown* punkSink,
  BSTR bstrLic)
{
  HRESULT hr = S_FALSE;
  // Used to keep track of whether we subclass the window

  bool bReleaseWindowOnFailure = false;
  // Release previously held control
  ReleaseAll();
```

---

[4] This is subclassing in the User32 sense, not the C++ sense.

```
...
if (::IsWindow(hWnd)) {
  if (m_hWnd != hWnd) { // Don't need to subclass the window
                        // if we already own it
    // Route all messages to CAxHostWindow
    SubclassWindow(hWnd);
    bReleaseWindowOnFailure = true;
  }
  ...
  bool bWasHTML = false;
  // Create control based on lpszTricsData
  hr = CreateNormalizedObject(lpszTricsData,
    __uuidof(IUnknown),
    (void**)ppUnk, bWasHTML, bstrLic);

  // Activate the control
  if (SUCCEEDED(hr)) hr = ActivateAx(*ppUnk, false, pStream);

  // Try to hook up any sink the user might have given us.
  m_iidSink = iidAdvise;
  if(SUCCEEDED(hr) && *ppUnk && punkSink) {
    AtlAdvise(*ppUnk, punkSink, m_iidSink, &m_dwAdviseSink);
  }
  ...

  // If raw HTML, give HTML control its HTML
  ...

  // If it's an URL, navigate the Browser control to the URL
  ...

  if (FAILED(hr) || m_spUnknown == NULL)    {
    // We don't have a control or something failed so release
    ReleaseAll();
    ...
  }
}
return hr;
}
```

How the control name is interpreted depends on another function, called `CreateNormalizedObject`. The actual COM activation process is handled by the `ActivateAx` function (discussed shortly).

CreateNormalizedObject

The `CreateNormalizedObject` function creates an instance of a COM object using strings of the form shown in Table 12.1.

Table 12.1. String Formats Understood by `CreateNormalizedObject`

Type	Example	CLSID of Created Object
HTML	mshtml:<body>Wow!</body>	`CLSID_HTMLDocument`
CLSID	{7DC59CC5-36C0-11D2-AC05-00A0C9C8E50D}	Result of `CLSIDFromString`
ProgID	ATLInternals.BullsEye	Result of `CLSIDFromProgID`
URL	http://www.awl.com res://htmlapp.exe/main.htm	`CLSID_WebBrowser`
Active document	D:\Atl Internals\10 Controls.doc file://D:\Atl Internals\10 Controls.doc	`CLSID_WebBrowser`

Because `CAxHostWindow` uses the title of the window to obtain the name passed to `CreateNormalizedObject`, you can use any of these string formats when creating an instance of the `AtlWinInit` window class.

If no license key is supplied, `CreateNormalizedObject` uses `CoCreateInstance` to instantiate the object. If there *is* a license key, `CreateNormalizedObject` instead calls `CoGetClassFactory` and uses the factory's `IClassFactory2::CreateInstanceLic` method to create the control using the given license key.

ActivateAx

The `ActivateAx` function is the part of the control-creation process that really performs the magic. Called after `CreateControlLicEx`[5] actually creates the underlying COM object, `ActivateAx` takes an interface pointer from the object that `CreateNormalizedObject` creates and activates it as a COM control in the parent window. `ActivateAx` is responsible for the following:

- Setting the client site—that is, the `CAxHostWindow`'s implementation of `IOleClientSite`—via the control's implementation of `IOleObject`.

---

[5] Despite the name, the `CreateControlLicEx` function handles the creation of COM controls with or without licensing information.

- Calling either InitNew or Load (depending on whether the pStream argument to AtlAxCreateControlEx is NULL or non-NULL) via the control's implementation of IPersistStreamInit.

- Passing the CAxHostWindow's implementation of IAdviseSink to the control's implementation of IViewObject.

- Setting the control's size to the size of the parent window, also via the control's implementation of IOleObject.

- Finally, to show the control and allow it to handle input and output, calling DoVerb(OLEIVERB_INPLACEACTIVATE) via the control's implementation of, again, IOleObject.

This process completes the activation of the control. However, creating an instance of CAxHostWindow via direct reference to the AtlAxWin80 window class is not typical. The implementation details of AtlAxWin80 and CAxHostWindow are meant to be hidden from the average ATL programmer. The usual way a control is hosted under ATL is via an instance of a wrapper class. Two such wrappers exist in ATL: CAxWindow and CAxWindow2.

CAxWindow

CAxWindow simplifies the use of CAxHostWindow with a set of wrapper functions. The initial creation part of CAxWindow class is defined as follows:

```
#define ATLAXWIN_CLASS    "AtlAxWin80"

template <class TBase /* = CWindow */> class CAxWindowT :
  public TBase {
public:
// Constructors
  CAxWindowT(HWND hWnd = NULL) : TBase(hWnd) { AtlAxWinInit(); }

  CAxWindowT< TBase >& operator=(HWND hWnd) {
    m_hWnd = hWnd; return *this;
  }

// Attributes
  static LPCTSTR GetWndClassName() { return _T(ATLAXWIN_CLASS); }

// Operations
  HWND Create(HWND hWndParent, _U_RECT rect = NULL, ...) {
    return CWindow::Create(GetWndClassName(), hWndParent,
      rect, ... );
```

```
  }
...
};


typedef CAxWindowT<CWindow> CAxWindow;
```

Notice that the `Create` function still requires the parent window and the name of the control but does not require passing the name of the `CAxHostWindow` window class. Instead, `CAxWindow` knows the name of the appropriate class itself (available via its static member function `GetWndClassName`) and passes it to the `CWindow` base class just like we had done manually. Using `CAxWindow` reduces the code required to host a control to the following:

```
class CMainWindow : public CWindowImpl<CMainWindow, ...> {
...
  LRESULT OnCreate(UINT uMsg, WPARAM wParam, LPARAM lParam,
    BOOL& lResult) {
    // Create the host window, the CAxHostWindow object, and
    // the BullsEye control, and host the control
    RECT rect; GetClientRect(&rect);
    LPCTSTR pszName = __T("ATLInternals.BullsEye");
    HWND hwndContainer = m_ax.Create(m_hWnd, rect,
        pszName, WS_CHILD | WS_VISIBLE);
    if( !hwndContainer ) return -1;
    return 0;
  }

private:
  CAxWindow m_ax;
};
```

The combination of a custom window class and a `CWindow`-based wrapper provides exactly the same model as the window control wrappers that I discussed in Chapter 10, "Windowing." For example, `EDIT` is a window class, and the `CEdit` class provides the client-side wrapper. The implementation of the `EDIT` window class happens to use the window text passed via `CreateWindow` as the text to edit. The `AtlAxWin80` class, on the other hand, uses the window text as the name of the control to create. The job of both wrapper classes is to provide a set of member functions that replace calls to `SendMessage`. `CEdit` provides member functions such as `CanUndo` and `GetLineCount`, which send the `EM_CANUNDO` and `EM_GETLINECOUNT` messages. `CAxWindow`, on the other hand, provides member functions that also send window messages to the `AtlAxWin80` class (which I discuss later). The only real difference between EDIT and AtlAxWin80 is that EDIT is provided with the operating system, whereas AtlAxWin80 is provided only with ATL.[6]

Two-Step Control Creation

You might have noticed that AtlAxCreateControlEx takes some interesting parameters, such as an IStream interface pointer and an interface ID/interface pointer pair, to specify an initial connection point. However, although the window name can be used to pass the name of the control, there are no extra parameters to CreateWindow for a couple interface pointers and a globally unique identifier (GUID). Instead, CAxWindow provides a few extra wrapper functions: CreateControl and CreateControlEx:

```
template <class TBase> class CAxWindowT : public TBase {
public:
  ...
  HRESULT CreateControl(LPCOLESTR lpszName,
    IStream* pStream = NULL,
    IUnknown** ppUnkContainer = NULL) {
    return CreateControlEx(lpszName, pStream, ppUnkContainer);
  }

  HRESULT CreateControl(DWORD dwResID, IStream* pStream = NULL,
    IUnknown** ppUnkContainer = NULL) {
    return CreateControlEx(dwResID, pStream, ppUnkContainer);
  }

  HRESULT CreateControlEx(LPCOLESTR lpszName,
    IStream* pStream = NULL,
    IUnknown** ppUnkContainer = NULL,
    IUnknown** ppUnkControl = NULL,
    REFIID iidSink = IID_NULL, IUnknown* punkSink = NULL) {
    ATLASSERT(::IsWindow(m_hWnd));
    // We must have a valid window!

    // Get a pointer to the container object
    // connected to this window
    CComPtr<IAxWinHostWindow> spWinHost;
    HRESULT hr = QueryHost(&spWinHost);

    // If QueryHost failed, there is no host attached to this
```

---

[6] Arguably, a window class whose function is to host COM controls should be part of the OS.

```
    // window. We assume that the user wants to create a new
    // host and subclass the current window
    if (FAILED(hr)) {
      return AtlAxCreateControlEx(lpszName, m_hWnd, pStream,
        ppUnkContainer, ppUnkControl, iidSink, punkSink);
    }

    // Create the control requested by the caller
    CComPtr<IUnknown> pControl;
    if (SUCCEEDED(hr)) {
      hr = spWinHost->CreateControlEx(lpszName, m_hWnd, pStream,
        &pControl, iidSink, punkSink);
    }

    // Send back the necessary interface pointers
    if (SUCCEEDED(hr)) {
      if (ppUnkControl) { *ppUnkControl = pControl.Detach(); }

      if (ppUnkContainer) {
        hr = spWinHost.QueryInterface(ppUnkContainer);
        ATLASSERT(SUCCEEDED(hr)); // This should not fail!
      }
    }
    return hr;
}

HRESULT CreateControlEx(DWORD dwResID, IStream* pStream = NULL,
  IUnknown** ppUnkContainer = NULL,
  IUnknown** ppUnkControl = NULL,
  REFIID iidSink = IID_NULL, IUnknown* punkSink = NULL) {
  TCHAR szModule[MAX_PATH];
  DWORD dwFLen =
    GetModuleFileName(_AtlBaseModule.GetModuleInstance(),
      szModule, MAX_PATH);
  if( dwFLen == 0 ) return AtlHresultFromLastError();
  else if( dwFLen == MAX_PATH )
    return HRESULT_FROM_WIN32(ERROR_INSUFFICIENT_BUFFER);

  CComBSTR bstrURL(OLESTR("res://"));
  HRESULT hr=bstrURL.Append(szModule);
  if(FAILED(hr)) { return hr; }
  hr=bstrURL.Append(OLESTR("/"));
  if(FAILED(hr)) { return hr; }
```

```
    TCHAR szResID[11];
#if _SECURE_ATL && !defined(_ATL_MIN_CRT)
    if (_stprintf_s(szResID, _countof(szResID),
      _T("%0d"), dwResID) == -1) {
      return HRESULT_FROM_WIN32(ERROR_INSUFFICIENT_BUFFER);
    }
#else
    wsprintf(szResID, _T("%0d"), dwResID);
#endif
    hr=bstrURL.Append(szResID);
    if(FAILED(hr)) { return hr; }

    ATLASSERT(::IsWindow(m_hWnd));
    return CreateControlEx(bstrURL, pStream, ppUnkContainer,
      ppUnkControl, iidSink, punkSink);
  }
  ...
};
```

CreateControl and CreateControlEx allow for the extra parameters that AtlAx-CreateControlEx supports. The extra parameter that the CAxWindow wrappers support beyond those passed to AtlAxCreateControlEx is the dwResID parameter, which serves as an ID of an HTML page embedded in the resources of the module. This parameter is formatted into a string of the format res://<module path>/<dwResID> before being passed to AtlAxCreateControlEx.

These functions are meant to be used in a two-stage construction of first the host and then its control. For example:

```
LRESULT
CMainWindow::OnCreate(UINT uMsg, WPARAM wParam, LPARAM lParam,
  BOOL& lResult) {
  RECT    rect; GetClientRect(&rect);
  // Phase one: Create the container (passing a null (0)
  // window title)
  // m_ax is declared in the CMainWindow class as:
  // CAxWindow m_ax;
  HWND    hwndContainer = m_ax.Create(m_hWnd, rect, 0,
    WS_CHILD | WS_VISIBLE);
  if( !hwndContainer ) return -1;

  // Phase two: Create the control
  LPCOLESTR pszName = OLESTR("ATLInternals.BullsEye");
```

```
  HRESULT hr = m_ax.CreateControl(pszName);
  return (SUCCEEDED(hr) ? 0 : -1);
};
```

I show you how to persist a control and how to handle events from a control later in this chapter. If you've already created a control and initialized it, you can still use the hosting functionality of ATL by attaching the existing control to a host window via the AttachControl function:

```
template <class TBase = CWindow> class CAxWindowT :
  public TBase {
public:
...
  HRESULT AttachControl(IUnknown* pControl,
    IUnknown** ppUnkContainer) {
    ATLASSERT(::IsWindow(m_hWnd));
    // We must have a valid window!

    // Get a pointer to the container object connected
    // to this window
    CComPtr<IAxWinHostWindow> spWinHost;
    HRESULT hr = QueryHost(&spWinHost);

    // If QueryHost failed, there is no host attached
    // to this window. We assume that the user wants to
    // create a new host and subclass the current window
    if (FAILED(hr))
      return AtlAxAttachControl(pControl, m_hWnd,
        ppUnkContainer);

    // Attach the control specified by the caller
    if (SUCCEEDED(hr))
      hr = spWinHost->AttachControl(pControl, m_hWnd);

    // Get the IUnknown interface of the container
    if (SUCCEEDED(hr) && ppUnkContainer) {
      hr = spWinHost.QueryInterface(ppUnkContainer);
      ATLASSERT(SUCCEEDED(hr)); // This should not fail!
    }

    return hr;
  }
...
};
```

AttachControl is used like this:

```
LRESULT
CMainWindow::OnCreate(UINT uMsg, WPARAM wParam, LPARAM lParam,
  BOOL& lResult) {
  RECT rect; GetClientRect(&rect);
  // Phase one: Create the container
  HWND hwndContainer = m_ax.Create(m_hWnd, rect, 0,
    WS_CHILD | WS_VISIBLE);
  if( !hwndContainer ) return -1;

  // Create and initialize a control
  CComPtr<IUnknown> spunkControl; // ...

  // Phase two: Attach an existing control
  HRESULT hr = m_ax.AttachControl(spunkControl);
  return (SUCCEEDED(hr) ? 0 : -1);
};
```

CAxWindow2 and the AtlAxWinLic80 Window Class

Earlier, I mentioned that ATL actually registers two window classes: AtlAxWin80 and AtlAxWinLic80. Why two window classes? AtlAxWinLic80 supports one feature that AtlAxWin80 does not: the creation of licensed controls.

This might sound odd at first. After all, the actual control-creation step is done by the CreateControlLicEx function, which handles the creation of controls with or without license keys. However, the AtlAxWin80 class never actually passes a license key, so CreateControlLicEx never uses the IClassFactory2 when AtlAxWin80 is the calling class.

The AtlAxWinLic80 window class, on the other hand, has a slightly different window proc:

```
static LRESULT CALLBACK AtlAxWindowProc2(HWND hWnd, UINT uMsg,
  WPARAM wParam, LPARAM lParam) {
  switch(uMsg) {
  case WM_CREATE: {
    // ... same as AtlAxWindowProc ...

    // Format of data in lpCreateParams
    // int nCreateSize;   // size of Create data in bytes
    // WORD nMsg;         // constant used to indicate type
    //                    // of DLGINIT data.
    //                    // See _DialogSplitHelper for values.
```

```
    // DWORD dwLen;         // Length of data stored for control
                            // in DLGINIT format in bytes.
    // DWORD cchLicKey;     // Length of license key in OLECHAR's
    // OLECHAR *szLicKey;   // This will be present only if
                            // cchLicKey is greater than 0.
                            // This is of variable length and will
                            // contain cchLicKey OLECHAR's
                            // that represent the license key.
    // The following two fields will be present only if nMsg is
    // WM_OCC_LOADFROMSTREAM_EX or WM_OCC_LOADFROMSTORAGE_EX.
    // If present this information will be ignored since
    // databinding is not supported.
    // ULONG cbDataBinding;     // Length of databinding
                                // information in bytes.
    // BYTE *pbDataBindingInfo  // cbDataBinding bytes that contain
                                // databinding information
    // BYTE *pbControlData;     // Actual control data persisted
                                // by the control.


    // ... Load persistence data into stream ...



    CComBSTR bstrLicKey;
    HRESULT hRet = _DialogSplitHelper::ParseInitData(spStream,
      &bstrLicKey.m_str);
    if (FAILED(hRet)) return -1;


    USES_CONVERSION_EX;
    CComPtr<IUnknown> spUnk;
    hRet = AtlAxCreateControlLic(T2COLE_EX_DEF(spName), hWnd,
      spStream, &spUnk, bstrLicKey);
    if(FAILED(hRet)) {
      return -1; // abort window creation
    }
    hRet = spUnk->QueryInterface(__uuidof(IAxWinHostWindowLic),
      (void**)&pAxWindow);
    if(FAILED(hRet)) return -1; // abort window creation
    ::SetWindowLongPtr(hWnd, GWLP_USERDATA,
      (DWORD_PTR)pAxWindow);
    // continue with DefWindowProc
  }
  break;


  // ... Rest is the same as AtlAxWindowProc ...
}
```

The difference is in the WM_CREATE handler. The CREATESTRUCT passed in can contain the license key information; if it does, AtlAxWinLic80 extracts the license key and passes it on to be used in the creation of the control.

Just as the CAxWindow class wraps the use of AtlAxWin80, the CAxWindow2 class wraps the use of AtlAxWinLic80:

```
template <class TBase /* = CWindow */>
class CAxWindow2T : public CAxWindowT<TBase> {
public:
// Constructors
  CAxWindow2T(HWND hWnd = NULL) : CAxWindowT<TBase>(hWnd) { }

  CAxWindow2T< TBase >& operator=(HWND hWnd);

// Attributes
  static LPCTSTR GetWndClassName() {
    return _T(ATLAXWINLIC_CLASS);
  }

// Operations
  HWND Create(HWND hWndParent, _U_RECT rect = NULL,
    LPCTSTR szWindowName = NULL,
    DWORD dwStyle = 0, DWORD dwExStyle = 0,
    _U_MENUorID MenuOrID = 0U, LPVOID lpCreateParam = NULL) {
    return CWindow::Create(GetWndClassName(), hWndParent, rect,
      szWindowName, dwStyle, dwExStyle, MenuOrID, lpCreateParam);
  }

  HRESULT CreateControlLic(LPCOLESTR lpszName,
    IStream* pStream = NULL,
    IUnknown** ppUnkContainer = NULL, BSTR bstrLicKey = NULL) {
    return CreateControlLicEx(lpszName, pStream, ppUnkContainer,
      NULL, IID_NULL, NULL, bstrLicKey);
  }

  HRESULT CreateControlLic(DWORD dwResID,
    IStream* pStream = NULL,
    IUnknown** ppUnkContainer = NULL, BSTR bstrLicKey = NULL) {
    return CreateControlLicEx(dwResID, pStream, ppUnkContainer,
      NULL, IID_NULL, NULL, bstrLicKey);
  }

  HRESULT CreateControlLicEx(LPCOLESTR lpszName,
    IStream* pStream = NULL,
```

```
    IUnknown** ppUnkContainer = NULL,
    IUnknown** ppUnkControl = NULL,
    REFIID iidSink = IID_NULL, IUnknown* punkSink = NULL,
    BSTR bstrLicKey = NULL);

  HRESULT CreateControlLicEx(DWORD dwResID,
    IStream* pStream = NULL,
    IUnknown** ppUnkContainer = NULL,
    IUnknown** ppUnkControl = NULL,
    REFIID iidSink = IID_NULL, IUnknown* punkSink = NULL,
    BSTR bstrLickey = NULL);
};

typedef CAxWindow2T<CWindow> CAxWindow2;
```

The first thing to note is that CAxWindow2 derives from CAxWindow, so you can use CAxWindow to create nonlicensed controls just as easily. CAxWindow2 adds the various CreateControlLic[Ex] overloads to enable you to pass the licensing information when you create the control.

For the rest of this chapter, I talk about CAxWindow and AtlAxWin80. Everything in the discussion also applies to CAxWindow2 and AtlAxWinLic80.

Using the Control

After you've created the control, it's really two things: a window and a control. The window is an instance of AtlAxWin80 and hosts the control, which might or might not have its own window. (CAxHostWindow provides full support for windowless controls.) Because CAxWindow derives from CWindow, you can treat it like a window (that is, you can move it, resize it, and hide it); AtlAxWin80 handles those messages by translating them into the appropriate COM calls on the control. For example, if you want the entire client area of a frame window to contain a control, you can handle the WM_SIZE message like this:

```
class CMainWindow : public CWindowImpl<CMainWindow, ...> {
...
  LRESULT OnSize(UINT, WPARAM, LPARAM lParam, BOOL&) {
    if( m_ax ) { // m_ax will be Create'd earlier, e.g. WM_CREATE
      RECT rect = { 0, 0, LOWORD(lParam), HIWORD(lParam) };
      m_ax.MoveWindow(&rect); // Resize the control
    }
    return 0;
  }
```

```
private:
  CAxWindow m_ax;
};
```

In addition to handling Windows messages, COM controls are COM objects. They expect to be programmed via their COM interfaces. To obtain an interface on the control, CAxWindow provides the QueryControl method:

```
template <class TBase = CWindow> class CAxWindowT :
  public TBase {
public:
  ...
  HRESULT QueryControl(REFIID iid, void** ppUnk) {
    CComPtr<IUnknown> spUnk;
    HRESULT hr = AtlAxGetControl(m_hWnd, &spUnk);
    if (SUCCEEDED(hr)) hr = spUnk->QueryInterface(iid, ppUnk);
    return hr;
  }

  template <class Q> HRESULT QueryControl(Q** ppUnk)
  { return QueryControl(__uuidof(Q), (void**)ppUnk); }
};
```

Like QueryHost, QueryControl uses a global function (AtlAxGetControl, in this case) that sends a window message to the AtlAxWin80 window to retrieve an interface, but this time from the hosted control itself. When the control has been created, QueryControl can be used to get at the interfaces of the control:

```
// Import interface definitions for BullsEye
#import "D:\ATLBook\src\atlinternals\Debug\BullsEyeCtl.dll" \
  raw_interfaces_only raw_native_types no_namespace named_guids

LRESULT
CMainWindow::OnCreate(UINT uMsg, WPARAM wParam, LPARAM lParam,
  BOOL& lResult) {
  // Create the control
  ...

  // Set initial BullsEye properties
  CComPtr<IBullsEye>  spBullsEye;
  HRESULT hr = m_ax.QueryControl(&spBullsEye);
  if( SUCCEEDED(hr) ) {
    spBullsEye->put_Beep(VARIANT_TRUE);
```

```
        spBullsEye->put_CenterColor(RGB(0, 0, 255));
    }

    return 0;
};
```

Notice the use of the `#import` statement to pull in the definitions of the interfaces of the control you're programming against. This is necessary if you have only the control's server DLL and the bundled type library but no original IDL (a common occurrence when programming against controls). Notice also the use of the `#import` statement attributes—for example, `raw_interfaces_only`. These attributes are used to mimic as closely as possible the C++ language mapping you would have gotten had you used `midl.exe` on the server's IDL file. Without these attributes, Visual C++ creates a language mapping that uses the compiler-provided wrapper classes (such as `_bstr_t`, `_variant_t`, and `_com_ptr_t`), which are different from the ATL-provided types (such as `CComBSTR`, `CComVariant`, and `CComPtr`). Although the compiler-provided classes have their place, I find that it is best not to mix them with the ATL-provided types. Apparently, the ATL team agrees with me because the ATL Wizard–generated `#import` statements also use these attributes (we talk more about the control containment–related wizards later).

Sinking Control Events

Not only are you likely to want to program against the interfaces that the control implements, but you're also likely to want to handle events fired by the control. Most controls have an event interface, which, for maximum compatibility with the largest number of clients, is often a `dispinterface`.[7] For example, the `BullsEye` control from the last chapter defined the following event interface:

```
const int DISPID_ONRINGHIT     = 1;
const int DISPID_ONSCORECHANGED = 2;

dispinterface _IBullsEyeEvents {
properties:
methods:
  [id(DISPID_ONRINGHIT)]
  void OnRingHit(short ringNumber);
  [id(DISPID_ONSCORECHANGED)]
  void OnScoreChanged(long ringValue);
};
```

---

[7] The scripting engines that Internet Explorer (IE) hosts allow you to handle only events defined in a `dispinterface`.

An implementation of IDispatch is required for a control container to handle events fired on a dispinterface. Implementations of IDispatch are easy if the interface is defined as a dual interface, but they are much harder if it is defined as a raw dispinterface.[8] However, as you recall from Chapter 9, "Connection Points," ATL provides a helper class called IDispEventImpl for implementing an event dispinterface:

```
template <UINT nID, class T, const IID* pdiid = &IID_NULL,
  const GUID* plibid = &GUID_NULL,
  WORD wMajor = 0, WORD wMinor = 0,
  class tihclass = CComTypeInfoHolder>
class ATL_NO_VTABLE IDispEventImpl :
  public IDispEventSimpleImpl<nID, T, pdiid> {...};
```

IDispEventImpl uses a data structure called a sink map, established via the following macros:

```
#define BEGIN_SINK_MAP(_class) ...
#define SINK_ENTRY_INFO(id, iid, dispid, fn, info) ...
#define SINK_ENTRY_EX(id, iid, dispid, fn) ...
#define SINK_ENTRY(id, dispid, fn) ...
#define END_SINK_MAP() ...
```

Chapter 9 explains the gory details of these macros, but the gist is that the sink map provides a mapping between a specific object/iid/dispid that defines an event and a member function to handle that event. If the object is a nonvisual one, the sink map can be a bit involved. However, if the object is a COM control, use of IDispEventImpl and the sink map is quite simple, as you're about to see.

To handle events, the container of the controls derives from one instance of IDispEventImpl per control. Notice that the first template parameter of IDispEventImpl is an ID. This ID matches the contained control via the child window ID—that is, the nID parameter to Create. This same ID is used in the sink map to route events from a specific control to the appropriate event handler. The child window ID makes IDispEventImpl so simple in the control case. Nonvisual objects have no child window ID, and the mapping is somewhat more difficult (although, as Chapter 9 described, still entirely possible).

So, handling the events of the BullsEye control merely requires an IDispEventImpl base class and an appropriately constructed sink map:

---

[8] ATL's IDispatchImpl can be used only to implement dual interfaces.

```
const UINT ID_BULLSEYE = 1;

class CMainWindow :
  public CWindowImpl<CMainWindow, CWindow, CMainWindowTraits>,
  public IDispEventImpl<ID_BULLSEYE,
                        CMainWindow,
                        &DIID__IBullsEyeEvents,
                        &LIBID_BullsEyeLib, 1, 0>
{
public:
...
  LRESULT OnCreate(...) {
    RECT rect; GetClientRect(&rect);
    m_ax.Create(m_hWnd, rect, __T("AtlInternals.BullsEye"),
                WS_CHILD | WS_VISIBLE, 0, ID_BULLSEYE);
    ...
    return (m_ax.m_hWnd ? 0 : -1);
  }

BEGIN_SINK_MAP(CMainWindow)
  SINK_ENTRY_EX(ID_BULLSEYE, DIID__IBullsEyeEvents,
    1, OnRingHit)
  SINK_ENTRY_EX(ID_BULLSEYE, DIID__IBullsEyeEvents,
    2, OnScoreChanged)
END_SINK_MAP()

  void __stdcall OnRingHit(short nRingNumber);
  void __stdcall OnScoreChanged(LONG ringValue);

private:
  CAxWindow m_ax;
};
```

Notice that the child window control ID (ID_BULLSEYE) is used in four places. The first is the IDispEventImpl base class. The second is the call to Create, marking the control as the same one that will be sourcing events. The last two uses of ID_BULLSEYE are the entries in the sink map, which route events from the ID_BULLS-EYE control to their appropriate handlers.

Notice also that the event handlers are marked __stdcall. Remember that we're using IDispEventImpl to implement IDispatch for a specific event interface (as defined by the DIID_IBullsEyeEvents interface identifier). That means that IDispEventImpl must unpack the array of VARIANTs passed to Invoke, push them on the stack, and call our event handler. It does this using type information at runtime, but, as mentioned in Chapter 9, it still has to know about the calling convention—

that is, in what order the parameters should be passed on the stack and who's responsible for cleaning them up. To alleviate any confusion, `IDispEventImpl` requires that all event handlers have the same calling convention, which `__stdcall` defines.

When we have `IDispEventImpl` and the sink map set up, we're not done. Unlike Windows controls, COM controls have no real sense of their "parent." This means that instead of implicitly knowing to whom to send events, as an edit control does, a COM control must be told who wants the events. Because events are established between controls and containers with the connection-point protocol, somebody has to call `QueryInterface` for `IConnectionPointContainer`, call `FindConnection-Point` to obtain the `IConnectionPoint` interface, and finally call `Advise` to establish the container as the sink for events fired by the control. For one control, that's not so much work, and ATL even provides a function called `AtlAdvise` to help. However, for multiple controls, it can become a chore to manage the communication with each of them. And because we've got a list of all the controls with which we want to establish communications in the sink map, it makes sense to leverage that knowledge to automate the chore. Luckily, we don't even have to do this much because ATL has already done it for us with `AtlAdviseSinkMap`:

```
template <class T>
inline HRESULT AtlAdviseSinkMap(T* pT, bool bAdvise)
```

The first argument to `AtlAdviseSinkMap` is a pointer to the object that wants to set up the connection points with the objects listed in the sink map. The second parameter is a Boolean determining whether we are setting up or tearing down communication. Because `AtlAdviseSinkMap` depends on the child window ID to map to a window that already contains a control, both setting up and tearing down connection points must occur when the child windows are still living and contain controls. Handlers for the `WM_CREATE` and `WM_DESTROY` messages are excellent for this purpose:

```
LRESULT CMainWindow::OnCreate(...) {
  ... // Create the controls
  AtlAdviseSinkMap(this, true); // Establish connection points
  return 0;
}


LRESULT CMainWindow::OnDestroy(...) {
  // Controls still live
  AtlAdviseSinkMap(this, false); // Tear down connection points
  return 0;
}
```

The combination of `IDispEventImpl`, the sink map, and the `AtlAdviseSinkMap` function is all that is needed to sink events from a COM control. However, we can further simplify things. Most controls implement only a single event interface and publish this fact in one of two places. The default source interface can be provided by an implementation of `IProvideClassInfo2`[9] and can be published in the `coclass` statement in the IDL (and, therefore, as part of the type library). For example:

```
coclass BullsEye {
  [default]           interface IBullsEye;
  [default, source] dispinterface _IBullsEyeEvents;
};
```

If `IDispEventImpl` is used with `IID_NULL` as the template parameter (which is the default value) describing the sink interface, ATL does its best to establish communications with the default source interface via a function called `AtlGetObject-SourceInterface`. This function attempts to obtain the object's default source interface, using the type information obtained via the `GetTypeInfo` member function of `IDispatch`. It first attempts the use of `IProvideClassInfo2`; if that's not available, it digs through the `coclass` looking for the `[default, source]` interface. The upshot is that if you want to source the default interface of a control, the parameters to `IDispEventImpl` are fewer, and you can use the simpler `SINK_ENTRY`. For example, the following is the complete code necessary to sink events from the `BullsEye` control:

```
#import "D:\ATLBook\src\atlinternals\Debug\BullsEyeCtl.dll" \
  raw_interfaces_only raw_native_types no_namespace named_guids

#define ID_BULLSEYE 1

class CMainWindow :
  public CWindowImpl<CMainWindow, CWindow, CMainWindowTraits>,
  // Sink the default source interface
  public IDispEventImpl< ID_BULLSEYE, CMainWindow> {
...
  LRESULT OnCreate(...) {
    RECT rect; GetClientRect(&rect);
    m_ax.Create(m_hWnd, rect, __T("AtlInternals.BullsEye"),
              WS_CHILD | WS_VISIBLE, 0, ID_BULLSEYE);
```

---

[9] The scripting engines that Internet Explorer hosts enable you to handle events only on the default source interface as reported by `IProvideClassInfo2`.

```
        AtlAdviseSinkMap(this, true);
        return (m_ax.m_hWnd ? 0 : -1);
    }


    LRESULT CMainWindow::OnDestroy(...)
    { AtlAdviseSinkMap(this, false); return 0; }

BEGIN_SINK_MAP(CMainWindow)
    // Sink events from the default BullsEye event interface
    SINK_ENTRY(ID_BULLSEYE, 1, OnRingHit)
    SINK_ENTRY(ID_BULLSEYE, 2, OnScoreChanged)
END_SINK_MAP()

    void __stdcall OnRingHit(short nRingNumber);
    void __stdcall OnScoreChanged(LONG ringValue);

private:
    CAxWindow m_ax;
};
```

Property Changes

In addition to a custom event interface, controls often source events on the IPropertyNotifySink interface:

```
interface IPropertyNotifySink : IUnknown {
  HRESULT OnChanged([in] DISPID dispID);
  HRESULT OnRequestEdit([in] DISPID dispID);
}
```

A control uses the IPropertyNotifySink interface to ask the container if it's okay to change a property (OnRequestEdit) and to notify the container that a property has been changed (OnChanged). OnRequestEdit is used for data binding, which is beyond the scope of this book, but OnChanged can be a handy notification, especially if the container expects to persist the control and wants to use OnChanged as an is-dirty notification. Even though IPropertyNotifySink is a connection-point interface, it's not a dispinterface, so neither IDispEventImpl nor a sink map is required. Normal C++ inheritance and AtlAdvise will do. For example:

```
class CMainWindow :
  public CWindowImpl<CMainWindow, ...>,
  public IPropertyNotifySink {
public:
  ...
```

```
// IUnknown, assuming an instance on the stack
STDMETHODIMP QueryInterface(REFIID riid, void** ppv) {
  if( riid == IID_IUnknown || riid == IID_IPropertyNotifySink )
    *ppv = static_cast<IPropertyNotifySink*>(this);
  else return *ppv = 0, E_NOINTERFACE;
  return reinterpret_cast<IUnknown*>(*ppv)->AddRef(), S_OK;
}

STDMETHODIMP_(ULONG) AddRef() { return 2; }
STDMETHODIMP_(ULONG) Release() { return 1; }

// IPropertyNotifySink
STDMETHODIMP OnRequestEdit(DISPID dispID) { return S_OK; }
STDMETHODIMP OnChanged(DISPID dispID) {
  m_bDirty = true; return S_OK;
}

private:
  CAxControl m_ax;
  bool       m_bDirty;
};
```

You have two choices when setting up and tearing down the IPropertyNoti-fySink connection point with the control. You can use AtlAdvise after the control is successfully created and AtlUnadvise just before it is destroyed. This requires managing the connection point cookie yourself. For example:

```
LRESULT CMainWindow::OnCreate(...) {
  ... // Create the control
  // Set up IPropertyNotifySink connection point
  CComPtr<IUnknown> spunkControl;
  m_ax.QueryControl(spunkControl);
  AtlAdvise(spunkControl, this, IID_IPropertyNotifySink,
    &m_dwCookie);
  return 0;
}

LRESULT CMainWindow::OnDestroy(...) {
  // Tear down IPropertyNotifySink connection point
  CComPtr<IUnknown> spunkControl;
  m_ax.QueryControl(spunkControl);
  AtlUnadvise(spunkControl, IID_IPropertyNotifySink,
    &m_dwCookie);
  return 0;
}
```

The second choice is to use the CAxWindow member function CreateControlEx, which allows for a single connection-point interface to be established and the cookie to be managed by the CAxHostWindow object. This simplifies the code considerably:

```
LRESULT CMainWindow::OnCreate(...) {
    ... // Create the control host
    // Create the control and set up IPropertyNotifySink
    // connection point
    m_ax.CreateControlEx(OLESTR("AtlInternals.BullsEye"), 0, 0, 0,
                         IID_IPropertyNotifySink, this);
    return 0;
}
```

The connection-point cookie for IPropertyNotifySink is managed by the CAx-HostWindow object; when the control is destroyed, the connection is torn down automatically. Although this trick works for only one connection-point interface, this technique, combined with the sink map, is likely all you'll ever need when handling events from controls.

Ambient Properties

In addition to programming the properties of the control, you might want to program the properties of the control's environment, known as ambient properties. For this purpose, CAxHostWindow implements the IAxWinAmbientDispatch interface:

```
interface IAxWinAmbientDispatch : IDispatch {
    [propput]
    HRESULT AllowWindowlessActivation([in]VARIANT_BOOL b);
    [propget]
    HRESULT AllowWindowlessActivation(
        [out,retval]VARIANT_BOOL* pb);

    // DISPID_AMBIENT_BACKCOLOR
    [propput, id(DISPID_AMBIENT_BACKCOLOR)]
    HRESULT BackColor([in]OLE_COLOR clrBackground);
    [propget, id(DISPID_AMBIENT_BACKCOLOR)]
    HRESULT BackColor([out,retval]OLE_COLOR* pclrBackground);

    // DISPID_AMBIENT_FORECOLOR
    [propput, id(DISPID_AMBIENT_FORECOLOR)]
    HRESULT ForeColor([in]OLE_COLOR clrForeground);
    [propget, id(DISPID_AMBIENT_FORECOLOR)]
```

```
    HRESULT ForeColor([out,retval]OLE_COLOR* pclrForeground);

    // DISPID_AMBIENT_LOCALEID
    [propput, id(DISPID_AMBIENT_LOCALEID)]
    HRESULT LocaleID([in]LCID lcidLocaleID);
    [propget, id(DISPID_AMBIENT_LOCALEID)]
    HRESULT LocaleID([out,retval]LCID* plcidLocaleID);

    // DISPID_AMBIENT_USERMODE
    [propput, id(DISPID_AMBIENT_USERMODE)]
    HRESULT UserMode([in]VARIANT_BOOL bUserMode);
    [propget, id(DISPID_AMBIENT_USERMODE)]
    HRESULT UserMode([out,retval]VARIANT_BOOL* pbUserMode);

    // DISPID_AMBIENT_DISPLAYASDEFAULT
    [propput, id(DISPID_AMBIENT_DISPLAYASDEFAULT)]
    HRESULT DisplayAsDefault([in]VARIANT_BOOL bDisplayAsDefault);
    [propget, id(DISPID_AMBIENT_DISPLAYASDEFAULT)]
    HRESULT DisplayAsDefault(
      [out,retval]VARIANT_BOOL* pbDisplayAsDefault);

    // DISPID_AMBIENT_FONT
    [propput, id(DISPID_AMBIENT_FONT)]
    HRESULT Font([in]IFontDisp* pFont);
    [propget, id(DISPID_AMBIENT_FONT)]
    HRESULT Font([out,retval]IFontDisp** pFont);

    // DISPID_AMBIENT_MESSAGEREFLECT
    [propput, id(DISPID_AMBIENT_MESSAGEREFLECT)]
    HRESULT MessageReflect([in]VARIANT_BOOL bMsgReflect);
    [propget, id(DISPID_AMBIENT_MESSAGEREFLECT)]
    HRESULT MessageReflect([out,retval]VARIANT_BOOL* pbMsgReflect);

    // DISPID_AMBIENT_SHOWGRABHANDLES
    [propget, id(DISPID_AMBIENT_SHOWGRABHANDLES)]
    HRESULT ShowGrabHandles(VARIANT_BOOL* pbShowGrabHandles);

    // DISPID_AMBIENT_SHOWHATCHING
    [propget, id(DISPID_AMBIENT_SHOWHATCHING)]
    HRESULT ShowHatching(VARIANT_BOOL* pbShowHatching);

    // IDocHostUIHandler Defaults
    ...
};
```

QueryHost can be used on a CAxWindow to obtain the IAxWinAmbientDispatch interface so that these ambient properties can be changed. For example:

```
LRESULT CMainWindow::OnSetGreenBackground(...) {
  // Set up green ambient background
  CComPtr<IAxWinAmbientDispatch> spAmbient;
  hr = m_ax.QueryHost(&spAmbient);
  if( SUCCEEDED(hr) ) {
    spAmbient->put_BackColor(RGB(0, 255, 0));
  }
  return 0;
}
```

Whenever an ambient property is changed, the control is notified via its implementation of the IOleControl member function OnAmbientPropertyChange. The control can then QueryInterface any of its container interfaces for IDispatch to obtain the interface for retrieving the ambient properties (which is why IAxWinAmbient-Dispatch is a dual interface).

Hosting Property Pages

If your container is a development environment, you might want to allow the user to show the control's property pages. This can be accomplished by calling the IOleObject member function DoVerb, passing in the OLEIVERB_PROPERTIES verb ID:

```
LRESULT CMainWindow::OnEditProperties(...) {
  CComPtr<IOleObject> spoo;
  HRESULT hr = m_ax.QueryControl(&spoo);
  if( SUCCEEDED(hr) ) {
    CComPtr<IOleClientSite> spcs; m_ax.QueryHost(&spcs);
    RECT rect; m_ax.GetClientRect(&rect);
    hr = spoo->DoVerb(OLEIVERB_PROPERTIES, 0, spcs,
      -1, m_ax.m_hWnd, &rect);
    if( FAILED(hr) )
      MessageBox(__T("Properties unavailable"), __T("Error"));
  }
  return 0;
}
```

If you want to add your own property pages to those of the control or you want to show the property pages of a control that doesn't support the OLEIVERB_PROPER-TIES verb, you can take matters into your own hands with a custom property sheet. First, you need to ask the control for its property pages via the ISpecifyProperty-

Pages member function GetPages. Second, you might want to augment the control's property pages with your own. Finally, you show the property pages (each a COM object with its own CLSID) via the COM global function OleCreatePropertyFrame, as demonstrated in the ShowProperties function I developed for this purpose:

```
HRESULT ShowProperties(IUnknown* punkControl, HWND hwndParent) {
  HRESULT hr = E_FAIL;

  // Ask the control to specify its property pages
  CComQIPtr<ISpecifyPropertyPages> spPages = punkControl;
  if (spPages) {

    CAUUID  pages;
    hr = spPages->GetPages(&pages);
    if( SUCCEEDED(hr) ) {
      // TO DO: Add your custom property pages here

      CComQIPtr<IOleObject> spObj = punkControl;
      if( spObj ) {
        LPOLESTR pszTitle = 0;
        spObj->GetUserType(USERCLASSTYPE_SHORT, &pszTitle);

        // Show the property pages
        hr = OleCreatePropertyFrame(hwndParent, 10, 10, pszTitle,
          1, &punkControl, pages.cElems,
          pages.pElems, LOCALE_USER_DEFAULT, 0, 0);

        CoTaskMemFree(pszTitle);
      }
      CoTaskMemFree(pages.pElems);
    }
  }

  return hr;
}
```

The ShowProperties function can be used instead of the call to DoVerb. For example:

```
LRESULT CMainWindow::OnEditProperties(...) {
  CComPtr<IUnknown> spunk;
  if( SUCCEEDED(m_ax.QueryControl(&spunk)) ) {
    if( FAILED(ShowProperties(spunk, m_hWnd)) ) {
```

```
        MessageBox(__T("Properties unavailable"), __T("Error"));
      }
    }
    return 0;
  }
```

Either way, if the control's property pages are shown and the Apply or OK button is pressed, your container should receive one `IPropertyNotifySink` call per property that has changed.

Persisting a Control

You might want to persist between application sessions. As discussed in Chapter 7, "Persistence in ATL," you can do this with any number of persistence interfaces. Most controls implement `IPersistStreamInit` (although `IPersistStream` is a common fallback). For example, saving a control to a file can be done with a stream in a structured storage document:

```
bool CMainWindow::Save(LPCOLESTR pszFileName) {
  // Make sure object can be saved
  // Note: Our IPersistStream interface pointer could end up
  // holding an IPersistStreamInit interface. This is OK
  // since IPersistStream is a layout-compatible subset of
  // IPersistStreamInit.
  CComQIPtr<IPersistStream> spPersistStream;
  HRESULT hr = m_ax.QueryControl(&spPersistStream);
  if( FAILED(hr) ) {
    hr = m_ax.QueryControl(IID_IPersistStreamInit,
      (void**)&spPersistStream);
    if( FAILED(hr) ) return false;
  }

  // Save object to stream in a storage
  CComPtr<IStorage>    spStorage;
  hr = StgCreateDocfile(pszFileName,
    STGM_DIRECT | STGM_WRITE |
    STGM_SHARE_EXCLUSIVE | STGM_CREATE,
    0, &spStorage);
  if( SUCCEEDED(hr) ) {
    CComPtr<IStream>    spStream;
    hr = spStorage->CreateStream(OLESTR("Contents"),
      STGM_DIRECT | STGM_WRITE |
      STGM_SHARE_EXCLUSIVE | STGM_CREATE,
      0, 0, &spStream);
```

```
    if( SUCCEEDED(hr) ) {
      // Get and store the CLSID
      CLSID clsid;
      hr = spPersistStream->GetClassID(&clsid);
      if( SUCCEEDED(hr) ) {
        hr = spStream->Write(&clsid, sizeof(clsid), 0);

        // Save the object
        hr = spPersistStream->Save(spStream, TRUE);
      }
    }
  }

  if( FAILED(hr) ) return false;
  return true;
}
```

Restoring a control from a file is somewhat easier because both the CreateControl and the CreateControlEx member functions of CAxWindow take an IStream interface pointer to use for persistence. For example:

```
bool CMainWindow::Open(LPCOLESTR pszFileName) {
  // Open object a stream in the storage
  CComPtr<IStorage>    spStorage;
  CComPtr<IStream>     spStream;
  HRESULT              hr;
  hr = StgOpenStorage(pszFileName, 0,
    STGM_DIRECT | STGM_READ | STGM_SHARE_EXCLUSIVE,
    0, 0, &spStorage);
  if( SUCCEEDED(hr) ) {
    hr = spStorage->OpenStream(OLESTR("Contents"), 0,
      STGM_DIRECT | STGM_READ | STGM_SHARE_EXCLUSIVE,
      0, &spStream);
  }

  if( FAILED(hr) ) return false;

  // Read a CLSID from the stream
  CLSID    clsid;
  hr = spStream->Read(&clsid, sizeof(clsid), 0);
  if( FAILED(hr) ) return false;

  RECT    rect; GetClientRect(&rect);
  OLECHAR szClsid[40];
```

```
StringFromGUID2(clsid, szClsid, lengthof(szClsid));

// Create the control's host window
if( !m_ax.Create(m_hWnd, rect, 0, WS_CHILD | WS_VISIBLE, 0,
                 ID_CHILD_CONTROL) {
  return false;
}

// Create the control, persisting from the stream
hr = m_ax.CreateControl(szClsid, spStream);
if( FAILED(hr) ) return false;
return true;
}
```

When a `NULL` `IStream` interface pointer is provided to either `CreateControl` or `CreateControlEx`, ATL attempts to call the `IPersistStreamInit` member function `InitNew` to make sure that either `InitNew` or `Load` is called, as appropriate.

Accelerator Translations

It's common for contained controls to contain other controls. For keyboard accelerators (such as the Tab key) to provide for navigation between controls, the main message loop must be augmented with a call to each window hosting a control, to allow it to pretranslate the message as a possible accelerator. This functionality must ask the host of the control with focus if it wants to handle the message. If the control does handle the message, no more handling need be done on that message. Otherwise, the message processing can proceed as normal. A typical implementation of a function to attempt to route messages from the container window to the control itself (whether it's a windowed or a windowless control) is shown here:

```
BOOL CMainWnd:: PreTranslateAccelerator(MSG* pMsg) {
  // Accelerators are only keyboard or mouse messages
  if ((pMsg->message < WM_KEYFIRST ||
    pMsg->message > WM_KEYLAST) &&
    (pMsg->message < WM_MOUSEFIRST ||
    pMsg->message > WM_MOUSELAST))
    return FALSE;

  // Find a direct child of this window from the window that has
  // focus. This will be AxAtlWin80 window for the hosted
  // control.
  HWND hWndCtl = ::GetFocus();
  if( IsChild(hWndCtl) && ::GetParent(hWndCtl) != m_hWnd ) {
```

```
  do hWndCtl = ::GetParent(hWndCtl);
  while( ::GetParent(hWndCtl) != m_hWnd );
}

// Give the control (via the AtlAxWin80) a chance to
// translate this message
if (::SendMessage(hWndCtl, WM_FORWARDMSG, 0, (LPARAM)pMsg) )
  return TRUE;

// Check for dialog-type navigation accelerators
return IsDialogMessage(pMsg);
}
```

The crux of this function forwards the message to the `AtlAxWin80` via the `WM_FORWARDMSG` message. This message is interpreted by the host window as an attempt to let the control handle the message, if so desires. This message is forwarded to the control via a call to the `IOleInPlaceActiveObject` member function `TranslateAccelerator`. The `PreTranslateAccelerator` function should be called from the application's main message pump like this:

```
int WINAPI WinMain(...) {
  ...
  CMainWindow wndMain;
  ...
  HACCEL haccel = LoadAccelerators(_Module.GetResourceInstance(),
    MAKEINTRESOURCE(IDC_MYACCELS));
  MSG msg;
  while( GetMessage(&msg, 0, 0, 0) ) {
    if( !TranslateAccelerator(msg.hwnd, haccel, &msg) &&
      !wndMain.PreTranslateAccelerator(&msg) ) {
      TranslateMessage(&msg);
      DispatchMessage(&msg);
    }
  }
  ...
}
```

The use of a `PreTranslateAccelerator` function on every window that contains a control gives the keyboard navigation keys a much greater chance of working, although the individual controls have to cooperate, too.

Hosting a Control in a Dialog

Inserting a Control into a Dialog Resource

So far, I've discussed the basics of control containment using a frame window as a control container. An even more common place to contain controls is the ever-popular dialog. For quite a while, the Visual C++ resource editor has allowed a control to be inserted into a dialog resource by right-clicking a dialog resource and choosing Insert ActiveX Control. As of Visual C++ 6.0, ATL supports creating dialogs that host the controls inserted into dialog resources.

To add an ActiveX Control to a dialog, you must first add it to the Visual Studio toolbox. This is pretty simple. Get the toolbox onto the screen, and then right-click and select Choose Items. This brings up the Choose Toolbox Items dialog box, shown in Figure 12.3.

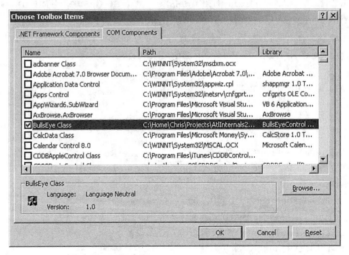

Figure 12.3   Choose Toolbox Items

Select the ActiveX controls you want, and they're in the toolbox to be added to dialogs. To add the control, simply drag and drop it from the toolbox onto the dialog editor.

The container example provided as part of this chapter has a simple dialog box with a `BullsEye` control inserted, along with a couple static controls and a button. This is what that dialog resource looks like in the `.rc` file:

```
IDD_BULLSEYE DIALOG DISCARDABLE  0, 0, 342, 238
STYLE DS_MODALFRAME | WS_POPUP | WS_CAPTION | WS_SYSMENU
CAPTION "BullsEye"
FONT 8, "MS Sans Serif"
```

```
BEGIN
    CONTROL "",IDC_BULLSEYE,
        "{7DC59CC5-36C0-11D2-AC05-00A0C9C8E50D}",
        WS_TABSTOP,7,7,269,224
    LTEXT "&Score:",IDC_STATIC,289,7,22,8
    CTEXT "Static",IDC_SCORE,278,18,46,14,
        SS_CENTERIMAGE | SS_SUNKEN
    PUSHBUTTON "Close",IDCANCEL,276,41,50,14
END
```

Control Initialization

Notice that the window text part of the CONTROL resource is a CLSID—specifically, the CLSID of the BullsEye control. This window text is passed to an instance of the AtlAxWin80 window class to determine the type of control to create. In addition, another part of the .rc file maintains a separate resource called a DLGINIT resource, which is identified with the same ID as the BullsEye control on the dialog: IDC_BULLSEYE. This resource contains the persistence information, converted to text format, that is handed to the BullsEye control at creation time (via IPersist-StreamInit):

```
IDD_BULLSEYE DLGINIT
BEGIN
    IDC_BULLSEYE, 0x376, 154, 0
0x0026, 0x0000, 0x007b, 0x0039, 0x0035,
...
0x0000, 0x0040, 0x0000, 0x0020, 0x0000,
    0
END
```

Because most folks prefer not to enter this information directly, the properties show up in the Visual Studio properties window. Simply click on the control and bring up the Property tab. Figure 12.4 shows the BullsEye properties window.

Also note that the RingCount property has an ellipsis button next to it. If you click that button, Visual Studio brings up the property page for that property.

The DLGINIT resource for each control is constructed by asking each control for IPersistStreamInit, calling Save, converting the result to a text format, and dumping it into the .rc file. In this way, all information set at design time is automatically restored at runtime.

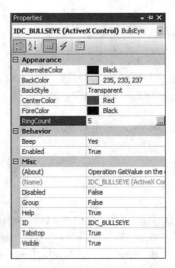

Figure 12.4   VS Dialog Editor properties window for `BullsEye` control

Sinking Control Events in a Dialog

Recall that sinking control events requires adding one `IDispEventImpl` per control to the list of base classes of your dialog class and populating the sink map. Although this has to be done by hand if a window is the container, it can be performed automatically if a dialog is to be the container. By right-clicking on the control and choosing Events, you can choose the events to handle; the `IDispEventImpl` and sink map entries are added for you. Figure 12.5 shows the Event Handlers dialog box.

The Event Handler Wizard adds the `IDispEventImpl` classes and manages the sink map. The `CAxDialogImpl` class (discussed next) handles the call to `AtlAdvise-SinkMap` that actually connects to the events in the control.

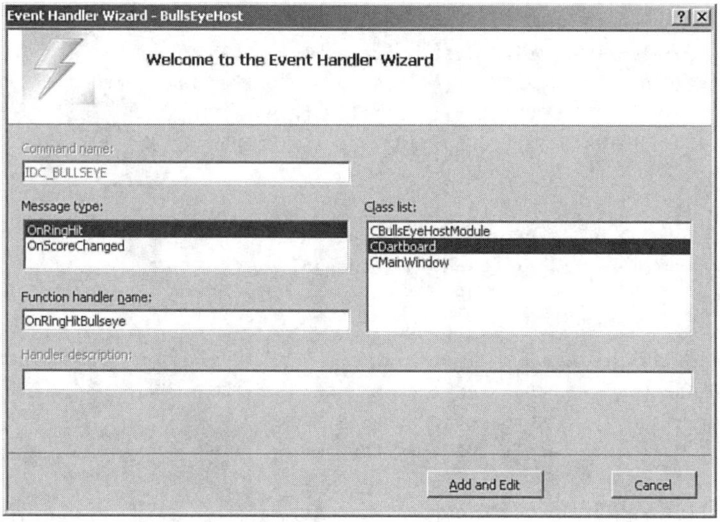

Figure 12.5   `BullsEye` Event Handlers dialog box

CAxDialogImpl

In Chapter 10, I discussed the `CDialogImpl` class, which, unfortunately, is not capable of hosting controls. Recall that the member function wrappers `DoModal` and `Create` merely call the Win32 functions `DialogBoxParam` and `CreateDialogParam`. Because the built-in dialog box manager window class has no idea how to host controls, ATL has to perform some magic on the dialog resource. Specifically, it must preprocess the dialog box resource looking for `CONTROL` entries and replacing them with entries that will create an instance of an `AtlAxWin80` window. `AtlAxWin80` then uses the name of the window to create the control and the `DLGINIT` data to initialize it, providing all the control hosting functionality we've spent most of this chapter dissecting. To hook up this preprocessing step when hosting controls in dialogs, we use the `CAxDialogImpl` base class:

```
template <class T, class TBase /* = CWindow */>
class CAxDialogImpl : public CDialogImplBaseT< TBase > {
public:
...
  static INT_PTR CALLBACK DialogProc(HWND hWnd, UINT uMsg,
    WPARAM wParam, LPARAM lParam);

  // modal dialogs
  INT_PTR DoModal(HWND hWndParent = ::GetActiveWindow(),
    LPARAM dwInitParam = NULL) {
```

```
    _AtlWinModule.AddCreateWndData(&m_thunk.cd,
      (CDialogImplBaseT< TBase >*)this);
      return AtlAxDialogBox(_AtlBaseModule.GetResourceInstance(),
        MAKEINTRESOURCE(static_cast<T*>(this)->IDD),
        hWndParent, T::StartDialogProc, dwInitParam);
  }

  BOOL EndDialog(int nRetCode) {
    return ::EndDialog(m_hWnd, nRetCode);
  }


  // modeless dialogs
  HWND Create(HWND hWndParent, LPARAM dwInitParam = NULL) {
    _AtlWinModule.AddCreateWndData(&m_thunk.cd,
      (CDialogImplBaseT< TBase >*)this);
    HWND hWnd = AtlAxCreateDialog(
      _AtlBaseModule.GetResourceInstance(),
      MAKEINTRESOURCE(static_cast<T*>(this)->IDD),
      hWndParent, T::StartDialogProc, dwInitParam);
    return hWnd;
  }


  // for CComControl
  HWND Create(HWND hWndParent, RECT&,
    LPARAM dwInitParam = NULL) {
    return Create(hWndParent, dwInitParam);
  }


  BOOL DestroyWindow() {
    return ::DestroyWindow(m_hWnd);
  }


  // Event handling support and Message map
  HRESULT AdviseSinkMap(bool bAdvise) {
    if(!bAdvise && m_hWnd == NULL) {
    // window is gone, controls are already unadvised
      return S_OK;
    }
    HRESULT hRet = E_NOTIMPL;
    __if_exists(T::_GetSinkMapFinder) {
      T* pT = static_cast<T*>(this);
      hRet = AtlAdviseSinkMap(pT, bAdvise);
    }
    return hRet;
  }


  typedef CAxDialogImpl< T, TBase > thisClass;
```

```cpp
  BEGIN_MSG_MAP(thisClass)
    MESSAGE_HANDLER(WM_INITDIALOG, OnInitDialog)
    MESSAGE_HANDLER(WM_DESTROY, OnDestroy)
  END_MSG_MAP()

  virtual HRESULT CreateActiveXControls(UINT nID) {
    // Load dialog template and InitData
    // Walk through template and create ActiveX controls
    // Code omitted for clarity
  }

  LRESULT OnInitDialog(UINT /*uMsg*/, WPARAM /*wParam*/,
    LPARAM /*lParam*/, BOOL& bHandled) {
    // initialize controls in dialog with DLGINIT
    // resource section
    ExecuteDlgInit(static_cast<T*>(this)->IDD);
    AdviseSinkMap(true);
    bHandled = FALSE;
    return 1;
  }

  LRESULT OnDestroy(UINT /*uMsg*/, WPARAM /*wParam*/,
    LPARAM /*lParam*/, BOOL& bHandled) {
    AdviseSinkMap(false);
    bHandled = FALSE;
    return 1;
  }

    // Accelerator handling - needs to be called from a message loop
    BOOL IsDialogMessage(LPMSG pMsg) {
        // Code omitted for clarity
    }
};

template <class T, class TBase>
INT_PTR CALLBACK CAxDialogImpl< T, TBase >::DialogProc(
  HWND hWnd, UINT uMsg, WPARAM wParam, LPARAM lParam) {
  CAxDialogImpl< T, TBase >* pThis = (
    CAxDialogImpl< T, TBase >*)hWnd;
  if (uMsg == WM_INITDIALOG) {
    HRESULT hr;
    if (FAILED(hr = pThis->CreateActiveXControls(
      pThis->GetIDD()))) {
      pThis->DestroyWindow();
      SetLastError(hr & 0x0000FFFF);
```

```
      return FALSE;
    }
  }
  return CDialogImplBaseT< TBase >::DialogProc(
    hWnd, uMsg, wParam, lParam);
}
```

Notice that the DoModal and Create wrapper functions call AtlAxDialogBox and AtlAxCreateDialog instead of DialogBoxParam and CreateDialogParam, respectively. These functions take the original dialog template (including the ActiveX control information that Windows can't handle) and create a second in-memory template that has those controls stripped out. The stripped dialog resource is then passed to the appropriate DialogBoxParam function so that Windows can do the heavy lifting. The actual creation of the ActiveX controls is done in the CreateActiveXControls method, which is called as part of the WM_INITDIALOG processing.

Using CAxDialogImpl as the base class, we can have a dialog that hosts COM controls like this:

```
class CBullsEyeDlg :
  public CAxDialogImpl<CBullsEyeDlg>,
  public IDispEventImpl<IDC_BULLSEYE, CBullsEyeDlg> {
public:
BEGIN_MSG_MAP(CBullsEyeDlg)
  MESSAGE_HANDLER(WM_DESTROY, OnDestroy)
  MESSAGE_HANDLER(WM_INITDIALOG, OnInitDialog)
  COMMAND_ID_HANDLER(IDCANCEL, OnCancel)
END_MSG_MAP()

BEGIN_SINK_MAP(CBullsEyeDlg)
  SINK_ENTRY(IDC_BULLSEYE, 0x2, OnScoreChanged)
END_SINK_MAP()

  // Map this class to a specific dialog resource
  enum { IDD = IDD_BULLSEYE };

  // Hook up connection points
  LRESULT OnInitDialog(...)
  { AtlAdviseSinkMap(this, true); return 0; }

  // Tear down connection points
  LRESULT OnDestroy(UINT uMsg, WPARAM wParam, LPARAM lParam,
    BOOL& bHandled)
  { AtlAdviseSinkMap(this, false); return 0; }
```

```
// Window control event handlers
LRESULT OnCancel(WORD, UINT, HWND, BOOL&);

// COM control event handlers
VOID __stdcall OnScoreChanged(LONG ringValue);
};
```

Notice that, just like a normal dialog, the message map handles messages for the dialog itself (such as WM_INITDIALOG and WM_DESTROY) and also provides a mapping between the class and the dialog resource ID (via the IDD symbol). The only thing new is that, because we've used CAxDialogImpl as the base class, the COM controls are created as the dialog is created.

Attaching a CAxWindow

During the life of the dialog, you will likely need to program against the interfaces of the contained COM controls, which means you'll need some way to obtain an interface on a specific control. One way to do this is with an instance of CAxWindow. Because ATL has created an instance of the AtlAxWin80 window class for each of the COM controls on the dialog, you use the Attach member function of a CAxWindow to attach to a COM control; thereafter, you use the CAxWindow object to manipulate the host window. This is very much like you'd use the Attach member function of the window wrapper classes discussed in Chapter 10 to manipulate an edit control. After you've attached a CAxWindow object to an AtlAxWin80 window, you can use the member functions of CAxWindow to communicate with the control host window. Recall the QueryControl member function to obtain an interface from a control, as shown here:

```
class CBullsEyeDlg :
  public CAxDialogImpl<CBullsEyeDlg>,
  public IDispEventImpl<IDC_BULLSEYE, CBullsEyeDlg> {
public:
...
  LRESULT OnInitDialog(...) {
    // Attach to the BullsEye control
    m_axBullsEye.Attach(GetDlgItem(IDC_BULLSEYE));

    // Cache BullsEye interface
    m_axBullsEye.QueryControl(&m_spBullsEye);
    ...
    return 0;
  }
...
```

```
private:
  CAxWindow            m_axBullsEye;
  CComPtr<IBullsEye>   m_spBullsEye;
};
```

In this example, I've cached both the HWND to the AtlAxWin80, for continued communication with the control host window, and one of the control's interfaces, for communication with the control itself. If you need only an interface, not the HWND, you might want to consider using GetDlgControl instead.

GetDlgControl

Because the CDialogImpl class derives from CWindow, it provides the GetDlgItem function to retrieve the HWND of a child window, given the ID of the child. Likewise, CWindow provides a GetDlgControl member function, but to retrieve an interface pointer instead of an HWND:

```
HRESULT GetDlgControl(int nID, REFIID iid, void** ppCtrl) {
  if (ppCtrl == NULL) return E_POINTER;
  *ppCtrl = NULL;
  HRESULT hr = HRESULT_FROM_WIN32(ERROR_CONTROL_ID_NOT_FOUND);
  HWND hWndCtrl = GetDlgItem(nID);
  if (hWndCtrl != NULL) {
    *ppCtrl = NULL;
    CComPtr<IUnknown> spUnk;
    hr = AtlAxGetControl(hWndCtrl, &spUnk);
    if (SUCCEEDED(hr))
      hr = spUnk->QueryInterface(iid, ppCtrl);
  }
  return hr;
}
```

The GetDlgControl member function calls the AtlAxGetControl function, which uses the HWND of the child window to retrieve an IUnknown interface. AtlAxGetControl does this by sending the WM_GETCONTROL window message that windows of the class AtlAxWin80 understand. If the child window is not an instance of the AtlAxWin80 window class, or if the control does not support the interface being requested, GetDlgControl returns a failed HRESULT. Using GetDlgControl simplifies the code to cache an interface on a control considerably:

```
LRESULT OnInitDialog(...) {
  // Cache BullsEye interface
  GetDlgControl(IDC_BULLSEYE, IID_IBullsEye,
```

```
      (void**)&m_spBullsEye);
   ...
   return 0;
}
```

The combination of the `CAxDialogImpl` class, the control-containment wizards in Visual C++, and the `GetDlgControl` member function makes managing COM controls in a dialog much like managing Windows controls.

Composite Controls

Declarative User Interfaces for Controls

There's beauty in using a dialog resource for managing the user interface (UI) of a window. Instead of writing pages of code to create, initialize, and place controls on a rectangle of gray, we can use the resource editor to do it for us. At design time, we lay out the size and location of the elements of the UI, and the ATL-augmented dialog manager is responsible for the heavy lifting. This is an extremely useful mode of UI development, and it's not limited to dialogs. It can also be used for *composite controls*. A composite control is a COM control that uses a dialog resource to lay out its UI elements. These UI elements can be Windows controls or other COM controls.

To a Windows control, a composite control appears as a parent window. To a COM control, the composite control appears as a control container. To a control container, the composite control appears as a control itself. To the developer of the control, a composite control is all three. In fact, if you combine all the programming techniques from Chapter 10 with the techniques I've shown you thus far in this chapter, you have a composite control.

CComCompositeControl

ATL provides support for composite controls via the `CComCompositeControl` base class:

```
template <class T>
class CComCompositeControl :
  public CComControl< T, CAxDialogImpl< T > > {...};
```

Notice that `CComCompositeControl` derives from both `CComControl` and `CAxDialogImpl`, combining the functionality of a control and the drawing of the dialog manager, augmented with the COM control hosting capabilities of `AtlAxWin80`. Both of the wizard-generated composite control types (composite control and lite composite control) derive from `CComCompositeControl` instead of `CComControl` and provide an `IDD` symbol mapping to the control's dialog resource:

```
class ATL_NO_VTABLE CDartBoard :
  public CComObjectRootEx<CComSingleThreadModel>,
  public IDispatchImpl<IDartBoard, &IID_IDartBoard,
    &LIBID_CONTROLSLib>,
  public CComCompositeControl<CDartBoard>,
  ...
  public CComCoClass<CDartBoard, &CLSID_DartBoard> {
public:
...
  enum { IDD = IDD_DARTBOARD };

  CDartBoard() {
    // Composites can't be windowless
    m_bWindowOnly = TRUE;

    // Calculate natural extent based on dialog resource size
    CalcExtent(m_sizeExtent);
  }
...
};
```

Notice that the construction of the composite control sets the `m_bWindowOnly` flag, disabling windowless operation. The control's window must be of the same class as that managed by the dialog manager. Also notice that the `m_sizeExtent` member variable is set by a call to `CalcExtent`, a helper function provided in `CComCompositeControl`. `CalcExtent` is used to set the initial preferred size of the control to be exactly that of the dialog box resource.

Composite Control Drawing

Because a composite control is based on a dialog resource, and its drawing will be managed by the dialog manager and the child controls, no real drawing chores have to be performed. Instead, setting the state of the child controls, which causes them to redraw, is all that's required to update the visual state of a control.

For example, the `DartBoard` example available with the source code of this book uses a dialog resource to lay out its elements, as shown in Figure 12.6.

This dialog resource holds a `BullsEye` control, two static controls, and a button. When the user clicks on a ring of the target, the score is incremented. When the Reset button is pressed, the score is cleared. The composite control takes care of all the logic, but the dialog manager performs the drawing.

Figure 12.6   DartBoard composite control dialog resource

However, when a composite control is shown but not activated, the composite control's window is not created and the drawing must be done manually. For example, a composite control must perform its own drawing when hosted in a dialog resource during the design mode of the Visual C++ resource editor. The ATL Object Wizard generates an implementation of OnDraw that handles this case, as shown in Figure 12.7.

Figure 12.7   Default CComCompositeControl's inactive OnDraw implementation

I find this implementation somewhat inconvenient because it doesn't show the dialog resource as I'm using the control. Specifically, it doesn't show the size of the resource. Toward that end, I've provided another implementation that is a bit more helpful (see Figure 12.8).

This implementation shows the light gray area as the recommended size of the control based on the control's dialog resource. The dark gray area is the part of the control that is still managed by the control but that is outside the area managed for the control by the dialog manager. The updated OnDraw implementation is shown here:

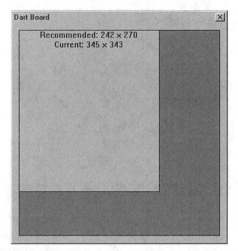

Figure 12.8 Updated `CComCompositeControl`'s inactive `OnDraw` implementation

```
// Draw an inactive composite control
virtual HRESULT OnDraw(ATL_DRAWINFO& di) {
  if( m_bInPlaceActive ) return S_OK;

  // Draw background rectangle
  SelectObject(di.hdcDraw, GetStockObject(BLACK_PEN));
  SelectObject(di.hdcDraw, GetStockObject(GRAY_BRUSH));
  Rectangle(di.hdcDraw, di.prcBounds->left, di.prcBounds->top,
            di.prcBounds->right, di.prcBounds->bottom);

  // Draw proposed dialog rectangle
  SIZE  sizeMetric; CalcExtent(sizeMetric);
  SIZE  sizeDialog; AtlHiMetricToPixel(&sizeMetric, &sizeDialog);
  SIZE  sizeBounds = {
    di.prcBounds->right - di.prcBounds->left,
    di.prcBounds->bottom - di.prcBounds->top };
  SIZE  sizeDialogBounds = {
    min(sizeDialog.cx, sizeBounds.cx),
    min(sizeDialog.cy, sizeBounds.cy) };
  RECT  rectDialogBounds = {
    di.prcBounds->left, di.prcBounds->top,
    di.prcBounds->left + sizeDialogBounds.cx,
    di.prcBounds->top + sizeDialogBounds.cy };
  SelectObject(di.hdcDraw, GetStockObject(LTGRAY_BRUSH));
  Rectangle(di.hdcDraw,
    rectDialogBounds.left, rectDialogBounds.top,
    rectDialogBounds.right, rectDialogBounds.bottom);
```

```
// Report natural and current size of dialog resource
SetTextColor(di.hdcDraw, ::GetSysColor(COLOR_WINDOWTEXT));
SetBkMode(di.hdcDraw, TRANSPARENT);

TCHAR sz[256];
wsprintf(sz, __T("Recommended: %d x %d\r\nCurrent: %d x %d"),
  sizeDialog.cx, sizeDialog.cy,
  sizeBounds.cx, sizeBounds.cy);

DrawText(di.hdcDraw, sz, -1, &rectDialogBounds, DT_CENTER);

return S_OK;
}
```

Using a dialog resource and deriving from `CComCompositeControl` are the only differences between a control that manages its own UI elements and one that leans on the dialog manager. A composite control is a powerful way to lay out a control's UI elements at design time. However, if you really want to wield the full power of a declarative UI when building a control, you need an HTML control.

HTML Controls

Generating an HTML Control

You create an HTML control via the ATL Control Wizard. On the Options page, choose DHTML Control (Minimal is also an option, as described in Chapter 11). The wizard-generated code creates a control that derives from `CComControl`, sets `m_bWindowOnly` to `TRUE`, and provides a resource for the layout of the UI elements of your control. This is similar to the resource that results from running the Object Wizard for a composite control, except that instead of using a dialog resource, an HTML control uses an HTML resource. The same `WebBrowser` control that provides the UI for Internet Explorer provides the parsing for the HTML resource at run-time. This allows a control to use a declarative style of UI development, but with all the capabilities of the HTML engine in Internet Explorer. The following are a few of the advantages that HTML provides over a dialog resource:

- Support for resizing via `height` and `width` attributes, both in absolute pixels and percentages
- Support for scripting when using top-level initialization code, defining functions, and handling events

- Support for extending the object model of the HTML document via an "external" object
- Support for flowing of mixed text and graphics
- Support for multiple font families, colors, sizes, and styles

In fact, pretty much everything you've ever seen on a web site can be performed using the HTML control.

By default, you get this HTML as a starting point in a wizard-generated string resource named IDH_<PROJECTNAME>:

```
<HTML>
<BODY id=theBody>
<BUTTON onclick='window.external.OnClick(theBody, "red");'>
Red
</BUTTON>
<BR>
<BR>
<BUTTON onclick='window.external.OnClick(theBody, "green");'>
Green
</BUTTON>
<BR>
<BR>
<BUTTON onclick='window.external.OnClick(theBody, "blue");'>
Blue
</BUTTON>
</BODY>
</HTML>
```

From here, you can start changing the HTML to do whatever you like.

HTML Control Creation

The magic of hooking up the WebBrowser control is performed in the OnCreate handler generated by the ATL Object Wizard:

```
LRESULT CSmartDartBoard::OnCreate(UINT, WPARAM, LPARAM, BOOL&) {
  // Wrap the control's window to use it to host control
  // (not an AtlAxWin80, so no CAxHostWindow yet created)
  CAxWindow wnd(m_hWnd);

  // Create a CAxWinHost: It will subclass this window and
  // create a control based on an HTML resource.
  HRESULT hr = wnd.CreateControl(IDH_SMARTDARTBOARD);
```

```
...
  return SUCCEEDED(hr) ? 0 : -1;
}
```

Because m_bWindowOnly is set to true, activating the HTML control creates a window. To give this window control-containment capabilities so that it can host an instance of the WebBrowser control, the HTML control's window must be subclassed and sent through the message map provided by CAxHostWindow, just like every other control container. However, because the HTML control's window is not an instance of the AtlAxWin80 class, the subclassing must be handled manually. Notice that the first thing the wizard-generated OnCreate function does is wrap an instance of CAxWindow around the control's HWND. The call to CreateControl creates an instance of CAxHostWindow. The CAxHostWindow object subclasses the HTML control's window, creates an instance of the WebBrowser control, and feeds it a URL of the form res://<module name>/<resource ID>, using CreateNormalizedControl. In effect, the HWND of the HTML control is a parent for the WebBrowser control, which then uses the HTML resource to manage the UI elements of the control. This is exactly analogous to the composite control, in which the HWND of the control was an instance of the dialog manager, using a dialog resource to manage the elements of the UI.

Element Layout

For example, the SmartDartBoard HTML control that is available with the source code of this book uses HTML to lay out its UI, just like the DartBoard composite control. However, in HTML, I can use the auto-layout capabilities of a <table> element to autosize the HTML control to whatever size the user wants, instead of limiting myself to a single size, as with the dialog resource. The following shows how the SmartDartBoard control's HTML resource lays out its elements:

```
<!- Use all of the control's area ->
<table width=100% height=100%>
<tr>
    <td colspan=2>
    <object id=objBullsEye width=100% height=100%
            classid="clsid:7DC59CC5-36C0-11D2-AC05-00A0C9C8E50D">
    </object>
    </td>
</tr>
<tr height=1>
    <td>Score: <span id=spanScore>0</td>
    <td align=right>
        <input type=button id=cmdReset value="Reset">
```

```
            </td>
        </tr>
    </table>
```

To test the UI of the HTML control without compiling, you can right-click the HTML file and choose Preview, which shows the HTML in the Internet Explorer. For example, Figures 12.9 and 12.10 show the control's UI resizing itself properly to fit into the space that it's given.

Figure 12.9   Small SmartDartBoard UI

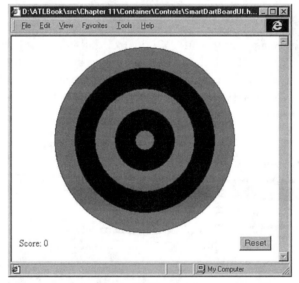

Figure 12.10   Large SmartDartBoard UI

Accessing the HTML from the Control

When you create an instance of the WebBrowser control, you're actually creating two things: a WebBrowser control, which knows about URLs, and an HTML Document control, which knows about parsing and displaying HTML. The WebBrowser control forms the core of the logic of Internet Explorer and lives in shdocvw.dll. The Web-Browser control implements the IWebBrowser2 interface, with methods such as Navigate, GoBack, GoForward, and Stop. Because the CAxWindow object is merely used to bootstrap hosting the WebBrowser control, and you'd need to be able to access the WebBrowser control in other parts of your code, the OnCreate code generated by the wizard uses QueryControl to cache the IWebBrowser2 interface:

```
LRESULT CSmartDartBoard::OnCreate(UINT, WPARAM, LPARAM, BOOL&) {
...
  // Cache the IWebBrowser2 interface
  if (SUCCEEDED(hr))
    hr = wnd.QueryControl(IID_IWebBrowser2,
        (void**)&m_spBrowser);
...
}
```

To display the HTML, the WebBrowser control creates an instance of the HTML Document control, which is implemented in mshtml.dll. The HTML Document represents the implementation of the Dynamic HTML object model (DHTML). This object model exposes each named element on a page of HTML as a COM object, each of which implements one or more COM interfaces and many of which fire events. Although the full scope and power of DHTML is beyond the scope of this book, the rest of this chapter is dedicated to showing you just the tip of the iceberg of functionality DHTML provides.

The HTML Document object implements the IHTMLDocument2 interface, whose most important property is the all property. Getting from the WebBrowser control to the HTML Document control is a matter of retrieving the IWebBrowser2 Document property and querying for the IHTMLDocument2 interface. Accessing any named object on the HTML page—that is, any tag with an id attribute—is done via the all property of the IHTMLDocument2 interface. Retrieving a named object on an HTML page in C++ can be accomplished with a helper function such as the GetHtmlElement helper shown here:

```
HRESULT CSmartDartBoard::GetHtmlElement(
    LPCOLESTR       pszElementID,
    IHTMLElement**  ppElement) {
    ATLASSERT(ppElement);
    *ppElement = 0;

    // Get the document from the browser
    HRESULT hr = E_FAIL;
```

```
    CComPtr<IDispatch> spdispDoc;
    hr = m_spBrowser->get_Document(&spdispDoc);
    if( FAILED(hr) ) return hr;

    CComQIPtr<IHTMLDocument2> spDoc = spdispDoc;
    if( !spDoc ) return E_NOINTERFACE;

    // Get the All collection from the document
    CComPtr<IHTMLElementCollection> spAll;
    hr = spDoc->get_all(&spAll);
    if( FAILED(hr) ) return hr;

    // Get the element from the All collection
    CComVariant        varID = pszElementID;
    CComPtr<IDispatch>  spdispItem;
    hr = spAll->item(varID, CComVariant(0), &spdispItem);

    // Return the IHTMLElement interface
    return spdispItem->QueryInterface(ppElement);
}
```

When you have the IHtmlElement interface, you can change just about anything about that element. For example, notice the <span> tag named spanScore in the SmartDartBoard HTML resource:

```
...
<td>Score: <span id=spanScore>0</span></td>
...
```

A span is just a range of HTML with a name so that it can be programmed against. As far as we're concerned, every named object in the HTML is a COM object that we can access from our control's C++ code. This span's job is to hold the control's current score, so after the WebBrowser control has been created, we need to set the span to the m_nScore property of the control. The SetScoreSpan helper function in the SmartDartBoard HTML control uses the GetHtmlElement helper and the IHTMLElement interface to set the innerText property of the span:

```
HRESULT CSmartDartBoard::SetScoreSpan() {
    // Convert score to VARIANT
    CComVariant varScore = m_nScore;
    HRESULT hr = varScore.ChangeType(VT_BSTR);
    if( FAILED(hr) ) return hr;

    // Find score span element
```

```
    CComPtr<IHTMLElement> speScore;
    hr = GetHtmlElement(OLESTR("spanScore"), &speScore);
    if( FAILED(hr) ) return hr;

    // Set the element's inner text
    return speScore->put_innerText(varScore.bstrVal);
}
```

Whenever the score changes, this function is used to update the contents of the HTML span object from the control's C++ code.

Sinking WebBrowser Events

You might be tempted to use the SetScoreSpan function right from the OnCreate handler to set the initial score value when the control is activated. Unfortunately, the architecture of the HTML Document object dictates that we wait for the document to be completely processed before the object model is exposed to us. To detect when that happens, we need to sink events on the DWebBrowserEvents2 interface. Specifically, we need to know about the OnDocumentComplete event. When we receive this event, we can access all the named objects on the page. Because DWeb-BrowserEvents2 is a dispinterface, sinking the events can be accomplished with IDispEventImpl and an entry in the sink map:

```
    typedef IDispEventImpl< 1, CSmartDartBoard,
      &DIID_DWebBrowserEvents2, &LIBID_SHDocVw, 1, 0>
      BrowserEvents;

    class ATL_NO_VTABLE CSmartDartBoard :
        public CComObjectRootEx<CComSingleThreadModel>,
        ...
        // Sink browser events
          public BrowserEvents {
        ...
    BEGIN_SINK_MAP(CSmartDartBoard)
      SINK_ENTRY_EX(1, DIID_DWebBrowserEvents2,
        0x00000103, OnDocumentComplete)
    END_SINK_MAP()

        void __stdcall OnDocumentComplete(IDispatch*, VARIANT*);
        ...
    };
```

The `OnCreate` handler and the `OnDestroy` handler are good places to establish and shut down the `DWebBrowserEvent2` connection point:

```
LRESULT CSmartDartBoard::OnCreate(UINT, WPARAM, LPARAM, BOOL&) {
  ...
  // Set up connection point w/ the browser
  if( SUCCEEDED(hr) )
    hr = BrowserEvents::DispEventAdvise(m_spBrowser);
  ...
  return SUCCEEDED(hr) ? 0 : -1;
}

LRESULT CSmartDartBoard::OnDestroy(UINT, WPARAM, LPARAM, BOOL&) {
  DispEventUnadvise(m_spBrowser);
  return 0;
}
```

In the implementation of the `OnDocumentComplete` event handler, we can finally access the HTML object:

```
void __stdcall CSmartDartBoard::OnDocumentComplete(IDispatch*,
  VARIANT*) {
  // Set the spanScore object's inner HTML
  SetScoreSpan();
}
```

Accessing the Control from the HTML

In addition to accessing the named HTML objects from the control, you might find yourself wanting to access the control from the HTML. For this to happen, the HTML must have some hook into the control. This is provided with the `window.external` property. The script can expect this to be another `dispinterface` of the control itself. In fact, the ATL Object Wizard generates two dual interfaces on an HTML control. The first, `I<ControlName>`, is the default interface available to the control's clients. The second, `I<ControlName>UI`, is an interface given to the `Web-Browser` control via the `SetExternalDispatch` function on the `CAxWindow` object:

```
HRESULT CAxWindow::SetExternalDispatch(IDispatch* pDisp);
```

The wizard-generated implementation of `OnCreate` sets this interface as part of the initialization procedure:

```
LRESULT CSmartDartBoard::OnCreate(UINT, WPARAM, LPARAM, BOOL&) {
...
  if (SUCCEEDED(hr))
    hr = wnd.SetExternalDispatch(static_cast<ISmartDartBoardUI*>(this));
...
  return SUCCEEDED(hr) ? 0 : -1;
}
```

In the SmartDartBoard example, the interface used by control containers is ISmartDartBoard:

```
[dual] interface ISmartDartBoard : IDispatch {
  [propget] HRESULT Score([out, retval] long *pVal);
  [propput] HRESULT Score([in] long newVal);
  HRESULT ResetScore();
};
```

On the other hand, the interface used by the HTML script code is ISmartDart-BoardUI:

```
[dual] interface ISmartDartBoardUI : IDispatch {
  HRESULT AddToScore([in] long ringValue);
  HRESULT ResetScore();
};
```

This interface represents a bidirectional communication channel. A script block in the HTML can use this interface for whatever it wants. For example:

```
<table width=100% height=100%>
...
</table>

<script language=vbscript>
    sub objBullsEye_OnScoreChanged(ringValue)
        ' Access the ISmartDartBoardUI interface
        window.external.AddToScore(ringValue)
    end sub

    sub cmdReset_onClick
        ' Access the ISmartDartBoardUI interface
        window.external.ResetScore
    end sub
</script>
```

In this example, we're using the `ISmartDartBoardUI` interface as a way to raise events to the control from the HTML, but instead of using connection points, we're using the window's external interface, which is far easier to set up.

Sinking HTML Element Events in C++

Notice that the previous HTML code handled events from the objects in the HTML itself. We're using the `object_event` syntax of VBScript; for example, `cmdReset_onClick` is called when the `cmdReset` button is clicked. It probably doesn't surprise you to learn that all the HTML objects fire events on an interface established via the connection-point protocol. There's no reason we can't sink the events from the HTML objects in our control directly instead of using the `window.external` interface to forward the events. For example, the `cmdReset` button fires events on the `HTMLInputTextElementEvents` dispinterface. Handling these events is, again, a matter of deriving from `IDispEventImpl` and adding entries to the sink map:

```
typedef IDispEventImpl<2, CSmartDartBoard,
  &DIID_HTMLInputTextElementEvents,
  &LIBID_MSHTML, 4, 0>
  ButtonEvents;

class ATL_NO_VTABLE CSmartDartBoard :
    public CComObjectRootEx<CComSingleThreadModel>,
    ...
    // Sink events on the DHTML Reset button
    public ButtonEvents {
    ...
BEGIN_SINK_MAP(CSmartDartBoard)
  ...
  SINK_ENTRY_EX(2, DIID_HTMLInputTextElementEvents, DISPID_CLICK,
                OnClickReset)
END_SINK_MAP()
  VARIANT_BOOL __stdcall OnClickReset();
  ...
};
```

Because we need to have an interface on the `cmdReset` button, we need to wait until the `OnDocumentComplete` event to establish a connection point with the button:

```
void __stdcall CSmartDartBoard::OnDocumentComplete(IDispatch*,
  VARIANT*) {
  // Set the spanScore object's inner HTML
  SetScoreSpan();
```

```
    // Retrieve the Reset button
    HRESULT hr;
    CComPtr<IHTMLElement> speReset;
    hr = GetHtmlElement(OLESTR("cmdReset"), &speReset);
    if( FAILED(hr) ) return;

    // Set up the connection point w/ the button
    ButtonEvents::DispEventAdvise(speReset);
}
```

When we've established the connection with the Reset button, every time the user clicks on it, we get a callback in our OnClickReset event handler. This means that we no longer need the cmdReset_onClick handler in the script. However, from a larger perspective, because we program and handle events back and forth between the C++ and the HTML code, we have the flexibility to use whichever is more convenient when writing the code. This is quite a contrast from a dialog resource, in which the resource is good for laying out the elements of the UI (as long as the UI was a fixed size), but only our C++ code can provide any behavior.

Extended UI Handling

It turns out that the external dispatch is but one setting you can set on the CAxHostWindow that affects the HTML Document control. Several more options can be set via the IAxWinAmbientDispatch interface implemented by CAxHostWindow:

```
typedef enum tagDocHostUIFlagDispatch {
    docHostUIFlagDIALOG                  = 1,
    docHostUIFlagDISABLE_HELP_MENU = 2,
    docHostUIFlagNO3DBORDER             = 4,
    docHostUIFlagSCROLL_NO              = 8,
    docHostUIFlagDISABLE_SCRIPT_INACTIVE = 16,
    docHostUIFlagOPENNEWWIN             = 32,
    docHostUIFlagDISABLE_OFFSCREEN = 64,
    docHostUIFlagFLAT_SCROLLBAR = 128,
    docHostUIFlagDIV_BLOCKDEFAULT = 256,
    docHostUIFlagACTIVATE_CLIENTHIT_ONLY = 512,
} DocHostUIFlagDispatch;

typedef enum tagDOCHOSTUIDBLCLKDispatch {
    docHostUIDblClkDEFAULT          = 0,
    docHostUIDblClkSHOWPROPERTIES = 1,
    docHostUIDblClkSHOWCODE         = 2,
} DOCHOSTUIDBLCLKDispatch;
```

```
interface IAxWinAmbientDispatch : IDispatch {
  ...
  // IDocHostUIHandler Defaults
  [propput, helpstring("Set the DOCHOSTUIFLAG flags")]
  HRESULT DocHostFlags([in]DWORD dwDocHostFlags);
  [propget, helpstring("Get the DOCHOSTUIFLAG flags")]
  HRESULT DocHostFlags([out,retval]DWORD* pdwDocHostFlags);

  [propput, helpstring("Set the DOCHOSTUIDBLCLK flags")]
  HRESULT DocHostDoubleClickFlags([in]DWORD dwFlags);
  [propget, helpstring("Get the DOCHOSTUIDBLCLK flags")]
  HRESULT DocHostDoubleClickFlags([out,retval]DWORD* pdwFlags);

  [propput, helpstring("Enable or disable context menus")]
  HRESULT AllowContextMenu([in]VARIANT_BOOL bAllowContextMenu);
  [propget, helpstring("Are context menus enabled")]
  HRESULT AllowContextMenu([out,retval]VARIANT_BOOL* pbAllowContextMenu);

  [propput, helpstring("Enable or disable UI")]
  HRESULT AllowShowUI([in]VARIANT_BOOL bAllowShowUI);
  [propget, helpstring("Is UI enabled")]
  HRESULT AllowShowUI([out,retval]VARIANT_BOOL* pbAllowShowUI);

  [propput, helpstring("Set the option key path")]
  HRESULT OptionKeyPath([in]BSTR bstrOptionKeyPath);
  [propget, helpstring("Get the option key path")]
  HRESULT OptionKeyPath([out,retval]BSTR* pbstrOptionKeyPath);
};
```

The DocHostFlags property can be any combination of DocHostUIFlagDispatch flags. The DocHostDoubleClickFlags property can be any one of the DOCHOSTUID-BLCLKDispatch flags. The AllowContextMenu property enables you to shut off the context menu when the user right-clicks on the HTML control.[10] The AllowShowUI property controls whether the host will be replacing the IE menus and toolbars. The OptionKeyPath property tells the HTML document where in the Registry to read and write its settings.

All these settings affect the CAxWindowHost object's implementation of IDocHost-UIHandler, an interface that the HTML Document control expects from its host to fine tune its behavior. If you want to control this interaction even more,

---

[10] There's no reason for the user to know you're just bootlegging IE functionality, is there?

CAxWindowHost enables you to set your own IDocHostUIHandlerDispatch interface[11] via the CAxWindow member function SetExternalUIHandler:

```
HRESULT CAxWindow::SetExternalUIHandler(
    IDocHostUIHandlerDispatch* pHandler);
```

The IDocHostUIHandlerDispatch interface is pretty much a one-to-one mapping to IDocHostUIHandler, but in dual interface form. When a CAxHostWindow object gets a call from the HTML Document control on IDocHostUIHandler, the call is forwarded if there is an implementation of IDocHostUIHandlerDispatch set. For example, if you want to replace the context menu of the HTML control instead of just turn it off, you have to expose the IDocHostUIHandlerDispatch interface, call SetExternalUIHandler during the OnCreate handler, and implement the ShowContextMenu member function. When there is no implementation of IDocHostUIHandlerDispatch set, the CAxHostWindow object uses the properties set via the IAxWinAmbientDispatch interface.

Hosting HTML Is Not Limited to the HTML Control

By hosting the WebBrowser control or the HTML Document control, you've given yourself a lot more than just hosting HTML. The HTML Document control represents a flexible COM UI framework called Dynamic HTML. The combination of declarative statements to lay out the UI elements and the capability to control each element's behavior, presentation style, and events at runtime gives you a great deal of flexibility.

Nor is this functionality limited to an HTML control. You can achieve the same effect by creating a CAxWindow object that hosts either the WebBrowser or the HTML Document control in a window, a dialog, or a composite control, as well as in an HTML control.[12]

ATL's Control Containment Limitations

ATL introduced COM control containment in Version 3.0. Although several significant bugs have been fixed and the control-containment code is very capable, it's not quite all you might like. Several limitations affect the way that ATL implements control containment:

---

[11] This interface is defined by ATL in atliface.idl.

[12] You can build entire applications using ATL as the glue code that initialized a first-tier thin client built entirely from HTML, but that's beyond the scope of this book.

- All the control-hosting interfaces are exposed by a single class, CAxHostWindow, which acts as the site, the document, and the frame. The actual implementations of some of the hosting interfaces are split into other classes, but there are no template parameters or runtime variables that you can change to pick a different implementation. If you contain multiple controls, you get duplicate implementation of interfaces that could have been shared. This is particularly cumbersome if the control asks for the HWND for the document or the frame. Instead of allowing the client application programmer to designate his own document or frame window, ATL creates a new window, resulting in potentially three container windows per control. If the control creates its own window, that's four windows instead of just one, to host a single control.

- Each control must have its own window on the container side for the CAxHostWindow object to work with. Even a windowless control has one window associated with it—not exactly the windowless-ness for which one would hope.

- Finally, unlike the rest of ATL, the control-containment architecture is not well factored. You can't easily reach in and change how one piece works without also changing the other pieces. For example, if you want to have a shared frame for all the control sites, you have to replace CAxHostWindow (probably by deriving from it) and also change how CAxWindow hooks up the control site so that it uses your new class. Ideally, we would like to override some CAxHostWindow members but still be able to use the rest of the containment framework as is.

What do these limitations mean to you? For a lot of the work you're likely to do with control containment, not much. This chapter has shown you the considerable use to which you can put ATL's control-containment framework. However, if you're looking for the C++ equivalent of a general-purpose, full-featured control container such as Visual Basic, ATL isn't quite there.[13]

Summary

ATL provides the capability to host controls in windows, dialogs, and other controls. Control containment under ATL is based on two new window classes, AtlAxWin80 and AtlAxWinLic80. As wrappers around these window classes, ATL provides the CAxWindow and CAxWindow2 classes, respectively. After a control hosting

---

[13] For more information about bringing ATL's COM control containment up to snuff, read "Extending ATL 3.0 Control Containment to Help You Write Real-world Containers" (*MSJ*, December 1999), at www.microsoft.com/msj/1299/Containment/Containment.aspx (http://tinysells.com/61).

window has been created, it can be treated as a window, using the functionality of the `CWindow` base class. It can also be used as a COM object, using the interfaces available with the `QueryControl` member function of the `CAxWindow` class. The interfaces of the control can be used to sink events, persist the control's state, or program against the control's custom interfaces.

Many objects in ATL can make use of these window classes to host controls. Windows can use them manually via the `CAxWindow` class. Dialogs can use them automatically when using the `CAxDialogImpl` class. Controls can contain other controls in ATL when derived from `CComCompositeControl`. Finally, HTML controls can host the `WebBrowser` control, combining the best of the dialog resource declarative model and a full-featured COM UI framework model.

CHAPTER

13 | Hello, ATL Server
A Modern C++ Web Platform

Throughout the previous 12 chapters, we've focused on ATL as a framework for building both COM components and user interfaces (via ATL's windowing classes and ActiveX control support). Now we look at ATL as a modern platform for building web applications. That framework is a set of classes known collectively as ATL Server.

Although most of the discussion thus far has involved ATL's COM support, ATL Server actually has very little to do with COM. Because its purpose is to handle Hypertext Transfer Protocol (HTTP) requests, the crux of ATL Server is built around Microsoft's Internet Service API (ISAPI). The library just happens to use COM inside. We start by briefly reviewing Microsoft's web platform. Then, we examine how ATL Server leverages that platform to provide a viable means of creating web applications and web services. There's much more to ATL Server than can be covered in this book, so we just hit the high points in this chapter.

The Microsoft Web Platform (Internet Information Services)

When the World Wide Web began taking root in the early 1990s, many sites were little more than collections of Hypertext Markup Language (HTML) files and perhaps some image files. Clients with Internet browsers surfed to various sites using Universal Resource Locators (URLs) that took a form like this: http://www.example.com.

After typing the URL and sending the request through a maze of routers, the request finally ended up at a server somewhere. In the earliest days of the Web, the server was probably a UNIX box. Web technologies soon evolved to handle more elaborate requests (not just file requests). Through the development of the Common Gateway Interface and the inclusion of HTML tags representing standard GUI controls (such as combo boxes, push buttons, and text boxes), the Web became capable of handling *interactive* traffic. That is, a client could carry on a two-way conversation with web servers that extended beyond simple file requests. Of course, this capability led to the great upsurge in web sites during the late 1990s, giving rise to such enterprises as Amazon.com and Google.

The earliest means of supporting interactive capabilities over the Web were made available through the Common Gateway Interface (CGI). CGI worked by handling separate incoming requests with a new process for each request. Although the Microsoft platform supports the CGI, it doesn't work quite as well as on a UNIX box. Starting new processes on a UNIX box is not as expensive as starting new processes on a Windows box. To compensate, Microsoft introduced the Internet Services API and its own new Internet server: Internet Information Services (IIS). The IIS strategy is that it's much faster to load a DLL to respond to an HTTP request than it is to start a whole new process.

IIS and ISAPI

The IIS component is the heart of Microsoft's web platform. Most modern web sites built around the Microsoft platform involve IIS and ISAPI DLLs. All the modern Microsoft web-based programming frameworks are extensions of the IIS/ISAPI architecture. Even classic ASP and the more modern ASP.NET rely on IIS and ISAPI at their core. And as you'll soon see, ATL Server depends upon IIS and ISAPI as well.

Regardless of the programming framework used (raw sockets programming, ASP, ASP.NET, or ATL Server), processing web requests is similar from framework to framework. A component listens to port 80 for HTTP requests. When a request, comes in, the component parses the request and figures out what to do with it. The request might vary from sending back some specific HTML, to returning a graphics file, or perhaps even to invoking a method of some sort.

When programming to the modern Microsoft web-based frameworks, IIS is the component that listens to port 80. IIS handles some requests directly and delegates others to specific ISAPI extension DLLs to execute the request. By default, IIS handles requests for standard HTML files directly. As an alternative, a custom file extension might be mapped to a handwritten ISAPI DLL that executes the request.

Classic ASP and ASP.NET integrate into IIS as ISAPI DLLs. IIS handles requests ASP files (`*.asp`) by mapping them to an ISAPI DLL named `ASP.DLL`, which handles the request by parsing the request string, loading the ASP file, parsing the contents of the file, and servicing the request according to the instructions given in the ASP file. ASP.NET files (`*.aspx`) are handled by an ISAPI DLL named `ASPNET_ISAPI.DLL`, which brings in the Common Language Runtime to help it process requests.

To set the stage for understanding ATL Server, let's take a look at how ISAPI extension DLLs work.

ISAPI Extension DLLs

Although IIS does a perfectly fine job responding to requests for standard web file types (such as HTML and JPG), its real power lies in the capability to extend your server by writing custom DLLs to respond to requests.

The core ISAPI infrastructure is actually fairly simple. ISAPI extension DLLs implement three entry points:

```
BOOL WINAPI GetExtensionVersion(HSE_VERSION_INFO* pVer);

DWORD WINAPI HttpExtensionProc(LPEXTENSION_CONTROL_BLOCK lpECB);

BOOL WINAPI TerminateExtension(DWORD dwFlags);
```

These three methods are the hooks for writing your web site using custom DLLs. GetExtensionVersion is called when IIS invokes the application for the first time. GetExtensionVersion must set the version number in the HSE_VERSION_INFO structure passed in and then return TRUE for IIS to be capable of using your ISAPI DLL.

IIS calls the TerminateExtension entry point when IIS is ready to unload the DLL from its process. If you don't need to do any cleanup, the TerminateExtension entry point is optional.

The heart of the extension is the HttpExtensionProc function. Notice that HttpExtensionProc takes a single parameter: an EXTENSION_CONTROL_BLOCK structure. The structure includes everything you'd ever want to know about a request, including the kind of request made, the content of the request, the type of content, a method for getting the server variables (for example, information about the connection), a method for writing output to the client, and a method for reading data from the body of the HTTP request. Here's the EXTENSION_CONTROL_BLOCK:

```
typedef struct _EXTENSION_CONTROL_BLOCK {
  DWORD cbSize;                // size of this struct.
  DWORD dwVersion;             // version info of this spec
  HCONN ConnID;                // Context number not to be modified!
  DWORD dwHttpStatusCode;      // HTTP Status code
  CHAR  lpszLogData[HSE_LOG_BUFFER_LEN]; // null terminated log
                               // info specific to this Extension DLL

  LPSTR lpszMethod;            // REQUEST_METHOD
  LPSTR lpszQueryString;       // QUERY_STRING
  LPSTR lpszPathInfo;          // PATH_INFO
  LPSTR lpszPathTranslated;    // PATH_TRANSLATED
  DWORD cbTotalBytes;          // Total bytes indicated from client
  DWORD cbAvailable;           // Available number of bytes
  LPBYTE lpbData;              // pointer to cbAvailable bytes
  LPSTR  lpszContentType;      // Content type of client data

  BOOL (WINAPI * GetServerVariable)(
```

```
     HCONN hConn, LPSTR lpszVariableName,
     LPVOID lpvBuffer, LPDWORD lpdwSize);

  BOOL (WINAPI * WriteClient)(HCONN ConnID, LPVOID Buffer,
     LPDWORD lpdwBytes, DWORD dwReserved);

  BOOL (WINAPI * ReadClient)(HCONN ConnID, LPVOID lpvBuffer,
     LPDWORD lpdwSize);

  BOOL (WINAPI * ServerSupportFunction)(HCONN hConn,
     DWORD dwHSERequest, LPVOID lpvBuffer, LPDWORD lpdwSize,
     LPDWORD lpdwDataType);
} EXTENSION_CONTROL_BLOCK, *LPEXTENSION_CONTROL_BLOCK;
```

When IIS receives a request, it packages the information into the
EXTENSION_CONTROL_BLOCK and passes a pointer to the structure into the ISAPI DLL
via the HttpExtensionProc entry point. The ISAPI extension's job is to parse the
incoming request into a useable form. After that, it's completely up to the ISAPI
DLL to do whatever it wants to with the request. For example, if the client makes
some sort of request using query parameters (perhaps a product lookup), the ISAPI
DLL might use those parameters to create a database query. The ISAPI DLL passes
any results back to the client using the pointer to the WriteClient method passed in
through the extension block.

If you've had any experience working with frameworks such as classic ASP or
ASP.NET, most of this structure will appear familiar to you. For example, when you
call Write through ASP's intrinsic Response object, execution eventually ends up
passing through the method pointed to by WriteClient.

The Simplest ISAPI Extension That Could Possibly Work[1]

Let's take a look at a simple "Hello, World" ISAPI extension. The result looks like
Figure 13.1.

Writing the Extension

Starting with a Win32 DLL project (not an ATL DLL project) named HelloISAPI,
including the HttpExt.h system header file in stdafx.h brings in the ISAPI extension types, which enables us to implement the GetExtensionVersion function:

---

[1] With apologies to Kent Beck.

```
BOOL WINAPI GetExtensionVersion(HSE_VERSION_INFO *pVer) {
  pVer->dwExtensionVersion = HSE_VERSION;
  strncpy_s( pVer->lpszExtensionDesc,
    HSE_MAX_EXT_DLL_NAME_LEN,
    "Hello ISAPI Extension", _TRUNCATE );
  return TRUE;
}
```

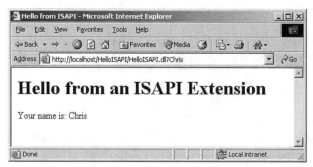

Figure 13.1   Hello World, ISAPI style

All I did here was set the ISAPI version number (HSE_VERSION is a constant defined in HttpExt.h) and fill in the description field for use by IIS. We use the HSE_VERSION constant because we're reporting the version of the ISAPI API that we're using, not the version number of our extension DLL. This way, as IIS and ISAPI changes, IIS can maintain backward-compatibility with older extensions.

The meat of the extension is the HttpExtensionProc function:

```
DWORD WINAPI HttpExtensionProc(EXTENSION_CONTROL_BLOCK *pECB) {
  char *header =
    "<html>"
      "<head>"
        "<title>Hello from ISAPI</title>"
      "</head>"
      "<body>"
        "<h1>Hello from an ISAPI Extension</h1>";

  DWORD size = static_cast< DWORD >( strlen( header ) );
  pECB->WriteClient( pECB->ConnID, header, &size, 0 );

  char *intro = "<p>Your name is: ";
  size = static_cast< DWORD >( strlen( intro ) );
  pECB->WriteClient( pECB->ConnID, intro, &size, 0 );
```

```
    size = static_cast< DWORD >(
       strlen( pECB->lpszQueryString ) );
    pECB->WriteClient( pECB->ConnID, pECB->lpszQueryString,
       &size, 0 );

    char *footer =
          "</p>"
        "</body>"
      "</html>";

    size = static_cast< DWORD >( strlen( footer ) );
    pECB->WriteClient( pECB->ConnID, footer, &size, 0 );

    return HSE_STATUS_SUCCESS;
}
```

This method simply builds up a series of strings and then sends them out to
the browser via the `pECB->WriteClient()` method. We also grab the query string
(the stuff in the URL after the ?) by using the `lpszQueryString` field in the
`EXTENSION_CONTROL_BLOCK`.

In this case, the `TerminateExtension` method doesn't need to do anything and,
thus, is technically optional, but adding a minimal stub for completeness looks like
this:

```
BOOL WINAPI TerminateExtension(DWORD dwFlags) {
    return TRUE;
}
```

Returning `TRUE` tells IIS that it can unload this extension. If we had loaded anything that needed to be cleaned up, the call to `TerminateExtension` would be the
place to do it.

There's one more thing we need to add to the project before we can deploy it:
We have to export the ISAPI entry points. Normal practice is to add
the `__declspec(dllexport)` declaration to each of the ISAPI functions; this tells the
compiler that we want the suitably decorated function to be exported from
the DLL. Unfortunately, when you do this with an ISAPI extension, you get this:

```
c:\helloisapi\helloisapi.cpp(24) : error C2375: 'GetExtensionVersion' :
redefinition; different linkage
        c:\program files\microsoft visual studio
8\vc\platformsdk\include\httpext.h(526) : see declaration of
'GetExtensionVersion'
```

```
c:\helloisapi\helloisapi.cpp(33) : error C2375: 'HttpExtensionProc' :
redefinition; different linkage
        c:\program files\microsoft visual studio
8\vc\platformsdk\include\httpext.h(527) : see declaration of
'HttpExtensionProc'
c:\helloisapi\helloisapi.cpp(65) : error C2375: 'TerminateExtension' :
redefinition; different linkage
        c:\program files\microsoft visual studio
8\vc\platformsdk\include\httpext.h(528) : see declaration of
'TerminateExtension'
```

If we look inside HttpExt.h on lines 526–528, we see the problem:

```
/****************************************************************
 *    Function Prototypes
 *    o  for functions exported from the ISAPI Application DLL
 ****************************************************************/

BOOL  WINAPI    GetExtensionVersion( HSE_VERSION_INFO  *pVer );
DWORD WINAPI    HttpExtensionProc(  EXTENSION_CONTROL_BLOCK *pECB );
BOOL  WINAPI    TerminateExtension( DWORD dwFlags );
```

The HttpExt.h file includes prototypes for the ISAPI entry points, but alas, the prototypes don't include __declspec(dllexport). When the compiler sees the prototype without the export directive and the actual implementation with the directive, it gives the error I just showed you.

To work around this, we need to do exports the old-fashioned way: Add a .def file to the project. This is a separate file that explicitly lists the functions we want exported from our DLL. As the number of exports grows, a .def file gets difficult to maintain, but we've got only three exports here, and they're the same for every ISAPI extension, so it's not too much of a burden.

The .def file looks like this:

```
;HelloISAPI.def : Declares the module parameters for the DLL.
LIBRARY    "HelloISAPI"

EXPORTS
    HttpExtensionProc
    GetExtensionVersion
    TerminateExtension
```

Configuring the Server

Next, we need to get the extension onto the server. Luckily, Visual Studio has some web-deployment tools built in to help, but when you're starting from scratch, they're not set up yet.

First things first: We need an IIS Virtual Directory. I recommend creating a directory that's separate from your build directory for this (you'll see why in a moment). The Internet Services Manager is a nice place to create virtual directories; the sample is called HelloISAPI.[2]

Next, we need to configure permissions on the directory so that the ISAPI extension will be executed and, more important, so we can debug it. In Internet Services Manager, right-clicking the HelloISAPI virtual directory and choosing Properties yields Figure 13.2.

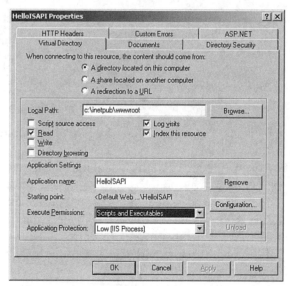

Figure 13.2   Virtual directory properties

We need to make sure two settings are correct in this dialog box. The first is the Execute Permissions drop-down list, which must be set to Scripts and Executables. (It defaults to Scripts Only.) Without this setting, instead of loading the extension and executing it, IIS attempts to download the DLL to your browser.

---

[2] To create a virtual directory, first create a directory via Windows Explorer. It's easiest to create it under C:\inetpub\wwwroot because permissions will be set correctly. Next, open the Internet Services Manager. Expand the treeview on the left until you see Default Web Site. Right-click this and choose New, Virtual Directory. Follow the wizard to name the virtual directory, and then choose the directory you just created. Click Next and then Finish.

The second setting is the Application Protection drop-down list. For easy debugging, you want this set to Low. This causes IIS to load an extension directly into the IIS process. This is generally a bad thing to do on a production server because misbehaving extensions can take the IIS process down with it, but for debugging, it just makes things easier. Do this only on a development server, not on your production boxes![3]

Configuring the Project

With a virtual directory created and configured to receive our ISAPI extension code, we want to configure Visual Studio to deploy the code on a successful build. In the project's property pages, there's an entry called Web Deployment (see Figure 13.3).

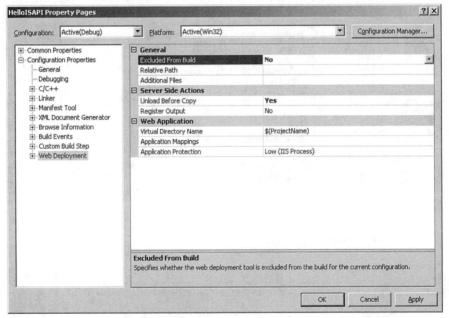

Figure 13.3   Web Deployment settings

By default, the Excluded From Build property is set to Yes, which means that web deployment won't happen. Changing it to No enables web deployment, which, by default, uses the name of the project at the IIS virtual directory name that will receive the result of a successful build—in this example, our `HelloISAPI.DLL` file.

---

[3] Some recommend that you debug in IIS out-of-process mode. Although I can see the appeal, setting that up involves mucking around with COM+ settings, which is often very complicated to get right. If you want to give it a try, take a look at http://www.west-wind.com/presentations/iis5Debug.htm (http://tinysells.com/53).

At this point, compiling the project and surfing to http://localhost/HelloISAPI/
HelloISAPI.dll?SomeName should get back a result that looks like Figure 13.1. If
you make changes to the project and rebuild, VS is smart enough to tell ISAPI to
unload our DLL so that it can be replaced. This is also the reason that we wanted a
separate build directory from our virtual directory. If we compile straight into the
virtual directory, IIS typically has the DLL locked. You would need to use a prebuild
step to shut down IIS so that Visual Studio could regenerate the .dll file after it
compiles. By using web deployment, you don't need to pay the compile-time speed
hit for resetting IIS until the compile succeeds.

If you click F5 to start a debugging session, by default, you get the helpful Executable for Debug Session dialog box. We want to configure Visual Studio to automatically attach to IIS when debugging. To do this, navigate to the Debugging page
of the project properties and set the options to match those shown in Figure 13.4.

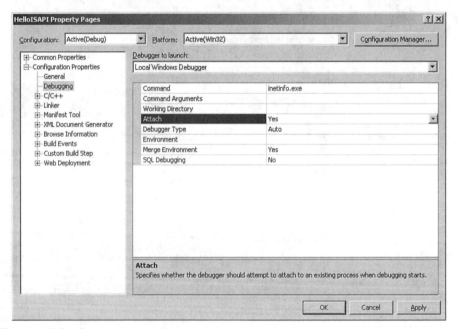

Figure 13.4 Debugging settings

You need to change these two fields:

- **Command.** Set this to inetinfo.exe, which is the name of the IIS process.
- **Attach.** Set this to Yes. If it is set to No, the debugger attempts to start a second copy of inetinfo.exe. Yes means "Attach to already running copy."

Now, to debug your extension, set your breakpoints wherever you want and click F5 to start the debugger. Visual Studio crunches for a while after it attaches to IIS and then looks like it's doing nothing. At this point, start a browser and point it at your extension's URL; your breakpoints should fire.

Wrapping ISAPI

You now have a simple extension written directly to ISAPI, but programming against raw ISAPI is rather awkward. It sure would be nice to have some more object-oriented wrappers. Luckily, ATL Server provides exactly that. The CServer-Context class is a COM object that provides a wrapper around the ECB.

```
class CServerContext :
    public CComObjectRootEx<CComMultiThreadModel>,
    public IHttpServerContext {
public:
    BEGIN_COM_MAP(CServerContext)
        COM_INTERFACE_ENTRY(IHttpServerContext)
    END_COM_MAP()

    void Initialize(__in EXTENSION_CONTROL_BLOCK *pECB);

    LPCSTR GetRequestMethod();
    LPCSTR GetQueryString();
    LPCSTR GetPathInfo();
    LPCSTR GetScriptPathTranslated();
    LPCSTR GetPathTranslated();
    DWORD GetTotalBytes();
    DWORD GetAvailableBytes();
    BYTE *GetAvailableData();
    LPCSTR GetContentType();
    BOOL GetServerVariable(
        LPCSTR pszVariableName,
        LPSTR pvBuffer,
        DWORD *pdwSize);

    BOOL WriteClient(void *pvBuffer, DWORD *pdwBytes);
    BOOL AsyncWriteClient(void *pvBuffer, DWORD *pdwBytes);
    BOOL ReadClient(void *pvBuffer, DWORD *pdwSize);
    BOOL AsyncReadClient(void *pvBuffer, DWORD *pdwSize);

    BOOL SendRedirectResponse(__in LPCSTR pszRedirectUrl);
```

```
BOOL GetImpersonationToken(__out HANDLE * pToken);

BOOL SendResponseHeader(
    LPCSTR pszHeader = "Content-Type: text/html\r\n\r\n",
    LPCSTR pszStatusCode = "200 OK",
    BOOL fKeepConn=FALSE);

BOOL DoneWithSession(__in DWORD dwHttpStatusCode);
BOOL RequestIOCompletion(__in PFN_HSE_IO_COMPLETION pfn,
    DWORD *pdwContext);

BOOL TransmitFile(
    HANDLE hFile,
    PFN_HSE_IO_COMPLETION pfn,
    void *pContext,
    LPCSTR szStatusCode,
    DWORD dwBytesToWrite,
    DWORD dwOffset,
    void *pvHead,
    DWORD dwHeadLen,
    void *pvTail,
    DWORD dwTailLen,
    DWORD dwFlags);

BOOL AppendToLog(LPCSTR szMessage, DWORD *pdwLen);

BOOL MapUrlToPathEx(LPCSTR szLogicalPath, DWORD dwLen,
    HSE_URL_MAPEX_INFO *pumInfo);
};
```

The CServerContext class provides a somewhat more convenient wrapper for the ISAPI interface. Before you use it, you need to add an ATL module object to your project and initialize it in DLL main. This code takes care of the housekeeping:

```
// Our module class definition
class CHelloISAPI2Module :
  public CAtlDllModuleT<CHelloISAPI2Module> {};

// Required global instance of module.
CHelloISAPI2Module _AtlModule;

// Initialize / shutdown module on DLL load or unload
BOOL APIENTRY DllMain( HMODULE hModule,
  DWORD  ul_reason_for_call, LPVOID lpReserved ) {
```

```
      // Set up shared data for use by CServerContext
      return _AtlModule.DllMain(ul_reason_for_call, lpReserved);
}
```

Having initialized shared data that `CServerContext` makes use of, we can now take advantage of `CServerContext`:

```
DWORD WINAPI HttpExtensionProc(EXTENSION_CONTROL_BLOCK *pECB) {
    CComObject< CServerContext > *pCtx;
    CComObject< CServerContext >::CreateInstance( &pCtx );
    pCtx->Initialize( pECB );
    // We use this smart pointer to ensure proper cleanup
    CComPtr< IUnknown > spContextUnk( pCtx );

    char *header =
      "<html>"
        "<head>"
          "<title>Hello from ISAPI</title> "
        "</head>"
        "<body>"
          "<h1>Hello from an ISAPI Extension</h1>";

    DWORD size = static_cast< DWORD >( strlen( header ) );
    pCtx->WriteClient( header, &size );

    char *intro = "<p>Your name is: ";
    size = static_cast< DWORD >( strlen( intro ) );
    pCtx->WriteClient( intro, &size );

    size = static_cast< DWORD >(
      strlen( pCtx->GetQueryString( ) ) );
    pCtx->WriteClient(
      const_cast< LPSTR >(pCtx->GetQueryString( )), &size );

    char *footer =
        "\r\n</body>\r\n"
      "</html>\r\n";

    size = static_cast< DWORD >( strlen( footer ) );
    pCtx->WriteClient( footer, &size );

    return HSE_STATUS_SUCCESS;
}
```

The bold lines show where we've replaced direct calls to the ECB with calls via the context. The `WriteClient` method is at least a little shorter, but we actually haven't gained much at this point. Luckily, there's more API wrapping to be done.

Request and Response Wrappers

Anyone who has done ASP or ASP.NET development is familiar with the Request and Response objects. The former gives access to the contents of the HTTP request: URL, query string, cookies, and so on. The latter gives you a way to write data to the output stream. ATL Server provides similar wrappers that make both reading and writing from the ECB much more pleasant.

The CHttpRequest object is a wrapper object that lets you get at the contents of the HTTP request:

```
class CHttpRequest : public IHttpRequestLookup {
public:
  // Constructs and initializes the object.
  CHttpRequest(
    IHttpServerContext *pServerContext,
    DWORD dwMaxFormSize=DEFAULT_MAX_FORM_SIZE,
    DWORD dwFlags=ATL_FORM_FLAG_NONE);

  CHttpRequest(IHttpRequestLookup *pRequestLookup);

  // Access to Query String parameters as a collection
  const CHttpRequestParams& GetQueryParams() const;

  // Get the entire raw query string
  LPCSTR GetQueryString();

  ... Other methods omitted - we'll talk about them later
}; // class CHttpRequest
```

The CHttpRequest object gives you easy access to everything in the request. Using the CHttpRequest object simplifies getting at query string variables. In the raw C++ extension code, I cheated and just passed data (such as ?Chris), to make using that data easier. However, typical web pages take named query parameters separated with the ampersand (&) and potentially containing special characters encoded in hex:

```
http://localhost/HelloISAPI2/HelloISAP2.dll?name=Chris&motto=I%20Love%20ATL
```

Unfortunately, decoding and parsing query strings in their full glory requires quite a bit of work to get right, which is where ATL Server really starts to shine via the CHttpRequest class:

```
DWORD WINAPI HttpExtensionProc(EXTENSION_CONTROL_BLOCK *pECB) {
  CComObject< CServerContext > *pCtx;
```

```
CComObject< CServerContext >::CreateInstance( &pCtx );
pCtx->Initialize( pECB );
// We use this smart pointer to ensure proper cleanup
CComPtr< IUnknown > spContextUnk( pCtx );

CHttpRequest request( pCtx );

char *header =
  "<html>"
    "<head>"
      "<title>Hello from ISAPI</title>"
    "</head>"
    "<body>"
      "<h1>Hello from an ISAPI Extension</h1>";

DWORD size = static_cast< DWORD >( strlen( header ) );
pCtx->WriteClient( header, &size );

CStringA name;
name = request.GetQueryParams( ).Lookup( "name" );
if( name.IsEmpty( ) ) {
  char *noName = "<p>You didn't give your name";
  size = static_cast< DWORD >( strlen( noName ) );
  pCtx->WriteClient( noName, &size );
}
else {
  char *intro = "<p>Your name is: ";
  size = static_cast< DWORD >( strlen( intro ) );
  pCtx->WriteClient( intro, &size );
  size = name.GetLength( );
  pCtx->WriteClient( name.GetBuffer( ), &size );
}

char *footer =
      "\r\n</p>\r\n"
    "\r\n</body>\r\n"
  "</html>\r\n";

size = static_cast< DWORD >( strlen( footer ) );
pCtx->WriteClient( footer, &size );

return HSE_STATUS_SUCCESS;
}
```

The bold lines show where we're calling into the CHttpRequest object and parsing the named query parameter name. If it's encoded with embedded spaces or other special characters, or if it's included with other query parameters, ATL Server parses it correctly.

One minor thing that might seem odd is the use of CStringA in the previous code sample. Why didn't I just use the plain CString? If you look in the documentation for CHttpRequestParams::Lookup (the method I used to get the query string values), you'll see this:

```
class CHttpRequestParams : ... {
  ...
  LPCSTR Lookup(LPCSTR szName) const;
  ...
};
```

Notice that the return type is LPCSTR, *not* LPCTSTR. In general, when dealing with strings coming in or going out via HTTP, ATL Server explicitly uses 8-bit ANSI character strings.

The CString class is actually a string of TCHARs. As you recall from Chapter 2, "Strings and Text," this means that the actual type of the underlying characters changes depending on your compile settings for Unicode. However, the return type for the Lookup method never changes: It's always ANSI. So, the sample code uses CStringA explicitly to say, "I don't care what the UNICODE compile setting is, I always want this to be 8-bit characters."

On the output side, ATL Server provides the CHttpResponse class:

```
class CHttpResponse :
  public IWriteStream,
  public CWriteStreamHelper {
public:
  // Implementation: The buffer used to store the
  // response before the data is sent to the client.
  CAtlIsapiBuffer<> m_strContent;

  // Numeric constants for the HTTP status codes
  // used for redirecting client requests.
  enum HTTP_REDIRECT {
    HTTP_REDIRECT_MULTIPLE=300,
    HTTP_REDIRECT_MOVED=301,
    HTTP_REDIRECT_FOUND=302,
    HTTP_REDIRECT_SEE_OTHER=303,
    HTTP_REDIRECT_NOT_MODIFIED=304,
    HTTP_REDIRECT_USE_PROXY=305,
```

```
   HTTP_REDIRECT_TEMPORARY_REDIRECT=307
};


// Initialization

CHttpResponse();
CHttpResponse(IHttpServerContext *pServerContext);
BOOL Initialize(IHttpServerContext *pServerContext);
BOOL Initialize(IHttpRequestLookup *pLookup);


// Writing to the output

BOOL SetContentType(LPCSTR szContentType);
HRESULT WriteStream(LPCSTR szOut, int nLen, DWORD *pdwWritten);
BOOL WriteLen(LPCSTR szOut, DWORD dwLen);


// Redirect client to another URL
BOOL Redirect(LPCSTR szUrl,
   HTTP_REDIRECT statusCode=HTTP_REDIRECT_MOVED,
   BOOL bSendBody=TRUE);
BOOL Redirect(LPCSTR szUrl, LPCSTR szBody,
   HTTP_REDIRECT statusCode=HTTP_REDIRECT_MOVED);


// Manipulate various response headers

BOOL AppendHeader(LPCSTR szName, LPCSTR szValue);
BOOL AppendCookie(const CCookie *pCookie);
BOOL AppendCookie(const CCookie& cookie);
BOOL AppendCookie(LPCSTR szName, LPCSTR szValue);
BOOL DeleteCookie(LPCSTR szName);

void ClearHeaders();
void ClearContent();

// Send the current buffer to the client
BOOL Flush(BOOL bFinal=FALSE);
... other methods omitted for clarity
}
}; // class CHttpResponse
```

The CHttpResponse class provides all the control you need to manipulate the response going back to the client. But the best thing about CHttpResponse isn't in this class definition—it's in the base class, CWriteStreamHelper:

```
class CWriteStreamHelper {
public:
  ... Other methods omitted for clarity

  CWriteStreamHelper& operator<<(LPCSTR szStr);
  CWriteStreamHelper& operator<<(LPCWSTR wszStr);
  CWriteStreamHelper& operator<<(int n);
  CWriteStreamHelper& operator<<(short int w);
  CWriteStreamHelper& operator<<(unsigned int u);
  CWriteStreamHelper& operator<<(long int dw);
  CWriteStreamHelper& operator<<(unsigned long int dw);
  CWriteStreamHelper& operator<<(double d);
  CWriteStreamHelper& operator<<(__int64 i);
  CWriteStreamHelper& operator<<(unsigned t64 i);
  CWriteStreamHelper& operator<<(CURRENCY c);
};
```

These `operator<<` overloads mean that `CHttpResponse` can be used much like C++ iostreams can, and they make it much, much easier to build up your output. Using `CHttpResponse`, our final `HttpExtensionProc` now looks like this:

```
DWORD WINAPI HttpExtensionProc(EXTENSION_CONTROL_BLOCK *pECB) {
  CComObject< CServerContext > *pCtx;
  CComObject< CServerContext >::CreateInstance( &pCtx );
  pCtx->Initialize( pECB );
  // We use this smart pointer to ensure proper cleanup
  CComPtr< IUnknown > spContextUnk( pCtx );

  CHttpRequest request( pCtx );
  CHttpResponse response( pCtx );

  response << "<html>" <<
    "<head>" <<
      "<title>Hello from ISAPI</title>" <<
    "</head>" <<
    "<body>" <<
      "<h1>Hello from an ISAPI Extension</h1>";


  CStringA name;
  name = request.GetQueryParams( ).Lookup( "name" );
  if( name.IsEmpty( ) ) {
    response << "<p>You didn't give your name";
```

```
  } else {
    response << "<p>Your name is: " << name;
  }

  response << "</p>" <<
      "</body>" <<
    "</html>";

  return HSE_STATUS_SUCCESS;
}
```

This use of the CHttpResponse object gives us a much simpler programming model. All those ugly casts are gone, and we don't need to worry about presizing anything.

The use of the CServerContext, CHttpRequest, and CHttpResponse objects does make the basics of request processing easier, but other issues haven't yet been addressed. IIS does some subtle work with threading, and if you don't handle threads properly, you'll destroy your server's performance. There's also dealing with form fields and form validation, something every web app has to do. Finally, does it really make sense that you have to recompile your C++ code every time you want to change some HTML?

To address these issues, let's take a look at how ATL Server implements the ISAPI extension.

ATL Server

ISAPI DLLs provide the necessary interface to build web applications, but ISAPI is an extremely low-level way to work. It forces the developer to manage every detail of the web application, even if the requirement is just to slap a username on a "Hello, World" HTML page. ATL Server is a set of classes that simplify the development of ISAPI DLLs in the same style that the rest of ATL simplifies COM development: reasonable implementations of default functionality, and the capability to override those defaults efficiently when needed.

Figure 13.5 presents a very high-level view of the typical ATL Server application architecture.

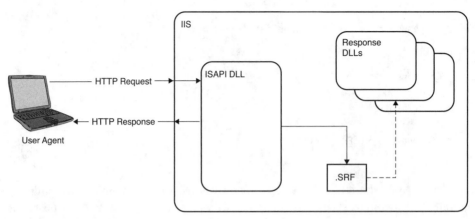

Figure 13.5   ATL Server architecture

The ATL Server architecture divides your web application into three parts:

- An ISAPI extension DLL
- Server Response Files (.SRF), also referred to as stencils
- Response DLLs

These three parts neatly divide up the details of implementing a web application. At the front of the stack is the ISAPI DLL. This is responsible for two things: interfacing with IIS (by implementing the ISAPI functions) and dispatching the incoming requests to the appropriate handler (more about handlers later).

In most cases, your application needs to return HTML that is a combination of static and dynamic content. ATL Server provides a custom extension mapping, .SRF, to a Server Response File. These files contain static text that's sent directly to the client, along with substitution markers that are evaluated at runtime to generate the dynamic content.

The Response DLLs contain the code that evaluates the substitution markers, and this is where your application logic typically resides.

Another way to look at the architecture is this: The ISAPI DLL handles the plumbing. The SRF files are your presentation. The Response DLLs contain your business logic. Each of these concerns is separated so that you work on each individually as needed.

Hello ATL Server

I next rebuilt the Hello ISAPI using ATL Server directly. The first step was to create a new ATL Server project (as shown in Figure 13.6).

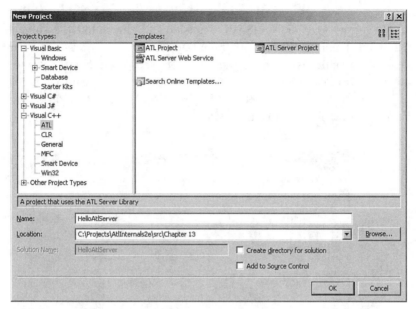

Figure 13.6 Creating an ATL Server project

The first page of the wizard is the usual "Welcome to the wizard" stuff. The next page, Project Settings (see Figure 13.7), is where things get interesting.

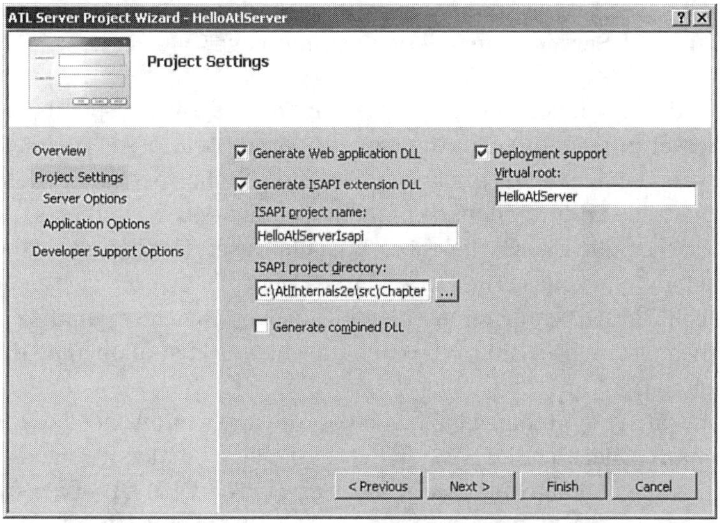

Figure 13.7 ATL Server Project Settings page

The Project Settings page lets you choose what the wizard generates. By default, you get two projects: an ISAPI extension DLL (much like the one I already wrote) and a web application DLL that contains the logic that drives the .srf file. This page also specifies what the virtual directory should be (and the wizard automatically creates and configures the virtual directory for us, saving a manual step).

The next page, Server Options (see Figure 13.8), lets you turn on various ATL Server services that the ISAPI DLL provides.

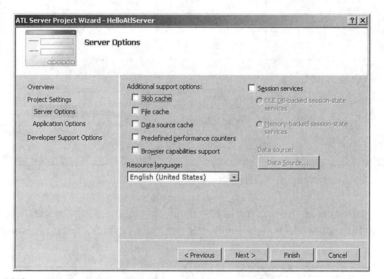

Figure 13.8   ATL Server project Server Options page

Each of the check boxes in the Server Options page corresponds to a service that ATL Server provides. One of the more important services is caching, and ATL Server provides several kinds of caches. The Blob Cache check box adds a service that lets you cache arbitrary chunks of memory (Binary Large OBjects) in memory in the web server. The File Cache check box adds a service that manages data that is stored in temporary files. The Data Source Cache check box adds a service that stores opened OLE DB connection objects. This way you can open the connection once and then just reuse it out of the cache, saving the cost of opening the connection on each request.

Session state is something else that most web applications need but that HTTP doesn't support. Checking the Session Services check box lets you add one of the two session-state implementations in ATL Server. The OLE DB—Backed Session-State Services uses a database (accessed via OLE DB) to store the session information. If a database is undesirable, you can instead choose Memory-Backed Session-State Services, which stores the session state in memory on the web server. This is much faster to access, but because the data is stored in the web server, it's not accessible from other machines; more specifically, if you've got a web farm, in-memory session state will be a problem.

The Predefined Performance Counters option causes the ISAPI DLL to automatically update Windows performance counters for the number of accesses, pages per second, and other such statistics.

The Browser Capabilities Support option turns on ATL Server's support for identifying the client's browser, which lets you, for example, output inline JavaScript only to browsers that support it.

I don't need any of the server options for this particular project, so I left everything unchecked.

The next page, Application Options (see Figure 13.9), lets you specify options for the generated application DLL.

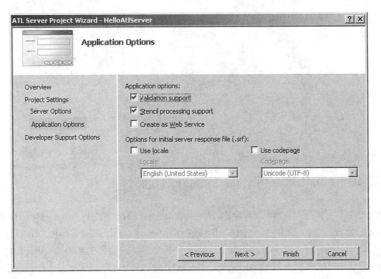

Figure 13.9   ATL Server Application Options page

Validation Support adds a skeleton implementation of the `ValidateAndExchange()` method to the request-handler class. This method is called once before the `.srf` file is processed; this is the place to put input validation code.

Stencil Processing Support provides a skeleton `REPLACEMENT_MAP` in the code and a sample replacement method. The stencil processor uses this map in the class declaration to find the proper method to execute when it hits a replacement token in the `.srf` file.

Create as Web Service adds a web service handler to the project instead of a regular HTML request handler (we discuss this one later).

The remaining two options affect the generated sample `.srf` file. The Use Locale and Use Codepage check boxes add a sample locale and codepage directive to the `.srf` file.

In the sample app I'm writing, the defaults are appropriate.

The final page, Developer Support (see Figure 13.10), gives a couple miscellaneous options that affect several files in the generated code.

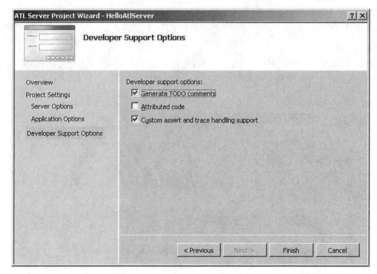

Figure 13.10   ATL Server Developer Support page

Generate TODO Comments tells the wizard to add TODO comments to the code to mark spots where you'll want to change things. Attributed Code tells the wizard to output code with ATL attributes. Custom Assert and Trace Handling Support adds extra code to the debug build of the project that allows trace messages to be output to the WinDbg debugger. Again, the defaults are fine for what I need for the sample.

After clicking Finish and waiting for Visual Studio to crunch, I had a solution containing two projects. The first contained the code for the new ISAPI extension. This project was already configured with an appropriate `.def` file to export the ISAPI methods and set up for web deployment.

The ISAPI DLL implementation was as follows:

```
// HelloAtlServerIsapi.cpp : Defines the entry point
// for the DLL application.


#include "stdafx.h"
```

```
// For custom assert and trace handling with WebDbg.exe
#ifdef _DEBUG
CDebugReportHook g_ReportHook;
#endif

class CHelloAtlServerModule
    : public CAtlDllModuleT<CHelloAtlServerModule> { };

CHelloAtlServerModule _AtlModule;

typedef CIsapiExtension<> ExtensionType;

// The ATL Server ISAPI extension
ExtensionType theExtension;


// Delegate ISAPI exports to theExtension

extern "C"
DWORD WINAPI HttpExtensionProc(LPEXTENSION_CONTROL_BLOCK lpECB) {
  return theExtension.HttpExtensionProc(lpECB);
}

extern "C"
BOOL WINAPI GetExtensionVersion(HSE_VERSION_INFO* pVer) {
  return theExtension.GetExtensionVersion(pVer);
}

extern "C"
BOOL WINAPI TerminateExtension(DWORD dwFlags) {
  return theExtension.TerminateExtension(dwFlags);
}

#ifdef _MANAGED
#pragma managed(push, off)
#endif

// DLL Entry Point

extern "C"
BOOL WINAPI DllMain(HINSTANCE hInstance,
  DWORD dwReason, LPVOID lpReserved) {
  hInstance;
  return _AtlModule.DllMain(dwReason, lpReserved);
}
```

```
#ifdef _MANAGED
#pragma managed(pop)
#endif
```

The ISAPI DLL provides the implementation of the three ISAPI exports, but the implementations here don't do any work. Instead, they forward the calls to a global instance of CIsapiExtension, which is the class that implements all the ISAPI plumbing.

The #pragma managed(push, off) line is there in case you're using managed C++. The DllMain entry point must be in native code for Windows to properly call it at load time. The #pragma turns managed code off the DllMain function, and then the second #pragma managed(pop) turns managed code back on. The mixture of managed and native code is beyond the scope of this book, but it is nice to know that the ATL engineers considered it.

For this particular project, I don't need to touch the ISAPI DLL. The interesting part is in the Application DLL project. This project contains two important things. The first is the HelloAtlServer.srf file:

```
<html>
{{// use MSDN's "ATL Server Response File Reference" to
learn about SRF files.}}
{{handler HelloAtlServer.dll/Default}}
<head>
</head>
<body>
This is a test: {{Hello}}<br>
</body>
</html>
```

Much as ASP files are HTML with the addition of <% %> markers, .srf files are HTML with the addition of {{ }} markers that indicate that substitutions should be performed at that point. Two kinds of substitution markers exist: directives (such as the {{hander.. }} marker) that control the execution of the stencil engine, and substitution markers that indicate where text should be replaced. Additionally, comments are also available (the {{// }} form) and are handy for putting notes into your code that don't get sent back to clients in the HTML.

To make this project's page match the output from my previous one, I edited the default .srf file to look like this instead:

```
<html>
{{handler HelloAtlServer.dll/Default}}
<head>
```

```
    <title>Hello from ATL Server</title>
</head>
<body>
<h1>Hello from ATL Server</h1>
{{if NameGiven}}
<p>Your name is {{Name}}
{{else}}
<p>You didn't give your name!
{{endif}}
</p>
</body>
</html>
```

This .srf file uses both flow control (the if block) and substitution (the Name block). An .srf file is connected to request handler classes via the handler marker. In this file, the handler marker says that the request-handler class is in the Hello-AtlServer.dll file, and it's marked with the name Default. The HelloAtlServer.cpp file shows how the name Default is mapped to an actual C++ class:

```
// HelloAtlServer.cpp
...


BEGIN_HANDLER_MAP()
    HANDLER_ENTRY("Default", CHelloAtlServerHandler)
END_HANDLER_MAP()
```

The HANDLER_MAP() in an ATL Server project serves the same purpose as the OBJECT_MAP()in an ATL project;[4] it maps a key (in this case, the handler name) to a specific class.

The CHelloAtlServer class is where we actually put the substitutions. The default version output from the wizard looks like this:

```
// HelloAtlServer.h : Defines the ATL Server
// request handler class

#pragma once

class CHelloAtlServerHandler
  : public CRequestHandlerT<CHelloAtlServerHandler> {
```

---

[4] Or at least, as the OBJECT_MAP() used to serve. Later, we talk about a macro that lets you avoid having to maintain the HANDLER_MAP(), but the wizard-generated code doesn't use it.

```
public:
  BEGIN_REPLACEMENT_METHOD_MAP(CHelloAtlServerHandler)
    REPLACEMENT_METHOD_ENTRY("Hello", OnHello)
  END_REPLACEMENT_METHOD_MAP()

  HTTP_CODE ValidateAndExchange() {
    // TODO: Put all initialization and validation code here

    // Set the content-type
    m_HttpResponse.SetContentType("text/html");

    return HTTP_SUCCESS;
  }

protected:
  // Here is an example of how to use a replacement
  // tag with the stencil processor
  HTTP_CODE OnHello(void) {
    m_HttpResponse << "Hello World!";
    return HTTP_SUCCESS;
  }
};
```

The REPLACMENT_METHOD_MAP() macros give the mappings between the markers in the .srf file and the actual methods in the class that get called at substitution time.

The class also includes the ValidateAndExchange() method. This method gets called once at the start of page processing, and this is the place where you can process and validate your inputs.

To implement our "Hello, World" page, we need to first check to see if a name parameter was passed on the query string, pull out the name, and provide implementations for the NameGiven and Name substitutions:

```
class CHelloAtlServerHandler
  : public CRequestHandlerT<CHelloAtlServerHandler> {

public:
  BEGIN_REPLACEMENT_METHOD_MAP(CHelloAtlServerHandler)
    REPLACEMENT_METHOD_ENTRY("NameGiven", OnNameGiven)
    REPLACEMENT_METHOD_ENTRY("Name", OnName)
  END_REPLACEMENT_METHOD_MAP()

  HTTP_CODE ValidateAndExchange() {
    m_name = m_HttpRequest.GetQueryParams( ).Lookup( "name" );
    return HTTP_SUCCESS;
  }
```

```
protected:
  HTTP_CODE OnNameGiven( ) {
    if( m_name.IsEmpty( ) ) {
      return HTTP_S_FALSE;
    }
    return HTTP_SUCCESS;
  }

  HTTP_CODE OnName( ) {
    m_HttpResponse << m_name;
    return HTTP_SUCCESS;
  }

private:
  // Storage for the name in the query string
  CStringA m_name;
};
```

The m_name member stores the name retrieved from the query string. To retrieve it, I used the m_HttpRequest member provided by the CRequestHandlerT base class. This is an instance of the CHttpRequest class that has already been initialized by the time ValidateAndExchange is called.

The OnName method is called when the {{Name}} substitution is hit in the .srf file. It uses the m_HttpResponse member from the base class, which is a ready-to-go instance of CHttpResponse. It simply writes the name to the output. All successful substitution methods must return HTTP_SUCCESS, or the processing will be aborted with an error.

The OnNameGiven method is slightly different. This is used from the {{if ...}} block and is used to control which chunk of HTML is actually output from the .srf file. For a method that must return true or false, true is indicated by an HTTP_SUC-CESS return code. HTTP_S_FALSE[5] indicates a false value. Any other return value aborts the processing. The HTTP code returned to the client depends on the actual return value. HTTP_FAIL is probably the most common; its returns an HTTP code 500 (Server Error).

Because the wizard enables web deployment, compiling the project automatically deploys it as well. Pressing F5 causes Visual Studio to automatically attach to

---

[5] This is analogous to the S_OK and S_FALSE return codes for HRESULTS. It would have been nice if the ATL Server team had simply reused HRESULTS for their error codes, but no such luck.

IIS, and brings up a browser showing the result of my .srf file processing[6] (see Figure 13.11). Tweaking the URL by adding ?name=Chris%20Tavares gave the result in Figure 13.12.

Figure 13.11 SRF processing, no name on query string

Figure 13.12 SRF processing with name on query string

So, what does the wizard-generated ATL Server project buy us? First, it saves a lot of effort in configuring the project: setting up virtual directories, configuring web deployment, and setting up for debugging. Next, we get a clean separation between the ISAPI plumbing and the business logic. ATL Server provides a high-performance implementation of ISAPI applications out of the box, one that would take a great deal of effort to do correctly by hand. Finally, we get a good separation of presentation and logic. We no longer need to recompile just to tweak the HTML; all we need to do is change the .srf file and redeploy that file to the web server.

---

[6] You might be wondering why the ATL Server project gives us a browser window when we debug, but the straight ISAPI project doesn't. The ATL Server implementation of the ISAPI extension has special hooks for debugging in the implementation. This is combined with Visual Studio's Web Services debugger to automatically attach to IIS and launch the browser. Without those (completely undocumented) hooks, we're stuck with attaching to IIS as previously described.

ATL Server also gave me something that is rather subtle but very important. Consider the URL that was used. For the "by hand" project, the URL was this:

```
http://localhost/HelloISAPI/HelloISAPI.dll
```

For the ATL Server project, the URL was this:

```
http://localhost/HelloAtlServer/HelloAtlServer.srf
```

Notice that the first URL references the DLL directly, whereas the second one goes to the .srf file. The big deal here is simply this: In the home-grown version, if I want multiple web pages, I need to provide the logic to map URLs (or query strings) to particular pages myself. ATL Server, on the other hand, automatically uses the appropriate DLLs when you reference an .srf file. If you want a new page, just drop in a new .srf file. The ATL Server Project Wizard configured the .srf extension to map to the ISAPI DLL, as shown in Figure 13.13.

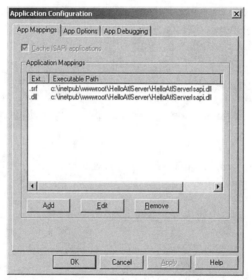

Figure 13.13 IIS extension mappings for an ATL Server project

IIS automatically routes any request for an .srf file in this virtual directory to the ISAPI extension; at that point, ATL Server takes over and routes the request to the correct .srf file and request handlers.

Web Services in ATL Server

ATL Server does more than generate HTML: It generates XML as well. More specifically, you can use ATL Server to implement web services using the same ISAPI infrastructure it uses to generate HTML pages.

Whenever I look at a new web services stack (which has happened quite frequently in recent years), I like to start by building a simple service that will convert strings to upper- or lowercase, and that will return the length of a string. This lets me concentrate on the plumbing without worrying much about the implementation.

I started by creating a new ATL Server project. Visual Studio shows two icons on the New Project dialog box (see Figure 13.6) for ATL Server. I used the ATL Server project icon in the previous example. It turns out that the two project wizards are almost identical. The only difference between the two is the Create as Web Service check box on the Application Options page (see Figure 13.9). With the ATL Server Web Service project, this check box is on by default.

One other important difference exists. The marshalling code between XML and C++ is complicated and requires a lot of code to be generated. Instead of swamping your projects with generated code that's hard to edit and update, the ATL Server team built the code generation into ATL attributes. This means that, for all practical purposes, web services are the only part of ATL that *requires* the use of attributed code. When the Create as Web Service check box is set, the Developer Support page (see Figure 13.10) has the Attributed check box set and disabled.[7]

I created a project called StringLib for my new web service and got the expected ISAPI and Application projects, just like my previous one. The ISAPI project contained this code:

```
// StringLibIsapi.cpp : Defines the entry point for
// the DLL application.
#include "stdafx.h"
// For custom assert and trace handling with WebDbg.exe
#ifdef _DEBUG
CDebugReportHook g_ReportHook;
#endif
[ module(name="MyStringLib", type=dll) ];
[ emitidl(restricted) ];

typedef CIsapiExtension<> ExtensionType;
```

---

[7] If you haven't already done so, you might like to read up on ATL attributes in Appendix D, "Attributed ATL."

```
// The ATL Server ISAPI extension
ExtensionType theExtension;
// Delegate ISAPI exports to theExtension
//
extern "C" DWORD WINAPI HttpExtensionProc(
  LPEXTENSION_CONTROL_BLOCK lpECB) {
  return theExtension.HttpExtensionProc(lpECB);
}

extern "C" BOOL WINAPI GetExtensionVersion(
  HSE_VERSION_INFO* pVer) {
  return theExtension.GetExtensionVersion(pVer);
}

extern "C" BOOL WINAPI TerminateExtension(DWORD dwFlags) {
  return theExtension.TerminateExtension(dwFlags);
}
```

The `module` attribute generates the type definition for the ATL module class. The `emitidl` attribute is used to prevent anything in that file after that point from going into the generated IDL file. The rest of the file is pretty much identical to the unattributed version. As with the HelloATLServer project, I didn't need to touch the ISAPI extension.

The interesting stuff ended up in the `StringLib.h` file in the application DLL project:

```
// StringLib.h
...
namespace StringLibService {
// all struct, enum, and typedefs for your web service
// should go inside the namespace

// IStringLibService - web service interface declaration
//
[ uuid("5CEAB050-F80B-4054-8E1B-43510E61B8CE"),
  object ]
__interface IStringLibService {
  // HelloWorld is a sample ATL Server web service method.
  // It shows how to declare a web service method and
  // its in-parameters and out-parameters
  [id(1)] HRESULT HelloWorld([in] BSTR bstrInput,
    [out, retval] BSTR *bstrOutput);
  // TODO: Add additional web service methods here
};
```

```
// StringLibService - web service implementation
//
[ request_handler(name="Default", sdl="GenStringLibWSDL"),
  soap_handler(
    name="StringLibService",
    namespace="urn:StringLibService",
    protocol="soap" ) ]
class CStringLibService :
  public IStringLibService {
public:
  // This is a sample web service method that shows how
  // to use the soap_method attribute to expose a method
  // as a web method
  [ soap_method ]
  HRESULT HelloWorld(/*[in]*/ BSTR bstrInput,
    /*[out, retval]*/ BSTR *bstrOutput) {
    CComBSTR bstrOut(L"Hello ");
    bstrOut += bstrInput;
    bstrOut += L"!";
    *bstrOutput = bstrOut.Detach();

    return S_OK;
  }
  // TODO: Add additional web service methods here
}; // class CStringLibService

} // namespace StringLibService
```

This default demonstrates quite well how you build web services with ATL Server. You start with an IDL interface and specify the inputs and outputs using various COM types.[8] Then, you create a class that implements that interface and add the `request_handler` and `soap_handler` attributes to tell the ATL Server plumbing that this is a web service implementation. Finally, you implement the interface methods, decorating each one with the `soap_method` attribute to wire up the incoming XML requests to the appropriate methods.

So, I removed the sample code, and created my interface:

```
[ uuid("5CEAB050-F80B-4054-8E1B-43510E61B8CE"),
  object ]
__interface IStringLibService {
  [id(1)] HRESULT ToUpper([in] BSTR bstrInput,
```

---

[8] Check the ATL Server documentation for details about which types are actually supported in web services. In general, scalars (numbers, strings) and arrays and structures of scalars are supported. Arbitrary interface pointers are *not* supported in web services.

```
      [out, retval] BSTR *pbstrOutput);
   [id(2)] HRESULT ToLower([in] BSTR bstrInput,
      [out, retval] BSTR *pbstrOutput );
   [id(3)] HRESULT GetLength([in] BSTR bstrInput,
      [out, retval] long *pResult );
};
```

And the implementation class:

```
[ request_handler(name="Default", sdl="GenStringLibWSDL"),
  soap_handler(
    name="StringLibService",
    namespace="urn:StringLibService",
    protocol="soap"
  ) ]
class CStringLibService :
  public IStringLibService {
public:

  [soap_method]
  HRESULT ToUpper( BSTR bstrInput, BSTR *pbstrOutput ) {
    CComBSTR result( bstrInput );
    HRESULT hr = result.ToUpper( );
    if( FAILED( hr ) ) return hr;
    *pbstrOutput = result.Detach( );
    return S_OK;
  }

  [soap_method]
  HRESULT ToLower( BSTR bstrInput, BSTR *pbstrOutput ) {
    CComBSTR result( bstrInput );
    HRESULT hr = result.ToLower( );
    if( FAILED( hr ) ) return hr;
    *pbstrOutput = result.Detach( );
    return S_OK;
  }

  [soap_method]
  HRESULT GetLength( BSTR bstrInput, long *pResult ) {
    *pResult = ::SysStringLen( bstrInput );
    return S_OK;
  }
};
```

Aside from the attributes, this code wouldn't look out of place in any COM server implementation.

To use the web service in question, you need a WSDL file. ATL Server automatically generates the WSDL; it's accessible at http://localhost/StringLib/StringLib.dll?Handler=GenStringLibWSDL.

Consuming a Web Service in C++

After my web service was deployed, I wanted to test it. You can call most web services from almost every language. Because this is a C++ book, I created a C++ client. Luckily, Visual Studio includes a code generator that makes it fairly easy to make calls on a web service.

I started by creating a Win32 Console application in Visual Studio. To bring in the web service, I used the Add Web Service feature of Visual Studio to read the WSDL file from the web service and generate a proxy class[9] that wraps access to the web service. The rest of the C++ code simply collected some input and called the web service:

```
#include <iostream>
#include <string>
#include <atlconv.h>

using namespace std;

class CoInit {
public:
  CoInit( ) { ::CoInitialize( 0 ); }
  ~CoInit( ) { ::CoUninitialize( ); }
};

void _tmain(int argc, _TCHAR* argv[]) {
  CoInit coInit;

  cout << "Enter a string: ";
  string input;
  getline( cin, input );

  StringLibService::CStringLibService proxy;

  CComBSTR bstrInput( input.c_str( ) );
```

---

[9] The Add Web Service function calls into a command-line utility named sproxy.exe. Look in the documentation for details on how to customize proxy-class generation.

```
CComBSTR bstrToLower;
HRESULT hr = proxy.ToLower( bstrInput, &bstrToLower );
if( FAILED( hr ) ) {
  cerr << "Call to ToLower failed with HRESULT " << hr;
  return -1;
}
cout << "This string in upper case is:" <<
  CW2A( bstrToLower ) << endl;

CComBSTR bstrToUpper;
hr = proxy.ToUpper( bstrInput, &bstrToUpper );
if( FAILED( hr ) ) {
  cerr << "Call to ToUpper failed with HRESULT " << hr;
  return -1;
}
cout << "This string in lower case is:" <<
  CW2A( bstrToUpper ) << endl;

int length;
hr = proxy.GetLength( bstrInput, &length );
if( FAILED( hr ) ) {
  cerr << "Call to GetLength failed with HRESULT " << hr;
  return -1;
}
cout << "This string is " << length <<
  " characters long." << endl;
}
```

The lines in bold show the calls to the web service. Calling via the proxy acts much like a call into a COM object: All calls return an HRESULT, the actual return value is given via an out parameter, and there are special rules for memory management (which are explained in the MSDN documentation). Because the web service client proxy uses the Microsoft XML 3.0 Server XMLHTTP object by default, I needed to initialize COM before making the calls.

This code simply calls all three of the methods in the web service. Figure 13.14 shows the result of running the test harness.

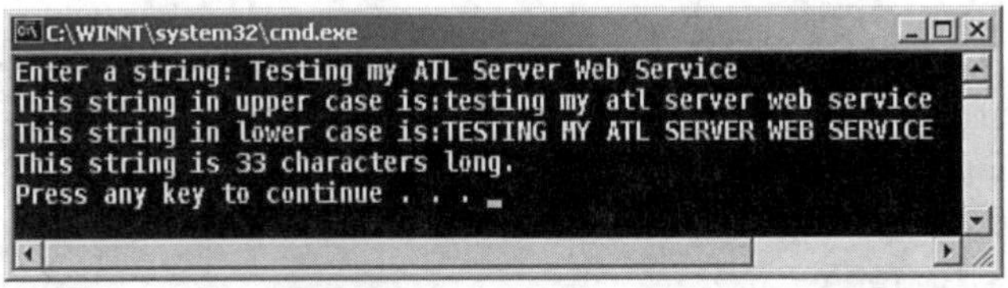

Figure 13.14   Output from Web Service test client

SOAP Box: Why ATL Server Does Web Services Poorly

So, it's possible to implement web services—and do so in a way that's fairly comfortable to COM developers. What's not to like? A lot, as it turns out.

When using ATL Server Web Services, you have absolutely no control over the actual XML that gets sent out. ATL Server maps your COM interface into RPC-encoded SOAP; you can't hand it an XML schema. You can't even tweak the WSDL after the fact. You're stuck with what ATL Server gives you.

Now, perhaps you're thinking that this isn't too bad. Maybe you're defining a new service and don't need to conform to an existing XML schema. Unfortunately, you might be in for problem even then.

SOAP uses two basic styles to map the XML in the SOAP document to the underlying programming model. ATL Server uses the RPC encoding. This is a set of rules defined in the SOAP specification that say how an integer, string, array, and so on is represented in XML. This encoding does not use the XML Schema definition (although it does use the XSD type system) because the XSD specification wasn't finished when the SOAP spec shipped.

You would think that the RPC style would be sufficient, but the SOAP spec was sufficiently ambiguous that different vendors implemented RPC encoding in different and incompatible ways. With ATL Server adopting RPC encoding, you're in for interop trouble.

The other option is to use document-literal encoding. With doc literal, you simply treat the body of the SOAP document as XML. This turns out to be much more flexible and interoperable than RPC encoding. In fact, in the current SOAP 1.2 specification,[10] Section 5 (which defines RPC encoding) is completely optional. More toolkits are moving toward doing doc literal–style web services and are leaving out RPC encoding altogether.[11]

---

[10] Available at www.w3.org/TR/soap12-part1/ (http://tinysells.com/54).

[11] See "The Argument Against SOAP Encoding," by Tim Ewald, at http://msdn.microsoft.com/library/default.asp?url=/library/en-us/dnsoap/html/argsoape.asp (http://tinysells.com/55), for more details about the evils of RPC encoding in web services.

As a result, I simply can't recommend using ATL Server Web Services in any serious application. It might be useful if you have existing C++ code that has to be exposed as a web service *now, now, now!* But for anything that needs to interop with other environments, you're better off choosing a web service layer that supports more modern web services styles such as doc-literal and XML Schema.

Summary

ATL Server is an extension of ATL that enables you to write ISAPI applications and bring your C++ skills to the World Wide Web. An ATL Server project consists of an ISAPI DLL that implements the ISAPI entry points for IIS, a set of .srf files that include the HTML to send back to the client, and an application DLL that provides request handlers that fill in the substitutions in the .srf files.

The ATL Server ISAPI implementation provides you with a built-in thread pool for high-performance web applications. ATL Server also provides optional caching mechanisms to further improve performance.

An ATL Server request handler is used to validate the incoming requests and (in concert with the .srf files) generate the output. ATL Server provides the CHttpRequest class that wraps the HTTP request. CHttpRequest provides access to query string parameters, form variables, cookies, and a whole lot more. CHttpResponse wraps the output and gives you the capability to easily generate output to the client in the style of a C++ iostream.

ATL Server can also be used for quick web service wrappers around existing COM code.

In the next chapter, we take a look at how ATL Server does all this under the hood.

CHAPTER 14

ATL Server Internals

ATL Server provides a robust implementation of an ISAPI extension right out of the box. It manages threading and IIS resources so you don't have to. You've already seen how to use ATL Server in Chapter 13, "Hello, ATL Server"; now let's take a look under the hood and see how it works.

Implementing ISAPI in ATL Server

The `CIsapiExtension` class is the heart of ATL's implementation of the ISAPI interface.

```
template <class ThreadPoolClass=CThreadPool<CIsapiWorker>,
  class CRequestStatClass=CNoRequestStats,
  class HttpUserErrorTextProvider=CDefaultErrorProvider,
  class WorkerThreadTraits=DefaultThreadTraits,
  class CPageCacheStats=CNoStatClass,
  class CStencilCacheStats=CNoStatClass>
class CIsapiExtension :
  public IServiceProvider,
  public IIsapiExtension,
  public IRequestStats {
protected:
  CIsapiExtension();

  DWORD HttpExtensionProc(LPEXTENSION_CONTROL_BLOCK lpECB) ;
  BOOL GetExtensionVersion(__out HSE_VERSION_INFO* pVer) ;
  BOOL TerminateExtension(DWORD /*dwFlags*/) ;

  // ...
};
```

As you can see, this class is heavily templated. Three of the template parameters (CRequestStatClass, CPageCacheStats, and CStencilCacheStats) are used for performance tracking and logging. The default template parameters result in no logging or performance counters being used; ATL Server provides other implementation that will gather statistics for you, but because that logging can have a significant performance impact, it's turned off by default.

The three `CIsapiExtension` methods contain the actual implementations of the three ISAPI functions. The `GetExtensionVersion` method is long but fairly straightforward. Because this is the method called when the ISAPI extension is first loaded, the class does most of its initialization here:

```
BOOL GetExtensionVersion( HSE_VERSION_INFO* pVer)  {
  // allocate a Tls slot for storing per thread data
  m_dwTlsIndex = TlsAlloc();

  // create a private heap for request data
  // this heap has to be thread safe to allow for
  // async processing of requests
  m_hRequestHeap = HeapCreate(0, 0, 0);
  if (!m_hRequestHeap) {
    m_hRequestHeap = GetProcessHeap();
    if (!m_hRequestHeap) {
      return SetCriticalIsapiError(IDS_ATLSRV_CRITICAL_HEAPCREATEFAILED);
    }
  }

  // create a private heap (synchronized) for
  // allocations.  This reduces fragmentation overhead
  // as opposed to the process heap
  HANDLE hHeap = HeapCreate(0, 0, 0);
  if (!hHeap) {
    hHeap = GetProcessHeap();
    m_heap.Attach(hHeap, false);
  } else {
    m_heap.Attach(hHeap, true);
  }
  hHeap = NULL;

  if (S_OK != m_WorkerThread.Initialize()) {
      return SetCriticalIsapiError(IDS_ATLSRV_CRITICAL_WORKERINITFAILED);
  }

  if (m_critSec.Init() != S_OK) {
      HRESULT hrIgnore=m_WorkerThread.Shutdown();
      return SetCriticalIsapiError(IDS_ATLSRV_CRITICAL_CRITSECINITFAILED);
  }
```

```
if (S_OK != m_ThreadPool.Initialize(
  static_cast<IIsapiExtension*>(this), GetNumPoolThreads(),
  GetPoolStackSize(), GetIOCompletionHandle())) {
  HRESULT hrIgnore=m_WorkerThread.Shutdown();
  m_critSec.Term();
  return SetCriticalIsapiError(
    IDS_ATLSRV_CRITICAL_THREADPOOLFAILED);
}


if (FAILED(m_DllCache.Initialize(&m_WorkerThread,
  GetDllCacheTimeout()))) {
  HRESULT hrIgnore=m_WorkerThread.Shutdown();
  m_ThreadPool.Shutdown();
  m_critSec.Term();
  return SetCriticalIsapiError(
    IDS_ATLSRV_CRITICAL_DLLCACHEFAILED);
}


if (FAILED(m_PageCache.Initialize(&m_WorkerThread))) {
  HRESULT hrIgnore=m_WorkerThread.Shutdown();
  m_ThreadPool.Shutdown();
  m_DllCache.Uninitialize();
  m_critSec.Term();
  return SetCriticalIsapiError(
    IDS_ATLSRV_CRITICAL_PAGECACHEFAILED);
}


if (S_OK != m_StencilCache.Initialize(
  static_cast<IServiceProvider*>(this),
  &m_WorkerThread,
  GetStencilCacheTimeout(),
  GetStencilLifespan())) {
  HRESULT hrIgnore=m_WorkerThread.Shutdown();
  m_ThreadPool.Shutdown();
  m_DllCache.Uninitialize();
  m_PageCache.Uninitialize();
  m_critSec.Term();
  return SetCriticalIsapiError(IDS_ATLSRV_CRITICAL_STENCILCACHEFAILED);
}

pVer->dwExtensionVersion = HSE_VERSION;
Checked::strncpy_s(pVer->lpszExtensionDesc,
  HSE_MAX_EXT_DLL_NAME_LEN, GetExtensionDesc(), _TRUNCATE);
```

```
    pVer->lpszExtensionDesc[HSE_MAX_EXT_DLL_NAME_LEN - 1] = '\0';

    return TRUE;
}
```

This method allocates two Win32 heaps for use during request process, sets up a thread pool, and initializes various caches.

The real action takes place in the HttpExtensionProc method. This is called for every HTTP request that IIS routes to our extension DLL. Before we look at the implementation of this method, we need to look at how to achieve high performance in a server environment.

Performance and Multithreading

Any production web server needs to handle many simultaneous network requests. In the original web extension platform, the Common Gateway Interface (CGI), each request was handled by spawning a new process. This process handled that one request and then exited. This worked acceptably on UNIX for small sites, but process creation overhead soon limited the number of simultaneous requests that could be processed.

This process-creation model was made even worse on Windows, where creating processes is much more expensive. However, there's a fairly obvious alternative in Win32: use a thread per request instead of a process. Threads are much, much cheaper to start. Unfortunately, the obvious solution is somewhat less obviously wrong in large systems. Threads might be cheap, but they're not free. As the number of threads increases, the CPU spends more time on thread management and less time actually doing the work of serving your web site.

The solution comes from the stateless nature of HTTP. Because each request is independent, it doesn't matter which specific thread processes a request. More usefully, when a thread is done processing a request, instead of dying, it can be reused to process another request. This design is called a *thread pool*.

IIS uses a thread pool internally to handle incoming traffic. Each request is handed off to a thread in the pool. The thread services the request (by either returning static content off the disk or executing the HttpExtensionProc of the appropriate ISAPI extension DLL). In general, this works well, but the thread has to finish its processing quickly. If all the threads in the IIS pool are busy, new requests start getting dropped. Serving static content is a low-overhead process. But when you start executing arbitrary code (to generate dynamic HTML, for example), suddenly the time it takes for the thread to return to the pool is much less predictable, and it could be much longer.

So, we need to return the IIS thread back to the pool as soon as possible. But we also need to actually perform our processing to handle the request. Instead of forcing every developer to micro-optimize every statement of the ISAPI extension to get the thread back to the pool, ATL Server provides its own thread pool. On a request, the `HttpExtensionProc` (which is running on the IIS thread) places the request into the internal thread pool. The IIS thread then returns, ready to process another request. The code follows:

```
DWORD HttpExtensionProc(LPEXTENSION_CONTROL_BLOCK lpECB) {
  AtlServerRequest *pRequestInfo = NULL;
  _ATLTRY {
    pRequestInfo = CreateRequest();
    if (pRequestInfo == NULL)
      return HSE_STATUS_ERROR;

    CServerContext *pServerContext = NULL;
    ATLTRY(pServerContext = CreateServerContext(m_hRequestHeap));
    if (pServerContext == NULL) {
      FreeRequest(pRequestInfo);
      return HSE_STATUS_ERROR;
    }

    pServerContext->Initialize(lpECB);
    pServerContext->AddRef();

    pRequestInfo->pServerContext = pServerContext;
    pRequestInfo->dwRequestType = ATLSRV_REQUEST_UNKNOWN;
    pRequestInfo->dwRequestState = ATLSRV_STATE_BEGIN;
    pRequestInfo->pExtension =
      static_cast<IIsapiExtension *>(this);
    pRequestInfo->pDllCache =
      static_cast<IDllCache *>(&m_DllCache);
#ifndef ATL_NO_MMSYS
    pRequestInfo->dwStartTicks = timeGetTime();
#else
    pRequestInfo->dwStartTicks = GetTickCount();
#endif
    pRequestInfo->pECB = lpECB;

    m_reqStats.OnRequestReceived();

    if (m_ThreadPool.QueueRequest(pRequestInfo))
      return HSE_STATUS_PENDING;

    if (pRequestInfo != NULL) {
      FreeRequest(pRequestInfo);
    }
```

```
    }
    _ATLCATCHALL() { }
    return HSE_STATUS_ERROR;
}
```

The `CreateRequest` method simply allocates a chunk of memory from the request heap to store the information about the request:

```
struct AtlServerRequest {
    // For future compatibility
    DWORD cbSize;

    // Necessary because it wraps the ECB
    IHttpServerContext *pServerContext;

    // Indicates whether it was called through an .srf file or
    // through a .dll file
    ATLSRV_REQUESTTYPE dwRequestType;
    // Indicates what state of completion the request is in
    ATLSRV_STATE dwRequestState;
    // Necessary because the callback (for async calls) must
    // know where to route the request
    IRequestHandler *pHandler;
    // Necessary in order to release the dll properly
    // (for async calls)
    HINSTANCE hInstDll;
    // Necessary to requeue the request (for async calls)
    IIsapiExtension *pExtension;
    // Necessary to release the dll in async callback
    IDllCache* pDllCache;

    HANDLE hFile;
    HCACHEITEM hEntry;
    IFileCache* pFileCache;

    // necessary to synchronize calls to HandleRequest
    // if HandleRequest could potentially make an
    // async call before returning. only used
    // if indicated with ATLSRV_INIT_USEASYNC_EX
    HANDLE m_hMutex;
    // Tick count when the request was received
    DWORD dwStartTicks;
    EXTENSION_CONTROL_BLOCK *pECB;
```

```
    PFnHandleRequest pfnHandleRequest;
    PFnAsyncComplete pfnAsyncComplete;
    // buffer to be flushed asynchronously
    LPCSTR pszBuffer;
    // length of data in pszBuffer
    DWORD dwBufferLen;
    // value that can be used to pass user data between
    // parent and child handlers
    void* pUserData;
};

AtlServerRequest *CreateRequest() {
    // Allocate a fixed block size to avoid fragmentation
    AtlServerRequest *pRequest = (AtlServerRequest *) HeapAlloc(
      m_hRequestHeap, HEAP_ZERO_MEMORY,
      __max(sizeof(AtlServerRequest),
        sizeof(_CComObjectHeapNoLock<CServerContext>)));
    if (!pRequest) return NULL;

    pRequest->cbSize = sizeof(AtlServerRequest);
    return pRequest;
}
```

As you can see, there's all the information that IIS supplies about the request
(the ECB pointer), plus a whole lot more.

The ATL Server Thread Pool

ATL Server provides a thread pool implementation in the CThreadPool class:

```
template <class Worker,
  class ThreadTraits=DefaultThreadTraits,
  class WaitTraits=DefaultWaitTraits>
class CThreadPool : public IThreadPoolConfig {
    // ...
};
```

The template parameters give you control over how threads are created and
what they do. The Worker template parameter lets you specify what class will actually do the processing of the request. The ThreadTraits class controls how a thread
is created. Depending on the ATL_MIN_CRT setting, DefaultThreadTraits is a typedef
to one of two other classes:

```
class CRTThreadTraits {
public:
  static HANDLE CreateThread(LPSECURITY_ATTRIBUTES lpsa,
      DWORD dwStackSize, LPTHREAD_START_ROUTINE pfnThreadProc,
      void *pvParam, DWORD dwCreationFlags, DWORD *pdwThreadId) {
    // _beginthreadex calls CreateThread
    // which will set the last error value
    // before it returns.
    return (HANDLE) _beginthreadex(lpsa, dwStackSize,
      (unsigned int (__stdcall *)(void *)) pfnThreadProc,
      pvParam, dwCreationFlags, (unsigned int *) pdwThreadId);
  }
};

class Win32ThreadTraits {
public:
  static HANDLE CreateThread(LPSECURITY_ATTRIBUTES lpsa,
      DWORD dwStackSize, LPTHREAD_START_ROUTINE pfnThreadProc,
      void *pvParam, DWORD dwCreationFlags, DWORD *pdwThreadId) {
    return ::CreateThread(lpsa, dwStackSize, pfnThreadProc,
      pvParam, dwCreationFlags, pdwThreadId);
  }
};

#if !defined(_ATL_MIN_CRT) && defined(_MT)
    typedef CRTThreadTraits DefaultThreadTraits;
#else
    typedef Win32ThreadTraits DefaultThreadTraits;
#endif
```

As part of initialization, the `CThreadPool` class uses the `ThreadTraits` class to create the initial set of threads. The threads in the pool all run this thread proc:

```
DWORD ThreadProc() {
  DWORD dwBytesTransfered;
  ULONG_PTR dwCompletionKey;

  OVERLAPPED* pOverlapped;

  // this block is to ensure theWorker gets destructed before the
  // thread handle is closed {
    // We instantiate an instance of the worker class on the
    // stack for the life time of the thread.
    Worker theWorker;
```

```
      if (theWorker.Initialize(m_pvWorkerParam) == FALSE) {
        return 1;
      }

      SetEvent(m_hThreadEvent);
      // Get the request from the IO completion port
      while (GetQueuedCompletionStatus(m_hRequestQueue,
        &dwBytesTransfered, &dwCompletionKey, &pOverlapped,
        INFINITE)) {
        if (pOverlapped == ATLS_POOL_SHUTDOWN) // Shut down {
          LONG bResult = InterlockedExchange(&m_bShutdown, FALSE);
          if (bResult) // Shutdown has not been cancelled
            break;

          // else, shutdown has been cancelled - continue as before
        }
        else {
          // Do work
          Worker::RequestType request =
            (Worker::RequestType) dwCompletionKey;

          // Process the request.  Notice the following:
          // (1) It is the worker's responsibility to free any
          // memory associated with the request if the request is
          // complete
          // (2) If the request still requires some more processing
          // the worker should queue the request again for
          // dispatching
          theWorker.Execute(request, m_pvWorkerParam, pOverlapped);
        }
      }

      theWorker.Terminate(m_pvWorkerParam);
    }

  m_dwThreadEventId = GetCurrentThreadId();
  SetEvent(m_hThreadEvent);

  return 0;
}
```

The overall logic is fairly common in a thread pool. The thread sits waiting on the I/O Completion port for requests to come in. A special value is used to tell the thread to shut down; if it's not shut down, the request is passed off to the worker object to do the actual work.

The worker class can be anything with a `RequestType` typedef and the appropriate `Execute` method.

At this point, ATL Server has already provided a greatly improved ISAPI development experience. The hard work to maintain the performance of the server has been done; all you need to do is write a worker class and implement your logic in the `Execute` method. This still leaves you with the job of generating the HTML to send to the client. This isn't too hard in C++,[1] but it is tedious, and building HTML in code means that you have to recompile to change a spelling error. What's really needed is some way to generate the HTML based on a template. ATL Server does this via Server Response Files.

Server Response Files

ATL Server provides a text-replacement system called Server Response Files (referred to in the ATL Server code and documentation occasionally as Stencil Files). An `.srf` file is an HTML file with some replacement markers. Consider this example, which is used to display the lyrics to a classic song:

```
<html>
{{handler Beverage.dll/Default}}
<head>
   <title>The Beverage Song</title>
</head>
<body>
{{if InputValid}}
{{while MoreDrinks}}
<p />
{{DrinkNumber}} bottles of {{Beverage}} on the wall, <br />
{{DrinkNumber}} bottles of {{Beverage}}.<br />
Take one down, pass it around,<br />
{{NextDrink}} bottles of {{Beverage}} on the wall.<br />
{{endwhile}}
{{else}}
<h1>You must specify a beverage and the number of them
 in the query string.</h1>
{{endif}}
</body>
</html>
<head>
```

---

[1] ATL Server actually provides a framework of classes to assist in HTML generation. Take a look at the `CHtmlGen` class in the documentation.

As we discussed in Chapter 13, the items within {{ }} are used for one of three purposes. They can be directives to the stencil processor (the handler directive), they can work as flow control (if and while), or they can be replaced at runtime by the request handler class. Any text outside the markers is simply passed straight to the output.

The actual replacements are handled by a class referred to a *request handler*. An example request handler for the song follows:

```
class CBeverageHandler
  : public CRequestHandlerT<CBeverageHandler> {

public:
  BEGIN_REPLACEMENT_METHOD_MAP(CBeverageHandler)
    REPLACEMENT_METHOD_ENTRY("InputValid", OnInputValid)
    REPLACEMENT_METHOD_ENTRY("MoreDrinks", OnMoreDrinks)
    REPLACEMENT_METHOD_ENTRY("DrinkNumber", OnDrinkNumber)
    REPLACEMENT_METHOD_ENTRY("Beverage", OnBeverage)
    REPLACEMENT_METHOD_ENTRY("NextDrink", OnNextDrink)
  END_REPLACEMENT_METHOD_MAP()

  HTTP_CODE ValidateAndExchange() {
    m_numDrinks = 0;
    m_HttpRequest.GetQueryParams().Exchange( "numdrinks",
      &m_numDrinks );
    m_beverage =
      m_HttpRequest.GetQueryParams().Lookup("beverage");

    m_HttpResponse.SetContentType("text/html");

    return HTTP_SUCCESS;
  }

protected:
  HTTP_CODE OnInputValid( ) {
    if( m_numDrinks == 0 || m_beverage.IsEmpty() ) {
      return HTTP_S_FALSE;
    }
    return HTTP_SUCCESS;
  }

  HTTP_CODE OnMoreDrinks( ) {
    if( m_numDrinks > 0 ) {
      return HTTP_SUCCESS;
    }
```

```
      return HTTP_S_FALSE;
  }

  HTTP_CODE OnDrinkNumber( ) {
      m_HttpResponse << m_numDrinks;
      return HTTP_SUCCESS;
  }

  HTTP_CODE OnBeverage( ) {
      m_HttpResponse << m_beverage;
      return HTTP_SUCCESS;
  }

  HTTP_CODE OnNextDrink( ) {
      —m_numDrinks;
      if( m_numDrinks > 0 ) {
        m_HttpResponse << m_numDrinks;
      } else {
        m_HttpResponse << "No more";
      }
      return HTTP_SUCCESS;
  }

private:
  long m_numDrinks;
  CStringA m_beverage;
};
```

Request handlers inherit from the CRequestHandlerT base class. A request handler needs to implement the ValidateAndExchange method, which gets called at the start of processing the HTTP request. In processing a form post, this is where you would process the submitted form fields. If this function returns HTTP_FAIL, the request is aborted and IIS sends back an HTTP 500 error to the client.

If, as you would usually prefer, ValidateAndExchange returns HTTP_SUCCESS, the stencil processor starts rendering the SRF file. Each time a replacement occurs, the processor calls back into the response-handler object.

The REPLACEMENT_METHOD_MAP() macros in the response-handler class are used to specify which methods should be called for which replacement. In the previous code, this line says that when the {{Beverage}} replacement is found in the .srf file, the OnBeverage method should be called:

```
REPLACEMENT_METHOD_ENTRY("Beverage", OnBeverage)
```

Actually generating the output is fairly simple using the `m_HttpResponse` member, which is inherited from the `CRequestHandlerT` base class. This is an instance of the `CHttpResponse` class, already initialized and ready to use. Figure 14.1 shows the result of this page running.

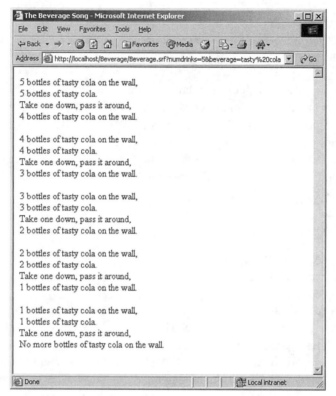

Figure 14.1   Some tasty beverages to sing about

Request-Handler Routing

How does the stencil processor know which response handler class to use? In the `.srf` file itself, you might have noticed this line:

```
{{handler Beverage.dll/Default}}
```

The `handler` directive says which DLL the handler is in (`Beverage.dll`, in this case) and what the name of the handler is (`Default`). This might seem strange because the name of our handler class isn't `Default`; it's `CBeverageHandler`. ATL Server isn't reading anybody's mind here. Instead, a global map in the response DLL provides the mapping between the name you use in the `handler` directive and the actual class. If you look in your request handler project's `.cpp` file, you'll see something like this at global scope:

```
// Beverage.cpp
...
BEGIN_HANDLER_MAP()
  HANDLER_ENTRY("Default", CBeverageHandler)
END_HANDLER_MAP()
```

This is one way to get your handler into the map: Simply add a new `HANDLER_ENTRY` macro to the map every time you add a new request-handler class. However, this global map is difficult to maintain over time. It sure would be nice to have the handler name with the class that handles it.

Much like the `COM_OBJECT_ENTRY_AUTO` macro for ATL COM classes, there's a macro that you can put in your `.h` file instead: `DECLARE_REQUEST_HANDLER`. You use it like this:

```
class CBeverageHandler : ... { ... };

DECLARE_REQUEST_HANDLER( "Default", CBeverageHandler,
  ::CBeverageHandler )
```

This macro uses similar linker tricks to the `COM_OBJECT_ENTRY_AUTO` macro to stitch together the tables at link time. The default project generated by the ATL Server project template uses `HANDLER_ENTRY`; for your own request-handler classes, I would recommend using `DECLARE_REQUEST_HANDLER` instead. Unfortunately, `DECLARE_REQUEST_HANDLER` is undocumented at this time. The parameters to the macro are, in order, the handler name, the name of the request-handler class without any namespaces, and the name of the request handler including the namespaces.

Now that you've seen the various pieces, let's look at the `.srf`-processing pipeline. The first stop for the HTTP request is IIS. IIS checks its configuration and finds that, for this virtual directory, it should route the request to our ATL Server ISAPI Extension DLL.

So IIS loads (on the first request) the extension DLL and calls the `HttpExtension-Proc` method. This immediately calls into the global instance of `CIsapiExtension`.

`CIsapiExtension` takes the request, builds a `CServerContext` object, places the request onto its internal thread pool, and releases the IIS thread back to handle another incoming request.

Meanwhile, the extension DLL's thread-pool threads are hungrily waiting for work to come in. The first one available pulls the request off the internal queue and hands it to the working class (which is, by default, `CIsapiWorker`).

The actual work is done in the `Execute()` method:

```
void CIsapiWorker::Execute(AtlServerRequest *pRequestInfo,
  void *pvParam, OVERLAPPED *pOverlapped) {
 _ATLTRY {
    (static_cast<IIsapiExtension*>(pvParam))->
      DispatchStencilCall(pRequestInfo);
  } _ATLCATCHALL() {
  ATLASSERT(FALSE);
  }
}
```

A pointer to the `CIsapiExtension` object is passed in via the `pvParam` parameter. The worker object then turns around and calls back into the `CIsapiExtension` via the `DispatchStencilCall` method. Why go back to the `CIsapiExtension` instead of doing the work within the worker class? The following chunk of the `DispatchStencilCall` method reveals the answer:

```
BOOL DispatchStencilCall(AtlServerRequest *pRequestInfo) {
  ...
    HTTP_CODE hcErr = HTTP_SUCCESS;
    if (pRequestInfo->dwRequestState == ATLSRV_STATE_BEGIN) {
      BOOL bAllowCaching = TRUE;
      if (TransmitFromCache(pRequestInfo, &bAllowCaching)) {
        return TRUE;
      }
    ...
    }
  ...
}
```

The results of processing the SRF file are stored in a cache and are regenerated only when needed. The cache is stored in the ISAPI extension object so that it is available to all the worker threads.

The `DispatchStencilCall` method takes care of the details of the various states in which a request can be. The request eventually ends up at a new instance of your request-handler object, and that's where we go next.

Request Handlers

All request handlers derive from the `CRequestHandlerT` template:

```
template < class THandler,
           class ThreadModel=CComSingleThreadModel,
           class TagReplacerType=CHtmlTagReplacer<THandler> >
```

```
class CRequestHandlerT :
    public TagReplacerType,
    public CComObjectRootEx<ThreadModel>,
    public IRequestHandlerImpl<THandler> {
public:
    // public CRequestHandlerT members
    CHttpResponse m_HttpResponse;
    CHttpRequest m_HttpRequest;
    ATLSRV_REQUESTTYPE m_dwRequestType;
    AtlServerRequest* m_pRequestInfo;

    CRequestHandlerT() ;
    ~CRequestHandlerT() ;

    void ClearResponse() ;

    // Where user initialization should take place
    HTTP_CODE ValidateAndExchange();

    // Where user Uninitialization should take place
    HTTP_CODE Uninitialize(HTTP_CODE hcError);

    // HandleRequest is called to perform default processing
    // of HTTP requests. Users can override this function in
    // their derived classes if they need to perform specific
    // initialization prior to processing this request or
    // want to change the way the request is processed.
    HTTP_CODE HandleRequest(
        AtlServerRequest *pRequestInfo,
        IServiceProvider* /*pServiceProvider*/);

    HTTP_CODE ServerTransferRequest(LPCSTR szRequest,
        bool bContinueAfterTransfer=false,
        WORD nCodePage = 0, CStencilState *pState = NULL);

    ...
}
```

The CRequestHandlerT class provides the m_HttpRequest object as a way of accessing the request data, and the m_HttpResponse object that is used to build the response to go back to the client. The previous code block shows some of the more useful methods of this class. Some, such as ServerTransferRequest, are available for you to call from your request handler. Others, such as ValidateAndExchange, exist to be overridden in your derived class.

The actual processing of the stencil file is handled via the `TagReplacerType` template parameter, which defaults to `ChtmlTagReplacer`. This class is itself a template:

```
template <class THandler, class StencilType=CHtmlStencil>
class CHtmlTagReplacer :
    public ITagReplacerImpl<THandler>
{ ... }
```

There's also a second layer of templates here. The `CHtmlTagReplacer` actually exists to manage the stencil cache. For each `.srf` file, a stencil object is created the first time. The `.srf` file is then parsed into a series of `StencilToken` objects, which are stored in an array in the stencil object. Rendering the HTML is done by walking the array and rendering each token. That stencil object is then stored in the cache for later use. This way the parsing is done only once.

By default, the type of stencil object created is `CHtmlStencil`. This class knows about all the replacement tags that can occur in `.srf` files. However, it is a template parameter and, as such, can be overridden to add new replacement tags. This is your opportunity to customize the stencil replacement system: Create a new stencil class (which should derive from `CStencil`) and override the parsing methods to add new tags to the processing.

An Example Request Handler

Let's see how this comes together. Here's an example `.srf` file that's part of a simple online forum[2] system, to provide a list of forums available:

```
<html>
{{handler SimpleForums.dll/ForumList}}
<head>
    <title>Forums</title>
</head>
<body>
<h1>ATL Server Simple Forums</h1>
<p>There are {{NumForums}} forums on this system.</p>
{{while MoreForums}}
    <h2><a href="{{LinkToForum}}">{{ForumName}}</a></h2>
    <p>{{ForumDescription}}</p>
```

---

[2] Thanks to Joel Spolsky of www.joelonsoftware.com for the original forums (written in classic ASP) that inspired this example, and for letting me steal—er, *borrow*—the idea for the book. He discusses his design decisions about the forums at www.joelonsoftware.com/articles/buildingcommunities-withso.html (http://tinysells.com/56).

```
    <p><a href="{{LinkToEditForum}}">Edit Forum Settings</a></p>
    <br />
{{NextForum}}
{{endwhile}}
</body>
</html>
```

This file uses not only the {{handler}} directive, but also textual replacements and the {{while}} loop.

So, we need a forum list handler. The handler class looks like this:[3]

```
class ForumListHandler :
  public CRequestHandlerT<ForumListHandler> {
public:
  ForumListHandler(void);
public:
  virtual ~ForumListHandler(void);

public:
BEGIN_REPLACEMENT_METHOD_MAP(ForumListHandler)
  REPLACEMENT_METHOD_ENTRY("NumForums", OnNumForums)
  REPLACEMENT_METHOD_ENTRY("MoreForums", OnMoreForums)
  REPLACEMENT_METHOD_ENTRY("NextForum", OnNextForum)
  REPLACEMENT_METHOD_ENTRY("ForumName", OnForumName)
  REPLACEMENT_METHOD_ENTRY("ForumDescription",
    OnForumDescription)
  REPLACEMENT_METHOD_ENTRY("LinkToForum", OnLinkToForum)
  REPLACEMENT_METHOD_ENTRY("LinkToEditForum",
    OnLinkToEditForum)
END_REPLACEMENT_METHOD_MAP()

  HTTP_CODE ValidateAndExchange();

private:

  HTTP_CODE OnNumForums( );
  HTTP_CODE OnMoreForums( );
  HTTP_CODE OnNextForum( );
  HTTP_CODE OnForumName( );
```

---

[3] The forum system uses ADO to access the database of forum information. Because this isn't a book about databases, I've omitted the database code from the chapter. The complete version is available with the sample downloads for this book.

```
   HTTP_CODE OnLinkToForum( );
   HTTP_CODE OnLinkToEditForum( );
   HTTP_CODE OnForumDescription( );

private:

   ForumList m_forums;
   CComPtr< _Recordset > m_forumsRecordSet;
};
```

The action starts for this class in the `ValidateAndExchange` method, which is called at the start of processing after the `m_HttpRequest` variable has been created.

```
#define AS_HR(ex) { \
   HRESULT_hr = ex; if(FAILED(_hr)) { return HTTP_FAIL; } }
HTTP_CODE ForumListHandler::ValidateAndExchange() {
    // Set the content-type
    m_HttpResponse.SetContentType("text/html");

    AS_HR( m_forums.Open( ) );
    AS_HR( m_forums.ReadAllForums( &m_forumsRecordSet ) );

    return HTTP_SUCCESS;
}
```

The return value, `HTTP_CODE`, is used to signal what HTTP return code to send back to the client. If this function returns `HTTP_SUCCESS`, the processing continues. On the other hand, if something is wrong, you can return a different value (such as `HTTP_FAIL`) to abort the processing and send an HTTP failure code back to the browser.

The `HTTP_CODE` type is actually a typedef for a `DWORD`, and it packs multiple data items into those 32 bits (much like `HRESULT` does). The high 16 bits contain the HTTP status code that should be returned. The lower 16 bits specify a code to tell IIS what to do with the rest of the request. Take a look at MSDN for the set of pre-defined `HTTP_CODE` macros.

In this example, we use the data layer object in the `m_forums` variable to go out to our forums database and read the list of forums. Assuming that this worked,[4] we store the list (an ADO recordset) as a member variable.

---

[4] The AS_HR macro used here is *not* part of ATL Server. It simply checks the returned HRESULT and, if it fails, returns HTTP_FAIL.

The replacement functions come in two varieties: textual replacement and flow control. The OnForumName method is an example of the former. When the {{ForumName}} token is found in the SRF file, this code is run:

```
HTTP_CODE ForumListHandler::OnForumName( ) {
    CComBSTR name;
    AS_HR( m_forums.GetCurrentForumName( m_forumsRecordSet,
        &name ) );
    m_HttpResponse << CW2A( name );
    return HTTP_SUCCESS;
}
```

Here, the m_HttpResponse member is used like a C++ stream class to output the name of the current forum. The CW2A conversion class is used because our data layer is returning Unicode, but the SRF file defaults to 8-bit characters.

The flow-control tokens use the same replacement map but work very differently. Within the replacement method, the return value is the important thing:

```
HTTP_CODE ForumListHandler::OnMoreForums( ) {
    VARIANT_BOOL endOfRecordSet;
    AS_HR( m_forumsRecordSet->get_adoEOF( &endOfRecordSet ) );
    if( endOfRecordSet == VARIANT_TRUE ) {
        return HTTP_S_FALSE;
    }
    return HTTP_SUCCESS;
}
```

Here, we're checking to see if we have any more records in our recordset. If so, we return HTTP_SUCCESS. If not, we return HTTP_S_FALSE. Much like S_FALSE is the "Succeeded, but false" HRESULT, HTTP_S_FALSE signals the stencil processor that the Boolean expression being evaluated is false, but the processing completed. In this case, the false return value causes the while loop to exit.

Handling Input

Let's get a little further into our example and look at how to process input. Consider this HTML form used to create or edit a forum in our system:

```
<html>
{{handler SimpleForums.dll/EditForum}}
  <head>
    <title>Edit Forum</title>
```

```html
  </head>
  <body>
    <h1>Edit Forum Information</h1>
    {{if ValidForumId}}
    <form action="editforum.srf?forumid={{ForumId}}"
     method="post">
      <table border="0" cellpadding="0">
        <tr>
          <td>
            Forum Name:
          </td>
          <td>
            <input type="text" name="forumName" id="forumName"
            maxlength="63" value="{{ForumName}}" />
          </td>
        </tr>
        <tr>
          <td>
            Forum Description:
          </td>
          <td>
            <textarea cols="50" rows="10" wrap="soft"
            id="forumDescription">
              {{ForumDescription}}
            </textarea>
          </td>
        </tr>
      </table>
      <input type="submit" />
      <a href="forumlist.srf">Return to Forum List</a>
    </form>
    {{else}}
    <p><b>You have given an invalid forum ID.
      Shame on you!</b></p>
    {{endif}}
  </body>
</html>
```

Here we're using both the standard ways to do input in HTML: The browser query string contains the forum ID that we're editing, and the post variables contain the new text and descriptions. ATL Server provides access to both of these via the m_HttpRequest object. This object is of the class CHttpRequest and provides a variety of ways to get access to server, query string, and form variables:

```
class CHttpRequest : public IHttpRequestLookup {
public:

  // Access to Query String parameters as a collection
  const CHttpRequestParams& GetQueryParams() const;

  // Access to Query String parameters via an iterator
  POSITION GetFirstQueryParam(LPCSTR *ppszName,
      LPCSTR *ppszValue);
  POSITION GetNextQueryParam(POSITION pos,
      LPCSTR *ppszName, LPCSTR *ppszValue);

  // Get the entire raw query string
  LPCSTR GetQueryString();

  // Access to form variables as a collection
  const CHttpRequestParams& GetFormVars() const;

  // Access to form variables via an iterator
  POSITION GetFirstFormVar(LPCSTR *ppszName,
      LPCSTR *ppszValue);
  POSITION GetNextFormVar(POSITION pos,
      LPCSTR *ppszName, LPCSTR *ppszValue);

  // Access to uploaded files
  POSITION GetFirstFile(LPCSTR *ppszName,
      IHttpFile **ppFile);
  POSITION GetNextFile(POSITION pos,
      LPCSTR *ppszName, IHttpFile **ppFile);

  // Get all cookies as a string
  BOOL GetCookies(LPSTR szBuf,LPDWORD pdwSize);
  BOOL GetCookies(CStringA& strBuff);

  // Get a single cookie by name
  const CCookie& Cookies(LPCSTR szName);

  // Access cookies via an iterator
  POSITION GetFirstCookie(LPCSTR *ppszName,
      const CCookie **ppCookie);
  POSITION GetNextCookie(POSITION pos,
      LPCSTR *ppszName, const CCookie **ppCookie);

  // Get the session cookie
```

```
const CCookie& GetSessionCookie();

// Get the HTTP method used for this request
LPCSTR GetMethodString();
HTTP_METHOD GetMethod();

// Access to various server variables and HTTP Headers
LPCSTR GetContentType();

BOOL GetAuthUserName(LPSTR szBuff, DWORD *pdwSize);
BOOL GetAuthUserName(CStringA &str);

BOOL GetPhysicalPath(LPSTR szBuff, DWORD *pdwSize);
BOOL GetPhysicalPath(CStringA &str);

BOOL GetAuthUserPassword(LPSTR szBuff, DWORD *pdwSize);
BOOL GetAuthUserPassword(CStringA &str);

BOOL GetUrl(LPSTR szBuff, DWORD *pdwSize);
BOOL GetUrl(CStringA &str);

BOOL GetUserHostName(LPSTR szBuff,  DWORD *pdwSize);
BOOL GetUserHostName(CStringA &str);

BOOL GetUserHostAddress(LPSTR szBuff, DWORD *pdwSize);
BOOL GetUserHostAddress(CStringA &str);

LPCSTR GetScriptPathTranslated();
LPCSTR GetPathTranslated();
LPCSTR GetPathInfo();

BOOL GetAuthenticated();

BOOL GetAuthenticationType(LPSTR szBuff, DWORD *pdwSize);
BOOL GetAuthenticationType(CStringA &str);

BOOL GetUserName(LPSTR szBuff, DWORD *pdwSize);
BOOL GetUserName(CStringA &str);

BOOL GetUserAgent(LPSTR szBuff, DWORD *pdwSize);
BOOL GetUserAgent(CStringA &str);

BOOL GetUserLanguages(LPSTR szBuff, DWORD *pdwSize);
BOOL GetUserLanguages(CStringA &str);
```

```
    BOOL GetAcceptTypes(LPSTR szBuff,DWORD *pdwSize);
    BOOL GetAcceptTypes(CStringA &str);

    BOOL GetAcceptEncodings(LPSTR szBuff, DWORD *pdwSize);
    BOOL GetAcceptEncodings(CStringA& str);

    BOOL GetUrlReferer(LPSTR szBuff, DWORD *pdwSize);
    BOOL GetUrlReferer(CStringA &str);

    BOOL GetScriptName(LPSTR szBuff, DWORD *pdwSize);
    BOOL GetScriptName(CStringA &str);

    // Raw access to server variables
    BOOL GetServerVariable(LPCSTR szVariable, CStringA &str) const;

}; // class CHttpRequest
```

For methods that return strings (that is, almost all of them), there are two overloads. The first one is the traditional "pass in a buffer and a DWORD containing the buffer length" style used so often in the Win32 API. The second overload lets you pass in a CStringA reference and stores the resulting string in the CString. The latter overload is much more convenient; the former gives you complete control over memory allocation if you need it for performance.

The query string and form variable access methods give you a variety of ways to get at the contents of these two collections of variables. For query strings, the easiest way to work if you know what query strings you're expecting is to use the GetQueryParams() method. This returns a reference to a CHttpRequestParams object. This object basically maps name/value pairs and is used to access the contents of the query strings. Usage is quite simple:

```
const CHttpRequestParams& queryParams =
    m_HttpRequest.GetQueryParams( );
CStringA cstrForumId = queryParams.Lookup( "forumid" );
```

If the query parameter you're looking for isn't present, you get back an empty string.

The CHttpRequestParams object also supports an iterator interface to walk the list of name/value pairs in the collection. Unfortunately, this is an MFC-style iterator rather than a standard C++ iterator. Here's an example that walks the list of form variables submitted in a post:

```
HTTP_CODE EditForumHandler::OnFormFields( ) {
  if( m_HttpRequest.GetMethod( ) ==
    CHttpRequest::HTTP_METHOD_POST ) {
    const CHttpRequestParams &formFields =
      m_HttpRequest.GetFormVars( );
    POSITION pos = formFields.GetStartPosition( );
    m_HttpResponse << "Form fields:<br>" << "<ul>";

    const CHttpRequestParams::CPair *pField;
    for( pField = formFields.GetNext( pos );
      pField != 0;
      pField = formFields.GetNext( pos ) ) {
      m_HttpResponse << "<li>" << pField->m_key <<
        ": " << pField->m_value << "</li>";
    }
    m_HttpResponse << "</ul>";
  }
  return HTTP_SUCCESS;
}
```

To use the iterator interface, you call the GetStartPosition( ) method on the collection to get back a POSITION object. This acts as a pointer into the collection and is initialized to one before the first element in the collection. The GetNext( ) method increments the POSITION to point to the next item in the collection and returns a pointer to the object at the new POSITION. When you get to the end, Get-Next( ) returns 0.

Because the CHttpRequestParams class stores name/value pairs, it makes sense that the GetNext() call returns a CPair object; this is a nested type defined within the map class. It has two fields: m_key and m_value, which should be self-explanatory.

It's up to you to choose which way to access your inputs. The Lookup method is much more convenient when you know in advance what form fields or query string parameters you're expecting. The iterator versions are useful if you can have a wide variety of inputs and don't know in advance what you're going to get (for example, some blog systems enable you to pass a variety of different parameters to bring up a single post, all posts in a month, or posts from a start/end date).

One thing to consider is what to do about parameters you don't expect and don't support. The easiest thing to do is simply ignore them. However, if somebody is sending you unexpected junk, it might be somebody trying to hack your system, so you might want to at least loop through the query string and form variables to check if there's anything in there you don't expect. Your response to these values is up to you: This could range from ignoring them to logging the invalid parameters or failing the request outright.

Data Exchange and Validation

So we have easy access to our query string and form variables, but that access is less than convenient. We need to check for empty strings when calling the Lookup() method to verify that the variable exists at all. We need to do data type conversions: In our example, the forum ID is an integer, but in the query string it's stored as a string. And when we've got the value, we need to do validation on it: Faulty input validation is the single biggest security flaw in web sites today.[5]

ATL Server includes some common validation and data-conversion functions to make life easier for the web developer. This is implemented via the CValidateObject< > template and the CValidateContext class.

The CValidateObject< > template is designed to be used as a base class; the CHttpRequestParams class derives from CValidateObject< >. It provides numerous overloads of two methods: Exchange and Validate:

```
template <class TLookupClass, class TValidator = CAtlValidator>
class CValidateObject {
public:
    template <class T>
    DWORD Exchange(
        LPCSTR szParam,
        T* pValue,
        CValidateContext *pContext = NULL) const;

    template<>
    DWORD Exchange(
        LPCSTR szParam,
        CString* pstrValue,
        CValidateContext *pContext) const;

    template<>
    DWORD Exchange(
        LPCSTR szParam,
        LPCSTR* ppszValue,
        CValidateContext *pContext) const;

    template<>
    DWORD Exchange(
        LPCSTR szParam,
        GUID* pValue,
        CValidateContext *pContext) const;
```

---

[5] See www.owasp.org/documentation/topten.html (http://tinysells.com/57).

```
    template<>
    DWORD Exchange(
        LPCSTR szParam,
        bool* pbValue,
        CValidateContext *pContext) const;


    template <class T, class TCompType>
    DWORD Validate(
        LPCSTR Param,
        T *pValue,
        TCompType nMinValue,
        TCompType nMaxValue,
        CValidateContext *pContext = NULL) const;

    template<>
    DWORD Validate(
        LPCSTR Param,
        LPCSTR* ppszValue,
        int nMinChars,
        int nMaxChars,
        CValidateContext *pContext) const;

    template<>
    DWORD Validate(
        LPCSTR Param,
        CString* pstrValue,
        int nMinChars,
        int nMaxChars,
        CValidateContext *pContext) const;

    template<>
    DWORD Validate(
        LPCSTR Param,
        double* pdblValue,
        double dblMinValue,
        double dblMaxValue,
        CValidateContext *pContext) const;
};
```

The Exchange( ) method takes in the name of a variable. If that variable exists in the collection you're using, it converts the string to the correct type (based on the type T you use) and stores the result in the requested pointer. The return value tells you whether the parameter was present:

```
HTTP_CODE ValidateAndExchange( ) {
  ...
  int forumId;
  m_HttpRequest.GetQueryParams().Exchange( "forumid",
    &forumId, NULL );
  ...
}
```

Thanks to the wonder of template type inference, by passing in the address of a variable of type int, the Exchange method knows that I want the string converted to type int. The Exchange( ) method properly works with these types: ULONGLONG, LONGLONG, double, int, unsigned int, long, unsigned long, short, and unsigned short. In addition, there are specializations for CString and LPCSTR, GUID, and bool.

This is a convenient way to check whether a parameter exists, copy it, and do data conversion all in one fell swoop. But that's usually not enough. You generally need to do more checking than "Is it an int?" The Validate( ) method and the various overloads give you some more checking. Specifically, when working with a numeric value, Validate lets you check that a parameter is within a particular numeric range. When validating strings, the Validate method can check for minimum and maximum string lengths (very helpful to avoid buffer overflows). For example, here's some code from the ValidateAndExchange method that checks the results of our form post:

```
HTTP_CODE ValidateAndExchange( ) {
  ...
  if( m_HttpRequest.GetMethod( ) ==
    CHttpRequest::HTTP_METHOD_POST ) {
    const CHttpRequestParams& formFields =
      m_HttpRequest.GetFormVars( );
    formFields.Validate( "forumName", &m_forumName,
      1, 50, &m_validationContext );
    formFields.Validate( "forumDescription",
      &m_forumDescription, 1, 255, &m_validationContext );
  }
  ...
}
```

Notice that I'm not actually checking the return values from the Validate method. That's one way to get the results of the Validate call, but having to do this repeatedly for every field gets tedious (and hard to maintain) quickly:

```
if( VALIDATION_SUCCEEDED( formFields.Validate(
   "forumName", &m_forumName, 1, 50, &m_validationContext ) )
{ ... }
```

Instead, we take advantage of another class: `CValidateContext`. The last parameter for the `Exchange()` and `Validate()` methods is an optional pointer to a `CValidateContext` object. This object acts as a collection—specifically, a collection of validation errors. If the `Exchange()` or `Validate()` call fails, an entry in the `CValidateContext` object is made. Using the validation context, you can do all your validation checks and not have to worry about the results until the end.

The easiest thing to do is check whether there were any validation failures, via the `ParamsOK()` method on the `CValidateContext` object. You can also walk the list of errors, like this:

```
HTTP_CODE EditForumHandler::OnValidationErrors( ) {
  if( m_validationContext.ParamsOK( ) ) {
    m_HttpResponse << "No validation errors occurred";
  }
  else {
    int numValidationFailures =
      m_validationContext.GetResultCount( );
    m_HttpResponse << "<ol>";
    for( int i = 0; i < numValidationFailures; ++i ) {
      CStringA faultName;
      DWORD faultCode;
      m_validationContext.GetResultAt( i, faultName,
        faultCode );
      m_HttpResponse << "<li>" << faultName << ": " <<
        faultCode << "</li>";
    }
    m_HttpResponse << "</ol>";
  }
  return HTTP_SUCCESS;
}
```

Here we're just printing the fault codes as integers. These are the possible fault codes:

- `VALIDATION_S_OK`. The named value was found and could be converted successfully.
- `VALIDATION_S_EMPTY`. The name was present, but the value was empty.
- `VALIDATION_E_PARAMNOTFOUND`. The named value was not found.

- VALIDATION_E_INVALIDPARAM. The name was present, but the value could not be converted to the requested data type.

- VALIDATION_E_LENGTHMIN. The name was present and could be converted to the requested data type, but the value was too small.

- VALIDATION_E_LENGTHMAX. The name was present and could be converted to the requested data type, but the value was too large.

- VALIDATION_E_FAIL. An unspecified error occurred.

It would have been nice if these were just custom HRESULT values, but, unfortunately, they're not. Luckily, there's also a VALIDATION_SUCCEEDED macro that tells you whether a particular error code is a success.

When validation for a particular variable fails, the Validate (or Exchange) method adds a name/value pair to the validation context. The name is the name of the variable that failed. The value is the fault code. These can be retrieved using the GetResultAt method, as shown earlier. You are also free to add your own error records to the validation context via the AddResult method. For example, we use the Exchange method to find out whether there's a forumid, but we still need to see if it's valid:

```
void EditForumHandler::ValidateLegalForumId( ){
  if( m_forumId != -1 ) {
    if( SUCCEEDED( m_forumList.ReadOneForum(
      m_forumId, &m_forumRecordset ) ) ) {
      bool containsData;
      if( SUCCEEDED( m_forumList.ContainsForumData(
        m_forumRecordset, &containsData ) ) ) {
        if( !containsData ) {
            m_validationContext.AddResult(
              "forumid", VALIDATION_E_FAIL );
            m_forumId = -1;
        }
      }
    }
  }
}
```

In this case, I'm using a generic VALIDATION_E_FAIL code, but there's no reason you can't make up your own DWORD error-validation codes.

If you have multiple records with the same name, only the last one in is recorded. So, if you check the same value multiple times, as we do with forumid, be aware that later validation failures could overwrite earlier records in the context.

The `CValidateContext` class gives you several options when adding records to the collection:

```
class CValidateContext {
public:
  enum { ATL_EMPTY_PARAMS_ARE_FAILURES = 0x00000001 };

  CValidateContext(DWORD dwFlags=0);
  bool AddResult(LPCSTR szName, DWORD type,
    bool bOnlyFailures = true);

  ...
};
```

When constructing the `CValidateContext` object, by default, empty parameters (ones that were in the request but have no data) are not considered an error by the `CValidateContext`. If you specify the `ATL_EMPTY_PARAMS_ARE_FAILURES` flag when constructing the context, empty parameters are treated as errors. In addition, you can pass a third, optional parameter to the `AddResult` method. If `true` (the default), the context ignores records that have the fault code `VALIDATION_S_OK` or `VALIDATION_S_EMPTY` (although the latter is ignored only if empty parameters are not errors). This optional parameter is useful when you call `AddResult` yourself; `Validate` and `Exchange` never pass `false` for this parameter.

When validation fails, you generally want to display something to the user. Nothing is built into ATL Server, but it's easy enough to display errors on your own. Here's the `.srf` file for my "edit forum" page:

```
<html>
{{handler SimpleForums.dll/EditForum}}
  <head>
    <title>Edit Forum</title>
  </head>
  <body>
    <h1>Edit Forum Information</h1>
    {{if ValidForumId}}
    <form action="editforum.srf?forumid={{ForumId}}"
      method="post">
      <table border="0" cellpadding="0">
        <tr>
          <td>
            Forum Name:
          </td>
          <td>
```

```
          <input type="text" name="forumName"
            id="forumName" maxlength="63"
            value="{{ForumName}}" />
        </td>
      </tr>
      <tr>
      <td>
        Forum Description:
      </td>
      <td>
        <textarea cols="50" rows="10"
          wrap="soft" name="forumDescription"
          id="forumDescription">
          {{ForumDescription}}
        </textarea>
      </td>
      </tr>
    </table>
    <input type="submit" />
    <a href="forumlist.srf">Return to Forum List</a>
  </form>
  {{else}}
  <p><b>You have given an invalid forum ID. Shame on you!</b>
  {{endif}}
  {{FormFields}}
  {{ValidationErrors}}
  </body>
</html>
```

The `ValidationErrors` substitution is handled by the `OnValidationErrors` method, which walks the validation context and outputs both the fields that have errors and the error code:

```
HTTP_CODE EditForumHandler::OnValidationErrors( ) {
  if( m_validationContext.ParamsOK( ) ) {
    m_HttpResponse << "No validation errors occurred";
  }
  else {
    m_HttpResponse << "Validation Errors:";
    int numValidationFailures =
      m_validationContext.GetResultCount( );
    m_HttpResponse << "<ol>";
    for( int i = 0; i < numValidationFailures; ++i ) {
      CStringA faultName;
```

```
        DWORD faultCode;
        m_validationContext.GetResultAt( i, faultName,
          faultCode );
        m_HttpResponse << "<li>" << faultName <<
          ": " << FaultCodeToString(faultCode) << "</li>";
      }
      m_HttpResponse << "</ol>";
    }
    return HTTP_SUCCESS;
}

CStringA EditForumHandler::FaultCodeToString(DWORD faultCode) {
    switch(faultCode) {
      case VALIDATION_S_OK:
        return "Validation succeeded";

      case VALIDATION_S_EMPTY:
        return "Name present but contents were empty";

      case VALIDATION_E_PARAMNOTFOUND:
        return "The named value was not found";

      case VALIDATION_E_LENGTHMIN:
        return "Value was present and converted, but too small";
      case VALIDATION_E_LENGTHMAX:
        return "Value was present and converted, but too large";

      case VALIDATION_E_INVALIDLENGTH:
        return "(Unused error code)";

      case VALIDATION_E_INVALIDPARAM:
        return "The value was present but could not be "
          "converted to the given data type";

      case VALIDATION_E_FAIL:
        return "Validation failed";

      default:
        return "Unknown validation failure code";
    }
}
```

This code simply walks through the validation context and displays the names of the failures (usually the field names) and the failure code, converted to a string. Figure 14.2 shows the results of validation failures. The fields in question weren't long enough to pass validation (because they need to be at least 1 character).

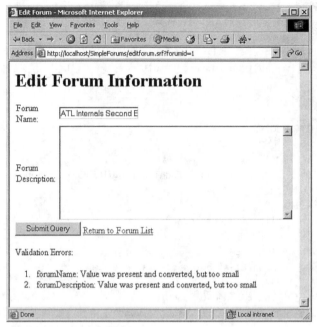

Figure 14.2   Results of validation failure

A small bug in the validation functions makes the ATL_EMPTY_PARAMS_ARE_FAIL-URES flag essential. The problem comes in when you have a post variable with an empty string. For example, Figure 14.3 shows our forum edit form; I cleared the forum name before clicking Submit.

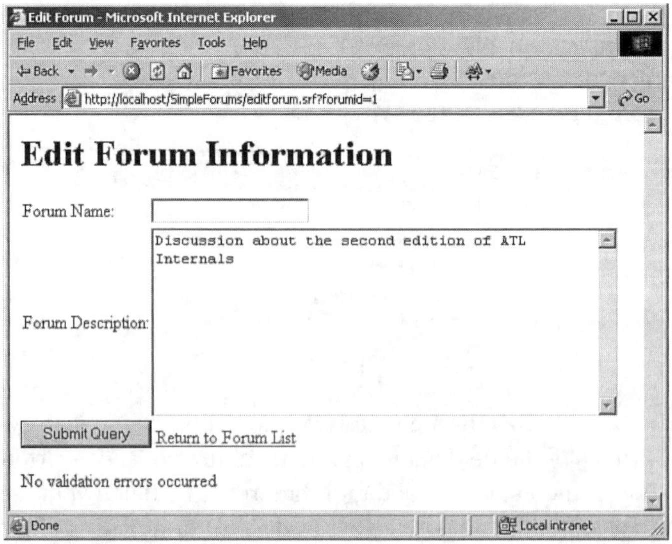

Figure 14.3   Edit Forum page with no forum name

When I click the Submit Query button, the `forumName` text field gets sent back in the HTTP post, but with no value. In the `ValidateAndExchange` method, we make use of ATL Server's validation functions to check our input:

```
HTTP_CODE EditForumHandler::ValidatePost( ) {
  ...
  if( m_HttpRequest.GetMethod( ) ==
    CHttpRequest::HTTP_METHOD_POST ) {
    const CHttpRequestParams& formFields =
      m_HttpRequest.GetFormVars( );
    formFields.Validate( "forumName", &m_forumName,
      1, 50, &m_validationContext );
  }


  return HTTP_SUCCESS;
}
```

The intention here is to require that the `forumName` variable exists and that it be from 1 to 50 characters in length. If we check the `ParamsOK` variable, it correctly returns false: The `forumName` variable is not within 1 and 50 characters in length. However, if we walk the list of errors in the validation context, there will be no record for the `forumName` field. What's going on here?

Let's take a look at the code for `CValidateObject::Validate` for strings:

```
template<>
DWORD Validate(
  LPCSTR Param,
  LPCSTR* ppszValue,
  int nMinChars,
  int nMaxChars,
  CValidateContext *pContext) const  {
  LPCSTR pszValue = NULL;
  DWORD dwRet = Exchange(Param, &pszValue, pContext);

  if (dwRet == VALIDATION_S_OK ) {
    if (ppszValue)
      *ppszValue = pszValue;
    dwRet = TValidator::Validate(pszValue, nMinChars, nMaxChars);
    if (pContext && dwRet != VALIDATION_S_OK)
      pContext->AddResult(Param, dwRet);
  }
  else if (dwRet == VALIDATION_S_EMPTY && nMinChars > 0) {
    dwRet = VALIDATION_E_LENGTHMIN;
    if (pContext) {
```

```
        pContext->SetResultAt(Param, VALIDATION_E_LENGTHMIN);
    }
  }
  return dwRet;
}
```

The two lines in bold are where the record is added to the validation context. Note that the first one calls the AddResult method. This is where we check for validation failures. Notice the second one: This code executes if the validation result is VALIDATION_S_EMPTY, and there's a minimum character length on the string. In this case, it calls the SetResultAt method on the validation context instead, using the name of the parameter.

Here's where the bug comes in. Let's look at the SetResultAt implementation:

```
class CValidateContext {
public:

  bool SetResultAt(__in LPCSTR szName, __in DWORD type) {
    _ATLTRY {
      if (!VALIDATION_SUCCEEDED(type) ||
        (type == VALIDATION_S_EMPTY &&
          (m_dwFlags & ATL_EMPTY_PARAMS_ARE_FAILURES))) {
        m_bFailures = true;
      }

      return TRUE == m_results.SetAt(szName,type);
    }
    _ATLCATCHALL() { }

    return false;
  }

  // Returns true if there are no validation failures
  // in the collection, returns false otherwise.
  __checkReturn bool ParamsOK() {
    return !m_bFailures;
  }

protected:
  CSimpleMap<CStringA, DWORD> m_results;
  bool m_bFailures;
}; // CValidateContext
```

The `SetResultAt` call sets the `m_bFailures` flag, which is used by the `ParamsOK` method, and then calls `m_results.SetAt`. And here's the source of the problem: `CSimpleMap::SetAt` sets the value only if the name you're using is *already in the map*. If the key isn't in the map, `SetAt` *silently fails*.

So what happens here is that, because an empty parameter isn't an error by default, it doesn't get added to the context in the `AddResult` call. Then, when the minimum-length validation fails, the call to `SetResultAt` tries to add using the `SetAt` call. But that fails because the parameter isn't already in the `m_results` map. As a result, the `m_bFailures` flag is set, but there's no actual record of the specific failure.

You can work around this bug in two ways. The first is to set the `ATL_EMPTY_PARAMS_ARE_FAILURES` flag when you create your validation-context object. This is best if you absolutely must have a value in the parameter in question. The other option is best used if the parameter is actually optional. In this case, be sure to set the minimum length in the `Validate` call to 0 instead of 1, as I did earlier.

Regular Expressions

Dealing with numeric values is made quite easy by the `Validate()` method, but for strings, you often need to do a lot more than just check for the maximum length. It's good security practice to enforce that your input contains only a known set of good characters, for example. Or what if you need to receive dates in a particular format? None of the `Validate` overrides helps you there.

The typical tool used in these kinds of string validation is the regular expression. UNIX programmers have been using them for years; one could argue that the popularity of the Perl programming language is mainly because of the ease of regular expression matching. Luckily, ATL Server provides a regular expression engine that we can use from the comfort of good old C++.

Unfortunately, a discussion of regular expression syntax and how to use regular expressions is beyond the scope of this book; see the documentation for details.[6]

Regular expressions are done in ATL Server via the `CAtlRegExp` class:

```
template <class CharTraits /* =CAtlRECharTraits */>
class CAtlRegExp {
public:
  CAtlRegExp();

  typedef typename CharTraits::RECHARTYPE RECHAR;

  REParseError Parse(const RECHAR *szRE,
```

---

[6] The standard text on regular expressions is *Mastering Regular Expressions* (O'Reilly Publishing, 2002), by Jeffrey E. F. Friedl.

```
     BOOL bCaseSensitive=TRUE);

  BOOL Match(const RECHAR *szIn,
    CAtlREMatchContext<CharTraits> *pContext,
    const RECHAR **ppszEnd=NULL);
};
```

The usage is fairly simple. For example, suppose we wanted to ensure that the forum name contains only alphabetical characters, spaces, and commas. The following does the trick:

```
void EditForumHandler::ValidateLegalForumName( ) {
  CAtlRegExp< CAtlRECharTraitsW > re;
  CAtlREMatchContext< CAtlRECharTraitsW > match;

  ATLVERIFY( re.Parse( L"^[a-zA-Z ,]*$" ) ==
    REPARSE_ERROR_OK );
  if( !re.Match( m_forumName.GetBuffer( ), &match ) ) {
    m_validationContext.AddResult( "forumName",
      VALIDATION_E_FAIL );
  }
}
```

First, you create the `CAtlRegExp` object. The template parameter is a *traits* class that defines various properties of the character set that the regular expression engine will be searching. ATL defines three of these traits classes: `CAtlRECharTraitsA` (for ANSI characters), `CAtlRECharTraitsMB` (for multibyte strings) and `CAtlRECharTraitsW` (for wide character strings). These traits classes are used much like the traits classes are in the `CString` class as discussed in Chapter 2, "Strings and Text."

After you've created the regex object, you need to feed in a regular expression by calling the `Parse` method. This method returns a value of type `REParseError`. `REPARSE_ERROR_OK` means that everything was fine; any other return code indicates a syntax error in the regular express. The documentation for `CAtlRegExp::Parse` gives the complete list of possible error codes.

Next, you create an object of type `CAtlREMatchContext`, which takes the same character traits template parameter as the regexp object did. Then, you call the `Match` method on the regular expression object, passing in the string to search and the match context object. `Match` returns `true` if the regular expression matched the string, and `false` if it did not. In some cases, this is all we need to know. In others, we might want to know more about what specifically matched. This information is stored in the match context object. The documentation and sample code give many examples on how to use the match context and more information about what you can do with regular expressions.

Session Management

The scalability of the Web comes directly from its stateless nature. As far as the web server is concerned, every HTTP request is independent. The stateless architecture means that server farms and load balancing are easy, caching can be added at many different places, and it's easy to add hardware to an existing system.

It also makes writing a shopping cart a real pain in the neck.

Nearly every web application needs to deal with state management. State can be on a per-session basis, a per-application basis, or a per-page basis. When thinking about state management, some standard questions need to be answered:

- What's the scope? From where is the state data available, and what's its lifetime?
- Where's the data stored? In memory? In a database? In a disk file? In a hidden form field?
- How do we find the state when processing a particular request?

One of the more difficult state-management pieces to build by hand is session state: per-user data that persists across HTTP request. Luckily for us, ATL Server, like all other serious web frameworks, provides a session-state service so we don't have to roll our own.

Using Session State

Before diving into the internals, let's take a quick look at how to use session state. In our ongoing forum example, I want to add a hit counter to each forum's page, so I can see how often I've gone to the page. It looks something like Figure 14.4.

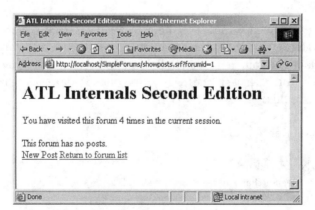

Figure 14.4   Forum page with a hit counter

The `.srf` file for this page is pretty simple:

```
<html>
{{handler SimpleForums.dll/ShowPosts}}
<head>
<title>{{ForumName}}</title>
</head>
<body>
<h1>{{ForumName}}</h1>
<p>You have visited this forum {{HitCount}} times in the
current session.</p>
<div>
<!- ... Post List content removed for clarity ->
</div>
<a href="newpost.srf?forumid={{ForumId}}">New Post</a>
<a href="forumlist.srf">Return to forum list</a>
{{endif}}
</body>
</html>
```

The trick is, how do we implement the `HitCount` replacement? We want the hit counter to stick around between page views; as the user moves from forum to forum on the site, we want each page's hit count to be independent and persistence.

Unlike classic ASP and ASP.NET, ATL Server does not automatically create a session for you. In the C++ tradition of "don't pay for what you don't use," you must explicitly create a session object when you need it.

Getting the Session Service

The first thing you need to do is get hold of an `ISessionStateService` interface pointer. This interface provides the capability to create and retrieve sessions. The object is available in your request handler via the `m_spServiceProvider` member that is inherited from `CRequestHandlerT< >`. In your `ValidateAndExchange` function, do something like this:

```
ShowPostsHandler.h:

class ShowPostsHandler :
    public CRequestHandlerT< ShowPostsHandler > {
...
private:
...
```

```
    CComPtr< ISessionStateService > m_spSessionStateSvc;
    CComPtr< ISession > m_spSession;
};
```

ShowPostsHandler.cpp:

```
HTTP_CODE ShowPostsHandler::ValidateAndExchange( ) {
  if( FAILED( m_spServiceProvicer->QueryService(
    __uuidof(ISessionStateService), &m_spSessionStateSvc ) ) ) {
    return HTTP_FAIL;
  }

  // Do rest of validation
  ...

  // Retrieve session data
  if( FAILED( RetrieveOrCreateSession( ) ) ) {
    return HTTP_FAIL;
  }

  if( FAILED( UpdateHitCount( ) ) ) {
    return HTTP_FAIL;
  }

  m_HttpResponse.SetContentType( "text/html" );
  return HTTP_SUCCESS;
}
```

The line in bold is the magic call that gets us the `ISessionStateService` interface pointer we need.

An Aside: The IServiceProvider Interface

The `IServiceProvider` interface is actually a standard interface that was introduced back in the IE4 days. It hasn't gotten a whole lot of attention, but implementing it can give you a surprisingly powerful system. The definition is actually quite simple:

```
interface IServiceProvider : IUnknown {
    HRESULT QueryService(
        [in] REFGUID guidService,
        [in] REFIID riid,
        [out, iid_is(riid)] IUnknown ** ppvObject);
};
```

The parameters of QueryService are essentially identical to those of QueryInterface, and QueryService acts a lot like QueryInterface: You ask for a particular IID, and you get back an interface pointer. There's a major difference, though: QueryInterface is required to return an interface pointer on the same object and obey all the rules of COM identity. QueryService, on the other hand, can (and usually does) return an interface pointer on a *different* COM object.

This explains the guidService parameter to the QueryService call: It's specifying which particular object we want to get the interface pointer to. This GUID doesn't need to be a CLSID, or an IID, or a CATID, or anything else. It's simply a predefined GUID that the developer chooses to represent that particular service.

The IServiceProvider interface is how ATL Server provides, well, services to the request handlers. When you create your project via the ATL Server Project Wizard and you choose session support, these lines get added to your ISAPI extension class:

```
// session state support
typedef CSessionStateService<WorkerThreadClass,
  CMemSessionServiceImpl> sessionSvcType;
CComObjectGlobal<sessionSvcType> m_SessionStateSvc;

public:

BOOL GetExtensionVersion(HSE_VERSION_INFO* pVer) {
  // ...
  if (S_OK != m_SessionStateSvc.Initialize(&m_WorkerThread,
    static_cast<IServiceProvider*>(this))) {
    TerminateExtension(0);
    return SetCriticalIsapiError(
      IDS_ATLSRV_CRITICAL_SESSIONSTATEFAILED);
  }
  return TRUE;
}

BOOL TerminateExtension(DWORD dwFlags) {
  m_SessionStateSvc.Shutdown();
  BOOL bRet = baseISAPI::TerminateExtension(dwFlags);
  return bRet;
}

HRESULT STDMETHODCALLTYPE QueryService(
  REFGUID guidService, REFIID riid, void** ppvObject) {
  if (InlineIsEqualGUID(guidService,
    __uuidof(ISessionStateService)))
    return m_SessionStateSvc.QueryInterface(riid, ppvObject);
  return baseISAPI::QueryService(guidService, riid,
    ppvObject);
}
```

The ISAPI extension creates a session-state service object as a "global" object; you might remember CComObjectGlobal from Chapter 4, "Objects in ATL." This object lives as long as the ISAPI extension object does and basically ignores AddRef and Release counts. The QueryService implementation checks to see if the guid-Service parameter is equal to the ISessionStateService method; if so, it simply calls QueryInterface on the member session state service object.

ATL Server uses this technique to provide several kinds of services to the request headers. If you have your own services that you want to provide across the application, this is a good way to do it.

Creating and Retrieving Sessions

So, we now have an ISessionService pointer. The next step is to use that pointer to look up our session, and to create one if it doesn't exist.

The first question is, how do we know which session to grab? ATL Server has built-in support for the standard approach (a session cookie) and the flexibility to let you do your own session identification, if you need to.

Here's how you retrieve a session using a session cookie:

```
HRESULT ShowPostsHandler::RetrieveOrCreateSession( ) {
  HRESULT hr;
  CStringA sessionId;
  m_HttpRequest.GetSessionCookie( ).GetValue( sessionId );
  if( sessionId.GetLength( ) == 0 ) {
    // No session yet, create one
    const size_t nCharacters = 64;
    CHAR szID[nCharacters + 1];
    szID[0] = 0;
    DWORD dwCharacters = nCharacters;
    hr = m_spSessionStateSvc->CreateNewSession(szID,
      &dwCharacters, &m_spSession) );
    if( FAILED( hr ) ) return hr;

    CSessionCookie theSessionCookie( szID );
    m_HttpResponse.AppendCookie( &theSessionCookie );
  }
  else {
    // Retrieve existing session
    hr = m_spSessionStateSvc->GetSession(sessionId,
      &m_spSession ) );
    if( FAILED( hr ) ) return hr;
  }
  return S_OK;
}
```

First, we grab the value of the cookie. This gives us our session ID. If there isn't a value, we create the session via the `ISessionService::CreateNewSession` method. This both creates the session and returns the ID for the session created. We then create a new session cookie and add it to the response. This step is important, and you can easily forget it if you're used to other web frameworks that create sessions for you automatically.

If there is a cookie value, we use the `ISessionService::GetSession` method to get an `ISession` interface pointer and connect back up to the session.

Storing and Retrieving Session Data

When we have our `ISession` pointer, we can store and retrieve values. `ISession` maps names (as ANSI strings) to `VARIANT`s. Usage is pretty much what you'd expect:

```
HRESULT ShowPostsHandler::UpdateHitCount() {
  CStringA sessionVarName = "mySessionVariable";
  CComVariant hits;
  if( FAILED(
    m_spSession->GetVariable( sessionVarName, &hits ) ) ) {
    // If no such session variable, GetVariable return E_FAIL.
    // Gotta love nice specific HRESULTS
    hits = CComVariant( 0, VT_I4 );
  }
  m_hits = ++hits.lVal;
  return m_spSession->SetVariable( sessionVarName, hits ) );
}
```

The `ISession` interface provides the `GetVariable` and `SetVariable` methods to get and save a single variable. There are also methods to enumerate the session variables and control session timeouts.

Session State Implementations

One question about session management hasn't been answered yet: Where is session data stored? The answer, as usual for ATL, depends on which template arguments you use.

Let's look back at that type declaration in the ISAPI extension:

```
typedef CSessionStateService<WorkerThreadClass,
  CMemSessionServiceImpl> sessionSvcType;
```

The `CSessionStateService` template takes two parameters: The first is the worker thread class for the ISAPI extension. The second is the class that implements the `ISessionService` interface. In this case, we use `CMemSessionServiceImpl`, which provides in-memory session storage. In-memory session-state storage has the advantage of being very fast, but because it is only in memory on the server, it doesn't work in a server farm.

ATL Server provides the `CDBSessionServiceImpl` as an alternative. This stores session state in a database instead. The access to a session is slower, but it can be shared across multiple machines in a farm. Choose the appropriate service implementation based on your requirements.

Data Caching

A smart caching strategy is often the difference between a site that comes up quickly and one that leave the users staring at the little spinning globe for the traditional 25 seconds before they go to anther site. ATL Server offers data-caching services to help you get below that magic time threshold.

Caching Raw Memory

The most basic caching service is the BLOB cache. No, this isn't a gelatinous alien that will try to digest your hometown. This cache handles raw chunks of memory. Getting hold of the cache is done just as when using the session service—that is, you use the `IServiceProvider` interface:

```
HTTP_CODE ShowPostsHandler::ValidateAndExchange( ) {
  ...
  HRESULT hr = m_spServiceProvider->QueryService(
    __uuidof(IMemoryCache), &m_spMemoryCache );
  if( FAILED( hr ) ) return HTTP_FAIL;
  ...
}
```

When you have an `IMemoryCache` interface pointer, you can stuff items into and pull them out of the cache. The cache items are stored as name/value pairs, just like session-state items. Instead of storing `VARIANT`s, however, the BLOB cache stores `void` pointers.

Retrieving an item requires two steps. First, you must get a *cache item handle*:

```
HRESULT ShowPostsHandler::GetWordOfDay(CStringA &result) {
  HRESULT hr;
  HCACHEITEM hItem;
```

```
    hr = m_spMemoryCache->LookupEntry( "WordOfDay", &hItem );
    if( SUCCEEDED( hr ) ) {
      // Found it, pull out the entry
      ...
    }
    else if( hr == E_FAIL ) {
      // Not in cache
      ...
    }
  }
```

The `LookupEntry` method returns `S_OK` if it found the item, and `E_FAIL` if it didn't.[7]

When we have the item handle, we can retrieve the data from the cache. This is done via the `GetData` method, which returns the `void*` that was stored in the cache, along with a `DWORD` giving you the length of the item:

```
HRESULT ShowPostsHandler::GetWordOfDay(CStringA &result) {
  ...
  // Found it, pull out the entry
  void *pData;
  DWORD dataLength;

  hr = m_spMemoryCache->GetData( hItem, &pData, &dataLength );
  if( SUCCEEDED( hr ) ) {
    result = CStringA( static_cast< char * >( pData ),
      dataLength );
  }
  m_spMemoryCache->ReleaseEntry( hItem );
  ...
}
```

The pointer that is returned from the `GetData` call actually points to the data that's stored inside the cache's data structure; it's not a copy. Because we don't want the cache to delete the item out from under us, we copy it into our result variable.

The final call to `ReleaseEntry` is essential for proper cache management. The BLOB cache actually does reference counting on the items stored in the cache. Every time you call `LookupEntry`, the refcount for the entry you found gets

---

[7] The ATL Server group made a mistake with this return code. A failed `HRESULT` is an exception: It means that something went wrong. A failed cache lookup is not an exception. This method should have returned `S_FALSE` instead on a cache miss.

incremented. `ReleaseEntry` decrements the refcount. Entries with a refcount greater than zero are guaranteed to remain in the cache. Because the whole point of using the cache is to pitch infrequently used data, properly releasing entries when you are finished with them is just as important as properly managing COM reference counts. Unfortunately, there's no `CCacheItemPtr` smart pointer template to help.[8]

If you get that `E_FAIL` error code, you typically want to load the cache with the necessary data for next time. Doing so is fairly easy; you just call the `Add` method:

```
HRESULT ShowPostsHandler::GetWordOfDay(CStringA &result) {
    ...

    // Not in cache
    char *wordOfTheDay = new char[ 6 ];
    memcpy( wordOfTheDay, "apple", 6 );
    FILETIME ft = { 0 };
    hr = m_spMemoryCache->Add( "WordOfDay", wordOfTheDay,
        6 * sizeof( char ), &ft, 0, 0, 0 );
    ...
}
```

This code allocates the memory for the item, specifies an expiration time (via the `FILETIME` value, where `0` means that it doesn't expire), and places it into the cache. The block of memory is now safely stored until the cache gets flushed or scavenged; at that point, we have a memory leak.

Why the memory leak? The cache is storing only `void` pointers; it knows nothing about how the memory it has been handed should be freed. It doesn't run destructors, either. To prevent memory leaks, there is a hook to provide a deallocator, and it's done on a per-entry basis. The last parameter in the call to the `Add` method is an optional pointer to an implementation of the `IMemoryCacheClient` interface, which has a single method:

```
interface IMemoryCacheClient : IUnknown {
    HRESULT Free([ in ] const void *pvData);
};
```

When an item is about to be removed from the cache, if you provided an `IMemoryCacheClient` implementation in the `Add` call, the cache calls the `Free` method to clean up. In this example, you'd just need to add a call to delete on the `void` pointer.

---

[8] Check out the `BlobCache` sample in MSDN. It includes some helper classes to manage the cache.

Unfortunately, there's no standard implementation of this interface for use in the BLOB cache.

Caching Files

The BLOB cache is useful for storing small chunks of arbitrary data, but sometimes you need to store *large* chunks. The file-caching service lets you create temporary files on disk; when the cache item expires, it automatically deletes the disk file.

The file cache operates much like the BLOB cache. You use `IServiceProvider` to get an `IFileCache` interface pointer. The file cache uses handles, just like the BLOB cache. The only major difference is that the file cache stores filenames instead of chunks of memory.

Summary

ATL Server is a set of classes to build ISAPI applications in C++. A typical ATL Server project is made up of three major components. The first is an ISAPI extension DLL that implements the required ISAPI methods. In addition, the ISAPI extension provides a thread pool and request-dispatching service to keep the web server responsive.

The second component is the `.srf` or stencil file. This is a file that contains replacements marked in {{ }} pairs. The `.srf` file is processed by a request-handler class, usually in a separate DLL. The third component, the request handler, actually processes the HTTP request and implements the replacements used in the `.srf` files.

ATL Server also provides utility functions to make web development easier. Input validation is supported for numeric ranges and string length, and a regular expression engine is included for sophisticated string analysis. Caching services are also provided to help improve performance in heavily loaded systems.

C++ Templates by Example

This chapter is meant to be a brief introduction to the basics of C++ templates using examples. It also shows some of the advanced template features that ATL uses, but without any ATL code cluttering up things. For a more thorough introduction to templates, see Stan Lippman's *C++ Primer* (Addison-Wesley, 2005).

The Need for Templates

Imagine a simple bounds-checked array class:

```
#define MAX_ELEMS 8

class Array {
public:
  long& operator[](size_t n) {
    if( n < 0 || n >= MAX_ELEMS ) throw "out of bounds!";
    return m_rg[n];
  }

protected:
  long  m_rg[MAX_ELEMS];
};
```

This class makes quiet, hard-to-find errors loud and easy to find:

```
void main(int argc, char* argv[]) {
  long rg[8]; // Built in array type
  rg[8] = 1;  // will corrupt the stack, but quietly

  Array array;  // Bounds-checked array type
  array[8] = 1; // will complain loudly
}
```

The bounds-checking part of the `Array` class really has nothing to do with the data being managed; using a little bit of C++ trickery, this is even easier to spot:

```
typedef long T;
class Array {
public:
  T& operator[](size_t n) {
    if( n < 0 || n >= MAX_ELEMS ) throw "out of bounds!";
    return m_rg[n];
  }

protected:
  T m_rg[MAX_ELEMS];
};
```

Notice that we've replaced the use of `long` with a generic type `T`. Unfortunately, this trick doesn't allow us to reuse the `Array` class with different types of `T`. When the compiler sees the `Array` class, it won't let us change `T` and compile it again with another type `T`. To get any reuse out of the `Array` class as it is, we have to do some cut-and-paste work and create different `Array` classes, one for each type we're interested in managing:

```
class ArrayOfChar {
public:
  char& operator[](size_t n);

protected:
  char m_rg[MAX_ELEMS];
};

class ArrayOfLong {
public:
  long& operator[](size_t n);

protected:
  long m_rg[MAX_ELEMS];
};
```

Besides the tedium involved with this technique, the developer of the `Array` family of classes would have to build an `Array` class for every type that the user of the class would want to manage. Because some of these types can be defined *after* the `Array` class is built, this is an especially difficult task. We'd like the compiler to step in and help us. And so it will, with templates.

Template Basics

Using template syntax, we can create an `Array` class that is parameterized on any number of parameters, including the type of data to manage and how large the internal buffer should be:

```
template <typename¹ T, size_t MAX_ELEMS>
class Array {
public:
  T& operator[](size_t n) {
    if( n < 0 || n >= MAX_ELEMS ) throw "out of bounds!";
    return m_rg[n];
  }

protected:
  T m_rg[MAX_ELEMS];
};
```

Notice that the only difference in this code is the use of the `template` statement before the class declaration. When the compiler sees a template, it knows to store the class declaration in its internal data structures, but not to generate any code. The compiler can't generate the code until it sees how the client would like to use it:

```
struct Point { long x; long y; };

void main(int argc, char* argv[]) {
  Array<long, 8>   a1; // Array of 8 longs
  Array<char, 256> a2; // Array of 256 chars
  Array<Point, 16> a3; // Array of 16 Points
  ...
}
```

The compiler uses the client's template parameters to generate the code for the class on demand, effectively creating a new member of the `Array` family of classes with each use.[2] Because the compiler is using the template parameters to generate the code, only parameters whose values are known at compile time are allowed.

---

[1] The ANSI C++ Standard allows the use of the keyword `class` instead of the keyword `typename`, but the use of `class` is deprecated.

[2] The linker makes sure that only one expansion per set of template parameters actually makes in into the final image.

However, that includes built-in types, user-defined types, constants, and even function pointers. To make the template even more convenient for the client to use, you're allowed to declare default values for template parameters, just as you would for functions:

```
template <typename T, size_t MAX_ELEMS = 8>
class Array {...};

void main(int argc, char* argv[]) {
  Array<long>      a1; // Array of 8 longs
  Array<char, 256> a2; // Array of 256 chars
  ...
}
```

Template Specialization

You might decide that for a specific combination of template parameters, the generic template expansion isn't good enough. For example, if you decide that an Array of 256 characters should have an equality operator, you might decide to override the Array general template using the template specialization syntax:

```
template <> // No template arguments here
class Array<char, 256> { // Template argument values here
public:
  // You are not required to provide the same functionality
  // as the general template (although it's a good idea)
  char& operator[](size_t n) {
    if( n < 0 || n >= 256 ) throw "out of bounds!";
    return m_sz[n];
  }

  // You may add functionality not in the general template
  bool operator==(const Array<char, 256>& rhs) {
    return strcmp(m_sz, rhs.m_sz);
  }

protected:
  char m_sz[256];
};
```

The client doesn't have to do anything new to use the specialized version of the template. When the compiler sees Array<char, 256>, the client automatically gets the specialized version.

Templates as Base Classes

Template specialization allows the addition of new functionality and optimized implementations based on specific template parameters. For example, the specialization I just showed specializes on all the parameters, both the type and the size of the array. It would probably be more useful to be able to specialize on the type of data held, but to expose additional functions for character strings of any size. This can be accomplished by using the Array as a base class:

```
template <size_t MAX_LEN>
class String : public Array<char, MAX_LEN+1> {
public:
  // Additional functionality
  bool operator==(const String<MAX_LEN>& rhs) {
    return strcmp(m_rg, rhs.m_rg);
  }
};
```

Notice that the String is still parameterized on length and that it passes arguments to the base Array class. The type is fixed because we're building a string, but the number of elements to store is based on the String template argument. In effect, this achieves a partial specialization, although the client code must use the String template instead of the Array template to make use of it.

A Different Kind of Polymorphism

Templates give us a different kind of reuse mechanism than inheritance. Inheritance means that we'd like to reuse the implementation and signature of a base class and extend it in a derived class. Inheritance is type-centric. The derived class is *type compatible* with the base class. Type compatibility means that an instance of the derived class can be used where an instance of the base class is required.

On the other hand, templates enable you to reuse the behavior of a class, but to divorce it from the types involved. If the type can fit where it's being used, the compiler doesn't care about the type. For example, all that was required of the type being passed to the Array template was that it had a default constructor so that it could be created in arrays. If the type couldn't live up to that requirement, the compiler would complain.

Because of the way the compiler generates code using template arguments, templates give us a different kind of polymorphism. Instead of polymorphism based on type compatibility, we've got polymorphism based on *signature compatibility*.[3] If the type has the appropriate function signatures available, the compiler

---

[3] This is often called *structural typing* these days.

is perfectly happy. This kind of polymorphism has some interesting properties, of which ATL makes heavy use.

Using Behavior Classes

Imagine modifying the `Array` class so that it does bounds checking only if you so desire:

```
template <typename T, size_t MAX_ELEMS = 8,
   bool bCheckBounds = true>
class Array {
public:
  T& operator[](size_t n) {
    if( bCheckBounds && (n < 0 || n >= MAX_ELEMS) )
      throw "out of bounds!";
    return m_rg[n];
  }

protected:
  T m_rg[MAX_ELEMS];
};
```

This allows a client to turn bounds checking on or off, based on its own requirements:

```
void main(int argc, char* argv[]) {
#ifdef _DEBUG
  bool bCheckBounds = true;
#else
  bool bCheckBounds = false;
#endif

  Array<long, 256, bCheckBounds>  array;
  array[256] = 1;
}
```

The intent here is that we skip the bounds checks in release mode because we have hopefully caught the out-of-bounds errors during development. However, we're still doing a check against bCheckBounds every time through the operator[] member function. We could hope for a good compiler that would optimize away the line because bCheckBounds is known at compile time, or we could remove all doubt and make use of a *behavior class*.

Behavior Classes Can Group Functions

A behavior class (also known as a trait class or a trait) is a class that contains some static member functions or some type definitions. Behavior classes are never meant to be created. Instead, by putting the functions and type definitions into a class, we've grouped them and can refer to them as a unit.

To solve our bounds-checking problem, imagine two behavior classes, one that checks the bounds and one that does not:

```
struct DebugBoundsChecker {
  static void CheckBounds(size_t n, size_t nMax) {
    if( n < 0 || n >= nMax ) throw "out of bounds!";
  }
};

struct ReleaseBoundsChecker {
  static void CheckBounds(size_t n, size_t nMax) {}
};
```

Notice that both the behavior classes have the same function with the same signature. The debug version does the bounds checking, and the release version doesn't do anything. And because both implementations are inline functions, the compiler can optimize easily. Given only the knowledge of the signature of the bounds-checking function, I can rewrite the Array class to use the CheckBounds function scoped by a type name passed as a template parameter:

```
template <typename T, size_t MAX_ELEMS = 8,
          typename BoundsChecker = DebugBoundsChecker>
class Array {
public:
  T& operator[](size_t n) {
    BoundsChecker::CheckBounds(n, MAX_ELEMS);
    return m_rg[n];
  }

protected:
  T m_rg[MAX_ELEMS];
};
```

The client can now take advantage of the bounds checking—or not, as decided at compile time:

```
void main(int argc, char* argv[]) {
#ifdef _DEBUG
```

```
    typedef DebugBoundsChecker BoundsChecker;
#else
    typedef ReleaseBoundsChecker BoundsChecker;
#endif

    Array<long, 256, BoundsChecker>  array;
    array[256] = 1;
}
```

In this case, I've used signature compatibility to make my decisions at compile time, resulting in potentially more efficient code. And if I want to add another kind of bounds-checking behavior class in the future, I can, if it has a CheckBounds function that lives up to the signature requirements of the caller.

Simulating Dynamic Binding

One of the benefits of inheritance is dynamic binding. A virtual function in the base class can be overridden in the derived class to extend or replace base class functionality. One especially powerful expression of this idea is the *pure virtual member function*. A pure virtual member function is a virtual member function that *must* be overridden in the deriving class. In fact, any class with a pure virtual member function is thought of as an *abstract base class (ABC)*, and no instance of that class can be created. To use the functionality of an ABC, it must be used as a base class, and the deriving class must implement all the pure virtual member functions. This is useful because it allows the base class to define functionality required by the deriving class:

```
template <typename T>
class Array {
public:
  ...
  virtual int Compare(const Array<T>& rhs) =0;

  bool operator< (const Array<T>& rhs)
  { return this->Compare(rhs) < 0; }

  bool operator> (const Array<T>& rhs)
  { return this->Compare(rhs) > 0; }

  bool operator== (const Array<T>& rhs)
  { return this->Compare(rhs) == 0; }

  T m_rg[1024];
};
```

By defining the Compare function as pure virtual, the Array class designer has decreed that Array can be used only as a base class and that the deriving class must provide some way of comparing two arrays of the same type so that the comparison operators can be implemented. For example, a String class must implement the Compare function:

```
class String : public Array<char> {
public:
  // the compiler requires this method:
  int Compare(const Array<char>& rhs)
  { return strcmp(m_rg, rhs.m_rg); }
};
```

The compiler uses the implementation of the pure virtual member function provided in the derived class to fill in the virtual function table entry for that member function (as it does with all virtual member function pointers). Using function pointers to invoke member functions is how C++ provides dynamic binding—that is, binding to the specific implementation at runtime based on the type of the variable.

However, we're paying the price of dynamic binding for our String class. The price of dynamic binding is a virtual function table, shared among all instances, an extra 4-bye virtual function pointer per object, and at least two extra pointer indirections to invoke the appropriate implementation. This seems a high price to pay, given perfect knowledge at compile time. We know how to compare two String objects. Why not make the compiler do the work and save us the overhead of dynamic binding? We can do that by using *simulated dynamic binding*.

Simulated dynamic binding enables us to provide the name of the deriving class to the base class. The base class casts itself to the deriving class to call the required function. Revising the Array to use simulated dynamic binding looks like this:

```
template <typename T, typename Deriving>
class Array {
public:
  ...
  bool operator< (const Array<T, Deriving>& rhs)
  { return static_cast<Deriving*>(this)->Compare(rhs) < 0; }

  bool operator> (const Array<T, Deriving>& rhs)
  { return static_cast<Deriving*>(this)->Compare(rhs) > 0; }

  bool operator== (const Array<T, Deriving>& rhs)
  { return static_cast<Deriving*>(this)->Compare(rhs) == 0; }
```

```
    T m_rg[1024];
};
```

Notice that the `Array` template takes an additional parameter: the name of the deriving class. It uses that class name to perform a static cast on itself. Because the compiler expands the code of the base class while instantiating the deriving class, the static cast performs a perfectly safe downcast (normally a contradiction in terms). The compiler uses the member functions of the deriving cast to resolve the address of the required function at compile time, saving us the cost of dynamic binding. The deriving class must implement the appropriate member function and pass its own name as a parameter to the base class template:

```
class String : public Array<char, String> {
public:
    // the compiler requires this method:
    int Compare(const Array<char, String>& rhs)
    { return strcmp(m_rg, rhs.m_rg); }
};
```

This technique gives us the look and feel of dynamic binding without using virtual member functions. The base class can require functionality of the deriving class. The base class cannot be instantiated by itself. The major difference is that because no virtual functions are required, we don't have the overhead of dynamic binding.

The Discovery of Simulated Dynamic Binding

It's my understanding that the ATL team members discovered simulated dynamic binding accidentally. When they did, they went immediately to the compiler team members, who claimed that the C++ Standard does not mandate or prohibit such behavior, but they promised to keep it working for ATL. Does that mean you should use simulated dynamic binding when you're writing your most portable code? Probably not. Should you still understand it because ATL is rife with it? Absolutely. Should you sneak it into your own bag of tricks? It's in mine.

Function Templates

Classes are not the only thing that can be parameterized; functions can be, too. The canonical example is the `min` function:

```
inline long min(long a, long b) { return (a < b ? a : b); }
inline float min(float a, float b) { return (a < b ? a : b); }
```

Because the code is the same for both overloaded `min` implementations, there's no reason not to make it into a template:

```
template <typename T>
inline T min(T a, T b) { return (a < b ? a : b); }
```

When the template is instantiated, the compiler generates the code on demand based on the use:

```
void main() {
  // produces: long min(long, long)
  long a = 1, b = 2, c = min(a, b);

  // produces: float min(float, float)
  float x = 1.1, y = 2.2, z = min(x, y);

  // produces: char *min(char *, char *)
  char *r = "hello", *s = "world", *t = min(r, s);
}
```

Notice that the compiler can figure out how to insatiate the `min` template implementation without any fancy angle brackets. However, also notice that sometimes, just as with class templates, function templates don't expand the way we'd like. For example, the `min` that takes two `char*` compares two pointer values, not the contents of the strings. A function template can be specialized by merely providing an implementation that takes the types involved:

```
inline char* min(const char* a, const char* b) {
  return (strcmp(a, b) < 0 ? a : b);
}
```

In this case, because a version of the function that takes two character pointers already exists, the compiler binds to that one instead of generating another implementation based on the `min` function template.

Member Function Templates

The fun of templates does not stop at global functions. Oh, no. You can create member function templates as well. As of Visual C++ 6.0, the definition of `IUnknown` has been augmented with a member function template for `QueryInterface`:

```
struct IUnknown {
...
  template <class Q>
  HRESULT STDMETHODCALLTYPE QueryInterface(Q** pp)
  { return QueryInterface(__uuidof(Q), (void**)pp); }
}
```

Before the member function template, all calls to `QueryInterface` had to be sure to match up the interface type and the interface identifier:

```
void Fly(IUnknown* punk) {
  IBird* pbird = 0;
  punk->QueryInterface(IID_ICat, (void**)&pbird); // Oops!
  punk->QueryInterface(IID_IBird, (void**)pbird); // Double oops!
  punk->QueryInterface(IID_IBird, (void**)&pbird); // OK
  pbird->Fly();
}
```

On the other hand, with the `QueryInterface` member function template, the type of the interface suffices:

```
void Fly(IUnknown* punk) {
  IBird* pbird = 0;
  punk->QueryInterface(&pbird); // __uuidof uses to determine IID
  pbird->Fly();
}
```

In effect, member function templates add new member functions of a class, just as function templates add new global functions based on use.

Summary

Templates provide two services. The first is code reuse, but in a different way than inheritance. Inheritance requires a certain type relationship. Templates require only that the compiler be capable of finding the functionality required of the specified type. Inheritance makes type requirements, whereas templates take what types we give them.

The other service that templates provide is efficiency. By mixing in types at compile time, we can use static binding to make decisions at runtime instead of at compile time. This is the key to the promise of smaller, faster code that templates make.

B | **ATL Header Files**

Assuming the default installation directory for Visual C++, ATL 8 source code is installed in the `C:\Program Files\Microsoft Visual Studio 8\VC\atlmfc\include` directory. At the time of this writing, this folder includes 297 files, so it's not practical to list all of them here. However, Table B.1 lists the ATL-specific header files in that folder, for your enjoyment.

Table B.1. ATL Header Files

`atlacc.h`	Accessibility support
`atlalloc.h`	Resource allocation helpers
`atlassem.h`	Libraries assembly version information
`atlbase.h`	ATL base services (threading helpers, interface debugging, and so on)
`atlbuild.h`	ATL and MFC build numbers
`atlcache.h`	ATL Server caching support
`atlchecked.h`	Secure (checked) CRT functions
`atlcoll.h`	Collection classes
`atlcom.h`	Core COM server support (such as `IPersist StreamInitImpl`)
`atlcomcli.h`	Core COM client support (such as `CComPtr`)
`ATLComMem.h`	OLE task memory-allocation support
`ATLComTime.h`	`COleDateTime`
`atlconv.h`	String conversion classes and macros
`atlcore.h`	Shared core types
`atlcrypt.h`	Cryptography wrappers
`atlctl.h`	COM control support
`atlcur.h`	`CComCurrency`
`atldb.h`	OLEDB provider support
`atldbcli.h`	Consumer code for OLEDB

`atldbgmem.h`	Tracked memory allocation
`atldbsch.h`	OLEDB Schema Rowset consumer support
`atldebugapi.h`	Tracing support
`atldef.h`	Common macro definitions (such as `ATLASSERT`)
`atlenc.h`	Data encoding/decoding algorithms (such as Base64 encoding)
`atlevent.h`	Support code for attributed event handling
`atlexcept.h`	Exception management
`atlextmgmt.h`	Thread pool management, stencil cache management, and DLL cache management
`atlfile.h`	File, temporary file, and memory-mapped file wrappers
`atlhost.h`	COM Control hosting support
`atlhtml.h`	HTML support
`atlhttp.h`	HTTP support
`atliface.h`	ATL-specific custom interface declarations, generated from `atliface.idl`
`atlimage.h`	HDC wrappers
`atlisapi.h`	Core ISAPI support
`atlmem.h`	Heap memory management
`atlmime.h`	MIME support
`atlpath.h`	File path support
`atlperf.h`	Performance Monitor support
`atlplus.h`	Registry script (RCS) support
`atlrc.h`	ATL resource IDs
`atlrx.h`	Regular expression parser
`atlsafe.h`	`CComSafeArray`
`atlsecurity.h`	Security wrappers
`atlserr.h`	HTTP status code definitions
`atlsession.h`	HTTP session support
`atlsharedsvc.h`	Shared cache support
`atlsiface.h`	Custom ATL Server interface declarations
`atlsimpcoll.h`	Simple collections
`atlsimpstr.h`	Support code for `CString`

`atlsmtpconnection.h`	SMTP connection management
`atlsmtputil.h`	SMTP utilities
`atlsnap.h`	MMC snap-in support
`atlsoap.h`	SOAP support
`atlsocket.h`	Network socket wrapper
`atlspriv.h`	Miscellaneous (very miscellaneous) internal support functions
`atlsrvres.h`	ATL Server resource IDs
`atlstdthunk.h`	Multi-CPU thunks
`atlstencil.h`	Stencil parser
`atlstr.h`	`CString` typedefs and character trait classes
`atlsync.h`	Critical section and mutex wrappers
`atltime.h`	Time and date format wrappers
`atltrace.h`	Tracing support
`atltypes.h`	Drawing wrapper classes (such as `CPoint`)
`atlutil.h`	Miscellaneous utility code
`atlwin.h`	Windowing wrappers

APPENDIX

C | Moving to ATL 8

This appendix covers the significant changes that ATL developers deal with when moving projects from ATL 3 to ATL 8. We talk specifically about externally visible changes—potential porting issues, bug fixes, and new features—rather than about internal changes (the rest of the book is for that). The changes from ATL 7 to ATL 8 are extremely minor (a couple of bug fixes and removal of some insecure string calls) and don't require any discussion; moving from ATL 7 to ATL 8 just works.

Strings, Character Sets, and Conversions

Several important changes have been made in the way that ATL handles strings. Everything you know from ATL 3 still works, but you should consider upgrading your code to use the new features.

Character-Conversions Macros

ATL 3 provided a set of macros that make it easier to convert among various character sets: ANSI, Multibyte, Wide, and the mutable TCHAR type. To use the macros, you first had to include the USES_CONVERSION macro in the code above the first use:

```
void PrintMessage( LPCTSTR lpszMessage ) {
  USES_CONVERSION;
  std::cout << "Your message is " << T2A(lpszMessage) << endl;
}
```

The conversion macros are convenient, but the implementation had a couple of problems. The storage for the conversion buffer was allocated on the program stack (via the _alloca function), which made cleanup automatic. Unfortunately, if you called the conversion macros in a loop, none of the memory was cleaned up until the function containing that loop returned. As a result, you could overrun your stack if you weren't careful. The use of _alloca also changed the stack layout enough that if you used a conversion macro inside a C++ catch { } block, your program would probably crash. Finally, if you forgot the USES_CONVERSION macro, you got some strange error messages.

To address these problems, ATL 7 introduced a new set of conversion *classes*. Each one has the same name as the old conversion macro, with a *C* on the front. The previous example becomes this with the class:

```
void PrintMessage( LPCTSTR lpszMessage ) {
  std::cout << "Your message is " << CT2A(lpszMessage) << endl;
}
```

The conversion classes do not require the USES_CONVERSION macro and are actually C++ classes instead of macro trickery. Each object has a small internal buffer that is used to store the converted string if the string is short; for longer conversions, a heap allocation is done. The conversion class's destructor makes sure to clean up any allocation.

Using the conversion classes instead of the macros avoids doing weird things to the stack, and as a result, you get more stable code and fewer weird corner cases (such as the crash in catch blocks). See Chapter 2, "Strings and Text," for more information on the new conversion classes.

Security Enhanced C Standard Library

This one isn't really an ATL change, but it's a new feature of Visual C++ 8. It's also something that all C and C++ developers should pay attention to, especially web developers, because this feature is now well supported in ATL via ATL Server. The Internet is a hostile place and is only getting more so as time goes on. One of the most common security holes in unmanaged code is the buffer overrun; data is copied into a fixed size array that's too small, and the data runs over the end of the array and puts carefully crafted bytes on the stack that do whatever the attacker wants them to do.

If you use the standard C library, particularly the string functions (the old standbys such as strcpy and strcat), it turns out to be remarkably difficult to avoid buffer overflows. These factors contribute to buffer overflows:

- **No buffer sizes.** strcpy provides no way to indicate how large the buffer is that you're copying into.

- **Inconsistent string termination.** strncpy does let you specify how long the destination buffer is, but if your buffer is too long, it doesn't actually put the \0 byte at the end to terminate the string. In general, the C string functions are either underspecified about string termination or just unpredictable.

- **Inadequate parameter checking.** Most of these functions handle NULL pointers unpredictably.

- **Interface inconsistency.** Some functions put the destination in the first parameter; others put it in the second. It's easy to mix up source and destination buffers because they're both variables of type char *.

As part of the recent security push at Microsoft, a new set of secure string functions was written and included in the C runtime library.[1] They're named with an "_s" suffix, so they are functions such as strcat_s, and strcpy_s.[2]

Why does this concern ATL developers? There are two reasons. The first, less interesting one is that the majority of changes from ATL 7 to ATL 8 were replacements of string function calls with these new secure string functions. The second, and more important, one is that when you compile your old code with ATL 8, you now get compiler warnings for calls to the old insecure functions saying that they're deprecated and what function to replace them with. For example, this code

```
void BuildUrl( char *dest, size_t dest_len, char *page ) {
  strncpy( dest, "http://localhost/Sample", dest_len );
  strncat( dest, page, dest_len );
  strncat( dest, "/default.srf", dest_len );
}
```

now results in these compile-time warnings:

```
c:\atlinternals2e\src\appendixc\unsafestringhandling\unsafestringhandling.c
pp
  (72) : warning C4996: 'strncpy' was declared deprecated
c:\program files\microsoft visual studio 8\vc\include\string.h(156) :
  see declaration of 'strncpy'
Message: 'This function or variable may be unsafe. Consider using
  strncpy_s instead. To disable deprecation, use _CRT_SECURE_NO_DEPRECATE.
  See online help for details.'
c:\atlinternals2e\src\appendixc\unsafestringhandling\unsafestringhandling.c
pp
  (73) : warning C4996: 'strncat' was declared deprecated
c:\program files\microsoft visual studio 8\vc\include\string.h(143) :
  see declaration of 'strncat'
Message: 'This function or variable may be unsafe. Consider using
  strncat_s instead. To disable deprecation, use _CRT_SECURE_NO_DEPRECATE.
```

---

[1] These functions have also been submitted to the C and C++ standardization committees, so expect to see them in other compilers as the language standards get revised.

[2] For details about the motivations and design of these functions, take a look at http://msdn.microsoft.com/library/default.asp?url=/library/en-us/dncode/html/secure03102004.asp.

```
See online help for details.'
c:\atlinternals2e\src\appendixc\unsafestringhandling\unsafestringhandling.c
pp
  (74) : warning C4996: 'strncat' was declared deprecated
c:\program files\microsoft visual studio 8\vc\include\string.h(143) :
  see declaration of 'strncat'
Message: 'This function or variable may be unsafe. Consider using
  strncat_s instead. To disable deprecation, use _CRT_SECURE_NO_DEPRECATE.
  See online help for details.'
```

You can turn off the deprecation warnings (using the _CRT_SECURE_NO_DEPRE-CATE preprocessor flag, as shown in the warning message), but it's generally a better idea to fix the code. For example, the previous code using the secure string functions looks like this:

```
void SafeBuildUrl( char * dest, size_t dest_len, char *page ) {
    // _TRUNCATE is a special value that tells the function to
    // copy as much of source as will fit in dest and still have a
    // \0 terminator.
    strncpy_s( dest, dest_len, "http://localhost/Sample",
      _TRUNCATE );
    strncat_s( dest, dest_len, page, _TRUNCATE );
    strncat_s( dest, dest_len, "/default.srf", _TRUNCATE );
}
```

The strncat_s function also has the nice feature of automatically figuring out how much room is left in the destination buffer, and it avoids many off-by-one (or off-by-many, in the case of the broken code shown previously) errors.

Chapter 2 discusses use of these functions more.

Shared Classes with MFC

The Supports MFC check box on the ATL Project Wizard was always a temptation to the ATL 3 developer. We generally didn't want the doc/view architecture, or windowing classes, or print preview framework, but we were sometimes willing to pay the price for them for the useful little utility classes, CString being first among them.

Thankfully, Microsoft has heard the ATL developer's pain. As of ATL 7, the classes in Table C.1 are all available for use in both MFC *and* ATL projects, without having to drag the rest of MFC along with them.

Table C.1   Shared MFC and ATL Classes

CFileTime	CFileTimeSpan	CImage	COleDateTime
COleDateTimeSpan	CPoint	CRect	CSize
CTime	CTimeSpan	CString	

Several new classes also are used in implementation or customization of CString. The CString class itself is now a template, CStringT, that can be parameterized by character type.

Implementing COM Servers

CComModule

Every ATL 3 project required a global instance of the CComModule class (or class derived from CComModule), and that global variable had to be named _Module. CComModule was responsible for maintaining global information about the COM server: what class factories were active, managing module handles to get resources, the lock count, the threading model, and so on. ATL 3 depended on the Project Wizard to generate specialized versions of the CComModule class through inheritance to handle an EXE versus a DLL versus a Windows Service.

In ATL 7, the CComModule was broken up, and several derived classes were introduced that reduced the amount of code that needed to be generated. Every ATL project still has a global module object; that object is now accessible through the _pAtlModule global variable (and, yes, the leading p indicates that this is now a pointer).

ATL 3 included a single CComModule class, and the ATL Project Wizard created a derived class in your project that handled being an EXE or DLL COM server. This was problematic because Microsoft can't fix or update the generated code when it ships new versions of ATL. Thus, several different module classes were introduced that pulled the COM server details into the library and out of the generated code (where it should have been in the first place).

These are the new module classes:

- CAtlModule. Base class for the COM server type-specific modules below
- CAtlExeModuleT. Module class for EXE COM servers
- CAtlDllModuleT. Module class for DLL COM servers
- CAtlServiceModuleT. Module class for Windows Service COM servers

The updated module classes take a burden off the Project Wizard. A typical starting file for an ATL 3 exe server looks like this:

```
// ATL3Project.cpp : Implementation of WinMain
#include "stdafx.h"
#include "resource.h"
#include <initguid.h>
#include "ATL3Project.h"
#include "ATL3Project_i.c"

const DWORD dwTimeOut = 5000; const DWORD dwPause = 1000;

// Passed to CreateThread to monitor the shutdown event
static DWORD WINAPI MonitorProc(void* pv) {
  CExeModule* p = (CExeModule*)pv;
  p->MonitorShutdown();
  return 0;
}

LONG CExeModule::Unlock() {
  LONG l = CComModule::Unlock();
  if (l == 0) {
    bActivity = true;
    SetEvent(hEventShutdown);  }
  return l;
}

// Monitors the shutdown event
void CExeModule::MonitorShutdown() {
  while (1) {
    WaitForSingleObject(hEventShutdown, INFINITE);
    DWORD dwWait=0;
    do {
      bActivity = false;
      dwWait = WaitForSingleObject(hEventShutdown, dwTimeOut);
    } while (dwWait == WAIT_OBJECT_0);
    // timed out
    if (!bActivity && m_nLockCnt == 0) { #if _WIN32_WINNT >= 0x0400 &
defined(_ATL_FREE_THREADED)
      CoSuspendClassObjects();
      if (!bActivity && m_nLockCnt == 0)
#endif
        break;
    }
  }
  CloseHandle(hEventShutdown);
```

```
    PostThreadMessage(dwThreadID, WM_QUIT, 0, 0);
}

bool CExeModule::StartMonitor() {
  hEventShutdown = CreateEvent(NULL, false, false, NULL);
  if (hEventShutdown == NULL) return false;
  DWORD dwThreadID;
  HANDLE h = CreateThread(NULL, 0, MonitorProc, this, 0,
    &dwThreadID);
  return (h != NULL);
}

CExeModule _Module;

BEGIN_OBJECT_MAP(ObjectMap)
END_OBJECT_MAP()

LPCTSTR FindOneOf(LPCTSTR p1, LPCTSTR p2) {
  while (p1 != NULL && *p1 != NULL) {
    LPCTSTR p = p2;
    while (p != NULL && *p != NULL) {
      if (*p1 == *p) return CharNext(p1);
      p = CharNext(p);
    }
    p1 = CharNext(p1);
  }
  return NULL;
}

extern "C" int WINAPI _tWinMain(HINSTANCE hInstance,
  HINSTANCE /*hPrevInstance*/,
  LPTSTR lpCmdLine, int /*nShowCmd*/) {
  lpCmdLine = GetCommandLine();

#if _WIN32_WINNT >= 0x0400 & defined(_ATL_FREE_THREADED)
  HRESULT hRes = CoInitializeEx(NULL, COINIT_MULTITHREADED);
#else
  HRESULT hRes = CoInitialize(NULL);
#endif
  _ASSERTE(SUCCEEDED(hRes));
  _Module.Init(ObjectMap, hInstance, &LIBID_ATL3PROJECTLib);
  _Module.dwThreadID = GetCurrentThreadId();
  TCHAR szTokens[] = _T("-/");
  int nRet = 0;
  BOOL bRun = TRUE;
```

```
    LPCTSTR lpszToken = FindOneOf(lpCmdLine, szTokens);
    while (lpszToken != NULL) {
      if (lstrcmpi(lpszToken, _T("UnregServer"))==0) {
        _Module.UpdateRegistryFromResource(IDR_ATL3Project, FALSE);
        nRet = _Module.UnregisterServer(TRUE);
        bRun = FALSE;
        break;
      }
      if (lstrcmpi(lpszToken, _T("RegServer"))==0) {
        _Module.UpdateRegistryFromResource(IDR_ATL3Project, TRUE);
        nRet = _Module.RegisterServer(TRUE);
        bRun = FALSE;
        break;
      }
      lpszToken = FindOneOf(lpszToken, szTokens);
    }

    if (bRun) {
      _Module.StartMonitor();
#if _WIN32_WINNT >= 0x0400 & defined(_ATL_FREE_THREADED)
      hRes = _Module.RegisterClassObjects(CLSCTX_LOCAL_SERVER,
        REGCLS_MULTIPLEUSE | REGCLS_SUSPENDED);
      _ASSERTE(SUCCEEDED(hRes));
      hRes = CoResumeClassObjects();
#else
      hRes = _Module.RegisterClassObjects(CLSCTX_LOCAL_SERVER,
        REGCLS_MULTIPLEUSE);
#endif
      _ASSERTE(SUCCEEDED(hRes));

      MSG msg;
      while (GetMessage(&msg, 0, 0, 0)) DispatchMessage(&msg);
      _Module.RevokeClassObjects();
      Sleep(dwPause); //wait for any threads to finish
    }

    _Module.Term();
    CoUninitialize();
    return nRet;
  }
```

All this code was output from the Project Wizard. It includes the logic for managing shutdown of multiple threads, the server object count, command-line parsing, and the main Windows message loop. Although it's nice to have the code out there to modify if you need it, it's really too much for code generation; most of this should have been part of the library.

The picture is much better in ATL 8, where an EXE server starts out as follows:

```
// ATL8Project.cpp : Implementation of WinMain
#include "stdafx.h"
#include "resource.h"
#include "ATL8Project.h"

class CATL8ProjectModule :
  public CAtlExeModuleT< CATL8ProjectModule > {
public :
  DECLARE_LIBID(LIBID_ATL8ProjectLib)
  DECLARE_REGISTRY_APPID_RESOURCEID(IDR_ATL8PROJECT,
    "{06CE2511-F6E0-4F80-9BC9-852A433E7B25}")
};

CATL8ProjectModule _AtlModule;

extern "C" int WINAPI _tWinMain(
  HINSTANCE /*hInstance*/, HINSTANCE /*hPrevInstance*/,
  LPTSTR /*lpCmdLine*/, int nShowCmd) {
  return _AtlModule.WinMain(nShowCmd);
}
```

As you can see, the ATL 8 module class does a lot more heavy lifting here; all the generated code does is declare a module class derived from CAtlExeModuleT, add the DECLARE_LIBID and DECLARE_REGISTRY_APPID_RESOURCEID macros to hook up some metadata, and declare a one-line _tWinMain function that calls into the module class. This makes the code we have to edit significantly shorter. The flexibility you need is still there, however, because CAtlExeModuleT has several functions that you can override to intercept various parts of the startup and shutdown process. This way, it's obvious what you're changing, and your changes aren't buried in 171 lines of generated code. Also, if you're using the ATL 8 module classes, if you need to move between an out-of-process server and an in-proc server, it's much easier to do.

Having said that, there's not much to be gained in removing your ATL 3 modules and replacing them with the ATL 8 modules when you migrate your project. With all the generated code, there's a good possibility that you've modified at least some of it, and it's hard to tell exactly what's changed. If you need (on moral or ethical grounds, let's say) to rewrite the module-related code in your ATL 3 server to match an ATL 8 server, your best bet is to run the new VS05 wizard with the names and settings you need and then move over your ATL 3 classes.

ATL 8 also includes several other module classes that deal with other common functionality, such as loading resources or managing window thunks. You typically don't need to touch them in your code; they're used as part of the internals of ATL 8.

You will never need to create instances of these module classes because they're defined as global variables and compiled into your project if they're needed.

These additional module classes include the following:

- **CAtlBaseModule**. Contains information that most applications need. The most important is the HINSTANCE of the module and the resource instance. Accessible as the global variable _AtlBaseModule.

- **CAtlComModule**. Contains information needed for all the COM classes in ATL. Accessible via the global variable _AtlComModule.

- **CAtlWinModule**. Contains information needed to manage window thunks created when you use CWindowImpl. Accessible via the global variable _AtlWinModule.

Take a look at the documentation for "ATL Module Classes" for more details on what each of these does—and, of course, read Chapters 4, "Objects in ATL," and 5, "COM Servers," of this book.

The OBJECT_MAP

ATL 3 projects required a global OBJECT_MAP in each COM server project. This map provided a central list of all the COM classes in the project and was used to drive both self-registration and the class factories.

The OBJECT_MAP worked, but it was yet another piece of metadata in an ATL 3 project. When you added a new COM object to your project, you had to remember to update the OBJECT_MAP. Forgetting meant lots of head-scratching trying to figure out why you were getting "class not registered" errors.

The centralized OBJECT_MAP also had a compile-time impact. To add the classes to the object map, you needed to include every header for every COM object to your project's main file. With the complexity of the average ATL header file, this could result in a significant compile-time slowdown.

ATL 8 rectifies all these problems with some clever linker tricks (described in Chapter 5). Instead of a central OBJECT_MAP, each class's header file has an OBJECT_ENTRY_AUTO macro in it. This macro is set up so that the linker automatically builds the OBJECT_MAP data structure.

Projects can have a combination of the old OBJECT_MAP and the OBJECT_ENTRY_AUTO macros. As you upgrade your code to ATL 8, it's a good idea to add the OBJECT_ENTRY_AUTO macros because it will make maintenance easier. After you add the last one, you can get rid of the OBJECT_MAP entirely.

ActiveX Controls and Control Hosting

ATL is still the best way to implement ActiveX controls, and you don't need to change anything to get your ATL 3 ActiveX controls to compile under ATL 8. In addition, the ActiveX control-hosting support has been improved significantly in ATL 8.

Readers of the previous edition of this book might remember that the chapters on ActiveX controls and control hosting spent several pages describing bugs in ATL 3, and the code downloads included functions and classes to work around these errors. I'm very happy to report that somebody at Microsoft apparently read a copy of *ATL Internals*—most of those bugs have been fixed.

Stock properties now provide a callback function that you can override to detect when the stock property is changed. This means that you no longer have to completely replace the put_XXXX stock property methods that the CStockPropImpl base class provides.

The AtlIPersistPropertyBag_Load method has been fixed, so you no longer need the updated function included with the first edition downloads.

The ActiveX hosting classes have been significantly cleaned up. The first edition of this book included a class named CAxWindow2 that fixed several memory leaks in the control hosting. These leaks have now been fixed. ATL 8 also includes a class named CAxWindow2; luckily, it's a drop-in replacement for the ATL Internals class of the same name, so all you need to do is remove the patched version from your project. ATL 8 ActiveX Hosting also now supports the creation of licensed ActiveX controls. The new CAxWindow2 class provides the support for creating licensed controls, but it works just fine for nonlicensed controls as well.

Take a look at Chapters 11, "ActiveX Controls," and 12, "Control Containment," in this edition for the full scoop on ActiveX controls.

ATL_MIN_CRT Changes

The infamous ATL_MIN_CRT preprocessor switch has been the source of controversy for many years. In ATL 7, Microsoft made some improvements to the ATL startup code that made ATL_MIN_CRT compile a little more useful. The most important change is that ATL_MIN_CRT builds now support correct construction and destruction of static and global C++ objects at module startup and shutdown.

Here's another important thing to note when starting an ATL project: In ATL 3, debug projects had ATL_MIN_CRT turned off, and release projects had it turned on. In ATL 8, both debug and release projects default to having ATL_MIN_CRT turned off. This is a useful change in my opinion—just about every ATL 3 project got the dreaded "cannot find _main" error the first time it did a Release mode build.

Summary

The ATL team has done a remarkable job in maintaining backward-compatibility, while improving the design and capabilities of ATL in Version 8. Most ATL 3 code simply compiles and works right out of the box. The projects that don't compile can be corrected very quickly, and ATL 8 offers significant new features to make building COM objects in C++ easier than ever.

D | **Attributed ATL**

ATL has always been the most powerful way to build COM objects in C++. Unfortunately, with that power comes complexity. ATL requires an advanced understanding of C++ to use it effectively. That advanced understanding took more effort than many people were willing to invest. Instead, many of those users used Visual Basic to do COM instead of C++. Unfortunately, there are some COM things VB 6 just doesn't do (including marshal-by-value, ActiveX controls with sophisticated drawing, and multithreading); when people hit those limits, they were forced back into the C++ world.

Even for those who are experienced C++ developers, building ATL projects can be a headache. Some of the most important information about your project isn't even in C++; it's in IDL and RGS files and resources. It can be a real effort to keep all these different parts in sync.

When Visual Studio .NET was released in 2002, the ATL team took an unusual approach in attempting to address these issues: They extended the C++ language. That extension is called *attributed ATL*.

Fundamentals of ATL Attributes

Introducing Attributes

C++ classes require a lot of help to become full-fledged COM objects. A coclass must be specified to expose the CLSID to clients so that instances of the class can be created. Interfaces must be defined in IDL and associated with a COM coclass. Registry entries must be created to specify the location of the server, the threading model of the class, and the ProgId, as well as other information. Of course, none of these is an inherent feature of standard C++ projects, so Visual Studio enlists the help of additional tools such as the MIDL compiler and RGS registration scripts. Consequently, much information that is logically part of the class definition is spread out across multiple different files. For instance, the CLSID for a component is specified in the coclass statement in the IDL file and also appears multiple times in the RGS script file used for component registration. Interfaces exposed from a COM coclass are listed in the IDL file as part of the coclass statement; they appear in the inheritance list in the C++ class definition and must be included in a special macro map used to implement `QueryInterface`. Having information about the class distributed in multiple places is inconvenient from a maintenance point of view and can even lead to obscure runtime errors if everything is not kept consistent.

ATL attributes are designed to consolidate the information that COM requires with the actual C++ class used to implement the COM component. After all, many of the various aspects of COM behavior are logically part of the C++ class definition, so it makes perfect sense to specify these aspects alongside the C++ class. Attributes can be applied to C++ classes, to files as a whole, or to special interface definitions that appear in the class header file. They appear in square brackets preceding the item to which they are applied (or anywhere in the file for attributes that apply to the entire file). The following code snippet shows how attributes appear in a class header file:

```
// CalcPi.h
...
[   coclass,
    threading("apartment"),
    uuid("86759049-8B8E-47F4-81F1-AE07D3F876C7"),
]
class ATL_NO_VTABLE CCalcPi :
    public ICalcPi
{ ... }
```

Applying the `[coclass]` attribute is all that is required to make the `CCalcPi` C++ class available as a COM coclass. The `[threading]` attribute indicates that the class supports the Apartment threading model and should be registered in the Windows Registry as such. The `[uuid]` attribute enables you to specify the CLSID to associate with the COM coclass, although the compiler generates one for you if it isn't provided. In previous versions of ATL, the information represented by these attributes was spread among IDL files, header files, and RGS script files. ATL attributes provide for a more concise specification of the exact same information.

Yet, the previous code certainly isn't suitable for consumption by any C++ compiler. How does this syntactic shorthand achieve the same result as many lines of IDL code and registration script? The answer is a fairly sophisticated code generator that works behind the scenes. When the C++ compiler sees an attribute in a source file, it passes the attribute and any parameters associated with it (such as the "apartment" parameter to the earlier `[threading]` attribute) to a special COM component called an *attribute provider*. The provider injects code into the compiler's internal parse tree to accomplish what the attribute and its parameters specified.

Code injected by the attribute provider affects your ATL projects in various ways. Some attributes produce IDL code to be consumed by the MIDL compiler, other attributes insert ATL base classes in your class definition, and still others insert macro maps in class header files. For example, the [threading] attribute applied to the CCalcPi class previously inserts the ATL base class CComObjectRoot-Ex<CComSingleThreadModel> to provide the level of thread safety that is appropriate for the "apartment" threading model value supplied to the attribute. It is important to note, however, that this code is *not* injected into the original source files. If this were the case, it would revive the same sort of maintenance hassles that ATL attributes were designed to alleviate in the first place. Instead, the code that the attribute provider injects is available only at compile time. Debug builds do include information about the injected code, enabling you to step into generated code while debugging.

Building an Attributed ATL COM Server

Creating the Project

As an example, I rebuilt the PiSvr project from Chapter 1, "Hello, ATL," as an attributed ATL project. To create the project, you simply run the ATL Project Wizard as normal. The only difference is to check the Attributed check box on the Application Settings page of the wizard. In Visual Studio 2005, this check box is not checked by default.

In a nonattributed project, a DLL server has a starter file with the definition of the ATL module class and the appropriate exports. With an attributed project, you instead get this:

```
// PiSvr.cpp : Implementation of DLL Exports.

#include "stdafx.h"
#include "resource.h"

// The module attribute causes DllMain,
// DllRegisterServer and DllUnregisterServer
// to be automatically implemented for you
[ module(dll,
  uuid = "{5247B726-8CB9-450C-9636-9C5781B69729}",
  name = "PiSvr",
  helpstring = "PiSvr 1.0 Type Library",
  resource_name = "IDR_PISVR") ]
class CPiSvrModule {
public:
// Override CAtlDllModuleT members
};
```

The attributed project is most notable for what it does not contain. There's no declaration of an ATL module class. There's no IDL file. Even the RGS file is extremely minimal:

```
HKCR
{
    NoRemove AppID
    {
        '%APPID%' = s 'ATL8Project'
        'ATL8Project.EXE'
        {
            val AppID = s '%APPID%'
        }
    }
}
```

In the attributed ATL project, the information that is scattered around the project is generated by the `module` attribute on the `CPiSvrModule` class. Did you notice the comment that says "Override `CAtlDllModuleT` members"? That's rather odd, considering that `CPiSvrModule` doesn't inherit from `CAtlDllModuleT`. Or does it? One of the things the module attribute does is add the `CAtlDllModuleT` class to `CPiSvr-Module`'s inheritance list. This is a common theme with ATL attributes. Instead of the gargantuan list of base classes that most unattributed ATL classes end up with, a single attribute can introduce one or more base classes.

Adding a Simple Object

My next step, of course, was to add an ATL Simple Object to the project, just like any other. There's no difference in running the Simple Object Wizard, with the exception that, in an attributed project, the Attributed check box on the Names page of the wizard is checked and disabled.

Running the wizard with an attributed project gives a significantly different output. First, we have two interface definitions in the `CalcPi.h` header file:

```
// CalcPi.h
...
 // ICalcPi
[ object,
  uuid("8E3ABD67-5075-4C38-BA00-8289E336E7F9"),
  dual,
  helpstring("ICalcPi Interface"),
  pointer_default(unique) ]
  __interface ICalcPi : IDispatch {
};
```

```
// _ICalcPiEvents
[ dispinterface,
  uuid("9822AB1A-8031-4914-BD73-3459A91B98A9"),
  helpstring("_ICalcPiEvents Interface") ]
__interface _ICalcPiEvents {
};
```

...

This looks a lot like IDL, but it's not; the __interface keyword is another compiler extension that lets you define IDL interfaces directly in your C++ code. The attributes on the interface provide the rest of the information (IID, helpstring, and so on) that ends up in the generated IDL file.

Next up is the class definition for our COM object:

```
// CalcPi.h
...
// CCalcPi

[ coclass,
  default(ICalcPi, _ICalcPiEvents),
  threading(apartment),
  support_error_info("ICalcPi"),
  event_source(com),
  vi_progid("PiSvr.CalcPi"),
  progid("PiSvr.CalcPi.1"),
  version(1.0),
  uuid("A892A09D-98C9-4AD4-98C5-769F7743F204"),
  helpstring("CalcPi Class") ]
class ATL_NO_VTABLE CCalcPi :
  public ICalcPi {
public:
  CCalcPi() { }

  __event __interface _ICalcPiEvents;

  DECLARE_PROTECT_FINAL_CONSTRUCT()

  HRESULT FinalConstruct() { return S_OK; }
  void FinalRelease() { }

};
```

Notice the shortness of the base class list. The only thing explicitly mentioned is the interface. Even though `ICalcPi` is a dual interface, there's no `IDispatchImpl` in sight.

I also cooked up a simple console application as a test client. This client works just like any other COM client application:

```
#include <iostream>

#import "../PiSvr/Debug/PiSvr.dll" no_namespace

using namespace std;

class CoInit {
public:
  CoInit( ) { CoInitialize( 0 ); }
  ~CoInit( ) { CoUninitialize( ); }
};

void _tmain(int argc, _TCHAR* argv[]) {
  CoInit coInit;

  ICalcPiPtr spPiCalc( __uuidof( CCalcPi ) );

  spPiCalc->Digits = 20;
  _bstr_t bstrPi = spPiCalc->CalcPi();

  wcout << L"Pi to " << spPiCalc->Digits << " digits is " <<
    bstrPi << endl;
}
```

The output of this application, shown in Figure D.1, indicates that the COM object is properly registered and working.

Figure D.1   Calling an attributed COM object

Visual Studio 2005 supplies a large number of attributes, and they're all fairly well documented in MSDN.[1] Instead of paraphrasing the documentation, let's take a look at how attributes work.

To do their magic, ATL attributes generate a *ton* of code within the compiler. It sure would be nice to see what code they actually are building. Unfortunately, that's where the trouble starts.

Expanding Attributed Code

The C++ compiler has a compiler switch (/Fx) that causes the compiler to output merge files that contain the original source code merged with the injected code. This is a useful mechanism for exploring and understanding exactly what the attribute providers are doing under the covers in response to attributes that we apply to our ATL code. IDL code that the attribute providers generate is output to a _<projectname>.idl. Merge files for objects appear as _<classname>.mrg.h and _<classname>.mrg.cpp. Merged code for the server as a whole is generated in _<projectname>.mrg.cpp. The /Fx switch is activated from the Expand Attributed Source property, located in the project property pages, shown in Figure D.2.

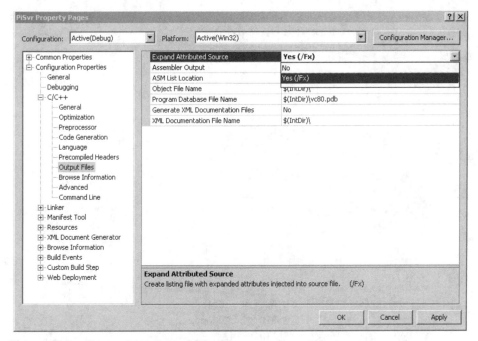

Figure D.2   Expand Attributed Source

---

[1] A good place to start is at http://msdn2.microsoft.com/en-us/library/f520z3b3(VS.80).aspx (http://tiny-sells.com/58).

Flipping this switch and compiling the project results in this code in the
_PiSvr.mrg.h file:

```
// CCalcPi

[ coclass,
  default(ICalcPi, _ICalcPiEvents),
  threading(apartment),
  support_error_info("ICalcPi"),
  event_source(com),
  vi_progid("PiSvr.CalcPi"),
  progid("PiSvr.CalcPi.1"),
  version(1.0),
  uuid("A892A09D-98C9-4AD4-98C5-769F7743F204"),
  helpstring("CalcPi Class") ]
class ATL_NO_VTABLE CCalcPi :
  public ICalcPi
,
    /*+++ Added Baseclass */ public ISupportErrorInfo
,
    /*+++ Added Baseclass */ public
IProvideClassInfo2Impl<&__uuidof(CCalcPi),
  &__uuidof(::_ICalcPiEvents)>
{
public:
  CCalcPi() { }

  __event __interface _ICalcPiEvents;


  DECLARE_PROTECT_FINAL_CONSTRUCT()

  HRESULT FinalConstruct() { return S_OK; }
  void FinalRelease() { }

public:

    // IDispatch methods
    virtual HRESULT STDMETHODCALLTYPE ICalcPi::Invoke(
            /* [in] */ DISPID dispIdMember,
            /* [in] */ REFIID riid,
            /* [in] */ LCID lcid,
            /* [in] */ WORD wFlags,
            /* [out][in] */ DISPPARAMS *pDispParams,
            /* [out] */ VARIANT *pVarResult,
```

```
              /* [out] */ EXCEPINFO *pExcepInfo,
              /* [out] */ UINT *puArgErr) {
// Implementation removed for clarity
}

virtual HRESULT STDMETHODCALLTYPE ICalcPi::GetIDsOfNames(
              /* [in] */ REFIID riid,
              /* [size_is][in] */ LPOLESTR *rgszNames,
              /* [in] */ UINT cNames,
              /* [in] */ LCID lcid,
              /* [size_is][out] */ DISPID *rgDispId) {
// Implementation removed for clarity
}

HRESULT TypeInfoHelper(REFIID iidDisp, LCID /*lcid*/,
  ITypeInfo** ppTypeInfo) {
...
}

virtual HRESULT STDMETHODCALLTYPE ICalcPi::GetTypeInfoCount(
  unsigned int*  pctinfo) {
...
}

virtual HRESULT STDMETHODCALLTYPE ICalcPi::GetTypeInfo(
  unsigned int iTInfo, LCID lcid, ITypeInfo** ppTInfo) {
...
}

BEGIN_CONNECTION_POINT_MAP(CCalcPi)
    CONNECTION_POINT_ENTRY(IID_IPropertyNotifySink)
    CONNECTION_POINT_ENTRY(__uuidof(::_ICalcPiEvents))
END_CONNECTION_POINT_MAP()

// Registration implementation

BEGIN_COM_MAP(CCalcPi)
    COM_INTERFACE_ENTRY(ICalcPi)
    COM_INTERFACE_ENTRY(IDispatch)
    COM_INTERFACE_ENTRY(IConnectionPointContainer)
    COM_INTERFACE_ENTRY(ISupportErrorInfo)
    COM_INTERFACE_ENTRY(IProvideClassInfo2)
    COM_INTERFACE_ENTRY(IProvideClassInfo)
END_COM_MAP()
```

```
        STDMETHOD(InterfaceSupportsErrorInfo)(REFIID riid) {
        ...
        }

};

OBJECT_ENTRY_AUTO(__uuidof(CCalcPi), CCalcPi)
```

The attribute providers generate code to implement Registry updates for this object. They also injected the `COM_MAP`, `CONNECTION_MAP`, `InterfaceSupportsError-Info` method, and all the other boilerplates that would normally have shown up in our header file.

There's just one problem: This output is wrong.

Look at the base class list. Where's `CComObjectRootEx`? `CComCoClass`? Also, the attributes are still in the file. You cannot feed the generated .mrg files into a C++ compiler and get code that works. Unfortunately, this limitation[2] makes it hard to trust the code that attributes generate because there's no way to actually see all of it.

The Future of Attributed ATL

When ATL 7 was released, Attributed ATL was a big new feature. All the wizards defaulted to generating attributed code, all the new help was about attributes, and everyone swore that this was the wave of the future. There was even talk of some-day opening up the compiler so that people could create their own attribute providers.

Things didn't work out that way. Attributed code suffers from several problems:

- **Difficulty debugging.** If there's a problem in the code generated by the attrib-ute or its interaction with your code, it's very difficult to debug.

- **Lack of control.** Attributes do a lot of work for you behind the scenes, but if you don't like the code the attribute is generating, you're out of luck. Because C++ is all about powerful tools that give you fine control over your code, this doesn't work so well for most C++ developers.

- **Bugs.** Some areas in attributed code (particularly around connection points) are just plain buggy.

---

[2] /Fx did generate correct output in Visual Studio.NET 2002 and 2003; it was broken in the 2005 release. Microsoft's response was that the switch was supposed to be only a quick check, and that it will not be fixed. See http://lab.msdn.microsoft.com/productfeedback/viewfeedback.aspx?feedbackid=a09357fe-32fa-43a1-9223-95bc2c38765e (http://tinysells.com/59).

It's very telling that in Visual Studio 2005, the ATL wizards now default to nonattributed code. The only part of ATL that requires attributed code is the Web Services portions of ATL Server (see Chapter 13, "Hello, ATL Server," for a discussion). Microsoft seems to be moving away from the attributed ATL experiment. It looks like the ATL community is stuck with templates, macros, IDL files, and RGS scripts.

Summary

Attributed ATL was an attempt to simplify the use of ATL through compiler extensions. Instead of using base classes, and scattering information through many different types of files (C++, IDL, RGS, and so on), attributed ATL used IDL-like attributes to provide extra information attached to the various type declarations in your ATL code.

At compile time, the attributes manipulate the compiler parse tree to add base classes, ATL maps, and sometimes entire interface implementations. Attributes also provide information that gets passed through to the MIDL compiler. This enables you to centralize all the information about a COM class with the C++ class declaration instead of having some in the class header, some in the IDL file, and some in RGS scripts.

Attributes were an interesting experiment, but it appears that Microsoft has abandoned the idea because the ATL wizards no longer default to attributed code.

Index

A

A, 50
ABC (abstract base class), 794
accelerator translations, control
    containment, 668-669
accessing
    controls from HTML, 690-692
    HTML from controls, 686-689
ActivateAx, 643-644
activation
    aggregated activation, CComObject,
        209-211
    alternative activation techniques,
        CComObject, 213- 218
    standalone activation, CComObject,
        207-209
Active Template Library. *See* ATL
ActiveX, 1
ActiveX controls, 28, 445
    control hosting and, 813
    functionality, 567-569
    keyboard handling, 627-630
    property page functionality, 569
    review of, 567
Add ATL control Wizard, 592
Add Web Service, 734
adding
    base classes to connectable
        objects, 447
    connection points, to connectable
        objects, 448
    custom properties and methods, to
        IDL (BullsEye), 594-595

events, 21-22
    marshal-by-value semantics using
        persistence, 376-379
    methods, 12-15
    persistence, 19-20
    properties, 12-15
    simple objects to attributed ATL
        COM servers, 818-820
    Windows message handler, 26
AddRef, 179-180
    tracing calls to, 239-242
AddRef method,
    IConnectionPointImpl, 475
AddResult, 768, 774
Advise method, 150
    IConnectionPointImpl, 475-477
aggregated activation, CComObject,
    209-211
aggregation, 328
    blind aggregation versus planned
        aggregation, 329-330
    FTM (Free Threaded Marshaler),
        335-336
    manual versus automatic creation,
        330-334
    planned aggregation versus blind
        aggregation, 329-330
    support for IUnknown, 197-198
alIndex, 134
_AllocStdCallThunk, 508
alternate message maps, CWindowImpl,
    536-537

O

object instantiation methods, CComPtr-
Base, 142-143
object maps, 246-247
CAtlModule class and, 245-246
class initialization and
uninitialization
ObjectMain method, 265-266
class registration support methods
category map macros, 261-262
component category maps, 260
GetCategoryMap method, 260
GetObjectDescription method, 253
UpdateRegistry method, 253-259
instantiation requests
CComClassFactory and DE-
CLARE_CLASSFACTORY,
276-277
CComCreator::CreateInstance,
272-275
CComObjectNoLock, 271-271
CCoomObjectCached, 271-272
class object registration, 266-269
_ClassFactoryCreatorClass,
269-271
_CreatorClass, 269-270
DECLARE_CLASSFACTORY, 270
DECLARE_CLASSFACTORY2 and
CComClassFactory2, 278-281
DECLARE_CLASSFACTORY_AUTO
_THREAD and CComClass-
FactoryAutoThread, 284-286
DECLARE_CLASSFACTORY_EX,
277-278
DECLARE_CLASSFACTORY_
SINGLETON and CComClass-
FactorySingleton, 282
macros
_ATL_OBJMAP_ENTRY, 247-248
OBJECT_ENTRY_AUTO, 248-251
OBJECT_ENTRY_NON_CREATE-
ABLE_EX_AUTO, 251

methods required for, 252-253
server registration, 262-263
inproc server registration, 263-264
local server and windows service
registration, 264
object models, 435-436
collection objects, implementing,
437-439
subobjects, implementing, 439-440
top-level objects, implementing,
436-437
using, 440
ObjectLock, 193
ObjectMain method, 265-266
objects
cached objects, 214
COM objects, 179
IUnknown, implementing, 175-177
scripting support, 199-203
supporting multiple dual
interfaces, 203-205
table-driven QueryInterface,
194-197
threads, 179-180
creating objects that are event
recipients, 457-458
callback methods, 464-465
connecting event sinks to event
sources, 465-468
event sink maps, 462-464
IDispEventImpl, 458-460
IDispEventSimpleImpl, 458-460
implementing event sinks, 460-461
global objects, 216
identity and lifetime options, 219
no-lock objects, 215
OBJECT_ENTRY_AUTO, 248-251
OBJECT_ENTRY_NON_CREATE-
ABLE_EX_AUTO, 251
OBJECT_MAP(), 725
implementing COM servers, 812
offsetofclass macro, 303

THIS BOOK IS SAFARI ENABLED

INCLUDES FREE 45-DAY ACCESS TO THE ONLINE EDITION

The Safari® Enabled icon on the cover of your favorite technology book means the book is available through Safari Bookshelf. When you buy this book, you get free access to the online edition for 45 days.

Safari Bookshelf is an electronic reference library that lets you easily search thousands of technical books, find code samples, download chapters, and access technical information whenever and wherever you need it.

TO GAIN 45-DAY SAFARI ENABLED ACCESS TO THIS BOOK:

- Go to **http://www.awprofessional.com/safarienabled**
- Complete the brief registration form
- Enter the coupon code found in the front of this book on the "Copyright" page

Addison
Wesley